The Crisi Wartegg System (CWS)

The Wartegg Drawing Completion Test (WDCT) is a semi-structured, graphic, performance-based personality test, created by Ehrig Wartegg in 1926 (Wartegg, 1939). With a foundation in Gestalt and Psychodynamic theory, the WDCT has been used widely throughout Europe, South America, and Japan, but only recently has become available in the United States. Initial scoring systems for the WDCT were considered cumbersome and lacked research-driven validation. In response to these factors, Alessandro Crisi, following years of clinical practice and research, developed the Crisi Wartegg System (CWS; 1998, 2007), a normed and standardized administration, scoring, and interpretation system for the WDCT. Over the past three decades, Dr. Crisi has refined and expanded the CWS through research, broadening the scope of the measure, and increasing the accessibility of the system to clinicians. This manual provides a comprehensive guide to the CWS, made available to English-speaking clinicians for the first time.

Alessandro Crisi is an Italian psychologist who lives in Rome where he works as a private professional and teaches at the Sapienza University of Rome. He has written numerous articles and book chapters, and presented at many professional conferences.

Jacob A. Palm is a licensed clinical psychologist, and founder of the Southern California Center for Collaborative Assessment in Long Beach, California. Dr. Palm is the United States representative of the *Istituto Italiano Wartegg.*

"This text is the quintessential resource for psychological assessors who wish to incorporate the Crisi Wartegg system of scoring and interpreting the Wartegg Drawing Completion Test into their resource bank of personality assessment instruments. It comprehensively describes the stages of implementing the Crisi Wartegg System from scoring through interpretation in children, adolescents, and adults, and provides a thorough exposition of the rapidly expanding research base for this enormously useful tool. Assessors from neophyte to expert will derive immeasurable benefit from welcoming this book into their libraries."

Virginia M. Brabender, *Ph.D., ABPP Professor, Widener University*

"Crisi and Palm's *The Crisi Wartegg System* is an eloquent, comprehensive step-by-step guide to the administration, scoring, and interpretation of a very important but underappreciated psychological test. Rich in theory, research, and historical context, this book should be required reading for practicing clinicians and researchers alike."

Robert F. Bornstein, *Ph.D., Professor of Psychology, Adelphi University*

"This book is a monumental gift to psychological assessment! It integrates the large body of research on the Wartegg Drawing Completion Test into a system (the Crisi Wartegg System) that is then itself thoroughly considered and researched. The result is a reliable, valid, and enormously useful performance-based measure that rivals the Rorschach Inkblot Method. The book is a well-organized, detailed, and accessible guide to administration, scoring, and interpretation, including instructive examples. The CWS will play a large role in the future of assessment."

Hale Martin, *Ph.D., Clinical Professor, University of Denver*

The Crisi Wartegg System (CWS)

Manual for Administration, Scoring, and Interpretation

Alessandro Crisi

English Adaptation and Additional Content by Jacob A. Palm

Routledge
Taylor & Francis Group
NEW YORK AND LONDON

First published in English 2018
by Routledge
711 Third Avenue, New York, NY 10017

and by Routledge
2 Park Square, Milton Park, Abingdon, Oxon, OX14 4RN

Routledge is an imprint of the Taylor & Francis Group, an informa business

English adaptation by Jacob A. Palm
Published in Italian by Magi Edizioni, Rome 1998

Library of Congress Cataloging-in-Publication Data
A catalog record for this book has been requested

ISBN: 978-1-138-56560-9 (hbk)
ISBN: 978-1-138-56688-0 (pbk)
ISBN: 978-1-315-12392-9 (ebk)

Typeset in Goudy
by Florence Production Ltd, Stoodleigh, Devon, UK

Visit the eResources: www.routledge.com/9781138566880

To my Father, Valentino Crisi

(1912: Highland Falls, NY, USA—1985: Rome, Italy)

Contents

Figures

Tables

Appendices

Contributors

Alessandro Crisi is an Italian psychologist who lives in Rome where he works as a private professional. He studied at Sapienza University of Rome where he received his Psychology Degree in 1976. Between 1976 and 1982, Dr. Crisi completed his psychotherapy training with Professor Lucio Pinkus of the D.G.G. Berlin (Germany). He had many periods of voluntary service (each lasting approximately one year) as assessment psychologist, including: the Psychiatric Hospital of "S. Maria della Pietà" in Rome; the "C. Forlanini" Hospital of Rome in the field of psychosomatic disorders; and the Institute of Neurology of the "A. Gemelli" Hospital of Rome in the field of multiple sclerosis.

In 1982 Dr. Crisi received a diploma in Sport Psychology from Sapienza University of Rome, subsequently working for many sporting leagues. After these initial training experiences, his career has mainly developed in three different directions: teaching, psychotherapy, and assessment.

Since 1999, Dr. Crisi has taught "Clinical Assessment" as adjunct professor at the Sapienza University of Rome and in other private Schools of Specialization in Rome. Trained as a psychodynamic psychotherapist, Dr. Crisi works primarily in assessment (including the clinical, forensic, selection, and career guidance fields).

Dr. Crisi has extensive experience working with performance-based personality tests, most significantly with the Wartegg Drawing Completion Test created by Ehrig Wartegg in 1926. Dr. Crisi has developed a new system of use and interpretation for the Wartegg Test, called the CWS (Crisi Wartegg System). The CWS is currently used in many fields of assessment in Italy. Since 2002, the Italian Armed Forces has consistently utilized the CWS in its Selection and Careers Guidance proceedings. Dr. Crisi authored the *Manuale del test di Wartegg* (Handbook of the Wartegg Test) published by E.S. Ma.Gi (1998, 2007) and co-authored with Bianchi and Di Renzo *Il test di Wartegg nell'età evolutiva* (The Wartegg Test in Childhood) published by E.S. Ma.Gi (1996). He has also written numerous articles and book chapters, and presented at numerous professional conferences.

Jacob A. Palm is a licensed clinical psychologist with extensive experience in collaborative/therapeutic psychological testing and assessment. Dr. Palm is a graduate of Fordham University, located in the Bronx, New York, where he received his Doctorate in Clinical Psychology. He completed his American Psychological Association (APA)-accredited Doctoral Internship at The Guidance Center, a non-profit community mental health agency, where he later supervised and trained clinicians in psychological assessment for nearly a decade (first as Assessment Supervisor, and later as Director of Doctoral Training).

Dr. Palm was licensed as a psychologist in California in 2005 and is the founder and director of the Southern California Center for Collaborative Assessment. He is currently affiliated with Miller Children's Hospital, where he provides neuropsychological assessments and consultation; Promises Treatment Center, where he conducts forensic personality assessments and evaluations; Hoag Hospital (Newport Beach) Neurosciences Institute where he assesses children and adolescents as part of the "Teen Brain" Program; the Alhambra Unified School District "Gateway to Success" Program, where he supervises and trains interns from multiple mental health disciplines; and Santiago Canyon College, where he provides short-term psychotherapy to college students. Dr. Palm is recognized as the United States representative of the *Istituto Italiano Wartegg*, serving as expert trainer, presenter, and consultant to English-speaking psychologists from around the world using the innovative Crisi Wartegg System (CWS) for the Wartegg Drawing Completion Test.

Foreword

In the history of psychological assessment we periodically see the emergence of highly talented individuals—such as Stark Hathaway and John Exner, Jr.—who combine great clinical acumen with creativity, determination, and methodological rigor to make a major impact on our field. Alessandro Crisi is one of these extraordinary individuals, and I am delighted that English-speaking readers will now have access to his work and to the test he has spent his life refining, the Wartegg Drawing Completion Test (WDCT).

The WDCT was almost unknown in the USA until recently, although it was published in 1926, only five years after the Rorschach. I myself had a passing acquaintance with the test because of my work in Sweden, where it is fairly widely used, but I was skeptical of the detailed interpretations attributed to clients' drawings to simple marks in eight square boxes on a piece of paper. As best I could glean, there was no theoretical or scientific basis for these interpretations. Then in 2009, I met Professor Alessandro Crisi in Prague at the Summer Seminar of the International Society for Rorschach and Projective Methods. I was quite taken with this humble man who kept saying insightful things about the Rorschach cases we were discussing and I decided I wanted to know him better. Soon we were discussing his Crisi Wartegg System (CWS). I learned that, just as Exner did with the Rorschach, Crisi had standardized the administration of the Wartegg, collected a large normative sample, developed a set of scores that made intuitive and scientific sense to me (Populars, Form Quality, Contents, Special Scores, etc.), and had conducted many validity studies to establish the construct validity of these scores. Crisi invited me to administer the WDCT to one of my clients and send him the protocol to interpret blind. I still remember my feeling of wonder when I read Crisi's report on the disturbed young man I was assessing, and the look of surprise and excitement on the faces of my colleagues at the Center for Therapeutic Assessment when I read it to them. Crisi's interpretation fit almost perfectly with my own impressions and with the results of the other tests I had given and it went beyond the other tests to offer some intriguing hypotheses about the client's relationship with his parents. For example, Crisi suggested that my client may have experienced some kind of violence from his father. I thought this idea was a test "miss" at the time, since the father had always seemed passive, submissive, and distant in my encounters with him and the family. When I interviewed the client, however, I found out that earlier in my client's life, his father had been a violent alcoholic. As a child, my client had witnessed many traumatic scenes of the father raging at the mother and breaking things in the house. I was impressed by Crisi's report, and this feeling only grew when I began reading his manual for the Crisi Wartegg System and saw the amount of work he had put into refining his system.

Not long after, my colleagues at the Center for Therapeutic Assessment and I invited Crisi to conduct an introductory training on the CWS in Austin, Texas; subsequently a core group completed the three levels of basic training and had a magical advanced CWS case conference in 2013 in Rome. Along the way, I became certified in the CWS, and it is now a regular part of the Therapeutic Assessments I do in Austin and elsewhere. I've had many cases where an extended inquiry of the WDCT or some information from the CWS protocol helped me understand some critical point about my clients' experience, and the clients have also been excited and moved by the insights afforded by the CWS. The test has been particularly useful in situations where self-report tests reveal little of the clients' problems and the Rorschach is constricted or highly defended. In my experience, in general the WDCT is not to be as emotionally arousing as the Rorschach, so clients are not as prone to "shut down" during the test. For these reasons the CWS is also extremely helpful with young children, who often seem to find the Rorschach too difficult.

Over the past five years, Crisi has conducted many CWS trainings in the USA, collected a US normative sample, and partnered with Dr. Jacob Palm to help make the CWS accessible to American psychologists. The publication of this manual in English will greatly help in this effort, and I enthusiastically recommend this book, the CWS, and Drs. Crisi and Palm to you. In skilled hands, the CWS is a particularly strong "empathy magnifying glass" and I am sure that if you learn it well, you and your clients will benefit.

Stephen E. Finn
Austin, Texas

Preface

It is with great pleasure that I present to American colleagues the first edition of the handbook for clinical use of the Wartegg Drawing Completion Test according to the method I began to create more than 30 years ago. Since the beginning, the Crisi Wartegg System (CWS) has gradually been expanded and refined through continuous use in clinical settings and significant clinical research with pathological populations.

In recent years, starting in 2008, I began to attend the Society for Personality Assessment (SPA) annual conventions in which I submitted many papers, participated in many symposia, two full-day workshops, and one half-day workshop on the CWS. In fact, I have noted that interest in this new tool is exponentially growing in American psychologists! In 2016, I also taught the CWS in the spring quarter at the GSPP in the University of Denver, CO.

I am sure that my American colleagues will find this book of great interest, given the characteristics of the CWS. It is easy to administer and score, it is easily comprehensible to the client, with software allowing efficient calculation of necessary computations. Above all, it provides the possibility of reaching, in a short time, an accurate and deep understanding of the assessed client's personality. All these characteristics (fast, easy, etc.) also make the CWS incredibly useful in the field of research.

The Wartegg test demonstrates an extraordinary concurrent validity with some of the most famous, widely respected, and frequently used tools: MMPI-2 and Rorschach. In particular, great incremental validity with the Rorschach has been noted. The two tests, although both projective, use different means to describe personality: the verbalization of the Rorschach, and the graphic gesture—the drawing—in the Wartegg. These different methods of examination allow us to observe the client by two very different points of perspective.

The CWS has proven to be particularly useful in childhood and its ease of administration is quite suitable in the evaluation of individuals with different abilities. Since many years, the CWS has also been used in forensic psychology and the Italian Armed Forces has included it in military Selection and Career Guidance proceedings.

I hope that this book will increase the use of the Wartegg test, and that soon we will have collected a comprehensive normative sample for the American population, leading to further research in all fields of assessment.

Alessandro Crisi, Rome, 2017

Acknowledgments

The purpose of this book is to introduce a personality test that has not been well known up to this point in the USA and to promote its use. Many people made direct or indirect contributions in support of this goal, and I wish to thank all of them.

First, I want to recognize my colleagues at the Center for Therapeutic Assessment in Austin, Texas for their friendship and support during and after the first CWS workshop in the USA: Stephen Finn, Marita Frackowiak, Melissa Lehmann, Dale Rudin, and Pamela Schaber. The interest and enthusiasm with which they welcomed the Wartegg was very important because it gave me greater confidence that my work was useful to American assessment practitioners. In addition to attending the initial CWS workshop, many of these individuals, together with other colleagues who attended the first CWS training in the USA, participated in collecting the first US nonpatient sample of more than 250 Warteggs (Sarah Avey, Diane Engelman, Maria Fishel, Christine Larson, Casey O'Neal, Jacob Palm, Tracy Zemansky).

A special thanks goes to all my colleagues in the Society for Personality Assessment (SPA). Since my first SPA annual meeting (New Orleans, 2008) I have been welcomed as an esteemed member of this prestigious Society. Everyone in the SPA has steadily encouraged me to promote Wartegg's test in the USA, and I want to affectionately recognize three SPA members, all former Presidents of the Society: Virginia Brabender, who encouraged me to attend the SPA annual meeting in New Orleans (2008); Robert Erhard, who did not hesitate to take the Wartegg himself in order to know it better; And Leonard Handler, who, together with Antoinette Thomas, included a chapter devoted entirely to the CWS in his final book.

Similar thanks go to my colleagues in the International Society of Rorschach and Projective Methods (ISR), whose interest in the CWS came to fruition when I was invited to hold a half-day workshop at the Rorschach Summer Seminar in Montreux, Switzerland (2010).

I am especially grateful to the Dean, teaching directors, administrative staff, and professors of the Graduate School of Professional Psychology at the University of Denver (DU). I was invited to teach a course on the CWS at DU during the

2016 spring quarter, and this was an unforgettable didactic, professional, and human experience. Really, thank you.

And speaking of Denver, one name comes immediately to my mind: E. Hale Martin. Many of the trainings I did in this beautiful city would not have been possible without Hale's support, interest, and organizational abilities. Over the years, our collegial relationship has slowly evolved into a deep friendship characterized by enormous mutual respect.

Many Italian and international colleagues contributed their impressive skills to the statistical analyses in this book. Therefore, I want to thank Enea Bonci, Francesco Dentale, Harald Janson, and Isabella Lops for their help elaborating and deepening the statistical aspects of this CWS manual.

Finally, if this book sees the light now, it is thanks to two people to whom I want to give special acknowledgment: Stephen E. Finn and Jacob A. Palm.

Stephen and I met in 1996 at the ISR Congress in Boston but we did not become better acquainted until many years later. It was at the ISR Rorschach Summer Seminar in Prague (2009) that, I discovered, to my great surprise, that Stephen was acquainted with the Italian language. After several lively discussions, Stephen became interested in the CWS, and during a visit to Rome shortly thereafter, he proposed to sponsor the first US workshop on the CWS, held in September, 2011 in Austin, Texas. From that point on, Stephen has consistently and courageously endorsed the validity of the CWS and its clinical utility in Therapeutic Assessment; his support was key in opening a gap in the skepticism that surrounded the Wartegg in the USA. Together, Stephen and I have presented symposia in the congresses of the SPA and ISR, and we have shared moments of joy and sadness that life has in the meantime brought to us. All this gave me the opportunity to appreciate Stephen's deep and wide professional competence, profound humanity, and sincere friendship.

Jacob Palm, who co-authored the first two chapters of this manual, was the key person in the success of this publication. Since he attended his first CWS training course in Austin in 2012, Jacob has shown great interest in this tool and a predisposition toward it. Then, at Stephen Finn's suggestion, Jacob began to refine an earlier English translation of the CWS manual undertaken by Silvia Fiammenghi. This final published English adaptation required an enormous amount of work; the difficulties of two languages, the complexity of some of the theoretical and technical aspects of the CWS, and the cultural differences between our countries have been major obstacles. All this required many hundreds of hours of meetings either by Skype or in person in Rome, at Jacob's home in Long Beach, CA, or at various professional conferences where both of us were present. Clearly, Jacob has also spent many hours working on the manuscript alone. Jacob has long been teaching and providing consultation on the CWS, and has proved himself to be a skilled and competent clinician and a brilliant lecturer. To my great pleasure, Jacob also agreed to be the representative of the Italian Wartegg Institute in the USA.

A Note about Adaptation

When I agreed to collaborate with Dr. Alessandro Crisi on the English adaptation of his 2007 Italian-language *Manuale del test di Wartegg*, I truly didn't know what I was getting into! Now, nearly five years later, having logged over a thousand hours on CWS-related activities (including hundreds of Skype-based consultations, thousands of emails, and multiple trans-Atlantic trips), this manual is the result. In the process, the CWS has taken root in the United States, with training materials simultaneously adapted for an English-speaking audience.

As many people have asked me what "adaptation" actually refers to in this context (as it is not a well-recognized term in the scientific community), I wanted to write a brief note about the process. To begin with, adaptation is far more than translation. While specific language considerations are inherent to the process (both in terms of commonly used psychological terms, but also in speech patterns and grammar between languages), the process of adaptation further takes into account differences in cultural expectations and learning style, as well as the specific needs of the intended audience and efforts to anticipate and facilitate the utility of the manuscript for that audience. Questions such as, "How do English-speaking clinicians learn?" or "What is the preferred format for presentation of this important information?" became critical to consider. Similarly, "What will make this manual clinically useful and efficient for clinicians?" was an important question to answer, leading to the creation of appendices containing both scoring and interpretation tables, for example. So, beyond translation, the process of adaptation considers learning style, presentational format, utility, and the needs and expectations of the intended audience.

As to the process, starting with a translated (Italian-to-English) draft of the previously published manual (2007), adaptation included re-organization and re-formatting for an English-speaking audience; polishing translated text for syntax and grammar; expansion of previous concepts reflecting advancements in the CWS over the past decade; clarification of discipline-specific language (given that Italian-speaking psychologists speak and write quite differently from English-speaking psychologists in terms of theory and psychological terminology); creation of figures and tables unique to the current version of the manual; addition and expansion of appendices (including scoring and interpretation tables to parallel other English-language test manuals); and writing of new examples, content, and clarifications to best communicate relevant information. In this case, the process of adaptation further included the creation of two new chapters, one focusing on history of the WDCT (given that less is known of the WDCT in the English-speaking world), and one reviewing statistical foundations of the CWS—both important considerations for today's clinician.

Of course, a substantial project such as this cannot happen without considerable assistance and input from others. Over the past five training sequences, suggestions and clarifications offered by skilled clinician–participants have been invaluable in shaping this manual and guiding the adaptation process. More specifically, during the initial review of the translated text, members of the first US training cohort—Diane Engelman, Steven Finn, Maria Fishel, Christine Larson, Melissa Lehmann, Casey O'Neal, Pamela Schaber and Tracy Zemansky—each provided comments on discreet "chunks" of Chapters 3–6. Later, Steve Finn's comments on an early draft of Chapter 2 proved invaluable, as did consultation with Dale Rudin regarding best practices for presentation of historical research results related to the Deaf community. Participants in subsequent training cohorts, Mitsugu Murakami provided information and translated Japanese-language publications related to the history of WDCT use in Japan, and Doreen Landrum reviewed scoring tables, offering a valuable perspective on usability and clinical utility. Jason Fletcher offered invaluable statistical consultation during the preparation of Chapter 2. Lastly, special thanks to Hale Martin for continued support of CWS training and research at the University of Denver. A debt of gratitude is owed to all clinical users of the CWS, who continue to refine our understanding of the unique challenges presented by English-speaking clinicians in training and communicating the intricacies of the CWS.

Lastly, I must, of course, express my deep appreciation to Alessandro Crisi, who has labored to bring his thoughtful, unique, and nuanced system for the WDCT to clinicians worldwide. I feel enormously thankful to have had the opportunity to collaborate so deeply with him on this and other CWS-related projects, and am truly fortunate to consider him a friend.

I hope you, the readers, find this manual as useful and enjoyable as I have found the process of adaptation.

Jacob A. Palm
Long Beach, California
June 2017

Abbreviations

The following abbreviations are used throughout this manual.

Italicized text below indicates abbreviations with multiple meanings, depending on context of use.

a	Active (direction of movement)
A	Animal (Primary Content)
A/F	Affective Stability Index ("A/F Ratio")
AAP	Adult Attachment Projective
ABS	Abstract (Primary Content)
AC	*Ambivalent Choice (Box Code)*
AC	*Archeology (Secondary Content)*
AD	*Ambivalent Delay (Box Code)*
AD	*Animal Detail (Content)*
ADP	Adaptive Area (Boxes 1, 3, 6, 8)
AFF	Affective Area (Boxes 2, 4, 5, 7)
AI	Anxiety Index
ANA	Anatomy (Primary Content)
AoS-1	Analysis of Sequence 1
AoS-2	Analysis of Sequence 2
AP	Arbitrary Performance (Special Score)
AQ	Affective Quality
ARC	Architecture (Primary Content)
AS	*Animal Simulacrum (Primary Content)*
AS	*Anxiety Stroke (Special Score)*
AST	Astronomy (Primary Content)
b	Blocked (direction of movement)
BD	Big Drawing, Protocol Level (Noted Phenomenon)
BIO	Biological (Primary Content)
BK	Blackening (Noted Phenomenon)
BOT	Botanical (Primary Content)
C	Choice (Box Code)
CB	Crossed Border (Special Score)

CG	Clothing (Secondary Content)
CJ	Conjoined Box (Noted Phenomenon)
CLD	Cloud (Primary Content)
CO	Contamination (Special Score)
CP	Color Projection (Noted Phenomenon)
CWS	Crisi Wartegg System
d	Double (direction of movement)
D	Delay (Box Code)
DB	Disproportion between Boxes (Noted Phenomenon)
DS	Disproportion (Special Score)
EC	Evocative (Primary Content)
EN	Encapsulation (Noted Phenomenon)
EXP	Explosion (Primary Content)
f	Female (gender of movement)
FA	Figurative Art (Secondary Content)
FD	Food (Primary Content)
FE	Facial Expression
FIR	Fire (Primary Content)
FM	Animal Movement
FQ	Form Quality
FT	Fairy Tale (Secondary Content)
GR	Global Rejection (Special Score)
H	Human (Primary Content)
HD	Human Detail (Primary Content)
HN	Human Content Negation (Noted Phenomenon)
HR	Heraldry (Secondary Content)
HS	Human Simulacrum (Primary Content)
i	Indeterminate (direction of movement, gender of movement)
ICC	Intraclass correlation coefficients
ICE	Ice (Primary Content)
ID	Incomplete Drawing (Special Score)
II	Inadequate Integration (Special Score)
IIT-1	Index of Inner Tension-1
IIT-2	Index of Inner Tension-2
IM	Impulsivity Index
IP	Improper Description (Noted Phenomenon)
IR	Impulse Response
IS	Interpreted Stimulus (Special Score)
ISR	International Society of Rorschach and Projective Methods
IST	Index of Suicidal Tendencies
IV	Validity Index
LD	Learning Difficulties
LSI	Low Symptoms and Impairments (Global Assessment)
m	*Secondary Movement*
m	*Male (gender of movement)*

M	Primary Movement
MI	Inanimate Movement
MIN	Mineral (Primary Content)
MK	Mask (Secondary Content)
MR	Morbid (Special Score)
MSI	Moderate Symptoms and Impairments (Global Assessment)
MT	Mythological (Secondary Content)
MU	Missing Union (Special Score)
NAT	Nature (Primary Content)
NC	Negative Compensation (Box Code)
NOP	Not Pathological (Global Assessment)
O	Original Response
(O)	Semi-Original Response
OA	"Or" Answer (Noted Phenomenon)
OBJ	Object (Primary Content)
OD	Opposite Direction (Special Score)
OoS	Order of Sequence
Or	Oral Impulse Response
OS	Opposite Sequence
p	Passive (direction of movement)
P	Popular Response
(P)	Semi-Popular Response
PA	Personalized Answer (Special Score)
PAT	Pathological (Primary Content)
PC	Positive Compensation (Box Code)
PIU	Problematic Internet Use
PP	Perseveration (Special Score)
PR	Partial Rejection (Special Score)
PS	Perspective Response (Noted Phenomenon)
PTL	Pathological (Global Assessment)
r	Rotary (direction of movement)
RB	Reversed Box (Special Score)
RE	Religious (Secondary Content)
SASS	Social Adaptation Self-Evaluation Score
SAT	Separation Anxiety Test
SC	Self-Criticism (Special Score)
SD	Small Drawing, Protocol Level (Noted Phenomenon)
SEX	Sexual (Primary Content)
SF	Science Fiction (Secondary Content)
SIG	Symbol (Primary Content)
SPA	Society for Personality Assessment
SR	Stimulus Repetition (Special Score)
SS	Special Score(s)
SSI	Severe Symptoms and Impairments (Global Assessment)
SSIRAD	Scale for the Rapid Dimensional Evaluation

TR	Transparency (Special Score)
TY	Toy (Secondary Content)
VI	Validity Index
WDCT	Wartegg Drawing Completion Test
WIP	Wartegg Index of Psychopathology
WP	Weapon (Secondary Content)

1 History and Development of the Crisi Wartegg System

Jacob A. Palm and Alessandro Crisi

The Crisi Wartegg System (CWS), developed by Alessandro Crisi over several decades of clinical practice and research, is a standardized system of administration, scoring, and interpretation for the Wartegg Drawing Completion Test. To fully understand the contributions of this methodology, including a normatively based quantitative scoring system, one must understand the history and origins of the Wartegg Test itself, including the life of its creator, Ehrig Wartegg. The aim of this chapter is to review the historical origins of the Wartegg Test, which laid the foundation for the development of Crisi's methodology, the Crisi Wartegg System, the focus of this manual.

The Wartegg Drawing Completion Test

The Wartegg Drawing Completion Test (WDCT; known historically as the *Wartegg Zeichen Test*, WZT, or simply the Wartegg Test) is a semi-structured, graphic, projective (performance-based) personality test. Created in 1926 by German psychologist Ehrig Wartegg (1897–1983), the first text related to the test was published in 1939, and the first test manual in 1953. Using the model proposed by Bornstein (2007) for the classification of personality measures, the Wartegg Test can be considered a stimulus-attribution test in which examinees attribute meaning through the characteristics of their stimulus interpretation. When taking the Wartegg Test, examinees are prone to project contents, dynamics, and organization of their personality (Rapaport, 1977). Moreover, the simplicity of the stimuli is likely to bypass the defensive mechanisms of the examinee (McCully, 1988), yielding rich information about the structure and functioning of personality. In regard to the WDCT, Kinget (1952) asserted, "Another merit of the test lies in the fact that the material used does not threaten the subject by the strangeness of its appearance or by its emotional implications, but rather appeals to him by its simple and neutral character" (p. xiv). As Schwartz (2016) wrote, "myriad clinical examples of the usefulness in understanding individual personality adds to the potential usefulness of this curious and interesting new (old) measure" (p. 12).

Until recently, the WDCT has remained mostly unknown to psychologists in North America. In fact, the test has been written about in only one English-language book (Kinget, 1952), and was featured in an article in *Life Magazine* ("Complete These Drawings," *Life Magazine*, Vol. 9 (1952), pp. 65–68). It was later described by Buros (1959) as "an interesting tool for its potential," although it failed to gain a foothold of use in the United States. While relatively unknown to primarily English-speaking clinicians, the WDCT is widely used in Northern European countries (i.e., Sweden, Finland, Denmark, Norway), Germany, Spain, Italy, and South America. It further has a long history of use in Japan. In these countries, particularly due to the work of notable scholars (see Caviglia, 2005; Falcone, Grasso, & Pinkus, 1986; Fontana, 1984, 2005, 2012, 2013; Mattlar, 2015; Scarpellini, 1962, 1964; Torazza, 1993; and Gardziella, 1985, to name a few), the test is widely used in the field of clinical evaluation, occupational selection, and educational and vocational screening and placement.

Several versions of the Wartegg Test exist. Lossen and Schott (1975) list seven versions, noting significant formatting and interpretation differences between the various methods. In this manual, the WDCT (as we will refer to the Wartegg Drawing Completion Test) will always indicate the version consisting of eight boxes, labeled 1 to 8, displayed in two parallel rows, with each row consisting of four boxes. Each box is delineated by a thick black margin and contains a different graphic stimulus or "mark" (see Figure 1.1, Client WDCT Form, below). The marks, in order of the boxes, include:

Box 1: A dot in the center;
Box 2: A curved dash in the upper left;
Box 3: Three parallel vertical lines, increasing in height from left to right;
Box 4: A small black square positioned at the top right of the box;
Box 5: Two opposite lines perpendicular to each other in the bottom left-hand corner;
Box 6: Two lines at right angles to each other, a horizontal line above a vertical line to the right;
Box 7: A series of dots arranged in a semi-circle open upward, positioned in the lower right-hand corner;
Box 8: A downward facing curve.

It is this version of the WDCT that is always utilized according to CWS guidelines.

The WDCT has several important advantages and benefits in comparison to other performance-based personality measures. As Kinget (1952) described, the WDCT provides a relatively unstructured modality for the examinee to complete (allowing ample space for projection and free association), while significant structure is simultaneously provided to the examiner (promoting standardization and consistent administration and scoring). Additional benefits, per Kinget, included the generation of multiple data points promoting the "crosschecking" of interpretive data, simple and non-threatening stimuli that do not affectively activate examinees, and practicality and efficiency of administration, scoring,

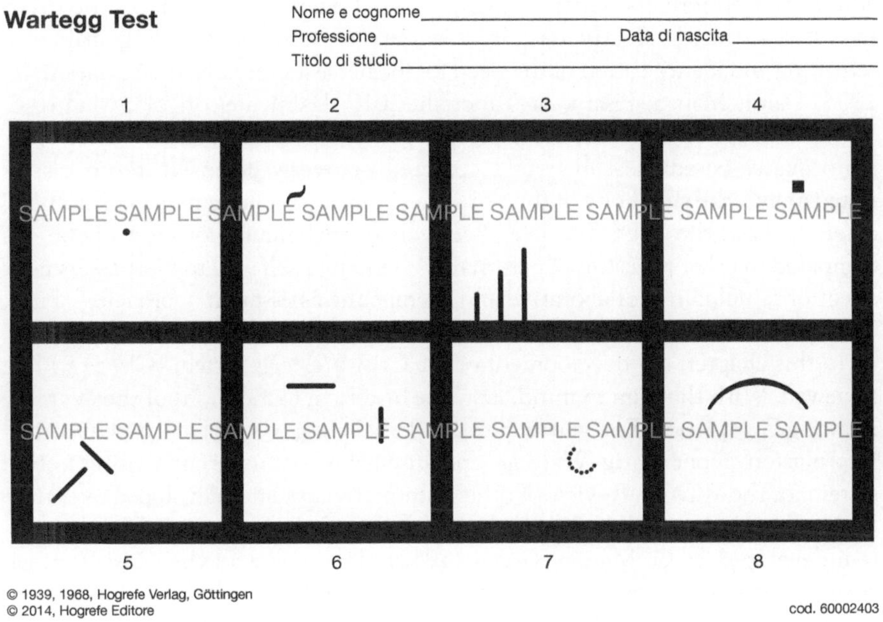

FIGURE 1.1 Client WDCT Form.

Figure 1.1 provides a sample copy of the WDCT form on which the client draws.

Source: Wartegg, E. (1953), *Schichtdiagnostik—Der Zeichentest (WZT)*, Hogrefe, Verlag für Psychologie. Copyright: 1957, Hogrefe, Verlag für Psychologie-Göttingen; 2014, Hogrefe Editore.
Please note that this test form is only a sample. Any kind of reproduction is strictly forbidden. A valid test result can only be obtained by a professionally qualified test administrator and using the original test materials. The test material can only be ordered at the Hogrefe Publishing Group (www.hogrefe.com). For any questions, please contact rights@hogrefe.com.

and interpretation. Lastly, Kinget wrote of the measure's "conduciveness to spontaneous verbal developments on the part of the subject" (p. xv). She noted the releasing or "opening" effect that drawing has on an individual's self-awareness, asserting that this process is especially conducive to the evaluation of personality.

In considering the Crisi Wartegg System (CWS) guidelines for the WDCT, these previously elaborated advantages persist, with additional benefits of the system noted. First, test instructions are easily understood by examinees of all ages and cognitive abilities, making it a useful test for assessment across the lifespan, including with those who demonstrate cognitive or developmental delays. Second, the WDCT is short to administer, with most subjects completing the test in 5–10 minutes. Third, the WDCT provides exceptional clinical efficiency, able to be scored in approximately 10–15 minutes by a proficient examiner, and taking only 30 additional minutes for interpretation. Fourth, a computer-scoring program is available (described in ►Appendix E) to facilitate reliable calculation of scores and indices. Fifth, the test may be administered in both individual and group administration formats (Crisi, in Handler & Thomas, 2014b). Sixth, the CWS has demonstrated effectiveness in a variety of settings including utility in screening and identification of the need for further assessment (Crisi & Carlesimo, 2008; Daini, Manzo, Pisani, & Tancredi, 2010; Daini, Petrongolo, Manzo, & Bernardini, 2012). Seventh, the WDCT is particularly useful in cases where other performance-based measures yield coarcted or overly defensive protocols; as noted above, the simplicity of the test stimuli oftentimes circumvents examinees' defenses. Last, the WDCT is less affectively overwhelming for most clients (as compared to other measures of personality), lending itself well to most assessment situations, including collaborative and therapeutic assessment approaches (Finn, 2014).

In this chapter, the development of the Crisi Wartegg System (CWS) will be reviewed. With that aim in mind, first, the historical foundations of the Wartegg Drawing Completion Test will be presented, including biographical and historical information about Ehrig Wartegg and discussion of his original interpretive system for the WDCT. Review of other interpretive systems, developed over time by various scholars, will be briefly discussed, including the English-language system developed by G. Marian Kinget (1952). The origins of the Crisi Wartegg System, including historical developments, early research, and development of the normative samples, will be presented. An overview of current developments in the CWS, including applications to Therapeutic Assessment (Finn, 2007) will be provided. Lastly, the organization of this manual will be reviewed.

Historical Foundations of the Wartegg Drawing Completion Test

The foundations and development of the Wartegg Drawing Completion Test parallel the life history of the test's creator, Ehrig Wartegg, and must be understood within the context of that history. Given the time period of Wartegg's professional development, as well as socio-political events in Europe during his lifetime, much about the life and work of Ehrig Wartegg is relatively unknown as compared to his contemporaries. For example, only one picture of Wartegg is known to exist, and until recently, his writings were generally unavailable with the exception of early publications (Wartegg, 1934, 1936, 1939, 1953). Most recently, a previously unpublished semi-autobiographical manuscript, "Sign of the times: The life and research of a psychodiagnostician" [translated], was published (Wartegg, 2000; in Bernhardt & Lockot, 2000). The majority of historical information reviewed in this chapter is summarized from two excellent biographical works on the life of Ehrig Wartegg, including the development of the WDCT, written by Eka Roivanen (2009) and Umberto Fontana (2013). Additional information comes from recollections by Wartegg's psychoanalyst, Therese Benedek, as well as interviews with Wartegg conducted by Peter Klemperer, published in 2000. A debt of gratitude is owed to these authors for their role in preserving the history and scientific contributions of Ehrig Wartegg.

A Brief Life History of Ehrig Wartegg

Born in Dresden, Germany on July 7, 1897, Ehrig Wartegg's life story is full of contradictions, struggles, and socio-cultural factors that required him to adapt to personal and professional frustrations, hide his true theoretical interests, and minimize his ambitious aspirations (Fontana, 2013). He was recognized as a hard-working, quiet, and well-respected academician (Bernhardt & Lockot, 2000), well esteemed by doctors and patients alike, and was considered a leader in the field and practice of psychoanalysis.

Fontana (2013) describes Wartegg's childhood as "unhappy," indicating that his parents separated shortly after his birth. While he remained with his mother, the pair moved in with a wealthy commercial businessman who became Wartegg's stepfather. Wartegg is reported to have felt like a "stranger" in his stepfather's home. While his upbringing was affluent, and he attended a prestigious school alongside children of nobility and high society, Wartegg is reported to have preferred socializing with everyday "normal" peers. He left home at 18, following in his father's footsteps, and entering the Austro-Hungarian army during the First World War (Roivanen, 2009). Having completed military academy training, Wartegg served on the Eastern Front, as a lieutenant of artillery, until he was seriously wounded in 1915. Serving in non-active duty positions following a lengthy recovery, Wartegg resigned from the military at the end of the war, entering "normal life" (Fontana, 2013).

Following his departure from the military, Wartegg was uncertain as to what career to pursue, demonstrating interest and aptitude in music, writing, art, and theatrical arts (Fontana, 2013). Initially deciding on music, Wartegg studied composition with famed German conductors, including Karl Böhm and Kurt Streigler. He further had opportunities to socialize with notable musicians of the time, given his family connections, including Gustav Mahler, Arturo Toscanini, Richard Strauss, and Igor Stravinski (Fontana, 2013; Roivanen, 2009). Along with his musical pursuits, Wartegg spent considerable time writing, heavily influenced by the writings of Indian poet, Rabindranath Tagore (Fontana, 2013).

While Wartegg maintained his interest in music and the arts throughout his life, he began frequenting lectures and symposia at the "School of Wisdom," influenced by the charismatic naturalist, philosopher, and mystic, Herman Keyserling. There, he had opportunities to attend workshops and interact with Carl Jung, Vassily Kandinsky, and Rabindranath Tagore (Roivanen, 2009). He was further exposed to psychoanalysis in 1923, during a seminar at the School of Wisdom. Per Fontana (2013), during this time period, three factors shaped Wartegg's life, moving him toward his later career in psychology. First, during a workshop with Richard Wilhelm, Wartegg was introduced to the ancient Chinese text, *I Ching*, or the "Classic of Changes." From this text, Wartegg began to consider the idea that simple signs and symbols could bring unconscious creative parts of the psyche to the surface, translating feelings into images. Per Fontana (2013), this idea was reinforced via Wartegg's interaction with Carl Jung, and exploration of the ideas of the collective unconscious inherent in universal symbols.

The second major influence on Wartegg's path into the field of psychology was his exposure to psychoanalysis at the School of Wisdom (Fontana, 2013). Following his reading of the early works of Sigmund Freud, Wartegg sought to enter into personal analysis, first working with Margaret Stegmann, and later, on the advice of Freud via written correspondence, with Therese Benedek. Wartegg had initially written to Freud in 1925, inquiring how to obtain training in psychoanalysis (Roivanen, 2009). While Wartegg did not possess a medical degree, Freud indicated that he did not believe only physicians could practice analysis (which was a commonly held opinion at the time), and encouraged Wartegg to pursue personal analysis (Fontana, 2013). In later correspondence, Freud discouraged Wartegg from synthesizing Gestalt psychology with psychoanalysis, indicating lack of knowledge of Gestalt theory (Horn & Lockot, 2000).

The third influence on Wartegg's career as a psychologist was personal in nature, the result of his mother's significant illness and subsequent unexplainable recovery (Fontana, 2013). When Wartegg was approximately 30 years of age, his mother contracted an unknown, undiagnosable nerve-related illness, leaving her completely paralyzed and near death. Over time, through what Wartegg would describe as sheer will, his mother recovered (to the surprise of her physicians), living 20 more years and working as a professional physiotherapist. Given this somewhat unexpected recovery, Wartegg began to believe that conventional medicine could not fully address internal maladies of the soul or psyche. He would later in his life be referred to as a "therapist of the spirit," reflecting this belief (Fontana, 2013).

Roivanen (2009) posits an additional influential factor on Wartegg and his eventual development of the WDCT, the influence of modern art. Given his interaction with Kandinsky, and the modern art movement that related graphic structure to internal concepts, Wartegg expanded his mystical psychological thoughts influenced by *I Ching*; that is, he began to further understand artistic expression as necessary for individuals, allowing the expression of unconscious attitudes, desires, and characteristics. This understanding likely contributed to his development of the WDCT in later years.

While Wartegg had been studying psychology at the Dresden University of Technology (1927), given these influences from the School of Wisdom and life experiences, he traveled to Leipzig in 1929, and entered the department of psychology at the University of Leipzig (Roivanen, 2009). His move to Leipzig was prompted by his desire to study with Felix Kreuger, who would become Wartegg's mentor, as well as to enter analysis with Therese Benedek, as recommended by Freud (Fontana, 2013). At the University of Leipzig, Wartegg adopted Gestalt Theory, primarily due to socio-political factors, while maintaining his interest in psychoanalysis. He began developing the Wartegg Zeichen Test, based upon Kreuger's and Freidrich Sander's theories, and was appointed assistant professor at the university in 1932. He completed his doctoral thesis, *Gestaltung and Charakter* (The Formation of Gestalts and Personality) in 1937, with the thesis published in 1939. During these years, authors note that Wartegg experienced both personal and professional setbacks given his heritage and participation in psychoanalysis, which were at odds with the rise of Nazism in Germany at that time. As Roivanen (2009) writes, "Wartegg had difficulties because of his 'contacts with "Jewish" psychoanalysis' and because of his Czechoslovakian citizenship. To secure his position, Wartegg claimed German nationality in 1922 and joined the National Socialist German Workers Party, the NSDAP (Lockot, 2000)" (p. 61). Despite joining the party, he was never trusted nor invited to participate, and was outspoken in his criticism of the actions and personality of Adolf Hitler (Fontana, 2013).

Due to these political leanings, Wartegg was asked to leave the University of Leipzig in 1939. Following his departure, he worked for the Ministry of Labor constructing tests for personnel recruitment until the end of the Second World War. After the war, given his membership in the NSDAP, Wartegg was brought before the "de-Nazification" committee, was sanctioned, and lost his right to practice as a psychologist until 1949 when he was pardoned due to testimony from former colleagues. It was later reported that Wartegg resisted Nazi politics in his work and private life, only taking party membership to preserve his job (Wartegg, 2000; Lockot, 2000; in Roivanen, 2009).

Following the conclusion of the war, Wartegg remained in communist East Germany, where he worked at a clinic in East Berlin beginning in 1950 (Roivanen, 2009). Little is known about this time in Wartegg's life, given his lack of contact with the West due to socio-political factors. It is known that he was married and was father to two daughters. Ehrig Wartegg retired in 1960, and died in 1983. As recounted by Fontana (2013), Wartegg's biographer, Peter Klemperer, recalled a meeting with him in 1957 or 1958:

> In winter 1957 or 1958, he was a short, old man, and he met me in a housecoat and slippers, but with a beautiful smile. We sat down and he offered me a cup of tea, smoking a cigar. I asked him if I could complete a didactic analysis with him. He was surprised by my request, as he was not a didactic analyst. He was not even a member of a psychoanalytic society. He told me immediately that I should tell him the details of my story, and should be administered the Wartegg. I agreed. And then we saw each other regularly once a week until 1960.
>
> (translated, p. 33)

The Ganzheit Psychological Framework—Wartegg's Theory of Personality

The system created by Ehrig Wartegg to score and interpret the WDCT appears to combine his interest in modern art with his training in Gestalt psychology. He specifically drew influence from the Ganzheit School of psychology as theorized by Felix Kreuger and Freidrich Sander at the University of Leipzig, referred to as the Psychology of Totality. As described in Roivanen (2009):

> According to Rosenthal (2004, 221–243), the Ganzheit School shared some of the basic tenets of Gestalt theory that were established by the Berlin school, as well as its phenomenological orientation. However, they focused on the detailed temporal dynamics of psychological processes, and on the categorical character of meaning and perception. Furthermore, the Ganzheit school postulated that perceptual experience is directly meaning-laden and intrinsically emotional, and that forms are inherently semantic and value laden.
>
> (p. 60)

Kinget (1952) further discussed the Theory of Totality, writing;

> According to "Ganzheit Psychologie" it is assumed that not only the object of experience but also the experiencing *subject* is to be conceived as a "structure." This structure is made up of a set of orientations and dispositions of a specific, dynamic nature which tend essentially toward "form-giving," that is, toward organizing whatever is afforded to experience. The supreme binding and all-pervading factor within the structure is emotion; it governs at any moment the configuration of the form-giving tendencies and determines the setting or significance of every element of experience. Experience thus being, as it were, molded by the individual structure, it follows that experience necessarily bears the marks of that structure; it must, therefore, be possible to infer the characteristics of the latter from those of the former.
>
> (p. 3)

Based upon these principles, Freidrich Sander (1962) developed an experimental method entitled the *Phantasie Test*. Described by Kinget (1952) as a precursor to the WDCT, Sander provided a form with "irregularly disposed lines which were to be organized in a free manner" to subjects. Graphic responses were considered to reflect the subjects' structural personality characteristics, made evident through their experience of the stimuli. Given his training with Sander, and the theoretical success of the *Phantasie Test* in identifying broad differences, Wartegg applied the fundamental tenets of the Psychology of Totality (as posited by Kreuger and Sander) to the development of the WDCT. These tenets, as described by Fontana (2013), included: 1) Subjective perception is the origin of all other experiences, with perception facilitating experiential growth; 2) Understanding of human perceptions and emotions must be studied and validated with rigorous scientific methods; 3) Good research methodology must include measurement of the tangible; and 4) Much within our perceptual awareness is connected with other processes occurring at deeper layers that we are not aware of. The WDCT, therefore, can be thought of as more than a simple drawing technique. Rather, it provides an opportunity to access these "deep layers of personality" through experimental methodology that measures the tangible, but is directed toward the acknowledgment of unseen, "deep," inner contents.

Wartegg's understanding of the personality as organized by layers was further influenced by the writings of Erich Rothacker, a noted German cultural anthropologist and philosopher, who described the context of humanity as organized on physiological, neurological, and biological layers, both at the individual and collective level (Rothacker, 1952). Rothacker described a stratilogical theory of hierarchically ordered layers of personality, including layers for intellect, will, emotion, and basic temperament (Ash, 1998). The aim of the layer theory was to distinguish between developmentally recent functions of personality as compared to older, more foundational aspects of personality. Together, the interaction between the recently developed and the primitive (older) functions was thought to provide an understanding of the global personality structure. The older foundational functions were seen as influencing the development of later layers, connected to emotional–perceptual consciousness in Gestalt terms, and subconscious/unconscious processes in psychoanalytic terms (Fontana, 2013). Given Rothacker's broadening of his theory to collective societal development, leading to potential pathologizing of entire groups based upon racial characteristics by political powers at the time (Biess and Gross, 2014), stratilogical theory was contextually influential on Wartegg's work.

Wartegg was further influenced by Lersch's (1938) structural–characterological theory, elaborated in *The Structure of Character*, which was integral to the development of portions of Wartegg's initial scoring system for his measure. In Lersch's theory, character "layers" were built upon "endothymic ground," the deepest and innermost source of emotional life. As quoted by Hillman (1961), Lersch wrote of the endothymic layer:

> Here belong above all those events and states of the soul which we habitually designate as affects, emotions, feelings, moods and passions, as well as drives, desires and tendencies. They all have the characteristic of the subterranean and of intimate inwardliness . . . Self-reflection gives witness that the endothymic contents of our experience present a special layer which we describe as the endothymic ground . . . The endothymic ground is thus the deepest and innermost sphere of experience, in so far as we look at it phenomenologically. Ontologically, the organic ground of life comes first, upon which all experience rests. (P. Lersch, *Aufbau der Person*,1952).
>
> (p. 91)

In considering layers of personality, and avoiding the perception of psychoanalytic foundations to his measure, Wartegg described the WDCT as an "experimental visual-graphic test." He elaborated several tenets of this graphoscopic technique, reviewed by Fontana (2013), including: 1) Conditions of the presented stimuli reflect and recall external reality; 2) Individual elaboration is made by the subject via drawing, linking graphic production with deeper layers of personality; 3) The personality type and structure of the client is evident via their response to the stimuli and approach to the drawings; 4) Meaning attributed to the drawings by subjects is a similar process to free association common to Freudian theory and psychoanalytic intervention; and 5) Different psychological types impact the reaction to the stimuli and determine creativity.

In developing the WDCT, and given the political climate of the time, Wartegg relied heavily on Sander's theory in his published thesis, *Gestaltung and Charakter* (Wartegg, 1939). Translated, Wartegg's thesis, *The Formation of Gestalts and Personality*, studied three personality types proposed by Sander via the WDCT: the analytical *A-type*, the synthesizing *S-type*, and the analytical-synthesizing *AS-type* (Kinget, 1952). As summarized by Roivanen (2009), Wartegg initially described differences in the process of drawing for each of the three personality types, later acknowledging that a more detailed understanding of personality is required for useful application of the measure. Wartegg expanded Sander's three formal personality types by integrating psychological content and interpretation. As described by Kinget (1952), Sander's synthesizing *S-type* became the *vital-emotional type*, described by Wartegg as determined by unconscious drives and elements, and characterized by a predominance of emotion and creativity. Sander's analytical *A-type* was described by Wartegg as the *rational-volitional type*, characterized by a predominance of analysis, thinking, cognitive function, and control. Lastly, Sander's *AS-type* evolved into Wartegg's *integrated type*, effectively balancing the characteristics of the other types, yielding personality integration and adaptive functioning.

Wartegg later expanded his description of personality further, positing a "four-dimensional schema [of personality] composed of more traditionally recognized basic functions: emotion, imagination, intellectual, and activity" (Wartegg, 1939, pp. 254–256; in Roivanen, 2009, p. 62). Each personality function was subsequently split into dyads of opposing characteristics: Emotion (Outgoing vs. Seclusive); Imagination (Combining vs. Creative); Intellect (Practical vs. Speculative); and Will (Dynamic vs. Controlled) (Kinget, 1952). Kinget later adopted this schema for her exploration of the WDCT, although modified the term "Will" to "Activity" in reflection of then current trends in psychological language and conceptualization.

Finally, in considering Wartegg's approach to personality understanding and evaluation, it should be noted that he discussed the Rorschach Inkblot Method in his thesis, drawing parallels between the technique and the contents elicited by the WDCT (Fontana, 2013). While avoiding psychoanalytic terms, Wartegg applied stratilogical theory to his discussion of the Rorschach and WDCT, referring to the "visualization of deep layers" within the personality, accessed through these assessment measures. While never referring to his technique as "projective" (Roivanen, 2009), Wartegg theorized that a subject's individual (ontogenetic) and collective (phylogenetic) development and experiences manifest in the completed drawing on the WDCT, reflecting an image full of experience that originates in the depth of personality. Through completion of the WDCT, and the subsequent verbalization of drawing content, the image emerges from the depths, reaching a level of personal awareness and meaning (Fontana, 2013).

Wartegg's Original Scoring System (1939)

To capture the complexities of personality typology and stratilogical personality theory, Ehrig Wartegg developed a complex and cumbersome system, by modern standards, for scoring and interpreting the WDCT. As stated by Fontana (2012), "The rules proposed by Wartegg for a numeric formal evaluation are very complicated and numerous, so almost no one uses them anymore" (p. 56). Similarly, Mattlar (2005) stated, referring to his original methodology for the WDCT: "The use of the test based on that created by Ehrig Wartegg—a very popular approach in the thirties and forties—is now abandoned since it does not work."

Wartegg's system of scoring (Wartegg, 1939) consisted of five general domains, each producing personality-related information, but typically considered qualitative (rather than quantitative). Within each domain, different elements of the produced drawings and examinees' approach to the drawings were considered and noted. Overall notations were interpreted qualitatively, considering each of the five evaluated domains as related to theoretical expectations. The five domains evaluated, each with their own tabular scoring system, included:

1. *Succession of Drawings*: In this domain, the order of sequence followed by examinees was noted, as compared to Wartegg's theoretical expectations for order of completion; that is, the examiner noted the order in which the examinee completed the boxes of the test. Per his writings, Boxes 1, 2, 3, and 8 were expected to occur within the first half of the test, whereas Boxes 4, 5, 6, and 7 were expected to occur within the second half of the test. In cases where the produced order differed from the expected pattern, notations were made related to advanced or delayed boxes. A sample scoring grid for the first domain of Wartegg's scoring system is provided in Figure 1.2.

2. *Stratigraphic Profile*: Based upon stratilogical ("layer") theory of personality, Wartegg posited eight developmental stages of graphic production that relate to the layers of personality formation. That is, earlier, more primitive layers are represented by less integration of the test stimuli, whereas later, more developed/functional layers are reflected by integration of the test stimulus, attributed meaning, and personalized projection. Performance on each test box was evaluated as to the developmental stage (I–VIII) of the drawing, with personality development and structure extrapolated from this.

   Each layer of graphic stage was divided into three sub-categories, generally measured by graphic indicators that identify the drawing as belonging to that level. For example, scribbling and blackening of the stimulus mark were considered as indicative of the first level of development. Failure to draw, understood as inhibition of impulses, was characteristic of the second stage. The third stage demonstrates response to the stimulus, generally without attributed meaning. The fourth stage is suggested by repetition and integration of the stimulus, similarly without clear meaning. The fifth and

1. Bildabfolge und Zeit

Reihenfolge:	1.	2.	3.	4.	5.	6.	7.	8.
Bild Nr.:								
Vershiebung +/–:								
Ausführungszeif (Minufen):								

FIGURE 1.2 Wartegg Scoring System (Wartegg, 1939)—1. Succession of Drawings.
Figure 1.2 provides a sample copy of the first domain of Ehrig Wartegg's original scoring system.

Source: Wartegg, E. (1953), *Schichtdiagnostik—Der Zeichentest (WZT)*, Hogrefe, Verlag für Psychologie.

sixth phases of development are indicated by increasing integration, whereas when a drawing reaches the seventh stage, clear meaning related to the examinees' experience is attributed. Lastly, the eighth stage elaborates motives and experiences via graphic drawing production.

As can be imagined, examining each response against a hierarchical 24-point developmental model required both time and attention. The resulting "stratigraphic profile" provided information regarding the examinees' graphic representation of internalized experiences, as well as the rationality of the approach an individual takes in interacting with the environment and reality. While this level of analysis provides the clinician with a starting point of understanding personality structure, more emphasis was placed on the qualitative profile, described below. A sample scoring grid for the second domain of Wartegg's scoring system is provided in Figure 1.3.

3. *Qualitative Profile*: The third of five domains evaluated by Wartegg's scoring system focuses on the degree of consistency between produced drawings and expected characteristics associated with each of the stimulus marks (or the evocative nature of the marks, based in Gestalt theory). For this reason, each box was examined against a specific set of criteria for that mark, with significant differences in evaluation existing between boxes. Specific criteria for "adequate quality" and "inadequate quality" were developed for each box, including the quality of the integration of the mark, the graphic nature of the drawing, and the content or meaning inherent to the box.

   For purposes of illustration, in considering Box 1, the evaluator rates the client's drawing as adequate in terms of stimulus quality (integration), expressive (graphic) quality, and meaning (content). Adequate integration is suggested in Box 1 via small, centered, and concentrated drawings, whereas

2. Schichtprofil

	I				II		III			IV			V				VI			VII			VIII					
	Rü	üb	kr	gs	ub	le	eg	eb	zg	gh	as	tö	Zn	Rn	Rp	gt	Rv	sy	fg	di	id	is	N+	N–	Np	O+	O–	Op
1																												
2																												
3																												
4																												
5																												
6																												
7																												
8																												

SAMPLE SAMPLE SAMPLE SAMPLE SAMPLE SAMPLE SAMPLE SAMPLE SAMPLE SAMPLE SAMPLE SAMPLE

SAMPLE SAMPLE SAMPLE SAMPLE SAMPLE SAMPLE SAMPLE SAMPLE SAMPLE SAMPLE SAMPLE SAMPLE

FIGURE 1.3 Wartegg Scoring System (Wartegg, 1939)—2. Stratigraphic Profile.

Figure 1.3 provides a sample copy of the second domain of Ehrig Wartegg's original scoring system.

Source: Wartegg, E. (1953), *Schichtdiagnostik—Der Zeichentest (WZT)*, Hogrefe, Verlag für Psychologie.

3. Qualitätenprofil

1		2		3		4		5		6		7		8	
+	–	+	–	+	–	+	–	+	–	+	–	+	–	+	–
kln	vgr	geb	ger	ger	geb	kln	vgr	ger	geb	ger	geg	kln	vgr	geb	ger
mit	vig	ott	ges	ster	falb	dkl	hell	vbnd	gtr	vbnd	gtr	bgr	vbr	agrd	abgs
konz	vstr	weit	eng	weit	eng	eck	rund	lgs	quer	ggl	ugl	ggl	ugl	ges	off
zrt	drb	vbr	bgr	ggl	ugl	bgr	vbr	rafw	labw	mit	vlg	zrt	drb	zrt	drb
stra	asw	lock	fest	stet	wchs	schw	lcht	dchz	awch	rml	flä	lock	fest	berg	bdro
org	mech	org	mech	ualf	übst	berg	bdro	fest	lack	mech	org	org	mech	org	mech
sta	dyn	dyn	sta	mech	org	sta	dyn	mech	org	sta	dyn	schn	abst	sta	dyn
phys	abst	phys	abst	sta	dyn	sach	phan	dyn	sta	abst	phys	phys	dyn	phys	abst

Qualitative Dominante:

Qualitatives Polverhältnis:

FIGURE 1.4 Wartegg Scoring System (Wartegg, 1939)—3. Qualitative Profile.

Figure 1.4 provides a sample copy of the third domain of Ehrig Wartegg's original scoring system.

Source: Wartegg, E. (1953), *Schichtdiagnostik—Der Zeichentest (WZT)*, Hogrefe, Verlag für Psychologie.

inadequate integration is noted through large, non-centered, and dispersed drawings. Adequate graphic quality is scored for drawings that are delicate and consistent, whereas unrefined and inconsistent drawings are considered inadequate. In terms of content meaning for Box 1, organic, stable, and natural content is considered adequate, whereas mechanical, dynamic, and abstract contents are considered inadequate.

In this manner, the drawing in each box is classified as adequate or inadequate, with two protocol-level mathematical indices calculated. The Qualitative Ratio (QR) represents the ratio of adequate to inadequate quality of drawings, thought by Wartegg to represent personality integration and maturation. The more integrated and mature the individual, the higher the ratio of adequate to inadequate quality would be evident. A second ratio, Quality Value (DomQ), was based upon the frequency or commonality of depicted drawings (frequent drawings/infrequent drawings). This ratio, per Wartegg, allowed evaluation of specific traits of personality depending on value and location of produced frequent drawings. A sample scoring grid for the third domain of Wartegg's scoring system is provided in Figure 1.4.

4. *Structure of Boxes*: In the fourth area of evaluation, structural elements of personality, as indicated by the presence of special phenomena, were noted. These phenomena, including perseverative tendencies, personal associations, divergence from the expected order of box completion, and adequate versus inadequate integration within each box were noted. Again, the presence of special structural phenomena was qualitatively analyzed by box, to determine personality difficulties within that area. A sample scoring grid for the fourth domain of Wartegg's scoring system is provided in Figure 1.5.

4. Bildgefüge

	Bild Nr.:	1	2	3	4	5	6	7	8	
Perseveration	Einzelperseveration									
	Eihenperseveration									
Assoziation	Einzelassoziation									
	Reihenassaziation									
Verlagerung	Reizverlagerung									
	Motivverlagerung									
Ergänzung	Adäquate Ergänzung									
	Inadäquate Ergänzuna									

FIGURE 1.5 Wartegg Scoring System (Wartegg, 1939)—4. Structure of Boxes.

Figure 1.5 provides a sample copy of the fourth domain of Ehrig Wartegg's original scoring system.

Source: Wartegg, E. (1953), *Schichtdiagnostik—Der Zeichentest* (*WZT*), Hogrefe, Verlag für Psychologie. Please note that this test form is only a sample. Any kind of reproduction is strictly forbidden. A valid test result can only be obtained by a professionally qualified test administrator and using the original test materials. The test material can only be ordered at the Hogrefe Publishing Group (www.hogrefe.com). For any questions, please contact rights@hogrefe.com.

5. Charakterologische Projektion der Darstellungs- und Sinnakzente

	Bild Nr.:	1	2	3	4	5	6	7	8	Strukturelles Gefüge
D	druckbreit—talgig, voll, geschwärzt									**Tr**
S	dynamisch—dramatisch: diffus—spielerisch—elementar, vital, tierhaft—derb, erotisch, phantastisch, abenteuerlich									
D	druckschwach—dünn—zart, leer, gentänt									**E**
S	stimmungsmäßig, atmosphärisch, pflanzenhalt, teirhaft—idyllisch, spielerisch									
D	groß, rund, gelockert, weif, raumlian—diffus, asymmetrisch									**A**
S	landschaftlich, physiognomisch—ganzheitlich, sozial befont, heiter									
D	klein, eng, geschlossen—gesammelt, fein-gliedrig									**I**
S	idyllisch—intim, physiognomisch—teilhaft, maskenhaft; ernst, märchenhaft, symbolisch, ornamenta—symbolisch, gemütsbefont									
D	aeffiällig übersteigert									
S	physiognomisch—geltungsbetont, schmuck-haft, sensationell, ornamental—dekorativ									**Gt**
S	symbolisch oder physiognomisch idealisierend, romantisch, kultisch									**Id**
D	druckfest—gerade—gerichtet									**W**
D	dynamisch—dramatisch: leistungsbetont									
D	druckfest—gerade—geschlossen—konturiert									**W**
S	statisch tenazitativ, halftungsbetont									
D	gerade—eckig—symmetrisch									**N**
S	stofflich, dinglich, architektonisch, schematisch									
D	sorgfältig, schraffiert, gegliedert, räumlich-perspektivisch									**G**
S	abstrakt, ornamental-abstrakt									
D	geschlossen—konzentriert, räumlich oder stilistirch präzisiert									**Gs**
S	vulgär—allgemein, schlagwortartig, reklame artig, karrikiert, formal, konventionell									**Ka, Fa**
S	eigenwillig—verschroben stilistisch—eigenschöpferisch									**Or**
	Punktzahl der Einzelbilder:									
	Gesamtpunktzahl:									**Gefügezeichen**

FIGURE 1.6 Wartegg Scoring System (Wartegg, 1939)—5. Characterological Profile.
Figure 1.6 provides a sample copy of the fifth domain of Ehrig Wartegg's original scoring system.

Source: Wartegg, E. (1953), *Schichtdiagnostik—Der Zeichentest (WZT)*, Hogrefe, Verlag für Psychologie.

5. *Characterological Profile*: Based on a structural personality theory of characterological layers proposed by Lersch (1938), the last domain of evaluation utilized both graphic and content indicators to arrive at a diagnostic interpretation of personality functioning. Similar to the Qualitative Profile, specific graphic and content markers were developed for each mark, resulting in a three-tiered evaluation system reflecting development and integration in the associated area of personality. Each drawing was evaluated against 22 specific criteria, established via stimulus-specific statistical tables. From this evaluation, interpretation was made regarding moods, feelings, affect, and drives, considered against a structural theory of personality. A sample scoring grid for the fifth domain of Wartegg's scoring system is provided in Figure 1.6.

Following completion of these five layers of analysis, overall qualitative interpretation was recommended by Wartegg, in attempts to understand the individual globally. With that in mind, each protocol was examined first on the basis of the formal evaluation and scoring (described above), second at the "expressive level" evidenced through quality of drawings and use of artistic medium, and third at the "analytical level" as suggested by interpretation of projected content (Fontana, 2012). In this manner, Wartegg's original system can be understood as both quantitatively and qualitatively based.

Socio-Political Factors Preventing Widespread Use of the WDCT

While Fontana (2013) refers to Ehrig Wartegg as a "pioneer" in the measurement of personality, he further notes that the WDCT has been largely "forgotten" since its development. Similarly, Crisi (2010), and Crisi and Palm (2016), refer to the WDCT as "the forgotten test," citing both socio-political and practical reasons for the WDCT's limited use outside of several geographic regions. Fontana (2013) and Roivanen (2009) list political influences and censorship on the work of Wartegg, as well as scientific bias against psychoanalytic theory at the time of test development, as contributing reasons for the WDCT's limited geographic use. These factors strongly influenced Wartegg's development of the measure, as well as the subsequent spread of the WDCT.

As biographers have noted, throughout his life, Wartegg demonstrated interest in psychoanalytic theories, studying and practicing psychoanalysis in the 1920s, engaging in his own analysis at several times throughout his life, communicating with Sigmund Freud regarding possible connectivity between analytic and Gestalt theories, and later in life returning to the practice of psychoanalysis in communist East Germany (against the official policy of the government). Socio-politically, given the time period and location in which Wartegg developed his measure, psychoanalysis and psychoanalytic theories were labeled as "non-scientific ideology," with clinicians who practiced these measures marginalized, terminated from academic positions, and ostracized by the scientific community. During the rise of Nazism in Germany in the 1930s, psychoanalysis was thought of negatively as "non-Arian ideology," and later in Wartegg's life in communistic East

Germany, analysis was further maligned due to its "American ideology" (Fontana, 2013). In both locations and contexts, Wartegg was unable to write about or promote the WDCT as having strong analytic foundations.

In reviewing Wartegg's writings, it appears likely that Wartegg thought about the WDCT in psychoanalytic terms, but wrote about the WDCT using Ganzheit terminology. As Fontana (2013) notes, the text is written in such a specific manner, one doesn't immediately grasp how much is based on psychoanalytic theory. Moreover, per Roivanen (2009), the majority of authors cited in Wartegg's thesis are Ganzheit scholars, stating:

> It is clear that political factors had a strong effect on Wartegg's writings. It is more difficult to judge to what extent his publications reflected his actual thoughts. Wartegg's censorship of psychoanalytic ideas from his thesis obviously did not reflect his real thinking.
>
> (p. 62)

Following the Second World War, when many European psychologists relocated to the United States, England, or Switzerland, interest in psychoanalysis again began to rise; however, for Wartegg, located in East Germany, few opportunities presented themselves. Forced to adopt Pavlovian psychology, deemed "ideologically correct" by Stalin, Wartegg "almost completely abandons his previous Ganzheit psychological ideas and tries to formulate a theoretical basis for the drawing test, combing 'Pavlovian sensory-physiological reflexology' with elements of depth psychology" (Wartegg, 1953; in Roivanen, 2009, p. 64). Wartegg's contact with international colleagues was further limited until his retirement in 1960. Despite this, the WDCT grew in use and reputation abroad, with an international conference devoted to the WDCT held in Switzerland (1947), attended by English, French, Swiss, Dutch, and Swedish clinicians. Following this conference, research began, promoted by translations of Wartegg's work into several languages; however, as Fontana (2013) points out, Wartegg's original technique began to lose comprehensiveness as the method spread throughout Europe, oftentimes due to inaccurate or incomplete translations.

Kinget's English WDCT Scoring System (1952)

In the United States, G. Marian Kinget built upon Wartegg's original scoring system in her 1952 text, based upon research with 383 normative subjects who were administered the WDCT concurrently with other measures, resulting in "an average of about 500 information points per subject" (Kinget, p. xiii). Kinget further conducted research with small samples of psychiatric patients, comparing their performance on the test to the normative sample to better understand characterological differences between groups. Designed as a "practical" system to understand the structure of personality, Kinget clarified, however, that the examination of psychopathology was not the initial goal of her work; rather, she acknowledged that practical use of the system in applied settings will likely focus on psychopathology. Acknowledging that no personality measurement technique can fully explain personality, Kinget wrote about her method for the WDCT:

> Its primary aim is to explore the structure of personality in terms of what are often called "basic functions," such as emotion, imagination, dynamism, control, reality-function, encountered in all human beings but with different intensity and with different interrelations. This structure is not static but changeable in varying degrees, and it determines to a large extent the individual's behavior. Consequently, a technique which explores the *structure* of personality provides at the same time insights into its *functioning*, whether normal or abnormal. Indeed, when one or several components strongly dominate, the structure is unbalanced and the subject's functioning is defective. When his emotional control function is overdeveloped, his behavior appears inhibited; when his imagination and ideation are excessively developed, his contact with reality and his social functioning may be impaired to the extent of suggesting serious disturbance.
>
> (p. xi)

With that aim, Kinget designed a system relying on the "language of drawings," a language free from the distorting influences of verbal communication, but more difficult to understand and evaluate. Kinget further elaborated that while most evaluative systems of drawing focused solely on *content*, to fully understand the interpretive language of drawing, one must also analyze *execution* of drawings (Kinget, 1952). Studying execution of single graphic elements for each box of the WDCT (for example, pressure, shading, size), Kinget noted that these elements had only previously been studied at the aggregate (or protocol) level. When taken as individual markers, more data points became available, and greater interpretive value resulted.

As mentioned above, Kinget drew from Wartegg's initial four-dimensional schema of personality organization (i.e., Emotion, Imagination, Intellect, Activity) in the development of her research, although noted this schema has "only typological value," limiting understanding of the individual to the broadest of interpretations until specific characteristics of personality have been linked with test results. To validate the WDCT in relation to this schema, Kinget reviewed the published illustrations in Wartegg's original thesis (1939), clarifying and formalizing specific scoring characteristics based on graphic qualities of drawings. Once a formal scoring system was developed, she compared WDCT test results to several other measures, including both forced-choice self-reports and clinician ratings to validate interpretive findings. Scores were considered at the aggregate level, by clusters presumed to associate with typological characteristics, and lastly at the individual level. Based upon results, Kinget proposed modification to her system, allowing for greater understanding at the individual level, as opposed to the typological level. Kinget acknowledged that her methodological procedures "however elaborate and lengthy, are far from realizing the scientific ideal of rigorous determination and treatment. However, they seem to represent the optimum procedure practicable to date" (p. 24).

In considering the structured administration and elaborate scoring system clarified by Kinget, only a summary will be presented here. Similar to Wartegg's original work, although somewhat simplified, three approaches to WDCT evaluation are suggested by Kinget (1952):

1. Symbolic connection of the drawings in relationship to the specific qualities evoked by the stimulus. Referred to by Kinget as "Stimulus-Drawing Relation," this evaluative aspect captures the participant's perceptive-associative processes, describing the affinity for the character of each stimulus. In Kinget's system, each stimulus (that is, each box), as originally described by Wartegg, was evaluated based upon the participant's indifference toward the stimulus, adaptation to the demands of the stimulus, or emphasis of the stimulus. Moreover, based upon Wartegg's original hypotheses regarding masculine boxes (referred to as *technical-constructive* boxes by Kinget) and feminine boxes (referred to as *organic* boxes by Kinget), particular attention was paid to the order in which individuals completed these boxes, whether they demonstrated preference for one group over the other, and whether their scores (based upon indifference, adaptation, and emphasis) differed significantly between groups.
2. Content evaluation of the drawing, or "what is drawn." This evaluative domain, per Kinget, captures the associative–projective elements inherent in the WDCT. Content was evaluated quantitatively based upon the client's produced drawings. Three categories were elaborated by Kinget, including 1) Scribblings (divided into motor, esthetic, or symbolic); 2) Abstractions (subtyped as symmetrical decorative, asymmetrical decorative, or technical); and 3) Pictures (with differentiation made between Realistic pictures, including natural or object phenomena, and Fantasy-based pictures). In this last Picture category, further scoring was undertaken based upon whether depicted content was animate or inanimate, utility and style of objects drawn, and elaboration, fantastical quality, or symbolism of fantasy drawings.
3. Execution, or "how is the thing drawn?" Per Kinget, this evaluative domain captures the active–expressive and fundamental characteristics of an individual's personality, including their patterns of reactivity, interests, and tendencies. Formal characteristics of the drawings were evaluated on several levels, based on graphic characteristics of produced test responses: 1) Quality of drawn lines, including pressure (strong, soft reinforced), type (straight, curved), and stroke (continuous, discontinuous); 2) "Covering" or use of available space provided by each test box (scant, full, expanded, constricted); 3) Shading (dark, light); and 4) Composition. The last evaluative characteristic, Composition, was composed of ten subsections, including: whole vs. part; context vs. isolation; level of detail; level of closure and orientation; repetition vs. variety; carefulness vs. casualness; movement; originality vs.

CRITERIA		Total Score	Drawings								Drawings								Total Score	CRITERIA	
			1	2	3	4	5	6	7	8	1	2	3	4	5	6	7				
NATURE	Animate																			Fancy	FANTASY
	Physiognomy																			Phantasm	
	Inanimate																			Symbolism	
	Atmosphere																			Original	
OBJECTS	Utility																			Symmetric	ABSTRACT
	Ornaments																			Asymetric	
Style																				Technical	
Movement																				Careful	
COVERAGE	Full																			Casual	
	Empty																			Light	SHADING
	Expanded																			Dark	
	Constricted																			Orientation	
Organization																				Closure	
Detail																				Parts	
LINES	Curved																			Scribbles	
	Straight																			Duplication	
	Strong																			Repetition	
	Soft																			Schematism	

SCORING BLANK

FIGURE 1.7 Kinget Scoring System (Kinget, 1952)—Scoring Blank.

Figure 1.7 provides a sample "Scoring Blank" developed by G. Marian Kinget for use with the Wartegg Drawing Completion Test.

Source: Reprinted with permission from: Kinget, G. M. (1952). *The Drawing-Completion Test: A projective technique for the investigation of personality*. New York: Grune & Stratton, p. 118.

Anim. Phys	Ina. Atm. Sof.	Phys. Orna.	Expa. FAN.	OBJECTS	Organized	Anim. Mov	Emp. Con. Strai.
Expan. Curv.	Sy. As. SHA. Po.	Styl. Organ.	Orig. Asy.	Detail	Technical	Ful. Strong	Stro. Clo. Rep
Casual	Scri. Sche.	Symmetr.	Dark			Dark, Orie.	Duplic. Caz.
Open	Seclusive	Combinative	Creative	Practical	Speculative	Dynamic	Controlled
EMOTION		IMAGINATION		INTELLECT		ACTIVITY	

INTERPRETATION BLANK

FIGURE 1.8 Kinget Scoring System (Kinget, 1952)—Interpretation Blank.

Figure 1.8 provides a sample "Interpretation Blank" developed by G. Marian Kinget for use with the Wartegg Drawing Completion Test.

Source: Reprinted with permission from: Kinget, G. M. (1952). *The Drawing-Completion Test: A projective technique for the investigation of personality*. New York: Grune & Stratton, p. 118.

popularity; clearness vs. vagueness; and consistency vs. inconsistency. While the majority of formal characteristics were evaluated quantitatively, some (due to infrequency) were evaluated on a qualitative level.

Scoring, per Kinget's system was undertaken quantitatively, utilizing a "scoring blank" that captured the three levels of evaluation listed above (including all their components and subtypes) for each box of the WDCT. A copy of Kinget's Scoring Blank is provided in Figure 1.7.

In scoring, each component was evaluated on a five-point scale (noting both presence and absence, but also quality), with totals derived for each category. Sum totals were aggregated according to their theoretical relationship to personality typology and characteristic, and subsequently plotted on an "Interpretation Blank" (see Figure 1.8), resulting in a structural personality profile as related to Wartegg's four-dimensional schema: Emotion (Outgoing vs. Seclusive), Imagination (Combining vs. Creative), Intellect (Practical vs. Speculative), and Activity (Dynamic vs. Controlled). The profile was subsequently analyzed, followed by consideration of personal factors (age, gender), evaluation of the order in which the boxes were completed, noted absent scoring categories, and qualitative observations. In this manner, per Kinget, a full understanding of the individual was afforded.

Additional Interpretive Systems for the Wartegg Drawing Completion Test

While Kinget's (1952) interpretive system was derived from Wartegg's original scoring system, significant divergence was evident, particularly in post-hoc modification of her system. Further, as noted previously, Kinget's system never gained traction or significant use in the United States or elsewhere.

Since Ehrig Wartegg developed the WDCT, several other scoring and interpretive systems have been developed, with varied research findings. In response to this issue, Soilevuo Grønnerød and Grønnerød (2012) published a comprehensive meta-analysis on the Wartegg test. The authors first draw differentiation between two schools of thought related to Wartegg interpretation: "the analytical systems of interpretation that see the printed signs as visual stimuli" and "dynamic systems which argue the printed signs have certain symbolic meaning representing certain areas of individual psychology" (Soilevuo Grønnerød and Grønnerød, 2012, p. 476). Of these two schools of thought, the CWS belongs to the latter. The authors assert that little published research exists regarding the reliability and validity of either type of interpretive system (i.e., analytical or dynamic), although specifically point to the dynamic models as lacking empirical verification (Tamminen & Lindeman, 2000, as cited in Soilevuo Grønnerød and Grønnerød, 2012). A scattered historical development of the Wartegg—across countries, psychological theories of personality, setting and usage, and assessment traditions were hypothesized to account for this perceived lack of clinical research.

Based upon these varied historical traditions, a second challenge in evaluating previously conducted Wartegg research was elaborated; that is, interpretation systems vary widely between authors. Some, including Erich Wartegg's original scoring methodology, emphasize qualitative interpretation. Others, including Kinget's (1952) efforts to bring the Wartegg to the United States, as well as the current CWS interpretive system, emphasize quantitative analysis. These differences, between not only scoring methodology, but also definitions of interpretive categories, result in challenges comparing results between authors and interpretive traditions (Soilevuo Grønnerød and Grønnerød, 2012). Further, while used throughout the world (including Brazil, Finland, Italy, Switzerland, Germany, Japan, Sweden, Spain, France, Argentina, Uruguay, Israel, Croatia, the Netherlands, and Indonesia, as cited in Soilevuo Grønnerød and Grønnerød, 2012), the authors assert that various interpretive systems have developed in isolation, with little contact between system developers and researchers. This lack of communication has resulted in difficulties locating and accessing published research on the test, as well as reduced the perception of empirical support for its continued clinical use. As stated by the authors, "Practicing psychologists, on the other hand, argue for the practical value of the method they feel they experience in their everyday work (Heiska, 2005; Kosonen, 1999)" (Soilevuo Grønnerød and Grønnerød, 2012, p. 481).

As noted by Roivanen (2009), a long-standing tradition of WDCT use, beginning in 1953 (Takala & Hakkarainen), and continuing to the present exists in Finland. Gardziella (1985) developed an interpretation method largely similar to Wartegg's original methodology, while also including suggested modifications by Kinget (1952) and Lossen and Schott (1952). This methodology, based upon the author's extensive clinical experience, operationalized personality characteristics based upon graphic qualities and contents of produced drawings. For example, as summarized by Mattlar (2015), who has facilitated trainings in the Gardziella system widely throughout Finland and Sweden: degree of line pressure indicates vitality; length of drawing time relates to spontaneity; frequency of popular responses indicates adaptability and conventionality; size of drawings relates to expansiveness and the need for containment; carefulness and specificity of drawings indicates self-control; drawing order and perseveration may indicate compulsiveness; linearity and contra-linearity may related to oppositionality; definitive use of the stimuli indicate ego strength; content and containment within the border of the boxes may relate to aggressivity and paranoia; organic content in Boxes 2 and 7 related to socialization, and many others. Using the Gardziella system, the client is further administered the WDCT twice in succession, the second time capturing the client's performance under conditions of stress, a major difference from the CWS. Additional differences, noted by Crisi during interview with The Wartegg Info Blog in 2013, include the CWS reliance on both graphic quality and client verbalization, a novel modification to most Wartegg systems relying only on drawings. Per Crisi, "In my scoring system, psychologists must score what their clients see in the signs and in their drawings. In this way, the scoring system becomes sensitive to detecting thinking disorders.

Psychologists should evaluate their clients, not themselves" ("Increase in Wartegg Education and Networking," 2013; www.wartegg.tumblr.com).

In South America, particularly in Brazil, the WDCT is used extensively in personnel selection, based upon the work of Biedma and D'Alfonso (1960, 1973). Along with this scoring system, initially based upon the translation of Wartegg's original work but incorporating 16 boxes rather than eight, several other systems have been developed in Brazil (see Roivanen, 2009, for a review), although these more recent systems have yet to be validated conclusively.

In Germany, the WDCT is still widely used, per Roivanen (2009), with interpretation based upon clinicians' clinical experience and Wartegg's originally published work. While contemporary authors have published new interpretation guidelines, it was noted that (similar to Brazilian systems), these guidelines have not conclusively been validated.

In Japan, as described by Murakami (2005), the Wartegg was introduced in the 1960s, with clinical cases published by several Japanese clinicians (Atsumi, 1960; Irie, 1966). The WDCT model of assessment published by Kinget was introduced to Japan by Takuma and Atsumi (1963), and subsequently used for hospital-based psychiatric assessment of psychosis. Iwabuchi (1970) conducted data on Japanese university students, although this research ceased before collection of normative sample data. A period of reduced WDCT use followed in Japan, with renewed interest and research later evident in the 1990s. At that time, the majority of WDCT studies focused on school counseling, particularly with younger students, utilizing the Avé-Lallemant (1994) method of interpretation (see Sugiura, Katsuki, & Sukigara, 2003; Yanagi, 2001). This method of interpretation relies on collaborative discussion with the client following drawing completion, with client's verbalizations utilized to reach applicable interpretation. This method, while not considered standardized, continues to be widely used in Japan.

In Italy, Wartegg's original work was translated shortly after publication, with widespread use developing since that time. Primary work in translating, clarifying, and modifying Wartegg's system was undertaken by Scarpellini (1962, 1964) and Fontana (1984, 2012) who has also written extensively about the life of Ehrig Wartegg (2005, 2013). Given continued use and interest in the WDCT in Italy, but little statistical validation of the current interpretive methods, the development of the Crisi Wartegg System began.

Development of the Crisi Wartegg System—An Empirical Methodology for the WDCT

The methodology of the Crisi Wartegg System, described in this manual, differs significantly from that initially proposed by Ehrig Wartegg or subsequently published by Marian Kinget. While commonalities exist in the understanding of the processes of unconscious content emerging via graphic production, and subsequently reaching conscious awareness via verbalization, significant administration, scoring, and interpretation divergence exists between the systems. Given this, Crisi commented in the initial Italian precursor to this manual,

"The differences between the two methods of interpretation are so significant that we can say the only common element remaining is the form used for administering the test!" (Crisi, 2007, p. 41).

The CWS was developed in the early 1980s by Alessandro Crisi, based upon extensive clinical assessment experiences, and particularly from his experience administering the Rorschach Inkbot Test. Per Crisi:

> It was my extensive experience with administering the Rorschach that gave me the idea of creating a new methodology for the Wartegg Test that would be easier to use, more efficient, and more accessible than the original methodology; and allow a comparison between the Wartegg and the Rorschach.
>
> (Crisi, 2011b)

The methodology presented in this manual has developed through ongoing clinical study and empirical research over the past 30 years, and has demonstrated not only clinical effectiveness but also its reliability and validity as an assessment tool (for a review of research, see Chapter 2).

Given the lack of consistent research related to the WDCT, as well as variability in administration, scoring, and interpretation of the measure across settings and geographic areas, the development of the CWS was predicated on several factors:

1. *Standardization*: The CWS provides guidelines for a standardized approach to both administration and scoring. Clear administration guidelines have been set forth for administration. Moreover, the development of specific and objective scoring criteria greatly improve consistency over previous scoring systems.
2. *Statistically derived normative comparison*: CWS interpretation is based upon comparison of individually derived scores and computations to an overall normative sample, allowing for statistically derived interpretations to be generated. Comparative samples for both child/adolescent and adult groups have been developed.
3. *Ease and efficiency of use*: As compared to previous scoring systems, the CWS allows clinicians to complete comprehensive scoring and interpretation with relative ease.

With these goals in mind, the development of the CWS began in the mid-1980s at the *Istituto di Ortofonologia* of Rome, an institution that provides assessment and intervention services to children with speech and language disorders. At that time, in response to a growing population of Deaf children in Italy, the WDCT was identified as an accurate and efficient means of assessment due to its graphic nature and reduced expressive and receptive speech demands. As Crisi (1998) wrote in the original CWS manual (translated):

> Due to its structural simplicity and graphic nature, the Wartegg Test was selected. On one hand, the test resulted in immediate results and easy administration; on the other hand, it required a complex scoring process and lacked an effective theoretical model for interpretation. Thus, the idea of creating a standardized scoring system for the Wartegg that would make it quicker and easier to interpret, and would provide, at the same time, an interpretative model anchored in a solid and viable theory of personality, was born.
>
> (p. 17)

Development of the Initial CWS Scoring System

Based on his extensive clinical experience of concurrent administration of the WDCT and Rorschach (according to the 1958 Bohm system of administration), Crisi applied commonly used and previously validated scoring categories from the Rorschach Test to the creation of a formal scoring system for the WDCT—what would become the Crisi Wartegg System. The initial CWS scoring system included five scoring categories similar to indices of the same name in various Rorschach scoring systems: Form Quality, Content, Frequency (similar to Popular responses on the Rorschach), Special Scores, and Movement. Additionally, psychoanalytically derived and interpreted Impulse Responses were noted.

Over time, two additional scoring categories were added to the formal CWS scoring system, both based upon clinical observations made by Crisi during administration of the test to over 800 children (in conjunction with Rorschach tests and other measures, including Human Figure Drawing). These two new scoring categories, Evocative Character (discussed in depth in Chapter 4) and Affective Quality (Crisi, 1998, 2007), provide a new foundation for the understanding of personality as compared to previous scoring systems for the WDCT. Evocative Character in the CWS, described in different terms and qualitatively scored by Wartegg (1939) and Kinget (1952), assesses the client's resonance and affinity with each stimulus mark, including his or her ability to effectively meet the Gestalt organizational demands inherent to each mark. Facility with and gravitation to specific WDCT stimuli are understood as representative of areas of personality strength and potential conflict. While other Wartegg scholars, including Wartegg himself, have discussed this evocative nature of the stimuli (see similarities to "Card Pull" below), the CWS is the first system to formally and quantitatively score and assess Evocative Character as foundational to the understanding of personality (Crisi, 1998, 2007). Similarly, Affective Quality, which empirically captures the positive, neutral, or negative emotional valence of test drawings, provides important diagnostic (and previously unmeasured) information related to affective functioning.

As Crisi's clinical experience with the WDCT continued, additional evaluative techniques were incorporated into the CWS, based upon clinical observation and empirical research. Similar to Wartegg's early supposition that certain boxes would be completed in the first half of the test, rather than the second half, Crisi investigated the test Order of Sequence, deriving a statistical model within the normative sample (see ►Appendix B for statistical analyses) to which test protocols could be compared. Divergence from the expected (statistical) Order of Sequence was subsequently understood as related to areas of personality strength and challenge, according to a theoretical model. Moving beyond simple order of test completion, two additional modes of analysis were developed by Crisi, referred to as Analysis of Sequence 1 and Analysis of Sequence 2. Based on normative scoring, these analyses quantitatively value the drawings in each box, assigning positive, neutral, or negative "Codes," and allowing interpretation of personality functioning based upon the codes associated with each functional domain (see ►Appendix B for statistical analyses). Through research, additional evaluative indices and constellations (discussed in detail throughout this manual) enhanced the CWS, including the Wartegg Index of Psychopathology (WIP), Index of Suicidal Tendencies (IST), a Validity Index (VI), and an overall Global Assessment classification providing estimation of functional impairment.

Like any personality assessment method, the Crisi Wartegg System continues to evolve, with current clinical use and empirical research shaping understanding of test results, normative data, differences between groups, and interpretive indications. Continued research will benefit use of the test in both clinical and selection fields.

Similarities between the CWS and the Rorschach (Crisi, 2008b)

While developing the CWS, which involved concurrent administration of over 3,000 WDCT and Rorschach Tests as noted above, Crisi noted similarities between the Evocative Character of the eight Wartegg boxes and the "Card Pull" of the ten Rorschach plates. As Wartegg (1953) described the "archetypal function" of the eight WDCT stimuli, indicating internal and universal ability to evoke unconscious shared experiences, many authors have similarly discussed the properties of specific Rorschach cards that pull for thematic responses (see Aronow & Reznikoff, 1976; Frank, 1977; Johnson, 2004; Merei, 1961; Weiner, 2003).

Based upon his clinical experience, Crisi (2008b) presented initial overlap between the measures, linking each WDCT box to specific Rorschach plates based upon shared evocative function. Results of this clinical comparison are presented in Table 1.1.

Noted similarities were based upon clinical observation of the concurrently administered measures, with particular attention paid to rejected Rorschach cards that corresponded to rejected Wartegg boxes. While Crisi encouraged caution in interpreting performance according to this schema, as well as verification of any derived hypotheses through formal normative scoring systems and inter-test correlations, he asserted the clinical value of observed within-test behaviors through the lens of these evocative expectations.

TABLE 1.1 Similarities Between WDCT Boxes and Rorschach Cards

Evocative Function	*WDCT Box*	*Rorschach Card*
Self-evaluation and self-concept	1	I, IX
Femininity, female object relations, and maternal figure	2	VII, IX
Instinctual energy; adaptive functionality	3	II, VI
Masculinity, male object relations, and paternal figure	4	IV
Aggressive energies, reactions to frustration	5	II
Clarity of thought, executive functions, judgment, learning, reality testing	6	V
Libidinal energies, intimacy	7	VI, VII, III
Sociability; ability to enter into relationship with environment	8	X

Note: Paper initially presented at Society for Personality Assessment Annual Convention, 2008 (New Orleans, Louisiana).

Standardization of Administration Procedures

Having formalized scoring procedures, the CWS further standardized administration procedures for the WDCT. With some similarities noted to experimental methods discussed by Wartegg (1953) and Kinget (1952), the CWS moved beyond solely graphic production, engaging the client in verbalization of depicted content that strongly influences scoring. As Soilevuo Grønnerød noted during interview with The Wartegg Info Blog (2013), "At the first sight, this may look like the non-verbal element of the method is not fully employed. However, the risk [in purely graphic WDCT traditions] is that psychologists may lean on their own projections of what the client has drawn" ("Increase in Wartegg Education and Networking," 2013; http://wartegg.tumblr.com). In this manner, the CWS—providing a relatively unstructured graphic production phase followed by a structured verbal interaction between examinee and examiner—allows for collection of a broader data set, while avoiding projection and over-interpretation by the examiner.

In standardizing administration procedures, specific language was developed by Crisi to provide the minimum necessary direction to clients in completing the task, reducing confusion, but allowing space for individual response style, elaboration of personal experience, and externalization and projection of unconscious contents (Crisi, 1998, 2007). Specific guidelines for clinicians are provided to ensure data required for scoring is captured, while at the same time balancing the potential for undue or "leading" influence on examinees. Lastly, to maximize the efficacy of analyses of the Order of Sequence in which the Wartegg boxes were completed, a formalized method of identifying preference and affinity for boxes (known as the Test of Sequence) was developed.

Collection of the Child/Adolescent Normative Sample (1993–1996)

Between the years 1985 to 1987, Crisi and colleagues Bianchi di Castelbianco and Di Renzo systemically administered the WDCT (according to CWS guidelines) to approximately 200 children at the *Istituto di Ortofonologia* of Rome. Initially, blindly administered WDCT results were crosschecked against children with well-known clinical pictures, having participated in treatment, medical examination, undergone evaluation and diagnosis, completed family interviews, and been administered other psychodiagnostic measures including the Rorschach and Human Figure drawing (Bianchi di Castelbianco, Crisi, & Di Renzo, 1996). Subsequently, over the next several years, 800 Rorschach and WDCTs were concurrently administered, honing and refining interpretive understanding of results.

With standardization of administration instructions complete, and refined knowledge of interpretive factors and scoring categories, normative data collection was begun to provide a non-clinical comparative population with which to contextualize test results. Between 1990 and 1992, 282 participants (159 male, 123 female), aged 6 to 14, were individually administered the WDCT. These children, randomly selected from central Italy, did not demonstrate any signs of psychological or medical disorder (including behavioral difficulties), with exclusion criteria based upon teacher, physician, and school psychologist ratings.

The normative sample was divided into three age bands: 6–7 (N = 110; 68 male, 42 female); 8–10 (N = 88; 52 male, 36 female); and 11–14 (N = 84; 49 male, 35 female). Normative ranges related to Order of Sequence, Analyses of Sequence 1 and 2, and calculated Indices and Computations for the CWS were established based upon distribution within this normative sample. Statistical data related to the child/adolescent normative sample, including descriptive demographic data, and differences between age and gender groups related to indices, content scores, and Analyses of Sequence are provided in ►Appendix A.

Exploratory Evaluation of Differences between Childhood Groups (1993–1996)

In conjunction with the child/adolescent normative sample data collection described above, Crisi and colleagues began exploratory analysis of differences within the childhood groups treated at the *Istituto di Ortofonologia* of Rome. Described in further detail in Chapter 2, three groups of children (N = 306) were compared to the normative sample data: 1) Children diagnosed with specific learning disorders; 2) Children demonstrating stuttering behaviors; and 3) Deaf children, including those who were Hard of Hearing (Bianchi di Castelbianco, Crisi, & Di Renzo, 1996).

Results of this early analysis suggested that the CWS was sensitive to differences between groups, and provided a clinically rich, efficient, and non-threatening manner in which to engage previously challenging-to-assess populations (i.e., children, individuals with differing communication abilities). The CWS was viewed as a tool allowing successful interaction with various developmental states and communication abilities, resulting in more appropriate (less pathologizing), sensitive, and effective assessment.

Summary results of these initial childhood studies utilizing the CWS are provided in Chapter 2.

Publication of First Edition of Crisi Wartegg System Manual (1998)

Given the standardization and development of the CWS administration and scoring system, the first edition of the CWS manual, *Manuale del Test di Wartegg* (Crisi, 1998), was published in Italian.

Development of CWS Scoring Software Platform (1999)

Shortly after publication of the first CWS manual, Crisi developed a computer software platform, focused both on the clinical and selection fields. Publication of both the manual and software prompted a significant moment in the history of the CWS: use of the measure as a selection tool within the Italian armed forces.

Founding of the Istituto Italiano Wartegg (IIW, 1999)

To facilitate research, training, and continued development of the CWS, the Istituto Italiano Wartegg (IIW) was founded in Rome, Italy in 1999. The IIW remains the international headquarters of CWS-related activities, including training and development, research, and publication. Since its founding, based upon international interest in the CWS, representative locations of the IIW have been established in both Sweden and the United States.

Initial Selection Evaluation Completed with Italian Armed Forces (1999–2000)

Between 1999 and 2000, the Italian Navy analyzed 331 candidates with the CWS, specifically utilizing the CWS Selection software package developed by the IIW. Global Assessment ratings contained in the CWS software (including five specific criteria required by the Italian government in selection assessments) were compared both to candidate performance on other assessment questionnaires and expert ratings (approximately 87% concordance rate; Ravecca, 2003). Since that time, the CWS has been consistently utilized by several branches of the Italian armed forces, assisting with selection, candidate placement, and identification of officer candidates (Crisi, 2009). The results of this research, comparing CWS scoring to both expert raters and concurrently administered personality testing, are fully reviewed in Chapter 2.

CWS Presentations at International Conferences (1999–present)

Beginning in 1999, the CWS began gaining use throughout Italy, and eventually in other countries, largely in part due to multiple presentations at conferences and conventions, including the International Rorschach Society (ISR), the Society for Personality Assessment (SPA), and others. Since that time, over 50 paper sessions, symposia, and workshops related to the CWS have been presented at these conferences by Crisi and colleagues. While too numerous to list here, those that presented experimental research results are summarized in Chapter 2 of this manual.

CWS International Trainings (2002–present)

Following the establishment of the IIW, international trainings of the CWS began in 2002, building upon a significant number of trainings facilitated across Italy. Since 2002, specific CWS trainings have been facilitated in Sweden, Austria, Spain, Finland, Argentina, and others, as well as the presentations and conferences noted above.

Collection of Adult Normative Sample (2003–2004)

Given previously collected child/adolescent normative sample, Crisi and the IIW undertook collection of an adult normative sample from 2003–2004. With the assistance of the Italian Navy, data was collected on 2,293 adults (1,953 male, 340 female), utilizing the CWS software platform to calculate normative data ranges. Additionally, frequency of responses was evaluated, with a list of Popular responses for the normative sample generated ($N = 1{,}017$). Statistical data related to the adult normative sample, including descriptive demographic data, and differences between age and gender groups related to indices, content scores, and Analyses of Sequence are provided in ►Appendix A.

Exploratory Analysis of Wartegg's Hypotheses related to Masculinity and Femininity (2008)

Continuing his development of the CWS, Crisi sought to experimentally investigate Wartegg's initial hypotheses regarding the "maleness" and "femaleness" of the eight test boxes. Wartegg posited that the eight stimuli of the Wartegg could be divided into two groups based upon their Gestalt characteristics: Boxes 1, 2, 7, and 8 were intuitively described as feminine, given their delicate, thin, organic, curved, and vital appearance. Boxes 3, 4, 5, and 6 were conversely described as masculine, given their mechanical, rigid, linear, static, and hard appearance. As Kinget (1952) had stated in response to this original supposition by Wartegg:

> These groups are also called the feminine and the masculine groups. As they are used here, these denominations do not refer to analytical symbolism, but

simply to the commonly accepted greater affinity of women for the organic–emotional sphere and that of men for material–technical things.

(p. 37)

In examining the anecdotal clinical evidence suggested by Wartegg related to perceived gender differences in test response style, Crisi investigated these differences empirically, presenting his findings at the 19th International Rorschach Society Convention in Leuven, Belgium (2008).

Crisi (2008a)

Given Wartegg's assertion of gender differences in test response, research was conducted to investigate the merits of this hypothesis. Two studies were conducted, the first with children and the second with adults. The first experiential group was composed of 1,000 school-aged children (ages 6–10); 200 students (100 male, 100 female) from each year contained in the sample completed the CWS. If Wartegg's hypothesis related to masculinity and femininity is true, it was assumed that female participants would (on average) produce higher Evocative Character percentages in feminine boxes, and male participants would (on average) produce higher Evocative Character percentages in masculine boxes. As presented in Table 1.2, this hypothesis was confirmed for both masculine and feminine boxes in the child sample.

The same hypothesis was tested with an adult population of 680 (340 male, 340 female, aged 18–25) subjects randomly selected from a sample of adults participating in the Italian Navy Selection process. As presented in Table 1.3, statistically significant differences were again noted in the feminine boxes, whereas no statistical difference was noted in the masculine boxes.

TABLE 1.2 Mean Evocative Character (EC+%) in Masculine and Feminine CWS Boxes by Gender in Child Sample

	Gender	*N*	EC+% $\bar{x}$	*SD*	*p*
Feminine Boxes	Male	521	65.75	21.77	.0001
(1 ,2, 7, 8)	Female	482	70.95	21.31	
Masculine Boxes	Male	521	63.07	21.38	.01
(3, 4, 5, 6)	Female	482	59.52	21.65	

TABLE 1.3 Mean Evocative Character (EC+%) in Masculine and Feminine CWS Boxes by Gender in Adult Sample

	Gender	*N*	EC+% $\bar{x}$	*SD*	*p*
Feminine Boxes	Male	340	75.29	15.86	.0001
(1, 2, 7, 8)	Female	340	80.26	14.17	
Masculine Boxes	Male	340	73.01	17.90	n.s.
(3, 4, 5, 6)	Female	340	74.56	16.78	

Given these results, Crisi (2008a) suggested post-hoc that Wartegg's original hypothesis appears generally accurate, although may appear less robust in an adult sample due to societal factors and evolving sensibilities over the past six decades. That is, while it may be more acceptable for women to engage in traditionally "masculine" endeavors, it remains less societally acceptable for men to engage in traditionally "feminine" endeavors. Additionally, a potential self-selection bias was noted, given that all participants were attempting to enlist in the military, and therefore may reflect a female group more inclined than the normative sample to engage in traditionally "masculine" activities and interests.

Crisi & Chianura (2013)

Continuing examination of gender differences on the WDCT, Crisi and Chianura conducted a pilot study with 27 transgender individuals (14 male-to-female transgender individuals; 13 female-to-male transgender individuals) participating in pre-surgical evaluation and treatment at a hospital-based treatment program. Participants were administered the MMPI-2 along with the WDCT according to CWS guidelines. Given the small number of participants, and the use of test data for clinical reasons, results were considered exploratory.

Consistent with MMPI-2 data, and previous research, the male-to-female transgender population demonstrated more discomfort and potential psychological symptoms than the female-to-male or normative sample comparison groups. Specifically, more negative performance was noted in Boxes 5, 1, 4, 2, and 3 for the male-to-female transgender participants, suggesting tendencies toward rationalization, repression of affect (particularly anger), challenges in relationships, discomfort with male identity, and insecurity. Consistent with literature, female-to-male transgender participants demonstrated negative performance in Boxes 5, 6, and 7, suggesting repression of affect (again, particularly aggressive energies), discomfort with feminine identity, and tendencies toward rationalization (Crisi & Chianura, 2013).

Overall, the CWS appeared sensitive to detecting discomfort and potential symptoms in transgender individuals. Moreover, specific discomfort in gender identity and relationship to others was noted; however, given the small sample size and exploratory nature of this study, the authors encouraged caution in interpreting results, and asserted the need for further research.

Development of Italian Scoring Online System (2009)

With the aim of improving the precision and accuracy in CWS scoring procedures, thereby increasing its reliability, the IIW created an online consultation service in 2009. Referred to as "Scoring Online," users may submit specific terms (nouns or verbs) to receive guidance on the scoring of Evocative Character (by box), Affective Quality, or direction of Movement (i.e., active, passive, double, blocked, rotary). Users receive an immediate response if their submitted query is already contained in the online database. If the query is a new term, a panel of expert CWS scorers independently rates the term, with consensus results determining the scoring rule. At the present time, the Italian Scoring Online database contains over 5,000 terms.

CWS Trainings in the United States (2011–present)

Beginning in 2011 (Crisi, 2011a), the IIW began offering English-language training on the CWS to clinicians in the United States. These trainings, co-sponsored by the Society for Personality Assessment (SPA), the Center for Therapeutic Assessment, the Southern California Center for Collaborative Assessment, and the Colorado Assessment Society, have been offered consistently since that time, with participants from across the United States, Canada, Japan, Finland, and other countries. Additionally, Crisi has offered graduate-level coursework on the CWS at the University of Denver, Graduate School of Professional Psychology.

United States Adult Normative Data Collection (2012–present)

Beginning in 2012, collection of a United States adult normative sample began, co-sponsored by the Center for Therapeutic Assessment (Austin, Texas) and the Southern California Center for Collaborative Assessment (Long Beach, California). An ongoing project, initial data analysis suggests few significant differences between Italian and American normative data, with some culturally based exceptions likely in Popular responses and Affective Quality scoring. Further analysis of these differences is currently being conducted.

Swedish Normative Data Collection (2013)

Given the frequent use of the CWS in selection proceedings in Sweden, adult normative sample data was collected, beginning in 2013 (Crisi & Holm, 2013). The current normative sample consists of 218 adults (102 male, 116 female).

CWS Applications to Collaborative/Therapeutic Assessment

The CWS came to the attention of clinicians in the United States largely in part due to collaboration between Crisi and Stephen Finn, founder of the Center for Therapeutic Assessment. Having met and discussed the CWS in 2009 at the European Rorschach Association meeting in Prague, Crisi later blindly scored and interpreted a CWS profile of a client Finn was therapeutically assessing. Known as "The Case of Samuel," and later presented by Crisi at the Society for Personality Assessment Annual Convention (Boston, 2011), Finn wrote of the results:

> Not only did Dr. Crisi's interpretation fit perfectly with the results of the MMPI-2, Rorschach, and Adult Attachment Projective (AAP) I had already

> collected, Dr. Crisi also made a number of intriguing hypotheses about issues I was struggling to understand.
>
> (Finn, 2014, p. 12)

The first US-based trainings on the CWS were organized shortly thereafter, co-sponsored by the Center for Therapeutic Assessment. Subsequent presentations involving use of the CWS in Therapeutic Assessment occurred at SPA annual conventions (Crisi, 2014a; Crisi, 2012, later published: Engelman, Allyn, Crisi, Finn, Fischer, & Nakamura, 2016). The CWS has since been identified as an acceptable performance-based personality measure for certification in Therapeutic Assessment.

In considering the C/TA practice of "Extended Inquiry," a process in which clients are asked to reflect on produced test materials as related to their personal assessment questions (Finn, 2007), the CWS has been noted as especially effective given the client's direct role in the production of their drawings, the evocative nature of the stimuli, the ease of drawings in the creation of metaphor, and the simple, non-threatening nature of the test (Crisi & Palm, 2016). Additionally, given the accessibility of drawings in creating metaphor, common language, and self-understanding, CWS content easily translates to provision and discussion of test feedback both during Summary and Discussion sessions and in written format via therapeutic letters, stories, or fables. For example, in the published case of Pippa, the client wrote of a therapeutic letter written by Crisi, "I've been giving a lot of thought to the Wartegg boxes and to the letter you shared with me. I'm amazed with his assessment of my drawings and the accuracy of what he said has unfolded gradually" (Engelman et al., 2016, p. 371).

English-language Scoring Online (2015)

With the aim of improving the precision and accuracy in CWS scoring procedures, thereby increasing its reliability, the IIW created an English-language version of its online consultation service in 2015. Referred to as "Scoring Online," users may submit specific terms (nouns or verbs) to receive guidance on the scoring of Evocative Character (by box), Affective Quality, or direction of Movement (i.e., active, passive, double, blocked, rotary). Users receive an immediate response if their submitted query is already contained in the online database. If the query is a new term, a panel of expert CWS scorers independently rates the term, with consensus results determining the scoring rule.

More information on English-language Scoring Online, including instructions regarding how to register and use the service, are presented in Chapter 5.

Organization of this Manual

The current Manual for the Administration, Scoring, and Interpretation of the Crisi Wartegg System (or the CWS, as it is referred to throughout this manual) is adapted from the Italian *Manuale del Test di Wartegg* (Crisi, 1998,

2007). The current publication reflects advancements in the Crisi Wartegg System since previous versions of the manual were published, as well as additional content reflecting historical development of the test and the CWS, statistical foundations of the CWS, and re-organized and re-formatted scoring and interpretation tables to assist clinicians in using the test in clinical and selection practices. An outline of the scope of each component of this manual is provided below.

As evident from this chapter, the current manual begins with a contextual history for the Crisi Wartegg System (Chapter 1), as well as thorough review of three decades of reliability and validity research, most of which is previously unpublished in the English language (Chapter 2). The remainder of the manual provides step-by-step administration, scoring, calculation, interpretation, and conceptualization guidelines, presented in the order in which clinicians will typically utilize the measure.

Chapter 3 provides standardized administration guidelines for use of the WDCT according to the Crisi Wartegg System. Chapter 4 elaborates the Evocative Character of each of the eight boxes of the test, providing foundational review of this important diagnostic and interpretive concept. Chapter 5 reviews scoring guidelines for the eight scoring categories of the CWS, with associated scoring tables presented at the back of this manual in Appendix F for convenience. Procedures for calculating diagnostic indices, constellations, and ratios are provided in Chapter 6. Chapter 7 focuses on interpretation of individual indices as compared to expected normative ranges, and Chapter 8 reviews conceptualization and integration of derived scores to best understand the assessed individual's functional intelligence, organization of thought processes, available energy, social skills, and emotional functioning (including symptoms associated with various clinical diagnoses).

In addition, several appendices provide additional statistical information, including review of statistics related to the CWS normative samples (►Appendix A), specifically to the Order of Sequence, Analysis of Sequence 1, and Analysis of Sequence 2 (►Appendix B) and exploratory analyses conducted related to correlates of Human, Cloud, and Food contents (►Appendix C). Sample administration forms, copyrighted and reprinted with permission, are provided in Appendix D. A brief description of the CWS software platform is reviewed in ►Appendix E. Last, Appendix F presents scoring tables for each of the eight primary scoring categories contained in the CWS.

References

Aronow, E., & Reznikoff, M. (1976). *Rorschach content interpretation*. New York: Grune & Stratton.

Ash, M. G. (1998). *Gestalt psychology in German culture, 1890–1967: Holism and the quest for objectivity*. New York: Cambridge University Press.

Atsumi, M. (1960). Wartegg drawing test (WZT) as one effective means for studying personality (translated). *Psychology Research, 31*(2), 121–125.

Avé-Lallemant, U. (1994). *Der Wartegg-Zeichentest in der Lebensberatung: Mit systematischer Grundlegung von August Vetter* [The Wartegg Drawing Completion Test in counseling: With systematic foundations by August Vetter] (2nd ed.). Munich, Germany: Ernst Reinhardt Verlag.

Bernhardt, H., & Lockot, R. (2000). *Mit ohne Freud: Zur Geschichte der Psychoanalyse in Ostdeutschland* [With without Freud: On the history of psychoanalysis in East Germany]. Giessen: Psychosozial-Verlag.

Bianchi di Castelbianco, F., Crisi, A., & Di Renzo, M. (1993). *Il Test di Wartegg nell'età evolutiva* [The Wartegg Test in childhood]. Rome: Armando.

Bianchi di Castelbianco, F., Crisi, A., & Di Renzo, M. (1996). *Il test di Wartegg nell'età evolutiva. Un contributo psicodiagnostico allo studio clinico della balbuzie, della sordità e dei disturbi dell'apprendimento* [The Wartegg Test in childhood. A clinical contribution to the study of stammering, deafness, and learning disorders]. Rome, Italy: Edizioni Magi.

Biedma, C. J., & D'Alfonso, P. G. (1960). *El lenguaje del dibujo: test de Wartegg-Biedman-D'Alfonso (version modificada del test de Wartegg, traduccion de Shuji Murata)* [The language of drawing: The Wartegg-Biedman-D'Alfonso Test (modified version of the Wartegg Drawing Completion Test, translation by Shuji Murata)]. Buenos Aires: Editorial Kapelusz.

Biedma, C. J., & D'Alfonso, P. G. (1973). *A Linguagem do Desenho* [The language of drawing]. São Paulo: Mestre Jou.

Biess, F., & Gross, D. M. (Eds.). (2014). *Science and emotions after 1945: A transatlantic perspective*. Chicago, IL: University of Chicago Press.

Bohm, E. (1958). *A textbook in Rorschach diagnosis*. New York: Grune & Stratton.

Bornstein, R. F. (2007). Toward a process-based framework for classifying personality tests: Comment on Meyer and Kurtz (2006). *Journal of Personality Assessment*, 89(2), 202–207.

Buros, O. K. (1959). *Anuario Quinto de medición mental*. [The fifth mental measurements yearbook]. Highland Park, NJ: Gryphon Press.

Caviglia, G. (2005), *Il lavoro diagnostico dello psicologo clinico: teoria, strumenti, competenze* [The work of the clinical psychologist: Theory, tools, competencies]. Caserta: Edizioni Melagrana.

Complete These Drawings. (1952). *Life Magazine*, Vol. 9, pp. 65–68.

Crisi, A. (1998). *Manuale del Test di Wartegg* [Manual for the Wartegg Test]. Rome, Italy: Edizioni Magi.

Crisi, A. (2007). *Manuale del test di Wartegg*, 2nd ed. [Manual for the Wartegg Test, 2nd Edition]. Rome, Italy: Edizioni Magi.

Crisi, A. (2008a, July). *Masculinity and femininity in The Wartegg Test*. Paper presented at the meeting of the International Rorschach Society Convention, Leuven, Belgium.

Crisi, A. (2008b, July). *Rorschach and Wartegg: Two twin tests*. Paper presented at the meeting of the International Rorschach Society Convention, Leuven, Belgium.

Crisi, A. (2009). Assessment in Italy. *SPA Exchange*, *21*(1), 7, 15.

Crisi, A. (2010, July). *The forgotten test: the Wartegg Drawing Completion Test*. Workshop presented at the meeting of the Rorschach Summer Seminars, Montreux, Switzerland.

Crisi, A. (2011a, March). *Meet the Wartegg Drawing Completion Test*. Workshop presented at the meeting of the Society for Personality Assessment, Boston, MA.

Crisi, A. (2011b). *Reliability and validity of the Crisi Wartegg System*. Unpublished manuscript.

Crisi, A. (2012, March). Using the CWS in case of Pippa. In C. T. Fischer, (Chair), "*Why am I so stuck?": A Collaborative/Therapeutic Assessment Case Discussion*. Symposium presented at the meeting of the Society for Personality Assessment, Chicago, Il.

Crisi, A. (2014a, March). The case of Samuel. In S. E. Finn, (Chair), *Using the Crisi Wartegg System in Therapeutic Assessment*. Symposium presented at the meeting of the Society for Personality Assessment, Arlington, VA.

Crisi, A. (2014b). The Wartegg Drawing Completion Test: A new methodology. In L. Handler & A. D. Thomas (Eds.), *Drawings in assessment and psychotherapy: Research and application* (pp. 148–163). New York: Routledge.

Crisi, A., & Carlesimo, S. (2008, July). *The Human, Food, and Cloud Contents: Their ability to discriminate in the clinical personality assessment*. Paper presented at the meeting of the International Rorschach Society, Leuven, Belgium.

Crisi, A., & Chianura, L. (2013, March). *A pilot study on a group of 27 transgender subjects: Results of the Wartegg Drawing Completion Test*. Paper presented at the meeting of the Society for Personality Assessment Annual Convention, San Diego, CA.

Crisi, A., & Holm, M. (2013). *Preliminary normative sample for the Crisis Wartegg System in Sweden*. Unpublished manuscript.

Crisi, A., & Palm, J. A. (2016, March). *A practical overview of the Wartegg Drawing Completion Test according to the Crisi Wartegg System*. Workshop presented at the meeting of the Society for Personality Assessment, Chicago, Il.

Daini, S., Manzo, A., Pisani, F., & Tancredi, A. (2010). Attempted suicide: Psychopathology and Wartegg Test indicators. *SIS Journal of Projective Psychology & Mental Health*, *17*(2), 171–177.

Daini, S., Petrongolo, L., Manzo, A., & Bernardini, L. (2012). Personality and nursing work: A comparison between professional and student nurses. *SIS Journal of Projective Psychology & Mental Health*, *19*(1), 18–24.

Engelman, D. H., Allyn, J. B., Crisi, A., Finn, S. E., Fischer, C. T., & Nakamura, N. (2016). "Why am I so stuck?": A Collaborative/Therapeutic Assessment Case Discussion. *Journal of Personality Assessment*, 98(4), 360–373.

Falcone, A., Grasso, M., & Pinkus, L. (1986). *Presupposti teorici per l'uso clinico del test di Wartegg* [Theoretical assumptions for the clinical use of the Wartegg test]. Firenze: Organizzazioni Speciali.

Finn, S. E. (2007). *In our clients' shoes: Theory and techniques of therapeutic assessment*. Mahwah, NJ: Erlbaum.

Finn, S. E. (2014). Using the Crisi Wartegg System in therapeutic assessment. *The TA Connection*, *2*(1), 12–16.

Fontana, U. (1984). *L'Uso del test di Wartegg nella pratica clinica* [Using Wartegg's test in clinical work]. Verona: CISERP.

Fontana, U. (2005). *Una tecnica da non dimenticare. Il WZT validato e allargato per il clinico di oggi* [A method not to be forgotten. Validation of the WZT for today's clinicians]. Venice: Edizioni Quaderni ISRE.

Fontana, U. (2012). *Il Wartegg-Zeichen Test originale* [The original Wartegg Test]. Libreriauniversitaria. It Edizioni.

Fontana, U., Giacopini, N., & Giacomazzo, M. (2016). *Lavoriamo con il Wartegg Zeichen Test* [Working with the Wartegg Test]. Libreriauniversitaria. It Edizioni.

Frank, G. (1977). On validity of hypotheses derived from the Rorschach: II. Interpretation of Card IV as "father" card and Card VII as "mother" card. *Perceptual and Motor Skills*, 45(3), 991–998.

Gardziella, M. (1985). *Wartegg-piirustustesti. K.sikirja* [The Wartegg Drawing Test. A Handbook]. Jyväskylä: Psykologien Kustannus Oy.

Heiska, J. (2005). *Projektiiviset testit—kyllä vai ei*. [Projective methods—yes or no.] *Psykologi*, 2005, 23.

Hillman, J. (1961). *Emotion: A comprehensive phenomenology of theories and their meanings for therapy*. Northwestern University Press.

Horn, M., & Lockot, R. (2000). Anmerkung zu zwei Briefen von Sigmund Freud an Ehrig Wartegg [Comments on Ehrig Wartegg's two letters to Sigmund Freud]. *Mit Ohne Freud. Zur Geschichte der Psychoanalyse in Ostdeutschland*, 112–117.

Increase in Wartegg education and networking. (2013, January 15). [web log post]. *The Wartegg Info Blog*. Retrieved from: http://wartegg.tumblr.com/post/40600782594/a-translation-now-available.

Irie, K. (1966). Clinical psychiatric study on drawings of schizophrenic patients: Free drawing with the Wartegg Drawing Test: Clinical drawing therapy (translated). *Journal of the Medical Society of Toho University*, *13*(4), 217–234.

Iwabuchi, T. (1970). Wartegg-Zeichen-Test: Trial application to normal people (translated). *Juntendo University Bulletin of Letters and Science*, *13*, 63–74.

Johnson, R. A. (2004). Stimulus pull in Rorschach inkblots. *Caribbean Journal of Psychology*, *1*(1), 5–12.

Kinget, G. M. (1952). *The Drawing-Completion Test: A projective technique for the investigation of personality*. New York: Grune & Stratton.

Klemperer, P. (2000). Eine Einstimmung auf Ehrig Warteggs autobiograpische Skizze: "Zeichen der Zeit" [A match for Ehrig Wartegg's autobiographical sketch: "Drawings of time"]. In H. Bernhardt and R. Lockot (Eds.), *Mit Ohne Freud: Zur Geschichte der Psychoanalyse in Ostdeutschland* [With without Freud: On the history of psychoanalysis in East Germany] (pp. 92–94). Giessen: Psychosozial-Verlag.

Kosonen, P. (1999). Tieteen papit ja käytännön työvälineet, eli miksi Wartegg toimii? [The high priests of science and the tools of practice. Why does the Wartegg work?]. *Psykologi*, 1999, 30–31.

Lersch, P. (1938). *Der Aufbau des Charakters*. [The structure of character]. Leipzig: JA Barth.

Lockot, R. (2000). Ehrig Wartegg's Selbstverwirklichung in der Andeutung [A look at Ehrig Wartegg's self-actualization]. In H. Bernhardt & R. Lockot (Eds.), *Mit ohne Freud: Zur Geschichte der Psychoanalyse in Ostdeutschland*. [With without Freud: On the history of psychoanalysis in East Germany] (pp. 118–127). Giessen: Psychosozial-Verlag.

Lossen, H., & Schott, G. (1952). *Gestaltung und Verlaufsdynamik* [Configuration and sequence dynamics]. Biel: Institut für Psycho-Hygiene.

Lossen, H., & Schott, G. (1975). *Wartegg: Analisi del processo percettivo* [Wartegg: Analysis of the perceptive process]. Turin: Centro Salesiano di Orientamento.

Mattlar, C.-E. (2005, July). *An overview of the Wartegg Zeichentest (WZT): The structure and use thereof, and of research supporting its utility*. Paper presented at the meeting of the International Rorschach Society, Barcelona, Spain.

Mattlar, C.-E. (2015). *A manual with respect to interpreting the Wartegg Zeichentest (WZT)*. Unpublished manuscript.

McCully, R. (1988). *Jung e Rorschach* [Jung and Rorschach]. Milan: Mimesis.

Merei, F. (1961). A Rorschach táblák felszólító jellege. [Card Pull in the Rorschach]. *Pszichológiai Szemle*, *16*, 115.

Murakami, M. (2005). *Characteristics of Wartegg Zeichen Test responses from the view point of Rorschach test* (translated). (Unpublished master's thesis). Seitoku University.

Rapaport, D. (1977). *Il modello concettuale della psicoanalisi: Scritti 1942–1960* [The conceptual model of psychoanalysis: Writings 1942–1960]. In M. M. Gill, M. Bolko, & E. Codignola (Eds.). Feltrinelli.

Ravecca, F. (2003, February). *Il processo di selezione del personale in una Forza Armata che cambia: sperimentazione del test Wartegg all'Accademia Navale di Livorno*. [The Selection proceeding in an Armed Force which is changing: Experimentation with the Wartegg test at the Navy Academy of Livorno]. Paper presented at the Annual Convention of Italian Society of Psychopathology (SOPSI).

Roivanen, E. (2009). A brief history of the Wartegg Drawing Test. *Gestalt Theory*, *31*(1), 55.

Rothacker, E. (1952). *Die Schichten der Persönlichkeit* [The Layers of Personality]. Bonn: H. Bouvier.

Sander, F. (1962). Experimentelle Ergebnisse der Gestaltpsychologie [Gestaltpsychological experiments]. In F. Sander & H. Volkelt (Eds.), *Ganzheitspsychologie* (pp. 23–88). Munich: Beck.

Scarpellini, C. (1962). *Diagnosi di personalità col reattivo di realizzazione grafica*. [Diagnosis of personality with the drawing completion test]. Contributi dell'Istituto di Psicologia dell'Università Cattolica del Sacro Cuore [Contributions from the Institute of Psychology of the Catholic University of the Sacred Heart], pp. 1–82.

Scarpellini, C. (1964). Diagnostic differentiel a travers deux tests de personalite: le Rorschach et le Wartegg. [Differential diagnostic through two personality tests: The Rorschach and the Wartegg.]. *Bulletin de Psychologie Scolaire et d'Orientation*, *13*, 79–92.

Schwartz, A. (2016). Special topics in assessment: The Wartegg Drawing Completion Test and the Crisi Wartegg System: A new introduction to an old test. *SPA Exchange*, *28*(2), 2, 11–12.

Soilevuo Grønnerød, J., & Grønnerød, C. (2012). The Wartegg Zeichen Test: A literature overview and a meta-analysis of reliability and validity. *Psychological Assessment*, *24*(2), 476–489.

Sugiura, K., Katsuki, N., & Sukigara, N. (2003). *Guidebook of Projective Drawing Tests* (translated). San-nou syuppan.

Takala, M., & Hakkarainen, M. (1953). Über Faktorenstruktur und Validität des Wartegg-Zeichentests [On the factor structure and validity of the Wartegg-Drawing test]. *Annales Academiae Scientiarum Fennicae*, *B 81*, 95–122.

Takuma, T., & Atsumi, R. (1963). Wartegg Drawing Test. In T. Imura (Ed.), *Clinical psychological assessment*. Igaku-syoin.

Tamminen, S., & Lindeman, M. (2000). Wartegg—Luotettava persoonallisuustesti vai maagista ajattelua? [The Wartegg: A valid personality test or magical thinking?] *Psykologia*, *35*(4), 325–331.

Torazza, B. (1993). *Contributi allo studio del Wartegg-Zeichentest (WZT)* [Contributions to the study of the Wartegg test]. Rome, Italy: Borla.

Wartegg, E. (1934). Ganzheit und Struktur: Gefühl [Totality and structure: Emotion]. *Neue Psychologische Studien*, *12*(1), 99–127.

Wartegg, E. (1936). Gefühl und Fantasiebild [Emotion and imagination]. *Industrielle Psychotechnik*, *13*(8), 251–255.

Wartegg, E. (1939). Gestaltung und Charakter [Formation of gestalts and personality]. *Zeitschrift für Angewandte Psychologie und Charakterkunde*, *84*, Beiheft 2.

Wartegg, E. (1953). *Schichtdiagnostik-Der Zeichentest* (WZT) [Differential diagnostics-The Drawing test]. Göttingen: Verlag für Psychologie.

Wartegg, E. (2000). "Zeichen der Zeit": Leben und Forschung eines Psychodiagnostikers. [Sign of the times: The life and research of a psychodiagnostician]. An unpublished manuscript from 1977. In H. Bernhardt & R. Lockot (Eds.), *Mit Ohne Freud. Zur*

Geschichte der Psychoanalyse in Ostdeutschland [With without Freud: A history of psychoanalysis in Eastern Germany] (pp. 95–111). Giessen: Psychosozial-Verlag.
Weiner, I. B. (2003). *Principles of Rorschach interpretation*. New York: Routledge.
Yanagi, M. (2001) Life experiences and emotional experiences in adolescence seen in university first grade students: Using Wartegg Drawing Test (translated). *Bulletin of the Faculty of Education, Ibaraki University*, 50, 195–208.

2 Statistical Foundations of the Crisi Wartegg System

Jacob A. Palm and Alessandro Crisi

As reviewed in Chapter 1, the Crisi Wartegg System developed over the course of 30 years, through a process of continuous refinement based upon clinical experience and empirical research. This chapter summarizes major research studies concerning the CWS. It should be noted that while many of these research studies have been published previously, this marks the first time they are presented for English publication. Additionally, much of the previous research has been presented at conferences and symposia during the previous two decades, including annual conventions of the Society for Personality Assessment (SPA) and the International Rorschach Society (ISR). As such, the collected data presented here is based upon translations of Italian publications, journal articles, and academic texts; summaries of data presented at conferences and symposia; review of recently published English-language peer-reviewed journal articles; and presentation of recent reliability data not previously published. In some cases, when possible, primary authors were contacted for further information about research design, clarification of statistical data, or broader explanation of findings. In some cases, when contact was not possible, the data summarized here is limited to that which was previously published or presented. It should be noted that all tables from previous publications are reproduced with the permission of the respective author or publisher.

Prior to research summarizing the specific validity and reliability of the CWS, the 2012 meta-analytic study conducted by Soilevuo Grønnerød and Grønnerød will be reviewed. Following this review, published and presented data related to the interrater and test–retest reliability of the CWS will be presented. Lastly, relevant convergent validity data will be summarized, beginning with early exploratory studies, and continuing chronologically, grouped by study focus, over the past several decades.

Meta-Analytic Study of the WDCT (Soilevuo Grønnerød & Grønnerød, 2012)

The varied interpretive systems and approaches for the Wartegg Drawing Completion Test that developed in isolation (described in Chapter 1), have resulted in limited comprehensive research. To address this limited integration of study data, a result of challenges in accessing previously conducted research due to geographic distance and publication language, Soilevuo Grønnerød and Grønnerød (2012) undertook analysis of available empirical studies on the reliability and validity of the Wartegg Test. In completing their meta-analytic review, the authors conducted a comprehensive literature search noting that advancements in online text access and databases yielded greater numbers of Wartegg-specific articles than previously conducted similar searches by several researchers. It was noted that some articles were unable to be retrieved, including dissertations from the United States, and unpublished works including Master's theses and conference presentations. Lastly, despite a long history of Wartegg use in Japan, studies published in Japanese were excluded due to translation challenges. The authors located 507 references of scholarly work from 31 countries. Following exclusion of non-empirical publications, 37 studies (containing 38 data sets) were determined to meet inclusion criteria for analysis. Full exclusion criteria, and case-by-case exclusion determination are well described in the authors' published article, and will not be summarized here (see Soilevuo Grønnerød & Grønnerød, 2012, for full details).

In terms of reliability, results of the 2012 meta-analysis appear quite favorable. Interrater reliability coefficients averaged in the excellent range ($r_w = .79$; 15 results from 12 samples). Similarly, internal consistency coefficients averaged in the satisfactory range ($r_w = .74$; 3 results from 2 samples). The authors noted that test–retest reliability coefficients were "disappointingly low" (page 14, $r_w = .53$; 3 results from 2 samples), although suggested that this weighted average is difficult to understand due to lack of clarity on the state versus trait aspects of included variables.

In terms of validity, the authors found similarly positive results from the analyzed research. Analysis of studies with a clearly stated research hypothesis yielded a large effect size ($r_w = .33$; 290 results from 14 samples). This effect size was noted to be slightly greater than meta-analytic results of both the Rorschach and the MMPI-2 (Hiller, Rosenthal, Bornstein, Berry, & Brunell-Neuleib, 1999; as cited in Soilevuo Grønnerød & Grønnerød, 2012). Overall, a lower magnitude effect size was found for all results ($r_w = .19$; 95% $CI = .14 - .26$); however, various factors (including scoring system, number of examined criteria, and scorer blindness) were determined to significantly impact results. For example, in considering scorer blindness during regression analysis, difference was noted between no scorer blindness ($r = .12$, predicted effect size) versus full scorer blinding ($r = .35$, predicted effect size). Given the small number of studies for each scoring system, including the CWS, effect sizes for each system were unable to be analyzed.

In their discussion of results, Soilevuo Grønnerød and Grønnerød (2012) noted "surprise" regarding the large effect size of studies involving specific clinical hypotheses. Based upon this result, and the comparability of this effect size with other performance-based and objective personality measures, the authors concluded, "the research on the WZT may reach levels comparable to other assessment methods, given sufficient focus on study quality" (p. 482). The authors further noted that based upon review, WDCT results appeared well correlated with other free-response methods and clinical observation, whereas were not well associated with self-report measures of personality. This lack of relationship was noted to occur with other commonly used free-response methods as well, as discussed in the assessment research literature (see Bornstein, 2009). In summation, the authors asserted:

> Based on our meta-analysis, we argue that there is no reason to dismiss the Wartegg method altogether as a method for personality evaluation. However, it is necessary to build a solid, cumulative research tradition to produce knowledge and create a basis for the use of the Wartegg method in psychological practice . . . We strongly encourage, however, more research built on previous studies that will cultivate the strongest part of the method.
> (p. 483)

Reliability and Validity of the Crisi Wartegg System

While the meta-analytic findings of Soilevuo Grønnerød and Grønnerød (2012) included research regarding several scoring and interpretation systems of the Wartegg Test, among them the Crisi Wartegg System (CWS), significant research has been conducted specifically on the CWS. In the last 20 years, studies have investigated the interrater and test–retest reliability, as well as the convergent validity of the CWS.

Reliability Studies

Projective and performance-based personality tests may be thought of as potentially reactive or subjective techniques, as their administration and scoring may be significantly impacted by factors related to the evaluator. These factors may include competence, training, relationship to the client, setting of test administration, and familiarity with the test being administered. While the WDCT according to the CWS is considered standardized, based upon an objective scoring and administration system, given the potentially subjective nature of the method it is crucial to evaluate agreement (interrater reliability) between scorers.

Once interrater reliability is established between professionals, it is then possible to examine consistency (test–retest reliability) between deferred administrations (Balboni & Cubelli, 2004). With this in mind, both interrater and test–retest reliability of the CWS have been researched, with consistently positive results. Eight studies on interrater reliability and one study on test–retest reliability are presented below.

Interrater Reliability

Many previously conducted studies involving the Wartegg Drawing Completion Test have demonstrated high levels of interrater agreement, including Kappa coefficients of .94 (Roivainen & Ruuska, 2005) to those ranging between .66 to 1.0 (Alves, Dias, Sardinha, & Conti, 2010). These studies have evaluated varied scoring methodologies, as discussed above. The interrater reliability of the Crisi Wartegg System is equally established, as described below in multiple studies.

Preliminary Interrater Reliability Analysis (Crisi, 1998, 2007)

Examination of the interrater reliability of CWS scoring was first undertaken in 1999, following basic standardization and formalization of the administration and scoring process. Initial research, published in the first and second editions of the Italian-language CWS Manual (Crisi, 1998, 2007), reviewed interrater reliabilities between three pairs of judges, each of whom independently reviewed and scored 18 CWS protocols randomly selected from the archives of the *Istituto Italiano Wartegg*. Data was collected under two conditions, to evaluate the effectiveness and impact of written CWS scoring and administration materials. First, judges were instructed to score the selected protocols without referencing published scoring guidelines; that is, scoring was based upon previous training and experience. In the second condition, the same judges were instructed to score selected protocols with the assistance of the instructional manual.

Interrater reliability was further evaluated based upon the experience level of the raters. Raters were divided into three categories: "Expert," indicating psychologists who had been practicing assessment with the CWS for at least five years; "Practical," indicating psychologists who had two years of experience; and "Novice," indicating psychologists who had only recently completed training on the use of the WDCT according to the CWS. Each dyad was examined using paired raters of similar or different experience levels, resulting in comparisons between Expert–Expert, Expert–Practical, and Expert–Novice.

In considering this initial interrater reliability research, it should be noted that indexes of agreement were calculated for only the most important scoring categories of the CWS. These categories included Evocative Character (EC), Affective Quality (AQ), Form Quality (FQ), and Special Scores (SS). Some scoring categories were not initially evaluated (Popular Responses, Content, Movement), given the objective scoring criteria for these scoring categories assures interrater agreement and might artificially inflate overall correlations of agreement. For example, Popular responses for each box are provided to users in list format, yielding near-perfect interrater agreement. Lastly, the theoretically derived category of Impulse Responses was not studied, given that depending upon the theoretical orientation of the examiner, this category can be scored or not scored without detracting from the overall quantitative or interpretive power of the test.

The degree of agreement between raters was calculated using Cohen's measure of agreement corrected for chance agreement (κ), between pairs of examiners for all possible combinations. That is, for each analyzed variable (i.e., EC, AQ, FQ), scores in each of the eight boxes, over a total of 18 rated protocols, were compared yielding a total of 432 points of comparison. These comparisons were analyzed for both condition #1 (scoring without referencing scoring manual) and condition #2 (scoring using formal scoring manual). For example, in comparing Expert–Expert ratings, identical ratings increased from the first condition (363 out of 432) to the second condition (380 out of 432), as further described below. Whereas the above-mentioned variables (i.e., EC, AQ, FQ) are mandatory in scoring (requiring a score in each of the eight boxes of every protocol), Special Scores are not mandatory and are only scored when warranted by the client's drawings or verbalizations. As such, the number of cases by which interrater agreement was calculated was determined independently by the presence of an assigned Special Score by any rater. That is, if one rater assigned a special score to Box 1 of a protocol, but another rater did not, the presence of a special score was considered possible (regardless of the degree of agreement or disagreement); therefore, interrater agreement was confirmed if both raters agreed on the presence or absence of a Special Score, and was not confirmed if either assigned a Special Score while the other did not.

Considering results from the first condition, in which the protocols were scored without reference materials, the highest degree of interrater reliability was obtained in the Expert–Expert comparison (κ = .84 to .88, "Almost Perfect"). As expected, agreement was lower between Expert–Practical (κ = .68–.78, "Substantial") and lowest between Expert-Novice (κ = .55–.59, "Moderate").

In the second condition, during which raters referenced written standardized scoring guidelines, interrater reliability was noted to significantly increase. Agreement between raters, on average, was high between Expert–Expert (κ = .91, "Almost Perfect") and Expert–Practical (κ = .84, "Almost Perfect") raters, and substantial between Expert–Novice (κ = .69, "Substantial").

In considering the results of this preliminary study, it is important to note that while a high level of agreement between expert examiners was discovered, the lower (yet still substantial) levels of interrater reliability found in this study would not significantly impact interpretation of the test results. Similar to other tests of this nature, including the Rorschach and MMPI-2, many of the indices obtained, as well as the resulting calculations and computations derived from these indices (i.e., in the CWS: EC+%, AQ+%, etc.; in the MMPI-2, the clinical scales), are interpreted via normative ranges of values. For example, in considering Evocative Character of the CWS, the EC+% (which is calculated by summing the individual EC scores for each box, dividing by 8, and converting into a percentage), has a "normal" range from 56% to 81%. Translated into raw scores derived from scoring, this equals 4.5 to 6.5 points. Considering that in each of the eight boxes of the Wartegg, a response can be assigned an EC raw score of 0, 0.5, or 1, let us imagine that a rater assigned 6 points (75%) to a CWS protocol. If a second rater assigns 5 points (62%), for interpretive purposes, the understanding of the client remains the same given that both calculated indices fall within the "normal" range (between 56% and 81%). While this is an important consideration, it should be noted that among experienced examiners, differences of more than one half a point are extremely rare.

Crisi (2011b)

CWS interrater reliability was further evaluated in a clinical sample randomly selected from the archives of the *Istituto Italiano Wartegg*. In this study, the protocols of 30 subjects were blindly evaluated by three independent judges certified in the Crisi Wartegg System. Intraclass correlation coefficients (ICC) were computed between the three judges on major CWS scoring categories. ICCs were calculated for all formal indices but not for specific Content, Movement and Special Score categories of scoring whose frequencies were too low for meaningful comparisons (i.e., those clinical phenomena that are captured by formal scoring, but occur in less than 2% of cases).

The majority of evaluated indexes exhibited excellent levels of ICC ranging from .77 to .97 ($p < .01$), as presented in Table 2.1. Several scoring categories, including Form Quality (ICC = .60), Original Responses (ICC = .68), and Popular Responses (ICC = .68) demonstrated substantial interrater agreement. Results are presented in Table 2.1.

Crisi (2011b)

Given that the Crisi Wartegg System introduced two new scoring categories to the evaluation of the WDCT—Evocative Character (EC) and Affective Quality

TABLE 2.1 Intraclass Correlation Coefficient (ICC) Values for Major CWS Indices

Index	*ICC**
Evocative Character (EC+%)	.77
Affective Quality (AQ+%)	.90
Form Quality (FQ+%)	.60
Popular Responses (P%)	.68
Original Responses (O%)	.68
Anxiety Index (AI)	.87
Impulsivity Index (IM)	.82
Primary Movement (M)	.90
Secondary Movement (m)	.79
Human Content (H%)	.98
Object Content (OBJ%)	.92
Animal Content (A%)	.93
Symbol Content (SIG%)	.89
Botanical Content (BOT%)	.95
Astronomical Content (AST%)	.93
Architecture Content (ARC%)	.94
Human Simulacrum Content (HS%)	.90
Nature Content (NAT%)	.88

Note: * $p < .01$ for all variables. ICC calculated between 3 independent raters.

(AQ)—interrater reliability analyses were conducted as specifically related to these categories to ensure consistent scoring. The AQ and EC of 30 protocols were reviewed. Both Cohen's kappa (κ) and Fleiss' kappa (K) were calculated, with the former examining each possible correlation between pairs of three (blind) independent raters, and the latter examining correlations between three independent evaluators concurrently.

In considering agreement at the scoring level (raw data level of agreement), independent raters can arrive at three levels of agreement: total agreement, partial agreement, or total disagreement. In both of the scored categories (Evocative Character and Affective Quality), possible scores are limited to 0, 0.5, or 1 in each box, for each rater. Therefore, in considering levels of agreement between three raters, the following possibilities exist:

1. *Total Agreement*: All raters assign the same score to a box (for example: 1, 1, 1);
2. *Partial Agreement*: One rater's score differs from the other two raters' scores (for example: 0, 1, 1);
3. *Total Disagreement*: All raters assign a different score to a box (for example: 1, 0.5, 0).

Preliminary analysis of the raw data found significant levels of total agreement. For Evocative Character, for example, 76.6% of boxes demonstrated total agreement (n = 191) between raters, 17.5% indicated partial agreement (n = 42), and only 2.9% demonstrated total disagreement (n = 7). Results for Affective Quality exceeded those of Evocative Character: 85.8% of boxes demonstrated total agreement (n = 206), 14.2% indicated partial agreement (n = 34), and 0% demonstrated total disagreement (n = 0).

Results of interrater reliability analyses for both Evocative Character and Affective Quality (by Box) are summarized in Table 2.2.

Crisi & Dentale (2016)

Crisi and Dentale investigated the interrater reliability of "three new scoring categories" introduced by the Crisi Wartegg System: Evocative Character (EC), Affective Quality (AQ), and Form Quality (FQ). Two independent scorers blindly reviewed 30 randomly selected clinical protocols. Intraclass correlation coefficients were calculated, with each variable demonstrating significant levels of agreement: EC (ICC = .74, F = 7.81, df = 29, p < .001), AQ (ICC = .92, F = 28.17, df = 29, p < .001), and FQ (ICC = .71, F = 5.77, df = 29, p < .001).

Crisi, Vari, Velotti, Carlesimo, Guzzi, & Zavattini (2014)

As part of a larger comparative study investigating depression and negative affect states in dermatology patients, interrater reliability analyses were conducted. Two independent raters scored 84 protocols (42 experimental, 42 control), blind to

TABLE 2.2 Interrater Reliability by WDCT Box—Evocative Character (EC) and Affective Quality (AQ)

Box	*Evocative Character*		*Affective Quality*	
	Fleiss' K	*Cohen's κ*	*Fleiss' K*	*Cohen's κ*
Box 1	.84	.85	.84	.87
Box 2	.44	.50	.56	.66
Box 3	.79	.85	.95	.96
Box 4	.59	.60	.66	.70
Box 5	.69	.69	.81	.79
Box 6	.24*	.18*	.79	.81
Box 7	.75	.76	.87	.88
Box 8	.80	.80	.96	.96
Mean	.64	.64	.81	.83

Note: * As initial analysis suggested poor results, scoring rules for Box 6 were specifically clarified, resulting in higher levels of agreement in subsequent studies. Despite this questionable result in Box 6, overall interrater reliability fell in the substantial range of classification (.61–.80).

TABLE 2.3 Interrater Reliability of Major CWS Indices—Evocative Character (EC), Affective Quality (AQ), Form Quality (FQ)

Variable	*ICC*	*F*	*df*	*p*
EC	.887	8.862	83	.000
AQ	.793	4.829	83	.000
FQ	.802	5.502	83	.000

Note: ICC calculated between two independent raters.

group membership. Intraclass correlation coefficients (ICC) were calculated for three CWS variables to determine mean consistency. On average, interrater reliability for the three investigated CWS variables (Evocative Character, EC; Affective Quality, AQ; and Form Quality, FQ) fell within the *almost perfect* range (ICC = .826).

More specifically, the ICC for each studied variable is presented in Table 2.3.

Overall, consistent interrater reliability (ranging from *substantial* to *almost perfect*) was demonstrated on three crucial CWS indices, including two indices original to the Crisi Wartegg System—Evocative Character and Affective Quality.

Daini, Lai, Festa, Maiorino, Pertosa, & De Risio (2006)

As part of a larger comparative study investigating affect states and impulsivity in patients being treated for eating disorders, interrater reliability analyses were conducted. Two independent raters scored 40 randomly selected protocols (from 181 protocols included in the research study). Interrater agreement on five specific scoring categories was studied: Evocative Character (EC), Affective Quality (AQ), Form Quality (FQ), Anxiety Index (AI), and the Index of Impulsivity (IM). Results for each comparison fell in the excellent range. For EC, AQ, and FQ, mean interrater reliability was reported by the authors (K *minimum* = .79; K *maximum* = .82; K *mean* = .80). Reliability coefficients for both the Anxiety Index (r = .80, $p < .0001$) and the Index of Impulsivity (r_w = .88, $p < .0001$) were found to be similarly adequate.

Daini, Petrongolo, Manzo, & Bernardini (2012)

As part of a larger comparative study investigating personality factors impacted by work as a professional nurse, interrater reliability analyses were conducted. Two independent evaluators scored 321 protocols (111 experimental, 210 control), blind to group membership. Interrater reliability coefficients were calculated for relevant indices, including Evocative Character, Affective Quality, Form Quality, Frequency (Popular Responses), Anxiety Index, Index of Impulsivity, Index of Inner Tension, and some Content category percentages. Overall mean interrater reliability was reported in the excellent range (*rw* = .95).

Crisi, Palm, & Lops (2016)[1]

Interrater reliability was further evaluated in an American sample of protocols, with clinicians trained in the United States serving as independent raters. In this study, 30 randomly selected protocols from the American normative sample were independently scored by five clinicians trained and certified in the CWS. Given training, certification, and experience, these clinicians were deemed experienced in the CWS, reflecting an advanced level of competence in both scoring and interpretation. A sixth judge, considered expert in Italy, additionally participated in the study. Interrater agreement was calculated at the individual scoring-decision level, the aggregate protocol-level of calculated indices and percentages, and overall evaluation of consistency between pairs of judges. Each will be discussed in turn below.

Agreement at the Scoring Level

Interrater agreement was calculated for the most common scoring elements of the CWS, including Evocative Character (EC), Affective Quality (AQ), Form Quality (FQ), Content (CONT), Popular Responses (P), Anxiety Stroke (AS), Crossed Border (CB), and Movement (M). Given that scores are assigned for each of eight boxes in a protocol, and 30 protocols were included in this study, interrater comparisons were calculated on a total of 240 data points (i.e., 30 protocols × 8 boxes = 240) for each scoring category evaluated.

In evaluating agreement between the six raters, Fleiss' kappa (K) was utilized. This statistic, typically used as an alternative to the Cohen's kappa in cases where more than three raters are evaluated, provides statistics relevant to level of agreement between judges while taking into account the probability of agreement due to chance. Moreover, given that for some CWS variables (i.e., FQ, AQ, EC) scoring values are limited to three alternatives on an ordinal scale (0, 0.5. and 1) for which the differences are weighted (i.e., the difference between 0 and 0.5 is different from that between 0 and 1), Fleiss' K is considered a better choice (Chiorri, 2011).

In considering overall agreement, a further consideration is relevant related to the paradox of high agreement concurrent with a low kappa (Randolph, 2005). Moreover, most statistical evaluations of interrater reliability assume that raters are limited in the manner in which cases may be distributed across categories, which, in the case of the CWS, is not true. Given that there are no limits placed on CWS raters regarding the frequency of assigned specific scores (i.e., raters can assign 0, 0.5, or 1 without limitation or expectation), the results of the Free Marginal Kappa are also presented because this coefficient may more accurately reflect interrater agreement under these circumstances. Brennan and Prediger (1981) recommend using free marginal kappa (K_{free})when raters are not forced to assign a certain number of cases to each category (as in the case of the CWS), and fixed marginal kappa (K_{fixed}) in cases where they are. Given this recommendation, two variations of kappa are presented in Table 2.4: Siegel and Castellan's (1988) fixed-marginal multirater kappa and Randolph's (2005) free marginal multirater kappa (Randolph, 2005; Warrens, 2010).

Given the occurrence of a paradoxically high level of overall agreement coupled with a low kappa, the scoring category Form Quality (FQ) must be examined. In this case, as presented in Table 2.4, the overall percentage of agreement appears high (87.1%), whereas the *kappa* appears low (K_{fixed} = .292). In understanding this, we must consider the FQ variable. FQ scoring, as compared to the other indices evaluated, demonstrates less variability. That is, while raters have the opportunity (as with other variables) to assign scores of 0, 0.5, or 1, the majority of ratings typically represent a score of 1, with relatively few scores of 0 assigned. Clinically, scores of 1 are expected and normative, whereas scores less than 1 are typically representative of difficulties, or in extreme cases, pathology. Given this distribution of scores, it is not surprising that there would be a high percentage of agreement between raters, but a corresponding low fixed marginal kappa (due to limited prevalence of scores based upon variable distribution). As such, the free marginal kappa appears a more reliable estimate of agreement corrected for chance (K_{free} = .807).

In considering the results presented in Table 2.4, specifically as related to free marginal kappa values, agreement for all variables falls above .7, with the majority (6 of 8 studied scoring variables) falling higher than .8. Relating these values to the interpretive scale devised by Landis and Koch (1977), three variables (EC, AS, FQ) demonstrate *substantial* agreement, and five variables demonstrate *almost perfect* agreement (AQ, Content, Popular, CB, Movement). These results provide strong support for consistent scoring between clinicians who have been trained and certified in the CWS. Considering that the CWS is a performance-based

TABLE 2.4 Interrater Reliability of Major CWS Scoring Categories

Variable	*% Overall Agreement*	K_{fixed}	K_{free}	$Z\ (K_{fixed})$	$p\ (K_{fixed})$
EC	82.2	.679	.733	31.09	.000
AQ	88.7	.809	.831	44.88	.000
FQ	87.1	.292	.807	12.37	.000
Content	88.7	.867	.882	44.91	.000
Popular Response (P)	91.5	.827	.873	33.31	.000
Anxiety Stroke (Special Score)	87.5	.617	.749	14.79	.000
Crossed Border (Special Score)	93.9	.875	.879	45.20	.000
Movement (M)	91.4	.770	.896	16.93	.000

Note: K_{fixed}: fixed-marginal multirater kappa (Siegel and Castellan, 1988); K_{free}: free marginal multirater kappa (Randolph, 2005).

or projective personality test, requiring complex scoring decisions based upon clinician judgment, these numbers are more compelling.

Agreement at the Protocol Level

Following analysis of individual scoring decisions made by the six judges, protocol-level calculations and indices were derived according to CWS guidelines. In general, the individual scoring data points spread over the eight boxes of the CWS are mathematically converted into approximately 60 calculated scores and indices on which interpretation is subsequently based. For the purposes of this study, the 17 most relevant scoring elements were studied with other calculated indices excluded due to low frequency or statistical rarity.

To evaluate the agreement between the six raters, intraclass correlation coefficients (ICC) were calculated, given that this technique is suitable for situations with more than two judges and rating scales with multiple points (Chiorri, 2011). A two-way random effects model was utilized taking into account that each of six raters evaluated each case, and these six raters are regarded as a sample of the entire population of clinicians certified in the CWS. Each studied index, presented in Table 2.5, was evaluated using the same parameters (random two-way effects model, absolute agreement definition, consistent estimator).

In evaluating results according to Cicchetti's guidelines (1994), as with previous findings, most indices on average demonstrate *good* to *excellent* levels of agreement.

Consistency Between Pairs of Judges

Lastly, aggregate correlations between each possible pair of judges were calculated for two scoring categories unique to the CWS: Evocative Character (EC) and Affective Quality (AQ). Calculated using Spearman rank order correlation (r_s),

TABLE 2.5 Interrater Reliability (ICC)—Major Calculated Indices of the CWS

Index	*Single Measures*	*p*	*Average Measures*	*p*
EC+%	.722	.000	.940	.000
AQ+%	.800	.000	.940	.000
FQ+%	.350	.000	.763	.000
P%	.680	.000	.860	.000
AI	.750	.000	.947	.000
IM	.928	.000	.987	.000
M	.881	.000	.978	.000
m	.656	.000	.920	.000
H%	.916	.000	.985	.000
OBJ%	.846	.000	.971	.000
A%	.987	.000	.998	.000
ARC%	.712	.000	.937	.000
SIG%	.863	.000	.974	.000
NAT%	.615	.000	.906	.000
BOT%	.932	.000	.988	.000
AST%	.839	.000	.969	.000
HS%	.823	.000	.965	.000

Note: ICC calculated based upon six independent raters.

TABLE 2.6 Correlations Between Rater Pairs—Evocative Character (EC)

	N	r_s	*t(n–2)*	*p*
Rater 1 & Rater 2	30	.9274	13.12187	.0000000
Rater 1 & Rater 3	30	.6836	4.957344	.0000312
Rater 1 & Rater 4	30	.7682	6.351255	.0000007
Rater 1 & Rater 5	30	.8119	7.359818	.0000001
Rater 1 & Rater 6	30	.7358	5.750079	.0000036
Rater 2 & Rater 3	30	.6249	4.235486	.0002228
Rater 2 & Rater 4	30	.7805	6.606388	.0000004
Rater 2 & Rater 5	30	.8342	8.004766	.0000000
Rater 2 & Rater 6	30	.7267	5.598184	.0000054
Rater 3 & Rater 4	30	.6075	4.047235	.0003702
Rater 3 & Rater 5	30	.7006	5.195174	.0000163
Rater 3 & Rater 6	30	.7302	5.655459	.0000046
Rater 4 & Rater 5	30	.7704	6.394437	.0000006
Rater 4 & Rater 6	30	.7529	6.053823	.0000016
Rater 5 & Rater 6	30	.8104	7.319362	.0000001

Note: r_s = Spearman rank order correlation.

TABLE 2.7 Correlations Between Rater Pairs—Affective Quality (AQ)

	N	r_s	$t(n–2)$	p
Rater 1 & Rater 2	30	.8501	8.542847	.0000000
Rater 1 & Rater 3	30	.7516	6.029415	.0000017
Rater 1 & Rater 4	30	.7803	6.602315	.0000004
Rater 1 & Rater 5	30	.7915	6.852993	.0000002
Rater 1 & Rater 6	30	.8306	7.893332	.0000000
Rater 2 & Rater 3	30	.7731	6.450924	.0000005
Rater 2 & Rater 4	30	.8616	8.981222	.0000000
Rater 2 & Rater 5	30	.7419	5.854662	.0000027
Rater 2 & Rater 6	30	.8451	8.365695	.0000000
Rater 3 & Rater 4	30	.7920	6.863811	.0000002
Rater 3 & Rater 5	30	.8935	10.52798	.0000000
Rater 3 & Rater 6	30	.7723	6.432695	.0000006
Rater 4 & Rater 5	30	.8078	7.251393	.0000001
Rater 4 & Rater 6	30	.8547	8.711901	.0000000
Rater 5 & Rater 6	30	.8344	8.009299	.0000000

Note: r_s = Spearman rank order correlation.

all resulting correlations ranged from *strong* to *very strong*. Results of correlations between raters for Evocative Character (EC) are presented in Table 2.6.

Results of correlations between raters for Affective Quality (AQ) are presented in Table 2.7.

It should be noted that these scoring categories, novel to the CWS, require judgment on the part of the clinician while scoring. Therefore, this strong agreement between raters underscores the effectiveness of CWS training, written guidelines, and scoring methodology. Overall, all components of this study demonstrated significant interrater reliability of the CWS at both the scoring level and the computational/interpretive level.

Test–Retest Reliability

While many studies have evaluated the interrater reliability of the CWS, less research has investigated the stability of CWS indices over time via formal analysis of test–retest reliability. Given the supposition that some variables of the CWS measure *state* personality characteristics and others personality *traits*, clinical experience suggests that not all CWS variables will remain consistent over time (similar to other personality measures). Further studies regarding the test–retest reliability of the CWS, both with normative and clinical populations (to assess the impact of psychotherapeutic intervention on functioning), are necessary (with several currently in process).

Crisi, Janson, & Palm (2016)[2]

Initial exploratory research into test consistency over time followed 38 normative study participants (non-clinical) recruited as volunteers from the general population. These individuals were administered the WDCT according to CWS standardized administration guidelines on two occasions, approximately 4–5 weeks apart ($\bar{x}$ = 31.2 days, *SD* = 2.7 days; minimum 28 days, maximum 45 days). The participants were all adults (26 women, 12 men) with a mean age of 37.7 years (minimum 18 years, maximum 71 years). The participants were tested solely for research, gave informed consent to participate in this study, and were not compensated for their participation. None of the participants had a known psychiatric diagnosis or disorder, and none had a history of psychiatric or psychotherapeutic treatment. Assessment took place individually at the offices of the *Istituto Italiano Wartegg*. The examiners included five psychologists proficient in the CWS. All protocols were coded by one expert coder.

Fourteen CWS variables were selected for analysis: EC+%, AQ+%, FQ+%, the Affective Stability Index (A/F Ratio), P%, Impulsivity Index (IM), Anxiety Index (AI), WIP Quadrant and Area (QUAD/AREA), Global Assessment classification, Index of Suicidal Tendencies (IST), H%, OBJ%, ARC%, and SIG%. These variables included the most central protocol-level aggregate variables as well as content code percentages with a frequency of >10% across the two administrations. Due to the small sample and the limited variation of some variables in this sample, test–retest reliability for low-frequency variables (including O%, less frequent Content codes, and Special Scores) or variables based on a subset of drawings (including P+% and O+%), were not investigated.

Two sets of analyses were performed, treating the variables as continuous and categorical, respectively. The analyses of the variables as continuous addresses the agreement between Times 1 and 2 for variable values. However, in clinical interpretation, interpretive ranges of variables are of primary importance, rather than absolute numeric values of variables. Thus, the agreement for the selected CWS variables was also analyzed in terms of time-to-time categorical agreement with categories representing interpretive ranges. The analyses of the categorized variables address the agreement between Times 1 and 2 in terms of stability within one interpretive range.

In regard to the Affective Stability Index (A/F Ratio), for which the interpretive ranges depend on both terms, the separate terms of the ratio (i.e., A and F) were included in the continuous analyses rather than the ratio. For the continuous evaluation of the WIP Quadrant and Area (QUAD/AREA), the separate terms that make up the basis for the evaluation (i.e., IIT-1 and the first term of the IIT-2 ratio) were included in the continuous analyses, as well as the Area. In the categorical analyses, the A/F ratio was analyzed as one categorical variable (but not the separate terms A and F). Likewise, for the categorical analyses, the WIP Quadrant and Area (QUAD/AREA) were analyzed as one categorical variable (but not the separate terms IIT-1, IIT-2, and Area).

Table 2.8 presents results for the selected variables analyzed as continuous. The table denotes means and standard deviations for variables at Times 1 and 2, with

TABLE 2.8 Test–Retest Reliability—CWS Continuous Variables

Variable	*Time 1*		*Time 2*		
	$\bar{x}$	*SD*	$\bar{x}$	*SD*	*r*
EC+%	73	9	76	12	.63
AQ+%	63	13	60	13	.47
FQ+%	95	6	98*	4	.72
A	2.7	.8	2.4	.8	.52
F	3.7	.4	3.9*	.3	.78
P%	24	12	24	13	.32
IM	.30	.21	.23*	.21	.81
AI	.80	.22	.83	.20	.83
IIT-1	1.2	.4	1.1*	.3	.80
IIT-2 (Term 1)	4.7	1.3	4.8	1.5	.66
Area	1.6	.6	1.5	.5	.68
Global Evaluation	1.8	1.3	1.3*	.9	.50
IST	2.4	1.8	1.8*	1.5	.45
H%	14	13	13	12	.55
OBJ%	32	19	37	20	.55
ARC%	16	10	17	9	.38
SIG%	10	13	10	13	.69

Note: * $p < .05$ for mean Time 2 – Time 1; difference by paired *t*-test.

t-test *p*, and Pearson test–retest-correlations (*r*). Results suggest overall small systematic shifts in variable means between Time 1 and Time 2 (paired *t*-test, $p < .05$ for 6 out of 18 variables, which is more than what would have been expected by chance, but the absolute size of systematic shifts were small and seemingly not important). The time-to-time-correlations were on the whole sizeable, with a mean Pearson *r* of .61. More than half of the correlations investigated found correlations > .60, 5 out of 17 reaching > .70, and three exceeding > .80. The lowest test–retest correlation was found for P% ($r = .32$).

Table 2.9 presents time-to-time agreement results for selected CWS variables recoded into interpretive ranges and treated as categorical. Test–retest agreement is presented as percent agreement (i.e., the proportion of participants who stayed within the same interpretive range from Time 1 to Time 2) and Cohen's (1968) kappa for chance-corrected test–retest agreement (κ). Results are presented both at the variable level (i.e., the agreement for classification in the same category out of all those possible at Times 1 and 2) and for each category (i.e., the agreement for having the same status—Present or Absent—for that specific category at both times). The overall proportion of agreement across times was generally high, averaging .78. With the exception of two variables (AQ+% and A/F Ratio), all test–retest agreement fell above .65, with results as high as .97 for

TABLE 2.9 Test–Retest Reliability—CWS Categorical Variables

Variable and Category	*Overall Proportion of Agreement*[a]	*Cohen's kappa (κ)*[b]	*Frequency*	
			Time 1	*Time 2*
EC+%	.76	.38		
1. 0 to 50%			2	3
2. 51 to 81%			33	26
3. 82 to 100%			3	9
AQ+%	.45	.10		
1. 0 to 49%			3	5
2. 50 to 63%			21	21
3. 64 to 75%			9	10
4. 76 to 100%			5	2
FQ+%	.97	.00		
1. 0 to 74%			0	0
2. 75%			1	0
3. 76 to 100%			37	38
A/F Ratio	.50	.17		
1. A < F			21	23
2. A < < F			2	7
3. A > F			10	7
4. A >> F			5	1
P%	.66	.35		
1. 0 to 12%			5	4
2. 13 to 31%			24	24
3. 32 to 100%			9	10
IM	.79	.57		
1. 0 to .25			20	26
2. .26 to 1.0			18	12
AI	.89	.79		
1. 0 to .37			1	1
2. .38 to .75			16	14
3. .76 to 1.0			21	23
Quadrant/Area	.92	.83		
1. Positive[c]			23	26
2. Negative[d]			15	12
Global Evaluation	.74	.31		
1. NOP + LSI			26	33
2. MSI			8	4
3. PTL + SSI			4	1
IST	.87	.23		
1. 0 to 4			33	36
2. 5 to 7			5	2
3. > 7			0	0
H%	.74	.53		
1. 0 to 12%			11	15
2. 13 to 25%			23	20
3. > 25%			4	3

TABLE 2.9 *continued*

Variable and Category	*Overall Proportion of Agreement*[a]	*Cohen's kappa* (κ)[b]	*Frequency*	
			Time 1	*Time 2*
OBJ%	.74	.26		
1. 0 to 12%			4	3
2. 13 to 50%			31	29
3. 51 to 100%			3	6
ARC%	.97	.65		
1. 0 to 25%			37	36
2. 26 to 100%			1	2
SIG%	.92	.62		
1. 0 to 25%			34	33
2. 26 to 100%			4	5

Notes:
a. The overall proportion of agreement for a variable describes the proportion of participants who were classified in the same category at Times 1 and 2.
b. *kappa* (κ) for a variable describes the chance-corrected agreement for the multi-category classification across Times 1 and 2.
c. Positive Quadrant/Area = Area alpha of all quadrants + Area beta of Quadrant A.
d. Negative Quadrant/Area = Area beta of Quadrants B, C, and D + Area gamma of all quadrants.

two variables (FQ+%, ARC%). Chance-corrected test–retest agreement was generally lower, averaging .41. Six variables fell between .50 and .84, whereas eight variables were lower than .50. An uneven distribution of participants over categories, with most participants classified in one single category—a condition that is known to be problematic for the estimation of chance-corrected agreement—was present for several variables, thereby making the interpretation of chance-corrected agreement results (i.e., kappa) more difficult.

Overall, the results of the current analyses suggest substantial time-to-time correlations for continuous variables, and high overall percent agreement (but moderate chance-corrected agreement) across time for variables when treated as categorical in interpretive ranges. Some Wartegg variables that are known to be more influenced by day-to-day fluctuations, including AQ+% and A/F Ratio (Crisi, 2007), were among those variables that showed less stability across the four- to five-week retest period. It was noted that given the small sample size, and the relatively normative population studied, limited variation in some variables may have further artificially decreased the chance-corrected consistency data (kappa). Given the exploratory nature of this study, and these limitations, further research on test–retest reliability is needed.

Validity Studies

With reliability established, it is important to evaluate the validity of test measures prior to clinical use. In evaluating validity, we address several important questions: Does the CWS measure what it purports to measure? Does the

CWS "agree" with other established personality measures (both self-report and performance-based)? Can the CWS discriminate between various clinical presentations, personality traits, or symptoms? Over the past 20 years, numerous published studies have addressed the validity of the Crisi Wartegg System, providing an empirical foundation with which we can begin to answer these questions.

In reviewing clinical research related to the validity of the CWS, we will first examine studies addressing construct validity, in particular the convergent validity (agreement with established personality tests) of the CWS. As the CWS is considered a projective test, performance-based measure, free-response task, or stimulus-attribution test, it is not designed to be (nor expected to be) face valid. Similarly, while informed by the theories of personality, the Wartegg Drawing Completion Test is not considered to demonstrate content validity. This lack of face validity and content validity results in reduction of clients' anxiety, skirting of defenses, and increased participation in assessment tasks. Following a review of convergent validity, published and presented case studies will be discussed, demonstrating the clinical utility of the CWS at the individual level.

Construct Validity

Construct validity, as first described by Cronbach and Meehl (1955), is "the degree to which a test measures what it claims, or purports, to be measuring" (Brown, 1996, p. 231). Convergent and discriminant validity are the two subtypes of validity that make up construct validity. Convergent validity refers to the degree to which two measures of constructs that theoretically should be related are, in fact, related. In contrast, discriminant validity tests whether concepts or measurements that are supposed to be unrelated are, in fact, unrelated (Campbell and Fiske, 1959).

Similarities between the Wartegg and other personality measures, including the Rorschach Inkblot Test (Rorschach, 1921/1942) and the MMPI-2 (Butcher, Graham, Ben-Porath, Tellegen, Dahlstrom, & Kaemmer, 1989), have been frequently described by numerous Wartegg scholars over the past two decades (see Crisi, 1999, 2008; Fontana, 1984, 2005; Gardziella, 1985; Mattlar, 2005; Scarpellini, 1962, 1964; for a review). These authors have generally affirmed the complementarity of the Wartegg with other measures of personality, even acknowledging surprise at the diagnostic capacity of the seemingly simple Wartegg stimuli (Fontana, 2013).

Concerning the CWS specifically, convergent validity has been studied as related to the MMPI-2, the Guilford–Zimmerman Temperament Survey (GZTS; Guilford & Zimmerman, 1949), the Rorschach Inkblot Test, the Separation Anxiety Test (SAT; Klagsbrun & Bowlby, 1976; Italian revision: Attili, 2001), the Adult Attachment Projective (AAP; George & West, 2012), and others. Convergent validity has further been evaluated as compared to independent psychiatric ratings, genetic testing, and expectations based upon client diagnosis, economic advantage, learning style, and psychiatric symptoms and impairments.

Early Exploratory Convergent Validity Studies

During the development of the CWS (see Chapter 1), several early exploratory validity studies were completed with children diagnosed with learning disabilities, children who exhibited articulation difficulties including stuttering, and Deaf children. For the purposes of these initial exploratory research studies, the term *Deaf* includes children who were deaf and Hard of Hearing. This term is capitalized in respect and reference to the Deaf population that is culturally Deaf and uses sign language. As explained by Padden and Humphries (1990):

> We use the lowercase deaf when referring to the audiological condition of not hearing, and the uppercase Deaf when referring to a particular group of deaf people who share a language and a culture. The members of this group have inherited their sign language, use it as a primary means of communication among themselves, and hold a set of beliefs about themselves and their connection to the larger society. We distinguish them from, for example, those who find themselves losing their hearing because of illness, trauma or age; although these people share the condition of not hearing, they do not have access to the knowledge, beliefs, and practices that make up the culture of Deaf people.
>
> (p. 2)

In total, four studies were completed by Crisi and colleagues, spanning over a decade, investigating differences between control group children and those who were deaf, demonstrated articulation difficulties, or were diagnosed with learning disorders. The purpose of these studies was to gather exploratory data regarding differences between groups, as well as determine the effectiveness and validity of the WDCT with populations that had previously been viewed as challenging to assess in a valid and fair manner. Some researchers, for example, have noted, that the dearth of appropriate psychological instruments to assess the Deaf population may contribute to previously reported findings of differences between groups (Iqbal & Hall, 1991). Moreover, authors have asserted that given potentially immature language abilities of Deaf children, rapport is difficult to establish and therefore, frustration and anxiety may be more common in assessment situations (Bailly, Dechoulydelenclave, & Lauwerier, 2003). Given these findings, the WDCT was identified as a potentially fair and inclusive test measure to use with Deaf, learning disabled, and stuttering children, given the reduced expressive language requirements.

The first set of studies, conducted as part of normative data collection at the *Istituto di Ortofonologia* of Rome (an institution that provides assessment and intervention services to children with speech and language disorders), focused on differences between all groups mentioned above. As the remainder of exploratory research summarized here focused solely on the Deaf population, a brief literature review is provided below summarizing previous research related to this topic.

Brief Literature Review of Mental Health Symptoms and Distress in the Deaf Population

In reviewing relevant research, authors have noted that Deaf and Hard of Hearing populations have often been associated with both psychological and neuropsychological disorders, but little agreement regarding etiology of these differences has existed between researchers. The World Health Organization cites negative functional, social, and emotional impact as prevalent within the Deaf community (WHO, 2017). Historically, Deaf individuals have been described as emotionally and socially immature, with characteristics of lability and behavioral explosiveness (Denmark, 1966). Hindley, Hill, McGuigan, and Kitson (1994) found the presence of psychological disorders in approximately 50% of the Deaf population studied. Further authors have consistently noted significant levels of psychological symptoms among Deaf individuals (Checinski, 1991, as cited in Fellinger et al., 2007; de Graaf & Bijl, 2002). These symptoms have included depression (Werngren-Elgström, Dehlin, & Iwarsson, 2003), suicide risk (Turner, Windfuhr, & Kapur, 2007), anxiety (Kvam, Loeb, & Tambs, 2007), impulsivity and externalizing behaviors (Barker, Quittner, Fink, Eisenberg, Tobey, & Niparko, 2009), obsessive and compulsive behaviors (Kitson & Fry, 1990; Marschark, Mouradian, & Halas, 1994), and social challenges (Ridgeway, 1997).

While these findings are assumed to be the multi-determined, including biological, environmental, and subjective causal factors, several authors have also offered specific theories as to the nature and etiology of these mental health symptoms. Hindley, Kitson, and Leach (2000) highlighted the difficulty of Deaf children in establishing emotional relationships with their mothers, whereas Palermo and Rhodes (2007) asserted that later psychopathology may stem from difficulties in recognizing the emotional facial expressions of others. Others (Vaccari & Marschark, 1997) have asserted that parent–child communication styles, and resulting frustration, may increase psychiatric symptoms, whereas Gallagher (1999) posits both interpersonal and intrapersonal language development as crucial to developmental of psychiatric symptoms. Further, authors suggest considerable heterogeneity within the Deaf population, including significant differences between Deaf children born into Deaf families as opposed to those born into hearing families (Rainer, 1963). As noted above, some of these etiological theories and research findings may stem from the lack of appropriate and effective psychological test measures to assess the Deaf population, historical biases, communication-based administration challenges, and cultural differences between assessors and individuals being assessed.

More recent literature review (Bailly, Dechoulydelenclave, & Lauwerier, 2003) suggests that deafness is a multifaceted condition with medical and social aspects, including developmental communication challenges and social–cultural–familial impact. Despite the assessment difficulties and potential biases described above, the authors listed several symptoms prevalent in the population of Deaf children studied, including delays in social maturity; however, the authors asserted that the prevalence of psychopathological disorders generally appears no higher in Deaf children when compared to their hearing counterparts. Exceptions to this include autism and attentional disorders, which appear more prevalent in the Deaf population.

Citing difficulties in assessment, Fellinger and colleagues (2007) assessed mental distress and quality of life in 233 Deaf research participants, using written measures paired simultaneously with computer-based sign language presentation. Results demonstrated significantly elevated levels of social distress in the Deaf population, as compared to the general population. Quality of life was found to be negatively impacted in the domains of physical and psychological functioning, whereas social relationships were not impacted (with results similar to those of the general population). Primary identified symptoms included emotional and conduct problems, "interpersonal sensitivity," insecurity, and feelings of inferiority. The authors suggested several potential reasons for higher levels of mental distress in the Deaf population, including lack of developmental communication opportunities, increased likelihood of victimization or trauma experienced by members of the Deaf community, ongoing cultural ostracism by those in a predominantly hearing culture, and associated cerebral pathology. The strong ties within the Deaf community, including sign language as a common communication and cultural system, were noted as robust protective factors for Deaf individuals.

Bianchi di Castelbianco, Crisi, & Di Renzo (1993, 1996)

Given previous research findings, a series of studies examining the ability of the CWS to distinguish between normal and historically challenging-to-assess experimental groups of children were conducted at the *Istituto di Ortofonologia* of Rome, beginning with the collection of the first childhood normative sample. In the current study, the authors reported significant differences between the childhood normative sample and three clinical groups of children.

The clinical groups were comprised of children who stutter (Stutter: $N = 98$; 29 female, age: $\bar{x} = 9.4138$, $SD = 2.822$; 69 male, age: $\bar{x} = 8.9565$, $SD = 2.825$; range: 7–14), children with diagnosed learning disabilities (LD: $N = 72$; 24 female, age: $\bar{x} = 9.25$, $SD = 2.418$; 48 male, age: $\bar{x} = 9.125$, $SD = 2.208$; range: 7–14), and Deaf children, including Hard of Hearing children (Deaf: $N = 102$; 48 female, age: $\bar{x} = 8.833$, $SD = 2.562$; 54 male, age: $\bar{x} = 9.277$, $SD = 2.149$; range: 7–14). Each experimental group was divided into three age bands: 6–7 years (Stutter: $N = 37$; LD: $N = 22$; Deaf: $N = 35$), 8–10 years (Stutter: $N = 31$; LD: $N = 29$; Deaf: $N = 42$), and 11–14 years (Stutter: $N = 30$; LD: $N = 21$; Deaf: $N = 25$). These clinical groups were compared to a control group comprised of children from the original childhood normative sample ($N = 282$; 113 female, age: $\bar{x} = 9.3602$, $SD = 2.6043$; 169 male, age: $\bar{x} = 9.0953$, $SD = 2.549$; range: 7–14; See ►Appendix A for further information). Three trained psychologists administered all control group evaluations, with two different clinicians administering experimental group protocols. All protocols were scored by an expert scorer, blind to group membership.

Initial investigation examined differences between the control group and the Deaf group. Specifically, mean differences between groups in 46 CWS interpretive data points were examined, including 22 Content categories, 17 Special Score frequencies, four movement categories, and three Impulse Response ratings. Differences were quantitatively tallied by the boxes in which they occurred. Statistically significant results ($p < .05$) were discovered for each age group studied. In the 6–7 year age group, the most statistically significant differences (four) were discovered in Box 6; that is, in Box 6, the Deaf group differed significantly from the control group on four investigated indices. Similar results were noted for the 8–10 year age group, with seven statistically significant differences noted in Box 6, and a high number of differences also noted in Box 1 (five) and Box 2 (five). The 11–14 year age group demonstrated the most statistically significant differences in Box 1 (four). The authors concluded that in the first two developmental age bands, differences in the Deaf group are related to interaction with the environment and perceptual challenges (evidenced by difficulties in Box 6). As they mature, Deaf students, consistent with research literature, may begin to experience feelings of inadequacy, inferiority, insecurity, and limited self-concept (as evidenced by differences in Box 1).

Similar analysis was subsequently undertaken with the sample of children diagnosed with learning disabilities. In the 6–7 year age group, the most statistically significant differences (nine) were discovered in Box 5. In the 8–10 year age group, the most statistically significant differences were noted in Boxes 4 (six) and 3 (five). Similarly, the 11–14 year age group demonstrated the most statistically significant differences in Box 4 (five). The authors concluded that students with learning disabilities initially react to the environment with frustration and anger (as evidenced by differences in Box 5), with this anger later converting into consistent difficulties interacting with authority figures and meeting environmental expectations (as evidenced by differences in Box 4). Some degree of inconsistency in performance and goal-achievement is likely (as evidenced by differences in Box 3).

Statistical analyses evaluated the differences between each clinical group and the control group, both overall and by corresponding age band. Specifically, mean differences between groups were investigated. Results of overall ANOVA analyses for major CWS indices are presented in Table 2.10.

As expected, control group subjects demonstrated significantly higher levels of Form Quality (FQ+%) and more balanced Affective Stability Indexes (A/F), suggesting a higher level of cognitive development and affective control. Control group subjects further demonstrated higher levels of Popular (P%) responses and lower Original (O%) responses, suggesting more conventional thinking. Lastly, the clinical groups demonstrated a significantly higher Index of Inner Tension (IIT-1) than control group subjects, indicating greater levels of internal tension, distress, state anxiety, and impulsivity. When investigating by age band, the highest number of significant differences was noted in the 8–10 year group, with lowest number of significant differences noted in the 11–14 year age

TABLE 2.10 Differences Between Control Group and Clinical Groups (All Ages)— Major CWS Indices

	AQ+% (*p*)	FQ+% (*p*)	A/F* (*p*)	P% (*p*)	P+% (*p*)	O% (*p*)	O+% (*p*)	*IIT-1* (*p*)	AS (*p*)	CB (*p*)
Stuttering	62 —	55 .001	1.25 .01	23 .05	65 .05	20 .001	38 —	.36 .001	.21 .05	.15 .001
Learning Disabled	65 —	50 .001	1.65 .01	24 —	53 .01	23 .001	35 —	.42 .001	.22 .05	.20 .001
Deaf	58 .05	51 .001	1.3 .001	17 .001	55 .01	20 .001	35 —	.32 .001	.22 .01	.09 .01
Control	62	65	1	26	72	12	34	.19	.15	.03
ANOVA**	.05	.0001	.0001	.0001	.0001	.0001	—	.0001	.0001	.001

Notes: * A/F calculated by converting ratio into decimal. ** *p* values for ANOVA.

TABLE 2.11 Comparisons Between Clinical and Control Groups—Missing Data Percentages and Statistically Significant Differences in Content, Special Scores, Movement (M/m), and Impulse Responses (IR)

Group	*Age Band*	*Missing Data%*[c]	*Statistically Significant Differences*			
			Contents[b]	*Special Scores*	*M/m*[b]	*I.R.*
Stuttering	6–7	3.7	ARC–, BOT+, FD–, HS+, SIG–	AS, CB, PP, AP, GR, PR	—	—
	8–10	0	ARC+, AST+, BOT–, FD–, OBJ–, SIG+	AS, CB, RB, II, PP, AP, SR, TR	M+ MI+	—
	11–14	2.9	A–, ARC+, AST+, BOT–, HS–, NAT+, OBJ–, SIG+	AS, CB, GR, SR	M+	—
Learning Disability	6–7	2.3	A–, ARC–, AST+, BOT+, CLD+, NAT+, SIG–	AS, CB, II, PP, AP, PR, SR	MI+	—
	8–10	1.3	A+, ARC+, BOT–, H+, NAT+, CLD+, OBJ–	AS, CB, II, PP, AP, GR, PR, SR	M+	—
	11–14	.6	A–, FD+, SIG+	AS, CB, PP, GR, PR, SR	M–	—
Deaf	6–7	16	ARC–, BOT+, OBJ–, SIG–	AS, CB, II, SR	M– MI+	—
	8–10	10	A+, ARC–, AST+, H–, OBJ–, SIG–	PA, AS, CB, II, AP, GR, PR, SR, TR	M–	—
	11–14	10.5	ARC+, AST+, BOT–, H–, OBJ–, NAT+, SIG–	AS, CB, II, AP, GR, PR, SR	M– MI+	—

Notes:
a. all differences at $p < .5$ level.
b. + = clinical group demonstrates higher level than control; – = clinical group demonstrates lower level than control group.
c. Missing Data % for Control Group: 6–7: .2%; 8–10: .2%; 11–14: .3%.

band. This suggests that with continued maturation, clinical group members may experience a decrease in symptoms and appear more similar to the control group.

Further analysis was conducted for each age band of each clinical group, as compared to the control group. These analyses were compounded by "missing data" in the clinical groups, due to Global Rejections, meaningless drawings, or incomprehensible explanations/verbalizations of depicted content. While these phenomena are rare in the normative population, the clinical groups demonstrated significantly higher percentages of missing data, which in and of itself is an important clinical finding. Table 2.11 notes missing data percentages and statistically significant differences from the control group for each age band of each clinical group.

Results suggested significant differences between control and clinical groups, primarily in content categories, presence of special scores, and movement responses. Overall, clinical groups generally demonstrated lower percentages of adaptive Content categories (i.e., Human [H], Object [OBJ], Symbol [SIG]), while simultaneously demonstrating higher levels of Content categories suggesting detachment and internal conflict (i.e., Astronomical [AST], Cloud [CLD]). Some tendencies toward distanced compensatory sensitivity to others (i.e., Nature [NAT] and Botany [BOT]) were noted in the clinical groups. Similarly, without exception, the clinical group at all age bands demonstrated higher frequency of Special Scores denoting cognitive difficulties (i.e., Perseveration [PP], Stimulus Repetition [SR], Inadequate Integration [II],), internal conflict (i.e., Global Rejection [GR], Partial Rejection [PR], Anxiety Stroke [AS], Crossed Border [CB], Reversed Box [RB]) and thinking challenges (i.e., Arbitrary Performance [AP], Personalized Answer [PA], Transparency [TR]). In terms of movement, clinical groups, in general, demonstrated higher presence of Secondary Movement (m), suggesting the presence of internal conflict and distress. The Deaf group, in particular, also demonstrated lower levels of Primary Movement (M) as compared to controls, suggesting potentially limited cognitive control, fewer internal cognitive resources, and a reduction in coping skills. No statistically significant differences were noted between groups in regard to Impulse Responses.

Overall, the authors concluded that the CWS identifies significant differences between groups, both in terms of box-by-box differences, as well as via aggregate differences in CWS indices, Content categories, Special Scores, and Movement responses.

Crisi (2002)

Extending the work of Bianchi di Castelbianco and colleagues (1993, 1996), this study further investigated differences in levels of psychopathology between Deaf and control groups. The goal of the study was to investigate the effectiveness of the CWS in detecting group differences, with the aim to determine the utility of the CWS in working effectively with the Deaf population in a valid and non-pathologizing manner.

One hundred participants were originally included in the clinical group, although 36 were subsequently excluded due to communication difficulties between the examinee and examiner or difficulties in comprehending the instructions of the CWS. The remaining 64 participants (39 male, 25 female) were divided into three age groups: 7–13 (N = 19, 9 female; 10 male, age: $\bar{x}$ = 9.895, SD = 1.9971); 14–19 (N = 23, 8 female, 15 male; age: $\bar{x}$ = 16.478, SD = 1.9038); 20 or above (N = 22, 8 female, 14 male; age: $\bar{x}$ = 25.273, SD = 4.4953). Level of hearing loss was determined as Severe in 23 participants, and Moderately Severe in 41 participants. In further analyses, no statistically significant differences were discovered between groups, related to either age or gender.

The clinical group described above was compared to a control group comprised of children, adolescents, and young adults (aged 7–19) from the original CWS normative sample (N = 282; 113 female, age: $\bar{x}$ = 9.3602, SD = 2.6043; 169 male, age: $\bar{x}$ = 9.0953, SD = 2.549; range: 7–19; See ▶Appendix A for further information). Initial analysis investigated the ability of the CWS to differentiate between groups based upon the Global Assessment classification assigned to each participant's protocol. In completing the CWS scoring mechanics, each protocol is assigned an overall Global Assessment classification, ranging from "No Pathology" (NOP) to "Pathological" (PTL). This classification rubric is divided into five levels of increasing severity (1) NOP, 2) LSI, 3) MSI, 4) SSI, 5) PTL), reflecting the degree of symptoms and functional impairment likely to be experienced by the examinee. Two of these five levels are considered positive classifications ("No Pathology" [NOP] + "Low Symptoms" [LSI]) reflecting limited pathology and functional impairment; one is considered indicative of moderate impairment ("Moderate Symptoms" [MSI]); and two are considered negative classifications ("Severe Symptoms" [SSI] and "Pathological" [PTL]) representing severe impairment in functioning. Clinical and control groups were compared based on their classification within this Global Assessment rubric. It was hypothesized that the experimental group would produce higher rates of negative classifications (i.e., SSI + PTL) as compared to control subjects. Results of chi-square analyses are presented in Table 2.12.

Results of chi-square analyses indicate significant differences between clinical and control groups, with the control group generally demonstrating a more positive global assessment, and the clinical group demonstrating a more negative global assessment as predicted. The author concluded from this initial analysis that a condition of impairment is present in the Deaf group, although asserted that this does not necessarily indicate that Deaf individuals demonstrate clinical psychopathology; rather, a level of inner tension or distress is present, which likely impacts personality development and everyday functioning. This heightened internal level of distress may limit a more functional and balanced development, as suggested by other research.

As follow-up to the initial investigation, differences between clinical and control groups were similarly investigated for each box of the WDCT. In the Analysis of Sequence 1, an interpretive strategy for the CWS, each of the eight test boxes is assigned a positive or negative Code computed mathematically by

TABLE 2.12 Differences in Positive, Neutral, and Negative Global Assessment Classifications—Deaf Group vs. Control Group

Global Assessment	*Group*	*Present*		*Absent*		χ^2	*p*	Φ^a
		N (%)	χ^2	*N (%)*	χ^2			
Positive	Deaf	19 (29.7)	62.56	45 (35)	20.03	99.42	.00001	.58
	Control	209 (89.3)	5.22	25 (10.7)	16.78			
Neutral	Deaf	17 (26.6)	8.32	47 (73.4)	1.28	12.21	.001	.20
	Control	23 (9.8)	2.26	212 (90.2)	.35			
Negative	Deaf	28 (43.8)	72.13	36 (56.2)	8.07	102.13	.00001	.59
	Control	2 (.9)	19.73	232 (99.1)	2.21			

Notes: Effect sizes calculated by current authors from previously published analyses; a. Φ effect sizes: small: .1–.29; medium: .3–.49; large: >.5 (Cohen, 1988).

summing the Evocative Character (EC) and Affective Quality (AQ) of each box. Six Codes are possible in each box, two considered positive (C, PC) and four considered negative (NC, AC, AD, D). Frequencies of positive versus negative Codes for both groups were analyzed by chi-square for each box of the WDCT. It was hypothesized that the control group would produce significantly more positive codes per box than the clinical group. Results of these analyses are presented in Table 2.13.

Overall, significant differences were noted between groups, with the Deaf population generally demonstrating more negative codes in all boxes. Boxes 1, 2, 3, 6, and 8 demonstrated statistically significant differences between groups in the expected direction. Boxes 4, 5, and 7 demonstrated this trend, albeit without significance. The author concluded that experimental hypotheses were confirmed.

As related to Box 1, 61.5% of Deaf participants produced negative codes, as compared to only 26.9% of control group subjects. This suggests that for the clinical group, self-evaluation is more likely to be based in insecurity, lower self-esteem, and lack of integration of ego functions. Significant differences in Box 2 indicated more negative codes in the clinical population (46.2%) as compared to the control group (17.5%). This, consistent with research conducted by Hindley, Kitson, and Leach (2000), suggests that the clinical group demonstrates greater challenge in entering into contact with the environment, which may stem (in part) from difficulties communicating with the maternal figure during development. Given the lack of significance in Box 4 (the box of the paternal figure), lack of verbal and non-verbal communication with the mother in particular appeared related to observed psychopathological indicators.

TABLE 2.13 Frequency of Negative and Positive Codes by WDCT Box—Differences Between Deaf (N = 39) and Control Groups (N = 234)

Box	*Group*	*Frequency [Negative] (χ^2)*	*% [Negative]*	*Frequency [Positive] (χ^2)*	*% [Positive]*	χ^2	p	Φ^a
Box 1	Deaf	24 (10.77)	61.5	15 (5.04)	39.5	18.44	.0001	.26
	Control	63 (1.80)	26.9	171 (.84)	73.1			
Box 2	Deaf	18 (10.87)	46.2	21 (3.00)	53.8	16.17	.0001	.24
	Control	41 (1.81)	17.5	193 (.50)	82.5			
Box 3	Deaf	16 (2.44)	41	23 (.94)	59	3.93	.05	.12
	Control	60 (.41)	25.6	174 (.16)	74.4			
Box 4	Deaf	18 (.13)	46.2	21 (.10)	53.8	.27	.6023	.03
	Control	98 (.02)	41.8	137 (.02)	58.2			
Box 5	Deaf	19 (1.35)	48.7	20 (.80)	51.3	2.50	.1133	.1
	Control	83 (.22)	35.4	151 (.13)	64.6			
Box 6	Deaf	9 (9.94)	23.1	30 (.91)	66.9	12.66	.001	.22
	Control	14 (1.66)	6.1	220 (.15)	93.9			
Box 7	Deaf	25 (.54)	64.1	14 (.67)	35.9	1.42	.2329	.07
	Control	126 (.09)	53.7	108 (.11)	46.3			
Box 8	Deaf	14 (7.91)	35.9	25 (1.64)	64.1	11.14	.001	.20
	Control	33 (1.32)	14.1	201 (.27)	85.9			

Notes: Positive Codes: C+PC; Negative Codes: NC+AC+AD+D. Effect sizes calculated by current authors from previously published analyses. a. Φ effect sizes: small: .1–.29; medium: .3–.49; large: > .5 (Cohen, 1988).

Box 3 illustrates the amount of energy available to individuals in service to the ego, facilitating adaptation to the environment; that is, the internal energy and drives available to the individual for productive use. Consistent with other results, the Deaf population produced significantly more negative codes (41.0%) as compared to the control group (25.6%). Considering the Jungian psychoanalytic understanding of affective complexes (see Jung, 1960 for a review), the authors hypothesized post-hoc that this lower score in Box 3 was likely related to the presence of affective difficulties draining available energy to ego functioning.

One of the most sensitive boxes on the WDCT, Box 6 relates to judgment, reality testing, one's capacity to structure and organize the environment, the ability to manage and resolve challenges, and general cognitive/rational processes. Similar to other studies, significant differences were noted, with the Deaf group demonstrating a higher frequency of negative codes (23.1%) as compared to the control group (6.1%). Confirming previous research, Box 6 appears one of the most sensitive differentiating measures between the Deaf and normative populations.

Lastly, Box 8, which measures areas of socialization, social skills, interactions with others, and the ability to enter into mature, socially flexible, and genuine relationships, differed significantly between groups. Again, the Deaf group produced a higher frequency of negative codes (35.9%) as compared to the control group (14.1%). On the basis of previous clinical literature citing interpersonal and social reciprocity challenges in the Deaf population, this finding was both expected and confirmed.

Overall, data from previous research studies was confirmed by the present research. Box 6 (rationality and cognitive processes) was the strongest differentiator between groups. Boxes 3, 4, and 8 indicate interruptions in interests and energy, as well as potential challenges in interpersonal relationships. Lastly, consistent with past studies, significant difficulties were noted in Box 2, suggesting sensory deficits may negatively impact both the relationship to mother and the sensitivity to others.

Given that these studies were conducted with children and adolescents, it is likely that these observed discrepancies may reduce or normalize during development (as suggested by previously reviewed CWS research). Citing the protective factors of the Deaf community, these differences are likely more visible during the childhood developmental period prior to full immersion in the Deaf culture and full acquisition of sign language abilities.

Bianchi di Castelbianco, Crisi, & Palermo (2002)

In continuing their research investigating the Deaf and Hard of Hearing population, Bianchi di Castelbianco and colleagues investigated differences within the Deaf community as compared to heterogeneous and homogeneous genotypes of the Serotonin Transporter Gene, linked to anxiety and internal distress via previous research.

In reviewing previous research, the authors noted a main objective of the study to include providing a description of Deaf individuals' personality via non-language-based assessment instruments, rather than potentially over-pathologizing the Deaf community through use of instruments designed for a hearing population. As such, the CWS was utilized, because of its reduced verbal language demands. Further, genetic studies were utilized, specifically focusing on polymorphism in genes that transmit serotonin, a neurotransmitter linked to mood disorders and stress, and believed to play an important role in brain development. While no definitive proof has been established between polymorphic gene-influenced serotonin-transmission and neuropsychological disease, authors (Melke et al., 2001) have described an association between S alleles (in the gene in question) and traits of anxiety. Therefore, the specific aim of the current study was to demonstrate that the presence of anxiety in some Deaf individuals is not due solely to the inability to hear, but rather also represents a genetic vulnerability at the polymorphic level.

More recent research highlights the link between the S allele of the S/S genotype and affective disorders, including major depressive disorder, unipolar or bipolar depression, and seasonal affective disorder (as described in Margoob & Mushtaq, 2011). In some of these cases, heterogeneous genotype (i.e., L/S) appeared to constitute a protective factor as related to environmental stress. Conversely, individuals with homogeneous genotype L/L who were exposed to environmental adversity displayed significantly higher rates of depressive and anxiety disorders (Laucht et al., 2009, replicated by Zhang et al., 2009). For comprehensive summary of current research on genetic sensitivity and the Serotonin Transporter Gene, see Caspi, Hariri, Holmes, Uher, and Moffitt (2010).

Fifty-four Deaf participants (36 male, 18 female) were included in the current study, representing a subset of the sample included in a larger study. Degree of hearing loss was distributed from mild to severe (Mild = 2, Moderate = 12, Severe = 24). Genetic testing related to the polymorphic Serotonin Transport Gene in question identified three types of alleles: L/S (heterogeneous; N = 32; 22 male, 10 female; age: $\bar{x}$ = 17.5), S/S (homogeneous; N = 4; 3 male, 1 female), and L/L (homogeneous; N = 18; 11 male, 7 female; age: $\bar{x}$ = 14).

To ascertain differences between allele groups, the authors evaluated categorical differences related to overall Global Assessment assigned to each participant's CWS protocol. As described above, in completing the CWS scoring mechanics, each protocol is assigned an overall Global Assessment classification, ranging from "No Pathology" (NOP) to "Pathological" (PTL). This classification rubric is divided into five categories, two of which are considered positive (NOP + "Low Symptoms" [LSI]) and three of which can be considered negative (PTL + "Moderate Symptoms" [MSI] and "Severe Symptoms" [SSI]). Clinical and control groups were compared based on their classification within this Global Assessment rubric. Given previous research, individuals with the L/L homogeneous genotype were expected to produce significantly more negative codes, as compared to heterogeneous L/S counterparts. For the purposes of analysis, the S/S

TABLE 2.14 Frequency of Distribution of Positive and Negative Global Assessment Classifications—Differences with the Deaf Group* Between Genotype L/S and Genotype L/L Groups

Group	*Frequency [Negative] (χ^2)*	*% [Negative]*	*Frequency [Negative] (χ^2)*	*% [Negative]*	χ^2	*p*	Φ^a
L/S	18 (.46)	56	14 (.89)	44	3.7656	.05	.27
L/L	15 (.82)	83	3 (1.59)	17			

Notes: Positive Global Assessment classification = NOP + LSI; Negative Global Assessment classification = MSI + SSI + PTL.

* When Genotype groups (L/S and L/L) were compared to matched adolescent control sample, statistically significant differences were noted ($\chi^2 = 8.2305$, $p = .016$) with clinical groups demonstrating greater frequency of negative Global Assessment.

Effect sizes calculated by current authors from previously published analyses. a. Φ effect sizes: small: .1–.29; medium: .3–.49; large: >.5 (Cohen, 1988).

group was not included due to small sample size. As expected, significant differences between the L/S and L/L groups were identified, presented in Table 2.14.

In examining the results, 83% of individuals with the homogeneous L/L genotype produced a negative global assessment classification, as compared to 56% of the heterogeneous L/S genotype. The authors concluded that this confirms the experimental hypotheses, and suggests the potentially protective factor of allele heterogeneity of the Serotonin Transport Gene. The authors further asserted that these findings support previous research identifying anxious characteristics within the Deaf community, specifically higher in the homogeneous allele group (Jorm et al., 2000). Additionally, while a small sample size, these findings give biological support to the utility of the CWS in diagnostic assessment and follow-up.

Bianchi di Castelbianco, Crisi, Palermo, Palladino, Sommaruga, Sgueglia, & Vichi (2002)

In further investigating differences between the Deaf and normative population, Bianchi di Castelbianco and colleagues conducted a pilot study with Deaf children. Citing literature indicating the presence of psychological discomfort and difficulty in the Deaf population (Hindley, Kitson, & Leach, 2000), the authors hypothesized that deprivation of hearing during preverbal development likely limits exposure to emotional content and information, which may impact relationships with primary attachment figures. Given this expectation, specific hypotheses of this study predicted that Deaf children, as compared to their matched control counterparts, would demonstrate more negative Codes in WDCT Boxes 2 and 4 (representing relationship to the maternal and paternal figure, respectively). Additional expectations, based upon previous literature and research, predicted more negative values in Boxes 1 and 6 for Deaf children, reflecting higher levels of self-doubt and recognition of greater difficulties, and less cognitive flexibility. The authors asserted that early intervention during this developmental period must focus not only on communication, but also include simulation of emotional and relational skills and abilities.

The pilot study included 33 participants, divided into three groups. The first group (N = 11) was comprised of children participating in language-based therapeutic intervention. The second group (N = 13) was comprised of children participating in gestural rehabilitation therapy, including therapeutic intervention provided via sign language. The third group (N = 9) was receiving a combination of the two above-mentioned therapeutic interventions. The three groups were compared to a matched control sample with no diagnosed hearing loss. Comparisons between the Code of each WDCT box were made between the four groups (3 clinical, 1 control). Given the small number of participants, the study was considered exploratory, and while significant findings were reported, no statistical data was provided by the authors in publication.

Overall results confirmed the experimental hypothesis, with clinical groups (specifically the first two groups, each of which received one form of intervention in isolation) demonstrating Codes that were less positive in the boxes of male (Box 4) and female (Box 2) relationships, related to parents when assessing children. Additionally, all three groups demonstrated significant differences in the predicted direction as compared to the control group, suggesting less positive self-concept in the clinical groups (Box 1), and a strong tendency toward rationality and rigidity of thought (Box 6). Additional findings, not hypothesized by the authors, indicated Codes that were less positive in Box 3 for Deaf children, suggesting potential difficulty in planning and maintaining a productive direction of psychic energies. Overall, these findings were noted to be consistent with literature and previous research.

Convergent Validity

More recent convergent validity studies have examined the CWS in relationship to a variety of symptoms, attachment styles, and diagnoses and conditions, in both the clinical and selection fields. Organized by focus, CWS convergent validity research will be reviewed as related to: learning disorders, general psychiatric conditions (including psychosis), depression and suicide, trauma and adjustment conditions (including work abuse), eating disorders, psychiatric symptoms associated with medical conditions, attachment, and test use within special situations (including infertility). CWS convergent validity in the selection field will be reviewed. Lastly, the ability of specific CWS content scores to indicate pathology and personality traits will be discussed.

Learning Disorders

Crisi (2006)

Following earlier research related to children with learning disabilities, Crisi hypothesized that children with learning disorders would produce more movement responses on the Wartegg, but also would produce a higher number of Global Rejections as compared to control group children. These hypotheses were based in the guiding beliefs of the *Istituto di Ortofonologia*, where the research was conducted, that observed learning disabilities often reflect emotional or psycho-affective symptoms, rather than organic cognitive deficits. Given this theory, it was hypothesized that children with learning disabilities would demonstrate average to above average cognitive abilities, as evidenced by average or above average primary movement scores (M) and positive codes in Box 6, the box of rational thought. At the same time, it was hypothesized that children with learning disabilities would demonstrate greater levels of internal tension and distress, indicated by above average secondary movement scores (FM, MI, FE) and higher levels of internal conflict, indicated by the presence of the special score Global Rejection (GR).

To investigate these hypotheses, 195 children (LD: 125 male, 70 female) independently diagnosed with learning disabilities were compared to 971 control group subjects (504 male, 467 female). The experimental group was divided into two age bands: 6–7 years old (CN: $N = 118$; 81 male, 37 female) and 8–10 years old ($N = 77$; 44 male, 33 female). No significant differences between groups were noted concerning age or gender.

In terms of overall cognitive abilities, the experimental group (LD) produced a higher number of primary movement (M) responses than the control group (CN), as predicted by the author (LD: 2.82; CN: 2.05, $p < .05$). While not statistically significant, the experimental group also produced higher levels of secondary movement, as predicted (FM: LD = .73, CN = .44; MI: LD = 5.06, CN = 4.68), with one exception (FE: LD = .83, CN = 1.78, $p < .01$). As Facial Expression (FE) movement responses are thought to reflect expressed emotion, the author hypothesized post-hoc that reduced FE scores in the experimental group may reflect the inability of children with learning disabilities to express their emotions, or a tendency to constrict or internalize these emotions leading to a deleterious impact on cognitive functioning. Additionally, as predicted, no significant differences were noted in Box 6 codes between experimental and control groups, suggesting that children in the learning disorder group demonstrated no more difficulties in rational thinking than their control group peers.

Along with secondary movement scores, the presence of Global Rejections was investigated with the clinical group producing a significantly higher percentage of this special score than their control group counterparts. Specific statistically significant differences were noted in Box 1 (LD: .19, CN: .04, $p < .05$), Box 2 (LD: .29, CN: .11, $p < .05$), Box 4 (LD: .49, CN: .2, $p < .01$), and Box 5 (LD: .44, CN: .17, $p < .01$). Given these findings, the author concluded that diminished cognitive performance resulting from psychoaffective disturbance is likely related to several factors, including self-concept (Box 1), general emotional sensitivity (Box 2), and reactions to authority (Box 4, Box 5). Overall, results suggested that children with learning disabilities demonstrate adequate cognitive abilities (M, Box 6 code), although may experience greater degrees of internal tension (FM, MI), may have a harder time expressing emotions (FE), and likely experience greater psychoaffective disturbance (GR).

General Psychiatric Conditions

Benedetti, Bologna, Crosato, Favretti, Giusti, Lestingi, Sangiorgi, & Crisi (2008)

Benedetti and colleagues conducted exploratory analysis regarding the ability of the CWS to differentiate between normative and clinical groups diagnosed with various psychiatric conditions. Fifty-six participants, 84% referred for clinical care and assessed while participating in inpatient psychiatric treatment, and 16% participating in medical-legal evaluation for forensic reasons, comprised the clinical group (age: $\bar{x}$ = 29.49, SD = 13.38; range = 10–55). No differentiation was made related to clinical diagnosis or mental health condition. The clinical group was 53.57% female (*N* = 30) and 46.43% male (*N* = 26). Educational level ranged from 5 years of academic instruction (17.8%), 6–8 years (44.6%), 9–13 years (33.9%), to over 13 years of academic instruction (3.57%). No significant differences were noted within the clinical group (in terms of age, gender, or education differences) as related to scores on CWS indices. The clinical group was compared with a group of control subjects (*N* = 299) matched in age, gender, and educational level from the Italian standardization sample.

Differences between clinical group and control group participants were examined related to 12 major CWS indices (EC+%, AQ+%, FQ+%, Affective Stability Index, P%, P+%, O%, O+%, IIT-1, IM, AI, and IIT-2). Additionally, 14 content categories were investigated (Human, Object, Architecture, Symbol, Astronomical, Nature, Botany, Animal Simulacrum, Biology, Food, Fire, Human Simulacrum, Pathology, and Cloud). Lastly, 17 Special Score categories were evaluated (Personalized Answer, Self-Criticism, Crossed Border, Reversed Box, Anxiety Stroke, Morbid, Incomplete Drawing, Inadequate Integration, Missing Union, Perseveration, Arbitrary Performance, Global Rejection, Partial Rejection, Interpreted Stimulus, Disproportion, and Transparency). Given the high number of comparisons undertaken, the Bonferroni post-hoc correction was applied (Bonferroni, .05: $p < .001$).

Presented in Table 2.15, significant differences between clinical and control groups were found in 4 out of 12 major scoring indices, one content category, and 7 out of 17 special score categories following Bonferroni correction.

As expected, CWS indices (FQ+%, O%, O+%, AI) demonstrated higher mean values in the control group as compared to the clinical group, reflecting more adequate adjustment to the environment and to reality, but also indicating higher awareness of experienced difficulties. Popular response percentage (P%) approached significance, suggesting greater ability of control group participants to engage in shared conceptual thinking than clinical groups participants.

TABLE 2.15 Significant Differences on Major CWS Indices, Content Categories, and Special Scores—Clinical (Psychiatric Diagnosis) Group vs. Control Group

Index, Content, Special Score	*Control* $\bar{x}$	*Control SD*	*Clinical* $\bar{x}$	*Clinical SD*	*t (354 df)*	*p*	d^a
Indices							
Form Quality (FQ+%)	99.76	1.576	87.15	13.19	16.044	.000*	1.70[b]
Popular Responses (P%)	19.38	10.83	23.72	11.45	–2.743	.006	.29[c]
Original Responses (O%)	.24	1.618	7.32	9.34	–12.233	.000*	1.30[c]
O% with Good Form (O+%)	2.34	15.14	40.49	42.78	–12.015	.000*	1.27[c]
Anxiety Index (AI)	.94	.15	.84	.20	4.372	.000*	.46[b]
Index of Inner Tension 2 (IIT-2)	5.22	1.34	4.79	1.58	2.152	.032	.22[b]
Content Categories							
Human Content (H%)	12.35	10.98	17.89	16.54	–3.185	.002	.33[c]
Object Content (OBJ%)	38.19	19.58	28.48	16.11	3.523	.000*	.37[b]
Symbol Content (SIG%)	4.90	9.31	8.82	13.42	–2.692	.007	.28[c]
Human Simulacrum (HS%)	12.50	.00	14.58	4.86	–1.986	.05	.21[c]
Special Scores							
Personalized Answer (PA)	.02	.16	.35	1.02	–5.267	.000*	.56[c]
Self-Criticism (SC)	.00	.00	.12	.38	–5.603	.000*	.56[c]
Anxiety Stroke (AS)	7.46	1.29	6.65	1.63	4.161	.000*	.44[b]
Incomplete Drawing (ID)	.02	.14	.18	.42	–5.037	.000*	.54[c]
Inadequate Integration (II)	.03	.19	.18	.42	–4.131	.000*	.44[c]
Missing Union (MU)	.16	.40	.00	.00	2.966	.003	.32[b]
Perseveration (PP)	.00	.00	.25	.60	–7.051	.000*	.79[c]
Arbitrary Performance (AP)	.02	.12	.23	.59	–5.508	.000*	.59[c]
Interpreted Stimulus (IS)	.00	.05	.11	.55	–3.096	.002	.33[c]

Notes: * Significance noted following Bonferroni ($p < .05$) post-hoc correction; $p < .001$.

Effect sizes calculated by current authors from previously published analyses. a. *d* effect sizes: small: .2–.49; medium: .5–.79; large: > .8 (Cohen, 1988). b. Control group values greater than clinical group. c. Clinical group values greater than control group.

Regarding primary Contents, results found lower levels of Object content (OBJ%) in clinical subjects, suggesting some disconnection from relationships in the environment. Lower levels of Human (H%) and higher levels of Human Simulacrum (HS%) were further noted in the clinical group, indicating the tendency to develop poor interpersonal relationships and to defensively avoid emotional contact. It should be noted that Animal Simulacrum (AS) content, Pathological content (PAT), Food content (FD), and Cloud content (CLD)—all of which have been linked to lower functioning and pathological conditions in other research— also approached significance in this study, with the clinical group demonstrating higher means than control group participants.

Lastly, referring to Special Scores, results demonstrate that the mean values of 7 out of 17 categories were significantly different between the clinical and control groups. In particular, clinical group members produced a higher frequency of: 1) Personalized Answer (PA), indicating an egocentric view of the world and potentially weakened self/world and reality/fantasy boundaries; 2) Self-Criticism (SC), indicating low self-esteem and insecurity; 3) Anxiety Stroke (AS), suggesting higher levels of internal tension and distress; 4) Incomplete Drawing (ID), suggesting marked insecurity and indecision, as well as possible detachment from reality; 5) Inadequate Integration (II), indicating an impaired sense of reality; 6) Perseveration (PP), indicating a stereotypical style of thinking; and 7) Arbitrary Performance (AP), indicating a reduced ability to perceive reality. It should be noted that two additional special scores approached significant, including Missing Union (MU), indicating psychoaffective inhibition of intelligence, and Interpreted Stimulus (IS), suggesting a tendency to avoid conflict with an associated high level of internal tension.

Individual box Codes were also analyzed by the investigators, to identify the ability of the Analysis of Sequence 1 to differentiate between clinical and control subjects. As described previously, in the Analysis of Sequence 1, each of the eight WDCT boxes are assigned a Code computed mathematically by summing the Evocative Character (EC) and Affective Quality (AQ) scores of each box. Six codes are possible in each box, two considered positive (C, PC) and four considered negative (NC, AC, AD, D). To analyze differences between clinical and control groups, the presence of positive codes (C and PC) in each group was investigated using *t*-test analysis. The control group demonstrated a statistically significant higher mean of positive codes per protocol ($\bar{x}$ = 5.22, SD = 1.34) as compared to the clinical group ($\bar{x}$ = 4.78, SD = 1.58; t = 2.152, df = 354, p = .032). From these results, the authors concluded that members of the clinical group produce significantly fewer positive box Codes, suggesting decreased relatedness to the environment and less positive affective experiences, and a higher number of negative codes.

Overall, the authors concluded that the CWS demonstrates preliminary ability to discriminate between clinical (psychiatric) and normative groups on several levels: normatively scored calculations and indices, presence of Special Scores, Content of drawings (scored per normative scoring rules), and Code of individual WDCT boxes (calculated per CWS guidelines). Given these findings, it was suggested that the CWS could serve as a sensitive, brief, and non-intrusive screening tool in a variety of clinical settings.

Crisi (2009)

The convergent validity of the Wartegg Index of Psychopathology (WIP) was investigated via comparison between normal (control group) subjects (*N* = 307), applicants deemed unfit for military service ("Unfit": *N* = 265), victims of workplace harassment and/or abuse ("Work-abused": *N* = 106), and individuals independently seeking outpatient psychotherapy ("Therapy-seeking": *N* = 57). To determine differences between groups, percentages of each group's distribution within the four quadrants of the WIP were calculated, with differences between groups subsequently investigated via chi-square analysis.

The Wartegg Index of Psychopathology (WIP) is a graphic representation of personality structure, plotting state anxiety and distress on the vertical axis and trait personality integration and flexibility on the horizontal access. Given the intersection of these continuous axes, four distinct personality descriptions, or "quadrants," may be derived:

Quadrant A: Low experienced state distress; High degree of flexibility and integration. Quadrant A generally represents autonomy and independence and lack of significant distress, tension, or dysphoria. Given the assumption of adaptation and health, it is expected that a significant proportion of the normal population will be categorized within Quadrant A.

Quadrant B: Low experienced state distress; Low degree of flexibility and integration. Quadrant B generally represents detachment, isolation, and in extreme cases, psychosis. These symptoms are generally not accompanied by awareness of suffering or discomfort. Given these symptoms and descriptions, it is expected that a higher percentage of individuals unfit for military service (including detachment, inability to work collaboratively with others, limited self-knowledge, antisocial attitudes, depressive symptoms, and difficulties in reality testing) might be categorized in Quadrant B.

Quadrant C: High experienced state distress; High degree of flexibility and integration. Quadrant C generally represents tendencies toward dependence. Moreover, given a well-functioning personality structure coupled with elevated state distress, trauma, adjustment, and adaptation disorders prevail in this quadrant. Given this, it is expected that individuals experiencing workplace harassment or abuse may more readily belong to Quadrant C.

Quadrant D: High experienced state distress; Low degree of flexibility and integration. Quadrant D generally represents long-standing and problematic patterns of ambivalence, discomfort, conscious distress, immaturity, and conflict. Anxious conditions and Cluster B personality disorders (Borderline, Histrionic, Narcissistic) are frequently found in this quadrant. Given the long-standing nature of symptoms, and the profoundly experienced distress experienced, it is expected that individuals seeking psychotherapy may frequently be categorized in Quadrant D.

TABLE 2.16 Differences in Percentage Distribution of WIP Quadrants Between Healthy, Unfit, Work-Abused, and Therapy-Seeking Groups

	Healthy %	*Unfit* %	*p*	*Work-Abused* %	*p*	*Therapy-seeking* %	*p*
Quadrant A%	45	43.1	—	10.3	.001	15.8	.001
Quadrant B%	17.3	32.1	.001	18.8	—	10.6	—
Quadrant C%	18.6	10.1	.01	36.9	.001	35.1	.01
Quadrant D%	19.3	14.6	.01	33.9	—	38.6	.01

In the normal population (Italian standardization sample, N = 2,300), distribution of subjects by Quadrant yielded the following results: Quadrant A (42.7%), Quadrant B (10.7%), Quadrant C (21.1%), and Quadrant D (25.4%).

Results of chi-square analysis are presented in Table 2.16.

In considering the results, the distribution of healthy (control group) subjects demonstrated no significant differences from the overall Italian normative sample. Statistically significant differences were noted between the control group and experimental groups. Individuals unfit for military service demonstrated a higher percentage of Quadrant B classifications as hypothesized, although also demonstrated a high percentage of classification in Quadrant A. This was explained by the authors, given that lack of fitness for military duty does not equate with psychopathology; rather, the "unfit" individuals who were classified in Quadrant A did not meet additional external criteria for military service (i.e., fitness level, military orientation, shared vision, etc.) that were unrelated to psychopathology.

Victims of work abuse and harassment demonstrated a higher percentage of trauma and adjustment difficulties (Quadrant C) as hypothesized, with a concurrent reduction in healthy adaptation (Quadrant A). Lastly, individuals seeking psychotherapy demonstrated lower levels of healthy adaptation (Quadrant A), higher levels of dependency (Quadrant C), and significantly higher levels of felt distress (Quadrant D) as hypothesized. Given these findings, the authors concluded that the CWS WIP is able to effectively discriminate between groups.

Crisi & Dentale (2016)

Crisi and Dentale investigated the convergent validity of three CWS indices—Evocative Character (EC), Affective Quality (AQ), and Form Quality (FQ)—by examining the ability of these scores to differentiate between normal ("healthy"), clinically anxious, and psychotic conditions. The CWS protocols of 564 participants (290 males, 274 females) were analyzed, with participants classified into three distinct groups based upon previous psychiatric evaluation using the DSM-IV-TR: healthy, anxious, and psychotic. The healthy group (N = 401) was comprised of 186 females and 215 males (age: $\bar{x}$ = 19.95, SD = 3.19). The anxious group (N = 56, 42 male, 14 female; age: $\bar{x}$ = 32.23, SD = 9.42) was comprised of individuals diagnosed with obsessive-compulsive disorder ($N = 18$), generalized anxiety disorder ($N = 24$), and panic disorder ($N = 14$). The psychotic group ($N = 107$, all female; age: $\bar{x} = 37.80$. $SD = 9.71$) was comprised of individuals diagnosed with paranoid schizophrenia ($N = 41$), schizo-affective disorder ($N = 11$), undifferentiated schizophrenia ($N = 6$), disorganized schizophrenia ($N = 13$), schizophrenia (no subtype) ($N = 6$), delusional disorder, erotomanic subtype ($N = 1$), bipolar psychosis ($N = 5$), and unspecified psychotic disorder ($N = 24$). Significant age [$F(2, 563) = 453.44$, $p < .001$] and gender [$\chi^2 = 31.38$, $p < .001$] differences were noted between the healthy, anxious, and psychotic groups, so these variables were included as covariates for subsequent analyses.

Two specific hypotheses were tested to assess the convergent validity of CWS indices. First, since healthy subjects are expected to demonstrate greater social sensitivity, balanced emotionality, and greater reality testing ability than psychopathological counterparts, it was hypothesized that subjects from the normative group would demonstrate higher mean Evocative Character (measuring social sensitivity), Affective Quality (measuring emotional balance), and Form Quality (measuring reality testing and connection to the environment) percentages than their psychopathological counterparts. Second, it was expected that subjects in the anxiety group would have higher averages on all three indices as compared to subjects in the psychotic group.

The power of EC and AQ in discriminating between groups was calculated using MANCOVA (controlling for age and gender). A non-parametric Quade test (controlling for age and gender) was conducted for FQ, as the distribution of scores demonstrated significant deviation from normal distribution. Significant age effects were noted for AQ ($p < .05$) and FQ ($p < .001$), but not for EC. Similarly, significant gender effects were noted for all categories (EC: $p < .05$; AQ: $p < .001$; FQ: $p < .001$). Sidak post-hoc comparisons were conducted for each category.

Results, summarized in Table 2.17, confirmed the first experimental hypotheses of the study, with mean scores of EC, AQ, and FQ significantly different between healthy, anxious, and psychotic groups in the expected directions. Specifically, healthy (normal) subjects demonstrated higher scores in all categories than pathological (anxious and psychotic groups), indicating better social adjustment (EC), more balanced emotionality (AQ), and adequate reality testing (FQ).

In regard to the second experimental hypothesis, anxious subjects were noted to exhibit higher scores on both EC and FQ categories than their psychotic counterparts, suggesting better social adaptability and reality testing. Although there was a trend in the predicted direction, no significant difference was discovered in terms of Affective Quality (AQ), suggesting less significant difference in emotional balance and regulation between the two groups.

The authors concluded that analyses support the convergent validity of EC, AQ, and FQ through demonstration of the indices' ability to differentiate between healthy and pathological groups. Further research regarding convergent and incremental validity was recommended.

TABLE 2.17 Evocative Character (EC), Affective Quality (AQ), and Form Quality (FQ) Comparisons Between Healthy, Anxious, and Psychotic Groups

Category	*Group*	$\bar{x}$	*SD*	*Skewness*	*Kurtosis*	F	*p*	*Partial eta squared*	d^{+*}
EC	Psychotic	$58.72^{a,c}$	15.69	–.41	–.20	33.70	< .001	.11	Psy/Hea = 1.66^{d}
	Anxious	$66.39^{b,c}$	16.71	–.41	–.29				Anx/Hea = $.91^{e}$
	Healthy	$77.17^{a,b}$	1.62	–.22	–.10				Psy/Anx = $.47^{f}$
AQ	Psychotic	57.92^{a}	14.12	.04	–.65	13.65	< .001	.05	Psy/Hea = $.59^{d}$
	Anxious	60.73^{b}	15.77	–.39	–.16				Anx/Hea = $.36^{e}$
	Healthy	$65.77^{a,b}$	12.07	–.05	–.04				Psy/Anx = $.18^{f}$
FQ	Psychotic	$68.50^{a,c}$	16.60	–.23	–.53	12.42	< .001	.30	Psy/Hea = 2.67^{d}
	Anxious	$85.93^{b,c}$	14.59	–1.39	2.50				Anx/Hea = 1.33^{e}
	Healthy	$99.79^{a,b}$	1.33	–6.98	52.10				Psy/Anx = 1.11^{f}

Notes: * Effect sizes calculated by current authors from previously published analyses via pair-wise comparisons between groups: Hea = healthy; Anx = anxiety; Psy = psychotic; + *d* effect sizes: small: .2–.49; medium: .5–.79; large: >.8 (Cohen, 1988):

Sidak adjustment for multiple comparisons: a. Mean difference significant at .01 level between Healthy and Psychotic groups. b. Mean difference significant at .01 level between Healthy and Anxious groups. c. Mean difference significant at .01 level between Anxious and Psychotic groups. d. Healthy group values greater than psychotic group. e. Healthy group values greater than anxiety group. f. Anxiety group values greater than psychotic group.

Psychosis

Crisi, Testa, Carlesimo, & Maio (2010)

Given the work of Benedetti et al. (2008, see above), further investigation of the ability of CWS indices and computations to differentiate between clinical and normative groups was undertaken by Crisi and colleagues (2010). The study began with 350 clinical patients who were initially assessed and diagnosed by qualified psychiatrists according to the DSM-IV-TR (American Psychiatric Association, 2000). Following evaluation, each patient was individually administered a battery of psychodiagnostic tests including the WDCT according to CWS administration guidelines. Thirty-four cases were excluded from the research, 14 (4%) due to falling outside the age range of inclusion (< 18 or > 60), and 20 due to the inability to produce a valid Wartegg protocol (5.7%). The research included 316 patients, 184 (58%) of which were hospitalized, and 132 (42%) of which were participating in day treatment programming or outpatient psychotherapy.

The researchers focused on a subset of the overall clinical sample, specifically those clients diagnosed with psychotic disorders ($N = 151$, 47.8% of the overall clinical sample); these 151 members of the Psychosis group (58 male, 93 female; age: $\bar{x} = 37.01$, $SD = 9.60$) were compared to a random sample of 299 subjects (150 male, 149 female; age: $\bar{x} = 20.94$, $SD = 2.82$) selected from the CWS standardization sample. As this constituted a preliminary data analysis, prior to investigating all clinical diagnostic groups, only differences between groups in terms of Order of Sequence (that is, the box order in which participants completed the test) and Content categories (that is, the presence or absence of specific contents, scored according to CWS guidelines) were investigated by the authors.

Two experimental hypotheses were developed, the first related to the Order of Sequence, and the second to specific Content categories. First, it was hypothesized that a higher number of psychosis group participants would follow the numerical Order of Sequence as compared to control group participants. This finding has been noted in previous research, suggesting that individuals without significant pathology are able to respond to the evocative character of the WDCT stimuli as they are generally in touch with and responsive to their internal psychoaffective dynamics. Individuals in the experimental psychosis group, by comparison, were expected to demonstrate reduced self-awareness, tendencies to insulate themselves from the evocative psychoaffective nature of the stimuli, and rigidity of thought process and behavior, as evidenced by inflexible adherence to a numerical Order of Sequence.

The second experimental hypothesis related to primary Content scoring categories. The authors hypothesized that contents related to human relationships, practical abilities and connection to the environment, sensitivity and relatedness to others (H, A, NAT, BOT, OBJ, ARC) would be higher in the control group, as compared to the experimental group. Conversely, contents connected to isolation, detachment, and withdrawal from the world and others

TABLE 2.18 Differences in Individualized and Numerical Orders of Sequence—Psychosis Group vs. Control Group

Group	*Numerical Order of Sequence*		*Individualized Order of Sequence*		χ^2	*p*	Φ^a
	N (%)	χ^2	*N (%)*	χ^2			
Psychosis	98 (65)	62.56	53 (35)	26.53	134.07	.00001	.55
Control	36 (12)	31.59	263 (88)	13.40			

Notes: Effect sizes calculated by current authors from previously published analyses; a. Φ effect sizes: small: .1–.29; medium: .3–.49; large: > .5 (Cohen, 1988).

(AS, ANA, HS, ICE, MIN, PAT, SIG) were hypothesized to occur more frequently in the experimental group.

In considering the first experimental hypothesis, related to the Order of Sequence, it is important to note that previous research has indicated that 92% of the normative sample follows an individualized Order of Sequence (Crisi, 1998, 2007); that is, when presented with the blank WDCT test form, the vast majority of test-takers follow a unique and personal system of completing the test, not bound by numerical or methodical order. In the normative sample, only 7% of test-takers followed a *numerical* Order of Sequence (i.e., Box 1, Box 2, Box 3, etc.). As such, it is expected that in a healthy, well-balanced and flexibly integrated individual, a unique Order of Sequence will be followed.

In evaluating results related to their first hypothesis, the authors noted significant differences in approach to the test between the psychosis group and the control group, presented in Table 2.18.

Given these results, the authors' first experimental hypothesis was confirmed. In considering Order of Sequence, generally speaking, healthy individuals (who are better able to access inner psychoaffective dynamics, and are therefore more responsive and adaptable) let themselves be led during test completion by the test stimuli, responding to the evocative character of each box (similar to the concept of "Card Pull" on the Rorschach Inkblot Test). As such, individualized Orders of Sequence would be expected, reflecting each participant's unique and personally driven response to the test. Conversely, results of the current study suggested that individuals in the psychosis group were less able to access internal dynamics, and were less self-aware. Moreover, a strong tendency to follow the numerical Order of Sequence was suggestive of an extreme defense against anxiety, as well as a cognitive rigidity that may serve to protect and insulate participants from disturbing evocative character.

In regard to the authors' second experimental hypothesis, differences between groups in terms of Primary Content categories were investigated. It should be noted that Content categories are rigorously scored according to CWS guidelines, and this process should not be mistaken for less structured "content analysis." In investigating the hypothesis, the frequency of protocols not containing any contents related to human relationships, practical abilities, connection to the

TABLE 2.19 Significant Differences in CWS Content Categories—Psychosis Group vs. Control Group

Index, Content, Special Score	*Control* $\bar{x}$	*Control SD*	*Psychosis* $\bar{x}$	*Psychosis SD*	*t (354 df)*	*p*	*d*+
Human Content (H%)	12.76	11.98	8.24	10.88	–3.492	.001	.37[a]
Object Content (OBJ%)	37.89	18.49	27.37	19.88	–5.87	.00001*	.62[a]
Architecture Content (ARC%)	19.58	11.27	11.82	11.21	–6.261	.00001*	.67[a]
Symbol Content (SIG%)	4.59	8.66	26.04	23.53	14.813	.0001*	1.57[b]
Pathological Content (PAT%)	1.40	3.95	3.64	8.02	4.020	.0001*	.43[b]

Notes: * Significance noted following Bonferroni ($p < .05$) post-hoc correction; $p < .0039$. Effect sizes calculated by current authors from previously published analyses; + *d* effect sizes: small: .2–.49; medium: .5–.79; large: > .8 (Cohen, 1988). a. Control group values greater than psychosis group. b. Psychosis group values greater than control group.

environment, and sensitivity and relatedness to others (H, A, NAT, BOT, OBJ, ARC) was calculated for each group. As expected, the control group (61.06%) differed significantly from the clinical group (48.20%, $\chi^2 = 6.41$, $p < .01$), producing more of these adaptive contents. Similarly, the same analysis was completed for contents connected to isolation, detachment, and withdrawal from the world and others (AS, ANA, HS, ICE, MIN, PAT, SIG). Again, significant differences were noted between groups, with the experimental group (26.4%) producing these contents more frequently than the control group (21.1%, $\chi^2 = 3.05$, $p < .01$).

In further examining these content category differences between groups at the individual category level (as opposed to the aggregate protocol level described above), four statistically significant results were noted following application of the Bonferroni correction for multiple comparisons. These results are presented in Table 2.19.

Out of the 13 Content categories investigated, four successfully differentiated between groups in the direction predicted by the experimental hypotheses. Most significantly, Object (OBJ%) and Architectural (ARC%) contents were noted as higher in the control group as compared to the psychosis group. Increased OBJ content likely indicates that the individuals of the control group demonstrate a greater ability to relate themselves to the concrete and practical aspects of reality (as compared to the psychosis group members). Similarly, ARC content (in the normative level, as seen here) can indicate a personality that is adequately structured and internally supported. Control group subjects were also noted to demonstrate higher Human (H%) content scores (approaching significance) suggesting greater interpersonal connectivity, and to the contrary, higher levels of isolation and detachment in the psychosis group.

Two additional Content domains demonstrated statistical significance, suggesting higher pathology and difficulty on the part of the Psychosis group. As compared to their control group counterparts, the psychosis group demonstrated significantly higher Symbol (SIG%) content. SIG content is typically indicative of an individual's mental representations (as opposed to concrete reality), and this heightened degree of SIG content is likely related to a rigid analog style, including primary process thinking (which would be more expected in a thought-disordered individual). Lastly, the psychosis group demonstrated higher levels of Pathological (PAT%) content, suggesting a tendency to imbue their internal world with negative experiences and bad objects. Overall, the authors concluded that their experimental hypotheses were supported with further research related to Primary Content categories recommended.

Crisi, Testa, Carlesimo, Lops, & Maio (2011)

Further investigation of the ability of CWS scores to differentiate between clinical and normative groups was undertaken by Crisi and colleagues (2011). Beginning with the same initial sample and procedures noted above (Crisi, Testa, Carlesimo, & Maio, 2010), 106 cases were excluded from the overall sample, 24 (6.9%) due to falling outside the age range of inclusion (< 18 or > 60), 28 for invalid CWS protocols (8.1%), and 54 (18.3%) due to failure to understand the test instructions. As it has been previously established that only .5% of the normative population experiences difficulty with test instructions (Crisi, 1998, 2007), the fact that 18.3% of clinical cases were unable to grasp the demands of the test indicate severe levels of affective distress and cognitive confusion. Over one quarter (26%) of individuals diagnosed as meeting criteria for a psychotic disorder, and 11% of individuals diagnosed was meeting criteria for a personality disorder were noted to experience difficulties comprehending test instructions, and were subsequently excluded from the study.

Following exclusions, 241 patients were included in the study, 136 (56%) of whom were hospitalized, and 105 (44%) of whom were participating in day treatment programming or outpatient psychotherapy. Clinical participants were grouped into five categories, based upon diagnostic features as determined by psychiatric evaluations: 1) Psychosis (N = 107, 44.4%; 74 female, 33 male; age: $\bar{x}$ = 37.8, SD = 9.706); 2) Personality Disorder (N = 54, 22.4%; 17 female, 37 male; age: $\bar{x}$ = 32.98, SD = 8.732); 3) Anxiety Disorder (N = 56, 23.2%; 14 female, 42 male; age: $\bar{x}$ = 32.23, SD = 9.416); 4) Mood Disorder (N = 19, 7.9%; 4 female, 15 male; age: $\bar{x}$ = 38.42, SD = 9.634), and 5) Other Disorder (N = 5, 2.1%; 2 female, 3 male; age: $\bar{x}$ = 2.758, SD = 6.943). It should be noted that a subset of the personality disorder group (N = 37, 15.3% of total group) was diagnosed with borderline personality disorder. For the purposes of the current study, only the first three groups were considered (psychosis, personality disorder, anxiety disorder) due to limited number of subjects falling within the remaining two categories. These three groups were compared to a random sample of 401 subjects (215 male, 186 female; age: $\bar{x}$ = 20.94, *SD* = 2.82) selected from the 2005 CWS standardization sample. Differences between groups were investigated in terms of Order of Sequence (that is, the box order in which participants completed the test), major indices of the CWS, Content categories, and Special Scores.

Six specific experimental hypotheses were investigated by the authors, each specifically in relationship to differences between the control and psychosis groups. While the anxiety disorder and personality disorder groups were included in analyses, given their relatively small sizes, inclusion was considered exploratory in nature, allowing only preliminary comparison between groups.

> *Hypothesis 1: Given previous research, the psychosis group would demonstrate a higher frequency of numerical Order of Sequence than the other groups. Moreover, all clinical groups would demonstrate a higher frequency of numerical Order of Sequence than the control group participants.*

Regarding Order of Sequence, similar to the study described above, significant differences (χ^2 = 108.321, $p < .00001$) were noted in the frequency of *numerical* Orders of Sequence between the control group and each of the clinical groups (psychosis, personality disorder, anxiety disorder). As predicted, the psychosis group demonstrated the highest frequency of *numerical* Orders of Sequence, followed by the personality disorder and anxiety disorder experimental groups. The authors asserted that the higher percentage of *numerical* (non-individualized) Orders of Sequence in the more pathological groups confirm the rigidity, internal distress, need for structure, heightened anxiety, and defensive attempts related to interpersonal protection from unwanted stimulation suggested by the included diagnoses. Results from chi-square analysis between the four groups are provided in Table 2.20.

TABLE 2.20 Frequency of Distribution of Numerical Order of Sequence Between Control, Psychosis, Anxiety Disorder, and Personality Disorder Groups

Group	*Frequency [Numerical OoS] (χ^2)*	*% [Numerical OoS]*	*Frequency [Individual OoS] (χ^2)*	*% [Individual OoS]*	χ^2	*p*	V^a
Control	31 (5.65)	7.7	370 (24.96)	92.3	108.1321	.00001	.41
Psychosis	54 (13.45)	50.5	53 (59.47)	49.5			
Anxiety Disorder	15 (.48)	25.9	41 (2.11)	74.1			
Personality Disorder	14 (.37)	26.8	40 (1.64)	73.2			

Notes: Effect sizes calculated by current authors from previously published analyses; a. *V* effect sizes: small: .1–.29; medium: .3–.49; large: >.5 (Cohen, 1988).

Hypothesis 2: Experimental groups will demonstrate more negative values on the main indices of the CWS as compared to the control group. Of the clinical groups, the psychosis group will produce the most negative values. In terms of Content scoring, results from the previous study (Crisi, Testa, Carlesimo, & Maio, 2010) were expected to be replicated.

In terms of comparisons between groups related to major CWS indices, exploratory analysis was conducted between groups with authors anticipating significant effect sizes. Highest discriminatory power was expected between the control group and psychosis group. In terms of specific indices of the CWS, it was expected that the control group (as compared to the psychosis group) would demonstrate: 1) higher Evocative Character (EC+%); 2) higher Affective Quality (AQ+%); 3) higher Form Quality (FQ+%); 4) higher Affective Stability Index (A/F Ratio); 5) lower Popular (P%) percentage; 6) higher Popular responses with good form (P+%); 7) lower Original responses (O%); 8) higher Original responses with good form (O+%); 9) higher Index of Inner Tension-1, Impulsivity Index (IM), and Anxiety Index (AI); 10) lower Index of Suicidal Tendencies; and 11) higher level of primary Movement (M) responses.

In terms of Content categories, similar to previous research, the authors hypothesized that control group participants would demonstrate greater frequency of Human (H%), Object (OBJ%), and Architecture (ARC%) content as compared to clinical groups, and lower frequency of Symbol (SIG%), Abstract (ABS%), and Pathology (PAT%) content.

Evaluation results demonstrated statistically significant differences in 30 out of 40 comparisons between the control group and experimental groups, following Bonferroni post-hoc correction. In terms of indices and computations, 15 statistically significant differences were noted, occurring in the expected direction, with effect size ranging from medium/large (EC+%, FQ+%, P%, P+%, O%, O+%, IIT-1, AI, IIT-2, and IST) to small (Affective Stability Index, M). Regarding Primary Contents, seven comparisons were significant and in the expected direction, with effect sizes ranging from large (OBJ%, ARC%, and SIG%) to medium/small (H%, ABS%, PAT%, and CLD%). Lastly, in terms of Special Scores, nine comparisons demonstrated significant differences between the control and clinical groups in the expected direction with effect sizes ranging from large/medium (ID, II, PP, AP, PR, MU) to small (PA, GR, IS, DS). Full results are presented in Table 2.21.

Regarding experimental hypothesis #2, 15 investigated variables demonstrated significant effect sizes (ranging from medium to large), with the psychosis group typically showing the most difference as compared to the control group. In examining the indices, the control group demonstrated: 1) higher Evocative Character (EC+%), generally suggesting greater relatedness and connection with the environment; 2) higher Affective Quality (AQ+%), indicating balanced affective regulation and integration; 3) significantly higher Form Quality (FQ+%), related to cognitive processes, control, and reality testing; 4) higher Affective Stability Index (A/F Ratio), indicating an appropriate level of affective openness and experience coupled with suitable levels of cognitive control and ego strength; 5) lower Popular (P%) responses suggesting the clinical groups demonstrated higher levels of stereotypical thinking; 6) higher Popular responses with good form (P+%), related to the ability to share in a common way of thinking with others while remaining connected to reality; 7) lower Original responses (O%), indicating the potential for the clinical groups to demonstrate idiosyncratic, unique, and divergent manners of thinking; 8) higher Original responses with good form (O+%), with similar interpretation as P+% above; 9) higher Index of Inner Tension-1, Impulsivity Index (IM), and Anxiety Index (AI), as these markers of internal distress are less apparent in psychotic clients as compared to the normative group; 10) lower Index of Suicidal Tendencies, suggesting increased likelihood of suicidal ideation or attempt in clinical groups; and 11) higher percentage of Primary Movement (M) as expected, reflecting greater levels of internal cognitive resources. The control group was further noted to demonstrate a significantly higher percentage of Facial Expression (secondary movement). While this effect was not predicted, previous studies have also demonstrated this tendency, suggesting facial expression responses may indicate greater awareness of internal emotional states on the part of the control/normative group (as compared to clinical groups).

Regarding Content categories, seven investigated contents indicated significant (medium or large) effect sizes. As predicted, control group subjects demonstrated greater frequency of Human (H%), Object (OBJ%), and Architecture (ARC%) content as compared to clinical groups, suggesting greater adaptability to the environment, social connectedness, and practicality. Conversely, clinical groups demonstrated more frequent Symbol (SIG%), Abstract (ABS%), and Pathology (PAT%) content, indicating tendencies toward primary process thinking, disconnection from the environment, increased levels of internal pain, and poor mental representations. Additionally, while not specifically hypothesized, it was noted that subjects in the personality disorder group demonstrated higher frequency in Cloud content (CLD%), suggesting greater internalized distress that is likely to have reached conscious awareness. Overall, the authors concluded that experimental hypothesis #2 was confirmed.

> *Hypothesis 3: Experimental groups will demonstrate higher frequency of CWS Special Scores as compared to the control group. Of the experimental groups, the psychosis group will demonstrate the highest frequency of Special Scores. Moreover, a specific constellation of Special Scores thought to be associated with thought disorder (Personalized Answer, Contamination, Arbitrary Performance, Disproportion, and Transparency) will occur with significantly higher frequency in the psychosis group as compared to the control group.*

Exploratory analysis was completed, investigating the frequency of all CWS Special Scores in the three clinical groups (psychosis, personality disorder, anxiety disorder) as compared to the control group. Results are presented in Table 2.22.

TABLE 2.21 Effect Sizes of Major CWS Indices and Content Categories in Psychosis, Anxiety Disorder, and Personality Disorder Groups as compared to Control Group

Index, Content [Control $\bar{x}$, SD]	*Psychosis*			*Anxiety Disorders*			*Personality Disorders*		
	$\bar{x}$ *(SD)*	*t (506) (p)*	*d Cohen*	$\bar{x}$ *(SD)*	*t (p)*	*d Cohen*	$\bar{x}$ *(SD)*	*t (p)*	*d Cohen*
Indices									
Evocative Character (EC+%) [77.17, 10.62]	58.72 (15.69)	−14.291 (.000*)	1.40[c]	66.39 (16.71)	−6.552 (.000*)	.079[b]	72.59 (13.96)	−2.855 (.005)	.48[a]
Affective Quality (AQ+%) [65.77, 12.06]	57.92 (14.12)	−5.761 (.000*)	.60[b]	60.73 (15.71)	−2.808 (.005)	.36[a]	57.20 (15.92)	−4.697 (.000*)	.76[b]
Form Quality (FQ+%) [99.79, 1.32]	68.50 (16.59)	−37.40 (.000*)	3.49[c]	85.93 (14.59)	−18.606 (.000*)	1.74[c]	86.65 (11.32)	−22.284 (.000*)	2.18[c]
Affective Stability Index: A [2.83, .67]	2.50 (.79)	−4.26 (.000*)	.44[a]	2.52 (.97)	−2.957 (.003)	.37[a]	2.44 (.98)	−3.699 (.000*)	.44[a]
Affective Stability Index: F [3.97, .19]	2.52 (.76)	−34.03 (.000*)	3.01[c]	3.28 (.71)	−15.700 (.000*)	1.51[c]	3.29 (.61)	−16.874 (.000*)	1.83[c]
Popular Responses (P%) [19.62, 10.69]	22.60 (12.38)	2.471 (.014)	−.26[a]	24.68 (13.31)	3.209 (.001*)	−.42[a]	25.48 (12.94)	3.681 (.000*)	−.57[b]
P% with Good Form (P+%) [99.82, 2.71]	83.98 (19.10)	−15.53 (.000*)	1.45[c]	91.53 (13.42)	−10.642 (.000*)	1.03[c]	91.44 (12.42)	−11.330 (.000*)	1.09[c]
Original Responses (O%) [.24, 1.59]	7.92 (10.35)	14.26 (.000*)	−1.29[c]	3.59 (7.57)	7.760 (.000*)	−.73[b]	7.91 (11.31)	12.745 (.000*)	−.94[c]
O% with Good Form (O+%) [100.00, .00]	42.67 (30.72)	−5.86 (.000*)	3.73[c]	61.54 (30.13)	−4.014 (.0001*)	2.55[c]	71.63 (28.96)	−3.070 (.004)	2.74[c]
Index of Inner Tension 1 (IIT-1) [1.22, .31]	.61 (.40)	−16.38 (.000*)	1.66[c]	.93 (.42)	−6.075 (.000*)	.78[b]	.99 (.45)	−4.586 (.000*)	.72[b]
Impulsivity Index (IM) [.28, .22]	.22 (.24)	−2.44 (.015)	.26[a]	.27 (.21)	−.342 (.0732)	.05	.29 (.26)	.131 (.896)	.07
Anxiety Index (AI) [.93, .17]	.39 (.28)	−24.66 (.000*)	2.37[c]	.65 (.29)	−10.087 (.000*)	1.19[c]	.70 (.30)	−8.046 (.000*)	1.03[c]
Index of Inner Tension 2 (IIT-2) (*first half of ratio*) [5.29, 1.32)	3.79 (1.40)	−10.29 (.000*)	1.10[c]	4.36 (1.73)	−4.772 (.000*)	.61[b]	4.65 (1.61)	−3.282 (.001*)	.59[b]

Index, Content *[Control* $\bar{x}$*, SD]*	*Psychosis*			*Anxiety Disorders*			*Personality Disorders*		
	$\bar{x}$ *(SD)*	*t* (506) *(p)*	*d* *Cohen*	$\bar{x}$ *(SD)*	*t* *(p)*	*d* *Cohen*	$\bar{x}$ *(SD)*	*t* *(p)*	*d* *Cohen*
Index of Suicidal Tendencies (IST) [1.98, 1.63]	5.93 (1.88)	21.45 (.000*)	–2.25[c]	4.46 (2.05)	10.273 (.000*)	–1.47[c]	4.63 (1.97)	10.866 (.000*)	–1.34[c]
Primary Movement (M) [.30, .68]	.07 (.34)	–3.44 (.001*)	.46[a]	.18 (.47)	–1.300 (.194)	.21[a]	.19 (.64)	–1.179 (.239)	.32[a]
Animal Movement (FM) [.10, .32]	.01 (.09)	–2.73 (.006)	.41[a]	.00 (.00)	–2.212 (.027)	.59[b]	.04 (.19)	–1.316 (.189)	.10
Inanimate Movement (MI) [.56, .77]	.37 (.57)	–2.31 (.021)	.27[a]	.46 (.63)	–.877 (.381)	.13	.52 (.74)	–.361 (.719)	.01
Facial Expression (FE) [.17, .41]	.03 (.16)	–3.55 (.000*)	.50[b]	.02 (.13)	–2.794 (.005)	.57[b]	.02 (.13)	–2.732 (.007)	.46[a]
Human Content (H%) [12.76, 11.96]	7.54 (11.41)	–4.04 (.000*)	.45[a]	8.96 (10.04)	–2.269 (.024)	.35[a]	10.75 (12.97)	–1.144 (.253)	.21[a]
Object Content (OBJ%) [37.89, 18.49]	26.95 (21.07)	–5.21 (.000*)	.55[b]	21.93 (16.57)	–6.120 (.000*)	.91[c]	26.05 (15.92)	–4.483 (.000*)	1.00[c]
Architecture Content (ARC%) [19.58, 11.27]	11.48 (11.90)	–6.53 (.000*)	.70[b]	12.41 (9.99)	–4.516 (.000*)	.67[b]	13.34 (11.24)	–3.823 (.000*)	.59[b]
Symbol Content (SIG%) [4.59, 8.66]	27.72 (26.91)	14.63 (.000*)	–1.30[c]	26.88 (26.97)	12.608 (.000*)	–1.25[c]	20.36 (21.15)	9.985 (.000*)	–1.34[c]
Astronomical Content (AST%) [3.72, 6.25]	5.91 (9.55)	2.84 (.005)	–.28[a]	4.45 (7.43)	.989 (.370)	–.12	3.94 (7.21)	.235 (.815)	–.15
Nature Content (NAT%) [5.49, 8.16]	3.19 (6.28)	–2.70 (.007)	.32[a]	4.63 (7.15)	–.742 (.458)	.11	4.86 (8.20)	–.528 (.598)	–.01
Botany Content (BOT%) [6.00, 8.12]	4.64 (9.09)	–1.50 (.134)	.16	8.40 (11.02)	1.976 (.049)	–.25[a]	5.85 (8.81)	–.127 (.899)	–.02
Abstract Content (ABS%) [.00, .00]	2.12 (7.40)	5.74 (.000*)	–.57[b]	.67 (3.70)	3.641 (.000*)	–.36[a]	.69 (3.77)	3.710 (.000*)	–.51[b]
Cloud Content (CLD%) [.47, 2.37]	1.00 (3.61)	1.84 (.066)	–.18	.22 (1.67)	–.744 (.457)	.12	1.73 (4.55)	3.200 (.001*)	–.38[a]
Pathological Content (PAT%) [1.40, 3.95]	2.34 (6.67)	1.83 (.066)	–.18	3.57 (7.80)	3.311 (.001*)	–.37[a]	3.27 (6.09)	3.032 (.003)	–.40[a]

Notes: Effect sizes calculated by current authors from previously published analyses: a. small effect size (.2–.49); b. medium effect size (.5–.79); c. large effect size (>.8; Cohen, 1988). * Significance noted following Bonferroni ($p < .05$) post-hoc correction; $p < .00125$.

TABLE 2.22 Effect Sizes of Major CWS Special Scores in Psychosis, Anxiety Disorder, and Personality Disorder Groups as compared to Control Group

Special Score	*Psychosis*			Anxiety Disorders			*Personality Disorders*		
[Control $\overline{x}$, SD]	$\overline{x}$ (*SD*)	*t* (506) (*p*)	*d* Cohen	$\overline{x}$ (*SD*)	*t* (*p*)	*d* Cohen	$\overline{x}$ (*SD*)	*t* (*p*)	*d* Cohen
Personalized Answer (PA) [.03, .18]	.23 (.90)	4.195 (.000*)	–.37[a]	.00 (.00)	–1.212 (.226)	.32[a]	.13 (.61)	2.521 (.012)	–.42[a]
Reversed Box (RB) [.16, .58]	.08 (.31)	–1.25 (.211)	.16	.07 (.32)	–1.080 (.281)	.19	.06 (.23)	–1.270 (.205)	.32[a]
Incomplete Drawing (ID) [.02, .17)	.31 (.53)	8.98 (.000*)	–.80[c]	.11 (.36)	2.812 (.005)	–.31[a]	.19 (.51)	4.623 (.000*)	–.43[a]
Inadequate Integration (II) [.05, .22]	.58 (.91)	10.48 (.000*)	–.93[c]	.32 (.60)	6.325 (.000*)	–.65[b]	.46 (.81)	8.074 (.000*)	–.89[c]
Missing Union (MU) [.18, .41]	.05 (.25)	–3.10 (.002)	.39[a]	.00 (.00)	–3.200 (.001*)	.86[c]	.00 (.00)	–3.143 (.002)	.86[c]
Perseveration (PP) [.00, .05]	.32 (.76)	8.24 (.000*)	–.78[b]	.07 (.26)	4.749 (.000*)	–.45[a]	.06 (.30)	3.226 (.001*)	–.44[a]
Arbitrary Performance (AP) [.02, .14]	1.13 (1.35)	16.08 (.000*)	–1.48[c]	.71 (.92)	13.796 (.000*)	–1.28[c]	.83 (1.20)	12.817 (.000*)	–1.39[c]
Global Rejection (GR) [.04, .25]	.21 (.65)	4.16 (.000*)	–.37[a]	.16 (.62)	2.533 (.000*)	–.26[a]	.13 (.43)	2.095 (.037)	–.35[a]
Partial Rejection (PR) [.01, .25]	.43 (.90)	8.10 (.000*)	–.72[b]	.41 (.91)	7.000 (.000*)	–.68[b]	.17 (.63)	3.235 (.001*)	–.44[a]
Interpreted Stimulus (IS) [.00, .05]	.04 (.23)	2.75 (.006)	–.24[a]	.05 (.22)	3.899 (.000)	–.37[a]	.00 (.00)	–.367 (.714)	.10
Disproportion (DS) [.01, .12]	.06 (.23)	2.49 (.013)	–.23[a]	.04 (.18)	1.108 (.268)	–.13	.09 (.04)	3.526 (.000*)	–.28[a]
Transparency (TR) [.01, .08]	.05 (.21)	2.91 (.004)	–.26[a]	.02 (.13)	.780 (.436)	–.09	.06 (.23)	2.928 (.004)	–.48[a]

Notes: Effect sizes calculated by current authors from previously published analyses; a. Small effect size (.2–.49); b. Medium effect size (.5–.79); c. large effect size (>.8; Cohen, 1988). * Significance noted following Bonferroni ($p < .05$) post-hoc correction; $p < .00125$.

Nine Special Scores demonstrated significant effect sizes when comparing the control group to each clinical group, with significance noted following Bonferroni post-hoc correction. As expected, the psychosis group demonstrated both the largest effect sizes and the most frequent differences from the control group. Specifically, clinical group members produced a higher frequency of: 1) Personalized Answer (PA), indicating their egocentric view of the world and their weakened self/world and reality/fantasy boundaries; 2) Incomplete Drawing, suggesting marked insecurity and indecision, as well as possible detachment from reality; 3) Inadequate Integration (II), indicating an impaired sense of reality; 4) Missing Union (MU), indicating potential psychoaffective inhibition of intelligence, noted solely in the anxiety disorder group; 5) Perseveration (PP), indicating a stereotypical style of thinking; 6) Arbitrary Performance (AP), indicating a reduced ability to perceive reality; 7) Global Rejection (GR), indicating areas of personality too conflictual, problematic, or "split off" to access; 8) Partial Rejection (PR), suggesting significant ambivalence and conflict in specific areas of functioning; and 9) Interpreted Stimulus (IS), suggesting a tendency to avoid conflict with an associated high level of internal tension, again noted only in the Anxiety Disorder group. As expected, in each case, Special Scores were significantly more frequent in clinical groups than the control group.

To further investigate experimental hypothesis #3, frequency of the presence of Special Scores indicating thought disorder (including Arbitrary Performance [AP], Personalized Answer [PA], Contamination [CO], Disproportion [DS], and Transparency [TR]) were summed across all WDCT boxes of the psychosis group and the control group. Chi-square analysis, presented in Table 2.23, indicates a statistically significant difference between groups in the frequency of these Special Scores related to thought disturbance. Protocols of 82% of psychosis group members contained problematic Special Scores, whereas only 7.5% of protocols of control group members contained these same Special Scores. Given these findings, experimental hypothesis #3 was considered fully supported.

TABLE 2.23 Frequency of Distribution of Special Scores Indicative of Thought Disturbance (AP, PA, CO, DS, & TR) Between Psychosis and Control Groups

Group	*Frequency [Present] (χ^2)*	*% [Present]*	*Frequency [Absent] (χ^2)*	*% [Absent]*	χ^2	*p*	Φ^1
Psychosis	88 (160.43)	82.2	19 (48.54)	17.8	264.73	.00001	.72
Control	30 (42.81)	7.5	371 (12.95)	92.5			

Notes: χ^2 computed for total WDCT boxes possible per group (Control: *N* = 401 multiplied by 8 boxes per protocol = 3,208 total boxes; Psychosis: *N* = 107 multiplied by 8 boxes per protocol = 856 total boxes). Effect sizes calculated by current authors from previously published analyses; 1Φ effect sizes: small: .1-.29; medium: .3-.49; large: >.5 (Cohen, 1988).

TABLE 2.24 Frequency of Distribution of Positive (+), Neutral (+/–) and Negative (–) Global Assessment Classifications Between Psychosis, Anxiety Disorder, Personality Disorder, and Control Groups

Group	*Fr.* + (χ^2)	% +	*Fr.* +/– (χ^2)	% +/–	*Fr.* – (χ^2)	% –	χ^2	*p*	*V*[a]
Control	365 (22.97)	91	32 (11.48)	8	4 (51.32)	1	299.6455	.00001	.49
Psychosis	25 (34.08)	23.4	21 (2.03)	19.6	61 (12.92)	57			
Personality Disorder	23 (7.02)	40.7	22 (24.06)	38.9	11 (.92)	20.4			
Anxiety Disorder	25 (4.60)	46.4	14 (4.98)	25	15 (6.25)	28.6			

Notes: + Positive Assessment; +/– Neutral Assessment; – Negative Assessment. Effect sizes calculated by current authors from previously published analyses; a. V effect sizes: small: .1–.29; medium: .3–.49; large: >.5 (Cohen, 1988).

Hypothesis 4: Control group will demonstrate more positive Global Assessment classification than experimental groups, with Psychosis group demonstrating more negative classifications than other experimental groups.

In addition to examination of Order of Sequence, Indices, Content categories, and Special Scores, the authors also examined overall Global Assessment of the protocols in each group to determine whether differences exist. It was hypothesized that experimental groups would demonstrate higher percentages of negative classifications as compared to the control group, with the psychosis group demonstrating the highest frequency of negative classifications.

As described earlier, in determining the Global Assessment, each protocol is assigned an overall classification based on specific CWS scores and indices, ranging from "No Pathology" (NOP) to "Pathological" (PTL). This classification rubric is divided into five categories, two of which are considered positive codes (NOP + "Low Symptoms" [LSI]), one of which is considered neutral ("Moderate Symptoms" [MSI]) and two of which are considered negative codes (PTL + "Severe Symptoms" [SSI]). Chi-Square analysis was conducted, indicating significant differences between groups existed ($\chi^2 = 299.6455$, $p < .00001$) in terms of Global Assessment. Results are presented in Table 2.24.

Results of analyses demonstrate statistically significant differences between groups in terms of distribution of Global Assessment classifications. As predicted, the control group was noted to demonstrate the highest percentage of positive codes, followed by the anxiety disorder group. The psychosis group was noted to demonstrate the highest percentage of negative codes, followed by the anxiety disorder group. Each group differed significantly from the control group, demonstrating the effectiveness of the Global Assessment in identifying pathological conditions.

Hypothesis 5:In terms of placement on the Wartegg Index of Psychopathology (WIP), the psychosis group will demonstrate higher frequency of classification in Quadrant B than other groups, and overall less positive placement (lower frequency in Quadrant A and alpha Area of all Quadrants).

As described previously, the CWS co-locates individuals on a graphic depiction of personality functioning, based upon the degree of currently experienced distress (vertical axis) and level of personality flexibility and integration (horizontal axis), known as the WIP. Four quadrants result, labeled A, B, C, and D, respectively. Quadrants A and C (reflecting high flexibility and integration) are generally considered less pathological and therefore more "healthy." Quadrant B reflects low personality integration and flexibility paired with absence of significant internal distress, whereas Quadrant D reflects low personality integration paired with significant levels of tension and distress. Given the expectation of personality inflexibility coupled with lower distress levels, it was hypothesized that a higher frequency of psychosis group members would be classified in Quadrant B.

TABLE 2.25 Frequency of Individuals Classified in WIP Quadrant B—Psychosis vs. Control Groups

Group	*Frequency [Qr. B] (χ^2)*	*% [Qr. B]*	*Frequency [Not Qr. B] (χ^2)*	*% [Not Qr. B]*	χ^2	*p*	Φ^a
Psychosis	67 (82.92)	62.62	40 (22.92)	37.38	134.07	.00001	.51
Control	43 (22.13)	10.72	358 (6.11)	89.28			

Notes: Effect sizes calculated by current authors from previously published analyses; a. Φ effect sizes: small: .1–.29; medium: .3–.49; large: >.5 (Cohen, 1988).

TABLE 2.26 Frequency of "Positive" WIP Classifications—Psychosis vs. Control Groups

Group	*Frequency [Positive] (χ^2)*	*% [Positive]*	*Frequency [Negative] (χ^2)*	*% [Negative]*	χ^2	*p*	Φ^a
Psychosis	41 (5.59)	38.32	66 (6.92)	61.68	15.84	.0001	.18
Control	240 (1.49)	59.85	161 (1.85)	40.15			

Notes: "Positive" WIP classification is considered placement in Quadrant A, or the *alpha* area of Quadrant B, C, and D. These areas represent adaptive functioning. Effect sizes calculated by current authors from previously published analyses; a. Φ effect sizes: small: .1–.29; medium: .3–.49; large: > .5 (Cohen, 1988).

As predicted, when compared to the control group, the psychosis group demonstrated a significantly higher frequency of classification in Quadrant B of the WIP. Results are presented in Table 2.25.

Overall frequency of classification in "positive" areas of the WIP was further compared between the psychosis and control groups. Positive classifications on the WIP are typically considered area *alpha* of all quadrants (the adaptive sphere of functioning), as well as all of Quadrant A. It was hypothesized that the psychosis group would demonstrate lower frequency of classification in these positive, adaptive areas of the WIP as compared to the control group. Results of chi-square analysis are presented in Table 2.26.

As predicted, the psychosis group demonstrated significantly fewer positive classifications on the WIP as compared to the control group. This suggests overall less flexible, integrated, and adaptive functioning on the part of the psychosis group.

Hypothesis 6: The psychosis group will demonstrate fewer overall positive box Codes (C or PC) than the control group.

In determining areas of integration, freedom from conflict, strength, and adaptive functioning, each box of the WDCT is assigned a positive or negative Code. As described previously, Codes are calculated via summation of Affective Quality and Evocative Character scores for each WDCT box, with six possible

Codes resulting. Two of these Codes are positive (C, PC) whereas four are considered negative (AC, AD, NC, D). A negative Code suggests less sensitivity, integration, and adaptive strength in the area of functioning in which it occurs.

To investigate experimental hypothesis #6, the presence of positive WDCT box Codes was investigated. That is, given the theory that individuals diagnosed with psychotic disorders demonstrate less flexibility, integration, and environmental sensitivity, it was hypothesized that psychosis group members would produce fewer positive box Codes. The number of positive box Codes (C and PC) was summed across protocols, with chi-square results presented in Table 2.27.

TABLE 2.27 Frequency of WDCT Boxes with Positive Codes—Psychosis vs. Control Groups

Group	*Frequency [Positive]* (χ^2)	*% [Positive]*	*Frequency [Negative]* (χ^2)	*% [Negative]*	χ^2	*p*	Φ^a
Psychosis	406 (30.13)	47.4	450 (49.64)	52.6	101.04	.00001	.16
Control	2123 (8.04)	66.2	1085 (13.24)	33.8			

Notes: Positive codes are considered C and PC. Effect sizes calculated by current authors from previously published analyses; a. Φ effect sizes: small: .1–.29; medium: .3–.49; large: > .5 (Cohen, 1988).

As predicted, members of the psychosis group produced fewer positive box Codes (47.4%) than control group members (66.2%), suggesting reduced flexibility, sensitivity, and adaptive functioning.

Overall, the authors concluded that all six experimental hypotheses were confirmed, with the CWS clearly differentiating between psychosis group and control group members in terms of index scores, Content scoring, Special Scores, Order of Sequence, Global Assessment, and box Codes. While exploratory, further differences were noted between the control group and remaining clinical groups (anxiety disorder, personality disorder). While these differences were significant, they were less robust as compared to noted differences between the control and psychosis groups. The authors concluded that more research was needed to clarify these differences.

Depression and Suicidality

Daini, Manzo, Pisani, & Tancredi (2010)

Daini and colleagues used the CWS to investigate differences between depressed subjects with no history of suicidal attempt, psychiatric patients who had attempted suicide, and matched control group subjects. Exploratory in nature, the authors reported their intention to assess whether the CWS demonstrates validity in assessing the risk of suicidality. No specific experimental hypotheses were reported. Per the authors, while self-reports are typically used in hospital settings, a projective methodology for determining risk of suicide was warranted, given the intersection of projective methods, psychopathology, and therapeutic intervention. Given this, the CWS was chosen given that it is "simpler and quicker to administer in emergency situations compared to other projective tests" (p. 173).

The current study comparatively analyzed responses to each box of the WDCT, as well as differences between group means related to major calculated indices of the CWS (including EC+%, AQ+%, FQ+%, P%, IIT-1, IM, AI, and Global Rejection) to determine whether the CWS is able to differentiate between psychiatric and control groups. While the CWS includes a computer-generated constellation of scores to indicate suicidal risk and intrapsychic indicators of suicidal tendencies (Index of Suicidal Tendencies, IST), review of this published study indicates that the authors did not include the IST as a variable to be studied in their research. Future studies related to suicidality will benefit from specific inclusion of the IST.

Three groups of subjects participated in the study, labeled as Attempted Suicide (AS), Depression (D), and Control (C). Subjects from the clinical groups (AS, D) were currently receiving hospital-based treatment, whereas control group subjects had never participated in psychiatric care. The attempted suicide (AS) group was comprised of 25 subjects (5 male, 20 female; age: $\bar{x}$ = 36.58, *SD* = 14.6) previously diagnosed with various psychiatric disorders, including depression, eating disorders, personality disorders, obsessive-compulsive disorder, or delirium. The depression (D) group was comprised of 29 subjects (5 male, 24 female; age: $\bar{x}$ = 37.28, *SD* = 10.48) presenting with clinically relevant states of depression, some comorbid with other mood and eating disorders. Lastly, the control (C) group was comprised of 29 subjects (9 male, 20 female; age: $\bar{x}$ = 39.95, *SD* = 11.26). No clinically significant differences in age or gender were noted between groups.

To evaluate differences between groups, as related to major indices of the CWS, analysis of variance (ANOVA) was conducted, with Duncan's post-hoc test utilized to explore differences in terms of group means. Results are presented in Table 2.28.

In evaluating results, significant differences were noted in terms of Affective Quality (AQ+%), Popular Responses (P%), and the number of special score Global Rejection (GR). In terms of Affective Quality, those who had attempted suicide demonstrated significantly lower AQ than matched control group subjects. When investigated further, the difference between groups occurred primarily in the area of ego functioning and thought (Adaptive Area, $F = 3.574$; $p < .5$), with no significant difference noted between groups in the more internal, psycho-affective domain (Affective Area). Similarly, the attempted suicide group demonstrated significantly higher levels of Popular responses (P%) than both the depression and control group. Again, these differences, when investigated further, depended solely on the area of ego functioning and rational thought (Adaptive Area, $F = 4.689$, $p < .01$). Lastly, the attempted suicide group was noted to demonstrate a significantly higher number of Global Rejections (GR, in which

TABLE 2.28 Mean Differences in CWS Indices—ANOVA by Group (Attempted Suicide, Depression, Control)

Variable	AS (N = 25) $\bar{x}$ (SD)	D (N = 29) $\bar{x}$ (SD)	C (N = 29) $\bar{x}$ (SD)	F	*Duncan Post-Hoc*	d+
Evocative Character (EC+%)	68.50 (17.07)	64.34 (16.18)	71.77 (16.33)	.293	—	.14
Affective Quality (AQ+%)	58.75 (17.68)	63.58 (13.16)	69.40 (12.08)	3.739	AS < C*	.56
Form Quality (FQ+%)	72.84 (19.87)	75.19 (22.97)	79.31 (13.37)	.800	—	.27
Popular Responses (P%)	37.25 (23.67)	25.86 (13.54)	24.35 (11.85)	4.640	AS > C** AS > D**	.40
Index of Inner Tension (IIT-1)	.52 (.47)	.61 (.57)	.59 (.43)	.240	—	.04
Impulsivity Index (IM)	.17 (.20)	.18 (.20)	.18 (.20)	.70	—	.07
Anxiety Index (AI)	.38 (.39)	.42 (.42)	.43 (.36)	.93	—	.10
Global Rejection (GR)	.52 (1.0)	.14 (.74)	.03 (.18)	3.387	AS > C*	.11

Notes: * $p < .05$; ** $p < .01$. Effect sizes calculated by current authors from previously published analyses; + *d* effect sizes: small: .2–.49; medium: .5–.79; large: >.8 (Cohen, 1988).

Table adapted from Daini, Manzo, Pisani, & Tancredi (2010).

nothing is drawn in a WDCT Box), reflecting a complete denial or avoidance of specific areas of personality, as compared to the control group. Analysis of the frequency of GR responses by box indicated no significant findings; that is, while AS group members were more likely than other groups to produce Global Rejections, there was no statistical trend related to which WDCT box the GR was produced within.

In considering these results, the authors posited that while depressed clients and those who have attempted suicide share many commonalities, the significant difference between them evident in this study appears related to thought process. That is, subjects who had previously attempted suicide appeared to gloss over internal thoughts about their lives, concerns, and feelings, instead subscribing to the conventional way of thinking (higher P%). To potentially counter negative affective states (lower AQ+%), this thinking style may reflect attempts at rationalization, divesting the self from both affective and interpersonal experiences. This hypothesis is further supported by all significant differences occurring in the area of ego functioning (ADP area, related to rational thought, view of self, and other-relatedness), as well as the higher number of Global Rejections presented by the attempted suicide group. The authors suggested that this last finding, the increase in GR responses, may indicate a tendency of participants to avoid relationships and self-disclosure of internal feeling states—a finding support by research conducted with suicide survivors.

Trauma and Adjustment Disorders

Crisi (2010a, in Bianchi di Castelbianco & Di Renzo)

Crisi and colleagues conducted exploratory analysis to investigate the impact of trauma on a group of adolescents, hypothesizing that the CWS would sensitively identify affective and interpersonal changes resulting from exposure to traumatic experiences; 104 adolescents (48 male, 56 female) aged 14–18 ($\bar{x}$ = 16.23, *SD* = 1.243) were included in the clinical sample. Each had been exposed to the significant earthquake that occurred in L'Aquila, Italy in April 2009, and had subsequently sought treatment at a mobile mental health clinic. Each participant was assessed within three months of the traumatic event, completing several self-report questionnaires along with the WDCT according to CWS administration guidelines.

Results of the clinical group CWS protocols were compared to a group of 400 subjects from the 2005 CWS standardization sample (186 male, 215 female; See ►Appendix A for a description of CWS standardization sample). In terms of major CWS indices, four primary and central scores were investigated, each relevant to clinical interpretation: 1) Evocative Character (EC+%), which measures an individual's sensitivity and engagement with the environment; 2) Affective Quality (AQ+%), which indicates an individual's affective receptivity and expression; 3) Form Quality (FQ+%), which illustrates a person's cognitive and rational functioning, thought processes, and commonality in thinking with others; and 4) Index of Suicidal Tendencies (IST), a constellation of scores and markers suggesting depressive tendencies, internal tension, limited coping, and heightened impulsivity. It was expected that the control group would demonstrate higher values of EC, AQ, and FQ, whereas the trauma-exposed group would demonstrate higher values on the IST. Results of *t*-test analyses are presented in Table 2.29.

Given that major CWS indices have been noted to stabilize at approximately age 14, no significant differences between the adolescent population and the young adult control group were expected; however, overall results suggested significant impact of trauma on the adolescents' functioning (as compared to expected normative values), as predicted. Specifically, lower Evocative Character (EC+%) is likely to reflect increased difficulty on the part of the clinical group subjects, in relating to the environment, engaging in reciprocal social interactions, and remaining open to affective situations. Similarly, lower Affective Quality (AQ+%) suggests adolescents in the clinical group were more likely to experience greater depressive symptoms, including limited spontaneity, reduced motivation, and higher levels of overall emotional constriction or avoidance.

A significant difference was noted in Form Quality (FQ+%) between groups, which typically relates to an individual's reality testing, judgment, cognitive self-control, and ego functions. As each of the assessed adolescents was in school at the time of assessment, with no notable learning difficulties or mental health diagnoses related to psychosis or thought disturbance, such a significant difference in Form Quality likely indicated a current condition related to high stress and difficulties in adjustment, potentially resulting in a relaxation of rational control mechanisms, and less cognitive ability to manage emotions and impulses. Lastly, the Index of Suicidal Tendencies (IST), which indicates a depressive state that may produce intrapunitive self-harm behaviors, was noted to be significantly higher in the clinical group. It should be noted that the average value for the IST in the normative population is 1.98, and the clinical group mean was equal to 3.42. This suggested a significantly higher level of depressive affect and internal discomfort in the clinical group, as compared to normative expectations.

In addition to examining major CWS indices, the authors further evaluated categorical differences between groups related to overall Global Assessment classifications assigned to each participant's CWS protocol. As discussed above, in completing the CWS scoring mechanics, each protocol is assigned an overall Global Assessment classification, ranging from "No Pathology" (NOP) to "Pathological" (PTL). This classification system is divided into five categories, two of which are considered positive (NOP + "Low Symptoms" [LSI]) and three of which are considered negative (PTL + "Moderate Symptoms" [MSI] and "Severe Symptoms" [SSI]). Clinical and control groups were compared based on their classification within this Global Assessment rubric. The authors hypothesized that the clinical (trauma-exposed) group would produce fewer positive Global Assessment classifications, and a higher frequency of negative classifications as compared to the control group. Results are presented in Table 2.30.

TABLE 2.29 Significant Differences on Major CWS Indices—Clinical (Trauma-Exposed) vs. Control Groups

Index	*Control* $\bar{x}$	*Control SD*	*Clinical* $\bar{x}$	*Clinical SD*	*t (503 df)*	*p*	*d*+
Evocative Character (EC+%)	77.17	10.62	64.58	18.51	–9.052	.0001	.80[a]
Affective Quality (AQ+%)	65.77	12.07	56.40	15.39	–6.638	.0001	.59[a]
Form Quality (FQ+%)	99.79	1.33	93.31	15.23	–8.427	.0001	.75[a]
Index of Suicidal Tendencies (IST)	1.98	1.64	3.42	2.24	7.362	.0001	.66[b]

Notes: Effect sizes calculated by current authors from previously published analyses; + *d* effect sizes: small: .2–.49; medium: .5–.79; large: >.8 (Cohen, 1988). a. Control group values greater than clinical group. b. Clinical group values greater than control group.

TABLE 2.30 Frequency of Distribution of Positive and Negative Global Assessment Classifications—Clinical (Trauma-Exposed) vs. Control Groups

Group	*Frequency [Positive]* (χ^2)	% *[Positive]*	*Frequency [Negative]* (χ^2)	% *[Negative]*	χ^2	*p*	Φ^a
Clinical	62 (4.52)	59.6	42 (16.3)	40.4	25.87	.00001	.23
Control	332 (1.17)	83.0	69 (4.16)	17.0			

Notes: Positive Codes: NOP+LSI; Negative Codes: MSI+SSI+PP. Effect sizes calculated by current authors from previously published analyses; a. Φ effect sizes: small: .1–.29; medium: .3–.49; large: >.5 (Cohen, 1988).

TABLE 2.31 Frequency of Distribution of Positive and Negative Codes by WDCT Box—Clinical (Trauma-Exposed) vs. Control Groups

Box	*Group*	*Frequency [Positive] (χ^2)*	*% [Positive]*	*Frequency [Negative] (χ^2)*	*% [Negative]*	χ^2	*p*	Φ^a
Box 1	Clinical	58 (2.82)	56	46 (6.43)	44	11.66	.0006	.15
	Control	293 (.73)	73	108 (1.67)	27			
Box 2	Clinical	50 (9.01)	48	54 (24.69)	52	42.43	.00001	.29
	Control	320 (2.34)	80	81 (6.40)	20			
Box 3	Clinical	44 (1.09)	42	60 (1.07)	58	2.71	.099	.07
	Control	206 (.28)	51	195 (.28)	49			
Box 4	Clinical	36 (9.29)	35	68 (12.43)	65	27.35	.00001	.23
	Control	253 (2.41)	63	148 (3.22)	37			
Box 5	Clinical	46 (7.66)	44	58 (15.10)	56	28.66	.00001	.24
	Control	289 (1.99)	72	115 (3.97)	28			
Box 6	Clinical	84 (.06)	81	20 (.30)	19	.449	.5027	.03
	Control	335 (.02)	84	62 (.08)	16			
Box 7	Clinical	42 (1.17)	40	62 (1.07)	60	2.82	.092	.07
	Control	199 (.30)	50	202 (.28)	50			
Box 8	Clinical	58 (.01)	56	46 (.07)	44	.040	.841	.01
	Control	228 (.00)	57	173 (.00)	43			

Notes: Positive Codes: C+PC; Negative Codes: NC+AC+AD+D. Effect sizes calculated by current authors from previously published analyses; a. Φ effect sizes: small: .1–.29; medium: .3–.49; large: >.5 (Cohen, 1988).

Results demonstrate a significant difference between the Global Assessment classifications of the clinical and control groups, with the clinical group demonstrating significantly more negative overall classifications. In considering interpretation of these categories, No Pathology (NOP) typically indicates adequate adjustment with the absence of significant symptoms or impairments. Similarly, while some mild affective difficulties may be present in a Low (LSI) classification, no considerable impairment is noted (due to the role of containing defenses). As expected, 83% of the control group, free from pathology, fell within these healthy categories. Conversely, the Medium (MSI) and Severe (SSI) codes indicate problematic affective, behavioral, and interpersonal symptoms that result in increasing levels of functional impairment until achieving a significant degree of mental health pathology (PTL). While only 17% of the control group fell within this most negative classification category, 40.4% of the clinical group were classified in the negative range (MSI+SSI+PTL) suggesting a significant increase in symptoms and impairment for adolescents exposed to trauma.

Given these findings, box-by-box analysis was conducted by the authors, investigating differences between clinical and control groups in terms of positive and negative Codes produced in each WDCT box. As described previously, Codes for each box are calculated by summing the Affective Quality and Evocative Character scores for each WDCT box. Six Codes are possible following this mathematical computation, two of which are considered positive (C, PC) and four of which are considered negative (AC, AD, NC, D). It was hypothesized that trauma-exposed adolescents would produce more negative codes in those areas likely to be impacted by trauma, including self-concept and self-esteem (Box 1), relationships and socialization (Boxes 2, 4, and 8), and functional energies (Boxes 3 and 5). Differences were not anticipated in Box 6, given no expected impact on cognitive ability and intellectual functioning, and Box 7, given that box values in this area tend overall to be low during adolescence due to developmental factors. Results of box-by-box analysis are presented in Table 2.31.

Results of the box-by-box comparison suggest overall lower functioning on the part of the clinical group, particularly in respect to psychoaffective issues, generally as predicted. It should be noted that Box 6, the box of rational thinking, intellect, and control (and therefore the most ego-driven of the CWS boxes), did not reach significance, suggesting the profound impact of trauma on affective experience (but not on intellect). Additionally, Box 7, which measures libidinal energies and ability to engage in emotionally intimate relationships, demonstrated no significant difference between groups; however, it should be noted that due to developmental tasks of adolescence (including questions of identity and intimacy), Box 7 Codes tend to be lower for all adolescents during this time.

In terms of the remaining boxes, a significant split between clinical and control groups was noted in Box 1, with the clinical group demonstrating significantly more negative Codes. Box 1 evokes an individual's feelings about the self and identity, with positive values linked to adequate ego functioning, harmony, and functioning in the environment. Lower scores, evidenced by the clinical group, in turn suggest lack of balance, disrupted sense of self, potential isolation and insecurity, and increased anxiety.

Box 3, which demonstrated a moderate (yet non-statistically significant) deficit on the part of the clinical group, reflects an individual's ability to productively direct psychic energy in the service of adaptation to the environment, including goal-directed behaviors. In the trauma-exposed group, this ability appeared diminished and variable, consistent with trauma-related literature indicating an increase in "blocked energy" or depressive affect. Similarly, Box 5, which represents an individual's integration of aggressive energy into the personality structure, appears significantly decreased in the clinical group as compared to matched controls. As might be expected based upon literature, lower Box 5 Codes may suggest limited frustration tolerance, limited effectiveness in dealing with negative feedback, pessimism, a view of the environment as dangerous and aggressive, and internalized aggressive impulses (intrapunitive thoughts and behaviors).

Boxes 2 and 4 suggest decreased sensitivity and relatedness in relationships, as expected. However, Box 8 demonstrated a unique and significant similarity between trauma-exposed and control group adolescents. This box relates to the social dimension of functioning, including social skills, interpersonal orientation, and the ability to engage in mutual relationships. As noted above, the adolescents in the clinical group produced a similar distribution of positive codes in this box as compared to their control group counterparts. While not predicted in the current study, several authors have suggested the reactive function trauma serves within communities—that resilient individuals impacted by disaster or difficulty may tend to band together, support each other, and look to others who have shared their experience. Higher degrees of social support, reliance on others, and sensitivity to the needs of others have been reported at the community-level post natural disaster (SAMHSA, 2014), which may, in part, suggest the reason behind the current findings. Given the exploratory nature of this study, further research in this area is recommended.

Crisi (2000)

The ability of the CWS to differentiate between groups was further evaluated in a study of children from economically disadvantaged neighborhoods versus matched children from the CWS normative sample. Given the higher rate of poverty, crime, and difficulties experienced by the experimental ("economically disadvantaged") group, it was hypothesized that these children's protocols would demonstrate higher levels of impairment and symptoms, and fewer indicators of overall positive health.

One thousand children (520 male, 480 female) aged 6–10 were included in the study, selected from an economically disadvantaged school within a poor urban neighborhood. Participants were divided into five equal bands, based upon age: 1) 6 years (N = 232, 23.2% of experimental group; males: N = 118, $\overline{x}$ = 6.42,

SD = .323; females: *N* = 114, $\bar{x}$ = 6.45, *SD* = .321); 2) 7 years (*N* = 227, 22.7% of experimental group; males: *N* = 129, $\bar{x}$ = 7.33, *SD* = .613; females: *N* = 98, $\bar{x}$ = 7.27, *SD* = .819); 3) 8 years (*N* = 248, 24.8% of experimental group; males: *N* = 123, $\bar{x}$ = 8.32, *SD* = .287; females: *N* = 125, $\bar{x}$ = 8.36, *SD* = .298); 4) 9 years (*N* = 172, 17.2% of experimental group; males: *N* = 85, $\bar{x}$ = 9.42, *SD* = .303; females: *N* = 87, $\bar{x}$ = 9.453 *SD* = .287); and 5) 10 years (*N* = 121, 12.1% of experimental group; males: *N* = 65, $\bar{x}$ = 10.40, *SD* = .315; females: *N* = 56, $\bar{x}$ = 10.34, *SD* = .311). No significant differences were discovered between groups regarding age and gender. The clinical group was compared to a sample of children selected from the CWS child normative sample (*N* = 282; 113 female, age: $\bar{x}$ = 9.3602, *SD* = 2.6043; 169 male, age: $\bar{x}$ = 9.0953, *SD* = 2.595; range: 6–14; see ►Appendix A for further information).

Initial analyses examined differences in overall Global Assessment classifications between the economically disadvantaged and control group children. As described elsewhere in this chapter, in completing the CWS scoring mechanics, each protocol is assigned an overall Global Assessment classification, ranging from "No Pathology" (NOP) to "Pathological" (PTL). This classification system is divided into five categories, two of which are considered positive codes (NOP + "Low Symptoms" [LSI]) and three of which are considered negative codes (PTL + "Moderate Symptoms" [MSI] and "Severe Symptoms" [SSI]). Clinical and control groups were compared based on their classification within this Global Assessment rubric. Results of this analysis are provided in Table 2.32.

Chi-square analysis clearly illustrates significant differences in overall level of impairment and mental health symptoms experienced by the experimental and control groups. To better understand these differences, investigation of differences in positive Global Assessment classifications (NOP + LSI) and negative Global Assessments (PTL + SSI + MSI) were further studied. Overall, the experimental group demonstrated a significantly higher percentage of negative codes (51.7%) as compared to the control group (31.9%), with statistically significant results (χ^2 = 35.5017, p < .00001). This suggests, as hypothesized, that the children of

TABLE 2.32 Distribution of Global Assessment Classifications Between Experimental (Economically Disadvantaged) and Control Groups

Global Assessment	*Control*		*Experimental*		χ^2 (*df* = 4)	*p*	V^a
	N	(%)	N	(%)			
NOP (No Pathology)	95	32.8	188	18.8			
LSI (Low Impairment)	102	35.3	295	29.5			
MSI (Medium Impairment)	60	20.8	234	23.4	51.95	.0001	.20
SSI (Severe Impairment)	26	8.9	191	19.1			
PTL (Pathological)	6	2.0	92	9.2			

Notes: Effect sizes calculated by current authors from previously published analyses; a. *V* effect sizes: small: .1–.29; medium: .3–.49; large: >.5 (Cohen, 1988).

the disadvantaged neighborhood demonstrated greater difficulties, symptoms, and impairments in their mental health functioning, as compared to their matched control group counterparts.

To further understand these findings, evaluation of differences occurring in each WDCT box was subsequently undertaken. It was noted that the experimental group demonstrated a higher than expected (as compared to normative data) number of Delay (D) and Negative Compensation (NC) box Codes. Negative Compensations have high diagnostic meaning, indicating strong internal conflict or difficulty, which have likely been "covered-up" or compensated for behaviorally. As such, difficulties may not be apparent at the behavioral level (given a demonstrated behavioral adaptation masking internal conflict). In the experimental group, the highest percentages of NC codes occurred in Boxes 2, 3, and 4, suggesting tendencies to overwork (without success), potential school phobia, possible conflict due to false assertiveness, and attachment challenges masked via social behaviors. Similarly, higher than expected levels of Delay (D) codes were discovered in the experimental group, specifically in Boxes 7 (24.4%), 5 (20.2%), 6 (18.7%), and 3 (18.7%). These findings suggest that children in dangerous and disadvantaged neighborhoods may demonstrate strong repression of affectivity, higher levels of rigidity, difficulties planning and organizing or making sense of the world, and ego-centric self-protection from intimacy. High levels of concurrent Delay in Boxes 5 and 7 are indicative of strong internal conflict, including neurotic personality organization.

Lastly, specific differences between groups in terms of negative Codes by box were investigated. The presence of the two most negative codes, described above (D + NC) were, studied for each box, with significant differences noted in 5 out of 8 boxes between the experimental and control groups. Results are presented in Table 2.33.

TABLE 2.33 Distribution of Negative Codes by Box Between Experimental (Economically Disadvantaged) and Control Groups

Box	*Control*		*Experimental*		χ^2 *(df = 1)*	*p*	Φ^a
	N	(%)	N	(%)			
1	47	16.2	151	15.1	.2332	.629	.01
2	40	13.8	188	18.8	4.676	.030	.06
3	27	9.4	480	38.0	140.411	.00001	.33
4	80	27.6	246	24.6	.5691	.4506	.02
5	38	13.2	120	12.0	.2751	.5999	.02
6	5	1.7	81	8.1	14.61	.0001	.10
7	54	18.6	317	31.7	20.988	.00001	.13
8	9	3.1	97	9.7	12.88	.0003	.10

Notes: Negative valuation includes presence of Delay (D) and Negative Compensation (NC) in each box. Effect sizes calculated by current authors from previously published analyses; a. Φ effect sizes: small: .1–.29; medium: .3–.49; large: >.5 (Cohen, 1988).

As evident from Table 2.33, children in the experimental group demonstrated significantly more negative Codes in the boxes related to sensitivity, social skills, and the ability to enter into mutual relationships (Box 2, Box 7, Box 8), and rational control, planning and organization, and achievement of goals (Box 3, Box 6). Taken with other results, experimental hypotheses were considered confirmed, with the author concluding that disadvantaged neighborhoods (including crime, poverty, and general struggle) results in less effective adaptation and a higher degree of conflict or manifest mental health symptoms. The CWS was determined to effectively discriminate between groups, highlighting behavioral symptoms and impairments (Delay), as well as more internal, behaviorally masked symptoms (Negative Compensation).

Crisi and Pastore (2006, 2010)

Crisi and Pastore, using CWS indices, examined the characteristics of work-abused victims compared to a group of control subjects. Estimates by the International Labor Organization (Harnois, Gabriel, & World Health Organization, 2000) at the time the study was completed indicated that approximately 9% of European workers (approximately 13 million) had been the victim of work-related abuses. Work abuse is defined as a systematic and long-standing (more than 6 months) pattern of psychological abuse inflicted on an individual by another individual or group in the workplace. Results of work abuse were documented to include lower self-esteem, high degree of personal distress, increased anxiety, social withdrawal, potential difficulties thinking and concentrating, and other affective impairments.

Given these previous findings, several experimental hypotheses were developed by the authors:

1. Participants in the work-abused group would demonstrate lower self-esteem as evident by less positive (and therefore more negative) Codes in Box 1, the box of self-concept.
2. Participants in the work-abused group will demonstrate tendencies toward social withdrawal, as evident by less positive Codes in Box 8.
3. Participants in the work-abused group would demonstrate difficulties reacting to frustrations and obstacles, similar to previous research with individuals who have experienced traumatic events, evidenced through lower Codes in Box 5.
4. Participants in the work-abused group will demonstrate a lower level of functioning in the social-affective environment, as evidenced by lower EC+%, and potentially decreased levels of rational control and logical thinking ability (as evidenced by lower FQ+%, higher P%, lower P+ and O+ percentages, and higher number of special scores, specifically Arbitrary Performance, Global Rejection, Partial Rejection).
5. Participants in the work-abused group will demonstrate higher levels of internal distress, as evidenced by higher Anxiety Index, higher Index of Inner

Tension-1, higher levels of Secondary Movement, and higher number of Special Scores related to tension (Self-Criticism and Anxiety Stroke).

Participants in the study included 107 individuals who had experienced work abuse (55 female, 52 male), divided between two age bands (35–45, 45–60). Participants were spread across four types of employment: civil servants (N = 25; 14 females, 11 males); civil management (N = 27; 13 females, 14 males); private employees (N = 28; 14 females, 14 males); and privately employed executives (N = 27; 14 females, 13 males). Each group was equally divided between age ranges. This experimental group was compared to 299 subjects (149 female, 150 male; $\bar{x}$ = 20.94, SD = 2.82) randomly selected from the 2005 CWS standardization sample. While few differences were noted within the experimental group, significant differences were noted between the experimental and control groups.

In regard to the first three experimental hypotheses, Codes of three specific boxes were analyzed, thought to be related to trauma: 1) Box 1, which relates to an individual's feelings regarding the self, the identity, and personal attributes; 2) Box 5, which indicates how an individual reacts to frustrations and the degree to which aggressive impulses are integrated into the personality structure; and 3) Box 8, which relates to the psychoaffective dynamics of socialization and the manner in which individuals successfully navigate their environment and those they encounter. For each box, chi-square analysis was completed, comparing the frequency of positive, ambivalent, and negative codes between groups.

As discussed earlier, using the CWS methodology, each box of a WDCT protocol is assigned a code based upon a mathematical summation of Affective Quality and Evocative Character scores. Six codes are possible in each box: two positive (C, PC), two ambivalent (AC, AD), and two negative (NC, D). Results of chi-square analysis for Boxes 1, 5, and 8 are provided in Table 2.34.

In regard to these three boxes, significant differences were noted in each box, with control group participants demonstrating more positive Codes in Box 1 and

TABLE 2.34 Distribution of Positive, Ambivalent, and Negative Codes in Boxes 1, 5, and 8—Work-Abused vs. Control Group

Box	*Valuation*	*Work-Abuse*		*Control*		χ^2
		N	(%)	N	(%)	*p*
Box 1	Positive	62	58.0	218	72.9	.01
	Ambivalent	36	33.6	72	24.0	.06
	Negative	9	8.4	9	3.1	.05
Box 5	Positive	50	46.7	212	70.9	.0001
	Ambivalent	34	31.8	76	25.4	—
	Negative	23	21.5	11	3.7	.001
Box 8	Positive	66	61.7	169	56.5	—
	Ambivalent	30	28.0	119	39.8	.05
	Negative	11	10.3	11	3.7	.05

TABLE 2.35 Distribution of Codes of All Boxes—Work-Abused vs. Control Group

Box Valuation	*Work-Abuse*		*Control*		χ^2
	N	(%)	N	(%)	*p*
Choice (C)	242	28.3	807	33.7	.005
Ambivalent Choice (AC)	134	15.6	328	13.7	—
Negative Compensation (NC)	51	5.9	61	2.6	.001
Positive Compensation (PC)	127	27.7	754	31.5	.05
Ambivalent Delay (AD)	116	13.6	318	13.3	—
Delay (D)	76	8.9	124	5.2	.001

Box 5, and work-abused individuals demonstrating more negative Codes in Box 1, Box 5, and Box 8. As predicted by the authors, this suggests lower self-esteem in individuals who have experienced work-abuse (Box 1), higher levels of internalized anger and tension (Box 5), and negatively impacted social relationships (Box 8). In general, differences in both statistical indices and box Codes suggested overall adaptation challenges to the situation or environment on the part of the work-abused participants, internal discomfort, challenges in thinking clearly and logically, and higher levels of anxiety. These findings are consistent with overall box Codes at the protocol level, as Table 2.35 details, suggesting general levels of dysfunction and higher levels of psychopathology.

As noted above, work-abused participants demonstrated a significantly lower number of positive Codes and a significantly higher number of negative Codes than their control group counterparts at the protocol level. This suggests the negative impact ongoing trauma may have on personality integration, flexibility, and adaptability. While statistically significant differences were noted in six CWS Boxes (1, 3, 4, 5, 6, and 8), the most pronounced impact appears in Boxes 1, 5, and 8 (as previously described in Table 2.34).

To investigate experimental hypotheses 4 and 5, differences between experimental and control groups were investigated regarding indices related to environmental functioning, logical thinking and rational control, and internal tension and distress. Results of these analyses are presented in Table 2.36.

Results suggest that work-abused subjects differ significantly from control subjects in several main indices in the expected direction. Primarily, work-abused subjects demonstrated a statistically lower EC+%, indicating a lower level of adjustment within the affective–relational environment, as well as decreased sensitivity to social context and situations. Additionally, work-abused subjects demonstrated lower FQ+%, potentially indicating a lower level of cognitive functioning (including possible concentration, thinking, and rational problem solving), likely connected to a traumatic condition in the workplace. Work-abused subjects were noted to produce protocols with higher P%, suggesting rigidity and conformity (with lower P+%), as well as innovative responses without

TABLE 2.36 Significant Differences on Major CWS Indices Between Work-Abused ("Work") and Control ("Control") Groups

Index, Content, Special Score	*Work* $\bar{x}$	*Work SD*	*Control* $\bar{x}$	*Control SD*	F (2,404)	*p*	d^+
Indices							
Evocative Character (EC+%)	70.56	15.81	77.14	11.95	19.95	.000**	.50[b]
Affective Quality (AQ+%)	60.07	12.01	64.48	11.88	10.80	.000**	.37[b]
Form Quality (FQ+%)	86.07	14.45	99.76	1.58	261.17	.000**	1.82[b]
Popular Responses (P%)	25.72	13.21	19.38	10.84	23.89	.000**	.55[a]
P% with Good Form (P+%)	91.68	15.00	99.82	3.02	73.31*	.000**	.96[b]
Original Response (O%)	4.82	7.03	.24	1.62	111.06	.000**	1.18[a]
O% with Good FQ (O+%)	71.71	25.09	100.00	.00	8.73*	.000**	.33[b]
Index of Inner Tension 1 (IIT-1)	1.14	.39	1.22	.29	4.44	.04	.23[b]
Anxiety Index (AI)	.82	.28	.94	.15	30.91	.000**	.63[b]
Secondary Movement (m)	.73	.83	.00	.95	4.12	.04	.22[a]
Special Scores							
Self-Criticism SS (SC)	1.10	1.61	.00	.00	141.37	.000**	1.33[a]
Anxiety Stroke SS (AS)	6.46	2.23	7.46	1.30	31.37	.000**	.63[a]
Arbitrary Performance (AP)	.22	.57	.00	.02	34.70	.000**	.66[a]
Global Rejection (GR)	.11	.44	.00	.07	20.28	.000**	.51[a]
Partial Rejection (PR)	.16	.73	.00	.02	8.79	.000**	.33[a]

Notes: * Cases excluded; ** Significance noted following Bonferroni ($p < .05$) post-hoc correction: $p < .003$. Effect sizes calculated by current authors from previously published analyses; + *d* effect sizes: small: .2–.49; medium: .5–.79; large: >.8 (Cohen, 1988). a. Work group values greater than control group. b. Control group values greater than work group.

TABLE 2.37 Exploratory Analysis of Significant Differences on Major CWS Indices Between Work-Abused ("Work") and Control ("Control") Subjects

Index, Content, Special Score	*Work $\overline{x}$*	*Work SD*	*Control $\overline{x}$*	*Control SD*	*F (2,404)*	*p*	*d*[1]
Indices							
Affective Stability Index (A/F): A	2.50	.68	2.81	.65	17.41	.000**	.47[b]
Affective Stability Index (A/F): F	3.23	.73	3.94	.35	171.04	.000**	1.47[b]
Index of Inner Tension 2 (IIT-2) *(first half of ratio)*	4.5	1.64	5.22	1.35	20.28	.000**	.51[b]
Index of Inner Tension 2 (IIT-2) *(second half of ratio)*	3.50	1.64	2.78	1.35	20.28	.000**	.51[a]
Content Categories							
Object Content (OBJ%)	31.07	18.84	38.09	19.68	10.25	.000**	.36[b]
Symbol Content (SIG%)	13.93	17.15	4.89	9.31	45.60	.000**	.76[a]
Nature Content (NAT%)	2.80	5.77	5.89	8.21	12.88	.000**	.40[b]
Abstract Content (ABS%)	3.97	11.97	.00	.00	33.07	.000**	.65[a]
Special Scores							
Personalized Answer (PA)	.26	.77	.02	.16	26.34	.000**	.58[a]
Inadequate Integration SS (II)	.13	.34	.03	.19	14.11	.000**	.42[a]
Perseveration (PP)	.11	.42	.00	.00	21.46	.000**	.52[a]
Stimulus Repetition (SR)	.31	.99	.00	.15	5.36	.02	.26[a]
ADP and AFF Areas							
ADP AQ+% (AQ+%[ADP])	58.66	14.22	64.86	14.58	14.41	.000**	.43[b]
ADP FQ+% (FQ+%[ADP])	87.87	14.29	99.84	1.74	202.22	.000**	1.60[b]
ADP: Affective Stability Index (A/F): A	1.19	.44	1.37	.47	11.26	.000**	.38[b]
ADP: Affective Stability Index (A/F): F	1.66	.044	1.98	.16	116.45	.000**	1.22[b]
ADP Popular (P%[ADP])	28.05	17.64	19.77	14.33	23.17	.000**	.54[a]
ADP Popular with Good FQ (P+%[ADP])	91.76	14.93	99.79	3.21	62.97*	.000**	.90

ADP Original (O%[ADP])	3.91	9.21	.00	.00	53.90	.000**	.83[a]
ADP IIT-1 (IIT-1[ADP])	1.13	.43	1.23	.35	6.33	.01	.28[b]
ADP AI (AI[ADP])	.79	.31	.93	.18	32.37	.000**	.64[b]
ADP Number of Special Scores	5.67	1.90	5.15	1.50	8.15	.000**	.32[a]
ADP Choice Codes (C)	1.35	.85	1.53	.80	3.87	.05	.22[b]
ADP Negative Compensation Codes (NC)	.21	.43	.11	.33	7.05	.01	.30[a]
AFF EC+% (EC+%[AFF])	64.99	19.75	79.12	17.39	48.31	.000**	.78[b]
AFF FQ+% (FQ+%[AFF])	84.36	17.89	99.71	2.36	210.94	.000**	1.63[b]
AFF: Affective Stability Index (A/F): A	1.30	.48	1.44	.50	5.78	.02	.27[b]
AFF: Affective Stability Index (A/F): F	1.57	.46	1.96	.22	129.84	.000**	1.28[b]
AFF Popular (P%[AFF])	23.65	2 .14	19.10	17.04	5.09	.02	.25[a]
AFF Popular+ (P+%[AFF])	92.61	16.75	100.00	.00	37.60	.000**	.69[b]
AFF Original (O%[AFF])	5.68	11.37	.48	3.20	51.45	.000	.80[a]
AFF Original+ (O+%[AFF])	72.00	25.33	100.00	.00	8.35*	.01	.33[b]
AFF AI (AI[AFF])	.85	.28	.95	.15	21.96	.000**	.53[b]
AFF IIT-2 (IIT-2[AFF]) *(first half of ratio)*	2.04	1.05	2.65	.97	30.06	.000**	.62[b]
AFF IIT-2 (IIT-2[AFF]) *(second half of ratio)*	1.96	1.05	1.35	.97	30.06	.000**	.62[a]
AFF Number of Special Scores	6.08	1.95	5.14	1.34	30.58	.000**	.62[a]
AFF Number of Rejections (GR/PR)	.21	.61	.07	.45	7.84	.01	.32[a]
AFF Primary Movement	.28	.61	.15	.45	5.70	.02	.27[a]
AFF Secondary Movement	.39	.63	.55	.75	3.89	.05	.22[b]
AFF Choice Codes (C)	.93	.68	1.17	.71	9.93	.000**	.36[b]
AFF Negative Compensation Codes (NC)	.26	.48	.10	.31	16.34	.000**	.46[a]
AFF Positive Compensation Codes (PC)	1.11	.87	1.47	.85	14.19	.000**	.42[b]
AFF Delay Codes (D)	.52	.69	.31	.54	10.70	.000**	.37[a]

Notes: * Cases excluded; ** Significance noted following Bonferroni ($p < .05$) post-hoc correction: $p < .009$. Effect sizes calculated by current authors from previously published analyses; [1]*d* effect sizes: small: .2–.49; medium: .5–.79; large: >.8 (Cohen, 1988). a. Work group values greater than control group. b. Control group values greater than work group.

an adequate interpretation of reality (Higher level of O% with negative Form Quality, lower O+%) suggesting some disconnection from the environment and internal retreat into fantasy. Work-abused participants further demonstrated high percentages of Special Scores related to general psychoaffective difficulty (Global Rejection, Partial Rejection). Lastly, work-abused subjects were noted to demonstrate significantly higher tendency to ruminate and interpret situations in an inadequate and potentially illogical manner (AP), suggesting a retreat from the environment and a developing idiosyncratic view of the world as a result of trauma.

In regard to hypothesis 5, specifically related to internal distress, results were mixed. No significant differences were noted between the experimental and control groups as related to special score Anxiety Stroke, Anxiety Index (AI), or Index of Inner Tension-1 (IIT-1). However, the work-abused participants produced higher rates of Secondary Movement and other Special Scores, as predicted. Specifically, higher frequency of Self-Criticism was noted in the work-abused sample, indicating pronounced feelings of insecurity, indecision, and fear. Moreover, while not predicted, Incomplete Drawing special scores were noted as higher in the work-abused subjects, further supporting the hypothesis related to insecurity and distress. This suggests that AI and IIT-1 are measuring trait anxiety, which may rise in the control group during test administration, and may not always effectively differentiate between characterologically anxious and transiently anxious individuals. Further exploration of this finding is recommended.

Overall, test results confirm experimental hypotheses 1–4, with mixed results noted for hypotheses 5. Given this, these results are generally consistent with previous literature related to work-abuse, demonstrating the Crisi Wartegg System's sensitivity in evaluating psychoaffective functioning.

Following investigation of the experimental hypotheses, further exploratory analysis was conducted on 78 additional CWS variables. Statistically significant differences were noted in 45 of 78 studied CWS variables following Bonferroni post-hoc correction, presented in Table 2.37.

Results suggested that work-abused subjects differ significantly from control subjects, with several post-hoc hypotheses put forth by the authors. In terms of Primary Content category percentages, work-abused subjects demonstrated a less pronounced disposition to practical abilities than control subjects (lower OBJ% and higher ABS%), a more defensive attitude toward the testing situation (Higher SIG%), and a lower adjustment to social demands (lower NAT%). They further demonstrated high percentages of Special Scores related to self-referential introspection and egocentrism (PA). Overall, more negative functioning was noted for the work-abused group in both the Adaptive (ADP) area, indicating challenges in social–environmental functioning, and the Affective (AFF) area, indicating deficits in emotional regulation, control, and integration. Given these findings, the impact of work abuse on individuals appears pervasive and significant, with the need for more research indicated.

Eating Disorders

Daini, Lai, Festa, Maiorino, Pertosa, & De Risio (2006)

Using the CWS, the psychological and psychopathological characteristics of individuals with eating disorders were evaluated by Daini and colleagues, focusing specifically on impulsivity. The WDCT, according to the CWS method was administered given the quantitative scoring system, relatively brief administration time, and proven validity of the coding system (D'Amore, 2004; in Daini et al., 2006). It was hypothesized that the CWS would differentiate between anorexic, bulimic, and control groups, with increased depression and impulsivity noted in the bulimic group, and affective over-control, perfectionism, and impulsivity noted in the anorexic group.

One hundred female pre-treatment outpatients selected to participate in hospital-based intervention for eating disorders were included in this study. Eating disorder diagnoses were established via psychiatric interview utilizing the DSM-IV (American Psychiatric Association, 1994) and the *Eating Disorder Evaluation Scale* (EDES, Vandereycken, 1993). The clinical (eating disorder) group was subdivided by diagnosis: anorexia, restricting type (ANrt, $N = 35$; age: $\bar{x} = 21.4$, $SD = 6.5$); anorexia, purging type (ANpt, $N = 22$; $\bar{x}$ and SD not reported), and bulimia (BL, $N = 43$; age $\bar{x} = 24.3$, $SD = 6.6$). The Control (CN) group (age: $\bar{x} = 24.4$, $SD = 6.5$) was comprised of 81 females matched to the clinical groups on educational and socioeconomic status. It was noted that the mean age of the ANrt group was significantly lower than the bulimia and control groups ($p < .01$), with age subsequently considered as a covariate in statistical analyses.

To determine differences between groups related to impulsivity and anxiety, three CWS indices were compared by MANCOVA: the Index of Inner Tension (IIT-1), which measures overall distress and internal discomfort; the Anxiety Index (AI), which measures general levels of internal and manifest anxiety; and the Impulsivity Index (IM), which measures cognitive, affective, and behavioral impulsivity. Results of these analyses are presented in Table 2.38.

Results demonstrated clear significant differences between clinical groups, as well as between clinical and control groups. In terms of overall inner tension and experienced distress and discomfort (IIT-1), the restricting anorexic (ANrt) group demonstrated significantly higher scores than both the purging anorexic (ANpt) and control (CN) group. Similarly, in terms of experienced anxiety, the restricting anorexic (ANrt) group demonstrated significantly higher scores than the purging anorexic (ANpt), bulimic (BL), and control (CN) groups. Lastly, both the restricting anorexic (ANrt) and bulimic (BL) groups demonstrated higher levels of impulsivity than the control (CN) group. These findings generally supported the authors' experimental hypotheses in that the bulimic group demonstrated higher impulsivity than the control group (although did not demonstrate higher levels of internal distress, as predicted), and the anorexic group demonstrated significant over-control (restricting type) and impulsivity.

TABLE 2.38 Mean Differences in CWS Indices [Index of Inner Tension (IIT-1), Anxiety Index (AI), and Impulsivity Index (IM)] MANCOVA by Group (Anorexic RT, Anorexic PT, Bulimic, Control)

Index	*Anorexic RT (ANrt)* $\bar{x}$ *(SD)*	*Anorexic PT (ANpt)* $\bar{x}$ *(SD)*	*Bulimic (BL)* $\bar{x}$ *(SD)*	*Control (CN)* $\bar{x}$ *(SD)*	*F (3,176)*	*LSD Post-Hoc*	*d+*
Index of Inner Tension (IIT-1)	1.20	.98	1.02	.91	4.0**	ANrt > ANpt**	.45
	(.4)	(.3)	(.5)	(.4)		ANrt > CN**	
Anxiety Index (AI)	.80	.66	.69	.62	4.1**	ANrt > ANpt*	
	(.2)	(.2)	(.3)	(.2)		ANrt > BL*	.39
						ANrt > CN**	
Impulsivity Index (IM)	.48	.37	.37	.28	5.5**	ANrt > CN**	.44
	(.3)	(.3)	(.3)	(.2)		BL > CN*	

Notes: * $p < .05$; ** $p < .01$. Effect sizes calculated by current authors from previously published analyses; + *d* effect sizes: small: .2–.49; medium: .5–.79; large: >.8 (Cohen, 1988). Table adapted from Daini, Lai, Festa, Maiorino, Pertosa, & De Risio (2006).

From this data, the authors concluded that the CWS clearly differentiates between clinical and control groups in terms of anxiety, impulsivity and experienced distress.

To investigate hypotheses related to increased presence of rationalization, perfectionism, and over-control in the ANrt population, the distribution of five Primary Contents (Human [H%], Animal [A%], Object [OBJ%], Nature [NAT%], and Abstract [ABS%]) and one Special Score (Global Rejection [GR]) was evaluated using chi-square to determine differences between groups. Results demonstrate higher frequency of Abstract (ABS%) content in restricting anorexic patients (ANrt) as compared to bulimic and control group participants ($\chi^2 = 15.4$, $p < .01$). Moreover, restricting anorexic participants further demonstrated fewer Global Rejections ($\chi^2 = 29.3$, $p < .01$). Together, per the authors, these results suggested that restricting anorexic patients demonstrate strong rationalization defenses and perfectionism, as supported by prior research and hypothesized in the current study. No additional differences between experimental and control groups were noted in regard to the Primary Contents analyzed.

To further investigate the overall hypotheses related to depression, the investigators further evaluated differences between groups in Affective Quality (AQ), Evocative Character (EC), and Form Quality (FQ) scores in each WDCT box, hypothesizing that significant differences might identify specific intrapsychic challenges or internal conflict experienced by the members of each group. Results are presented in Table 2.39.

Results indicated that relatively few differences occurred in the scoring domain of Evocative Character (EC), which measures ego processes in relation to the environment. The authors concluded that little difference exists between individuals diagnosed with eating disorders as compared to the normal population in this perceptual and goal-directed domain. The notable exception to this occurred in Box 3, which measures the individual's ability to utilize psychic resources to reach goals and objectives. In this box, restricting anorexics (ANrt) demonstrated statistically significant higher scores than all other groups (ANpt, BL, CN). This suggests that in the domain of planning capacity, restricting anorexics may demonstrate greater ability.

Contrary to the Evocative Character, the Affective Quality scores significantly differentiated between groups. Overall, control (CN) group participants presented with higher AQ scores than clinical groups, confirming research indicating higher rates of depressive and negative affect in patients with eating disorders. Specifically in this area, bulimics (BL) demonstrated statistically lower AQ in Box 1 (related to self-evaluation and esteem), and Box 3 (related to planning capacity and goal achievement). Purging anorexics (ANpt) demonstrated statistically lower AQ in Box 2 (related to femininity, vitality, and sensitivity).

As related to Form Quality, or the ability to practically and conventionally represent the reality of one's thoughts and ideas, significant differences occurred between groups. In total, control (CN) group participants demonstrated the highest Form Quality, with purging anorexics (ANpt) demonstrating significantly lower FQ scores than all other groups. Specifically, restricting anorexics (ANrt),

TABLE 2.39 Mean Differences in CWS Indices (EC+%, AQ+%, FQ+%) by Box MANCOVA by Group (Anorexic RT, Anorexic PT, Bulimic, Control)

Box	*Index*	*Anorexic RT (ANrt)* $\bar{x}$ *(SD)*	*Anorexic PT (ANpt)* $\bar{x}$ *(SD)*	*Bulimic (BL)* $\bar{x}$ *(SD)*	*Control (CN)* $\bar{x}$ *(SD)*	*F (3,176)*	*LSD Post-Hoc*	d^+
Box 1	**EC+%**	.80 (.4)	.82 (.3)	.83 (.3)	.89 (.3)	.6		.19[a]
	AQ+%	.76 (.4)	.66 (.3)	.69 (.4)	.81 (.3)	2.1	CN > BL* CN > ANpt*	.32[a]
	FQ+%	.86 (.3)	.77 (.4)	.88 (.3)	.93 (.2)	2.0		.29[a]
Box 2	**EC+%**	.77 (.4)	.77 (.4)	.80 (.3)	.74 (.4)	.2		.10[b]
	AQ+%	.67 (.7)	.60 (.6)	.74 (.7)	.78 (.8)	1.5	CN > ANpt*	.24[a]
	FQ+%	.86 (.3)	.82 (.3)	.94 (.2)	.91 (.2)	1.4		.10
Box 3	**EC+%**	.61 (.3)	.79 (.3)	.60 (.3)	.56 (.3)	3.4*	ANpt > ANrt* ANpt > BL* ANpt > CN**	.28[b]
	AQ+%	.64 (.3)	.57 (.2)	.58 (.2)	.68 (.2)	1.9	CN > BL*	.31[a]
	FQ+%	.90 (.2)	.73 (.4)	.76 (.3)	.89 (.2)	4.2**	ANrt > ANpt* ANrt > BL* CN > ANpt* CN > BL**	.33
Box 4	**EC+%**	.53 (.5)	.68 (.4)	.64 (.4)	.52 (.5)	1.1		.19[b]
	AQ+%	.59 (.3)	.48 (.3)	.46 (.3)	.58 (.3)	1.8		.21
	FQ+%	.81 (.3)	.73 (.4)	.84 (.3)	.88 (.3)	1.4	CN > ANpt*	.23[a]

Box 5	EC+%	.82 (.3)	.74 (.3)	.80 (.3)	.85 (.3)	1.4		.24[a]
	AQ+%	.54 (.2)	.54 (.1)	.55 (.3)	.59 (.2)	.5		.18[a]
	FQ+%	.77 (.4)	.73 (.4)	.79 (.3)	.92 (.2)	4.8**	CN > BL* CN > ANrt* CN > ANpt**	.55[a]
Box 6	EC+%	.83 (.3)	.77 (.4)	.89 (.3)	.89 (.3)	1.4		.17[a]
	AQ+%	.56 (.2)	.48 (.2)	.60 (.2)	.59 (.2)	1.5	CN > ANpt*	.12
	FQ+%	.86 (.3)	.79 (.4)	.87 (.3)	.92 (.2)	1.8	CN > ANpt*	.28[a]
Box 7	EC+%	.50 (.4)	.51 (.5)	.49 (.5)	.51 (.5)	.2		.08[a]
	AQ+%	.73 (.3)	.57 (.3)	.64 (.4)	.68 (.3)–.23	1.2		.07
	FQ+%	.91 (.2)	.75 (.4)	.81 (.3)	.90 (.3)	2.4	CN > ANpt* ANrt > ANpt*	.23
Box 8	EC+%	.73 (.3)	.80 (.3)	.79 (.3)	.75 (.3)	.4		.07
	AQ+%	.64 (.4)	.61 (.3)	.65 (.4)	.73 (.8)	.8		.22[a]
	FQ+%	.97 (.1)	.86 (.3)	.95 (.1)	.97 (.1)	3.0*	ANrt > ANpt* BL > ANpt* CN > ANpt**	.20[a]
Total	EC+%	.70 (.1)	.74 (.2)	.73 (.1)	.71 (.1)	.5		.08
	AQ+%	.64 (.2)	.56 (.1)	.61 (.1)	.68 (.2)	4.1**	CN > ANpt**	.45[a]
	FQ+%	.87 (.2)	.77 (.3)	.86 (.1)	.92 (.1)	6.1**	ANrt > ANpt* BL > ANpt* CN > ANpt**	.51[a]

Notes: * $p < .05$; ** $p < .01$. Effect sizes calculated by current authors from previously published analyses; + *d* effect sizes: small: .2–.49; medium: .5–.79; large: >.8 (Cohen, 1988). a. Control group values greater than (or equal to) all clinical groups. b. All clinical group values greater than control group. Table adapted from Daini, Lai, Festa, Maiorino, Pertosa, & De Risio (2006).

TABLE 2.40 Relative Strengths and Deficits within the Eating Disorder Clinical Groups

Box	*Anorexic-Restricting (ANrt)*	*Anorexic-Purging (ANpt)*	*Bulimic (BL)*
Box 1			Deficit (AQ)
Box 2		Deficit (AQ)	
Box 3		Strength (EC)	Deficit (AQ)
Box 4			
Box 5	Strength (FQ)	Deficit (FQ)	Deficit (FQ)
Box 6			
Box 7	Strength (FQ)		
Box 8	Strength (FQ)		

Note: Table prepared through analysis of relative strengths presented in Table 2.38 *within* the clinical group. Without exception, control group scores exceeded clinical group scores.

bulimics (BL), and purging anorexics (ANpt) demonstrated significantly lower FQ in Box 5, related to regulation adaptive and integration of aggressive impulses. These results, as well as other significant findings, are summarized in Table 2.40.

Considering the results from the current study, the authors reached several conclusions. First, given the lack of variability in Evocative Character (EC), the adaptive and associative processes necessary for participation in psychotherapy were presumed equal between individuals diagnosed with eating disorders and the normal population, confirming research supporting successful therapeutic intervention in these diagnostic areas. Significant indications of depression were noted (AQ) in the clinical groups, with depressive affect linked to personality identity, self-realization and goal achievement, and respecting social norms in the bulimic group. Additionally, both anorexic and bulimic participants demonstrated difficulty in adaptively utilizing aggressive and assertive impulses to overcome obstacles (FQ, Box 5). Purging anorexic patients demonstrated deficits as related to femininity and sexuality (Box 2), and a higher level of rational functioning (Box 3).

Both anorexic and bulimic members of the clinical group demonstrated greater internal distress, anxiety, and impulsivity as compared to the control group, with restricting anorexic patients appearing more anxious and perfectionistic (AI, ABS content, GR), and bulimic patients demonstrating higher levels of depression (AQ) and impulsivity (IM), as initially hypothesized. Overall, the authors asserted that their experimental hypotheses were confirmed.

Psychiatric Symptoms Related to Medical Conditions

Crisi, Vari, Velotti, Carlesimo, Guzzi, & Zavattini (2014)

Convergent validity of the CWS was further assessed in a sample of dermatology patients affected by psoriasis (a chronic skin disease) in regard to their experience

TABLE 2.41 Descriptive Statistics (Age, Gender, Education, Relationship Status, Smoking Habits)—Clinical Group vs. Control Group

	Clinical Group (N = 42)		*Control Group (N = 42)*		*Analysis*
	$\bar{x}$	*SD*	$\bar{x}$	*SD*	*p*
Age	42.05	11.21	37.90	14.21	.142[a]
Gender					
Male	24	57.1	16	38.1	.126[b]
Female	18	42.9	26	61.9	
Education					
Secondary School	10	23.8	1	2.4	
High School	19	45.2	17	40.5	.005[b]
University	13	31.0	24	57.1	
Relationship Status					
Yes	30	71.4	35	83.3	.192[b]
No	12	28.6	7	16.7	
Smoking Habits					
Yes	17	40.5	12	28.6	.251[b]
No	25	59.5	30	71.4	

Notes: a. *t*-test. b. Chi Square.

of depression and negative affective states; 42 adult patients diagnosed with psoriasis and receiving treatment at the Dermatology Unit of the Policlinico Umberto I-Sapienza University, Rome were compared with 42 matched control group participants. As presented in Table 2.41, no significant demographic differences were noted between groups, with the exception of educational level (with experimental group demonstrating less education than control).

In reviewing research related to psychopathology in dermatological patients, the authors noted that depression, anxiety, and suicidal ideation are common in patients affected by skin diseases (Kurd & Gelfand, 2009; Olivier et al., 2010; Picardi, Lega, & Tarolla, 2013). Additionally, authors have found that patients with psoriasis experienced increased thoughts of suicide (21.2%) as compared to health control subjects (6.8%; Zacharie, Zacharie, Lei, & Pedersen, 2004).

Participants were administered the WDCT according to CWS guidelines, with tests independently scored by two trained coders (interrater reliability coefficient, $r_w = .826$). In considering previous research findings, CWS indices (AQ+%, FQ+%, EC+%, Affective Stability Index) and the presence of CWS Special Scores were examined. These indices were selected given their relative ease in calculation (i.e., possible to do by hand quickly and easily), with the goal of developing an efficient screening tool for use in the hospital setting as an alternative to potentially minimizing self-report measures. With this aim in mind, only these specific indices, as well as the presence of Special Scores, were investigated.

TABLE 2.42 CWS Indices (AQ+%, FQ+%, EC+%, Affective Stability Ratio)—Comparison Between Clinical and Control Group

	AQ+%		FQ+%		EC+%	
	Median (IR)	*p*	*Median (IR)*	*p*	*Median (IR)*	*p*
Clinical (Psoriasis)	56.00 (19)	.004[a]	92.50 (18)	.015[a]	63.00 (25)	.160[a]
Control	63.00 (13)		100.00 (6)		69.00 (18)	

	Affective Stability Index: A			*Affective Stability Index: F*		
	Mean	*SD*	*p*	*Mean*	*SD*	*p*
Clinical (Psoriasis)	2.40	.64	<.05[b]	3.29	.78	<.05[b]
Control	2.71	.64		3.74	.41	

Notes: a. Mann-Witney U test. b. *t*-test.

Given research on individuals with dermatological conditions, it was hypothesized that clinical group participants would demonstrate lower values on all investigated indices as compared to control group participants, indicating depressive affect, increased sensitivity, and reduced cognitive control. Moreover, a higher percentage of Special Scores, specifically Global Rejections, was predicted for the clinical group, suggestive of increased levels of internal distress and psycho-affective conflict, as compared to the control group.

Results of analyses, presented in Table 2.42, demonstrated lower AQ+% and FQ+% in the clinical group, as well as a lower Affective Stability Index, as predicted. Contrary to expectations, while the control group demonstrated a higher mean value of EC+% than the clinical group, no significant difference was noted.

Additionally, of the 19 CWS Special Scores evaluated, two demonstrated significant differences between clinical and control groups. As predicted, Global Rejection (GR) was noted to be scored more frequently in the clinical group ($\bar{x}$ = 47.00) as compared to the control group ($\bar{x}$ = 38.00; U = 1.071, p = .002). Arbitrary Performance (AP) was also noted to be scored more frequently in the clinical group ($\bar{x}$ = 47.57) as compared to the control group ($\bar{x}$ = 37.43; U = 1.095, p = .025). Using the post-hoc Bonferroni correction for multiple comparisons ($p < .002$), only Global Rejection remained statistically significant following correction, as predicted by the authors.

In considering the results, the authors suggested that the current research utilizing the CWS is consistent with previous research suggesting increased depression in patients with chronic skin diseases. This is evidenced by lower AQ+% in the clinical group as compared to the control group. Similarly, the clinical group evidenced more Global Rejections, which has been linked to depressive symptoms and suicidal ideation in previous research (Daini, Manzo, Pisani, & Tancredi, 2010). Tendencies toward suicidal ideation are also confirmed via lower Affective Stability Ratios in the clinical group, suggesting attempts at emotional suppression and limited self-control. Lastly, a higher rate of Arbitrary Performance in the clinical group, coupled with a lower FQ+%, may indicate difficulties in thinking clearly, potentially due to intrusive affective experiences; however, as AP differences did not reach significance, this finding requires further investigation. No significant difference between groups was noted related to Evocative Character (EC+%), suggesting similar levels of defensiveness and sensitivity to the environment in the clinical and control groups. Given these findings, the authors concluded that the specific CWS indices studied appear sensitive in the measurement of negative affective states and anxiety, which a patient may be unwilling or unable to self-report on standard questionnaires used within the hospital setting.

CWS and Attachment

Maio, Ricci, & Crisi (2008)

In another study of convergent validity, the relationship between attachment-related personality traits, as measured by the Wartegg Index of Psychopathology (WIP) Quadrant and styles of attachment as measured by the Separation Anxiety Test (SAT; Klagsbrun & Bowlby, 1976; Italian revision: Attili, 2001) were explored. In consideration of the WIP, each subject may be classified as falling within one of four "Quadrants" (as described above; see Crisi, 2009) by graphically plotting state anxiety and distress on a vertical axis and trait personality flexibility and integration on a horizontal access. This overlay of state versus trait characteristics results in four quadrants (labeled A, B, C, and D, respectively), each of which corresponds to particular personality traits and attachment styles, as described below:

Quadrant A: In Quadrant A, characteristics of autonomy and independence predominate, indicative of a Secure attachment classification.

Quadrant B: In Quadrant B, characteristics of detachment and isolation predominate, indicative of an Insecure-Dismissing attachment classification.

Quadrant C: In Quadrant C, characteristics of dependency predominate, indicative of an Insecure-Preoccupied attachment classification.

Quadrant D: In Quadrant D, characteristics of conflict and confusion predominate, indicative of an Unresolved attachment style.

CWS and SAT results of 30 clinically referred female subjects (aged 6–14) were evaluated; 47% of subjects (N = 14) were referred for mental health intervention subsequent to school difficulties, including school refusal or learning disorders; 53% of subjects (N = 16) were referred for emotional disturbances, including anxiety, depression, or relational difficulties. No significant differences in age, socioeconomic status, or intellectual ability were noted between groups. Experimental hypotheses asserted that subjects' attachment classification (as determined by the SAT) would be correlated with the CWS WIP Quadrant reflective of that attachment style. Specifically, SAT Secure classifications were predicted to be correlated with WIP Quadrant A; SAT Avoidant classifications with QIP Quadrant B; SAT Ambivalent classifications with WIP Quadrant D; and SAT Disorganized classifications with WIP Quadrants B and C. Moreover, it was hypothesized that individuals with high coping abilities (as indicated by the SAT) would demonstrate greater interpersonal sensitivity and lower levels of anxiety and distress, as measured by CWS indices. That is, high coping individuals would demonstrate higher EC+%, lower Index of Inner Tension-1 scores (IIT-1) and lower Anxiety Index (AI scores), as compared to low coping ability counterparts.

Results, summarized in Table 2.43, demonstrate that the greatest percentage of subjects classified as having a Secure attachment style on the SAT (50%) fell within CWS WIP Quadrant A, indicating autonomy, independence, and security of attachment. Similarly, the greatest number of subjects (72%) who were classified as having an Insecure-Disorganized attachment style on the SAT fell within the CWS WIP Quadrants B (36%) suggesting detachment/dismissing styles and C (36%) suggesting dependent/preoccupied styles. Given the small number of participants in this pilot study ($N = 30$), no statistically significant differences were noted ($\chi^2 = 9.727$, $p = .373$).

While preliminary data, these percentages suggest that the greatest number of individuals classified with Secure attachment styles fall within Quadrant A, whereas the greatest number of individuals with Insecure attachment styles fall within Quadrants B and C. While more research is needed on the relationship between WIP Quadrant and attachment classification, initial results support the clinical interpretation of the CWS WIP classification schema.

Significant differences in CWS indices were discovered between individuals with high and low coping abilities as determined by the SAT. Specifically, individuals classified as having high coping abilities demonstrated higher levels of EC+%, suggesting greater interpersonal and social sensitivity. While this difference did not reach statistical significance, likely due to small sample size, a preliminary trend is noted that would benefit from further study. Moreover, individuals rated as having higher coping skills demonstrated lower levels of

TABLE 2.43 Relationship Between SAT Attachment Style and CWS WIP Quadrant—Percentage of Agreement

	SAT Attachment Classification			
	Secure (%)	*Insecure-Avoidant* (%)	*Insecure-Ambivalent* (%)	*Insecure-Disorganized* (%)
Quadrant A ("Autonomy")	50	70	50	19
Quadrant B ("Detachment")	38	15	25	36
Quadrant C ("Dependency")	—	—	25	36
Quadrant D ("Unresolved")	12	15	—	9

Note: Shaded areas indicate findings supportive of experimental hypotheses.

TABLE 2.44 Relationship Between Coping Skills and CWS Indices—Evocative Character (EC+%), Index of Inner Tension-1 (IIT-1), Anxiety Index (AI)

Index	*Coping Style*	*N*	$\bar{x}$	*SD*	*F*	*t*	*df*	*p*	*d*+
EC+%	high	20	73.8	16.39	.171	.898	28	.377	.35[a]
	low	10	68.3	14.50					
IIT-1	high	20	.82	.36	1.324	−1.838	28	.077*	.67[b]
	low	10	1.12	.50					
AI	high	20	.54	.28	.109	−1.743	28	.092*	.68[b]
	low	10	.73	.25					

Notes: * approaching significance. Effect sizes calculated by current authors from previously published analyses; + *d* effect sizes: small: .2–.49; medium: .5–.79; large: >.8 (Cohen, 1988). a. High coping group values greater than low coping group. b. Low coping group values greater than high coping group.

experienced distress on the CWS Index of Inner Tension-1 (IIT-1, *p* approaching significance) and lower levels of anxiety as measured by the CWS Anxiety Index (AI, *p* approaching significance). Statistical analyses are presented in Table 2.44.

Initial results of this pilot study supported the proposed experimental hypotheses, specifically those regarding the relationship between CWS and SAT indices. The authors suggested that these findings support preliminary construct and convergent validity of the CWS in relation to attachment classification and description of coping skills.

Di Riso, Crisi, Bianchi di Castelbianco, di Renzo, Vichi, Racinaro, & Morellini (2013)

In this study, the authors investigated CWS-derived personality factors of parents classified by the Adult Attachment Projective Picture System (AAP; George & West, 2012) as falling within the Pathological Mourning framework (Bowlby, 1980; George and West, 2012), as compared to a normative sample. As George and West describe:

> When mourning is incomplete, representational models of the self and attachment figures remained unchanged and failures of the past continue to "haunt" the present. The failure to accomplish reintegration, in which the individual's internal works is experienced as incoherent and chaotic, begets helplessness, futility, and isolation. Bowlby referred to this state as *pathological mourning* and described two main forms that he believed were powerful explanatory tools of understanding debilitating psychiatric and physical symptoms.
>
> (p. 199)

Fifty parents (35 mothers, 15 fathers) of children diagnosed with learning disabilities were initially included in a larger study investigating the emotional availability of parents as predictive of learning challenges in children. Parents were administered the Adult Separation Anxiety Checklist (ASA-CL; Manicavasaga, Silove, & Curtis, 1997), Child Behavior Checklist (CBCL; Achenbach, 1991), and the AAP.

Results of initial analysis suggested the following attachment classifications: 56% (*N* = 28) of parents were classified as Unresolved/Disorganized, 21% (*N* = 10) Dismissing, 11.5% (*N* = 6) Preoccupied, and 11.5% (*N* = 5) Secure. Twenty-six of 50 parents (50.9%) of learning disabled children fell within the framework for Pathological Mourning with 58% demonstrating exaggerated distortions of healthy mourning (unresolved pathological mourning and/or pathological mourning with personal suffering) and 42% utilizing defensive processes to block the course of healthy mourning (failed mourning). In describing these 26 parents, traumatic experiences, feelings of helplessness, emotional dysregulation, and impaired capacity to make and maintain social relationships were noted.

Following classification based upon the AAP, specific CWS indices were next examined to determine differences between the Pathological Mourning parent group and the normal population. Studied indices included the CWS Global Assessment classification, Index of Inner Tension-2 (IIT-2), Wartegg Index of Psychopathology (WIP), WIP Quadrant, Form Quality Percentage (FQ+%), Popular Response Percentage (P%), practical Content percentages (OBJ%+ ARC%), and the Index of Suicidal Tendencies (IST). Each index is discussed in turn below.

CWS Global Assessment Code: As discussed earlier, using a constellation of CWS indices and calculations, each individual can be classified in one of five incremental Global Assessment categories, ranging from no pathology to significant psychopathology. In order from highest functioning to highest level of symptoms/impairment, the five categories are: Not Pathological (NOP), Low level of symptoms (LSI), Moderate symptoms and impairment (MSI), Severe symptoms and impairment (SSI) and Pathological (PTL).

Index of Inner Tension-2 (IIT-2): The IIT-2 measures the degree of integration and flexibility evident in an individual's personality structure. The more positive the IIT-2, the better able the subject is to utilize various aspects and strengths of personality, solve problems, regulate emotions, consistently navigate relationships, and meet the obstacles of daily life.

Wartegg Index of Psychopathology (WIP): The WIP (described earlier in this chapter, see Crisi 2009), graphically plots state anxiety and distress on a vertical axis and trait personality flexibility and integration on a horizontal access. An individual's WIP may be considered "positive" if falling within adaptive areas of functioning (appropriate flexibility, average distress) or "negative" if significantly inflexible, dis-integrated, and/or distressed.

WIP Quadrant: Based upon the calculation of the WIP, each individual is classified as falling within one of four diagnostic Quadrants: A (low distress, high integration, characterized by autonomy and independence); B (low distress, low integration; characterized by detachment); C (high distress, high integration; characterized by dependency); and D (high distress, low integration; characterized by conflict and ambivalence). Each quadrant further relates to a specific attachment style: A (Secure); B (Dismissing); C (Preoccupied); D (Unresolved/ Disorganized).

Form Quality (FQ+%): FQ+% provides a global indication of an individual's cognitive efficiency, rational control, reality testing, and planning and organizational abilities.

Popular Response (P%): P% reflects a client's ability to share a common worldview and conventional way of thinking with others.

Practical Contents (OBJ%+ARC%): OBJ% and ARC% suggest an individual's ability to think practically and functionally.

Index of Suicidal Tendencies (IST): The IST is a constellation of symptoms that together arrive at a numerical value indicating risk of suicidal ideation or behavior. The IST can range from 0–23, with a clinical cutoff of 8. In the normative population, the mean IST score equals 1.98.

Results of chi-square analysis examining the differences between groups in terms of Global Assessment classifications are presented in Table 2.45. Results of further analyses examining the differences in categorical and numerical CWS Indices between normal and pathological mourning parent groups are presented in Tables 2.46 and 2.47, respectively.

TABLE 2.45 Difference in Global Assessment Classifications Between Pathological Mourning Parent Groups and Control Group

Index	*Group*	N *Present*	% *Present*	N *Absent*	% *Absent*	χ^2 *(df = 4)*	*p*	V[a]
Global Assessment								
NOP	Pathological Mourning	3	11.5	23	88.5	11.025	.026	.30
	Control	37	39.8	82	60.2			
LSI	Pathological Mourning	9	34.6	17	65.4			
	Control	34	36.6	85	63.4			
MSI	Pathological Mourning	8	30.8	18	69.2			
	Control	12	12.9	107	87.1			
SSI	Pathological Mourning	4	15.4	22	84.6			
	Control	7	7.5	112	92.5			
PTL	Pathological Mourning	2	7.7	24	92.3			
	Control	3	3.2	116	96.8			

Notes: Effect sizes calculated by current authors from previously published analyses; a. *V* effect sizes: small: .1–.29; medium: .3–.49; large: >.5 (Cohen, 1988).

TABLE 2.46 Difference in Categorical Classifications on CWS Indices Between Pathological Mourning Parent and Control Groups

Index	*Group*	*n Present*	*% [Present]*	*n Absent*	*% [Absent]*	χ^2 *(df = 1)*	*p*	Φ^a
Positive Global Assessment	Pathological Mourning	12	46.1	14	53.9	8.77	.003	.27
(NOP+LSI)	Control	71	76.4	22	23.6			
IIT-2 (Positive)	Pathological Mourning	7	26.9	19	73.1	13.17	.000	.33
	Control	62	66.7	31	33.3			
WIP (Positive)	Pathological Mourning	7	26.9	12	73.1	8.45	.004	.26
	Control	55	59.1	38	40.9			
WIP: Quadrant A (Secure)	Pathological Mourning	8	30.7	18	69.3	3.18	.07	.16
	Control	46	49.4	47	50.6			
WIP: Quadrant B (Dismissing)	Pathological Mourning	6	23.1	20	76.9	4.10	.042	.18
	Control	8	8.9	85	91.1			
WIP: Quadrant C (Preoccupied)	Pathological Mourning	5	19.2	21	80.8	.01	.9120	.009
	Control	17	18.9	76	81.1			
WIP Quadrant D (Unresolved)	Pathological Mourning	7	26.9	19	73.1	.02	.731	.009
	Control	22	23.7	71	76.3			

Notes: Effect sizes calculated by current authors from previously published analyses; a. Φ effect sizes: small: .1–.29; medium: .3–.49; large: >.5 (Cohen, 1988).

Results are suggestive of significant differences between the pathological mourning group, as compared to the normative population. Specifically, both the AAP and CWS suggested less secure (Dismissing, Unresolved) patterns of attachment. That is, the pathological mourning group demonstrated less Secure attachment classifications (Quadrant A) and a greater percentage of Dismissing classifications (Quadrant B). Moreover, parents who met pathological mourning criteria demonstrated higher levels of emotional distress and impairment as evidenced by the Global Assessment classification (lower NOP and LSI, higher MSI, SSI, PTL), IIT-2 (significantly less positive), and Index of Suicidal Tendencies (significantly more negative, see Table 2.47).

In general, the pathological mourning group demonstrated lower levels of coping resources as evidenced by less cognitive efficiency (lower FQ+%), less

TABLE 2.47 Differences in CWS Numerical Indices (Means) Between Pathological Mourning Parent and Control Groups

Index	*Normal Group*	*Pathological Mourning*	*t*	*df*	*p*	*d*+
Form Quality (FQ+%)	99.9	93.54	−8.832	117	.00001	1.63[a]
Popular Percentage (P%)	19.71	29.27	4.024	117	.00001	.74[b]
Practical Content (OBJ%+ARC%)	62.62	48.07	−3.683	117	.00001	.07[a]
Index of Suicidal Tendencies (IST)	2.04	3.96	4.819	117	.00001	.73[b]

Notes: Effect sizes calculated by current authors from previously published analyses; + *d* effect sizes: small: .2–.49; medium: .5–.79; large: >.8 (Cohen, 1988). a. Normal group values greater than pathological mourning group. b. Pathological mourning group values greater than normal group.

conventional thinking and relationships (lower P%), and limited practical thinking and problem solving (OBJ%+ARC%). Overall, while concordance between the CWS and the AAP had been noted in numerous individual clinical case studies, these results statistically validate the convergence of the AAP and the CWS in the assessment of attachment attributes.

Special Topics of Study

Daini, Bernardini, & Panetta (2007)

Daini and colleagues investigated psychological aspects of infertility utilizing the CWS, citing that most previous studies had relied on self-report questionnaires to gain access to the inner world of women experiencing challenges in becoming pregnant. Sixty-one women, divided into three groups based upon cause of infertility, were studied: women experiencing consecutive miscarriages (CM, $N = 21$; age: $\bar{x} = 30.81$, $SD = 1.18$); women diagnosed with organic sterility (OS, $N = 20$; age: $\bar{x} = 28.50$, $SD = 1.48$); and women with unexplained sterility (US, $N = 20$; age: $\bar{x} = 28.40$, $SD = 1.16$). These three groups of women were compared to a control group (CO, $N = 30$; age: $\bar{x} = 30.03$, $SD = .78$). Clinical groups were selected from an urban hospital, where they were assessed with the CWS pre-treatment. Control group participants were selected at random from women presenting at the same hospital for an outpatient gynecological visit. No significant differences related to age or socioeconomic status between groups were noted.

Statistical analyses investigated differences between groups using MANCOVA procedures, specifically as related to scores on major CWS indices, including Evocative Character (EC+%), Affective Quality (AQ+%), Form Quality (FQ+%), Index of Inner Tension (IIT-1), Anxiety Index (AI), and Impulsivity Index (IM). Additionally, responses to each WDCT Box were analyzed, as well as the Order of Sequence followed by each participant. It was noted that while

76% of the Control group completed Box 1 first in the Order of Sequence, only 50% of the two sterility groups and 24% of the Consecutive Miscarriage (CM) group completed Box 1 first ($\chi^2 = 13.36$, $p = .004$). Per the authors, this may indicate the negative impact of infertility on a woman's self-esteem, as well as a potential defensive tendency to avoid thinking about the self.

Multivariate analysis demonstrated significant differences (F: 3.218, $p < .001$) between groups as related to Form Quality (FQ+%, $p = .0001$) and Evocative Character (EC+%, $p = .006$). No significant differences were noted in terms of Affective Quality, with observed trends indicating lower mean scores in the consecutive miscarriages (CM) group. This lack of significant difference in AQ+% was hypothesized to relate to research linking infertility to alexithymia. The authors note that the differences in FQ+% and EC+% mean scores (lower in the clinical groups as compared to control groups) confirm the emotional impact of infertility on the imaginative life, engagement with the environment, and rational ability to plan.

Additional differences between clinical groups were noted. The unexplained sterility (US) group appeared generally commensurate with the control group in most indices, although demonstrated higher levels of anxiety (AI: CM: $\bar{x} = .01 \pm .04$; OS: $\bar{x} = .04 \pm .1$, US: $\bar{x} = .14 \pm .2$; CO: $\bar{x} = .07 \pm .1$; $F = 3.27$, $p = .05$). This may suggest generally adequate integration and functioning, with underlying tension related to currently unclear etiological issues of sterility. The organic sterility (OS) group demonstrated less adaptation, integration of self, and ability to enter into social relationships (lower EC+% in Boxes 4, 5, 6, and 7, $p < .05$). The consecutive miscarriage (CM) group appeared most impacted by challenges in maintaining a positive self-identify (EC+% Box 1: CM: $\bar{x} = .78 \pm .04$; OS: $\bar{x} = .95 \pm .1$, US: $\bar{x} = .87 \pm .03$; CO: $\bar{x} = .94 \pm .1$; $F = 2.15$, $p = .05$);. Lastly, women impacted by organic sterility and consecutive miscarriages demonstrated lower affective stability (A/F Ratio: CM: $\bar{x} = .81 \pm 1.0$; OS: $\bar{x} = .75 \pm 1$, US: $\bar{x} = .02 \pm 1.2$; CO: $\bar{x} = .19 \pm 1$; F = 2.96, $p = .05$). This likely indicates greater affective reactivity coupled with less apparent mental control. The utility of the CWS to access internal functioning that might not otherwise be apparent via self-report was noted.

Daini, Petrongolo, Manzo, & Bernardini (2012)

In this study, the authors investigated similarities and differences between student and professional nurses, hypothesizing that the length of time spent in professional practice increases empathy in professional nurses; that is, professional nurses are more empathic, whereas student nurses are more practical. Moreover, it was hypothesized that professional nurses may demonstrate higher rates of stress and or anxiety as related to student nurses. Given this higher stress level, professional nurses were predicted to demonstrate higher rates of depression as evidenced by previous research on the topic. The CWS was selected for use in this study, given its ease of administration, and the likelihood it would "offer a wide range of personality features" (p. 19).

Two groups of individuals participated in this study: Professional nurses (N = 111; 49 male, 62 female; age: $\bar{x}$ = 33, SD = 5.19) working in an Italian hospital and Student nurses (N = 210; 102 male, 108 female; age: $\bar{x}$ = 24.46, SD = 4.37) selected from two graduate programs in nursing. The majority of participants in both groups were of Italian descent, with less than 3% of each group originating outside the country.

In comparing groups, the authors investigated differences between groups on major CWS indices (Evocative Character [EC+%], Affective Quality [AQ+%], Form Quality [FQ+%], Index of Inner Tension-1 [IIT-1], Impulsivity Index [IM], Anxiety Index [AI], and Popular percentages [P%]) and Content categories (Architecture [ARC%], Nature [NAT%], Object [OBJ%], and Symbol [SIG%]). Professional nurses' scores exceeded Student nurses' scores on five statistically significant indices. Evocative Character (EC+%; Pro: $\bar{x}$ = 74.10±12; Stu: $\bar{x}$ = 66.79±15, F = 5.78, p = .01), Popular Responses (P%; Pro: $\bar{x}$ = 21.33±12.49; Stu: $\bar{x}$ = 10.39±10.61, F = 25.52, p = .000), Architecture content (ARC%; Pro: $\bar{x}$ = 8.05±10.23; Stu: $\bar{x}$ = 5.74±7.66, F = 7.02, p = .008), Nature content (NAT%; Pro: $\bar{x}$ = 4.09±7.68; Stu: $\bar{x}$ = 2.72±5.98, F = 3.98, p = .048), and Symbol content (SIB%; Pro: $\bar{x}$ = 12.31±12.91; Stu: $\bar{x}$ = 9.66±11.50, F = 3.67, p = .05). Conversely, Student nurses' scores exceeded Professional nurses' scores on Object content (OBJ%; Stu: $\bar{x}$ = 49.21±21.01, Pro: $\bar{x}$ = 39.63±20.05; F = 12.74, p = .000).

Further analysis demonstrated that Boxes 1, 2, and 4 accounted for the most differentiation between groups in terms of Evocative Character scores, with professional nurses scoring higher than student nurses. Professional nurses were further found to produce higher Affective Quality scores in boxes 1, 6, and 7 than their student counterparts. Lastly, in investigating Order of Sequence, it was noted that professional nurses tended to select Box 1 as the first box drawn as compared to student nurses (χ^2 = 16.75, p = .02).

The authors concluded that the test results suggest that professional nurses tend to possess more defenses than student nurses. While both groups' EC+% fell within the normal range, suggesting connection and responsiveness to the environment and intact associative processes, significantly higher scores in the professional group demonstrate increased sensitivity and receptivity. This heightened sensitivity appears particular to the professional nurses' sense of self (Box 1), vitality (Box 2), and relationship to authority or external expectations (Box 4). To counteract this increased sensitivity (also evidenced by higher NAT%, higher ARC%), an important component of their caregiving capacity, professional nurses demonstrated tendencies toward rational detachment and self-protection (increased P%, increased SIG%, higher AQ in Box 6). Lastly, higher percentages of Object (OBJ%) content (associated with lower Human content percentage) observed in student nurses may indicate a practical, task-based approach to their work and those they encounter, possibly due to their limited professional experience.

Summarizing, the authors reported that the data of the current study converges with that of previous studies among health care workers, primarily that emotional detachment serves as a protective factor. In terms of the second hypothesis, no significant depressive tendencies were noted in the professional nursing group.

CWS *in Selection Settings*

Ravecca (2003)

Ravecca and colleagues in the Italian Navy investigated the convergent validity of the CWS in an applied setting, specifically focused on the selection of appropriate candidates for the Italian armed forces. Drawing from a sample of military applicants, 331 male subjects (aged 19–29) were selected for evaluation. All candidates were Caucasian, and had successfully completed a high school education. Convergent validity related to both clinical/personality factors relevant to military selection and aptitude for military service was investigated.

CWS AGREEMENT WITH OTHER TEST MEASURES

To better understand the utility of the CWS in military selection, comparisons at the global level were studied to determine agreement between measures regarding clinical/personality factors of candidates. Overall CWS Global Assessment classifications (derived from the clinical scoring software) were compared to global ratings of both the MMPI-2 (Butcher et al., 1989) and the Guilford–Zimmerman Temperament Survey (GZTS; Guilford & Zimmerman, 1949). To facilitate such a comparison, independent psychiatrists rated each subject's performance on the MMPI-2 and GZTS as falling in one of five categories. Categories were derived using pre-established criteria related to MMPI-2 and GZTS test scores indicative of low, moderate, or severe symptoms. This five-point categorization schema corresponded to that of the computer-generated five-category CWS Global Assessment, derived from scored CWS indices and calculations, allowing easy comparison between test results and psychiatric ratings.

For the purposes of this study, the five ordinal categories included:

1. NOP (Non-Pathological), characterized by appropriate individual and social adaptive processes. This category corresponds to a judgment of general adequacy for military service.
2. LSI (Low Symptoms/Impairments), characterized by psychoaffective difficulties that are ameliorated by the presence of appropriate defenses and result in little negative impact on individual global functioning. Without other negative results, this category corresponds to a judgment of general adequacy for military service, similar to NOP.
3. MSI (Medium Symptoms/Impairments), indicating problematic and conflicting aspects of personality that likely impair the psychoaffective balance of the individual. This category suggests the need for further psychodiagnostic evaluation prior to making a selection decision.
4. SSI (Severe Symptoms/Impairments), indicating severely problematic and conflicting aspects of personality that likely negatively influences the

individual's behavior. This category corresponds to a judgment of inadequacy for military service.

5. PTL (Pathological), characterized by the presence of overt psychopathology and significant impairment in functioning, especially if other indices suggest negative outcomes. This category corresponds to a judgment of inadequacy for military service.

In comparing the classifications between tests, concordance was determined between the CWS and the MMPI-2 in 76.1% of cases. Similarly, agreement was noted between the CWS and the GZTS in 74.6% of cases. Given the overall goal of selection, the five categories were subsequently condensed into three categories (Select, Further Investigation Needed, and Don't Select), with significant improvement in concordance between measures noted. In considering three classification categories, agreement between the CWS and MMPI-2 rose to 98.5%, whereas agreement between the CWS and the GZTS rose to 98.2%. The author concluded that results of this study support the convergent validity of the CWS with both the MMPI-2 and Guilford–Zimmerman test.

CWS AGREEMENT WITH EXPERT RATINGS

In terms of aptitude for military service, additional analysis was undertaken, comparing candidates' rating in five qualitative domains derived from the CWS clinical software: 1) Overall maturity level; 2) Emotional regulation; 3) Cognitive abilities; 4) Interpersonal skills; and 5) Group affiliation. Independent psychiatrists concurrently rated candidates on these categories, blind to the evaluations derived from the CWS. Each candidate was rated on each domain qualitatively as positive (+), neutral (+/–), or negative (–). Given that 331 candidates were included in the research, and each was rated on five domains, 1,655 points of comparison were analyzed. Of these, 84.2% demonstrated agreement between the CWS and independent psychiatric ratings.

In evaluating results, positive and negative predictive values were calculated to determine the extent of agreement between the CWS Global Assessment and expert psychiatric ratings. Results strongly validated the utility of the test in screening and selection based upon the Global Assessment ratings. Positive and neutral ratings were combined, resulting in a dichotomous decision rating (positive/neutral vs. negative). Utilizing this approach, both Positive and Negative Predictive Values were excellent for the CWS (PPV = .969; NPV = 1.0; sensitivity = 1.00; specificity = .33).

Overall, the study suggested increased flexibility and efficiency of selection via inclusion of the CWS with self-report measures. Further, results were noted to suggest that the utility of the CWS is high when each derived component is analyzed separately, but demonstrates higher incremental validity when clinical/personality, aptitude, and descriptive components are fully integrated to inform the global process of selection.

CWS Content Categories

Crisi & Carlesimo (2008)

Crisi and Carlesimo (2008) examined differences in personality profiles between subjects whose WDCT protocols were positive for Human (H), Food (FD) and Cloud (CLD) contents as compared to subjects that did not depict these content categories. Similar to scoring systems developed for the Rorschach Inkblot Method, the presence or absence of specific content categories on the CWS are hypothesized to be indicative of important elements of personality structure and interpersonal relatedness. For each content studied, specific experimental hypotheses were developed, described below. In examining the experimental hypotheses, 2,293 male subjects (aged 18–25; a subsection of the Italian CWS normative sample) were included in analyses.

In conducting analyses, specific indices and classifications contained within the CWS were utilized. Care was taken to study scores and indices demonstrating limited overlap with investigated content areas, although it must be considered that some degree of relationship is inherent in all test variables. Specifically studied variables included, but were not limited to:

Global Assessment: As previous described, each CWS protocol is assigned an overall Global Assessment classification, ranging from "No Pathology" (NOP) to "Pathological" (PTL). This classification system is divided into five categories, two of which are considered positive (NOP + "Low Symptoms" [LSI]), one of which is considered to represent moderate difficulties ("Moderate Symptoms" [MSI]), and two of which are considered negative (PTL + "Severe Symptoms" [SSI]). During evaluation, the presence of positive and negative classifications was considered for each content area;

WIP Quadrant: As described previously (see Crisi, 2009), the CWS co-locates individuals on a graphic depiction of personality functioning, based upon the degree of currently experienced distress (vertical axis) and level of personality flexibility and integration (horizontal axis). Four quadrants result, labeled A, B, C, and D, respectively. Quadrants A and C (reflecting high flexibility and integration) are generally considered less pathological and therefore more "healthy";

Box Codes: As noted above, in each Box on the CWS, a Code is assigned based upon the mathematical summation of Evocative Character and Affective Quality scores. Two Codes (C and PC) are considered positive, whereas four Codes (NC, AC, AD, and D) are considered negative;

Affective Stability Index (A/F Ratio): The A/F Ratio depicts affective levels ("A", left side of ratio) as compared to cognitive resources and control ("F", right side of the ratio). Based on normative data, it is expected that F will be greater than A by 1–2 points, indicating sufficient cognitive control to modulate affective reactions to the environment. Higher levels of affect ("A") are typically related to higher expressed emotion, immaturity, overwhelming emotions, and reactivity to the environment;

Index of Suicidal Tendencies (IST): The IST is a constellation of CWS scores and calculations that are indicative of internal tension, depressive affect, low frustration tolerance, self-punitive thinking style, and poor affect regulation. Normative values range from 0–3, with higher values suggesting increased distress and pathology;

Index of Inner Tension-2 (IIT-2): The IIT-2 numerically measures the degree of flexibility and integration inherent in an individual's personality structure. To calculate the IIT-2, each box in a protocol is assigned a Code based upon a numerical formula combining Affective Quality and Evocative Character scores. Six Codes are possible per box, with two considered positive (C, PC) and four considered negative (NC, AC, AD, D). The IIT-2 creates a ratio of positive Codes on the left to negative Codes on the right. The higher the value on the left, the more general levels of health and integration are anticipated. Normatively, the left side of the ratio exceeds the right.

In general, as summarized below, overall results confirmed experimental hypotheses, supporting the usefulness and the construct validity of CWS Content categories.

HUMAN CONTENT

In evaluating the hypotheses related to the presence of Human content, 1,518 males with Human content present in their protocols were compared to 775 males without Human content. Overall, the authors hypothesized that the presence of Human (H%) content is an important factor in the CWS and is able to effectively discriminate between subjects. Specific hypotheses included the following:

1. The presence of Human (H%) content will be associated with greater social skills as assessed by analyzing other CWS indices, including higher Popular (P%), lower Object content (OBJ%) and higher frequency of positive Code of Box 8 (the box of social skills and relatedness).
2. Individuals with Human (H%) content are more likely to demonstrate healthy functioning overall, as evident by a higher frequency of positive Global Assessment classification.
3. Individuals with Human (H%) content are more likely to demonstrate healthier attachment style, as evident by higher frequency of classification in WIP Quadrants A and C.

Results of analyses, related to the three Human (H%) content experimental hypotheses, are presented in Table 2.48.

In each case, the experimental hypothesis was confirmed as predicted by the authors, suggesting that the absence of Human content in a CWS protocol is likely indicative of affectively driven interpersonal difficulties, and may contribute to overall reduced functioning in individuals.

TABLE 2.48 Differences Between Groups on Select CWS Indices—Clients with Human ("H%") Content vs. Those without Human Content ("No H%")

Scoring Phenomena	"No H" (%)	"H" (%)	χ^2	*p*	Φ^+
Global Assessment (Positive Classification: NOP + LSI)	55	82	189.88	.00001	.29
WIP Quadrant (Positive Placement: A + C)	52	61	17.06	.0001	.08
Box 8 Valuation (Positive: C + PC)	50	63	35.26	.00001	.14

Index	"No H" $\bar{x}$	"No H" *SD*	"H" $\bar{x}$	"H" *SD*	*t* (2,291 *df*)	*p*	d^{++}
Popular Responses (P%)	13.29	9.09	19.60	11.34	–13.417	.000	.56[a]
Object Content (OBJ%)	47.56	20.00	38.45	17.88	11.079	.000	.46[b]

Notes: Effect sizes calculated by current authors from previously published analyses; + Φ effect sizes: small: .1–.29; medium: .3–.49; large: >.5; ++ *d* effect sizes: small: .2–.49; medium: .5–.79; large: >.8 (Cohen, 1988). a. "No H" group values greater than "H" group. b. "H" group values greater than "No H" group.

Additionally, for each protocol, 103 calculations and indices inherent to the CWS interpretation strategy were calculated for exploratory analytical purposes, with independent samples *t*-test used to analyze differences between "H" and "No H" groups. Results, presented in ►Appendix C, suggested that the presence of Human content differentiates to a statistically significant level between the "H" group and the "No H" group in 59 out of 103 evaluated indices. In evaluating results, it is important to note that all indices demonstrating significant differences were related to affective and interpersonal functioning. That is, no indices measuring cognitive difficulties were found to be significantly different between groups. The authors noted that this constellation of differences suggests that the presence or absence of Human content differentiates well between clients experiencing interpersonal and affective difficulties as compared to those who are not.

FOOD CONTENT

Experimental investigation of the ability of Food (FD) content alone to discriminate between individuals was investigated with a subset of the overall sample; 195 male participants who depicted Food content in the CWS protocols were compared to 209 matched participants without Food content. Overall, the authors hypothesized that the presence of Food (FD%) content is an important factor in the CWS and is able to effectively discriminate between subjects in terms of overall health and attachment style; however, when the positive Global Assessment classification of participants with Food content (79%) was compared to those without Food content (79%), no statistical significance was noted. Similarly, when positive WIP Quadrant placement of those with Food content (64%) was compared to those without Food content (62%), no statistical significance was noted. These results suggest that Food content alone does not discriminate between subjects. Given these initial results, further hypotheses were elaborated:

1. The presence of Food (FD%) content will be associated with passivity, dependence, and immaturity as evidenced by increased Anxiety Index (AI), higher frequency of Architectural content (ARC%), and higher frequency of Human contents (H%).
2. The presence of Food (FD%) content will be associated with reduced autonomy and challenges in managing relationships with authority, as indicated by the increased frequency of negative Codes in Box 4 (the box of autonomy and relation to authority).

Results of the analyses related to the Food content experimental hypotheses are presented in Table 2.49.

Given these findings, individuals who produce Food content responses on the CWS appear to exhibit greater tendencies toward dependence, insecurity, and anxiety than those who produce no Food responses; however, these findings are less robust and less evident at the overall protocol level (given the lack of significance in differences in Global Assessment and WIP classification between groups) than other studied Content categories.

TABLE 2.49 Differences Between Groups on Select CWS Indices—Clients with Food ("FD") Content vs. Those without Food Content ("No FD")

Index	*"No FD" $\bar{x}$*	*"No FD" SD*	*"FD" $\bar{x}$*	*"FD" SD*	*t (402 df)*	*p*	*d+*
Anxiety Index (AI)	.91	.16	.95	.14	2.666	.01	.26[b]
Architectural Content (ARC%)	19.69	11.86	16.55	10.53	4.050	.000	.50[a]
Human Content (H%)	12.35	11.87	9.89	9.71	3.197	.001	.32[a]
Scoring Phenomena	*"No FD" (%)*		*"FD"(%)*		χ^2	*p*	Φ^{++}
Box 4 Valuation (Positive: C + PC)	33		24		5.22	.01	.22

Notes: Effect sizes calculated by current authors from previously published analyses; + *d* effect sizes: small: .2–.49; medium: .5–.79; large: >.8; ++ Φ effect sizes: small: .1–.29; medium: .3–.49; large: >.5 (Cohen, 1988). a. "No FD" group values greater than "FD" group. b. "FD" group values greater than "No FD" group.

Additionally, for each protocol, 103 calculations and indices inherent to the CWS interpretation strategy were calculated for exploratory analytical purposes, within independent samples *t*-test used to analyze differences between "FD" and "No FD" groups. Results, presented in ►Appendix C, suggest that Food content is less able to discriminate between participants in isolation with only 33 of 103 analyzed indices demonstrating statistically significant differences.

CLOUD CONTENT

Experimental investigation of the hypotheses related to the presence of Cloud content was analyzed utilizing a subset of the overall Italian normative sample; 117 male participants' protocols containing Cloud content were compared to 2,176 matched participants without Cloud content. Overall, the authors hypothesized that the presence of Cloud (CLD%) content is an important factor in the CWS and is able to effectively discriminate between subjects in terms of overall health, anxiety states, internal tension, and distress. Specific hypotheses included the following:

1. The presence of Cloud (CLD%) content will be associated with less positive overall health and functioning, as evidenced by fewer positive Global Assessment classifications, fewer classifications in WIP Quadrants A and C, and fewer overall positive box Codes as compared to the control group.
2. The presence of Cloud (CLD%) content will be associated with indicators of affective distress and tension, including a more negative IIT-2, higher Index of Suicidal Tendencies (IST), and lower Human (H%) content.
3. The presence of Cloud (CLD%) content will be associated with higher anxiety and lower ability to enter into mutual relationships, as evidenced by higher frequency of negative Codes in Box 2 (related to sensitivity, relatedness, and vulnerability). As the experimental sample was comprised only of males, it was noted by the authors that Box 2 (generally thought of as specifically representing relationships with women) would likely be most sensitive to discerning anxiety and distress.

Results of analyses related to the Cloud content experimental hypotheses are presented in Table 2.50.

In general, experimental hypotheses were confirmed, with the presence of Cloud content discriminating between normal and pathological protocols. Findings suggest that individuals who produce Cloud content are more likely to present with traits of pathological personality organization, accompanied by high levels of anxiety, difficulties in navigating affective relationships, and potential deficits in their ability to control feelings and emotions.

Additionally, for each protocol, 103 calculations and indices inherent to the CWS interpretation strategy were calculated for exploratory analytical purposes, with independent samples *t*-test used to analyze differences between "CLD" and

TABLE 2.50 Differences Between Groups on Select CWS Indices—Clients with Cloud ("CLD") Content vs. Those without Cloud Content ("No CLD")

Scoring Phenomena	"No CLD" (%)	"CLD" (%)	χ^2	*p*	Φ^+
Global Assessment (Positive Classification: NOP + LSI)	82	67	16.0047	.0001	.08
WIP Quadrant (Positive Placement: A + C)	47	39	2.8989	.08	.03
Overall Positive Box Codes (C+ PC)	61	54	18.7084	.00001	.09
Box 2 Valuation (Positive: C + PC)	76	35	96.666	.00001	.20

Index	"No CLD" $\overline{x}$	"No CLD" CLD" *SD*	"CLD" $\overline{x}$	"CLD" *SD*	*t* (2,291 *df*)	*p*	d^{++}
Affective Stability Index: Affective Quality	2.67	.72	2.06	.72	8.809	.000	1.14[a]
Human Content (H%)	12.27	11.67	8.41	11.14	3.487	.000	.50[a]
Popular Responses (P%)	17.63	11.09	14.44	9.74	3.047	.002	.43[a]
Index of Suicidal Tendencies (IST)	1.8	.12	4.8	.42	68.97	.0001	9.80[b]
Index of Inner Tension-2 (*left side: positive codes*)	4.91	1.42	4.34	1.41	4.220	.000	.60[a]
Index of Inner Tension-2 (*right side: negative codes*)	3.08	1.42	3.65	1.41	–4.220	.000	.60[b]

Notes: Effect sizes calculated by current authors from previously published analyses; + Φ effect sizes: small: .1–.29; medium: .3–.49; large: >.5; ++ *d* effect sizes: small: .2–.49; medium: .5–.79; large: > .8 (Cohen, 1988). a. "No CLD" group values greater than "CLD" group. b. "CLD" group values greater than "No CLD" group.

"No CLD" groups. Results, presented in ►Appendix C, suggest that Cloud content is less able than Human content to discriminate between participants at the individual index level, with only 34 of 103 analyzed indices demonstrating statistically significant differences. However, Cloud content was noted to differentiate between pathological and non-pathological at the overall protocol level (i.e., WIP, Global Assessment, overall Box Codes), indicating its usefulness in identifying pathology and symptomatology.

Overall, Human content and Cloud content appear to discriminate between subjects, whereas Food content does not in isolation. Absence of Human content is related to greater difficulties in social relationships; presence of Food content suggests passivity, insecurity, and dependence; and presence of Cloud content indicates higher levels of pathology including anxiety and difficulties regulating emotions. Future research on the relationship of these Content areas to external measures (rather than other CWS indices) is recommended.

Clinical Utility of the CWS—Published and Presented Case Studies

In addition to the research presented above, several case studies utilizing the CWS have been presented and/or published, suggesting the clinical utility of the CWS. These case studies have investigated convergences between the CWS and the Rorschach Comprehensive System (Exner, 1997, 2003), the CWS and the Adult Attachment Projective (AAP), the CWS and the MMPI-2, and the CWS and the Social Adaptation Self-Evaluation Scale (SASS; Bosc, Dubini, & Polin, 1997) and Scale for the Rapid Dimensional Evaluation (SSIRAD; Pancheri, Biondi, Gaetano, & Picardi, 1999). Overall, these case studies have suggested incremental validity of the CWS in conjunction with other measures, highlighting the utility of the measure to assess clients with affective disturbance, suicidal ideation, pre-psychotic thinking, and varied levels of psychopathology.

Crisi & Shorey (2009)

The convergence between the CWS and the Rorschach Comprehensive System (CS, Exner, 1997, 2003) results was presented by Crisi and Shorey. In this case, the primary author assessed a 19-year-old male who had recently attempted suicide, administering both the Wartegg according to CWS guidelines and the Rorschach according to Comprehensive System guidelines. The primary author independently scored the CWS whereas the second author independently scored the Rorschach. Only after written interpretations were prepared were the interpretive findings integrated.

Given the markedly different methods of information gathering inherent to the two tests (i.e., the Rorschach relies primarily on verbalization, whereas the WDCT relies primarily on drawing), the authors noted a potential lack of clarity in the extent of "convergence and divergence" between the two measures. Results of the independent interpretations are summarized in Table 2.51.

TABLE 2.51 Comparisons Between Rorschach Comprehensive System and CWS Interpretation in a 19-year-old Male Client

Comparative Domain	*Rorschach CS Results*	*CWS Interpretive Results*
Ideation	This client has a pessimistic view of the world that appears to be intruding into his thought processes and he prefers to deal with his negative affect through intellectualization. He also has difficulty thinking logically or coherently, and as a result, may arrive at faulty conclusions, which he then clings to in an inflexible manner.	This client is inclined to face situations with a strong tendency to rationalization and to rigidity. Such tendency should decline in highly emotional situations and his performances might suffer. At present it is important to highlight the presence of pessimistic polarizations of thought.
Cognitive Mediation	This client is capable of recognizing conventional modes of responding but he has difficulty in reality testing, may misperceive events, and may form mistaken impressions about the motives of other people.	His thought is appropriate and adequate to the common way of thinking with emphasis of conformism because of strong traits of dependency. It is possible that the client actively avoids his anxiety with characteristics of repetition and compulsion.
Information Processing	This client takes in less information than is needed to avoid arriving at hasty ill-conceived conclusions. As a result he may be careless in his approach to problems, and not be flexible enough to make needed corrections. By extension, he may perform well below his ability.	
Capacity for Control and Stress Tolerance	This client lacks a consistent and well-defined coping style and currently has fewer psychological resources than are needed to cope with the demands of everyday life in other than a very restricted repertoire of behaviors and situations.	The Index of Suicidal Tendencies is positive (> 8): This client has a very low and weak tolerance for stress. There is a depressive condition that, together with a marked tendency to intropunitive reactions, make real the risk that this client should have strong self-aggressive or self-punitive behaviors.
Affect	This client is prone to depression and mood disturbances. He then copes with his emotional distress through intellectualization. This may further interfere with the clarity of his thinking in affect-laden situations.	The client has deep traits of immaturity arising from a structure of personality characterized by conflict and neuroticism with high and intense states of anxiety. The behavior of the client is mainly characterized by reactivity.

continued

TABLE 2.51 *Continued*

Comparative Domain	*Rorschach CS Results*	*CWS Interpretive Results*
Self-Perception	This client appears to have a defensive tendency to over-value himself to the detriment of attending to the needs of others. Having some awareness that his inflated self-esteem is not reality-based, and having underlying feelings of inadequacy, he avoids close self-examination.	Under an apparent tendency to overestimate and overvalue the self, the subject is very insecure and indecisive. This client likely doesn't share the interests of his peers.
Interpersonal Perception	This client shows interest in other people and generally expects positive interactions with others, but may have limited capacity to form close and lasting attachments.	The client shows a deep social dependency. He does not share sincere and genuine interests of his peer group. His relationships with women are the origin of strong anxiety and fears.

Comparisons of the Rorschach and Wartegg data, and resulting independent interpretations, revealed a high level of concordance in relation to affective experience, negative intrusive ideation, coping strategies, and ability to recognize conventional reality. The authors noted that this convergence between the tests is impressive, given the different modes of response inherent to the two tests (spoken language vs. drawing).

Reports from the two measures diverged, however, in relation to information about thought processes and ideation. The Rorschach protocol identified problems with thinking and reality testing that were not identified with the Wartegg. The Wartegg, in contrast, was more sensitive in detecting a risk for suicide with this client (Rorschach S-CON = 5; Wartegg Index of Suicidal Tendencies > 8). The authors concluded that the data from this single case study is compelling enough to warrant further larger scale and better-controlled research.

Toivakka & Crisi (2014)

Similarities between the CWS and the Rorschach Comprehensive System (CS; Exner, 1997, 2003) were further presented by Toivakka and Crisi. In this case, the CWS was evaluated with minimal information about the client (14-year-old female), with results of the CWS compared to that of the Rorschach. Independently generated interpretive results from each test were evaluated in terms of five comparisons: 1) Diagnosis; 2) Affect; 3) Interpersonal Relationships; 4) Conventionality of Thinking; and 5) Constellations of Scores. In each comparison, a strong degree of clinical concordance was discovered. Conclusions are summarized in Table 2.52, with Rorschach Comprehensive System data presented in the left-hand column, and CWS interpretation presented on the right.

TABLE 2.52 Comparisons Between Rorschach Comprehensive System and CWS Interpretation in a 14-year-old Female Client

Comparative Domain	*Rorschach CS Results*	*CWS Interpretive Results*
Diagnosis	"In the RCS the main clinical impression is of an acute depression with posttraumatic features and developmental risk for a borderline personality disorder."	"In the CWS, clear signs of a reactive depression appeared and many elements indicate that the depressive condition is likely connected with a traumatic event (including sexual or physical violence)."
Affect	FC:CF+C = 8:2 Pure C = 0 SumC:WSumC = 2:6.0 Afr = .33 S = 2 Blends:R = 11:28 CP = 0	This client presents as "in control" emotionally; however, underneath this presentation, she is likely very immature (AQ+% = 75 and Ratio A/F = 4/4) and shows a high level of impulsivity (Impulsivity Index = .75). Traits of egocentrism, tendency to be "explosive," and gross immaturity result in a tendency toward attempted over-control. Such a condition could be the origin of psychosomatic troubles. We should say that this girl "fights against her own dependency from others" but she's not aware of her dependency.
Interpersonal Relationships	COP = 1 AG = 0 GHR:PHR = 4:9 a:p = 11:5 Food = 0 SumT = 0 Human Content = 10 Pure H = 8 PER = 1 Isolation Index = .36	Regarding social skills, we can say that we have found a strong need to lean on others, including marked dependency traits. Moreover, she seeks confirmation and support from others (resulting in reduced autonomy). This girl is very sensitive (she shows an elevated value in the Evocative Character, EC+% = 94). Such a high score is generally found in severely disturbed subjects, who show excessive sensitivity and receptivity to external stimuli. Therefore, these individuals may lack filters, or, in other words, lack intact defense mechanisms. So she is likely to have her feelings easily hurt by the words or actions of others. Traits of hypervigilance are possible.
Conventional Thinking	XA% = .75 WDA% = .67 X–% = .25 S– = 1 P = 4 X+% = .36 Xu% = .39	Generally, high scores in Popular and Human Responses are found in highly conformistic individuals who demonstrate an excessive adherence to conventional thinking. In the present case, the high score obtained (P% = 63% and H% = 50%) appears more

continued

TABLE 2.52 *Continued*

Comparative Domain	*Rorschach CS Results*	*CWS Interpretive Results*
		correlated with depression and strong dependency on others and a strong need for approval. Another element is consistent with this observation: the high percentage of Architectural contents (= 38%).
Constellations of Scores*	PTI = 3 DEPI = 5 CDI = 3 S-CON = N/A HVI = YES OBS = NO	PTI = NO DEPI = YES CDI = YES S-CON = N/A HVI = YES OBS = NO

Note: *While the CWS does not incorporate the Comprehensive System constellations, the primary author extrapolated from CWS indices, estimating whether the client would meet criteria for each cluster based upon performance on the test.

The authors concluded that the Rorschach and CWS demonstrate a high level of convergence in relation to overall clinical description of clients across multiple domains. Given the differences in information gathering inherent in the tests (i.e., verbalization versus drawing), this concordance reinforces the validity of both measures in the complex assessment of personality.

Crisi (2011a)

As part of a larger presentation, a pilot study evaluating the concordance between the CWS and the Adult Attachment Projective (George & West, 2012) was presented at the Society for Personality Assessment annual convention (2011). Two main questions were proposed by the researchers: 1) Is there concordance between the AAP and the CWS in terms of attachment classification; and 2) Is there incremental validity inherent in using both the AAP and CWS in the same assessment battery?

In considering the AAP, attachment classification is generally divided into four categories: Secure, Dismissing, Preoccupied, and Unresolved. This classification is arrived at via standardized scoring at the linguistic level. High convergence between the AAP and the Adult Attachment Interview (AAI) has been reported by George and West (2011). More specifically, 97% convergence between AAP and AAI for secure versus insecure classifications (*kappa* = .80, *p* = .000) and 92% convergence for the four major attachment groups (*kappa* = .89, *p* = .000) has been reported.

In regard to the CWS, attachment style is evident via examination of the Wartegg Index of Psychopathology (WIP). As described elsewhere, the WIP is a

TABLE 2.53 Comparison of AAP Coding Dimension and CWS Clinical Indices

AAP Coding	*Presence/ Absence*	*Corresponding CWS Scoring*	*Presence/ Absence*
Discourse			
Personal Experience	NO	Personalized Answer (PA)	YES (*Box 4*)
Content			
Agency of Self	ABSENT	Valuation Box 3 & 5	ABSENT (*Poor value, Box 3 & 5)*
Connectedness	LOW	H%, Positive AQ+%	LOW (*Low H%, Neg. AQ+%)*
Synchrony	LOW	Valuation of Box 8	LOW (*Box 8 Ambivalent)*
Defenses			
Deactivation	YES	Quadrant B	YES (*Quadrant B)*
Cognitive Disconnection	YES	Quadrant C, High FQ+%, Incomplete Drawing (ID)	NO (*No Quadrant C, Average FQ+%, No ID)*
Segregated Systems	YES	Valuation Box 2 & 4	YES (*Ambivalence in 2 & 4)*

graphic plotting of a client's experienced distress and internal tension (vertical axis) as related to the degree of personality integration, flexibility, and adaptability (horizontal axis). Upon plotting this data, clients are classified into one of four quadrants, each with accompanying attachment style: A) Adaptation (Secure), B) Detachment (Dismissing), C) Dependency (Preoccupied), and D) Ambivalence (Unresolved).

To examine the concordance between AAP classification and CWS quadrant, a case study was evaluated. In addition, examination of several additional factors was considered to determine incremental validity, identifying coding dimensions of the AAP and indices of the CWS that measure similar constructs. First, the presence or absence of verbalized personal experience was noted. Second, content was analyzed for the presence of Agency of Self, Connectedness, and Synchrony, concepts specific to the evaluation of attachment. Lastly, attachment defenses (Deactivation, Cognitive Disconnection, and Segregated Systems) were analyzed. Table 2.53 presents results of this analysis.

Given these preliminary results, concordance between AAP attachment classification (Dismissing) and CWS quadrant (Quadrant B, Detachment) was discovered. Moreover, incremental validity of both measures is suggested, given unique information provided by both. That is, while the AAP better captured the client's thinking related to behaviors and attitudes, as well as tendencies toward cognitive disconnection, the CWS provided clinically relevant affective information related to the client's emotional experiences with parental figures (via analysis of Boxes 2 and 4).

Crisi (2010b)

Convergence between the CWS and the MMPI-2 (Butcher et al., 1989) was presented in a case study focusing on a 38-year-old female client. During the course of an evaluation, the client was administered both the CWS and the MMPI-2, with resulting MMPI-2 code-types compared to CWS scores and indices.

Based upon MMPI-2 results (considered valid), the client produced a "2–7–8" code-type, oftentimes related to depression with psychotic features or thought disturbance. The 2–7–8 code-type has been described by Nichols (2001) as:

> Moderate to severe depression with suicidal ideation, anxiety, fearfulness and phobias, anhedonia, obsessional worry and rumination, compulsions, self-depreciation, pessimism . . . Feelings of worthlessness, helplessness, hopelessness, inadequacy . . . Markedly intropunitive; may be compulsively self-critical and self-accusatory . . . Look for manifest psychotic ideation, thought disorder, hallucinations and delusional ideations; a history of social isolation; and identity and sexual concerns. Maybe severe suicide risk.
>
> (pp. 258–259)

Similar to the description of the 2–7–8 code-type, based upon CWS scoring, the client was noted to meet criteria for 9 out of 13 indicators of psychotic depression, presented in Table 2.54.

In this case, significant concordance was noted between MMPI-2 and CWS interpretation, suggesting the convergence of the measures. Given the strong agreement evident, further studies are recommended.

TABLE 2.54 CWS Criteria Met for Psychotic Depression

Criterion	*Client Score*	*Classification*
EC+% ⩽ 50	50	MET
AQ+% ⩽ 44	44	MET
Box 3 valuation: NC, AD, or D	NC	MET
IIT-1 negative	positive	NOT MET
IIT-2 negative	1/7 (neg)	MET
Quadrant B, area B	B, beta	MET
# of Primary Contents < 4	1	MET
H% low	0%	MET
P% high	0%	NOT MET
OBJ% ⩾ 63	100	MET
Presence of GR or PR	Not present	NOT MET
IST ⩾ 8	9	MET
Opposite Direction (OD)	Not present	NOT MET

Rizzo, Della Villa, & Crisi (2015)

Published in *Computers in Human Behavior*, this case study investigated the utility of the CWS with a 17-year-old boy suffering from Problematic Internet Use (PIU) as described by Young (1996). Convergence of the CWS with both the Social Adaptation Self-Evaluation Scale (SASS; Bosc, Dubini, & Polin, 1997) and the Scale for Rapid Dimensional Assessment (SSIRAD; Pancheri, Biondi, Gaetano, & Picardi, 1999) was investigated. The analysis of the CWS and self-report (SASS) and expert report (SSIRAD) questionnaires included in the study, along with collected life history data, suggested that the client's withdrawal and cyber-dependence likely represented initial symptoms of a pre-psychotic state.

In this study, the WDCT was individually administered, per CWS guidelines, with resulting descriptive, categorical, and attitudinal calculations generated. The Social Adaptation Self-Evaluation Score (SASS) was completed as a self-report instrument by the client, measuring behavior in four broad areas of

TABLE 2.55 Comparisons Between CWS, SASS, and SSIRAD Results

SASS	*SSIRAD*	*CWS*
Social Relationships significantly lower than normal. Relationships likely restricted to family members.	Inability to be reassured by others. Decreased interest and initiative.	Marked difficulties in social interaction; Inability to form close relationships with peers. Behavior based on isolation and detachment. Potentially disorganized attachment classification.
Self-Esteem significantly lower than normal Feelings of inadequacy are likely.	Distrust of himself and his abilities. Feeling of imminent danger.	Feelings of insecurity, inferiority, inadequacy likely to present in interactions with authority.
Evidence of Frustration	Sense of constraint.	Intrapunitive reactions toward frustration; Inability to adequately (adaptively) express frustration.
	Severe psychic anxiety and tension.	Internal tension and distress.
	Reduction of creativity and energy; pessimism; decreased pleasure. Affective constriction.	Basic depressive state, resulting in discomfort, and limiting performance and behavior.
	Stereotypical, rigid, and de-realized thinking. Idiosyncratic and unusual beliefs, thoughts, decisions.	Formal, rigid, closed ideational process. Synthesis and judgment are decidedly inadequate.

social functioning: 1) Work; 2) Spare time; 3) Family; and 4) Ability to cope with resources/finances. The SASS further assesses motivation, self-perception, and satisfaction. The Scale for the Rapid Dimensional Evaluation (SSIRAD) was compiled by a psychologist, based upon review of client's life history data. The SSIRAD evaluates clients on ten dimensions: 1) Apprehension-fear; 2) Sadness-demoralization; 3) Rage-aggressiveness; 4) Obsessionality; 5) Apathy; 6) Impulsiveness; 7) Reality distortion; 8) Thought disorganization; 9) Somatic preoccupation-somatization; and 10) Activation.

Interpreted results of the three instruments are summarized in Table 2.55.

The authors noted the similarities between the client-report (SASS), clinician-report (SSIRAD), and projective methodology (CWS), suggesting both the convergent validity of the measures, as well as the incremental validity of the CWS. Additional strengths of the CWS were noted, in particular, that given this client's affective interference in communicating, the CWS provided a clear and comprehensive manner in which to better understand his personality structure, symptoms, strengths, and current functioning.

Conclusions

In reviewing presented data on the reliability of the CWS, interrater agreement has been clearly established in multiple studies, both in Italian and English. Preliminary test–retest reliability data is promising, and similar to that of other performance-based personality measures, although more conclusive research is needed.

Summarized studies further suggest the convergent validity of the CWS with other established measures, including the MMPI-2, the Rorschach Inkblot Test, the AAP, the Guilford–Zimmerman Temperament Survey, and others. Moreover, the CWS has demonstrated the ability to differentiate between normal and clinical groups, with studies focusing on a variety of ages, conditions, and mental health diagnoses. High levels of concordance with expert ratings have further been noted. As with any measure, further validity research is recommended.

Lastly, clinical experience with the CWS suggests practical advantages to the measure, incremental validity, and therapeutic applications. These advantages have been elaborated in presented and published case studies, as well as through formal case consultations with clinicians using the measure. With continued use, and the development of a vibrant CWS community of clinicians, further research, development, and growth of the measure is anticipated.

Notes

1. We are thankful to Isabella Lops who contributed with data analysis and suggestions for the text in this section.
2. We are thankful to Harald Janson who contributed with data analysis and suggestions for the text in this section.

References

Achenbach, T. M. (1991). *Child behavior checklist/4–18*. University of Vermont, Department of Psychiatry.

Alves, I. C. B., Dias, A. R., Sardinha, L. S., & Conti, F. D. (2010). Precisão entre juízes na avaliação dos aspectos formais do teste de Wartegg [Accuracy among judges in evaluating the formal aspects of the Wartegg test]. *Aletheia*, (31), 54–65.

American Psychiatric Association. (1994). *Diagnostic and statistical manual, 4th ed. (DSM-IV)*. Washington, DC: American Psychiatric Association.

American Psychiatric Association. (2000). *Diagnostic and statistical manual, 4th ed., Text Revision (DSM-IV-TR)*. Washington, DC: American Psychiatric Association.

Attili, G. (2001). *Ansia da separazione e misura dell'attaccamento normale e patologico: versione modificata e adattamento italiano del Separation anxiety test (SAT) di Klagsbrun e Bowlby (12 tavole per la somministrazione del test)*. [Anxiety from separation and measurement of normal and pathological attachment: Modified version and Italian adaptation of the Klagsbrun and Bowlby Separation Anxiety Test (SAT) (12 tables for the administration of the test)]. Milan: Unicopli.

Bailly, D., Dechoulydelenclave, M. B., & Lauwerier, L. (2003). Hearing impairment and psychopathological disorders in children and adolescents. Review of the recent literature. *L'Encephale*, *29*(4, pt.1), 329–337.

Balboni, G., & Cubelli, R. (2004). La specificità delle tecniche proiettive ei limiti del dibattito sulle loro proprietà psicometriche [The specificity of projection techniques and the limits of the debate on their psychometric properties]. *Psicologia Clinica dello Sviluppo*, 8(2), 195–216.

Barker, D. H., Quittner, A. L., Fink, N. E., Eisenberg, L. S., Tobey, E. A., & Niparko, J. K. (2009). Predicting behavior problems in deaf and hearing children: The influences of language, attention, and parent–child communication. *Development and Psychopathology*, *21*(2), 373–392.

Benedetti, A., Bologna, M., Crosato, S., Favretti, L., Giusti, E., Lestingi, L., Sangiorgi, A. M., & Crisi, A. (2008). Il test di Wartegg nei servizi di consulenza [The Wartegg test in the Consultant services], *Psichiatria e Psicoterapia*, *27*(2), 128–132.

Bianchi di Castelbianco, F., Crisi, A., & Di Renzo, M. (1993). *Il Test di Wartegg nell'età evolutiva* [The Wartegg Test in childhood]. Rome, Italy: Armando.

Bianchi di Castelbianco, F., Crisi, A., & Di Renzo, M. (1996). *Il test di Wartegg nell'età evolutiva. Un contributo psicodiagnostico allo studio clinico della balbuzie, della sordità e dei disturbi dell'apprendimento* [The Wartegg Test in childhood. A clinical contribution to the study of stammering, deafness, and learning disorders]. Rome, Italy: Edizioni Magi.

Bianchi di Castelbianco, F., Crisi, A., & Palermo, M. T. (2002). Ansia, sordità e serotonina [Anxiety, deafness and serotonin]. *Babele, anno VI* (21), 32–35.

Bianchi di Castelbianco, F., Crisi, A., & Palermo, M. T., Palladino, G., Sommaruga, L., Sgueglia, F., & Vichi, P. (2002). Ilrischio psicopatologico nella sordità [The psychopathological risk in deafness]. *Babele, anno VI* (21), 36–40.

Bornstein, R. F. (2009). Heisenberg, Kandinsky, and the heteromethod convergence problem: Lessons from within and beyond psychology. *Journal of Personality Assessment*, *91*(1), 1–8.

Bosc, M., Dubini, A., & Polin, V. (1997). Development and validation of a social functioning scale, the Social Adaptation Self-evaluation Scale. *European Neuropsychopharmacology*, *7*(1), S57–S70.

Bowlby, J. (1980). *Attachment and loss: Vol. 3. Loss: Sadness and depression*. New York: Basic Books.

Brennan, R. L., & Prediger, D. J. (1981). Coefficient kappa: Some uses, misuses, and alternatives. *Educational and Psychological Measurement, 41*(3), 687–699.

Brown, J. D. (1996). *Testing in language programs*. Upper Saddle River, NJ: Prentice Hall Regents.

Butcher, J., Graham, J., Ben-Porath, Y., Tellegen, A., Dahlstrom, W. G., & Kaemmer, B. (1989). *The Minnesota Multiphasic Personality Inventory, Second Edition (MMPI-2)*. Minneapolis, MN: University of Minnesota Press.

Campbell, D. T., & Fiske, D. W. (1959). Convergent and discriminant validation by the multitrait-multimethod matrix. *Psychological Bulletin*, 56(2), 81.

Caspi, A., Hariri, A. R., Holmes, A., Uher, R., & Moffitt, T. E. (2010). Genetic sensitivity to the environment: The case of the serotonin transporter gene and its implications for studying complex diseases and traits. *American Journal of Psychiatry*, *167*(5), 509–527.

Checinski, K. (1991). Preliminary findings of the study of the prevalence of psychiatric disorder in prelingually deaf adults living in the community. In *Proceedings of the Mental Health and Deafness conference*, St. George's Hospital Medical School, London.

Chiorri, C. (2011). *Teoria e tecnica psicometrica: costruire un test psicologico* [Psychometric theory and technique: Build a psychological test]. New York: McGraw-Hill.

Cicchetti, D. V. (1994). Guidelines, criteria, and rules of thumb for evaluating normed and standardized assessment instruments in psychology. *Psychological Assessment*, 6(4), 284.

Cohen, J. (1968). Weighted kappa: Nominal scale agreement provision for scaled disagreement or partial credit. *Psychological Bulletin*, 70(4), 213.

Cohen, J. (1988). *Statistical power analysis for the behavioural sciences*. Hillsdale, NJ: Lawrence Erlbaum Associates.

Crisi, A. (1998). *Manuale del Test di Wartegg* [Manual for the Wartegg Test]. Rome, Italy: Edizioni MaGi.

Crisi, A. (1999, July). *Similitudes between the Evocative Character of the Wartegg panels and those of Rorschach plates*. Paper presented at the meeting of the International Rorschach Society, Amsterdam, the Netherlands.

Crisi, A. (2000). Test di Wartegg [The Wartegg test]. In F. Bianchi di Castelbianco & M. Di Renzo (Eds.), *Vivere bene la scuola: Esplorazione del disagio infantile nel mondo scolastico* [Living well the school: Exploring childhood discomfort in the scholastic world] (pp. 41–50). Rome, Italy: ES MaGi.

Crisi, A. (2002). La valutazione psicodiagnostica Wartegg nell'ambito della sordità [The clinical assessment of deafness with the Wartegg Test]. *Babele, anno VI* (21), 26–31.

Crisi, A. (2006, October). *Il test di Wartegg: un contributo allo studio dei Disturbi dell' Apprendimento* [The Wartegg Test: Contributions to the study of learning disorders]. Paper presented at the meeting of the *Istituto di Ortofonologia*, Rome, Italy.

Crisi, A. (2007). *Manuale del test di Wartegg, 2nd ed.* [Manual for the Wartegg Test, 2nd Edition]. Rome, Italy: Edizioni MaGi.

Crisi, A. (2008, July). *Rorschach and Wartegg: Two twin tests*. Paper presented at the meeting of the International Rorschach Society Convention, Leuven, Belgium.

Crisi, A. (2009, March). *The Wartegg Index of Psychopathology*. Poster presented at the meeting of the Society for Personality Assessment, Chicago, IL.

Crisi A. (2010a). Il Test di Wartegg applicato ad un gruppo di adolescenti de L'Aquila [The Wartegg test applied to a group of adolescents of L'Aquila]. In F. Bianchi di Castelbianco & M. Di Renzo (Eds.), *Le 398 meravigliose maestre de L'Aquila* [The 398 wonderful teachers of L'Aquila] (pp. 257–264). Rome, Italy: Edizioni MaGi.

Crisi, A. (2010b, July). *The forgotten test: The Wartegg Drawing Completion Test*. Workshop presented at the meeting of the Rorschach Summer Seminars, Montreux, Switzerland.

Crisi, A. (2011a, March). AAP and Wartegg: A pilot study on attachment. In A. Lis (Chair), *Adult Attachment Projective Picture System (AAP): New Perspectives in the Assessment of Adult Attachment Pattern*. Symposium conducted at the meeting of the Society for Personality Assessment, Boston, MA.

Crisi, A. (2011b). *Reliability and validity of the Crisi Wartegg System*. Unpublished manuscript.

Crisi, A., & Carlesimo, S. (2008, July). *The Human, Food, and Cloud contents: Discriminative ability in clinical personality assessment*. Paper presented at the meeting of the International Rorschach Society, Leuven, Belgium.

Crisi, A., & Dentale, F. (2016). The Wartegg Drawing Completion Test: Inter-rater agreement and criterion validity of three new scoring categories. *International Journal of Psychology and Psychological Therapy, 16*(1), 85–92.

Crisi, A., Janson, H., & Palm, J. (2016). *Test–Retest reliability of the Crisi Wartegg System: Initial analysis*. Unpublished research.

Crisi, A., Palm, J., & Lops, I. (2016). *Interrater reliability of the Crisi Wartegg System: An initial United States sample*. Unpublished research.

Crisi, A., & Pastore, L. (2006). La valutazione psicodiagnostica: Uno studio pilota condotto con il test di Wartegg [The clinical assessment: A pilot study with the Wartegg test]. In L. Pastore (Ed.), *Il fenomeno del Mobbing. Aspetti psicologici e strumenti di ricerca-intervento* (pp. 131–158). Milan: Franco Angeli.

Crisi, A., & Pastore, L. (2010, March). *Main characteristics of work-abused clients examined through the Wartegg Test*. Paper presented at the meeting of the Society for Personality Assessment, San Jose, CA.

Crisi, A., & Shorey, H. (2009, March). *Comparing projective measures: A case study using the Wartegg and the Rorschach*. Poster presented at the meeting of the Society for Personality Assessment, Chicago, IL.

Crisi, A., Testa, F., Carlesimo, S., Lops, I., & Maio, S. (2011, March). *The Wartegg Drawing Completion Test in a Sample of 350 Psychiatric Clients: The indices*. Paper presented at the meeting of the Society for Personality Assessment, Boston, MA.

Crisi, A., Testa, F., Carlesimo, S., & Maio, S. (2010, March). *Psychopathology and projective techniques: Content analysis through the Wartegg Drawing Completion Test in a sample of 350 psychiatric clients*. Paper presented at the meeting of the Society for Personality Assessment, San Jose, CA.

Crisi, A., Vari, C., Velotti, P., Carlesimo, S., Guzzi, C., & Zavattini, G. C. (2014, July). *Depression and negative affect in dermatology patients: The use of the WDCT according to the Crisi Wartegg System*. Paper presented at the meeting of the International Rorschach Society, Istanbul, Turkey.

Cronbach, L. J., & Meehl, P. E. (1955). Construct validity in psychological tests. *Psychological Bulletin, 52*(4), 281.

D'Amore, G. (2004). *Comparison between some Rorschach Inkblot Test indexes and Wartegg Test*. Proceedings of the 35th annual meeting of the Society for Psychotherapy Research.

Daini, S., Bernardini, L., & Panetta, C. (2007). A personality perspective on female infertility: An analysis through Wartegg test. *SIS Journal of Projective Psychology & Mental Health, 14*(2), 135–144.

Daini, S., Lai, C., Festa, G. M., Maiorino, F., Pertosa, M., & De Risio, S. (2006). Impulsivity in eating disorders: Analyzed through Wartegg test. *Journal of Projective Psychology & Mental Health, 13*(2), 107–117.

Daini, S., Manzo, A., Pisani, F., & Tancredi, A. (2010). Attempted suicide: Psychopathology and Wartegg Test indicators. *SIS Journal of Projective Psychology & Mental Health, 17*(2), 171–177.

Daini, S., Petrongolo, L., Manzo, A., & Bernardini, L. (2012). Personality and nursing work: A comparison between professional and student nurses. *SIS Journal of Projective Psychology & Mental Health, 19*(1), 18–24.

de Graaf, R., & Bijl, R. V. (2002). Determinants of mental distress in adults with a severe auditory impairment: Differences between prelingual and postlingual deafness. *Psychosomatic Medicine, 64*(1), 61–70.

Denmark, J. C. (1966). Mental illness and early profound deafness. *British Journal of Medical Psychology, 39*(2), 117–124.

Di Riso, D., Crisi, A., Bianchi di Castelbianco, F., Di Renzo, M., Vichi, P., Racinaro, L., & Morellini, D. (2013, March). *Attachment, personality and learning disabilities: A study of learning disabled children and their parents.* Symposium presented at the meeting of the Society for Personality Assessment, San Diego, CA.

Exner, J. (2003). *The Rorschach: A Comprehensive System. Volume 1: The Rorschach, basic foundations and principles of interpretation.* New York: Wiley & Sons.

Fellinger, J., Holzinger, D., Dobner, U., Gerich, J., Lehner, R., Lenz, G., & Goldberg, D. (2007). Mental distress and quality of life in the hard of hearing. *Social Psychiatry and Psychiatric Epidemiology, 40*, 737–742.

Fontana, U. (1984). *L'Uso del test di Wartegg nella pratica clinica* [Using Wartegg's test in clinical work]. Verona: CISERP.

Fontana, U. (2005). *Una tecnica da non dimenticare. Il WZT validato e allargato per il clinico di oggi* [A method not to be forgotten. Validation of the WZT for today's clinicians]. Venice: Edizioni Quaderni ISRE.

Fontana, U. (2013). *La psicoanalisi imbavagliata* [Psychoanalysis gagged]. Libreria-universitaria. It Edizioni.

Gallagher, T. M. (1999). Interrelationships among children's language, behavior, and emotional problems. *Topics in Language Disorders, 19*(2), 1–15.

Gardziella, M. (1985). *Wartegg-piirustustesti. K.sikirja* [The Wartegg Drawing Test. A Handbook]. Jyväskylä: Psykologien Kustannus Oy.

George, C., & West, M. L. (2011). The adult attachment projective picture system: Integrating attachment into clinical assessment. *Journal of Personality Assessment, 93*(5), 407–416.

George, C., & West, M. L. (2012). *The Adult Attachment Projective Picture System: Attachment theory and assessment in adults.* New York: Guilford Press.

Guilford, J. P., & Zimmerman, W. S. (1949). *The Guilford–Zimmerman Temperament Survey: Manual.* Beverly Hills, CA: Sheridan Supply Co.

Harnois, G., Gabriel, P., & World Health Organization. (2000). *Mental health and work: Impact, issues and good practices.* International Labor Organization. WHO: Geneva, Switzerland. Retrieved from: www.ilo.org/wcmsp5/groups/public/---ed_emp/---ifp_skills/documents/publication/wcms_108152.pdf

Hiller, J. B., Rosenthal, R., Bornstein, R. F., Berry, D. T., & Brunell-Neuleib, S. (1999). A comparative meta-analysis of Rorschach and MMPI validity. *Psychological Assessment, 11*(3), 278.

Hindley, P. A., Hill, P. D., McGuigan, S., & Kitson, N. (1994). Psychiatric disorder in deaf and hearing impaired children and young people: A prevalence study. *Journal of Child Psychology and Psychiatry, 35*(5), 917–934.

Hindley, P., Kitson, N., & Leach, V. (2000). Forensic psychiatry and deaf people. *Mental Health and Deafness*, 206–231.

Iqbal, Z., & Hall, R. (1991). Mental health services for deaf people: A need identified. *Public Health, 105*(6), 467–473.

Jorm, A. F., Prior, M., Sanson, A., Smart, D., Zhang, Y., & Easteal, S. (2000). Association of a functional polymorphism of the serotonin transporter gene with anxiety-related temperament and behavior problems in children: A longitudinal study from infancy to the mid-teens. *Molecular Psychiatry*, *5*(5), 542.

Jung C. G. (1960). A review of the complex theory. *Collected Works, Vol. VIII*. Bollingen Series XX. Princeton, NJ: Princeton University Press.

Kitson, N., & Fry, R. (1990). Prelingual deafness and psychiatry. *British Journal of Hospital Medicine*, *44*(5), 353.

Klagsbrun, M., & Bowlby, J. (1976). Responses to separation from parents: A clinical test for young children. *British Journal of Projective Psychology & Personality Study*, *2*, 7–27.

Kurd, S. K., & Gelfand, J. M. (2009). The prevalence of previously diagnosed and undiagnosed psoriasis in US adults: Results from NHANES 2003–2004. *Journal of the American Academy of Dermatology*, *60* (2), 218–224.

Kvam, M. H., Loeb, M., & Tambs, K. (2007). Mental health in deaf adults: Symptoms of anxiety and depression among hearing and deaf individuals. *Journal of Deaf Studies and Deaf Education*, *12*(1), 1–7.

Landis, J. R., & Koch, G. G. (1977). The measurement of observer agreement for categorical data. *Biometrics*, 159–174.

Laucht, M., Treutlein, J., Blomeyer, D., Buchmann, A. F., Schmid, B., Becker, K., & Banaschewski, T. (2009). Interaction between the 5-HTTLPR serotonin transporter polymorphism and environmental adversity for mood and anxiety psychopathology: Evidence from a high-risk community sample of young adults. *International Journal of Neuropsychopharmacology*, *12*(6), 737–747.

Maio, S., Ricci, C., & Crisi, A. (2008, July). *Attachment styles in projective techniques: A pilot study*. Paper presented at the meeting of the International Rorschach Society, Leuven, Belgium.

Manicavasaga, V., Silove, D., & Curtis, J. (1997). Separation anxiety in adulthood: A phenomenological investigation. *Comprehensive Psychiatry*, *38*(5), 274–282.

Margoob, M. A., & Mushtaq, D. (2011). Serotonin transporter gene polymorphism and psychiatric disorders: Is there a link? *Indian Journal of Psychiatry*, *53*(4), 289.

Marschark, M., Mouradian, V., & Halas, M. (1994). Discourse rules in the language productions of deaf and hearing children. *Journal of Experimental Child Psychology*, *57*(1), 89–107.

Mattlar, C.-E. (2005, July). *An overview of the Wartegg Zeichentest (WZT): The structure and use thereof, and of research supporting its utility*. Paper presented at the meeting of the International Rorschach Society, Barcelona, Spain.

Melke, J., Landén, M., Baghei, F., Rosmond, R., Holm, G., Björntorp, P., Westberg, L., Hellstrand, M., & Eriksson, E. (2001). Serotonin transporter gene polymorphisms are associated with anxiety-related personality traits in women. *American Journal of Medical Genetics*, *105*(5), 458–463.

Nichols, D. (2001). *Essentials of MMPI-2 assessment*. New York: Wiley & Sons.

Olivier, C., Robert, P. D., Daihung, D., Urbà, G., Catalin, M. P., Hywel, W., Kurd, S., Troxel, A. B., Crits-Christoph, P., & Gelfand, J. M. (2010). The risk of depression, anxiety, and suicidality in patients with psoriasis: A population-based cohort study. *Archives of Dermatology*, *146*(8), 891–895.

Padden, C. A., & Humphries, T. (1990). *Deaf in America: Voices from a culture*. Cambridge, MA: Harvard University Press.

Palermo, R., & Rhodes, G. (2007). Are you always on my mind? A review of how face perception and attention interact. *Neuropsychologia*, *45*(1), 75–92.

Pancheri, P., Biondi, M., Gaetano, P., & Picardi, A. (1999). Costruzione della "SSIRAD", una scala per la valutazione rapida dimensionale [Construction of the "SSIRAD", a scale for rapid dimensional evaluation]. *Riv. Psichiatria, 34*, 72–83.

Picardi, A., Lega, I., & Tarolla, E. (2013). Suicide risk in skin disorders. *Clinics in Dermatology, 31*(1), 47–56.

Rainer, J. D. (1963). *Family and mental health problems in a deaf population. Final report of the Mental Health Project for the Deaf.* New York: New York State Psychiatric Institute, Department of Medical Genetics.

Randolph, J. J. (2005). Free-Marginal Multirater Kappa (multirater K [free]): An Alternative to Fleiss' Fixed-Marginal Multirater Kappa. *Online Submission*. Retrieved from: http://files.eric.ed.gov/fulltext/ED490661.pdf.

Ravecca, F. (2003, February). *Il processo di selezione del personale in una Forza Armata che cambia: sperimentazione del test Wartegg all'Accademia Navale di Livorno.* [The selection proceeding in an Armed Force which is changing: Experimentation with the Wartegg test at the Navy Academy of Livorno]. Paper presented at the Annual Convention of Italian Society of Psychopathology (SOPSI).

Ridgeway, S. M. (1997). Deaf people and psychology: Some preliminary findings. *Deaf Worlds, 13*, 9–18.

Rizzo, A., Della Villa, L., & Crisi, A. (2015). Can the Problematic Internet Use evolve in a pre-psychotic state? A single case study with the Wartegg. *Computers in Human Behavior, 51*, 532–538.

Roivainen, E., & Ruuska, P. (2005). The use of projective drawings to assess alexithymia. *European Journal of Psychological Assessment, 21*(3), 199–201.

Rorschach, H. (1942). *Psychodiagnostics: A diagnostic test based on perception.* Bern, Switzerland: Verlag Hans Huber. (Original work published 1921.)

Scarpellini, C. (1962). *Diagnosi di personalità col reattivo di realizzazione grafica* [Diagnosis of personality with the drawing completion test]. Contributi dell'Istituto di Psicologia dell'Università Cattolica del Sacro Cuore [Contributions from the Institute of Psychology of the Catholic University of the Sacred Heart], pp. 1–82.

Scarpellini, C. (1964). Diagnostic differentiel a travers deux tests de personalite: le Rorschach et le Wartegg [Differential diagnostic through two personality tests: The Rorschach and the Wartegg]. *Bulletin de Psychologie Scolaire et d'Orientation, 13*, 79–92.

Siegel, S., & Castellan, N. J. (1988). *Nonparametric systems for the behavioural sciences.* New York: McGraw Hill International Editions.

Soilevuo Grønnerød, J., & Grønnerød, C. (2012). The Wartegg Zeichen Test: A literature overview and a meta-analysis of reliability and validity. *Psychological Assessment, 24*(2), 476–89.

Substance Abuse and Mental Health Services Administration (SAMHSA), Center for Substance Abuse Treatment, US (2014). *Trauma-Informed Care in Behavioral Health Services.* Treatment Improvement Protocol (TIP) Series, No. 57. Rockville, MD. Retrieved from: www.ncbi.nlm.nih.gov/books/NBK207191/.

Toivakka, H., & Crisi, A. (2014, March). *Rorschach and Wartegg as tools in a case of adolescent assessment.* Paper presented at the meeting of the Society for Personality Assessment, Arlington, VA.

Turner, O., Windfuhr, K., & Kapur, N. (2007). Suicide in deaf populations: A literature review. *Annals of General Psychiatry*, 6(1), 6–26.

Vaccari, C., & Marschark, M. (1997). Communication between parents and deaf children: Implications for social-emotional development. *Journal of Child Psychology and Psychiatry*, 38(7), 793–801.

Vandereycken, W. (1993). The Eating Disorder Evaluation Scale (EDES). *Eating Disorders, 1*(2), 115–122.

Warrens, M. J. (2010). Inequalities between multi-rater kappas. *Advances in Data Analysis and Classification, 4*(4), 271–286.

Werngren-Elgström, M., Dehlin, O., & Iwarsson, S. (2003). Aspects of quality of life in persons with pre-lingual deafness using sign language: Subjective wellbeing, ill-health symptoms, depression and insomnia. *Archives of Gerontology and Geriatrics, 37*(1), 13–24.

World Health Organization. (2017). *Fact sheet: Deafness and hearing loss*. Retrieved from: www.who.int/mediacentre/factsheets/fs300/en/.

Young, K. S. (1996). Psychology of computer use: XL. Addictive use of the Internet: A case that breaks the stereotype. *Psychological Reports, 79*(3), 899–902.

Zacharie, R., Zacharie, C. O., Lei, U., & Pedersen, A. F. (2004). Medication and health care service utilization related to depressive symptoms in older adults with psoriasis. *Journal of Drugs in Dermatology, 3*(6), 661–666.

Zhang, K., Xu, Q., Xu, Y., Yang, H., Luo, J., Sun, Y., Sun, N., Wang, S., & Shen, Y. (2009). The combined effects of the 5-HTTLPR and 5-HTR1A genes modulates the relationship between negative life events and major depressive disorder in a Chinese population. *Journal of Affective Disorders, 114*(1), 224–231.

3 Administration

The WDCT, according to the Crisi Wartegg System guidelines, can be administered to clients four and a half years of age and older, either individually or in a group setting.

Individual Administration with Adults

Administration of the WDCT is divided into four distinct phases:

1. the Drawing Phase, during which the client produces drawings;
2. the Picture Gallery, during which the client is asked to verbally describe his/her drawings;
3. the Choice of Drawings and Boxes, during which the client identifies preferences, likes, and dislikes related to their drawings and test stimuli;
4. the Test of Sequence, in which the client's preference for WDCT stimuli is recorded. (In some cases, this is not necessary, as discussed later in this chapter.)

Each phase of WDCT administration will be described below. An overview of Individual Administration Instructions to be used with adult clients, according to the Crisi Wartegg System, is provided in Figure 3.1.

PHASE of ADMINISTRATION	STANDARDIZED INSTRUCTIONS	ASSESSOR TASKS/INFORMATION RECORDED
The **Drawing Phase**	*"As you can see, this form is divided into eight boxes. In each box there is a little mark. Using the mark as a starting point, make a drawing in each box that means something, preferably the first thing that comes to mind, trying to avoid abstract drawings. You do not need to follow numerical order. Work at your own pace; there's no time limit."* **If client is confused about the phrase "a drawing that means something":** *"By a 'drawing that means something' I mean a drawing that represents something like an object, a person, a building, and so on. Avoid drawings without meaning, like lines, dots, or simple repetitions of the mark."* **If the client is still confused, see Figure 3.8 for Additional Instructions** **If necessary, provide further instructions when:** 1) Client produces protocol with four or more abstract or symbol drawings; 2) Client begins to explain drawings during Drawing Phase; 3) Client completes a box, later returning to modify/change the original drawing; 4) Client rejects one or more boxes (verbally or through non-completion).	1) Record the order in which the client completed the drawings; 2) Record the Drawing Completion Time (exact length of time it takes the client to complete the initial phase of the test); 3) Record *verbatim*: a) Everything the client says; b) Client's questions; c) Client's comments or critiques; d) All interruptions and pauses; e) Significant verbal or non-verbal behavior the client demonstrates during the administration. 4) Record presence of Reversed Boxes; 5) Record if Additional Instructions were required.
The **Picture Gallery**	*"Very good. Now, in numerical order, tell me what you drew in each box."* **In seven specific instances, the assessor questions the client for clarification:** 1) Client's use of stimulus is not clear or easy to understand; 2) Gender of produced figures is not clear *("Is that a male or female?")*; 3) Drawings accompanied by: a) verbalizations such as: "A strange human figure" or "A scary scene." *("Why is it strange?"* or *"Why is it scary?")*; or b) by descriptions that do not match the drawing; 4) Content of depicted figure can be interpreted in multiple ways (i.e., a pyramid may be a geometric shape or an architectural object); 5) Abstract drawing produced (e.g., "happiness") and the connection between the drawing and the client's verbal description is unclear. *("Yes, but what exactly did you draw?")*; 6) Drawing is not completely described. (e.g., "an object") requiring clarification. *("What does the object represent?")*; 7) Client changes the meaning of a drawing by returning to it and modifying drawing later in Order of Sequence *(What did you draw first?)*.	1) Record *verbatim* the client's descriptions of each drawing produced. 2) Avoid asking leading questions. Question only in the seven specific instances listed at left.

PHASE of ADMINISTRATION	STANDARDIZED INSTRUCTIONS	ASSESSOR TASKS/INFORMATION RECORDED
The **Choice of Drawing and Boxes**	**With the completed protocol visible to both client and assessor, the assessor asks the client:** *"Which of your drawings do you like the most?"* (Following client's response): *"Why?"* *"Which of your drawings do you like the least?"* (Following client's response): *"Why?"* **The completed Client WDCT form is set aside, and a blank Client WDCT form is provided, visible to both client and assessor. The assessor asks the client:** *"Which of these marks do you like the most?"* (Following client's response): *"Why?"* *"Which of your marks do you like the least?"* (Following client's response): *"Why?"* **Careful attention must be paid to obtain complete answers, without leaving anything open to interpretation.** (e.g., if client says: "I like this one the best, because it's so strange!", the assessor must ask, *"Strange?"*)	3) Record *verbatim*: a) Drawing client likes the most and why; b) Drawing client likes the least and why; c) Symbol client likes the most and why; d) Symbol client likes the least and why.
The **Order of Sequence** and **Test of Sequence**	**The Test of Sequence is <u>only administered</u> if:** 1) The client uses one of the four non-individualized Orders of Sequence (Numerical, Reversed, Numerical Circular, Reversed Circular). This may be done in a "pure" way or when there is <u>only one</u> alteration in the box-order. 2) When the first 4 boxes used by the client are Boxes 1, 2, 3, and 4, <u>regardless of the order in which they were drawn.</u> 3) The assessor observes a methodical Order of Sequence (i.e., all even boxes first, etc.). **To Complete the Test of Sequence:** 1) Record most-liked and least-liked symbol on the Examiner Administration Form. The box number of the most-liked symbol is recorded next to the "+" sign; The box number of the least-liked symbol is recorded next to the "–" sign. 2) Using pre-prepared small squares of paper, cover the most-liked and least-liked boxes, saying: *"I am now covering Boxes X and Y and would like you to choose which you like most and least from the remaining boxes."* 3) Record the box number of the most-liked symbol to the right of the previously indicated most-liked symbol, on the spaces provided on the Examiner Administration Form. The box number of the least-liked symbol is recorded to the left of the previously indicated least-liked symbol on the space provided on the Examiner Administration Form. 4) Continue this pattern until two boxes remain. At that point, say: *"Very good. Now, for the last two boxes, which mark do you like the most, and which do you like least?"* Record remaining box numbers in the remaining spaces.	1) Evaluate whether client has completed unique/individualized Order of Sequence. If ***yes,*** administration is complete; If ***no,*** administer the Sequence Test. 2) Record results of Sequence Test on Examiner Administration Form using the eight blank lines provided between the "+" and "–" signs. When completed, the numbers of the 8 Boxes should be listed (left to right) from Most-liked to Least-liked symbol.

FIGURE 3.1 Summary of CWS Administration Instructions for Adult Clients.

Figure 3.1 provides a general overview of administration instructions for use with adult clients. Please refer to Chapter 3 of this manual for further information regarding administration, special instructions, and use of the CWS with special populations.

The Drawing Phase

To begin individual administration with adult clients, the assessor hands the client the Client WDCT Form (see Figure 3.2), and a well-sharpened #2 pencil, without an eraser. Erasers are not allowed.

The assessor says:

> *"As you can see, this form is divided into eight boxes. In each box there is a little mark. Using the mark as a starting point, make a drawing in each box that means something, preferably the first thing that comes to mind, trying to avoid abstract drawings. You do not need to follow numerical order. Work at your own pace. There is no time limit."*

Usually, these instructions are sufficient for the client to begin drawing without needing any further explanation. Sometimes, the client may object that he/she cannot draw, that he/she is not a good artist, or offer similar verbalizations

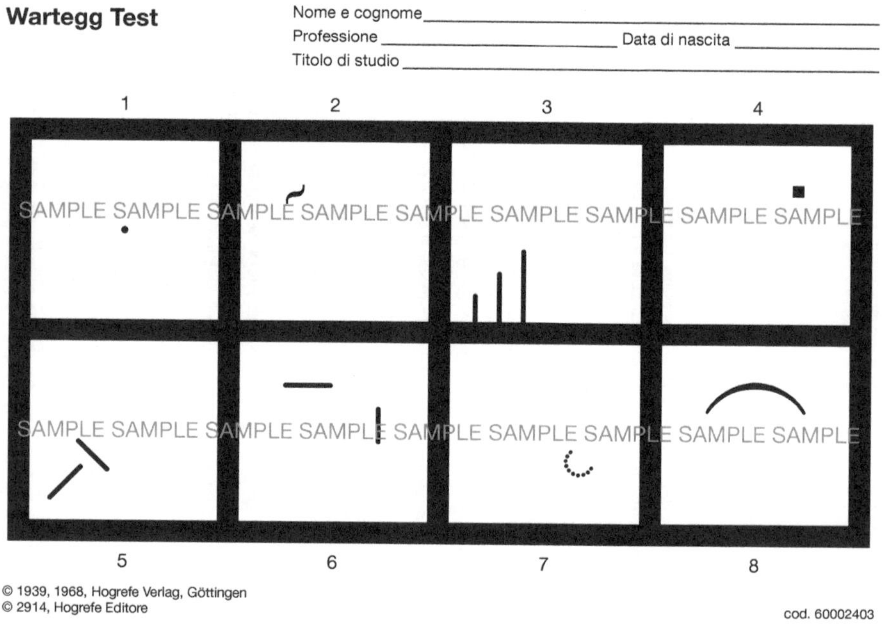

FIGURE 3.2 Client WDCT Form.

Figure 3.2 provides a sample copy of the WDCT form on which the client draws.

Source: Wartegg, E. (1953) *Schichtdiagnostik – Der Zeichentest (WZT)*, Hogrefe, Verlag für Psychologie. Copyright: 1957, Hogrefe, Verlag für Psychologie-Göttingen; 2014, Hogrefe Editore.

related to perceived artistic ability. In this case, the assessor should reassure the client that drawing skills do not matter for the purposes of this test and that anything he/she draws will be fine.

Only in cases when a client seems confused about the specific phrase "a drawing that means something," the assessor should add:

> "By '*a drawing that means something*' *I mean a drawing that represents something like an object, a person, a building, and so on. Avoid drawings without meaning, like lines, dots, or simple repetitions of the mark.*"

If the client is still confused, the specific procedure for Additional Instructions should be followed (discussed later in this chapter).

Once the client begins drawing, the examiner should start timing and keep track of the order in which the client completes the boxes.

Examiner Administration Form

During administration, the assessor will use the Examiner Administration Form (see Figure 3.3; A copy of the complete CWS *Form for Administration, Scoring, and Computation* is provided in Appendix D) to:

1. record the order in which the client completed the drawings;
2. record the Drawing Completion Time (exact length of time it takes the client to complete the initial phase of the test) in the space provided;
3. record the following, verbatim, in the note-column (located on the right side of the form):
    a) everything the client says;
    b) any of the client's questions for the assessor;
    c) all of the client's comments or critiques;
    d) all interruptions and pauses; and
    e) any other significant verbal or non-verbal behavior the client demonstrates during the administration.

The Picture Gallery

Once the Drawing Phase is completed, the assessor asks the client to describe what he/she drew in each box and transcribes it verbatim on the Examiner Administration Form. To accomplish this, the assessor says the following:

"*Very good. Now, in numerical order, tell me what you drew in each box.*" This is called the Picture Gallery (in Italian, the "*pinacoteca*") phase and is a critical element for accurate scoring. Because this phase of the Wartegg administration is one of the few occasions to ask for the client's verbalizations, it is recommended that the assessor record the client's responses verbatim, making sure not to miss

	I	II	III	IV	V	VI	VII	VIII
Order of Sequence								

(Write here the order in which the client completed the 8 boxes)

Time of performance		

PICTURE GALLERY
(In numerical order, write here what the client drew in each box)

NOTES
(Starting on the first line, write here in chronological order everything that happens during the administration)

B1 ....

B2 ....

B3 ....

B4 ....

B5 ....

B6 ....

B7 ....

B8 ....

Which drawing do you like the most?........... Why?....................

Which drawing do you like the least?........... Why?....................

(Using a new blank form) Which mark do you like the most?........... Why?....................

Which mark do you like the least?........... Why?....................

Test of sequence: + ____ ____ ____ ____ ____ ____ –

Did the subject turn the Wartegg form during the administration? YES – NO

If YES, which panels?......... ....

Were the additional instructions necessary? YES – NO

FIGURE 3.3 CWS Examiner Administration Form.

Figure 3.3 provides a sample CWS Examiner Administration Form.

Source: Copyright by IIW, Rome, Italy. Reproduction of any kind is strictly forbidden. The administration form can be ordered at the Istituto Italiano Wartegg (www.wartegg.com). For inquiries, please contact: iiw@wartegg.com.

any detail. Often, in his/her verbalization, the client expresses and conveys a great deal of information about his/her way of being, thinking, and behaving. It is extremely important that the assessor avoid asking leading questions, intervening as little as possible.

In order to standardize the Picture Gallery phase of the administration, the assessor only asks questions in seven specific instances, essentially conducting a brief investigation of particular drawings. This is allowed *only* when:

1. The client's use of the stimulus (mark) is not clear and easy to understand. For example, the client says that he/she drew a building in Box 1. However, objectively assessing the drawing, it is not clear what the stimulus (the black dot) represents in relation to the building. The assessor would ask, "*What does the mark represent?*"
2. The gender of a drawn human figure is not clear. For example, a client says, "Here, I drew a face," or "This is a person." In both cases, the assessor should ask, "*Is it a male or a female face?*" or "*Is it a male or female?*" It is important not to ask questions that may encourage self-references or personalized answers such as, "Whose face is this?" or "Who is it?" This is particularly true when the client is a child. It should be noted that this question is not asked in response to human simulacrum response (i.e., emoticons) or pathological content (i.e., isolated human or animal body parts; see Chapter 5 for further information on these Content categories).
3. The drawings are accompanied by: A) Types of verbalizations including unclear descriptive adjectives, such as: "A *strange* human figure" or "A *scary* scene." (The assessor would then ask, "*Why is it strange?*" or "*Why is it scary?*"); or B) by descriptions that do not match the drawing. For example, a client draws a rectangle and verbalizes, "A triangle." In this case, the assessor repeats the verbalization, "A *triangle?*" to allow the client to clarify or correct his or her response. If the client does not modify his or her verbalization, the response would be considered an Improper Description (see Special Noted Phenomena, Chapter 5);
4. The client's drawing can be interpreted in more than one way, requiring clarification. For example:

    - "a pyramid" can be either an architectural building or a geometric figure;
    - "a geometric figure" could be any type of geometric figure;
    - "an arrow" could be a traffic sign, a directional symbol, or a weapon.

    In these cases, the examiner asks for clarification, stating, for example, "*What kind of arrow did you draw?*"
5. The client draws something abstract, for example "happiness," and the connection between the drawing and the client's verbal description is unclear. For example, a client draws a dog, but states, "happiness." In this case, the assessor asks in response to the verbalization, "*Yes, but what exactly did you draw?*"

6. The client does not completely describe the drawing. For example, he/she says something excessively vague, such as "an object." In these cases the assessor must ask, "*What does the object represent?*"
7. The client initially draws a specific content in a WDCT box, returning later during the Drawing Phase and seemingly changing the content. (There should be a specific change of depicted object, rather than simple embellishment of the same content through added detail or elements). In this case, where drawn content has been significantly changed, the assessor should ask, "*What did you draw first?*"

The Choice of Drawings and Boxes

Once the Picture Gallery is complete, the assessor asks the client to indicate which one of the produced drawings he/she likes the most, which one he/she likes the least, and why (transcribing the answers verbatim). This begins the Choice of Drawings and Boxes phase.

After the client chooses which of the drawings he/she likes best and which he/she likes least, the assessor sets aside the client's completed Client WDCT form, and presents the client with a new blank WDCT form. The assessor asks the client to indicate which stimulus (mark) he/she likes the most, which stimulus (mark) he/she likes the least, and why. Again, the assessor transcribes all responses verbatim. In recording these verbalizations, careful attention must be paid to obtain complete answers, without leaving anything open to interpretation. For example, if the client says: "I like this one the best, because it's so strange!" the assessor must ask, "*Strange?*"

In summary, at the end of the Choice of Drawings and Boxes phase, the assessor should have noted the client's four selections (listed below) and his/her verbalized reasons for those specific choices, recording these verbatim on the Examiner Administration Form in the designated location.

1. most-liked drawing;
2. least-liked drawing;
3. most-liked stimulus (mark);
4. least-liked stimulus (mark).

The Order of Sequence and the Test of Sequence

As explained below, a great majority of clients (approximately 92%) do not complete the drawings in numerical order, but instead follow a unique, Individualized Order of Sequence (Crisi, 1998, 2007). It is this characteristic that gives the Order of Sequence diagnostic importance (discussed further in Chapter 6). Thus, specific procedures are carried out regarding the Order of Sequence. These procedures are known as Analysis of Sequence 1 and Analysis of Sequence 2, both of which provide relevant information about the client.

Approximately 8% of clients complete the test using one of the following four sequences:

NUMERICAL (going in order from Box 1 to Box 8); this is the most frequent model, used by approximately 7% of adult clients and 15% of child clients), depicted in Figure 3.4.

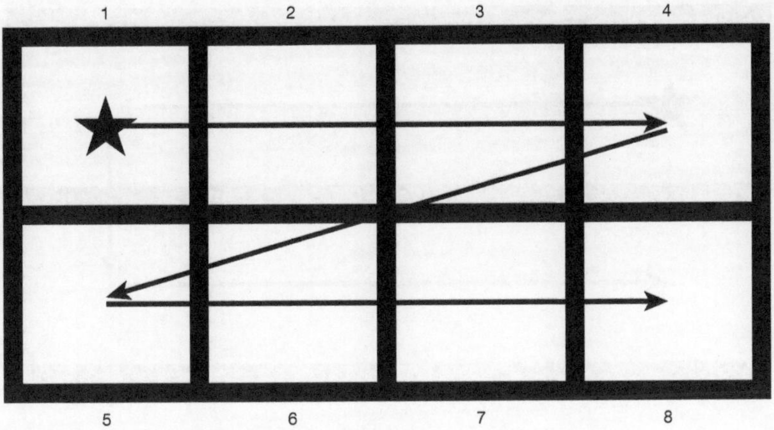

FIGURE 3.4 Numerical Order of Sequence.

Graphic representation of Numerical Order of Sequence. When clients produce this Order of Sequence, the Test of Sequence must be administered.

REVERSED (going backwards in order from Box 8 to Box 1), used by approximately .3% of clients), depicted in Figure 3.5.

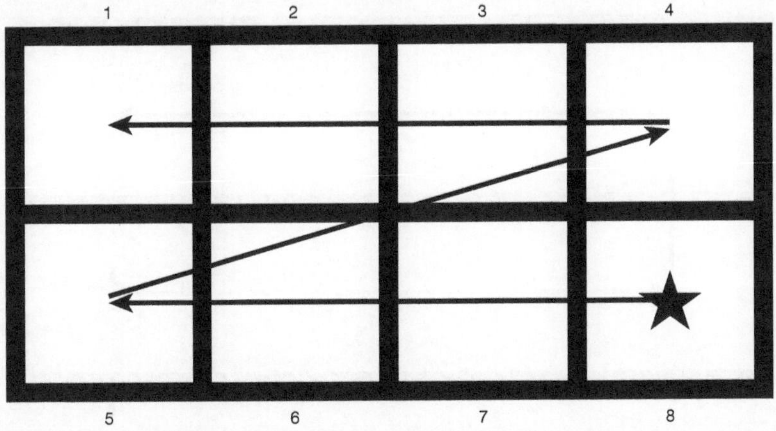

FIGURE 3.5 Reversed Order of Sequence.

Graphic representation of Reversed Order of Sequence. When clients produce this Order of Sequence, the Test of Sequence must be administered.

NUMERICAL CIRCULAR (going in order clockwise: starting with Box 1–2–3–4–8–7–6–5), used by approximately .2% of clients), depicted in Figure 3.6.

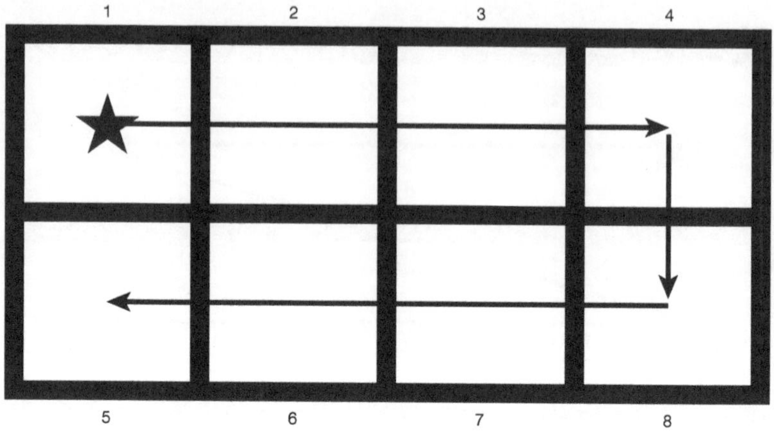

FIGURE 3.6 Numerical Circular Order of Sequence.

Graphic representation of Numerical Circular Order of Sequence. When clients produce this Order of Sequence, the Test of Sequence must be administered.

REVERSED CIRCULAR (going in order clockwise: starting at Box 8–7–6–5–1–2–3–4), used by approximately .1% of clients), depicted in Figure 3.7.

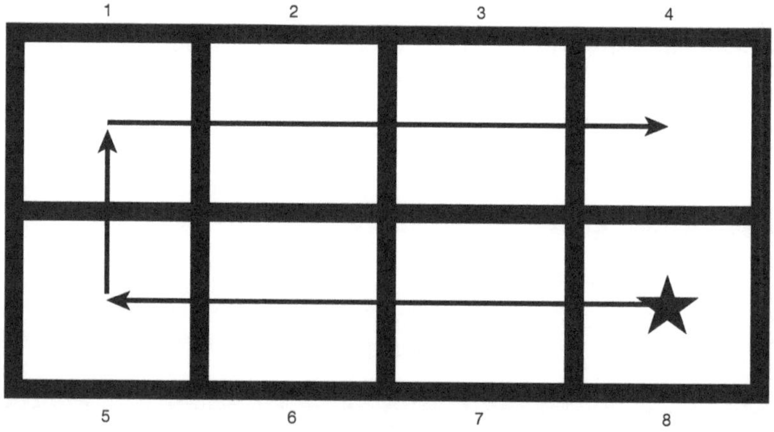

FIGURE 3.7 Reversed Circular Order of Sequence.

Graphic representation of Reversed Circular Order of Sequence. When clients produce this Order of Sequence, the Test of Sequence must be administered.

In these four instances, the Analysis of Sequence 1 and Analysis of Sequence 2 cannot be completed, causing significant interpretive data loss. In order to compensate for this loss, an additional task is used in order to provide an individualized Order of Sequence, based on the client's choices. This task, known as the "Test of Sequence," is *administered if the client has used one of the four Orders of Sequence listed above*, whether this is done in a "pure" way (exactly as noted above) or when there is *only one* alteration in box order sequence. That is, for example, when the client completes the boxes in Numerical Order except that Boxes 4 and 5 are switched (1–2–3–5–4–6–7–8), the Test of Sequence is performed. Similarly, another example could be when the client uses Circular Order, but shifts the placement of Box 6 with Box 7 (1–2–3–4–8–6–7–5).

The Test of Sequence is also administered if the first four boxes used by the client are boxes 1, 2, 3, and 4, or boxes 5, 6, 7, and 8 regardless of the order in which they were drawn (for example: 1, 3, 4, and 2, *or* 4, 1, 3, and 2, *or* 8, 5, 7, and 6, *or* 6, 7, 5, and 8, etc.). Lastly, the Test of Sequence is administered whenever the assessor observes a logical or methodical pattern of completion by the client. This may include completion of the even-numbered boxes, followed by the odd-numbered boxes; completion of the left-hand four boxes prior to the right-hand four boxes, etc. In each of these cases, the Test of Sequence should be administered.

The Test of Sequence must be completed after the Choice of Drawings and Boxes phase. As described above, this is when the assessor provides the client with a new, blank Client WDCT Form, and inquires as to which are his/her most and least preferred drawings and which are his/her most and least preferred stimuli (marks). For example, if the client indicates Box 1 as his most-liked stimulus and the Box 5 as his least-liked stimulus, the assessor would record this on the Examiner Administration Form:

Which mark do you like the most?	**1**
Which mark do you like the least?	**5**

Then, using pre-prepared small squares of paper—the same size as the boxes on the Client WDCT Form—the assessor covers both identified Boxes (1 and 5), while saying something like:

> "*I am now covering Boxes 1 and 5 and would like you to choose which box you like most and least from the remaining boxes.*"

If the client then chooses, for example, the mark in Box 3 (as next most-liked) and that in Box 2 (as next least-liked), the assessor puts a "3" to the right of the "+" side and a "2" to the left of the "–" side, as demonstrated below.

+ 3 __ __ __ __ 2 –

The assessor then covers Boxes 3 and 2 and asks the client to continue choosing his most- and least-liked marks among the four remaining boxes. If, for example, the client then chooses Box 4 as next most-liked stimulus and Box 6 as next least-liked stimulus, the assessor will put a "4" to the right of the "3" on the "+" side and a "6" to the left of the "2" on the "–" side, as demonstrated below.

+ 3 **4** ___ ___ **6** 2 –

The assessor then covers these boxes indicated, and asks the client to finish by saying:

> "*Very good. Now, for the last two boxes, which mark do you like the most, and which do you like least?*"

If the client choses the stimulus in Box 8 as next most-liked and that in Box 7 as next least-liked, the assessor would write an "8" to the right of the "4" on the "+" side and a "7" to the left of the "6" on the "–" side, as demonstrated below.

+ 3 4 **8 7** 6 2 –

In this example, the complete Order of Sequence (obtained via the Test of Sequence) would be [+ 1–3–4–8–7–6-2–5 –] and at this point, would be used for both calculations and interpretation of the Analysis of Sequence (see Chapter 6 and 7). Thus, the client's choices are placed along a continuum from the stimulus in the box that he/she liked the most (Box 1) to the stimulus in the box that he/she liked the least (Box 5).

Reversed Boxes

The assessor should record the presence or absence of responses where the client has drawn something that he/she intends to be viewed either sideways or upside down. This does not apply in instances when the client has turned the paper in some other direction in order to draw more comfortably—such as if a left-handed individual slants the paper in a particular manner, or if someone turns the protocol upside down for ease of drawing.

The best place to record this information is on the Examiner Administration form, following the question: "Did the subject turn the Wartegg form during the administration?" If the client turned the form simply for ease of drawing (and did not intend the figure to be viewed from an alternative perspective, for example, sideways or upside down) the assessor should mark "NO." If the client has produced a Reversed Box (RB)—that is, the box *is* intended to be viewed with a different orientation on the Client WDCT Form—the assessor should mark "YES" and indicate the boxes in which this occurred. (More discussion of the special score Reversed Box is provided in Chapter 5.)

The Additional Instructions

In cases when the client does not understand the initial instructions, and appears unsure how to proceed, additional instructions may be offered using the formalized sequence described below. While rare in the normative population, the additional instructions are primarily needed when working with clients of limited cognitive ability or severe psychopathology.

The assessor must note whether or not Additional Instructions (see below) were necessary (using the designated space on the Examiner Administration Form).

First Additional Instructions

On a blank piece of paper, the assessor draws the mark "ʌ" and uses it to draw a house.

Then, on another sheet of paper, the assessor makes the same mark "ʌ" and asks the client to draw something other than a house using the mark.

If the client draws something other than a house (and incorporates the mark), the assessor proceeds to administration.

If the client also draws a house, the assessor, makes the same mark "ʌ" on the same piece of paper and asks the client to draw something different than a house; if the client is now able to draw something other than a house, the assessor proceeds directly to administration. If the client again draws a house, the assessor provides the second additional instructions (below).

Second Additional Instructions

Continuing to use the same piece of paper, the assessor once again draws the same mark "ʌ" and using it, draws a pair of cherries.

Then, on a new, clean sheet of paper, the assessor draws the same mark "ʌ" again and asks the client to complete the drawing with something other than cherries.

If the client draws something other than cherries (and incorporates the mark), the assessor proceeds to standard administration of the WDCT. If the client repeats the drawing of the cherries or doesn't draw anything at all, *the administration must be stopped.*

The Additional Instructions are further summarized in Figure 3.8.

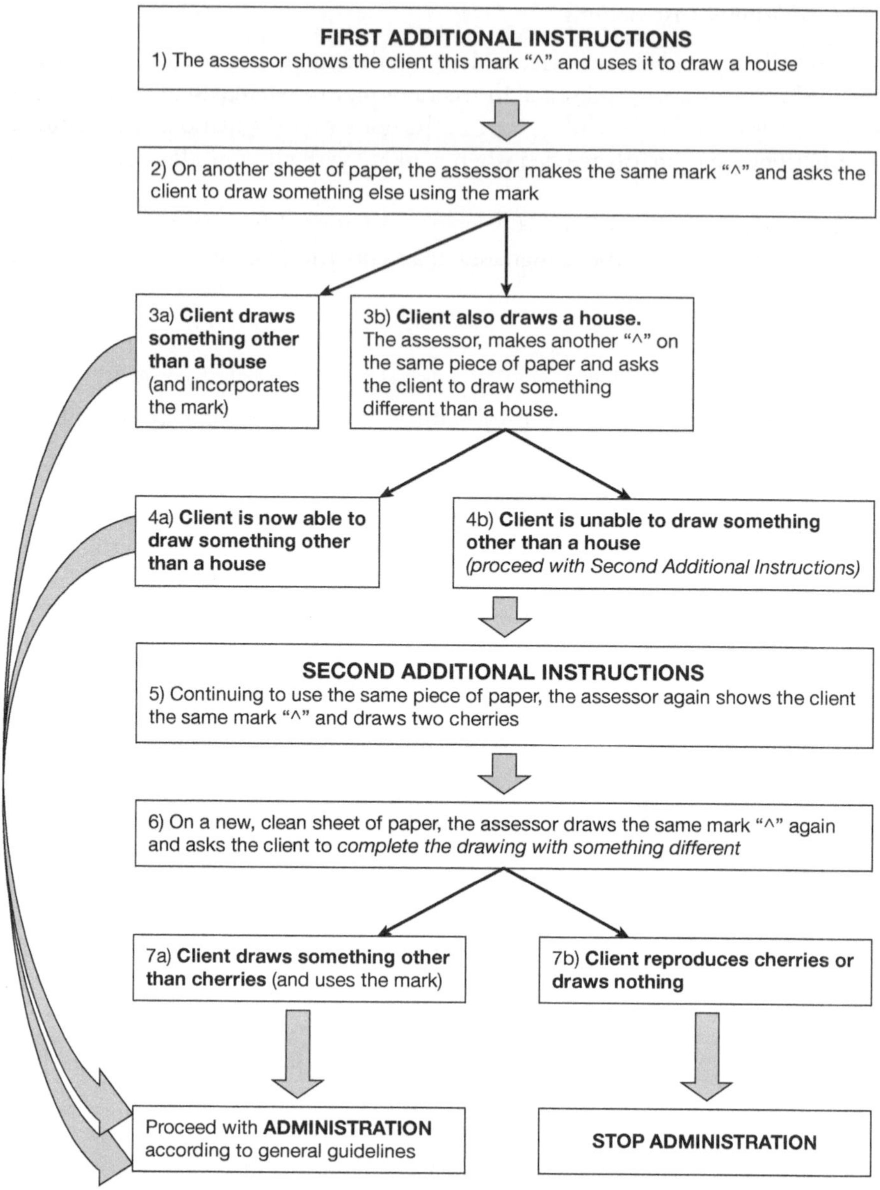

FIGURE 3.8 Summary of CWS Additional Instructions.

These instructions are administered to clients if they appear confused or unable to complete the task following provision of the standardized instructional set.

Special Cases When Further Instructions Should Be Used

In certain, specific cases, further administration instructions are required.

4+ Abstract (ABS) or Symbol (SIG) Drawings

One specific case in which further instructions are required is when a client completes the Client WDCT Form with abstract drawings in four (or more) boxes, or SIG content (signs or symbols) in four or more boxes. In either of these cases, after finishing the Picture Gallery phase, the assessor should remove the completed Client WDCT Form and provide a new form to the client, inviting him/her to specifically avoid abstract or symbol drawings, while being careful not to convey that his/her initial attempt at the task was inadequate.

For example, while handing the client a new Client WDCT Form, the assessor might say:

> "*Very good. Now, I would like you to do this a second time, but this time I would like you to draw people, things, or animals.*"

The second administration is carried out exactly like the first one, making sure to record all required information on the Examiner Administration Form.

Verbalizations during Drawing Phase

A second special case requiring further instructions is when the client begins to explain his or her drawings during the Drawing Phase (that is, while drawing). If this occurs, the examiner should say:

> "*We'll talk about the drawings at the end. For now, just focus on completing your drawings.*"

Changed Meaning of Drawings

A third special case requiring further instructions is when the client draws something in a box and later returns to the box and changes the meaning of his or her drawing during the Drawing Phase. This special circumstance was addressed earlier in this chapter.

Rejection of Boxes

A fourth special case requiring further instructions is that of clients who reject one or more boxes. This phenomenon, rare for non-pathological clients, usually happens in one of two situations:

1. *The client explicitly communicates* his/her difficulty in completing a drawing for one or more boxes by saying something like, "I can't think of anything

for this one"; "Here I cannot draw anything"; or "Do I have to draw something in every box?" In this case, the assessor should encourage the client one time to complete the task by saying, "*Take all the time that you need; most people eventually think of something to draw.*" This encouragement is only provided once per administration.

2. *The client does not say anything to the assessor* and indicates they have finished drawing by returning an incomplete Client WDCT Form to the assessor, or by saying something like, "I'm done." When this happens, an "Interpreted Stimulus" special score (see Chapter 5) might be present; thus, the assessor does not question this lack of drawn content and proceeds to the next phase of test administration with the client, the Picture Gallery.

Administration with Children

When administering the test to children, the procedures are identical to those described for adult administration. Of course, the environment in which children are tested is especially important. Generally speaking, other people (parents, caregivers, or relatives) should not be present in the assessment room, so as not to alter the child's performance. Nonetheless, in special cases (with children who are excessively anxious, insecure, or afraid of strangers), a third person may be allowed in the room, after this person has been given explicit instructions on how to behave. The presence of a third person in the assessment room should be recorded on the Examiner Administration Form.

Historically, in their administration methodology, Lossen and Schott (1975) invited children and cognitively limited clients to take the WDCT by using the following instructions: "Someone started working on each one of these boxes, and then lost interest in finishing. You must finish the drawings they began" (p. 22).

Using the Crisi Wartegg System, children under twelve years of age receive the following instructions:

> *"On this sheet there are eight boxes. In each box, someone has started a drawing but then did not finish the drawing. Do you want to try to complete them?*
>
> *"To complete them, try to turn them into a drawing that means something by adding anything you want. Remember do not make doodles or drawings that do not represent anything. The mark that is in each box must be part of your design. Start wherever you like and follow the order you prefer. You have as much time as you need."*

As mentioned above, other than the difference in the wording used for the instructions, the administration procedure for children is identical. Should the client not understand the phrase, "a drawing that means something," assessors clarify (see instructions for Individual Administration with Adults, earlier in this chapter) as they would with adult clients. Should clients experience significant challenges, the *Additional Instructions* should be utilized as described above.

Clinical experience demonstrates that for children aged four and a half and above, no particular problems arise in terms of comprehension or ability to complete the task (Caricchia, D'Angerio, & Lonoce, 2000). However, it must be noted that, at times, difficulties may arise when the assessor asks the necessary questions for the Picture Gallery and Choices of Drawings and Boxes phases. This is especially true with younger children, when an attempt to clarify the drawing's meaning may embarrass the child or hurt his/her feelings. Thus, in a tactful manner, when the child reports having drawn something unrecognizable (for example a specific animal), the assessor should gently clarify it, saying, for example, "*You know, I do not know this animal. How big is it? Does it look more like X or more like Y?*" It might happen, for example, that a child says "a spider," when he/she really means to say "a crab." These differences are important to clarify, as they may impact scoring.

Administration with Differently Abled Clients

In the case of clients with sensory-motor disabilities, cognitive or developmental delays, or comprehension difficulties caused by emotional challenges, the *Additional Instructions*, described above, may be utilized prior to formal administration to ensure comprehension and avoid potential difficulties or embarrassment.

Group Administration

The WDCT can be administered either individually or in the group setting. The following factors are critical for proper group administration of the WDCT and must be appropriately addressed:

- the way the space in the room is used;
- the number of professionals needed for test administration;
- any alterations or changes in test administration procedure.

One assessor for every 8–10 examinees is recommended as an appropriate ratio for CWS group administration.

After having the clients sit in a way that removes any possibility of confusion, comparison, cheating, or offering suggestions, each client is provided with test materials (consisting of a #2 pencil without an eraser, the Group Administration/Transcription Form, and the WDCT Client Form inside the folder). One of the assessors gives the instructions to the clients, while briefly showing them the Client WDCT Form and saying:

> "*Inside each folder, you will find this form. Take it out and place it in front of you. As you can see, in each box there is a small mark. Using this mark, you will draw something in each box that means something, preferably the first thing that comes to mind, trying to avoid abstract drawings. You do not need to follow numerical order. Once you are done with your first drawing, on the inside of the folder is a*

PLEASE WRITE USING CAPITAL LETTERS

A – Number of Box completed first: ....

I've drawn: ....

....

B – Number of Box completed second: ....

I've drawn: ....

....

C – Number of Box completed third: ....

I've drawn: ....

....

D – Number of Box completed fourth: ....

I've drawn: ....

....

E – Number of Box completed fifth: ....

I've drawn: ....

....

F – Number of Box completed sixth: ....

I've drawn: ....

....

G – Number of Box completed seventh: ....

I've drawn: ....

....

H – Number of Box completed last: ....

I've drawn: ....

....

FIGURE 3.9 CWS Group Administration/Transcription Form.

Sample CWS Group Administration/Transcription Form.

> *Transcription Form* [Examiner shows the inside of the folder to the clients]. *Here at letter A, where it says* 'Number of the box drawn first,' *write the number of the box in which you drew first. In the line below, where it says, 'I drew,' write what you drew. Do the same thing each time you are done with one of the eight boxes. Take your time, you have enough time to complete the test.*"

The assessors should answer any questions in the same way described above and then, going around the room, will discretely verify that instructions are being followed correctly.

Special attention must be paid to making sure that clients sequentially write down each box number and the meaning of their drawing *as they proceed through the test.* Ten minutes after announcing the instructions, the assessor says aloud: "*We are half way through.*" Five minutes later, the assessor says: "*You have five more minutes to complete the test.*" In total, examinees are given 20 minutes to complete the test.

Before turning in their Group Administration/Transcription Forms with their Client WDCT Forms inside, the assessors ask clients to complete the biographical section at the top of the Client WDCT Form, then to put the Client WDCT Form inside their folder, close it, and leave it on the top right-hand corner of their desk or table. At this point, the assessor walks around the room and checks to see that the Client WDCT Forms and the Transcription Forms were completed correctly. On a case by case basis, and only when necessary, the assessor can ask specific clients for more detail as described above for individual administration (e.g., the assessor notes that a client has written "a person" without specifying the gender. In this case, the assessor would ask, "*Male or female?*" and have the client add that to his/her Transcription Form).

A copy of the CWS Group Administration/ Transcription Form is provided in Figure 3.9.

References

Caricchia, F., d'Angerio, S., & Lonoce, G. (2000). Il bambino in età prescolare all'esame del test di Wartegg [The preschool child examined by the Wartegg Drawing Completion Test]. *Babele*, 14.

Crisi, A. (1998). *Manuale del Test di Wartegg* [Manual for the Wartegg Test]. Rome, Italy: Edizioni MaGi.

Crisi, A. (2007). *Manuale del test di Wartegg, 2nd ed.* [Manual for the Wartegg Test, 2nd Edition]. Rome, Italy: Edizioni MaGi.

Lossen H., & Schott, G. (1975). *Wartegg: Analisi del processo percettivo* [Wartegg: Analysis of the perceptive process]. Turin, Italy: Centro Salesiano di Orientamento.

4 Evocative Character

Characteristics of the Wartegg Test

In order to fully understand the Wartegg Drawing Completion Test (WDCT), it is necessary to reflect on two fundamental concepts. *First*, in choosing among the stimuli of the eight WDCT boxes, the client is faced with "very few quantitative options, which are, however, qualitatively extremely poignant" (Wartegg, 1953, p. 20). For this reason, the WDCT can be defined as an actual projective test, in which the graphic stimuli of each box are semi-structured (or partially structured) stimuli on which the client "tends to project contents and specific personality dynamics that are revealing of personality organization" (Rapaport, 1977, p. 187). *Second*, "Wartegg's stimuli carry two levels of interpretation: a perceptive–gestaltic one and an interpretive–symbolic one. These two levels of interpretation are closely related by the emotional dynamic that underlies the *Gestaltung*" (Scarpellini, 1962, p. 26). *Gestaltung* is an integrated whole, representing properties that are more than a simple sum of its parts.

First, the perceptive aspects involved in the test are reviewed, followed by the central topic of this chapter, the Evocative Character of the eight boxes.

Perceptive Aspects

The principle of simplicity is the logical criteria of this test. "The more primitive the structures are, the more they relate to emotional dynamics and tend to evoke projected meaning" (A. Scarpellini, 1962, p. 26). McCully (1988) further asserted, "Stimulus' simplicity is one of many ways to trick defenses" (p. 97).

Each of the WDCT boxes is perceived by the client according to the laws of perceptual organization. Specifically:

- **Boxes 1, 2, 4 and 7**: The stimuli in these boxes are perceived in relationship to space, according to the law of "Good Form";
- **Boxes 3 and 5**: The three incremental lines are perceived according to "Common Fate," "Proximity," and "Similarity" laws;
- **Box 6**: "Closure," "Similarity," "Shared Destiny," and "Proximity" laws;

- **Box 8**: "Closure"; this stimulus does not impose itself, but instead tends to be elaborated through highly individualized drawings.

The Evocative Character

A separate issue is that of the Evocative Character of each WDCT box. This matter was the object of debate among scholars, particularly with regard to the interpretation of certain boxes; however, most authors have reached consensus through research (see Chapter 2) and clinical practice. Evocative Character can be defined as the stimulus' ability to evoke and foster the projection of certain categories of concepts. This ability originates from the stimulus' perceptive characteristics (which the client perceives consciously, subconsciously, and unconsciously); it is linked almost instantaneously to the conceptual categories that relate to these perceptual characteristics.

Wartegg (1972) believed that the stimuli that he chose respectively evoked the following:

- **Box 1**, a dot in the center: evokes something delicate, unapparent, though determined, perceptually centered;
- **Box 2**, a small wavy line: evokes affect, softness, movement, or excitement;
- **Box 3**, three incremental lines: evokes either the dynamic raise of the parallel lines or an architectural partition of space;
- **Box 4**, a small black square: evokes spikiness, darkness, and heaviness;
- **Box 5**, two opposite lines: stimulates the dynamic joining of lines, in the simultaneous overcoming of a moment of tension;
- **Box 6**, two horizontal and vertical lines: compels to choose between merging and separation of the lines in the stimulus;
- **Box 7**, the dotted half-circle: fosters the emotional perception of delicate structures;
- **Box 8**, the arch of a circle: suggests harmonic closure and roundness (pp. 37–38).

Evocative Character in the CWS

Over the last 30 years, through the development of the CWS, the WDCT was administered to well over 30,000 subjects. Concurrently, the Rorschach was administered to 3,000 subjects. In the context of this prolonged psychodiagnostic experience, drawing a continuous and constant comparison between Wartegg and Rorschach data (Crisi, 1999), specific evocative characteristics for each box were identified. Other authors also have looked at evocative character in the Rorschach (Mérei, 1947; Andronikof-Sanglade, 1995; Exner, 1997, 2003), although no one has assigned it a specific scoring category.

Before discussing this interesting topic, and in order to better understand it, some brief observations on the theoretical aspects of the Wartegg response process are reviewed.

The Wartegg Response Process

When a client is administered the WDCT, he/she is faced with unfamiliar, semi-structured, and non-organized material. We define the measure as *semi-structured* because the various stimuli hold a precise identity. For example, the stimulus in the first box is a dot, while in the fourth it is a black square. Thus, in the Wartegg, the initial level of stimulus definition is shared by all individuals. Such characteristics (non-familiarity, semi-structure, and lack of organization) bring about a process of organization within the client that results in a response.

The response itself is an independent behavioral segment. It is an entity capable of unveiling certain dynamics, which reveal aspects of the client's personality organization. Therefore, in response to the WDCT, the client organizes the material by the decisions he/she makes. This process is guided by different coexisting motives, organized hierarchically:

1. On the one hand are *immediate motives*, led by Gestalt-ruled perceptive factors and by the Evocative Character of the different boxes;
2. On the other hand are *remote motives*, highly organized and governed by unconscious dynamics.

In other words, when the client is administered the WDCT, perceptive factors are initially at play; these factors are strictly determined and guided by the laws of visual perception (e.g., the client perceives the stimulus as a dot in the center of Box 1). The perceived object (the dot in the center) is then linked in the client's mind to what he/she associates with being a "central point." The idea of centrality, of being in the center, represents the Evocative Character of the first box.

Only at this point does the client develop associative links that are unique and characteristic of the idea of centrality to him/her. Based on the client's individual characteristics at the time of administration, he/she elaborates and organizes the perceptive and evocative stimulus into an actual response (the drawing). The response, by its very nature, can move freely on a continuum that consists of form and superficial attributes on one hand and highly individualized and personalized attributes on the other. If the latter attributes prevail, in essence, we can distinguish two different levels of projection: *externalization* and *projection* (as it is commonly defined).

Externalization is a process through which "images that are moderately repressed, but organized so to be easily recalled" (Abt & Bellak, 1967, p. 37) are expressed as a response to the test. The client can externalize a situation that can vary by the degree to which it is conflictual. He or she may not even be aware, at the time of the test, of such a conflictual situation. Nevertheless, in completing the test, he/she can easily recognize something of his/her own, either spontaneously or with the psychologist's help.

An example from the Rorschach can illustrate the characteristics of externalization: A client, who is in the process of separating from his spouse, says in response to Card III, "Two people, a man and a woman, who are violently fighting over an object." At the time of the inquiry for Card III, the client spontaneously states, "It's incredible: I did not think about it before, but in these two, I see my wife and me, who cannot resolve our separation in a calm and civilized manner." It's evident, in this case, that the term "projection" here would be overstated, to say the least (Cridsi 1998, 2007). Therefore, the object of the externalization consists of emotions, feelings, sensations, thoughts, and conflicts that are conscious or preconscious in nature.

The *projection* mechanism works differently. It acts unconsciously and represents a process through which the individual reflects his/her impulses, feelings, and affects toward others and the external world. This allows the client to remain unaware of some phenomena, usually unpleasant ones, that reside within him/her.

When this unconscious mechanism becomes active during the administration of the WDCT it does so in a spontaneous, non-conscious (automatic) manner. Therefore, the client cannot link the drawing with his/her internal dynamics. If anything, in most cases, the client would respond with decisive denial to any attempt to increase his/her awareness. The object of projection consists completely of *unconscious* emotional dynamics.

Based on the information above, a distinction can be made among the different response process levels for each of the Wartegg boxes at the time of evaluation and interpretation of the test. Each of these levels can guide the response process (i.e., the client's drawing) in each of the boxes.

More often than not, different levels of response coexist within the same WDCT protocol. For example, considering Box 1:

- When *perceptive* elements prevail, they represent primitive, immediate, relatively poorly integrated modalities, which are defined as Level I of response. In this case, the drawings are simple, at times mere repetition of the stimulus.
- However, when *evocative* aspects prevail, they represent more differentiated response modalities, further connected to experiential factors and defined as Level II of response. In this case, the drawings are more sophisticated and not simply based on the "dot," but, instead, on the concept that stems from the dot (i.e., centrality). In this case, the responses are often Popular, and related to daily life.
- If *externalization* prevails, it represents a high level of integration and differentiation, known as Level III of response. In this case, we are facing a more specifically intrapsychic dimension, characterized by aspects such as self-esteem, confidence, self-image, the relationship with the environment, experience, etc. The responses begin to show highly individualized elements, represent metaphorical meanings, and, at times, may present Original features.
- Finally, when *projection* prevails, it represents the most differentiated of the levels of response, defined as Level IV, because it allows for unconscious representations. In this case, the response is almost certainly an Original one, which most often represents an element of the client's unconscious dynamics.

Thus, the response process starts with a perceptive stimulus that immediately brings with it the associated Evocative Character relating to the client's experience and socio-cultural background. Further associative links are formed that range within the client's psyche from immediate motivations (i.e., *externalization*) to deeper, unconscious ones (i.e., *projection*). In a client that is free from significant distress, the response process is a fluid one that continuously fluctuates between these various levels, providing information related to personality functioning.

The four levels of response process for each box of the WDCT are described in Table 4.1.

TABLE 4.1 Four Levels of Response Process in the Wartegg Drawing Completion Test

Box	*Level I* *Perception*	*Level II* *Evocative Character*	*Level III* *Externalization*	*Level IV* *Projection*
1	A central point/ Dot	Centrality, Relevance	Self-Evaluation	
2	A wavy line with rounded edges	Vitality, Movement	Female Object Relation	
3	Three progressive lines of increasing height	Directionality, Progression	Available Energies	
4	A little black square	Stability, Heaviness	Male Object Relations	Highly individualized contents or unconscious dynamics
5	Two contraposed perpendicular lines	Overcoming an obstacle (or block)	Aggressive Energies	
6	Two lines at right angles	Synthesis, Structure (Union)	Relation to Reality, Rationality, Planning	
7	A dotted semi-circle	Delicacy	Libidinal Energies	
8	A curved line turned downward	Roundness, Closure	Social Skills	

Evocative Character of the Wartegg Boxes

When speaking about the Evocative Character of a box and of its psychodiagnostic meaning, it is not implied that the theme of each client's drawing in an individual box is invariably consistent with the meaning that has been attached to the box in general. Instead, clinical experience suggests that a client's drawings will often connect back to the box's specific psychodiagnostic theme (e.g., Box 4 might be considered "the father box").

Below, the Evocative Character of each box will be discussed.

Box 1

Box 1 immediately evokes the idea of *centrality*, being placed at the center of a situation. Generally, the center of everything is related to ourselves.

The Evocative Character of this box can be related to that of Card I of the Rorschach, which Mérei (1947) defines as the "Who are you?" card. Indeed, quite often, inadequate or negatively framed responses or contents in this box correspond to equally negative responses provided on Card I of the Rorschach. For example, a 20-year-old male who was assessed after he had attempted suicide drew "a mannequin" in Box 1, and on Card I of the Rorschach responded, "A torn up dress, all broken."

A key point is that this box primarily evokes the client's feelings and self-evaluations about his/her identity (when externalization prevails) or about the self (when projection prevails). On one hand, the wide space that surrounds the dot placed in the center stresses the impression of centrality. On the other hand, it represents the living space, the environment in which the client lives, moves, and acts. The word "environment" is here intended in its more literal connotation, including constructs external to the client. For children in particular, family is considered as "environment."

When externalization prevails, this box might elicit responses such as the one provided by a 12-year-old boy who was helplessly witnessing the continuous fights and separation of his parents; this conflict led to inevitable arguments about his custody. In Box 1, this boy drew two tennis players, where the central dot was the ball.

When projection prevails, Box 1 shows highly individualized responses that are connected to the self. In these cases, Box 1 seems to be more closely connected to Card IX of the Rorschach. For example, a 53-year-old woman with panic disorder drew "A ring" in Box 1; the identical content was provided in her only response to Card IX of the Rorschach.

Box 2

Box 2 evokes dynamics of *movement*, *vitality*, *the origin of existence*, and ultimately *female objects*.

Several clues, currently under research investigation, tend to connect the Evocative Character of Box 2 with Cards VII and IX of the Rorschach, which some authors (Loosli-Usteri, Brameri, & Davy, 1969) define as "maternal." Clients tend to project onto this box the primary experiences and modalities that characterized the maternal object relation. In Wartegg protocols of adopted children and children whose mothers are deceased, for example, rejections or clearly dysphoric responses to Box 2 are frequently produced. These clients quite often complete this box last or second to last, and during the Analysis of Sequence, this box is coded "Delay."

Box 3

With its three incremental lines, Box 3 evokes *dynamism*, *impulse to action*, and *direction*.

In dynamic terms, Box 3 indicates the amount of psychoaffective energy available to the client. This energy, if sublimated, is at the service of the ego: of its aspirations, activity levels, and process of adaptation to the environment. This box indicates the client's ability to invest his/her energy into daily life endeavors in a more or less functional way.

Proof of the above is found in the protocols of depressed or neurotic clients where we discover responses that do not continue the lines vertically and that represent cages, nets, and sometimes prisons. At present, no relevant elements have emerged to allow pairing of this box with one of the Rorschach cards. A possible route, yet to be followed, could be that of pairing it with Cards II and VI, which several authors respectively associate to aggressive and libidinal dynamics.

Box 4

Box 4 evokes themes of *heaviness*, *solidity*, and *stability*.

The symbolic aspects linked to the square are extremely complex. The square in the WDCT evokes everything that is profound, heavy, and unconscious; but at the same time, it also suggests what is stable, solid, and a point of reference. This box strongly affects the client with its poignant character, and, in it, the highest variability of contents is recorded. Because of its unique characteristics, Box 4 predominantly evokes the client's experience or relationship to authority figures, including the father. For example, a 9-year-old girl drew a male figure in the Draw-A-Person (DAP; Goodenough, 1963) test, first stating that she had drawn, "My dad." Then, on Card IV of the Rorschach, she responded, "A king sitting on his throne." In Box 4 of the WDCT, she drew a vignette with a female figure extending her hand toward an apple on a tree (the apple being the black square). During the WDCT Picture Gallery, the girl reported that she drew "A girl that would like to get the apple, but knows that she cannot." Many children with fathers who are absent or who lack authority produce drawings with a strongly negative or devaluing connotation (e.g., clown, broken homes, etc.) or indicative of tensions or blockages (e.g., walls, masks, robots).

Several connections have also been recorded between Box 4 of the WDCT and Card IV of the Rorschach. In this box, for example, a 9-year-old boy with a violent father drew "A stick of dynamite," and on Card IV of the Rorschach responded, "An atomic explosion." A 44-year-old client drew "DNA" in this box, and on Card IV of the Rorschach responded, "An old family tree."

Box 5

Box 5 evokes the theme of *opposite positions* and the *overcoming of an obstacle*. The two opposite lines represent the obstacle, the unforeseen. Meanwhile, their perceptive structure suggests the overcoming of an obstacle and invites the client's attention to that aspect of it.

Consequently, what the client draws in this box provides information about 1) the primary mode in which aggressive energy was channeled within his or her personality organization over the course of the person's development; and 2) the person's main patterns of reacting to frustration.

Based on clinical data, this box can be paired with Card II of the Rorschach, which became apparent while assessing a large number of stuttering clients. These clients are known to experience conflict in managing aggression. Stuttering clients were found to respond 1) with notable shock to the color red on Card II of the Rorschach (this data is statistically significant not only in the comparison with the normative sample but also with the other clinical groups); and 2) with increased inadequate, dysphoric, negative responses to Box 5 of the WDCT (producing the most of these responses of all Wartegg clinical groups).

Box 6

Box 6 evokes the concepts of *union* and *synthesis*. With its linear and geometric structure, Box 6 stimulates the ability for Gestalt perception, as well as for organizing, solving, and practically managing problems and difficulties posed by the environment.

By virtue of its structural simplicity, Box 6 seems able to provide information about judgment (reality testing), foresight, and planning functions. This is the most cognitive box of the WDCT, indicated by the reduced form accuracy and increased number of Special Scores found in the responses of clients diagnosed with learning disabilities and mental retardation in this box. These clients (i.e., those diagnosed with learning disabilities and/or mental retardation) produce drawings in Box 6 with negative indices (mainly FQ and EC) that significantly differed from the performance of the clients in the control group (Bianchi di Castelbianco, Crisi, & Di Renzo, 1993; see Chapter 2).

Because of its obvious features, Box 6 can be paired with Card V of the Rorschach, the so-called "reality card." This comparison is supported by the fact that 1) often work-related responses are provided in this box (e.g., a bartender drew a shaker and a glass; a carpenter drew a nail and a hammer); and 2) this is the box with the highest number of Popular responses.

Box 7

Box 7 represents all that is *light*, *related to aesthetics*, *delicate*, *soft*, and *harmonious*. It allows assessment of 1) delicacy, sensitivity, and plasticity; and 2) the interpersonal relationship with female objects (for both men and women), and also with sexuality.

This box shares many commonalities with several Rorschach cards and especially Card VI, where sexually charged responses are often found. Often responses of distress to Card VI of the Rorschach are paired with mechanical or clearly dysphoric drawings in the WDCT on Box 7 that reject the delicate nature of the box (see the clinical case described in Chapter 8).

Box 8

Box 8 evokes the theme of *expansion*, *rounding*, and *closure*. Emotional dynamics that are evoked by the arch in the box relate to social interactions and to the client's primary ways of relating to others in the environment (intended in its widest connotation).

The Evocative Character of Box 8 can sometimes by paired with that of Card X of the Rorschach, the so-called "environment card." Comparing verbalization for this card with the Wartegg drawings, clients presenting with relational difficulties show decreased performance in this box. For example, a young man with severe social phobia drew a turtle in Box 8 of the WDCT and rejected Card X of the Rorschach. Additionally, clients that are markedly dependent on others and on their environment often draw parachutists, food, umbrellas, and other contents suggesting dependency. Recently a child that had been labeled at school as clumsy and uncoordinated drew "an elephant" in this box, which is an Original response.

References

Abt, L. E., & Bellak, L. (1967). *La Psicología Projettiva. Introduzione Clinica alla Personalita Totale*. Milan: Longanesi.

Andronikof-Sanglade, A. (1995). Interpretation and the response process. *Rorschachiana*, *20*(1), 49–63.

Bianchi di Castelbianco, F., Crisi, A., & Di Renzo, M. (1993). *Il Test di Wartegg nell'età evolutiva* [The Wartegg Test in childhood]. Rome, Italy: Armando.

Crisi, A. (1998). *Manuale del Test di Wartegg* [Manual for the Wartegg Test]. Rome, Italy: Edizioni MaGi.

Crisi, A. (1999, July). *Similitudes between the Evocative Character of the Wartegg panels and those of Rorschach plates*. Paper presented at the meeting of the International Rorschach Society, Amsterdam, the Netherlands.

Crisi, A. (2007). *Manuale del test di Wartegg, 2nd ed.* [Manual for the Wartegg Test, 2nd Edition]. Rome, Italy: Edizioni MaGi.

Exner, J. (2003). *The Rorschach: A comprehensive system. Volume 1: The Rorschach, basic foundations and principles of interpretation*. New York: Wiley & Sons.

Goodenough, F. L. (1963). *Goodenough-Harris drawing test*. New York: Harcourt Brace Jovanovich.

Loosli-Usteri, M., Brameri, M. T., & Davy, M. (1969). *Manuale pratico del test di Rorschach* [A practical handbook for the Rorschach test] Florence: OS Organizzazioni Speciali.

McCully, R. (1988). *Jung e Rorschach* [Jung and Rorschach]. Milan: Mimesis.

Mérei, F. (1947). *Az együttes élmény*. Budapest: Officina.

Rapaport, D. (1977). Theoretical implications of psychodiagnostic procedures. In M. M. Gill, M. Bolko, & E. Codignola (Eds.), *Il modello concettuale della psicoanalisi: Scritti 1942–1960* [The Collected Papers of David Rapaport 1942–1960] (pp. 181–205). New York: Basic Books.

Scarpellini, C., (1962), *Diagnosi di personalità col reattivo di realizzazione grafica*. [Diagnosis of personality with the drawing completion test]. Contributi dell'Istituto di Psicologia dell'Università Cattolica del Sacro Cuore [Contributions from the Institute of Psychology of the Catholic University of the Sacred Heart], pp. 1–82.
Wartegg, E. (1953): *Schichtdiagnostik-Der Zeichentest* (WZT) [Differential diagnostics – The Drawing test. Göttingen: Verlag für Psychologie.
Wartegg, E. (1972). *Il reattivo di disegno*. Florence: Organizzazioni Speciali.

5 Scoring

This chapter reviews proper scoring of the WDCT according to Crisi Wartegg System scoring guidelines. Figure 5.1 (CWS Scoring Form) provides a sample scoring grid that guides how each box is scored according to eight specific scoring categories.

A copy of the complete WDCT *Form for Administration, Scoring, and Computation* is provided in Appendix D. Appendix F contains scoring tables for each of the eight scoring categories for convenient use in clinical scoring.

An overview of CWS scoring categories and scoring options is provided in Table 5.1.

As described later in this manual, each scoring category is used in determining particular calculations and/or formal indices (see Chapter 6), and contributes to a description of the client's personality structure via comparison to normative ranges (see Chapter 7).

Independent scoring elements include the *Choice of Drawings and Boxes*, and the *Picture Gallery* (see Chapter 3). In order to assist the reader, the scoring process will be described in the same order in which it is performed while scoring a completed WDCT protocol.

Evocative Character (EC)

Theoretical considerations relating to Evocative Character were reviewed in Chapter 4. At this time, it is sufficient to understand that experienced clinicians who use the Wartegg agree that each of the eight WDCT stimuli has a certain evocative or symbolic power. This has further been evaluated via research (reviewed in Chapter 2). This is somewhat comparable to "Card Pull" in the Rorschach, and is called Evocative Character in the Wartegg. Each stimulus in the eight Wartegg Boxes "pulls for" certain types of drawings, or suggests certain kinds of graphic or conceptual responses.

Box	EC	AQ	FQ	CONT. PR.	CONT. SE.	Fr.	SPECIAL SCORES					M/m M/m	M/m g	M/m d	IR
1															
2															
3															
4															
5															
6															
7															
8															

AoS 1 & 2	I	II	III	IV	V	VI	VII	VIII
Order of Sequence								
Evocative Character								
Affective Quality								
Code								
Form Quality								
Ratio A/F								
Impulse Response								

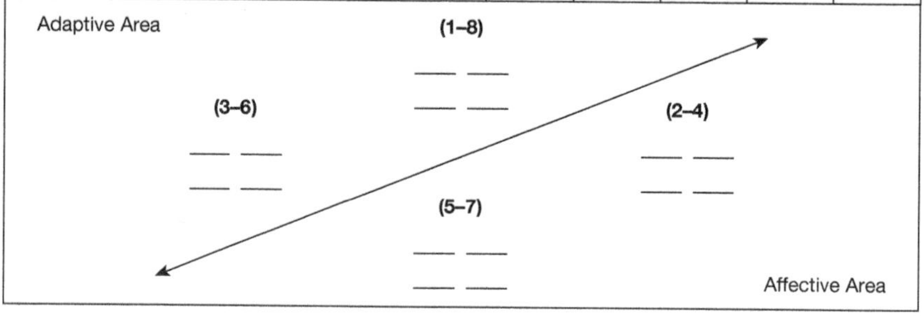

W.I.P.: Quadrant A B C D   Area: α β γ

Notes

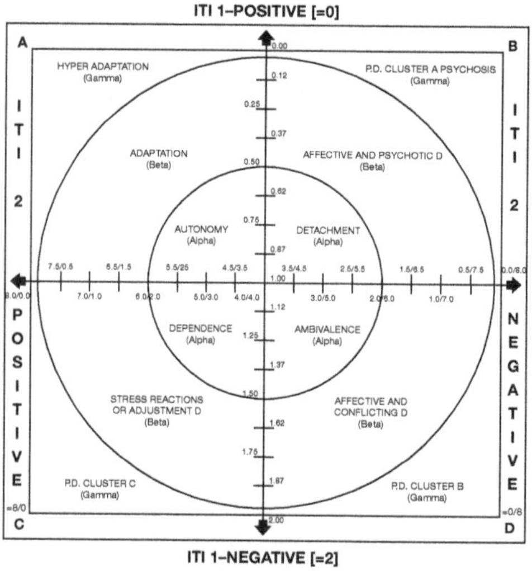

FIGURE 5.1 CWS Scoring Form.

Figure 5.1 provides a sample of the CWS Scoring Form, which allows the clinician to record scores by box in the upper section, complete the Analyses of Sequence in the middle section, and plot the Wartegg Index of Psychopathology (WIP) at the bottom.

TABLE 5.1 Overview of CWS Scoring Categories and Scoring Options

*Order of Sequence**	*Evocative Character**	*Affective Quality**	*Form Quality**	*Contents**	*Frequency*	*Special Scores*	*Movement*	*Impulse Responses*
• Individualized • Numerical • Reversed • Numerical Circular • Reversed Circular • Other Methodical	• **1**: Fully captured • **0.5**: Partially captured • **0**: Not captured	• **1**: Positive • **0.5**: Neutral • **0**: Negative	• **1**: Immediately Recognizable • **0.5**: Recognized with verbal-ization • **.0**: Unrecog-nizable (with or without verbalization)	***Primary*** • **A** (Animal) • **ABS** (Abstract) • **AD** (Animal Detail) • **ANA** (Anatomy) • **ARC** (Architecture) • **AS** (Animal Simulacrum) • **ASD** (Animal Simulacrum Detail) • **AST** (Astronomy) • **BIO** (Biology) • **BOT** (Botanical) • **CLD** (Cloud) • **EXP** (Explosion) • **FD** (Food) • **FIR** (Fire) • **H** (Human) • **HD** (Human Detail) • **HS** (Human Simulacrum) • **HSD** (Human Simulacrum Detail) • **ICE** (Ice) • **MIN** (Mineral) • **NAT** (Nature) • **OBJ** (Object) • **PAT** (Pathological) • **SEX** (Sexual) • **SIG** (Symbol) ***Secondary*** • **AC** (Archeology) • **CG** (Clothing) • **FA** (Figurative Art) • **FT** (Fairy Tale) • **HR** (Heraldry) • **MK** (Mask) • **MT** (Mythological) • **RE** (Religion) • **SF** (Science Fiction) • **TY** (Toy) • WP (Weapon)	***Popular*** • **P**: Popular • **(P)**: Semi-Popular ***Original*** • **O**: Original • **(O)**: Semi-Original	***Level 1*** • **AP** (Arbitrary Performance) • **CO** (Contamination) • **DS** (Disproportion) • **PA** (Personalized Answer) • **TR** (Transparency) ***Level 2*** • **ID** (Incomplete Drawing) • **II** (Inadequate Integration) • **MU** (Missing Union) • **PP** (Perseveration) • **SR** (Stimulus Repetition) • **AP** (Arbitrary Performance) ***Level 3*** • **AS** (Anxiety Stroke) • **CB** (Crossed Border) • **GR** (Global Rejection) • **ID** (Incomplete Drawing) • **IS** (Interpreted Stimulus) • **MR** (Morbid) • **OD** (Opposite Direction) • **PR** (Partial Rejection) • **RB** (Reversed Box) • **SC** (Self-Criticism) ***Noted Phenomena*** • **BK** (Blackening) • **CJ** (Conjoined Boxes) • **CP** (Color Projection) • **DB** (Disproportion between Boxes) • **EN** (Encapsulation) • **HN** (Human Content Negation) • **IP** (Improper Description) • **OA** ("Or" Response) • **PS** (Perspective Response) • **BD** (Big Drawing) • **SD** (Small Drawing)	***Primary*** • **M** (Primary Movement) ***Secondary*** • **FE** (Facial Expression) • **FM** (Animal Movement) • **MI** (Inanimate Movement) ***Gender*** • **f** (female) • **m** (male) • **i** (indeterminate) ***Direction*** • **a** (active) • **b** (blocked) • **d** (double) • **p** (passive) • **r** (rotary) • **i** (indeterminate)	• OR (Oral) • AN (Anal) • PH (Phallic)

Note: * Must be scored for each WDCT box.

Box 1: Responses where the mark is centered and/or highly relevant to the drawing, either graphically or thematically.
Box 2: Responses that suggest vitality or movement.
Box 3: Responses that continue the sense of direction indicated by the three existing marks, showing a progression from bottom left to top right, from shorter to taller.
Box 4: Responses that express a sense of heaviness, weight, and/or stability.
Box 5: Responses that suggest overcoming an obstacle by showing a sense of direction toward the center of the box. (Note that the line starting at the lower left corner is being "blocked" by a second, nearly perpendicular line.)
Box 6: Responses where the two marks are joined in some type of synthesis and/or structure.
Box 7: Responses that represent a sense of delicacy.
Box 8: Responses that show a rounding and closure of the curved mark.

The Evocative Character of each mark is derived from Gestalt perceptual rules, and informs the clinically interpreted meaning as described in Table 5.2.

As a general rule, a box receives an Evocative Character score of 1 if the client's drawing and/or verbalization fits with the "pull" or suggestion of the stimulus. A score of 0.5 is given when the client's response only partially aligns with the mark's "suggestion" (i.e., a client captures a sense of "heaviness" in Box 4, but not "stability"). A score of 0 is given when the client completely ignores or does not seem to understand a box's particular Evocative Character.

In addition, based on perceptual and gestalt characteristics, each of the eight boxes, can be described as either "simple" (when the stimulus consists of

TABLE 5.2 Perceptual Appearance, Evocative Character, and Clinical Meaning of WDCT Stimuli

Box	*Perceptual Appearance*	*Evocative Character*	*Clinical Meaning*
1	A central point/ Dot	Centrality, Relevance	Self-Evaluation
2	A wavy line with rounded edges	Vitality, Movement	Female Object Relations
3	Three progressive lines of increasing height	Directionality, Progression	Available Energy
4	A little black square	Stability, Heaviness	Male Object Relations
5	Two contraposed perpendicular lines	Overcoming an Obstacle (or Block)	Aggressive Energies
6	Two lines at right angles	Synthesis, Structure (Union)	Relation to Reality, Rationality, Planning
7	A dotted semi-circle	Delicacy	Libidinal Energies
8	A curved line turned downward	Rounding, Closure	Social Skills

only one mark, as in Boxes 1, 2, 4, and 8) or "complex" (when the stimulus consists of two or more marks, as with Boxes 3, 5, 6, and 7).

This factor influences and determines the scoring criteria of Evocative Character. As noted above, "simple" boxes receive a score of 1, 0.5, or 0, based on how well the client does or does not capture the box's Evocative Character. However, for "complex" boxes, in order to give a score of 1 or 0.5, a *necessary, but not sufficient condition* must be met, with the client conceiving of the two (or more) marks in the box as part of the same entity. For example, the three lines of Box 3 must be graphically related (i.e., part of a staircase or a building) or conceptually related (i.e., three flowers, three trees, three telephone poles).

Only after this *necessary* condition is satisfied, can the Evocative Character of the box be scored in a manner similar to that of "simple" boxes (i.e., if the drawing and/or verbalization captures the Evocative Character). If the *necessary* condition is not satisfied, the score for that specific box must be 0.

General review of the Evocative Character related to each box is elaborated below. Scoring tables, to guide specific scoring of Evocative Character by box, are provided in Appendix F. Scoring tables contain scoring rules and examples to guide reliable scoring. The descriptions in this chapter are not considered comprehensive, and clinicians are referred to the scoring tables in Appendix F for comprehensive scoring guidance.

Box 1 (Simple)—Centrality and Relevance

In considering the Evocative Character of Box 1, centrality or relevance, a 1-point response is one in which the client grasps the centrality or relevance (importance) of the mark and depicts responses where the stimulus is central and/or a major element in the drawing. The central placement of the stimulus must be appropriate based on either graphic or conceptual criteria (for example, the center of a target).

A 0.5-point response is one in which the client only partially understands the mark's centrality or importance, drawing something that includes the mark in a non-centralized way or attributing less important or of secondary meaning to the mark (for example, a star in a constellation or a button on a shirt). To ensure interrater reliability, a quantitative aspect to scoring EC in Box 1 was further developed: drawings that include *between 2 and 5 items* (5 apples, 5 windows, etc.) earn an EC score of 0.5. Drawings that include more than five items (showing even less centrality or importance to each item) earn EC scores of 0.

Lastly, a 0-point response is one in which the client does not seem to understand the centrality or the importance of the stimulus and draws. This is evident in several response styles, including responses in which the stimulus is simply repeated, without any meaning attributed to it; responses that alter the stimulus itself (i.e., the mark is thickened to make it bigger); and responses that include the stimulus in such a way that any sense of centrality or importance is lost (for example, a freckle on a face).

Box 2 (Simple)—Vitality and Movement

In considering the Evocative Character of Box 2, vitality and movement, a 1-point response is one in which the client understands the mark's "pull" for movement and vitality and draws things that include the stimulus; that is, the client draws human figures or animals (including faces), living objects (including botanical content), or inanimate objects in motion (for example, rain, wind, or a waving flag).

A 0.5-point response is one in which the client does not understand the suggestion of movement and vitality, but produces a drawing that includes the stimulus and a sense of plasticity, flexibility, or curviness (for example, an arch, the curve of a road, the outline of a leaf).

A 0-point response is one in which the client does not seem to understand the mark's movement or vitality, and does not even grasp a sense of plasticity or curviness. In these cases, the client draws rigid, mechanical, static drawings (for example, square buildings, geometric figures). Additionally, isolated human or animals body details earn an EC of 0 in Box 2.

Box 3 (Complex)—Directionality and Progression

Recall that for complex Boxes, the *necessary, but not sufficient condition* requires that the client perceives the two or more marks in each complex box as belonging to the same entity, either conceptually or graphically. If this condition is not met, an EC score of 0 is automatic. Once the necessary condition has been met (i.e., the marks are graphically and/or conceptually linked to each other) scoring proceeds in the following manner.

In considering the Evocative Character of Box 3, directionality and progression, a 1-point response is one that demonstrates a sense of direction and of dynamic progression toward the top right corner (for example, buildings of increasing height, and objects in a perspective view). In order for the drawing to receive a 1-point EC score, the direction of the drawing must be *clearly oriented* (either structurally or dynamically or both) toward the top right corner of the box. Examples of clear orientation include buildings that get taller and taller as they are closer to the top right-hand side of the box (structural), stairs going up toward the upper right side of the box (structural), cars going up a hillside toward the upper right side of the box (dynamic).

A 0.5-point response in Box 3 is one in that integrates the three consecutive lines of the stimulus without demonstrating any sense of vertical progression (for example, three trees), integrates the three marks continuing horizontally after the third mark (for example, stairs leading to a landing), or responses that turn downward (for example, the roof of a building).

In Box 3, a 0-point response is one in which a Reversed Box special score is assigned (see later in this chapter); the three lines are not integrated and represent unrelated objects for example, a broom, a cigarette, and a fishing pole); the lines are extended primarily vertically (for example, a person's legs); a sense of progression or directionality is totally lost although the drawing may use the entire box (for example, prison bars); and a response in which a special score of Opposition Direction (see later in this chapter) is assigned. In this last case, the drawing is clearly oriented toward the bottom left corner of the box (for example, a hill with a car driving toward the bottom left corner). In these cases, the sense of directionality and progression is completely lost, and therefore the EC = 0.

Note that in scoring the EC for Box 3, special attention must be paid to the client's age. As the skill of drawing in perspective only develops around 11–12 years of age, the younger the child is, the more leniently EC should be scored.

Box 4 (Simple)—Heaviness and Stability

In considering the Evocative Character for Box 4, heaviness and stability, a 1-point response is one in which the client draws something that includes the mark simultaneously representing heaviness, great weight, and/or stability—expressed in either a literal or symbolic manner. Examples of literal 1-point responses include architectural structures, whereas symbolic responses refer to cognitively challenging (and complicated) objects or activities that "make you think" (for example, a chess or checkerboard). In Box 4, a 0.5-point response is one in which the client demonstrates partial understanding of a sense of heaviness and/or stability (for example, a piece of furniture); responses that represent heaviness, but not stability (for example, a rolling boulder); and responses that represent stability, but not heaviness (for example, a camera tripod). 0-point responses typically grasp neither the concepts of heaviness or stability (for example, a kite or a person).

Box 5 (Simple)—Overcoming of an Obstacle/Dynamic Directionality toward Center of the Box

Recall that for complex Boxes, the *necessary, but not sufficient condition* requires that the client perceives the two or more marks in each complex box as belonging to the same entity, either conceptually or graphically. If this condition is not met, an EC score of 0 is automatic. Once the necessary condition has been met (i.e., the marks are graphically and/or conceptually linked to each other) scoring proceeds in the following manner.

In considering the Evocative Character for Box 5, overcoming of an obstacle, the directionality of the client's drawing must be considered. That is, it is expected that the client's drawing will suggest dynamic directionality toward the center of the box, past the contraposed mark. In Box 5, a 1-point response includes drawings that point (even slightly) past the contraposed line and extend toward the center of the box (for example, a tool or flashlight); and drawings of objects that are separate, but conceptually related (for example, a nail and hammer). Due to their high frequency, the following responses are exceptions to the above rules and are scored as 1-point responses in Box 5 only: the letter "T," a hammer, and a steering wheel with a driver.

Examples of 0.5-point responses in Box 5 are those that don't demonstrate directionality, including all responses in which the drawing is confined to the bottom left corner of the box (for example, a teepee; and responses in which the marks, although part of the same object, are graphically disconnected (for example, an arrow in which the point is disconnected from the shaft). This "disconnect" rule also applies to the common responses noted above (that is, the letter "T," a hammer, and a steering wheel with a driver), which are scored 0.5 if the two marks remain graphically disconnected.

Lastly, 0-point responses in Box 5 occur when the client fails to integrate or relate the marks to each other, loses or reverses the expected dynamic directionality of the box, or depicts situations in which the contraposed mark (or obstacle) is not overcome. More specifically, 0-point responses include all responses involving a Reversed Box (see Special Scores later in this chapter); responses in which the drawing is oriented laterally, either toward the right or toward the left (for example, a person doing sit-ups); responses in which the two marks are not integrated, graphically OR conceptually (for example, a match and a nail; see Missing Union special score, later in this chapter); responses that express a total block of movement (for example, a car stopped at a stop sign) and all responses that focus toward the bottom left corner of the box. These drawings may integrate the two marks and point toward the center of the box; however, the directional focus of the depicted objects is toward the bottom left corner (for example, a syringe oriented toward the lower left-hand corner, where the needle is the lower diagonal stimulus mark. This type of drawing meets criteria for the special score Opposite Direction (see later in this chapter).

Box 6 (Complex)—Synthesis and Structure (Union)

Recall that for complex Boxes, the *necessary, but not sufficient condition* requires that the client perceives the two or more marks in each complex box as belonging to the same entity, either conceptually or graphically. If this condition is not met, an EC score of 0 is automatic. Once the necessary condition has been met (i.e., the marks are graphically and/or conceptually linked to each other) scoring proceeds in the following manner.

As Box 6 has particular diagnostic relevance, it has specific rules for Evocative Character scoring. Sometimes, on Box 6, when the client conceptually and/or graphically joins the two marks, the structural quality of the drawing is insufficient (for example, the two marks are utilized as rays of the sun, which is not a structured use of the mark). Thus, once the necessary condition is met, the assessor must closely evaluate the *type* and *quality of the synthesis* drawn by the client in order to properly score this box.

In considering the Evocative Character of Box 6, synthesis and structure, a 1-point response is one in which the client grasps the ideas of "shared destiny," "proximity," and "similarity" of the two marks and demonstrates this either graphically and/or symbolically. That is, the marks are literally or symbolically integrated and synthesized, often with a sense of graphic structure or union.

Examples of graphically demonstrated 1-point responses include a geometric figure or building, whereas a symbolically demonstrated 1-point response might include two geometric figures or a hammer and nail.

In Box 6, 0.5-point responses are those in which the client understands synthesis, but leaves the structure partially incomplete or unstructured by leaving a disconnection, gap, or break in the two lines (for example, a perspective view of a road left open as it comes "forward." Additionally, all drawings that deserve a score of 1, but that are not completely graphically closed (for example, squares that are clearly left with gaps at the corners) are scored 0.5 in Box 6. This is due to the lack of structure or union evident in these drawings. Lastly, given Box 6's relation to rational thinking, planning, and organization, drawings receiving the special score Incomplete Drawing (discussed later in this chapter) receive a score of 0.5 in Box 6.

Several types of drawings are scored as 0-point responses in Box 6. This include drawings involving a Reversed Box (see Special Scores, later in this chapter); drawings that do not satisfy the necessary condition of graphic and/or conceptual linking (for example, a telephone pole and a spoon; see Missing Union special score); and responses that ignore the "pull" of synthesis and structure, resulting in clear alterations of the stimulus and rounded shapes (for example, clouds, faces, or whole human figures). Drawings such as these would generally earn the special scores Inadequate Integration or Arbitrary Performance, discussed later in this chapter, and are always scored 0.

Box 7 (Complex)—Delicacy

Recall that for complex Boxes, the *necessary, but not sufficient condition* requires that the client perceives the two or more marks in each complex box as belonging to the same entity, either conceptually or graphically. If this condition is not met, an EC score of 0 is automatic. Once the necessary condition has been met (i.e., the marks are graphically and/or conceptually linked to each other) scoring proceeds in the following manner.

In considering the Evocative Character of Box 7, delicacy, both the concept of delicacy and the affective tone (that is, the positive or negative affective indications of the drawing content) must be considered. In this latter consideration, the Affective Quality of the depicted content must factor into the EC scoring decision. This consideration of AQ in the scoring of EC is limited to Box 7, and does not apply to other WDCT boxes.

Generally 1-point responses in Box 7 include responses that grasp delicacy along with sophistication, sensitivity, and aesthetic sense, either literally or symbolically, and are paired with an AQ of 1 (positive). This can include positive "dotted drawings" (that mimic the stimulus). Examples of 1-point responses include figurative art (anything evoking aesthetics and artistic appreciation), faces, and flowers. Due to the high frequency in which they are depicted, round geometric figures and wheels (either in isolation or as part of a vehicle) receive a score of 1.

A 0.5-point response generally captures a similar sense of delicacy as a 1-point response; however, the Affective Quality associated with the depicted content is considered neutral (AQ = 0.5). Examples of 0.5-point responses include a snail, a light bulb, or dotted drawings (that mimic the stimulus) associated with an AQ = 0.5.

A 0-point response in Box 7 generally includes the stimulus without grasping any sense of delicacy, and instead incorporates the mark as something coarse, rigid, or hard (for example, weapons, mechanical objects, and food objects characterized by a hard exterior). Additionally, delicate objects with an associated AQ = 0 receive an EC score of 0 in Box 7 (for example, spider, tears, sad face), including dotted drawings (that mimic the stimulus).

Box 8 (Simple)—Rounding and Closure

In considering the Evocative Character of Box 8, rounding and closure, 1-point responses include those in which the client produces pictures depicting rounding and closure (for example, a circle, a face, or the sun. Additionally, the following frequently provided responses in Box 8 are assigned an EC of 1: a parachute *with the parachutist*, an umbrella, the sun partially covered by mountains or by the ocean, a half-moon, and an isolated eye.

A 0.5-point response in Box 8 includes those in which the client does not fully capture both Evocative Character criteria (that is rounding *and* closure), but rather only communicates one criterion via the produced drawing. That is, the client understands the sense of rounding, but only partially captures that of closure and draws things that close the stimulus either partially (for example, a rainbow) or only at its base (for example, a helmet); or, the client fully captures the idea of closure, but only partially emphasizes the rounding of the stimulus (for example, a curved-roof hut).

Lastly, a 0-point response in Box 8 is one in which the client demonstrates no sense of closure or rounding (for example, square objects). Additionally, in Box 8, when the special score Reversed Box (see Special Scores, later in this chapter) is assigned to a drawing, the EC is scored as 0.

Impact of Verbalizations During the Picture Gallery on Evocative Character Scoring

During the Picture Gallery phase, when clients describe what they drew in a manner that does not clarify the *specific* meaning of the mark/stimulus (e.g., the client draws something abstract, and says: "Mardi Gras"), this should prompt the assessor to ask: "*What does the mark mean?*" The client's answer should ideally help to score the EC according to the general guidelines as outlined in this chapter.

The assessor must pay careful attention to the client's verbalization of what he/she drew, as it is diagnostically important. The exact words the client uses can change the EC score. For example, in Box 2, if the client draws a complete human face and verbalizes, "A face," the EC score is 1. However, if, for the same drawing, the client says: "An eyebrow on a face," the EC score is 0.5. Similarly, if a client draws a complete face, but verbalizes only "An eyebrow," the EC is scored as 0.5, as the client has graphically (but not verbally) captured the Evocative Character for the box. Lastly, if the client draws only an isolated eyebrow and says: "An eyebrow," the EC score is 0. This same rationale is used, for example in Box 4, if a client uses the stimulus as a window incorporated into a house. If the client verbalizes "A house," the EC = 1; however, if the client verbalizes "a window" (but draws a complete house) or "a window in a house," the EC = 0.5.

Scoring tables for Evocative Character, by box, are provided in Appendix F (Tables F.1 through F.8). Additional scoring guidelines for Evocative Character, as well as the relationship of EC to AQ, FQ, P, and Special Scores, are provided here.

BOX 5.1 ADDITIONAL SCORING GUIDELINES FOR EVOCATIVE CHARACTER (EC)

The following are additional guidelines for accurate EC scoring as well as for other aspects of reliable scoring. Readers should carefully review this information and refer to applicable sections throughout this chapter.

Clarity of Drawing/The Relationship between EC and FQ

If the client draws something that is well defined and clear (generally associated with a high FQ), scoring is based on the general rules listed for each box. When the drawing is unclear, vague, or confusing, the EC score is generally 0.

The Relationship between EC and Frequency [P, (P)]

In *most* cases, responses that fall into the category of Popular ["P"] or Semi-Popular ["(P)"] will receive an EC score of 1; however, some exceptions to this guideline exist (for example, a "staircase" in Box 3 which only include three steps will receive an EC = 0.5, but is still considered P; or, a "hammer" in Box 5 that is left disconnected will receive and EC = 0.5, but is still considered P).

The Relationship between EC and Special Scores

- **Inadequate Integration (II) in Box 6 (only)**: All responses showing the Level II Special Score Inadequate Integration (II) in Box 6 will receive an EC score of 0.
- **Missing Union (MU) in Boxes 3, 5, 6, and 7 (only)**: All responses showing the Level II Special Scores Missing Union (MU) will receive an EC score of 0.

- **Reversed Box (RB):** When the Special Score Reversed Box (RB) is assigned in *Boxes 3, 5, 6, and 8*, these drawings will receive EC scores of 0. *In the case of Boxes 1, 2, 4, and 7, given the graphic stimulus, an RB would either be less meaningful and not significantly alter the "pull" of the stimulus (as with Box 1), or the RB would only slightly impact the "demand" of the stimulus (such as with Boxes 2, 4, and 7). Thus, when a Reversed Box is recorded in Boxes 1, 2, 4, or 7, the general rules of EC scoring apply.*
- **Partial Rejection (PR):** In the event of a Partial Rejection, the EC is scored based on the drawing's content and the EC scoring rules for the box in which the PR occurs. (See Evocative Character, for further discussion).
- **Interpreted Stimulus (IS):** When the Special Score Interpreted Stimulus (IS) is present, EC is scored according to the rules of the box in which it occurs. For example, in Box 2, should the client indicate the stimulus is a snake, the EC = 1. Conversely if the client verbalizes that the stimulus is a lead pipe, the EC = 0.

Affective Quality (AQ)

Affective Quality scores (AQ) are based solely on the affective connotation and emotional tone that the client assigns to his/her drawings. Thus, AQ scoring is completely independent from other formal characteristics (e.g., darkened areas, things that are crossed out, drawings of very unusual things), which are accounted for using other scoring categories. As with the EC scoring category, drawings in each box are assigned a score of either 1, 0.5, or 0, depending on the positive/pleasant, neutral, or negative/unpleasant connotation of that box's content.

Generally speaking:

Positive AQ (score = 1) refers to drawings of humans (H), animals (A), constructs related to Nature (NAT), botanical content (BOT), and food (FD).

Neutral AQ (score = 0.5) refers to drawings of objects (OBJ), signs and numbers (SIG), minerals (MIN), and architecture or constructions (ARC).

Negative AQ (score = 0) refers to anatomy (ANA), weapons (OBJ, WP), explosions (EXP), adverse meteorological conditions including clouds and rain (CLD), and pathological content (PAT).

Applying these rules in clinical practice, it became clear that the scoring of AQ could not be approached in a completely linear manner, given the intersubjectivity of scorers. Given this, it was determined that AQ needed to be scored according to a specific list of contents, to ensure interrater reliability. Given the difficulties and hazards of thematic analysis (see Schafer, 1971), the initial list of the contents was based on clinical experience. This list of contents was further based, in part, on the psychodynamic interpretation of content provided by several authors (Schafer, 1953, 1954; Brown, 1953; Scarpellini, 1962) and in part on socio-cultural factors. When faced with ambiguous contents (that is, content open to multiple interpretations) or when the client's explanation of what he/she drew failed to clarify the emotional tone of the drawing (either in the Picture Gallery phase or subsequent phases of administration), that particular drawing was assigned an AQ score of 0.5. This is true for contents including the moon, ashes, a sunset, a cat, night, a clown, a cross, and others. Additionally, a mechanism has been implemented by the Istituto Italiano Wartegg (IIW) that allows clinicians to submit contents to a panel of experts, who independently rate and assign Affective Quality scores for uncertain, unfamiliar, or unusual contents (see "Scoring Online Service," below). This service is now available in both Italian and English.

Scoring AQ does not require or imply subjective analysis of drawing content; clearly, the same content can assume or take on different meanings depending on age, sex, and status of the client, as well as the perspective and experience of the examiner. Therefore, for consistency, it is necessary to first approach the scoring of AQ with a standardized guide, necessitating the development of the AQ list of positive, neutral, and negative values contained in this manual. However, through clinical application, it became clear that the decisive factor in scoring AQ should not simply depend on the value contained in the list, but also must take into account the verbalization of the atmosphere and emotional tone of the drawings made by the client. For example, a flower, because it belongs to the content category Botany, is generally assigned an AQ score of 1; however, verbalizations such as "A beautiful exotic flower," and "a wilted flower with no petals," describe completely different internal realities from each other. Therefore, these two flower responses are assigned different AQ scores: AQ = 1 for the exotic flower, based upon its description in pleasant, positive terms; and AQ = 0 for the "wilted" flower, based upon its description as damaged and negative. The critical, determining factor for AQ is, therefore, twofold: First, the "base AQ" as listed in this manual, which is primary; and second, modifications in either the positive or negative direction based upon descriptive client verbalizations.

In addition, anything explicitly described by the client in a negative manner (for example, "a cold and desolate landscape," "a vicious dog," "a sad face," "a crumpled leaf," "an abandoned house," "a broken toy"), or described in a derogatory or pejorative manner (preceded by adjectives such as "ugly," "bad," etc.), will be assigned an AQ score of 0, (even though if described otherwise the same drawing would usually receive a score of AQ = 1 or AQ = 0.5). Conversely, neutral or negative contents can have positive connotations if described using terms of endearment. For example, "pig or tiger" would receive an AQ score of 0, but "piggy" and "tiger cub" receive an AQ of 1. For contents such as drawings, maps, paintings, photographs, and television shows, the AQ score will depend on the specific content represented. For example, in Box 6, if the verbalization is "a painting" the AQ score is 0.5, but if the verbalization is "a painting of flowers," then the AQ score is 1. Conversely, "a portrait of a sad person" receives an AQ of 0. Similarly, "a geographic map" receives an AQ score of 0.5, whereas a "treasure map" receives an AQ of 1.

Content classification is thus based on scholarly work (e.g., Schafer, Scarpellini), on knowledge of the culture, tradition, and collected wisdom of the Italian cultural frame in which the test was developed, as well as on environmental context. With time, modifications appropriate to normative samples of different nationalities will be available. While these are being developed, CWS users are encouraged to utilize the Affective Quality charts contained in this manual. Adopting this relatively conservative approach will allow for increased reliability and validity and for comparison across research carried out in different contexts. Given these potential cross-cultural differences in Affective Quality, further research is currently being conducted in the United States.

Scoring Tables for positive, neutral, and negative AQ are provided in Appendix F (Table F.9).

Form Quality (FQ)

In order to effectively score client drawings in a qualitative manner, it was clear that the aesthetics of the drawings or the client's artistic skill could not be solely relied upon as this would reward few individuals and penalize most. After considering this issue at length, an "*evidence criterion*" was adopted, defined as "immediate visual clarity and complete understanding" (Devoto & Oli, 1971, p. 852), or as "characteristics of any idea, perception, or sensation that appears to have such a manifest sense of truth that the mind automatically agrees without the need for demonstration or proof" (Battaglia, 1968, pp. 526–527).

In this context, Form Quality is not intended to measure the ability to draw well, but rather the ability to make clear and obvious the drawing to the eyes of the assessor. This skill is strictly linked to the client's level of cognitive functioning, as it is based on the ability to recognize and represent the whole from a part. For example, the key elements of a face are the eyes and the mouth, regardless of how skillfully or artistically they are drawn. That is, we recognize the concept of a whole face through these two key elements (i.e., two parts), as in the case of the smiley face symbol. Conversely, we often only see the outline (devoid of key elements) of the face in WDCT drawings completed by children with serious physical, cognitive, or emotional limitations.

Form Quality is scored according to the following criterion:

— *An FQ score of 1 is assigned when the meaning of the drawing is obvious and immediately clear to the assessor, in most cases requiring no explanation or clarification by the client*. Thus, generally speaking, these are drawings with no important parts missing, no major disproportions, no arbitrary spatial shifts, or other noticeable graphic or conceptual defects. The assessor must pay special attention to those drawings that, while not immediately clear, are then explained by the client in a way that describes them clearly, making

BOX 5.2 SCORING ONLINE SERVICE

The following provides information to clinicians seeking to enroll and utilize the Scoring Online service offered by the Istituto Italiano Wartegg. Scoring Online is offered both in Italian and English languages.

With the aim of improving the precision and accuracy in CWS scoring procedures, thereby increasing its reliability, the IIW has created an online consultation service referred to as "Scoring Online."

What is Scoring Online?

Scoring online is a service developed by the IIW to facilitate more accurate and reliable scoring consistency within the CWS community. To use the service, one must first register (i.e., create an account). Following registration, users may submit specific terms (nouns or verbs) to receive guidance on the scoring of Evocative Character (by box), Affective Quality, or Direction of Movement (i.e., active, passive, double, blocked, rotatory, etc.).

For example, upon administering the Wartegg, a clinician finds that a client drew a "doctor holding a stethoscope" in Box 2, with the stethoscope incorporating the stimulus mark. Unsure of how to score the EC, the clinician may login to the Scoring Online system, select Evocative Character, and submit "Stethoscope" (with a scan of the drawing). Similarly, this term could be submitted for Affective Quality (generally no scan required). If the verbalization accompanying the drawing was "A doctor using a stethoscope," the verb "to use" could be submitted to receive guidance on the Direction of Movement.

Once submitted, clinicians will receive an immediate scoring guideline (if the submitted word is in the online database). If the term has not been previously submitted, a scientific committee of certified CWS users will review the submitted terms. Consensus results will be entered into the online database. The more that clinicians use this service, the more terms will be entered, and the more useful it will become. (By way of example, currently in the Italian version of this service, there are more than 5,000 terms available.) As this service is new to the United States, the database is not as large, but is growing with your help.

How to Register

There is currently no fee to participate in the Online Scoring service, and all CWS users are encouraged to do so. To register, please visit: http://en.wartegg.com/login.php.

Should you have difficulty registering for Online Scoring, please contact the secretary of the IIW at iiw@wartegg.com for further assistance.

their specificity and/or originality quite evident, and justifying that these are appropriate and accurate drawings of the object or person. This is similar to cases where the client draws something unique to their personal area of interest or experience that the assessor may not be familiar with (and therefore the content of the drawing may not be immediately recognizable). Upon verbalization, if the drawing represents well the verbalized answer, the client should not be penalized for the assessor's failure to recognize the object when drawn.

— *An FQ score of 0.5 is assigned when the meaning of the drawing is not immediately apparent or is open to multiple interpretations and requires client's explanation or description in order to be understood.* For example, in Box 8 the client draws a circle with no other distinctive marks and in the Picture Gallery phase he says he drew the sun. With the verbalization, the drawing is recognizable, but prior to verbalization, the content of the drawing was unclear (and could have been several objects, including the sun, a ball, an orange, etc.); therefore, this would be scored 0.5. It should be further noted that the Form Quality for a box in which the special score Inadequate Integration (II) is coded will always equal 0.5 in adults.

— *An FQ score of 0 is assigned when the meaning of the drawing is unintelligible, totally incorrect or arbitrary. In these cases, nothing (including the client's verbalizations) makes the drawing identifiable or recognizable.*

In order to not to be influenced by the verbal explanations clients give in the Picture Gallery phase, it is recommended that the assessor tries to understand what each drawing means as the client draws and completes it. This same criterion should also apply to children. Children's WDCT drawings should not be scored in a more lenient manner, as this approach introduces subjectivity into scoring (i.e., an assessor who is "lenient" versus the "more strict" assessor), making it impossible to compare data from different assessors.

It is unusual for clinicians, when scoring Form Quality, to experience difficulty differentiating between scores of 0 and 1, as 0 FQ scores are typically quite obvious. The occasional challenges arise, however, in differentiating between FQ scores of 0.5 and 1. In these circumstances, clinicians must remain aware of several decision scoring guidelines. First, if a drawn content is not immediately recognizable, or is subject to multiple interpretations, the clinician must ask, "Is there anything that could have been *quickly* and *easily* drawn by the client (in addition to what they have drawn) to clarify the content?" The key words here are "quickly" and "easily" as there is no expectation that clients have exceptional artistic ability or spend significantly long periods of time attempting to represent their intentions. If the answer to this question is "yes," it is likely that the FQ of this drawing equals 0.5. On the other hand, if the answer is "no," (i.e., the client could not have added anything quickly or easily to clarify their drawing), the FQ is likely to be scored as 1. Using the example above of a client who draws a circle in Box 8, given the verbalization of "the sun," the client's drawing would be assigned a score of FQ = 0.5 as the "rays" of the sun could have quickly and easily been added to the drawing to clarify the content. Conversely, if the client verbalized the drawing as "a circle," there is nothing required to clarify this content, and the drawing would be assigned a score of FQ = 1 (despite the fact that it was not immediately recognized by the clinician).

An additional category that can be quite difficult to score is that of "abstract" drawings (ABS). These drawings require the assessor to distinguish between actual abstract drawings and masked Partial Rejections (PR), which are discussed later in this chapter. A masked Partial Rejection (PR) is usually recognizable in the Picture Gallery phase as the client remains vague and imprecise, and oftentimes says he/she drew "something," "a strange thing," "one of those modern drawings," or a similar description. When asked by the assessor about the exact meaning of the drawing, the client may answer, "nothing really," or "nothing in particular." In these cases the response will receive a FQ score of 0.

However, a true abstract (ABS) drawing is usually accompanied by more precise client verbalizations that inform the scoring of FQ. In these cases, FQ scores of 1 are assigned when the link between the drawing and the title given to the box is completely clear (for example, the client draws a smiley face and then in the Picture Gallery states: "happiness"). Keep in mind (see Chapter 3 for review), that when Abstract content is verbalized, the examiner must clarify the content of the depicted object. FQ scores of 0 are assigned when the link between the drawing and the title, even in light of the client's explanation, is not immediately apparent (for example, the client draws some unspecific doodles, and in the Picture Gallery states: "Fall").

Scoring tables for Form Quality are provided in Appendix F (Table F.10).

Contents

Content scoring captures the category and type of drawing produced by clients, and falls into two major categories: Primary Contents and Secondary Contents.

Primary Content Categories

Primary Contents are the most important content categories and represent the principal factor in identifying what the client drew. CWS drawings can be coded into 24 separate Primary Content categories. Scoring guidelines for these categories of primary content are provided in Table F.11 of Appendix F.

Content scores are primarily based on the exact words the client uses to describe what he/she drew. Thus, for example, if a client draws the muzzle of a dog (i.e., the nose and mouth), but in the Picture Gallery says "a dog," the drawing will be scored as A (Animal) content as opposed to AD (head of an animal) content. Similarly, it is common in Box 5 for clients to draw a person's profile at the wheel of a car, and then to say, "A steering wheel" in the Picture Gallery. In this case, the response is scored as OBJ (Object) as opposed to H (Human), matching the client's verbalization. This same rule applies to content that is drawn by the client, but not mentioned during the Picture Gallery. For example, a client draws a kite in the sky, with both sun and clouds behind it. In the Picture Gallery, the client states, "I drew a kite." As neither the sun nor the clouds were verbalized, they would not be captured by content scoring. In this case, the only content scored would be Object (OBJ) for "kite."

When drawings include multiple elements, a hierarchy of contents applies. Within this hierarchy, Human (H) contents come first, followed by Animal (A) contents, followed by all other contents, depending on how the client verbalizes the relative importance of each content element in the Picture Gallery phase. In other words, when multiple elements coexist as part of one response, if a Human content is present ("A dog being walked by a man"), the primary content is H. If Animal content is present ("A park with a dog running"), the primary content is A. *If contents other than H and A are verbalized*, the primary content is the *first* content that the client verbalizes in the Picture Gallery. For example, if the client says, "A flower on a deck in the sun," the primary content is BOT (Botany, for "flower"). If instead, the client says, "A deck with flowers in the sun," the primary content is ARC (Architecture, for "deck"). For content scoring, the primary factor is always the client's verbalization; scoring is based on whatever content the client makes most important in his/her response during the Picture Gallery.

Secondary Content Categories

Secondary Contents are supplemental scoring elements that mostly refer to H, HD, OBJ, A, and AD contents, but that can be applied to any primary content, if necessary. The role of Secondary Contents is to clarify or specify Primary Contents. The CWS contains 11 Secondary Content categories, with scoring guidelines provided in Table F.12 (Appendix F).

In the case of especially elaborate and complex drawings, all categories of Primary Contents can be listed on the Examiner Form in the Secondary Content scoring section. For example, "A man walking along a river in a typical mountain scene" would be scored: H and NAT, respectively (H as primary and NAT as secondary content). However, it should be noted that a Secondary Content can never be scored as a Primary Content.

In some cases, it might be difficult to distinguish primary and secondary content. For example, in Box 3, if the client draws a factory with smokestacks emitting smoke, but simply verbalizes, "a factory," the smoke would not be scored. That is, if the client says, "A factory," the content score would simply be ARC (Architecture, for "factory"). However, if the client says, "A factory with pollution," the content scoring would be ARC first (Architecture, for "factory"), then CLD (Cloud, for "pollution") as Secondary Content. Lastly, if the client says, "Smoke coming from a factory," the content scoring would be CLD first (as it was verbalized first), followed by ARC.

Special attention must be paid to cases when, for example, the client draws a coat and in the Picture Gallery phase verbalizes an abstract interpretation such as "Winter." In cases like this, the content scoring would be ABS/OBJ: "Winter" is coded as Abstract (ABS) content and Object (OBJ) captures that a "coat" is considered an object.

It is strongly recommended that assessors not focus on excessive scoring of Secondary Contents. In general, Secondary Contents should only be scored when the client stresses the importance of several elements.

Frequency

Wartegg drawings are also scored according to the statistical frequency of similar responses in the normative sample. Frequency scoring falls on a spectrum with high and low frequency responses denoted respectively as: "Popular" responses (i.e., drawings that are quite frequent) and "Original" responses (i.e., drawings that are rarely found).

Most responses fall somewhere between Popular [P] and Original [O] responses and as a result, no Frequency scoring is attributed to these responses; that is, they are neither frequent (Popular) nor infrequent (Original). Additionally, there are categories for somewhat less common Popular responses, referred to as "Semi-Popular" responses and indicated by "(P)," as well as slightly more common Original responses, referred to as "Semi-Original" and indicated by "(O)." It should be noted that both Popular and Original responses may not be scored in the same box. Additionally, as these scores are derived from statistical frequency, Popular and Original responses may not be scored in the case of the Reversed Box special score (as this special score occurs too rarely to calculate statistical frequencies).

Popular responses, "P," are found in more than 18% of cases; Semi-Popular responses, "(P)" are found in 10% to 17.9% of cases. To be scored as a Popular or Semi-Popular response, a drawing must meet two criteria: 1) Reach statistical frequency described above (and referenced in Tables F.13 and F.14, presented in Appendix F); and 2) Integrate the stimulus into the Popular or Semi-Popular Content. For example, in Box 8, a human face is generally scored as a Popular response because this content occurs in 21% of responses; however, to be scored Popular, the stimulus mark must be incorporated into the drawing as the dome of the head or face (as this is the manner in which it is frequently depicted). If, for example, the mark is instead utilized as a "frowning mouth" (part of a larger face), this would not correctly incorporate the mark, and would therefore not be scored as Popular.

Original responses, "O," are found in less than 1% of cases; Semi-Original responses, "(O)," are found in 1% to 3% of cases. While it is possible to provide an exhaustive list of Popular and Semi-Popular responses, it is not possible to create a list of Original and Semi-Original responses, given their unique nature and statistical infrequency. Only experience and extensive practice administering the test allow the assessor to utilize the "O" and "(O)" scoring category. Until such experience is obtained, clinicians are encouraged to consult with more experienced clinicians prior to coding O or (O).

Table F.14 Popular Responses in Italy (2005): Adult					
Male Adult (18+ years)			Female Adult (18+ years)		
Box 1	Human being (whole or face)	(P)		Flower	P
				Human being (whole or face)	(P)
Box 2	Human being (whole or face)	P		Human being (whole or face)	P
	Animal	(P)		Animal	(P)

For each box, Popular and Semi-Popular contents are indicated by the abbreviations P [Popular] and (P) [Semi-Popular]. For example, in Box 1 (the top row of the table), human beings (either in whole form or just a face) are considered Semi-Popular for both males (left-hand column) and females (right-hand column). Additionally, flowers are noted as Popular content for females only.

In Box 2, human beings (again, either in whole form or just a face) are Popular responses for both males and females, whereas animal content is considered Semi-Popular for both males and females.

FIGURE 5.2 Guidelines for Use of CWS Frequency Tables.

Figure 5.2 demonstrates how to interpret CWS Frequency Tables, presenting a sample from Table F.14, found in Appendix F.

For scoring purposes, Popular and Semi-Popular response tables, by box, are provided in Appendix F. Table F.13 lists Popular and Semi-Popular responses for children and adolescents. Table F.14 lists Popular and Semi-Popular responses for adults, by gender. Guidelines for use of CWS Frequency tables are provided in Figure 5.2.

Special Scores (SS)

Several special occurrences can happen while administering the Wartegg. These phenomena are accounted for in the scoring system by assigning a class of scores known as Special Scores. Special Scores are noted for each box on the test, when they occur. It is possible for a box to have no Special Scores. Conversely, it is possible to score several Special Scores within the same box. It should be noted that the same Special Score may only be scored once per box. That is, should a client's drawing extend beyond the borders of the box on every side (seemingly producing four Crossed Border special scores), only one CB may be assigned to that box.

The two most common categories of Special Scores relate to graphic qualities of the actual drawings produced by the client: Anxiety Stroke (AS) and Crossed Border (CB).

- *Anxiety Stroke (AS)*: Related to the graphic quality of the response, AS is scored when the response entirely or partially consists of areas that are emphasized with deliberately doubled or shaded pencil strokes, including even minimally darkened areas of the drawing, thickened lines, shading, and shadows that are drawn. This special score does not apply to adopting a single heavy line.
- *Crossed Border (CB)*: CB is scored when the client's drawing crosses over or touches the inside black border, or edge, of the box. Sometimes this is very evident, such as when the drawing literally enters into part of a neighboring box. In other cases, the thick black border is only barely touched. The decision whether or not to assign a CB score can easily be made by closely examining the Wartegg form sideways in good light. While consistency in scoring requires that even minimal border crossing (or part of the drawing simply touching the edge of the thick black border) be notated as CB, such slight CB scores are interpreted in a different manner (addressed in Chapter 7) than more obvious or dramatic border crosses.

  Specific rules regarding the scoring of Crossed Border are considered in relationship to Box 3. That is, if a Wartegg protocol contains *only a single Crossed Border* at the bottom of Box 3, CB will *not* be scored. This rule takes into account that Box 3 is the only box in which the stimulus touches the edge of the box, and therefore if the client mimics the stimulus in this box (but only this box) and touches the edge of the box, no CB is scored. However, if the client concurrently produces a Crossed Border response in any other box in the protocol, the CB for Box 3 will be subsequently coded. Similarly, if the client crosses the right, left, or top border in Box 3, this is scored as a Crossed Border.

Additional Special Scores scored in the CWS, listed here in alphabetical order, include:

- *Arbitrary Performance (AP)*: This special score applies to drawings that show a degree of arbitrariness, inadequacy, dissonance, or randomness. This can be evident in the drawing's position in space, the graphic quality of the drawing itself, or through unusual verbalizations. (In this last case, the AP score is similar to a FABCOM code in the Rorschach.) An example of an AP manifested in a client's verbalization would include: In Box 4 the client uses the mark as a window in a house, something that is frequently drawn. However, in the Picture Gallery phase, the client verbalizes: "A house where someone recently died and the black window was left open to let out the filth that accumulated over the years." An example of a graphic, non-verbal AP could include: In Box 6, the client uses both marks to draw a "table and chair," but the table is drawn from an overhead perspective while the chair is drawn from the side. Given the complexity of coding AP, several "subtypes" have been identified to guide review of protocols and assist with scoring:

Subtypes of Arbitrary Performance (AP)

Arbitrary Performance (AP)—Based on Graphic Nature of Drawing

1. Different perspectives are used for different elements within the same drawing.

   Examples:

   > *Box 6*: The facade of a building is drawn using one mark; the other mark is used to draw a building as if seen from an aerial view;
   >
   > *Box 4*: A house, with walls drawn from different points of view;
   >
   > *All boxes*: All eight boxes are joined together to be "a window" but several boxes are disproportionate with the perspective that could be seen from a single window.

2. The drawing shows incongruence with the laws of the physical world.

   Examples:

   > *Box 5*: A tilted wine glass, but the client does not comment on this;
   >
   > *Box 6*: House and sun, with the sun drawn in the lower right corner;
   >
   > *Box 4*: Flower growing upside down losing petals;
   >
   > *Box 5*: Slanted drawing of a room with a bed, a rug, and a mirror.

3. Strange representations of familiar objects.

   Examples:

   > *Box 1*: A clock with 4 hands;
   >
   > *Box 2*: A face with eyes drawn below the mouth;
   >
   > *Box 8*: The sun is drawn and shaded black.

4. Multiple objects are represented with no conceptual connection (in the absence of special score Missing Union).

   Example:

   > *Box 7*: A necklace, a mirror, a hair comb, and a pair of eyeglasses all drawn in the box together without a meaningful explanation.

Arbitrary Performance (AP)—Based on Client's Verbalizations

1. The client describes imagined elements not justified by the drawing itself.

   Examples:

   > *Box 4*: "An apartment building that allows pets and the black door is so cats can go outside and watch the clouds."
   >
   > *Boxes 6 + 7* (combined into one drawing): "Answer machine 5000—you put in the question and the answer comes out."

Box 5: A syringe, "A magic potion that you inject and become a spider for a day."

2. Familiar objects in impossible or implausible relationships.

   Examples:

   Box 1: "An eye watching other eyes."

   Box 6: "Two cars talking to each other."

   Box 4: "A turkey eating Pilgrim pie."

3. Verbalizations that don't fit with the picture the client drew.

   Example:

   Box 7: (a flower), "The pain of life."

4. Tangential, and off-topic verbalizations.

   Example:

   Box 7: "A car, the car I drove to California with friends when I was 18 and I met a beautiful girl who I stayed with for 2 days. She had red hair and made really wonderful lasagna that I can still remember to this day. Boy, that lasagna was delicious."

5. Unreal or bizarre drawings.

   Example:

   Box 8: "A princess that is talking with death."

Note: In some cases, a drawing assigned an Arbitrary Performance (AP) score can also be scored as Inadequate Integration (II, see below). An example of this could include: In Box 4, "a night scene with the sun, moon and stars" (AP is scored because there is no sun at night; also II is scored because the sun does not resemble a black square).

- *Contamination (CO)*: Contamination is usually scored in two circumstances:

  1) *When a client draws two things that are interwoven or overlapping.* For example: "a man with a wolf's head," "a dog with wings"; or
  2) *When part of the drawing holds two different meanings at the same time (and is verbalized as such)*. For example, in Box 5, the two marks are simultaneously "the letter T for Thomas and a microphone."

  Half-human and half-animal mythological figures, coats of arms, and heraldic badges are also considered CO, but are viewed as much less pathological than the CO examples mentioned above. In general, the more incompatible the joined contaminated elements, the more disturbed or pathological the interpretation of the CO score.

- *Disproportion (DS)*: The DS response includes notably disproportionate elements within the same box. For example, the dot in Box 1 is the head of a man that takes up the entire bottom half of the box.

- *Global Rejection (GR)*: GR is scored when the client does not draw anything in one or more boxes. This is the most blatant expression of a psychological "shock" and is therefore very valuable diagnostically. Additional guidelines for scoring Boxes in which a Global or Partial rejection have occurred are provided at the end of this section.
- *Incomplete Drawing (ID)*: ID is scored when a drawing is missing important parts, is unfinished or left incomplete, or only the outline of a figure was drawn without internal details (i.e., the outline of a person missing all identifying features). For example, an ID would be scored when a face is missing important elements, such as eyes or a mouth. Similarly, in Box 5, an unfinished arrow (that is, an arrow where the marks have not been connected, and therefore part of the shaft is missing) would be assigned an ID special score. In cases where especially significant or important components of a drawing are missing, Arbitrary Performance (AP) may also be scored to capture the absurdity, violation of reality, or implausibility of the drawing. The older and more educated the client, the more diagnostically relevant the ID special score becomes.
- *Inadequate Integration (II)*: II is scored when the stimulus in the box is included in the drawing in an inadequate manner, which contradicts reality. In viewing these pictures, the observer will have the impression that the stimulus has been "forced" into the client's drawing. For example, the mark in Box 4 (a small black square), is used as a bird's eye (without being modified in any way); or the mark in Box 4 is the center of a flower. For adults, this special score is always associated with a FQ of 0.5.
- *Interpreted Stimulus (IS)*: IS is scored when, in the Picture Gallery phase, the client attributes meaning to the mark(s) in a box, without having drawn anything. For example, Box 4 is "a cube," or Box 2 is "an eyebrow."
- *Morbid Contents (MR)*: The Morbid special score in the CWS is similar to the Morbid special score in both the Rorschach Comprehensive System (Exner, 1997, 2003) and the Rorschach-Performance Assessment System (R-PAS; Meyer, Viglione, Mihura, Erard, & Erdberg, 2011). Specifically, as in these other systems, this score captures two distinct response phenomena: 1) When the client draws or verbalizes objects, people, or situations that are objectively damaged, abnormal, destroyed, deteriorated, or decomposing (often containing terms including, "broken," "ruined," "dead," "sick," "diseased," "mutated," "disabled," and/or "misshapen"; and 2) Indications of sadness, pain, distress, dysphoric mood or overt depression, gloominess, pessimism, or hopelessness. It should be noted that MR is not scored for aggressive or angry content. Further, caution should be made in assigning the special score MR in response to a client's negative commentary regarding their drawings or drawing ability (e.g., "I didn't draw that well," "That doesn't look right," or "The way I drew it looks deformed.") In these cases,

the special score Self-Criticism (SC) is assigned, whereas MR is not. Lastly, the morbidity of the drawing must be clearly verbalized; that is, clinicians must avoid interpreting drawings based upon visual characteristics (for example, a sad face verbalized as "a face" would not be assigned a MR special score, due to lack of verbalization of sadness or dysphoria).

- *Missing Union (MU)*: The MU Special Score can occur in Complex Boxes only, generally in Boxes 5 and 6, and sometimes in Box 3. (Although it is theoretically possible to have an MU in Box 7, it is extremely rare.) MU is scored when the client uses the marks as part of his/her drawing but does not conceptually connect the separate elements of the marks. For example, in Box 5, one stimulus is "a matchbox" and the other is "a nail"; or in Box 3, the shortest mark on the left is "a flower," the second, medium height mark is "a street lamp," and the third, tallest mark is "a sword."
- *Opposite Direction (OD)*: This special score only applies to Boxes 3 and 5. It is scored when the client draws something *opposite or contrary* to that suggested by the box's Evocative Character.

    Box 3: Recall that in Box 3, an accurate (*not* OD) drawing would include increased vertical direction from the lower left-hand corner to the upper right-hand corner (such as a stairway going up). In the case of an OD, the client might draw something that *emphasizes energy going down toward the lower left corner of the box* (such as a child's slide facing left). Another OD example in Box 3 includes a car on a street that slants upward toward the top right corner, but the car itself is pointing downward, toward the bottom left corner.

    Box 5: Examples of accurate (*non*-OD) drawings in Box 5 include those that "continue" the lower left-hand mark so that it "goes past the obstacle" of the more central, perpendicular mark (such as a fork with the tines going up toward the upper right-hand corner of the box, or a bow and arrow where the tip of the arrow is pointed toward the upper right-hand corner). An example of a Box 5 OD is a drawing in which the client draws a syringe with the needle *pointing downward toward the bottom left corner*, or where the client draws a person facing the left side of the box, pushing a mop in that same direction. Due to the frequency in which it occurs, one specific drawing—a steering wheel with a driver or cyclist on a bicycle or motorcycle—will not be scored OD, even though it seems to fulfill OD scoring criteria.

- *Personalized Answer (PA)*: PA is scored for responses in which the client introduces highly personal elements about his/her life, either while drawing or while describing the drawing. For example, "This is a drawing of me" or "My mom has a necklace like this one I just drew." Of note, comments such as, "I can't draw" or "Drawing was never my thing" are not scored as Personalized Answers (PA), but instead as Self-Criticism (SC).

- *Partial Rejection (PR)*: PR is scored in two circumstances:

  1) When the client draws something in a given box, but essentially ignores the stimulus and does not incorporate it into his/her drawing or in the Picture Gallery verbalization. For example, in Box 2 the client draws "a dog" in the lower half of the box, without including the curved stimulus in any way.
  2) The client draws something that graphically includes the stimulus, but states that he/she did not draw anything. For example, the client includes the mark in his/her drawing, but does not attribute any meaning to it.

  Additional guidelines for scoring Boxes in which a Global or Partial Rejection have occurred are provided at the end of this section.

- *Perseveration (PP)*: PP is scored when the same content appears in two or more boxes. An example of PP scoring is when the client draws a horse in Boxes 1 and 2. In assigning a PP score, the assessor must take into account the frequency (Popularity) of the contents. *PP does NOT apply for Popular or frequently drawn content*. For example, "Human faces" are Popular, or Semi-Popular, in Boxes 1, 2, and 8; therefore, drawings of faces in all three boxes would *not* be considered or scored as PP. This guideline also applies for drawings of "buildings or constructions" that are common in Boxes 3, 4, and 6 and geometric figures drawn in Boxes 4, 5, 6, 7, and 8. However, if a response is considered Popular for Box 1, but is not considered Popular for Box 8, and the same response is drawn in both of those boxes, PP is scored in Box 8 (where it is *not* Popular or Semi-Popular).

  Perseveration is scored in the order in which it occurs, according to the Order of Sequence. PP is not coded in the first instance of a repeated content, but is coded on all subsequent iterations (according to the rules above).

- *Reversed Box (RB)*: The RB special score is assigned only when the drawing produced is made and/or intended to be viewed with the Client WDCT Form turned upside down or sideways. For example, in Box 8, the client draws a face using the stimulus at the top as a smiling mouth and adds in eyes at the bottom. Given this drawing, the expectation is that the face will be viewed correctly by rotating the Client WDCT Form 180 degrees, and RB is coded. The same is true if the client describes the drawing, during the Picture Gallery, as "an upside-down smiley face."

  If the client turns the paper to be comfortable while drawing, but the drawing itself is accurately viewed with the Client WDCT Form in the expected ("right-side up") orientation, then an RB score would *not* be assigned.

- *Self-Criticism (SC)*: SC is scored when, at any point in the Wartegg administration, the client *spontaneously* expresses his/her inability to draw or finish the task, saying things such as, "Is this any good?," "I don't have much imagination," "I'm a total disaster at this, aren't I?" or other similar self-critical expressions. SC is scored whenever the client criticizes himself/herself, his or her ability to draw, and/or the drawings produced. Only spontaneous verbalizations are scored SC; that is, if a client self-criticizes in response to the examiner's questions, or during the Choice of Drawings and Boxes, SC is not scored.

- *Stimulus Repetition (SR)*: SR is scored when the client simply re-draws or copies (one or more times) the stimulus provided in the box and gives no meaning to the drawing. For example, in Box 2, the stimulus is repeated many times and the client verbalizes, "Lots of quotation marks," "I just copied the mark that's in the box a bunch of times," or "I don't know, just something random." However, SR is *not* scored if the client re-draws the mark many times but ascribes meaning to the drawings. For example, he/she makes many curved marks in Box 2, and verbalizes, "Swallows," "Seagulls," or "A flock of flying birds." Another *non*-SR response would include, in Box 7, when the small dots of the stimulus are repeated, and the client verbalizes "a necklace."
- *Transparency (TR)*: TR is scored when the drawing includes visible elements that would not be visible in reality. Examples include a clothed human figure with his heart showing through his clothing; or, in Box 6, the client draws a house with an interior visible through the exterior walls. Certain Popular drawings can be exceptions to this scoring guideline. For example, in Box 5, the two marks are often drawn to be a steering wheel as part of a side view of the inside of the car. Because of its high frequency, this response is *not* scored for transparency and has lower psychodiagnostic value.

Other Noted Phenomena

In addition to the Special Scores that are included as part of the formal scoring process, a few less common phenomena must also be noted in the clinician's interpretive notes while scoring. The majority of these phenomena are noted by box, whereas several are attributed to the overall CWS protocol.

Phenomena Noted by Box

- *Blackening (BK)*: Blackening is noted when the client obscures or "blackens" the stimulus mark in a box completely without attributing meaning to the drawing.
- *Color Projection (CP)*: Color Projection is a rare noted phenomenon in which the client attributes color qualities to the drawing based on the client verbalizations. For example, "A painting with colorful fall leaves," or "A red ladybug." Frequently drawings (i.e., sun, rainbow, tree) are not considered Color Projections unless color is specifically verbalized and emphasized by the client (i.e., "The sun shining yellow rays").

- *Conjoined Boxes (CJ)*: This is an infrequent occurrence that happens when the client graphically joins two or more boxes within the same drawing. Conjoined Boxes are almost always also Crossed Border (CB) drawings; however, sometimes only the verbalized meaning joins the boxes.
    - *An example of Conjoined Boxes with accompanying CB special scores*: The client connects Box 4 and Box 8 by drawing a man's face; the eyes are in Box 4 and the mouth curves downward in Box 8. The outline of the face starts in Box 4 and continues in Box 8.
    - *An example of Conjoined Boxes without a CB score:* in Box 2, the client draws a monster moving toward Box 3; in Box 3, the client draws the scared spectators that see the monster coming out of the movie theater in Box 2.
- *Disproportion between Boxes (DB)*: For example, in a Wartegg protocol of small/medium size drawings, one drawing completely fills an entire box.
- *Encapsulation (EN)*: Encapsulation is noted when the client circles or encloses the stimulus marks without attributing meaning to the drawing.
- *Human Content Negation (HN)*: Human Content Negation is noted when the client depicts one or more human contents without verbalizing the presence of these human contents in the picture gallery. For example, a client draws two people flying a kite and states, "A kite flying in the wind."
- *Improper Description (IP)*: Improper Description is noted when during the Picture Gallery the client gives an incorrect or inaccurate description of the completed drawing in a box (for example, a client draws a rectangle and states, "It's a triangle").
- *"Or" Answer (OA)*: "Or" Answers are noted when during the Picture Gallery the client points out at least two meanings for the same drawing, often separated by the word "or." For example, the client may state, "I drew a cat OR a tiger." (Scoring note: When this occurs, whichever content the client verbalizes *first* is the content that is scored.)
- *Perspective Response (PS)*: Perspective Responses are noted when the client's drawing is characterized by a perspective view, with strong emphasis on depth. For example, a client depicts a road disappearing into the distance (Box 1) or a long hallway (Box 4). A significant sense of perspective (similar to "Vista" responses on the Rorschach) is required.

Phenomena Noted for Overall Protocol

Two additional tendencies are noted in reference to the overall client protocol (and are not noted in each box). These descriptors capture the client's overall approach to the task. That is, when the majority of client drawings are either overly large or small, the protocol is described as:

- *Big Drawing (BD)*: Big Drawing is noted for the protocol when the majority of drawings take up all or most of the box. This often occurs in conjunction with Crossed Border (CB).
- *Small Drawing (SD)*: Small Drawing is noted for the protocol when the majority of drawings are extremely tiny, almost microscopic; the area used for drawings are minimal.

Scoring tables for Special Scores and Other Noted Phenomena are provided in Appendix F (Table F.15).

BOX 5.3 ADDITIONAL SCORING GUIDELINES FOR BOXES CONTAINING GLOBAL OR PARTIAL REJECTIONS

The following are additional guidelines for accurate scoring of responses containing GR and PR special scores. Readers should carefully review this information and refer back to previous sections in this chapter.

Responses Containing Global Rejections

Global Rejections (GR) are the most blatant indication of shock or conflict in the psychic area in which they occur. When a Global Rejection occurs in a given box, holding in mind the negative implications of this special score, Evocative Character (EC), Affective Quality (AQ), and Form Quality (FQ) are all scored as equal to 0. When scoring by hand, a question mark ("?") is generally entered into the Content field. Of course, GR is noted as a Special Score. When utilizing the CWS Clinical Software package, the clinician indicates that a Global Rejection has occurred, and these scoring decisions are thereafter automatically applied.

Responses Containing Partial Rejections

As noted earlier in this chapter, generally two types of Partial Rejections may occur in a protocol. Each is discussed below.

1) Client draws something in the box, but does not include the stimulus as part of the drawing

In this case, the general rules of scoring are followed for the box. That is, Evocative Character, Affective Quality, Form Quality, Content, Frequency, and Movement are scored based upon what the client drew.

Example: In Box 2, the client draws a human figure (that does not integrate the mark). When questioned during administration as to what the mark represents, the client indicates, "I didn't use it." This is a Partial Rejection. Scoring proceeds according to guidelines, with EC = 1 (as a human figure meets EC criteria in Box 2), AQ = 1 (again, as human figures are considered positive unless verbalized otherwise), and FQ = 1 (assuming the figure is recognizable and well drawn). Content would be scored as H. Given that the mark was not incorporated into the drawing, it is unlikely that this human figure would be considered Popular. PR would be noted as a special score.

2) Client draws an abstract design that incorporates the mark, but is not given specific meaning.

Cases like this are generally accompanied by Picture Gallery verbalizations including, "I don't know," "an abstract drawing," "modern art," or "just a design." When questioned as to what the mark represents, the client typically responds, "Nothing" or "I don't know." In this case, specific scoring rules are followed: EC = 0.5, AQ = 0.5, FQ = 0, and Content = SIG. PR is scored as a special score.

Differences between Abstract (ABS) Drawings and Partial Rejections (PR)

In the case of #2 above, some confusion may occur regarding the difference between abstract drawings (requiring an ABS content code) and Partial Rejections (requiring a PR special score). To differentiate between these types of responses, the precise verbalization of the client must be considered. True abstract responses (scored as ABS) generally utilize representational language, including descriptors such as, "Spring" or "Sadness" (in which case a flower or a dark room is drawn, respectively). In these cases, a Partial Rejection is typically not scored; however, the clinician is reminded to ask, "But what exactly did you draw?" to understand the graphic representation and ensure accurate scoring.

Movement (M)

Movement (M) is scored in drawings that depict human figures, animals, or objects in overt motion, as well as when moving in a more subtle way. Movement scores are extremely important and are generally scored *only when the client explicitly verbalizes movement in the Picture Gallery phase*. For example, movement *is* scored for the verbalization, "A man walking," but it *is not* scored for those cases in which the client simply says "A man," even if the movement in the drawing seems obvious to the assessor.

Movement is also scored when the description verbalized by the client during the Picture Gallery *implicitly* indicates movement (for example, "a basketball player," "a dancer," "a paratrooper," "a motorcyclist," "sadness" as the title for a face, "a trip to the moon" for a rocket ship, or "a volcano eruption" for a mountain).

TABLE 5.3 Implicit Movement Scoring—Inanimate Objects Coded as in Motion

Astronomical objects in motion (meteor, comet); Solar System (*if drawn with rings representing orbit*)
Balloon (child's or hot air balloon)
Candle or Torch (*if flame is drawn*)
Carnival, Mardi Gras
Circus
Confetti
Escalator
Flag (*if drawn waving*)
Flames, Fire, Fireworks
Fountain
Hourglass
Kite
Natural elements (lightening, rain, snow blizzard, wind, avalanche)
Pinwheel
Roller coaster (if car is drawn on track)
Soap bubbles
Sunrise, Sunset, Solar eclipse
Top (toy)
Water elements (ocean, waves, ripples in water, typhoon, waterfall, whirlpool, river)
Windmill

Note: Movement is scored as inanimate (MI) for these objects.

There are also specific object contents that clearly imply movement by definition, and *are* therefore scored for movement in almost all cases. These objects are listed in Table 5.3.

Based on their diagnostic value, movement responses are divided into two categories: *Primary* movement and *Secondary* movement. Guidelines for scoring movement are provided in Figure 5.3.

Primary Movement (M)

Primary Movement includes only the category of response representing human movement. All M responses must include coding for:

a) The *gender* of the person represented as being in movement (recorded on the Examiner Administration Form in the designated box next to M).

- **m** = male
- **f** = female
- **i** = indeterminate, when client does not know or report the person's gender

Scoring of movement is completed, by box, using three columns on the CWS Scoring Form (pictured below, left). Guidelines for use of these columns in scoring are provided below.

M/m		
M/m	g	d

Column 1: M/m
Here, the clinician enters "M" if Primary Movement (i.e., Human) is scored for the box in question. Lowercase "m" refers to Secondary Movement. Should Secondary Movement be present, the clinician enters the *type* of Secondary Movement (i.e., FE, FM, or MI) in the column labeled M/m. (The clinician does not need to enter "m" as FE, FM, and MI indicate the presence of Secondary Movement.)

Column 1: g
For Primary Movement (M) responses, the clinician enters the *gender* of the human figure (i.e., "m" for male, "f" for female, or "i" for indeterminate).

Column 3: d
For both Primary (M) and Secondary (FE, FM, or MI) Movement responses, the clinician enters the *direction* of movement in this column (i.e., "a" for active, "b" for blocked, "d" for double, "p" for passive, "r" for rotary, or "i" for indeterminate).

FIGURE 5.3 Guidelines for the Scoring of Movement.

Figure 5.3 provides instructions for the 3-column process of scoring both Primary and Secondary Movement according to CWS guidelines.

b) The *direction* of movement:

- **Ma** = active movement. Examples include:
  - "two men lifting something"
  - "two women dancing"
  - "a girl playing with her dog."
- **Mp** = passive movement. Examples include:
  - "two people laying down"
  - "a man who's sleeping"
  - "a seated woman."
- **Mb** = blocked movement. Examples include:
  - "two people fighting over something, both pulling on it"
  - "people playing tug-of-war"
  - "two wrestlers pushing on each other."
- **Md** = double movement. Examples include:
  - "two men squatting down then standing up"
  - "kids on a teeter-totter"
  - "a man doing sit-ups."
- **Mr** = rotary movement. Examples include:
  - "two friends on a merry-go-round"

– "a ballerina doing pirouettes"
– "children playing ring-around-the-rosy."

- **Mi** = indeterminate movement. Examples include:
  – "something moving."

When neither the gender of the person, nor the direction of the movement can be determined, the response is scored as **Mii** (indeterminate gender, indeterminate movement direction).

Secondary Movement (m)

Secondary Movement is divided into three separate categories:

- **FM** = Animal Movement. Examples include: dogs running, climbing monkeys, flying birds;
- **MI** = Movement of inanimate objects. Examples include: flags waving, explosions, fireworks, racing cars, flowing rivers, spraying fountains;
- **FE** = Facial Expressions of Humans or Animals. Examples include: happy or sad faces, fierce or scared animal faces.

A Note about Facial Expression: Movement scores are based upon client verbalizations, as mentioned above. In the case of facial expressions, if the client only draws a face, but verbalizes "A smiling lady," the response is scored as Mfa (human movement, female/active); however, if the client verbalizes, "A smiling face," the response is scored as FE (Secondary facial expression, active).

With Secondary Movement responses, gender is not scored. Only the direction of the movement is recorded:

Active

- **FMa** = active animal movement. Examples include:
  – "fighting tigers"
  – "the head of a growling wolf."
- **MIa** = active inanimate movement. Examples include:
  – "a volcano erupting"
  – "a shooting star."
- **FEa** = active facial expression. Examples include:
  – "a smiling baby face"
  – "an angry face."

Passive

- **FMp** = passive animal movement. Examples include:
  - "two sleeping elephants"
  - "a cow standing in a field."
- **MIp** = passive inanimate movement. Examples include:
  - "a ball rolling down hill"
  - "a waterfall"
  - "a parachute" (assuming the parachutist is not drawn or mentioned).
- **FEp** = passive facial expression. Examples include:
  - "a bored face"
  - "the face of someone crying."

Blocked

- **FMb** = blocked animal movement. Examples include:
  - "two dogs pulling on a bone."
- **MIb** = blocked inanimate movement. Examples include:
  - "a hot air balloon that is tied-down."
- **FEb** = blocked facial expression. Examples include:
  - "an embarrassed face"
  - "a perplexed face"
  - "a woman's face. The face indicates that she's trying to not show her emotions."

Double

- **FMd** = double animal movement. Examples include:
  - "a frog sitting on a lily pad or maybe he's about to jump onto another lily pad."
- **MId** = double inanimate movement. Examples include:
  - "a plane taking off and landing."
- **FEd** = double facial expression. Examples include:
  - "a face that might be about to laugh or cry."

A Note about Double Movement: A double movement response can happen in two different ways. The first is when the movement goes "back and forth," essentially "negating" itself (e.g., "a tiger walking back and forth in the zoo."). A double movement response can also occur when a client uses the word "or" in his/her verbalization, suggesting that the action is both happening *and* not happening, a diagnostic indication of indecision. In this case, double movement "or" responses are clinically important and *unlike the use of "or" for Contents*, are recorded as such.

Rotary

- **FMr** = rotary animal movement. Examples include:
  - "a dog chasing his tail in a circle."
- **MIr** = rotary inanimate movement. Examples include:
  - "a spinning top."
- **FEr** = rotary facial expression is never scored, as it does not exist.

It is important to note that *only one movement response can be scored for each box*. When multiple movements are depicted, the movement with higher diagnostic value is scored. Thus, in the example, "A man driving a car," Primary Movement (M) is scored rather than Inanimate Movement (MI). In all cases, due to higher diagnostic value, M responses take priority over other responses (FE, FM, or MI).

Drawings in which the client attributes movement to human or animal "stand-ins" or replicas are very rare, but extremely meaningful from a psychodiagnostic point of view. This relates only to the four contents categories, AS, ADS, HS, and HDS. Examples of this rare type of movement include: "The face of a sad doll," "A painting of a galloping horse," or "A robot walking around." These particular cases are not scored as overt movement, but rather as a "tendency" toward movement, marked with the symbol "→". Therefore, "The face of a sad doll" would be scored "→FE"; "A painting of a galloping horse" would be scored "→FM"; and "A robot walking around" would be scored "→M."

While noted "tendencies" are not included in formal scoring, clinicians should make note of these phenomena in the Notes section of the CWS Administration, Scoring, and Computation Form. Tendencies of this type (as well as in other cases; for example, when a response is not formally coded for a specific Special Score, although there are clear indications, albeit subthreshold, of characteristics of that Special Score) are interpretively important, and are considered during interpretation and conceptualization (see Chapters 7 and 8).

Scoring tables for Movement are provided in Appendix F (Table F.16).

Impulse Response (IR)

The category of *Impulse Response* scores is based in Levine and Spivack's (1964) work on the Repression Index of the Rorschach Inkblot Test. According to these authors:

> Any direct reference to sexuality, hostility, anality or dependency in a response reflects lessened repressive functioning. It is assumed that repressions are maintained to keep just such impulse derivates from consciousness. The presence of such ideation in the Rorschach thus implies a lessening of repressive functioning. This lessening of repressive functioning may take

> place when the individual accepts and incorporates the idea, when there is a defensive failure, or when there is isolation of the thought from its affect. Because repressive defenses are generally directed against such direct representation, the appearance of impulse material "in the raw" is weighted in the scoring system.
>
> (p. 25)

Levine and Spivack's statement can be generalized to responses provided in the context of other assessment measures with high psychodynamic meaning. In the context of the CWS, therefore, Impulse Responses can be considered indicative of highly individualized elements that reveal specific dynamics, as well as conflicting areas or domains present in the client. Or, in more closely psychoanalytic terms, Impulse Reponses can indicate the presence of fixations at certain stages of psychoaffective development, and therefore constitute a unique source of information based in the psychoanalytic model of personality.

In the CWS, the following categories of Impulse Responses (IR) are scored:

- *Or (Oral Impulse Response)*: Or IR are scored for all direct and/or indirect references to food and nutrition, sources of food, objects containing food, organs connected with food, and situations related to food. In considering oral Impulse Responses, we must keep in mind the classical distinction between oral-receptive and oral-aggressive responses (Schafer, 1954). That is, we can identify two main types of oral Impulse Responses—oral-receptive (for example, "someone who is eating") and oral-aggressive (for example, "the mouth of a shark")—each with different implications for interpretation.
- *An (Anal Impulse Response)*: An IR is scored for all direct and/or indirect references to excretory functions of the human and animal body, but also associated details such as rashes, mud, diapers, people or animals seen from behind, puddles, dirt, trash, dirty objects or unintentional messes (for example, paint splotches, a spot of sauce, an oil stain), sewer, volcano, gas, etc.
- *Ph (Phallic Impulse Response)*: Ph IR is scored for all direct references to male or female sexual organs (human or animal), as well as references to human and/or animal sexuality.

The presence of Impulse Responses (Oral, Anal, Phallic), while not considered in the calculations discussed in Chapter 6, may be addressed in both content analysis and report writing. This suggests that assessors should mark the presence or absence of Impulse Responses on the Examiner Administration Form (see Chapter 3, Figure 3.3). Later, in the notes and on the Computation Form (see Chapter 6, Figure 6.7), the assessor will specify the type of Impulse Response (Oral, Anal, Phallic) and the content category to which it belongs. For practical and theoretical support, Schafer's (1971) work on the Rorschach is recommend, along with classical psychoanalytic literature.

Scoring tables for Impulse Responses are provided in Appendix F (Table F.17).

Scoring Examples for Drawings with Several Elements

In general, most scores refer to the graphic manner in which the client uses or incorporates the mark into his/her drawing. However, sometimes clients verbalize a box as a scene consisting of several elements. In these cases scoring should be based on *whichever elements the client stresses most in his/her verbalization.*

For example, in Box 7, a client uses the stimulus to draw a side view of a bench and also draws the sun, a tree, and a patch of grass with flowers. Scoring will differ, depending on how the client describes his drawing in the Picture Gallery phase of administration.

If during the Picture Gallery the client says:

1. "A park" (Q. What does the mark represent?) "A bench."

   Scoring: EC = 0 **AQ = 1** FQ = 1 Content = **NAT**

EC	=	0	(*The stimulus was used for the bench, which is not delicate*);
AQ	**=**	**1**	(*"A park" is considered to be pleasant*);
FQ	=	1	(*Assuming the drawing is clear and/or relatively obvious at first glance*);
Content	=		**NAT** (*Nature; The client verbalized "a park," which is associated with Nature*).

2. "A bench"

   Scoring: EC = 0 **AQ = 0.5** FQ = 1 Content = **OBJ**

EC	=	0	(*The stimulus was used for the bench, which is not delicate*);
AQ	**=**	**0.5**	(*"A bench" is a neutral object*);
FQ	=	1	(*Assuming the drawing is clear and/or relatively obvious at first glance*);
Content	=		**OBJ** (*Object; The client verbalized "a bench," which is an Object*).

3. "A sad autumn landscape" (Q. What does the mark represent?) "A bench."

   Scoring: EC = 0 **AQ = 0** FQ = 1 Content = **NAT**

EC	=	0	(*The stimulus was used for the bench, which is not delicate*);
AQ	**=**	**0**	(*"A sad autumn landscape" is affectively unpleasant*);
FQ	=	1	(*Assuming the drawing is clear and/or relatively obvious at first glance*);
Content	=		**NAT** (Nature; The client's words emphasized the landscape, which is associated with Nature).

As this example shows, EC scoring primarily relates to how the client graphically uses the stimulus, while other elements of the scoring (i.e., AQ, Content) may vary depending on the client's verbalizations.

"Give to the ones that have; take from the ones that do not"

This chapter concludes by discussing a fundamental concept of the scoring process. The scoring guidelines explained in this chapter likely seem quite complicated, especially to the first-time reader. In fact, practice and experience will become the reader's best instructors, with both scoring and interpretation becoming progressively easier with time and experience. It is in light of this that the reader must remember this fundamental rule of psychodiagnostic scoring: "*Give to the ones that have; take from the ones that do not.*"

For example, if a client tends to provide movement responses (although the same guideline applies to all scoring categories: Content, Affective Quality, etc.), and the assessor is uncertain whether a response should be coded as M, it is sufficient to look at the rest of the protocol. If the client provided other M responses, this box should be scored as well (i.e., "*Give to the ones that have.*"). To the contrary, if there are no other M responses in the protocol, it would be best not to score in the uncertain box (i.e., "*Take from the ones that do not.*"). Similarly, if while evaluating the AQ of a specific box, the assessor experiences difficulty in deciding between assigning an Affective Quality score of 1 and one of 0.5, he/she must look at what scores the client obtained on the other seven boxes. If scores of 1 prevail, then the assessor should grant a score of 1 on this box as well; otherwise, a score of 0.5 should be assigned.

References

Battaglia, S. (1968). *Grande dizionario della lingua italiana* [Great Dictionary of the Italian language, Vol. V]. Turin: UTET.

Brown, F. (1953). An exploratory study of dynamic factors in the content of the Rorschach protocol. *Journal of Projective Techniques, 17*(3), 251–279.

Devoto, G., & Oli, G. C. (1971). *Dizionario della lingua italiana* [Dictionary of the Italian language]. Florence: Le Monnier.

Exner, J. (2003). *The Rorschach: A comprehensive system. Volume 1: The Rorschach, basic foundations and principles of interpretation.* New York: Wiley & Sons. (1st edition, 1997).

Levine, M., & Spivack, G. (1964). *The Rorschach index of repressive style.* Oxford, UK: Charles C. Thomas.

Meyer, G. J., Viglione, D. J., P., Mihura, J. L., Erard, R. E., & Erdberg (2011). Rorschach Performance Assessment System: Administration, coding, interpretation, and technical manual. Rorschach Performance Assessment System, LLC, P.O. Box 12699, Toledo, OH 43606.

Scarpellini, C. (1962). *Diagnosi di personalità col reattivo di realizzazione grafica* [Diagnosis of personality with the drawing completion test]. Contributi dell'Istituto di Psicologia dell'Università Cattolica del Sacro Cuore [Contributions from the Institute of Psychology of the Catholic University of the Sacred Heart], pp. 1–82.

Schafer, R. (1953). Content analysis in the Rorschach test. *Journal of Projective Techniques, 17*(3), 335–339.

Schafer, R. (1954). *Psychoanalytic interpretation in Rorschach testing: Theory and application.* New York: Grune & Stratton.

Schafer, R. (1971). *L'interpretazione psicoanalitica del Rorschach* [Psychoanalytic interpretation in Rorschach Testing]. Turin: Boringhieri.

6 Computation

In preparing to interpret a CWS protocol, a methodical strategy is recommended to ensure that all available interpretive data are considered. First, procedures known as the Analyses of Sequence 1 and 2 are undertaken, interpreting not only the values assigned to each box, but the sequence order in which the test was completed. These initial analyses form the foundation on which interpretation of a clinical profile is based.

Following completion of the Analyses of Sequence, additional calculations must be performed. These calculations, ratios, and indices guide interpretation and provide a statistical framework for understanding and interpreting client responses. It should be noted, as the Wartegg is a graphic test, along with the scoring elements described below, additional elements that are commonly used to score graphic tests are also used in scoring the WDCT.

To provide examples illustrative of the scoring and calculation process, two cases (complete with scoring and calculations) are provided at the conclusion of this chapter.

Order of Sequence

The WDCT instructions explicitly direct the client to complete the drawings in the eight boxes in whatever order he/she chooses. The assessor must record the client's exact order of sequence on the Examiner Administration Form (see Chapter 3, Figure 3.3).

In both children and adults, the majority of clients complete the WDCT following an individualized Order of Sequence. The remaining subset of individuals follows a logical or methodical Order of Sequence. Of these, four specific recurrent Order of Sequence patterns occur in both clinical practice and research settings. For both adults and children, the most common non-individualized order of sequence is the Numerical Sequence (1–2–3–4–5–6–7–8). In completing the WDCT, approximately 15% of children in the normative population follow this Numerical Sequence. The other three specific patterns occur with lower frequencies: Reversed Sequence (8–7–6–5–4–3–2–1) in approximately .5% of cases; Numerical Circular (1–2–3–4–8–7–6–5) in approximately 3% of cases); and Reversed Circular (8–7–6–5–1–2–3–4) in approximately 1.5% of cases.

In adults, the Numerical Sequence is only produced by 7% of clients, while Reversed Sequence, Numerical Circular, and Reversed Circular patterns are also found, but with much lower frequencies (less than .4% of cases, combined; see Tables B.2 and B.20 in ►Appendix B for more information).

Approximately 80% of children and 92% of adults follow Individualized Orders of Sequence in completing the WDCT. Various studies demonstrate that the WDCT Order of Sequence is a highly personal and individualized "pathway" that can be interpreted for each client. Interpretation of these unique Orders of Sequence is referred to as the Analysis of Sequence, and is divided into two parts.

Analysis of Sequence

Research on the significance of the Order of Sequence has led Wartegg scholars (Crisi, 1998, 2007; Kinget, 1952; Lossen & Schott, 1975; Wartegg, 1953) to examine not only the Order of Sequence of the boxes as a whole, but also the significance of each box's placement within the sequence. Thus, it is possible to analyze the Order of Sequence in great detail. Over the last few years, two complementary sequential analysis techniques have been developed to score the WDCT Order of Sequence, known as Analysis of Sequence 1 and Analysis of Sequence 2.

Analysis of Sequence 1

In discussing the Analysis of Sequence, it is important to clarify the differences in notation between box numbers and position within the Order of Sequence. When Arabic numerals are utilized (i.e., Box 1, Box 2), this will always refer to the specific box as labeled on the WDCT Client Form (i.e., "Box 1" is the box with a dot in the center). When Roman numerals are utilized (i.e., I, II), this will always refer to *position* within the Order of Sequence (i.e., I is the first box completed, VI is the sixth box completed). Therefore, if an individual completes the WDCT with the following sequence: 1, 3, 5, 4, 2, 6, 8, 7, we can denote this as follows: I = 1, II = 3, III = 5, IV = 4, V = 2, VI = 6, VII = 8, and VIII = 7.

The first four boxes completed (I, II, III, and IV) in the Order of Sequence, and particularly in positions I and II, are viewed as representing *choices*. In contrast, boxes completed in the second half of the test (V, VI, VII, and VIII) in the Order of Sequence, and particularly in positions VII and VIII, are viewed as *delays*. That is, these general terms suggest a degree of affinity ("choices") or aversion ("delays") on the part of the individual, as related to the Evocative Character of each box. The terms "choice" and "delay" are used here to indicate affinity of the client to these boxes, but should not be confused with formal box Codes discussed later in the chapter.

Using the Examiner Administration Form, the assessor must first record the client's exact Order of Sequence in completing the drawings (generally in all eight boxes). If the client follows an Individualized Order of Sequence, this will be used to conduct the Analyses of Sequence 1 and 2. Occasionally (see Chapter 3), the assessor may have also needed to complete the Test of Sequence (in those cases where a methodical Order of Sequence is completed by the client), with the resulting sequence used for the Analyses of Sequence 1 and 2 when administered.

Figure 6.1 demonstrates how to begin the Analysis of Sequence 1 by recording an individual Order of Sequence on the Examiner Administration Form. In this example, the client began by drawing Box 6, followed by Box 7, Box 4, and so on. If the Test of Sequence had been administered, results would be indicated here as the client's individualized Order of Sequence.

ANALYSIS OF SEQUENCE 1								
	I	II	III	IV	V	VI	VII	VIII
Order of Sequence	6	7	4	5	8	2	1	3

FIGURE 6.1 Example of Analysis of Sequence 1—Recording the Order of Sequence.
Figure 6.1 provides an example of the first step in completing the Analysis of Sequence 1, recording the Order of Sequence (reflecting the client's Individualized Order of Sequence or the results of the Test of Sequence when applicable).

Following recording of the Order of Sequence (or insertion of the results from the Test of Sequence), the assessor records the Evocative Character and the Affective Quality scores corresponding to each box in the two rows below the Order of Sequence. Therefore, in the example above, if in Box 6 (the first completed box), the client obtained an EC score of 0.5 and an AQ score of 0.5, the scores would be entered as demonstrated in Figure 6.2.

ANALYSIS OF SEQUENCE 1								
	I	II	III	IV	V	VI	VII	VIII
Order of Sequence	6	7	4	5	8	2	1	3
Evocative Character	0.5	0	0	1	1	1	1	0.5
Affective Quality	0.5	0.5	0.5	0.5	0	0	1	0.5

FIGURE 6.2 Example of Analysis of Sequence 1—Recording EC and AQ.
Figure 6.2 continues the example presented in Figure 6.1, demonstrating the second step in completing the Analysis of Sequence 1. Here, the EC and AQ of each box, according to the Order of Sequence, is entered.

Once this procedure has been completed for each box, each drawing can be assigned one of six Codes. Codes are calculated by summing the Evocative Character and Affective Quality for each box, with the resulting values deterring the assigned Code according to the following guidelines:

If the box is completed in the first half of the test (positions I–IV), it is coded as one of the following:

Choice (C): when EC + AQ > 1;

Ambivalent Choice (AC): when EC + AQ = 1;

Negative Compensation (NC): when EC + AQ < 1.

If the box is completed in the second half of the test (Positions V–VIII), it is coded as one of the following:

Delay (D): when EC + AQ < 1;

Ambivalent Delay (AD): when EC + AQ = 1;

Positive Compensation (PC): when EC + AQ > 1.

A Note about Global Rejections (GR): In the event that one or more boxes are scored as a Global Rejection (GR), for Analysis of Sequence purposes, these boxes are coded as Delays. They are reported in the last place(s) in the Order of Sequence on the CWS Scoring Form, and are scored as 0 for Evocative Character (EC), Affective Quality (AQ), and Form Quality (FQ). Conventionally, in the case of two or more Global Rejections, the rejected boxes are listed on the CWS Scoring Form in numerical order. That is, if Boxes 2 and 7 were rejected, they would be listed in positions VII and VIII in the Order of Sequence, in numerical order: 2, 7.

Returning to the above example, Figure 6.3 demonstrates the calculated Code for each of the eight WDCT boxes.

ANALYSIS OF SEQUENCE 1								
	I	II	III	IV	V	VI	VII	VIII
Order of Sequence	6	7	4	5	8	2	1	3
Evocative Character	0.5	0	0	1	1	1	1	0.5
Affective Quality	0.5	0.5	0.5	0.5	0	0	1	0.5
Code	**AC**	**NC**	**NC**	**C**	**AD**	**AD**	**PC**	**AD**

FIGURE 6.3 Example of Analysis of Sequence 1—Calculating Box Codes.

Figure 6.3 continues the example presented previously in Figures 6.1 and 6.2, demonstrating the third step in completing the Analysis of Sequence 1. Here, the evaluative Code for each box is entered, following computational guidelines presented in this chapter.

To complete Analysis of Sequence 1, the client's scores for three other scoring categories are also reported for each box (Form Quality, Affective Stability Index, Impulse Responses), as shown below. To denote the A/F Ratio, the ratio of AQ to FQ for each box is recorded. An example of the completed Analysis of Sequence 1 is provided in Figure 6.4.

ANALYSIS OF SEQUENCE 1								
	I	**II**	**III**	**IV**	**V**	**VI**	**VII**	**VIII**
Order of Sequence	6	7	4	5	8	2	1	3
Evocative Character	0.5	0	0	1	1	1	1	0.5
Affective Quality	0.5	0.5	0.5	0.5	0	0	1	0.5
Code	AC	NC	NC	C	AD	AD	PC	AD
Form Quality	**1**	**1**	**1**	**1**	**1**	**1**	**1**	**0.5**
A/F Ratio	**0.5:1**	**0.5:1**	**0.5:1**	**0.5:1**	**0:1**	**0:1**	**1:1**	**0.5:0.5**
Impulse Response				*				

FIGURE 6.4 Example of Analysis of Sequence 1—Recording FQ, A/F Ratio, and IR.
Figure 6.4 concludes the example presented previously in Figures 6.1, 6.2, and 6.3, demonstrating the final step in completing the Analysis of Sequence 1. Here, the Form Quality, A/F Ratio, and presence of Impulse Responses are recorded for each WDCT box.

Analysis of Sequence 2

As discussed in Chapter 7, clinical experience with the WDCT led to the development of a theoretical model to explain the sequence that clients adopt in completing the boxes. Specifically, clients are expected to complete Boxes 1, 8, 3, and 6 in the first half of the test; the remaining boxes are expected to follow in the second half of the test. This theory has been demonstrated through statistical analyses (see ►Appendix B, Tables B.25 through B.30 for further details).

Based upon these statistical analyses, which confirmed a theoretical sequence model, the WDCT boxes are expected to be completed in the following manner:

Boxes 1–8: *first* and *second* (I, II) positions in the Order of Sequence;
Boxes 3–6: *third* and *fourth* (III, IV) positions in the Order of Sequence;
Boxes 2–4: *fifth* and *sixth* (V, VI) positions in the Order of Sequence;
Boxes 5–7: *seventh* and *eighth* (VII, VIII) positions in the Order of Sequence.

According to this theoretical model, examining how significantly the client's individualized Order of Sequence differs from the model's expected order holds great diagnostic power. To assist in comparing the two, the clinician undertakes the Analysis of Sequence 2, utilizing the model depicted on Figure 6.5, and contained on the CWS Scoring Form. In this diagram, the numbers in parentheses represent the expected theoretical sequence model; that is, it is expected that Boxes 1 and 8 will be completed in the first (I) and second (II) position of the Order of Sequence. As the diagram is read from top to bottom, left to right, Boxes 3 and 6 are expected to be completed in the third (III) and fourth (IV) positions, Boxes 2 and 4 as the fifth (V) and sixth (VI) positions, and Boxes 5 and 7 as the seventh (VII) and last (VIII) positions in the Order of Sequence.

Referring to the example from the Analysis of Sequence 1 above, the assessor enters the relevant information into the Analysis of Sequence 2. Beneath the numbers in parentheses that represent the theoretical sequence model, the

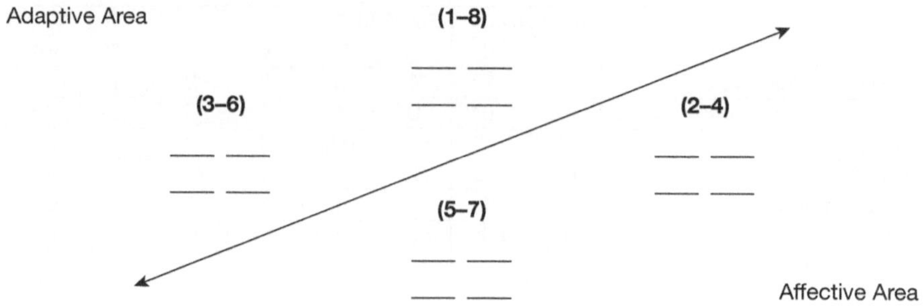

FIGURE 6.5 Example of Analysis of Sequence 2—Theoretical Order of Sequence Diagram.

Figure 6.5 provides a graphic description of the Analysis of Sequence 2, with parenthetically indicated numbers representing expected Order of Sequence according to the theoretically derived statistical model.

assessor enters the Order of Sequence produced by the client. Beneath the client's Order of Sequence, the Code for each box (i.e., C, AC, NC, PC, AD, or D) is recorded. Thus, in this example, the client completed Boxes 6 and 7 as drawings I and II (coded AC and NC, respectively), rather than completing Boxes 1 and 8, as expected. As the second pair (drawings III and IV), the client completed Boxes 4 and 5 (coded NC and C), as compared to the expected theoretical sequence of Boxes 3 and 6. Full results of the Analysis of Sequence are presented in Figure 6.6.

At the end of the process of sequence analyses, the assessor holds a powerful psychodiagnostic tool that is the core interpretive element of the WDCT. For the time being, we can summarize the above by saying that the study of sequence relies on two different types of evaluation. The first type of evaluation focuses on the

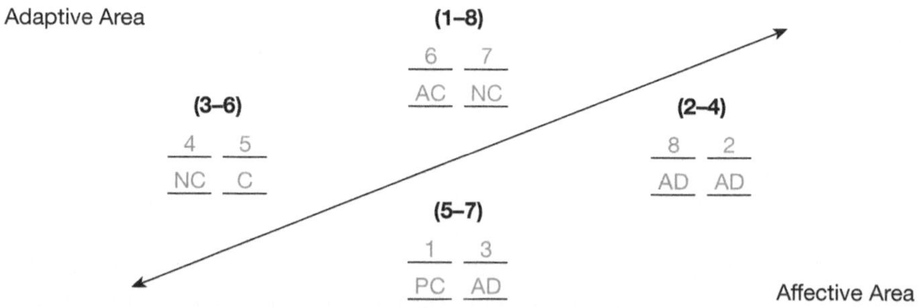

FIGURE 6.6 Example of Analysis of Sequence 2—Completed Analysis with Codes.

Figure 6.6 demonstrates completion of the Analysis of Sequence 2, utilizing the clinical example previously described in Figures 6.1–6.4. Here, box numbers and Codes are entered according to the Order of Sequence, allowing comparison between expected order and actual order, as well as qualitative evaluation of each box.

Order of Sequence as a whole (i.e., Individualized, Numerical, Reversed, etc.); that is, the order in which the client approaches the test provides information related to his/her functioning. The second type of evaluation allows for a more thorough analysis, known as "Analysis of Sequence," and is performed for each box. This Analysis of Sequence examines the Code of each box as informed by the scoring (*Analysis of Sequence 1*) and the relative position of each box in the Order of Sequence as compared to the theoretical model (*Analysis of Sequence 2*). These two types of evaluation will be further discussed in Chapter 7 of this manual.

Computation of CWS Indices

Many diagnostic indices can be derived from the scoring elements introduced in the previous chapter. These indices are presented here in the same order in which they appear on the CWS Computation Form (see Figure 6.7; A copy of the complete WDCT *Form for Administration, Scoring, and Computation* is provided in Appendix D).

Table 6.1 provides an overview of major CWS indices and computations, including abbreviations and descriptions, indicating the order in which they will be presented in this chapter, and equations numbered for reference.

Each diagnostic index is discussed below, including how calculations are derived and computed.

Calculations

1. The Analysis of Sequence

This topic was reviewed at the beginning of this chapter.

2. EC+%

The EC+% describes the percentage of responses aligned with the Evocative Character demands of the boxes. That is, how well the client grasped the Evocative Character of the stimuli while completing his or her drawings.

The EC+% is obtained by dividing the sum (Σ) of the EC scores (1 and 0.5) by 8 (number of WDCT boxes), and then multiplying by 100.

Therefore, the EC+% formula (6.1) is written as:

$$EC+\% = \frac{\sum EC}{8} \times 100 \qquad (6.1)$$

INDICES

EC+% ____ AQ+% ____ FQ+% ____ A/F ____

P% ____ P+% ____ O% ____ O+%% ____

I.I.T.–1 ____ IM ____ AI ____ I.I.T.–2 ____

W.I.P.: Quadrant A B C D Area: α β γ M/m=

AC ___ NC ___ AD ___ D ___

NUMBER OF PRIMARY CONTENT CATEGORIES (# = ______)

H% _____ A% _____ OBJ% _____

ARC% _____ SIG% _____ AST% _____

NAT% _____ BOT% _____ ....% _____

........% _____ ....% _____ ....% _____

NUMBER OF SECONDARY CONTENT CATEGORIES (# = ______)

.... % _____ .... % _____ .... % _____

.... % _____ .... % _____ .... % _____

TOTAL NUMBER OF SPECIAL SCORES (# = ______)

Type: ___ Number: ___ Type: ___ Number: ___ Type: ___ Number: ___

Type: ___ Number: ___ Type: ___ Number: ___ Type: ___ Number: ___

Type: ___ Number: ___ Type: ___ Number: ___ Type: ___ Number: ___

TOTAL NUMBER OF IMPULSE RESPONSES (# = ______)

Type: ________ Box: _____ Type: ________ Box: _____

Type: ________ Box: _____ Type: ________ Box: _____

Type: ________ Box: _____ Type: ________ Box: _____

COMPARISON Adp-A / Aff-A	Boxes 1-3-6-8	Boxes 2-4-5-7
EC+%		
AQ+%		
FQ+%		
A/F		
P%		
P+%		
O%		
O+%		
I.I.T.-1		
IM		
IA		
I.I.T.-2		
QR. Area		
H%		
# Sp.Sc		
# GR/PR		
M		
m		
# I.R.		
C		
AC		
NC		
PC		
AD		
D		

PRIMARY MOVEMENT (# = ______)

	m	f	i	Total
Active				
Passive				
Blocked				
Double				
Rotary				
Intermediate				
Total				

SECONDARY MOVEMENT (# = ______)

	FM	MI	FE	Total
Active				
Passive				
Blocked				
Double				
Rotary				
Intermediate				
Total				

FIGURE 6.7 CWS Computation Form.

Figure 6.7 provides a sample CWS Computation Form.

TABLE 6.1 Major CWS Indices and Computations—Order of Calculation, Abbreviation, Description, and Equation Numbers

Order	*Abbreviation*	*Description*	*Equation #*
1	AoS-1, AoS-2	Analyses of Sequence 1 and 2	—
2	EC+%	Percentage of responses aligned with Evocative Character demand	6.1
3	AQ+%	Percentage of positive Affective Quality responses	6.2
4	FQ+%	Percentage of positive Form Quality responses	6.3
5	A/F Ratio	Affective Stability Index: AQ to FQ Ratio	6.4
6	P%	Percentage of Popular responses	6.5
7	P+%	Percentage of Popular responses *with positive Form Quality*	6.6
8	O%	Percentage of Original responses	6.7
9	O+%	Percentage of Original responses *with positive Form Quality*	6.8
10	IIT-1	Index of Inner Tension-1; Level of currently experienced distress and tension	6.9
11	IM	Impulsivity Index	6.10
12	AI	Anxiety Index	6.11
13	IIT-2	Index of Inner Tension-2; Level of personality flexibility and integration	6.12
14	WIP	Wartegg Index of Psychopathology; Integration and comparison between IIT-1 and IIT-2 • Adjusted IIT-1 • Adjusted IIT-2	6.13
15	M/m	Ratio of Primary to Secondary Movement	6.14
16	# Pr. Contents	Number of Primary Content categories	—
17	% Pr. Contents	Percentage of each individual Primary Content category	6.15
18	# Sec. Contents	Number of Secondary Content categories	—
19	% Sec. Contents	Percentage of each individual Secondary Content category	6.15
20, 21	# SS	Total *number* and *type* of Special Scores	—
22, 23	# IR	Total number of Impulse Responses, and *box* in which they were scored	—
24, 25	M	Total number of Primary Movement responses, including *gender* and *direction*	—
26, 27	m	Total number of Secondary Movement responses, including *type* and *direction*	—
28	Adp-A vs. Aff-A	Comparison between Adaptive Area indices (Adp-A) and Affective Area indices (Aff-A)	6.16—6.28

3. AQ+%

The AQ+% describes the percentage of responses with positive affect content.

The AQ+% is obtained by dividing the sum (Σ) of the Affective Quality scores (1 and 0.5) by 8 (number of WDCT Boxes), and then multiplying by 100.

Therefore, the AQ+% formula (6.2) may be written as:

$$AQ+\% = \frac{\sum AQ}{8} \times 100 \tag{6.2}$$

4. FQ+%

Similarly, the FQ+% describes the percentage of responses with positive Form Quality.

The FQ+% is obtained by dividing the sum (Σ) of Form Quality scores (1 and 0.5) by 8 (number of WDCT Boxes), and then multiplying by 100.

Therefore, the FQ+% formula (6.3) may be written as:

$$FQ+\% = \frac{\sum FQ}{8} \times 100 \tag{6.3}$$

5. *The Affective Stability Index ("A/F Ratio")*

The A/F ratio describes the ratio of Affective Quality (AQ) to Form Quality (FQ).

The A/F ratio is not calculated using all AQ and FQ scores from all boxes, due to the nature of the individual boxes. That is, as some boxes (3, 4, 5, and 6) primarily evoke neutral content categories and rarely obtain an Affective Quality score of 1, including these scores in the calculations would result in a disproportionate ratio between the two indexes (which would for the most part lean to the FQ side of the ratio). For this reason, an abbreviated calculation is utilized to calculate the A/F Ratio.

- The first term (A) consists of the sum (Σ) of *Affective Quality* scores for **Boxes 1, 2, 7, and 8;**
- The second term (F) consists of the sum (Σ) of *Form Quality* scores for **Boxes 3, 4, 5, and 6.**

Therefore, the A/F Ratio formula (6.4) may be written as:

$$\frac{A}{F} = \frac{\sum AQ_{(1,2,7,8)}}{\sum FQ_{(3,4,5,6)}} \tag{6.4}$$

6. P%

The P% describes the percentage of Popular content responses produced by the client.

P% is obtained by assigning numerical values to each P and (P) response, multiplying these values by the number of each P and (P) response respectively, taking the sum (Σ), dividing by 8 (number of WDCT Boxes), and then multiplying by 100.

— Each Popular response—P—is assigned a score of 1;
— Each Semi-Popular response—(P)—is assigned a score of 0.5.

Therefore, the P% formula (6.5) may be written as:

$$P\% = \frac{N_P + .5n_{(P)}}{8} \times 100 \qquad (6.5)$$

(N_P = the number of Popular responses; and $n_{(P)}$ = the number of Semi-Popular responses.)

7. P+%

The P+% describes the percentage of Popular responses with positive Form Quality.

P+% is obtained by considering *P* and (*P*) responses in terms of their associated positive, neutral, or negative Form Quality (*FQ*) values.

In calculating *P*+%:

- Each *P* response with an *FQ* score of 1 obtains a score of 1; the number of these responses is indicated with $N_P(1)$;
- Each *P* response with an *FQ* score of 0.5 obtains a score of 0.5; the number of these responses is indicated $N_P(0.5)$;
- Each (*P*) response with an *FQ* score of 1 obtains a score of 0.5; the number of these responses is indicated with $n_{(P)}(1)$;
- Each (*P*) response with an *FQ* score of 0.5 obtains a score of .25; the number of these responses is indicated with $n_{(P)}(0.5)$
- All *P* and (*P*) responses with an *FQ* score of 0 obtain a score of 0.

The sum (Σ) of the scores (numerator of the formula below) is divided by the sum of Popular content scores (not by the number of boxes, like it is for the previous percentages) and multiplied by 100.

Therefore, the *P*+% formula (6.6) may be written as:

$$P+\% = \frac{N_{P(1)} + .5N_{P(.5)} + .5n_{(P)(1)} + .25n_{(P)(.5)}}{N_P + .5n_{(P)}} \times 100 \qquad (6.6)$$

(N_P = the number of Popular responses; and $n_{(P)}$ = the number of Semi-Popular responses.)

8. O%

The O% describes the percentage of Original content responses.

O% is calculated similarly to P% (see #6 above). O% is obtained by assigning numerical values to each O and (O) response, multiplying these values by the number of each O and (O) response respectively, taking the sum (Σ), dividing by 8 (number of WDCT Boxes), and then multiplying by 100.

— Each Original Response—O—is assigned a score of 1;
— Each Semi-Original Response—(O)—is assigned a score of 0.5.

Therefore, the O% formula (6.7) may be written as:

$$O\% = \frac{N_O + .5n_{(O)}}{8} \times 100 \tag{6.7}$$

(N_O = the number of O responses; and $n_{(O)}$ = the number of (O) responses.)

9. O+%

The O+% describes the percentage of Original responses with positive Form Quality.

O+% is obtained by considering O and (O) responses in terms of their associated positive, neutral, or negative Form Quality (*FQ*) values.

In calculating O+%:

- All O responses with an FQ score of 1 receive a score of 1; the number of these responses is indicated with $N_O(1)$;
- All O responses with an *FQ* score of 0.5 receive a score of 0.5; the number of these responses is indicated with $N_O(0.5)$;
- All *o* responses with an *FQ* score of 1 receive a score of 0.5; the number of these responses is indicated with $n_{(O)}(1)$;
- All *o* responses with an *FQ* score of 0.5 receive a score of .25; the number of these responses is indicated with $n_{(O)}(0.5)$;
- All O and *o* responses with an *FQ* score of 0 receive a score of 0.

The sum (Σ) of the scores (numerator of the formula below) is divided by the sum of Original content scores (not by the number of Boxes, like it is for the previous percentages) and multiplied by 100.

Therefore, the O+% formula (6.8) may be written as:

$$O+\% = \frac{N_{O(1)} + .5N_{O(.5)} + .5n_{(O)(1)} + .25n_{(O)(.5)}}{N_O + .5n_{(O)}} \times 100 \tag{6.8}$$

(N_O = the number of O responses; and $n_{(O)}$ = the number of (O) responses.)

Author's Note: It is worth mentioning that, while the distinction between O% and O+% is also present in the scoring of other tests, the distinction between *P*% and *P*+% described here is an original contribution of the CWS.

10. The IIT-1(Index of Inner Tension-1)

The IIT-1 describes the frequency of Crossed Border (CB) and Anxiety Stroke (AS) Special Scores produced by the client.

The IIT-1 is calculated by assigned a score of 1 to each Crossed Border (CB) and Anxiety Stroke (AS) special score, calculating the sum (Σ) of these scores, and dividing the sum by 8.

Therefore, the IIT-1 formula (6.9) may be written as:

$$IIT\text{-}1 = \frac{\sum CB + \sum AS}{8} \tag{6.9}$$

The value of this index ranges from 0 to 2.

For both the IIT-1 and the IM (see #11, below), only *evident* cases of Crossed Border (CB) must be included in the calculation.

Computations of the adjusted IIT-1, used in calculating the WIP, are provided in #14 below.

11. The IM (Impulsivity Index)

The Impulsivity Index (IM) describes the frequency of Crossed Border (CB) Special Scores produced by the client.

The Impulsivity Index (IM) is calculated by assigning a score of 1 to each Crossed Border (CB) special score, calculating the sum (Σ) of these scores, and dividing the sum by 8.

Therefore, the IM formula (6.10) may be written as:

$$IM = \frac{\sum CB}{8} \tag{6.10}$$

The value of this index ranges from 0 to 1.

12. The AI (Anxiety Index)

The Anxiety Index (AI) describes the frequency of Anxiety Stroke (AS) Special Scores produced by the client.

The Anxiety Index (AI) is calculated by assigning a score of 1 to each Anxiety Stroke (AS) Special Score, calculating the sum (Σ) of these scores, and dividing the sum by 8.

Therefore, the AI formula (6.11) may be written as:

$$AI = \frac{\sum AS}{8} \tag{6.11}$$

The value of this index ranges from 0 to 1.

13. The IIT-2 (Index of Inner Tension-2)

The IIT-2 describes the ratio of positive valuations to negative valuations of the completed Wartegg Boxes.

The IIT-2 is a ratio obtained from the Analysis of Sequence 1 Codes in the following manner:

— On the left side of the ratio, the number of boxes that have been coded C and PC is noted;
— On the right side of the ratio, the number of boxes that have been coded AC, NC, AD or D is noted.

First Term = $N_C + N_{PC}$
Second Term = $N_{AC} + N_{NC} + N_{AD} + N_D$

Therefore, the IIT-2 formula (6.12) may be written as:

$$IIT\text{-}2 = \frac{(N_C + N_{PC})}{(N_{AC} + N_{NC} + N_{AD} + N_D)} \tag{6.12}$$

On the Computation Form (see Figure 6.7), next to the second term of the ratio, is a curved bracket that includes the four negative codes (AC, NC, AD, D). This allows the clinician to further assess the qualitative value of the IIT-2. The assessor records in this bracket the number of each valuation found in the protocol.

Computations of the adjusted IIT-2, used in calculating the WIP, are provided in #14 below.

14. WIP (Wartegg Index of Psychopathology)

The WIP describes the result of the comparison of two indexes: the IIT-1 and the IIT-2

For computation of the WIP, an adjusted formula for both the IIT-1 and IIT-2 is used.

Adjusted IIT-1

The adjusted IIT-1 is computed beginning with the formula (6.9) described above (see #10):

$$IIT\text{-}1 = \frac{\sum CB + \sum AS}{8} \tag{6.9}$$

To adjust the formula, and take into account other signs of internal tension present in CWS protocols, several other scores are added to the sum (Σ) of AS and CB. Specifically, a score of 1 is assigned to each Secondary Movement response (FE, MI and FM), each cloud (CLD) content, and for each ID (Incomplete Drawing) special score (when the FQ+% is ≥81). These additional scores are added to the basic IIT-1 formula.

Therefore, the formula (6.13) for the *adjusted IIT-1* may be written as:

$$IIT\text{-}1_{(adj)} = \frac{\left(\sum CB + \sum AS\right) + \sum\left(FE + MI + FM\right) + \sum CLD + \sum ID}{8} \tag{6.13}$$

Adjusted IIT-2

Similarly, the formula for the IIT-2 is adjusted in computing the WIP. For the adjusted IIT-2 we proceed according to the following steps:

1. We compute the IIT-2 formula (6.12) as described above (see #12), prior to making adjustments as described in steps 2–5 below;

$$IIT\text{-}2 = \frac{\left(N_C + N_{PC}\right)}{\left(N_{AC} + N_{NC} + N_{AD} + N_D\right)} \tag{6.12}$$

2. For each AC (Ambivalent Choice), we deduct .25 from the second term and add it to the first term (e.g., IIT-2 = 6/2; Where the negatives valuations of the second term are 2 AC, the adjusted computation will be: 6.5/1.5);
3. For each AD (Ambivalent Delay), we deduct 0.5 from the first term and add it to the second term (e.g., IIT-2 = 6/2; When the negatives valuations of the second term are 2 AD, the adjusted computation will be: 5/3);
4. For each D (Delay), we deduct .65 from the first term and add it to the second term (e.g., IIT-2 = 6/2; When the negatives valuations of the second term are 2 D, the adjusted computation will be: 4.7/3.3);
5. No adjustments are made in the case of NC (Negative Compensation).

Once the adjusted IIT-1 and IIT-2 have been calculated, the WIP is determined by plotting these two figures on a four-quadrant "map" of personality and functioning. The IIT-1, describing anxiety and impulsivity, is plotted on the *y-axis* (vertical axis); the IIT-2, describing overall integration of personality, is plotted on the *x-axis* (horizontal axis). The intersection of these two points, falling in one of four quadrants (A, B, C, D) and three areas within those quadrants (α, β, γ), provides an estimation of the overall level of personality integration and psychopathology currently experienced by the client.

Graphic illustration of the Wartegg Index of Psychopathology (WIP) is presented in Figure 6.8.

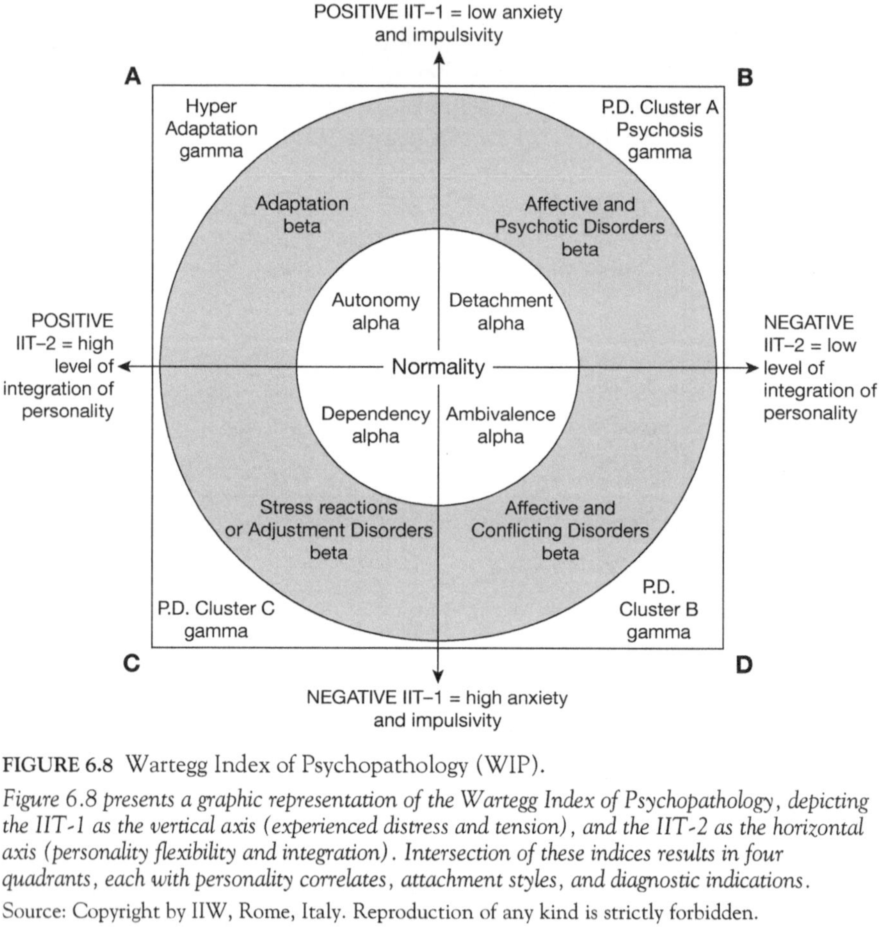

FIGURE 6.8 Wartegg Index of Psychopathology (WIP).

Figure 6.8 presents a graphic representation of the Wartegg Index of Psychopathology, depicting the IIT-1 as the vertical axis (experienced distress and tension), and the IIT-2 as the horizontal axis (personality flexibility and integration). Intersection of these indices results in four quadrants, each with personality correlates, attachment styles, and diagnostic indications.

As the illustration presents, the highest levels of adaptive functioning are present at the intersection (mid-point of each axis) of the IIT-1 and IIT-2, falling within the *alpha* (α) area. As the WIP moves toward more extreme values, difficulties in functioning increase with affective, psychotic, and stress reaction

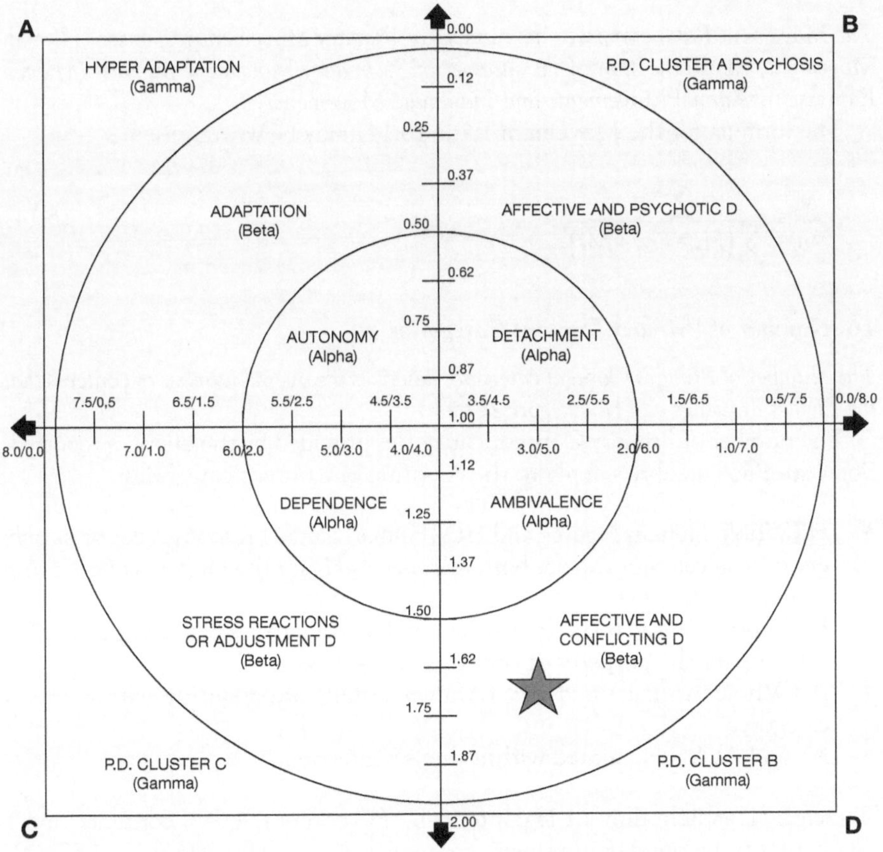

FIGURE 6.9 Wartegg Index of Psychopathology (WIP)—Example.

Figure 6.9 presents an example of plotting a client's IIT-1 and IIT-2 scores to arrive at a WIP placement and classification. In this example, the client's IIT-1 (adjusted) = 1.75, and IIT-2 (adjusted) = 5.5/2.5. Plotting the intersection of these scores, this client's functioning falls within the beta (β) band of Quadrant C, identified by a star on the WIP diagram.

disorders present in the *beta* (*β*) area, and personality disorders noted in the *gamma* (*γ*) area. Additional interpretive information related to the WIP is provided in Chapter 7.

To further illustrate the WIP, the following example is considered. Following computation, a client's IIT-1 (*adjusted*) = 1.75, and his IIT-2 (*adjusted*) = 5.5/2.5. Plotting the intersection of these scores, this client's functioning falls within the *beta* (*β*) band of Quadrant C, as shown in Figure 6.9.

15. Movement Ratio

The Movement Ratio compares the number of Primary Movement responses (Human Movement, M) to the sum of the number of Secondary Movement responses (Facial Expression, Animal Movement, and Inanimate Movement).

The formula for the Movement Ratio (6.14) may be written as:

$$\frac{M}{m} = \frac{\sum M}{\sum (FE + FM + MI)} \tag{6.14}$$

16. Number of Primary Content Categories

The Number of Primary Content categories describes the overall number of contents that the client's drawings can be categorized into.

The number of Primary Content categories provided by the client is reported. Some specific guidelines apply to the counting of Content categories:

- *H* (Whole Human Figure) and *HD* (Human Detail) responses count as *only one content category* and are both recorded as *H* (for the purposes of counting content categories).
- *HS* responses and *HDS* responses are both considered as belonging to the *HS* category for the purposes of counting categories.
- A (Whole Animal) and *AD* (Animal Detail) are counting within the *A* category.
- *AS* and *ADS* are counted within the *AS* category.

Therefore, if a client draws 1 *H* content, 1 *ARC* content, 4 *OBJ* contents, and 1 *SIG* content, the number of primary contents is 4 = *H* (*H* + *HD* = 1), *ARC* (1), *OBJ* (1) and *SIG* (1).

17. Percentage of Primary Contents

The Percentage of Primary Contents provides information on the extent to which each Primary Content category is present in the test.

To calculate the Percentage of Primary Contents, the frequency (i.e., number) that each content category appears is recorded, with the total divided by 8 and multiplied by 100. (Note: In the event of 1 or more rejections, the instructions provided in the *Special Cases* section at the end of this chapter apply.)

In considering Human content, for example, the *H*% formula (6.15) is written as follows:

$$H\% = \frac{N_{WP}}{8} \times 100 \tag{6.15}$$

(N_H = the number of Human responses.)

This formula is modified for each Content category contained in the protocol, with percentages calculated for each Content category. For example, in a protocol with 4 *OBJ* responses, 2 *BOT* responses, 1 *ARC* response, and 1 *H* response, the respective percentages are: *OBJ* = 50%, *BOT* = 25%, *ARC* = 12.5%, and *H* = 12.5%.

As with the scoring of the Number of Content Categories (see #15 above), the following exceptions to this calculation apply:

- *H* (Whole Human Figure) and *HD* (Human Detail) are grouped into the *H*% category;
- *HS* and *HDS* are grouped into the *HS*% category;
- A (Whole Animal) and *AD* (Animal Detail) are grouped into the *A*% category;
- *AS* and *ADS* are grouped into the *AS*% category.

For example, if a WDCT protocol has two human face responses (*HD*) and 1 whole person response (*H*), the *H*% equals equal 37.5 (that is, (3 ÷ 8) × 100).

In general, the most frequent content categories in the WDCT are: A%; ARC%; *BOT*%; *H*%; *NAT*%; *OBJ*%; and *SIG*%.

18. *Number of Secondary Content Categories*

The Number of Secondary Content categories describes the overall number of Secondary Contents that the client's drawings can be categorized into.

Similar to the number of Primary Contents, the number of Secondary Content categories provided by the client is reported.

For example, if a client draws 3 *OBJ/CG* (Primary Content = Object, Secondary Content = Clothing) and 1 *H/FT* (Primary Content = Human, Secondary Content = Fairy Tale), the total number of Secondary Contents equals 2 (i.e., Clothing, Fairy Tale).

19. *Percentage of Secondary Contents*

The Percentage of Secondary Contents provides information on the extent to which each secondary content category is present in the test.

To calculate the Percentage of Secondary Contents, the same procedure followed for Primary Contents applies. As the percentage of Secondary Contents is obtained over eight Boxes (in the absence of rejections; for more information on calculations in protocols containing rejections, see *Special Cases* at the end of this chapter), the sum of Secondary Contents is *always divided by 8 and multiplied by 100*. The same formula used to calculate Primary Contents is used for Secondary Contents (formula 6.15), with the specific Content categories present in the protocol substituted for *H*.

$$H\% = \frac{N_{WP}}{8} \times 100 \qquad (6.15)$$

(N_{WP} = the number of Weapon responses.)

Using the above example (in a protocol with 4 *OBJ* responses, 2 *BOT* responses, 1 *ARC* response, and 1 *H* response), if two of the four *OBJ* responses have a Secondary Content of *WP* (Weapon) and the *H* contents include a Secondary Content of *FT* (Fairy Tale), the percentages of primary contents would remain unchanged (see #16 above). The percentage of Secondary Contents would be calculated at: *WP* = 25% [(2 ÷ 8) × 100] and *FT* = 12.5% [(1 ÷ 8) × 100].

Table 6.2 provides a summary of the mathematical computation formulas for the major calculated CWS indices.

20. *Total Special Scores*

The Total Special Scores describes the total number of Special Scores present in the client protocol.

In recording the total number of Special Scores, each incidence of a Special Score is counted, with the total number reported on the CWS Computation Form.

For example, in a protocol with 6 *AS* (Anxiety Stroke), 4 *CB* (Crossed Border), and 1 *AP* (Arbitrary Performance) special scores, the Total Special Scores = 11 (i.e., 6 + 4 + 1).

21. *The Number and Type of Special Scores*

The Number and Type Special Scores numerically describe the frequency of each type of Special Score present in the client protocol.

In the spaces provided on the CWS Computation Form, each category (type) of Special Score present in the client's protocol is recorded, with the number of occurrences indicated. Using the above example: *AS* = 6; *CB* = 4; *AP* = 1.

22. *Total Number of Impulse Responses*

The Total Number of Impulse Responses describes frequency of IR present in the client protocol.

The total number of Impulse Responses are reported on the CWS Computation Form, with a score of 1 is assigned to each. For example, in a protocol containing one Oral IR and one Phallic IR, the total number of IR = 2.

23. *Number and Type of Impulse Responses*

The Number and Type Impulse Reponses numerically describe the frequency of each type of IR present in the client protocol.

TABLE 6.2 Formulas for Major CWS Indices and Calculations

Evocative Character %	EC+%	$EC+\% = \frac{\sum EC}{8} \times 100$
Affective Quality %	AQ+%	$AQ+\% = \frac{\sum AQ}{8} \times 100$
Form Quality%	FQ+%	$FQ+\% = \frac{\sum FQ}{8} \times 100$
Affective Stability Index	A/F	$\frac{A}{F} = \frac{\sum AQ_{(1,2,7,8)}}{\sum FQ_{(3,4,5,6)}}$
Popular %	P%	$P\% = \frac{N_P + .5n_{(P)}}{8} \times 100$
Popular % with Good Form	P+%	$P+\% = \frac{N_{P(1)} + .5N_{P(.5)} + .5n_{(P)(1)} + .25n_{(P)(.5)}}{N_P + .5n_{(P)}} \times 100$
Original %	O%	$O\% = \frac{N_O + .5n_{(O)}}{8} \times 100$
Original % with Good Form	O+%	$O+\% = \frac{N_{O(1)} + .5N_{O(.5)} + .5n_{(O)(1)} + .25n_{(O)(.5)}}{N_O + .5n_{(O)}} \times 100$
Index of Inner Tension-1	IIT-1	$IIT\text{-}1 = \frac{\sum CB + \sum AS}{8}$
Index of Inner Tension-1 (adjusted)	IIT-1 (adjusted)	$IIT\text{-}1_{(adj)} = \frac{\left(\sum CB + \sum AS\right) + \sum\left(FE + MI + FM\right) + \sum CLD + \sum ID}{8}$
Impulsivity Index	IM	$IM = \frac{\sum CB}{8}$
Anxiety Index	AI	$AI = \frac{\sum AS}{8}$
Index of Inner Tension-2	IIT-2	$IIT\text{-}2 = \frac{\left(N_C + N_{PC}\right)}{\left(N_{AC} + N_{NC} + N_{AD} + N_D\right)}$
Movement Ratio	M/m	$\frac{M}{m} = \frac{\sum M}{\sum\left(FE + FM + MI\right)}$
Content %* (Primary or Secondary)	H%	$H\% = \frac{N_H}{8} \times 100$

Note: * Content percentages calculated for each Primary and Secondary Content. Example calculation for Human content (*H*) is provided here.

Similar to the manner in which the number and type of Special Score is recorded, the frequency (i.e., number) and category (i.e., oral, anal, phallic) of Impulse Response is specified. In addition, *the box number for each IR is recorded.*

24. Number of Primary Movement Responses

The Number of Primary Movement Responses describes frequency of Primary Movement present in the client protocol.

Each Primary Movement Response present in the client protocol is counted, with the total number reported in the space provided on the CWS Computation Form.

25. Type and Direction of Primary Movement Responses

The Type and Direction of Primary Movement Responses describes the frequency of the gender and direction of Primary Movement Reponses present in the client protocol.

The gender type (i.e., Male, Female, Indeterminate) and direction (i.e., Active, Passive, Blocked, Rotary, Indeterminate) for each M response is recorded, indicating the total of each sub-category on the CWS Computation Form.

26. Number of Secondary Movement Responses

The Number of Secondary Movement Responses describes frequency of Secondary Movement present in the client protocol.

As with the Primary Movement Responses, each Secondary Movement Response is counted, with the total number recorded on the Computation Form. For example, in a protocol containing 1 FM response and 2 FE responses, the Total Number of Secondary Movement Responses = 3.

27. Direction of Secondary Movement Responses

The Direction of Secondary Movement Responses describes the frequency of the direction of Secondary Movement Reponses present in the client protocol.

As with the Primary Movement Responses, the assessor counts and records the direction (i.e., Active, Passive, Blocked, Double, Rotary) of each Secondary Movement response by category (i.e., FE, FM, MI).

28. Comparison between Adaptive Area and Affective Area Indices

Clinical practice demonstrates that comparing the Adaptive Area (1, 3, 6, 8) to the Affective Area (2, 4, 5, 7) indices provides highly significant diagnostic elements.

The calculation process for the Adaptive and Affective Areas indices is comparable to the procedures used to calculate the overall WDCT indices; however, instead of referring to all eight WDCT boxes these calculations are limited to four boxes:

TABLE 6.3 Formulas for Major CWS Indices and Calculations—Adaptive Area (ADP)

Evocative Character %	EC+%	$EC+\% = \frac{\sum EC_{(1,3,6,8)}}{4} \times 100$
Affective Quality %	AQ+%	$AQ+\% = \frac{\sum AQ_{(1,3,6,8)}}{4} \times 100$
Form Quality%	FQ+%	$FQ+\% = \frac{\sum FQ_{(1,3,6,8)}}{4} \times 100$
Affective Stability Index	A/F	$\frac{A}{F} = \frac{\sum AQ_{(1,8)}}{\sum FQ_{(3,6)}}$
Popular %	P%	$P\% = \frac{N_{P(1,3,6,8)} + .5n_{(P)(1,3,6,8)}}{4} \times 100$
Popular % with Good Form	P+%	$P+\% = \left(\frac{N_{P(1)} + .5N_{P(.5)} + .5n_{(P)(1)} + .25n_{(P)(.5)}}{N_P + .5n_{(P)}}\right)_{(1,3,6,8)} \times 100$
Original %	O%	$O\% = \frac{N_{O(1,3,6,8)} + .5n_{(O)(1,3,6,8)}}{4} \times 100$
Original % with Good Form	O+%	$O+\% = \left(\frac{N_{O(1)} + .5N_{O(.5)} + .5n_{(O)(1)} + .25n_{(O)(.5)}}{N_O + .5n_{(O)}}\right)_{(1,3,6,8)} \times 100$
Index of Inner Tension-1	IIT-1	$IIT\text{-}1 = \frac{\sum CB_{(1,3,6,8)} + \sum AS_{(1,3,6,8)}}{4}$
Impulsivity Index	IM	$IM = \frac{\sum CB_{(1,3,6,8)}}{4}$
Anxiety Index	AI	$AI = \frac{\sum AS_{(1,3,6,8)}}{4}$
Index of Inner Tension-2	IIT-2	$IIT\text{-}2 = \frac{(N_C + N_{PC})_{(1,3,6,8)}}{(N_{AC} + N_{NC} + N_{AD} + N_D)_{(1,3,6,8)}}$
Content %* *(Primary or Secondary)*	H%	$H\% = \frac{N_{H(1,3,6,8)}}{4} \times 100$

Note: * Content percentages calculated for each Primary and Secondary Content. Example calculation for Human content (*H*) is provided here.

- Boxes 1, 3, 6, 8 for the Adaptive Area;
- Boxes 2, 4, 5, 7 for the Affective Area.

For the purpose of explanation, only the calculations for the Adaptive Area column will be described below (summarized in Table 6.3). The calculations for the Affective Area column are calculated in the same manner using the applicable boxes (with formulas provided in Table 6.4).

Each calculation is described briefly below.

EC+% (*percentage of responses aligned with the Evocative Character demands of the boxes*) is obtained by summing (Σ) the scores for boxes 1, 3, 6, and 8, dividing the result by 4, and multiplying by 100. Therefore, the EC+%$^{(Adp)}$ formula (6.16) may be written as:

$$EC+\% = \frac{\sum EC_{(1,3,6,8)}}{4} \times 100 \tag{6.16}$$

AQ+% (percentage of responses with positive affect content):

$$AQ+\% = \frac{\sum AQ_{(1,3,6,8)}}{4} \times 100 \tag{6.17}$$

FQ+% (percentage of responses with positive form quality):

$$FQ+\% = \frac{\sum FQ_{(1,3,6,8)}}{4} \times 100 \tag{6.18}$$

A/F Ratio (*Affective Quality/Form Quality ratio*) describes the sum (Σ) of Affective Quality for boxes 1 and 8 as the numerator, and the sum (Σ) of Form Quality for boxes 3 and 6 as the denominator:

$$\frac{A}{F} = \frac{\sum AQ_{(1,8)}}{\sum FQ_{(3,6)}} \tag{6.19}$$

Note: The above formula describes calculating the A/F for the Adaptive Area; when calculating the A/F Ratio for the Affective Area, boxes 2 and 7 are used in calculating of the Affective Quality sum (numerator), while boxes 4 and 5 are used in calculating the Form Quality sum (denominator). Following calculation, both sides of the ratio should be multiplied by 2 to allow comparison with the normative ranges

P% (*percentage of responses with popular content*) is calculated by applying formula 6.5 (see above) to boxes 1, 3, 6, and 8:

$$P\% = \frac{N_{P(1,3,6,8)} + .5n_{(P)(1,3,6,8)}}{4} \times 100 \tag{6.20}$$

P+% *(percentage of responses with popular content with good form quality)* is calculated by applying formula 6.6 (see above) to boxes 1, 3, 6, and 8:

$$P+\% = \left(\frac{N_{P(1)} + .5N_{P(.5)} + .5n_{(P)(1)} + .25n_{(P)(.5)}}{N_P + .5n_{(P)}} \right)_{(1,3,6,8)} \times 100 \tag{6.21}$$

O% *(percentage of responses with original content)* is calculated by applying formula 6.7 (see above) to boxes 1, 3, 6, and 8:

$$O\% = \frac{N_{O(1,3,6,8)} + .5n_{(O)(1,3,6,8)}}{4} \times 100 \tag{6.22}$$

O+% *(percentage of responses with original content with good form quality)* is calculated by applying formula 6.8 (see above) to boxes 1, 3, 6, and 8:

$$O+\% = \left(\frac{N_{O(1)} + .5N_{O(.5)} + .5n_{(O)(1)} + .25n_{(O)(.5)}}{N_O + .5n_{(O)}} \right)_{(1,3,6,8)} \times 100 \tag{6.23}$$

The **IIT-1** *(Index of Inner Tension-1)* is obtained by assigning a score of 1 to each Crossed Border (CB) and Anxiety Stroke (AS) special score in boxes 1, 3, 6, and 8. This sum (Σ) is then divided by 4:

$$IIT\text{-}1 = \frac{\sum CB_{(1,3,6,8)} + \sum AS_{(1,3,6,8)}}{4} \tag{6.24}$$

The **IM** *(Impulsivity Index)* is obtained by assigning a score of 1 to each Crossed Border (CB) special score in boxes 1, 3, 6, and 8. This sum (Σ) is then divided by 4:

$$IM = \frac{\sum CB_{(1,3,6,8)}}{4} \tag{6.25}$$

Similarly, the **AI** *(Anxiety Index)* is obtained by assigning a score of 1 to each Anxiety Stroke (AI) special score in boxes 1, 3, 6, and 8. This sum (Σ) is then divided by 4:

$$AI = \frac{\sum AS_{(1,3,6,8)}}{4} \tag{6.26}$$

The **IIT-2** *(Index of Inner Tension-2)* is obtained by assigning a score of 1 to each code in the Analysis of Sequence-1 and then by examining the ratio of total positive valuations (C and PC) to total negative valuations (AC, NC, AD, and D) for boxes 1, 3, 6, and 8.

$$IIT\text{-}2 = \frac{(N_C + N_{PC})_{(1,3,6,8)}}{(N_{AC} + N_{NC} + N_{AD} + N_D)_{(1,3,6,8)}} \quad (6.27)$$

WIP *(Wartegg Index of Psychopathology)* may be calculated for both the ADP and AFF areas. To calculate for the Adaptive area, follow the instructions provided above (#14) using only Boxes 1, 3, 6, and 8. Once you will have calculated IIT-1 and IIT-2 in boxes 1, 3, 6, and 8, both indices must be multiplied by 2 and may subsequently be plotted on the WIP graph. The same process may be repeated with the Affective Area boxes (2, 4, 5, 7).

The **H%** *(percentage of Human Content responses)* is calculated by summing (Σ) the number of H and HD responses for Boxes 1, 3, 6, and 8, dividing the sum (Σ) by 4, and multiplying the product by 100. Therefore, the formula may be written as:

$$H\% = \frac{N_{H(1,3,6,8)}}{4} \times 100 \quad (6.28)$$

Additional Calculations

In addition, the following indices must be computed for Boxes 1, 3, 6, and 8:

- Special Scores;
- Global or Partial Rejections;
- Primary (M) and Secondary Movement (m) Responses;
- Impulse Responses (IR);
- boxes coded as Choice (C), Ambivalent Choice (AC), Negative Compensation (NC), Positive Compensation (PC), Ambivalent Delay (AD), and Delay (D).

In the event of one or more rejections, the EC+% and the AQ+% are still calculated on all four boxes. All other percentages (with the exception of P% and O%) are calculated based on four minus the number of rejections obtained for that area (see *Special Cases* below for more guidance in this area). It should be noted that the presence of any rejection reduces the number of boxes included in comparisons, and therefore negatively impacts the utility of the calculated indices. The clinician must keep this in mind when faced with protocols containing rejections. This limitation is especially true of the A/F ratio in that its diagnostic value is significantly reduced, if not completely annulled, by the presence of a rejection.

TABLE 6.4 Formulas for Major CWS Indices and Calculations—Affective Area (AFF)

Evocative Character %	EC+%	$EC+\% = \frac{\sum EC_{(2,4,5,7)}}{4} \times 100$
Affective Quality %	AQ+%	$AQ+\% = \frac{\sum AQ_{(2,4,5,7)}}{4} \times 100$
Form Quality%	FQ+%	$FQ+\% = \frac{\sum FQ_{(2,4,5,7)}}{4} \times 100$
Affective Stability Index	A/F	$\frac{A}{F} = \frac{\sum AQ_{(2,7)}}{\sum FQ_{(4,5)}}$
Popular %	P%	$P\% = \frac{N_{P(2,4,5,7)} + .5n_{(P)(2,4,5,7)}}{4} \times 100$
Popular % with Good Form	P+%	$P+\% = \left(\frac{N_{P(1)} + .5N_{P(.5)} + .5n_{(P)(1)} + .25n_{(P)(.5)}}{N_P + .5n_{(P)}}\right)_{(2,4,5,7)} \times 100$
Original %	O%	$O\% = \frac{N_{O(2,4,5,7)} + .5n_{(O)(2,4,5,7)}}{4} \times 100$
Original % with Good Form	O+%	$O+\% = \left(\frac{N_{O(1)} + .5N_{O(.5)} + .5n_{(O)(1)} + .25n_{(O)(.5)}}{N_O + .5n_{(O)}}\right)_{(2,4,5,7)} \times 100$
Index of Inner Tension-1	IIT-1	$IIT\text{-}1 = \frac{\sum CB_{(2,4,5,7)} + \sum AS_{(2,4,5,7)}}{4}$
Impulsivity Index	IM	$IM = \frac{\sum CB_{(2,4,5,7)}}{4}$
Anxiety Index	AI	$AI = \frac{\sum AS_{(2,4,5,7)}}{4}$
Index of Inner Tension-2	IIT-2	$IIT\text{-}2 = \frac{(N_C + N_{PC})_{(2,4,5,7)}}{(N_{AC} + N_{NC} + N_{AD} + N_D)_{(2,4,5,7)}}$
Content %* *(Primary or Secondary)*	H%	$H\% = \frac{N_{H(2,4,5,7)}}{4} \times 100$

Note: * Content percentages calculated for each Primary and Secondary Content. Example calculation for Human content (*H*) is provided here.

Special Cases

In the case of one or more rejected boxes, all calculations are based on the total number of boxes (8) *minus the number of rejections*. Thus, when calculating ratios and indexes, the number (8) appearing in the formulas must be replaced with 8 *minus the number of rejections*. That is, in the case of a protocol with one Global Rejection, 7 (that is, 8 boxes minus 1 rejection) will be used as the denominator of select formulas.

Similarly, the calculations required for the comparison between the Adaptive and the Affective Areas are based on the total number of boxes in each area (4) minus the number of rejections. Thus, when calculating the comparative ratios and indexes, the number (4) appearing in the formulas must be replaced with (4 *minus the number of rejections*).

However, some exceptions to this substitution rule exist. Both in the general calculations and in the comparison between Adaptive and the Affective Areas, the following calculations are *not modified* to account for rejected boxes:

- P+%;
- O+%;
- EC+%;
- AQ+%;
- A/F Ratio;
- Analysis of Sequence-1 and -2;
- Index of Inner Tension-2 (IIT-2).

More specifically:

1. *The P+% and the O+%* formulas are not modified in the case of rejections because these percentages are not calculated based on the total number of boxes (either 8 or 4), but rather on the total number of popular (P) or original (O) responses contained in the protocol.
2. *The AQ+% and the EC+%* formulas are not modified in the case of rejections. In calculating the AQ+% and the EC+%, due to their nature and diagnostic meaning, even in the event of one or more rejections, the percentage is always derived from the 8 or 4 boxes. This decision is based on the fact that a rejection is always the result of an emotional blockage that takes place in the client's perceptive-associative processes during the Drawing Phase of the test. As this blockage is due to an activation of conflict caused by the evocative character of the rejected box, it indicates:
    - negative or unpleasant contents in terms of Affective Quality; the box, therefore, is coded an AQ score of 0; and/or
    - content with non-grasped Evocative Character in terms of EC+% (see Chapter 4 for more discussion on this point) and is, therefore, coded an EC score of 0.

Therefore, for the calculation of AQ+% and EC+%, the number of boxes to be used is always either 8 or 4, depending on the type of calculations that are being performed.

3. *The A/F Ratio* is not modified in the case of rejections. In calculating the A/F ratio, in the event of one or more rejections in Boxes 1, 2, 7, and 8 (the numerator), the same considerations that were made for AQ+% apply (i.e., a rejection is given a score of 0 when calculating AQ+%). However, in the event of one or more rejections in boxes 3, 4, 5, and 6 (the denominator), the clinician does not include these boxes for the FQ+ sum in the calculation of the A/F Ratio, but instead includes them as part of the psychodiagnostic assessment by assigning the average score of the FQ+ to the rejected boxes.

   For example, let us consider a protocol that has a rejection in Box 2 and in Box 6, in which the client obtained the following scores:

   Affective Quality: Box 1 = 1; Box 7 = 1; Box 8 = 0.5; Box 2 = rejection

   Form Quality: Box 3 = 1; Box 4 = 1; Box 5 = 0; Box 6 = rejection

   The A/F ratio is calculated as follows:

   AQ sum = 1 + 1 + 0.5 + 0 = 2.5

   FQ sum = 1 + 1 + 0 + 0 = 2

   Thus, the A/F Ratio equals: 2.5 / 2.

   However, in properly calculating the ratio to maximize its diagnostic meaning, the clinician must attribute the client's average FQ score (calculated across all the Boxes in which it could be scored) to Box 6. For the purposes of the above example, if this value equals 4, then the average FQ (calculated as: 4 divided by the total number of usable Boxes, in this case: 6) equals .66 (4 ÷ 6 = .66). Therefore, in the psychodiagnostic assessment, the clinician must keep in mind that the actual value of this ratio is more realistically: 2.5 / 2.66.

4. In assessing the *Analyses of Sequence*, as calculations are mostly based on Affective Quality and Evocative Character, the same rules provided above in #2 (EC+% and AQ+%) apply to both Analysis of Sequence 1 and 2. The rejected box is recorded on the CWS Computation Form in the last place of the Analysis of Sequence. In the case of more than one rejection, the rejected boxes are placed in the Order of Sequence in numerical order. That is, if a client rejects Boxes 7 and 3, these are placed respectively at the last and second-to-last places in the Order of Sequence.

   When comparing the Adaptive and the Affective areas, only the Analysis of Sequence 1 is taken into account, and rejections are coded as D.

5. The *IIT-2*. Because this index is calculated according to the coding of the Analysis of Sequence 1 (C, AC, NC, PC, AD, D), it is always calculated based on either 8 or 4 boxes.

Additional CWS Indices Available in the Clinical Software Package

Several additional indices and constellations are not able to be calculated by hand, and rather, are provided within the CWS Software package. These indices require complex calculations and decision rules, and due to the complicated nature of these, are included only in the software. The three specific additional indices include the Index of Suicidal Tendencies (IST), the Index of Validity (IV), and the Global Assessment classification. (Interpretation of these indices is reviewed in Chapter 7.)

Examples of Scoring

Two examples, including scoring and calculations, are provided in the figures below. Figures 6.10–6.12 demonstrate scoring and calculations for a WDCT protocol that does not contain rejections.

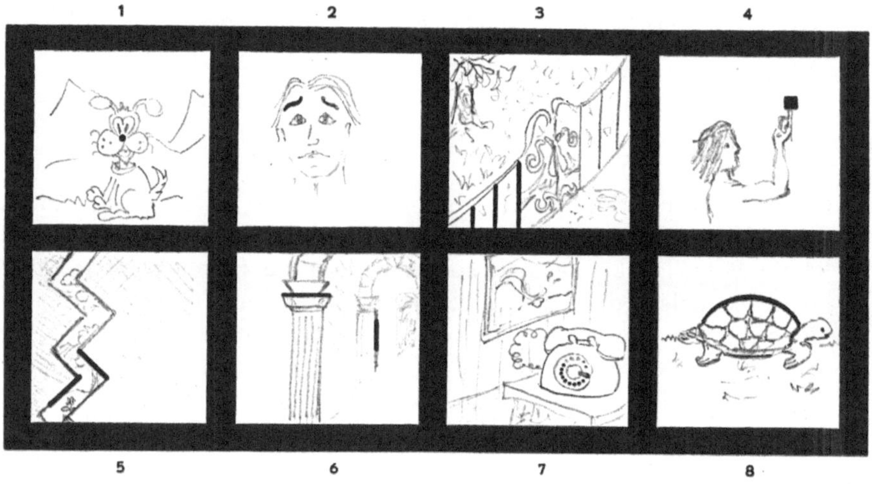

FIGURE 6.10 Example of CWS Protocol *Without Rejections*—WDCT Client Form.
Figure 6.10 provides an example of a WDCT Client Form completed by a 19-year-old female client.

	I	II	III	IV	V	VI	VII	VIII
Order of Sequence	1	2	3	4	5	6	7	8

(Write here the order in which the client completed the 8 boxes)

Total Time of performance: 6'

PINACOTECA	NOTES
B1. A cartoonish dog.	
B2. A sad face. (Q gender.) Male.	
B3. A gate into a garden.	
B4. A person with a cube on the finger. (Q gender.) Male.	
B5. From a slit in a metal fence, you see the sun and a planet.	
B6. The remains of an ancient Greek temple. You see the arches and columns.	
B7. A telephone.	
B8. A turtle.	

Which drawing do you like the most? **4** Why? **I'm surprised to have done this type of drawing.**

Which drawing do you like the least? **7** Why? **The telephone is commonplace.**

(Using a new blank form) Which stimulus do you like the most? **4** Why? **It gave me an opportunity to do something special.**

Which stimulus do you like the least? **1** Why? **It does not inspire me.**

Succession Test: + 3 8 6 2 5 7 –

Did the subject turn the Wartegg during the performance? ☐ Yes ☒ No

If YES, which panels? n/a

Was it necessary to provide the additional instructions? ☐ Yes ☒ No

FIGURE 6.11 Example of CWS Protocol *Without Rejections*—Administration Transcript. *Figure 6.11 provides the administration transcript of the WDCT protocol completed by a 19-year-old female client (presented in Figure 6.10).*

02/10/2016

Group	CWS	Code	6

Name	WOMAN 19 YRS	SCHOOL GUIDANCE	Sex	F

SCORING

	I	II	III	IV	V	VI	VII	VIII
Order of sequence	**4**	**3**	**8**	**6**	**2**	**5**	**7**	**1**
ORIGINAL ORDER OF SEQUENCE PERFORMED	1	2	3	4	5	6	7	8

TEST execution time 6 Minutes **# Boxes completed** 8

BOX	E.C.	A.Q	F.Q.	Content		FR.	SPECIAL SCORES								Movement			I.R.
				PR.	SE.										M/m	g	d	
1	1.0	1.0	1.0	AS	FA		AS											
2	1.0	0.0	1.0	HD		P	AS	MR							FE		p	
3	1.0	0.5	1.0	OBJ	BOT		AS	CB										
4	0.0	1.0	1.0	H	SIG	O	AP	AS							M	m	a	
5	0.0	1.0	1.0	OBJ	NAT	O	AS	CB										
6	1.0	1.0	1.0	ARC	AC	(P)	AS	CB										
7	0.5	0.5	1.0	OBJ			AS	CB										
8	0.5	0.5	1.0	A			AS	CB										

ANALYSIS OF SEQUENCE 1

	I	II	III	IV	V	VI	VII	VIII
Order of Sequence	4	3	8	6	2	5	7	1
Evocative Character	0.0	1.0	0.5	1.0	1.0	0.0	0.5	1.0
Affective Quality	1.0	0.5	0.5	1.0	0.0	1.0	0.5	1.0
Code	AC	C	AC	C	AD	AD	AD	PC
Form Quality	1.0	1.0	1.0	1.0	1.0	1.0	1.0	1.0
A/F Ratio	1.0 : 1.0	0.5 : 1.0	0.5 : 1.0	1.0 : 1.0	0.0 : 1.0	1.0 : 1.0	0.5 : 1.0	1.0 : 1.0
Impulse Responses								

ANALYSIS OF SEQUENCE 2

Adaptive area
(1–8)
4 AC 3 C

Adaptive area
(3–6)
8 AC 6 C

Affective area
(2–4)
2 AD 5 AD

Affective area
(5–7)
7 AD 1 PC

Istituto Italiano Wartegg

FIGURE 6.12 Example of CWS Protocol *Without Rejections*—Scoring and Computations

Figure 6.12 provides the scoring and calculations of the WDCT protocol completed by a 19-year-old female client (presented in Figures 6.10 and 6.11).

02/10/2016

Group	CWS	Code	6

Name	WOMAN 19 YRS	SCHOOL GUIDANCE	Sex	F

 # Boxes completed 8

INDICES

EC+%	63	AQ+%	69	FQ+%	100	A/F	2.0/4.0	P%	19	P+%	100	AC = 2 AD = 3
0%	25	O+%	100	I.I.T.–1	1,750	IM	0.63	AI	1.00	I.I.T.–2	3.0:5.0	NC = 0 D = 0

W.I.P. : Quadrant **D** Area β Beta

UNRESOLVED

M/m = **1 / 1**

Index of Suicidal Tendency

5 / 23

SPECIAL SCORE MR PRESENT = 1

Validity Index

1 / 18

PRIMARY CONTENTS	# 5		
H%	25	A%	13
OBJ%	38	ARC%	13
SIG%		AST%	
NAT%		BOT%	
ABS%		ANA%	
AS%	13	BIO%	
FD%		EXP%	
FIR%		ICE%	
HS%		MIN%	
CLD%		PAT%	
SEX%			

SECONDARY CONTENTS				# 5	
AC%	13	H%		A%	
HR%		OBJ%		ARC%	
FG%	13	SIG%	13	AST%	
TY%		NAT%	13	BOT%	13
MT%		ABS%		ANA%	
CG%		AS%		BIO%	
WP%		FD%		EXP%	
FR%		FIR%		ICE%	
SF%		HS%		MIN%	
MK%		CLD%		PAT%	
RE%		SEX%			

IMPULSE RESPONSES # 0

SPECIAL SCORES										# 15	
SC		SC		CB	5	CO		RB		AS	8
MR	1	ID		II		MU		PP		AP	1
GR		PR		SR		IS		DS		TR	
		Box 3 OD						Box 5 OD			

PRIMARY MOVEMENT

# M	GENDER m	f	i	DIRECTION a	p	b	d	r	i
1	1	0	0	1	0	0	0	0	0

SECONDARY MOVEMENT

# m	MI	FE	FM
1		1	

Istituto Italiano Wartegg

FIGURE 6.12 *Continued*

02/10/2016

Group	CWS	Code	6

Name	WOMAN 19 YRS	SCHOOL GUIDANCE	Sex	F

Boxes completed 8

INDICES

INDEX	boxes 1-3-6-8	boxes 2-4-5-7
EC+%	88	38
AQ+%	75	63
FQ+%	100	100
A/F	3.0/4.0	1.0/4.0
P%	13	25
P+%	100	100
O%	0	50
O+%	0	100
I.I.T–1	1,750	1,750
IM	0.75	0.50
AI	1.00	1.00
I.I.T. –2	3.0:1.0	0.0:4.0
WIP [Q/A]	C b	D g
H%	0	50
N. Sp.Sc.	7	8
N. GR, PR	0	0
M	0	1
m	0	1
N. IR	0	0
C	2	0
AC	1	1
NC	0	0
PC	1	0
AD	0	3
D	0	0

INDEX	boxes I–III III–IV	boxes V–VI VII–VIII
EC+%	63	63
AQ+%	75	63
FQ+%	100	100
A/F	3.0/4.0	2.5/4.0
P%	13	25
P+%	100	100
O%	25	25
O+%	100	100
I.I.T–1	1,750	1,750
IM	0.75	0.50
AI	1.00	1.00
I.I.T. –2	2.0:2.0	1.0:3.0
WIP [Q/A]	C b	D g
H%	25	25
N. Sp.Sc.	8	7
N. GR, PR	0	0
M	1	0
m	0	1
N. IR	0	0
C	2	0
AC	2	0
NC	0	0
PC	0	1
AD	0	3
D	0	0

INDEX	boxes 1-2-7-8	boxes 3-4-5-6
EC+%	75	50
AQ+%	50	88
FQ+%	100	100
A/F	2.0/4.0	3.5/4.0
P%	25	13
P+%	100	100
O%	0	50
O+%	0	100
I.I.T–1	1,750	1,750
IM	0.50	0.75
AI	1.00	1.00
I.I.T. –2	1.0:3.0	0.0:2.0
WIP [Q/A]	D b-	D b
H%	25	25
N. Sp.Sc.	7	8
N. GR, PR	0	0
M	0	1
m	1	0
N. IR	0	0
C	0	2
AC	1	1
NC	0	0
PC	1	0
AD	2	1
D	0	0

Istituto Italiano Wartegg

FIGURE 6.12 *Continued*

02/10/2016

Group	CWS	Code	6

Name	WOMAN 19 YRS	SCHOOL GUIDANCE	Sex	F

BOX VALUES

Boxes	Val.	Personality Description
Box 1 Self-evaluation	PC	Possible feelings of insecurity and lack of confidence in his/her abilities are limited but there is also great potential for emotional maturity.
Box 2 Female O.R.	AD	Introverted and ambivalent in relationships with others. Personality dominated by inhibition, withdrawal, and reactive responses.
Box 3 Available Energies	C	Energy level is good and effectively directed to attain desired goals. Assertive and able to persevere.
Box 4 Male O.R.	AC	Self-confident when confronting difficulties or obstacles and able to overcome them. Relationships with authority figures are generally good, although there may be some difficulty in this area of which the person is aware.
Box 5 Aggressive Energies	AD	The subject's limited abilities to manage aggression result in maladaptive attempts to manage conflict, consequently leading to reactive, immature behaviors.
Box 6 Relation to reality	C	Able to structure and synthesize thoughts and actions. Reality testing is solid and effective. Judgment and logic is good (capable of mature decision making, rational thinking, and logic). Able to understand and interpret situational and emotional nuance. Original and creative thinker.
Box 7 Sexual Energies	AD	Sexually inhibited with marked interpersonal difficulties, the subject has a strong tendency to be rigid and lacks sensitivity.
Box 8 Social skills	AC	Relationships with others are generally satisfying and mature. Difficulties in this context are generally mild, contained, and limited to specific situations.

Istituto Italiano Wartegg

FIGURE 6.12 *Continued*

02/10/2016

Group	CWS	Code	6

Name	WOMAN 19 YRS	SCHOOL GUIDANCE	Sex	F

GLOBAL ASSESSMENT

ASSESSMENT CODE	PTL	Quadrant	D	Area	β	Beta

I1)	Overall maturity level	:	Well-balanced personality structure	–
I2)	Emotional regulation	:	Self-controlled and mood stability	+
I3)	Cognitive abilities	:	Critical analysis and judgment	+
I4)	Interpersonal skills	:	Effectiveness as a group member	+
I5)	Group affiliation	:	Flexibility and adaptiveness	±

Istituto Italiano Wartegg

FIGURE 6.12 *Continued*

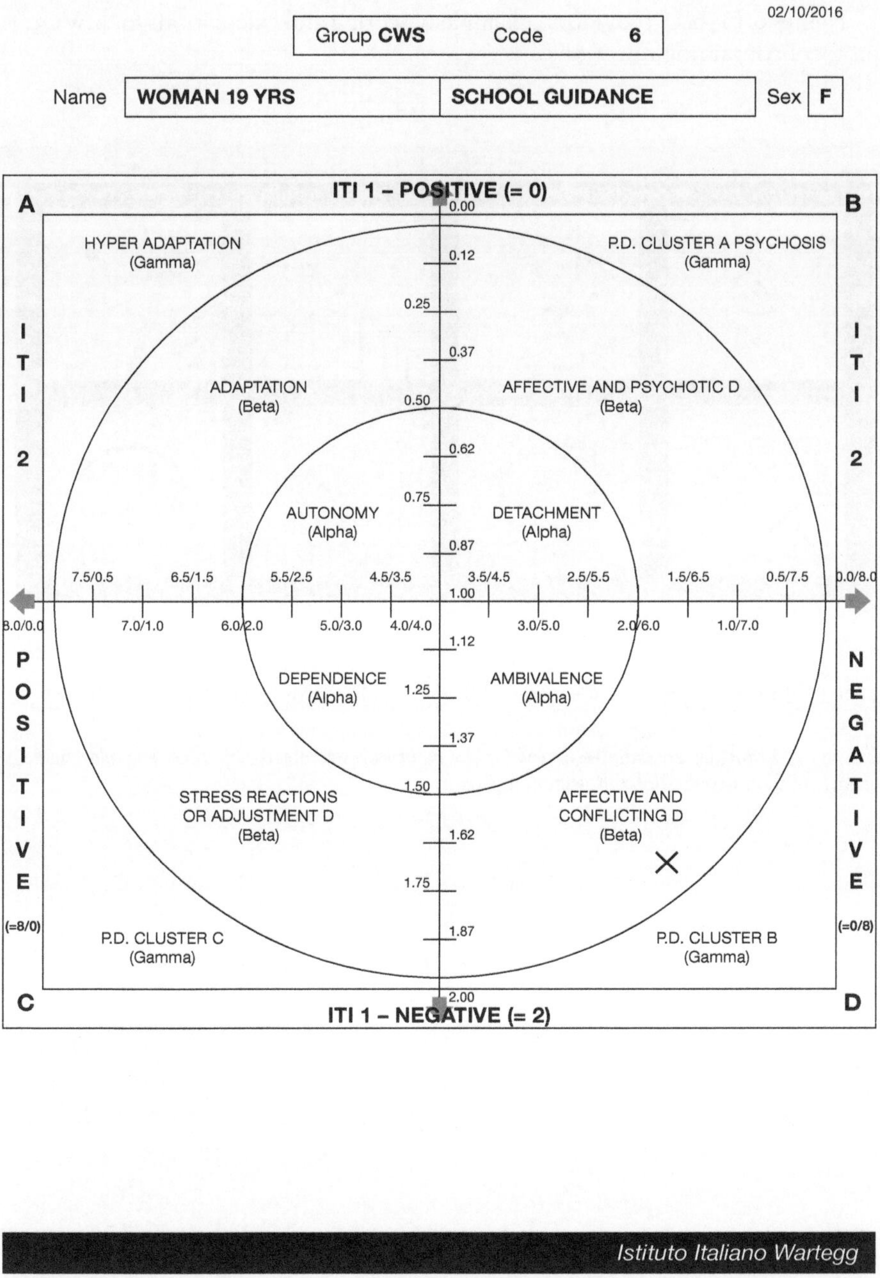

FIGURE 6.12 *Continued*

Figures 6.13–6.15 provide an example of scoring and calculations for a WDCT protocol containing rejections.

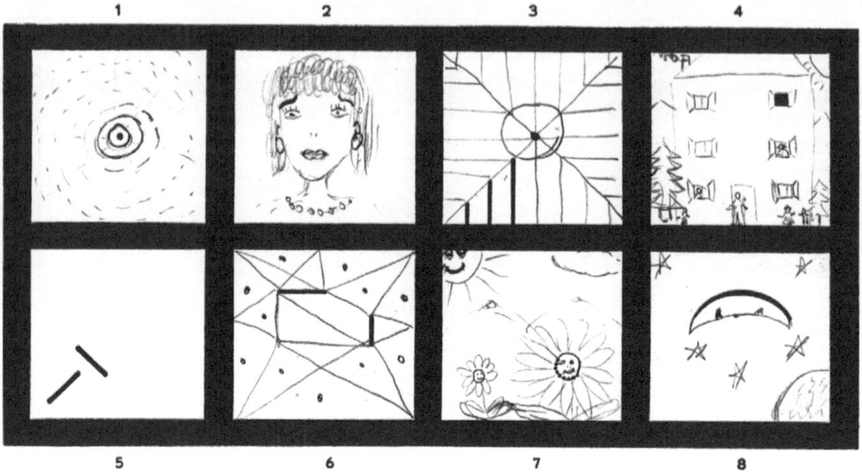

FIGURE 6.13 Example of CWS Protocol *With One Global Rejection*—WDCT Client Form.

Figure 6.13 provides an example of a WDCT Client Form completed by a 37-year-old female client, containing one Global Rejection in Box 5.

	I	II	III	IV	V	VI	VII	VIII
Order of Sequence	4	1	6	2	7	3	8	5

(Write here the order in which the client completed the 8 boxes)

Total Time of performance: 7'

PINACOTECA	NOTES
B1. The origin of the universe, the big bang. (Q mark) The point from which the explosion originated.	
B2. A woman.	
B3. Lines. Only geometrical lines.	
B4. The house where I was born, but I don't like it. The dark window makes me think of my father's room, empty after his death.	
B5. I don't know.	
B6. It could be like a star in the sky … I'm not able to draw …	
B7. Little flowers.	
B8. A rotated moon.	

Which drawing do you like the most? **6** Why? **It is a star. It's strange, but it is a star.**

Which drawing do you like the least? **5** Why? **I did not know what to do with it.**

(Using a new blank form) Which stimulus do you like the most? **None.** Why? **They all seem a bit strange to me.**

Which stimulus do you like the least? **5** Why? **As I told you before, I didn't know what to do with it.**

Succession Test: +

Did the subject turn the Wartegg during the performance? ☐ Yes ☒ No

If YES, which panels? n/a

Was it necessary to provide the additional instructions? ☐ Yes ☒ No

FIGURE 6.14 Example of CWS Protocol *With One Global Rejection*—Administration Transcript.

Figure 6.14 provides the administration transcript of the WDCT protocol completed by a 37-year-old female client, containing one Global Rejection in Box 5 (presented in Figure 6.13).

02/10/2016

Group	CWS	Code	7

Name	WOMAN 37 YRS	CLINICAL ASSESSMENT	Sex	F

SCORING

	I	II	III	IV	V	VI	VII	VIII
Order of sequence	4	1	6	2	7	3	8	5 R

* TEST OF SEQUENCE NOT PERFORMED *

TEST execution time 7 Minutes **# Boxes completed** 7

BOX	E.C.	A.Q.	F.Q.	Content		FR.	SPECIAL SCORES							Movement			I.R.
				PR.	SE.									M/m	g	d	
1	1.0	1.0	1.0	AST	EXP	(O)	AS	CB						MI		a	
2	1.0	1.0	1.0	H		P	AS										
3	0.0	0.5	0.5	SIG			AS	CB									
4	1.0	0.0	1.0	ARC		P	AS	CB	MR	PA							
5	Global rejection						GR										
6	0.0	1.0	0.5	AST		(O)	AS	CB	II	SC							
7	1.0	1.0	1.0	BOT		(P)	AP	AS	CB								
8	1.0	0.5	1.0	AST			AS	CB									

ANALYSIS OF SEQUENCE 1

	I	II	III	IV	V	VI	VII	VIII
Order of Sequence	4	1	6	2	7	3	8	5
Evocative Character	1.0	1.0	0.0	1.0	1.0	0.0	1.0	0.0
Affective Quality	0.0	1.0	1.0	1.0	1.0	0.5	0.5	0.0
Code	AC	C	AC	C	PC	D	PC	D
Form Quality	1.0	1.0	0.5	1.0	1.0	0.5	1.0	0.0
A/F Ratio	0.0 : 1.0	1.0 : 1.0	1.0 : 0.5	1.0 : 1.0	1.0 : 1.0	0.5 : 0.5	0.5 : 1.0	0.0 : 0.0
Impulse Responses								

ANALYSIS OF SEQUENCE 2

Adaptive area
(1–8)
4 1
AC C

Adaptive area
(3–6)
6 2
AC C

Affective area
(2–4)
7 3
PC D

Affective area
(5–7)
8 5
PC D

Istituto Italiano Wartegg

FIGURE 6.15 Example of CWS Protocol *With One Global Rejection*—Scoring and Computations.

Figure 6.15 provides the scoring and calculations of the WDCT protocol completed by a 37-year-old female client, with one Global Rejection in Box 5 (presented in Figures 6.13

02/10/2016

Group **CWS** Code **7**

Name **WOMAN 37 YRS** **CLINICAL ASSESSMENT** Sex **F**

 # Boxes completed 7

INDICES

EC+%	63	AQ+%	63	FQ+%	86	A/F	3.5/2.0	P%	36	P+%	100	AC = 2 AD = 0
0%	14	O+%	75	I.I.T.–1	2,000	IM	0.86	AI	1.00	I.I.T.–2	4.0:4.0	NC = 0 D = 2

W.I.P. : Quadrant **D** Area γ Gamma

UNRESOLVED

M/m = **0 / 1**

Index of Suicidal Tendency

5 / 23

SPECIAL SCORE MR PRESENT = 1

Validity Index

2 / 18

PRIMARY CONTENTS # 5

H%	14	A%	
OBJ%		ARC%	14
SIG%	14	AST%	43
NAT%		BOT%	14
ABS%		ANA%	
AS%		BIO%	
FD%		EXP%	
FIR%		ICE%	
HS%		MIN%	
CLD%		PAT%	
SEX%			

SECONDARY CONTENTS # 1

AC%		H%		A%	
HR%		OBJ%		ARC%	
FG%		SIG%		AST%	
TY%		NAT%		BOT%	
MT%		ABS%		ANA%	
CG%		AS%		BIO%	
WP%		FD%		EXP%	14
FR%		FIR%		ICE%	
SF%		HS%		MIN%	
MK%		CLD%		PAT%	
RE%		SEX%			

IMPULSE RESPONSES # 0

SPECIAL SCORES # 19

SC	1	SC	1	CB	6	CO		RB		AS	7
MR	1	ID		II	1	MU		PP		AP	1
GR	1	PR		SR		IS		DS		TR	
		Box 3 OD						Box 5 OD			

PRIMARY MOVEMENT

# M	GENDER m	f	i	DIRECTION a	p	b	d	r	i
0	0	0	0	0	0	0	0	0	0

SECONDARY MOVEMENT

# m	MI	FE	FM
1	1		

Istituto Italiano Wartegg

FIGURE 6.15 *Continued*

and 6.14). Given the Global Rejection in Box 5, many calculations are modified to account for the presence of this Special Score (described fully in this chapter).

Source: CWS Scoring Platform;

02/10/2016

Group **CWS**	Code **7**

Name **WOMAN 37 YRS** | **CLINICAL ASSESSMENT** | Sex **F**

 # Boxes completed 7

INDICES

INDEX	boxes 1-3-6-8		boxes 2-4-5-7	
EC+%	50		75	
AQ+%	75		50	
FQ+%	75		100	
A/F	3.0/2.0		4.0/2.0	
P%	0		83	
P+%	0		100	
O%	25		0	
O+%	75		0	
I.I.T–1	2,000		1,250	
IM	1.00		0.67	
AI	1.00		1.00	
I.I.T. –2	2.0:2.0		2.0:2.0	
WIP [Q/A]	D	g	D	a-
H%	0		33	
N. Sp.Sc.	10		9	
N. GR, PR	0		1	
M	0		0	
m	1		0	
N. IR	0		0	
C	1		1	
AC	1		1	
NC	0		0	
PC	1		1	
AD	0		0	
D	1		1	

INDEX	boxes I–III III–IV		boxes V–VI VII–VIII	
EC+%	75		50	
AQ+%	75		50	
FQ+%	88		83	
A/F	3.0/3.5		2.0/2.5	
P%	50		17	
P+%	100		100	
O%	25		0	
O+%	75		0	
I.I.T–1	2,000		2,000	
IM	0.75		1,00	
AI	1.00		1.00	
I.I.T. –2	2.0:2.0		2.0:2.0	
WIP [Q/A]	C	g	D	g
H%	25		0	
N. Sp.Sc.	11		8	
N. GR, PR	0		1	
M	0		0	
m	1		0	
N. IR	0		0	
C	2		0	
AC	2		0	
NC	0		0	
PC	0		2	
AD	0		0	
D	0		2	

INDEX	boxes 1-2-7-8		boxes 3-4-5-6	
EC+%	100		25	
AQ+%	88		38	
FQ+%	100		67	
A/F	3.5/4/0		1.5/2.0	
P%	38		33	
P+%	100		100	
O%	13		17	
O+%	100		50	
I.I.T–1	2,000		1,500	
IM	0.75		1.00	
AI	1.00		1.00	
I.I.T. –2	4.0:0.0		0.0:4.0	
WIP [Q/A]	C	g	D	g
H%	25		0	
N. Sp.Sc.	8		11	
N. GR, PR	0		1	
M	0		0	
m	1		0	
N. IR	0		0	
C	2		0	
AC	0		2	
NC	0		0	
PC	2		0	
AD	0		0	
D	0		2	

Istituto Italiano Wartegg

FIGURE 6.15 *Continued*

02/10/2016

Group	CWS	Code	7

Name	WOMAN 37 YRS	CLINICAL ASSESSMENT	Sex	F

BOX VALUES

Boxes	Val.	Personality Description
Box 1 Self-evaluation	C	Positive self-image, stability, self-assurance, confidence and awareness of one's abilities. Ability to adapt to the environment.
Box 2 Female O.R.	C	Appropriately adaptive to the environment, vital, and engaged with life. Socially skilled, extroverted, spontaneous, and comfortable expressing emotion.
Box 3 Available Energies	D	Activity level totally blocked due to passivity, lack of focus and inability to effectively direct energy. Psycho affective inhibition and limited ambition.
Box 4 Male O.R.	AC	Self-confident when confronting difficulties or obstacles and able to overcome them. Relationships with authority figures are generally good, although there may be some difficulty in this area of which the person is aware.
Box 5 Aggressive Energies	D	Passive, indecisive, and inhibited, aggressive energy is often repressed. Frustration is often directed toward others.
Box 6 Relation to reality	AC	Able to structure and synthesize thoughts and actions. Reality testing is solid and effective. Judgment and logic is good (capable of mature decision making, rational thinking, and logic). Able to understand and interpret situational and emotional nuance. In highly emotionally charged situations, these abilities may fluctuate and decrease in effectiveness.
Box 7 Sexual Energies	PC	The subject is emotionally perceptive with a good sense of aesthetics, and is able to understand and engage effectively with the environment. Difficulties in interpersonal or sexual relationships are generally mild, contained, and limited to specific situations.
Box 8 Social skills	PC	Good ability to relate to others, with generally mature, adaptive and stable interactions. May demonstrate ambivalent and/or reactive behaviors, in more meaningful, important, or intimate relationships.

Istituto Italiano Wartegg

FIGURE 6.15 *Continued*

02/10/2016

Group **CWS** Code **7**

Name **WOMAN 37 YRS** | **CLINICAL ASSESSMENT** Sex **F**

GLOBAL ASSESSMENT

ASSESSMENT CODE PTL Quadrant **D** Area **γ** Gamma

I1)	Overall maturity level	:	Well-balanced personality structure	–
I2)	Emotional regulation	:	Self-controlled and mood stability	–
I3)	Cognitive abilities	:	Critical analysis and judgment	+
I4)	Interpersonal skills	:	Effectiveness as a group member	+
I5)	Group affiliation	:	Flexibility and adaptiveness	+

Istituto Italiano Wartegg

FIGURE 6.15 *Continued*

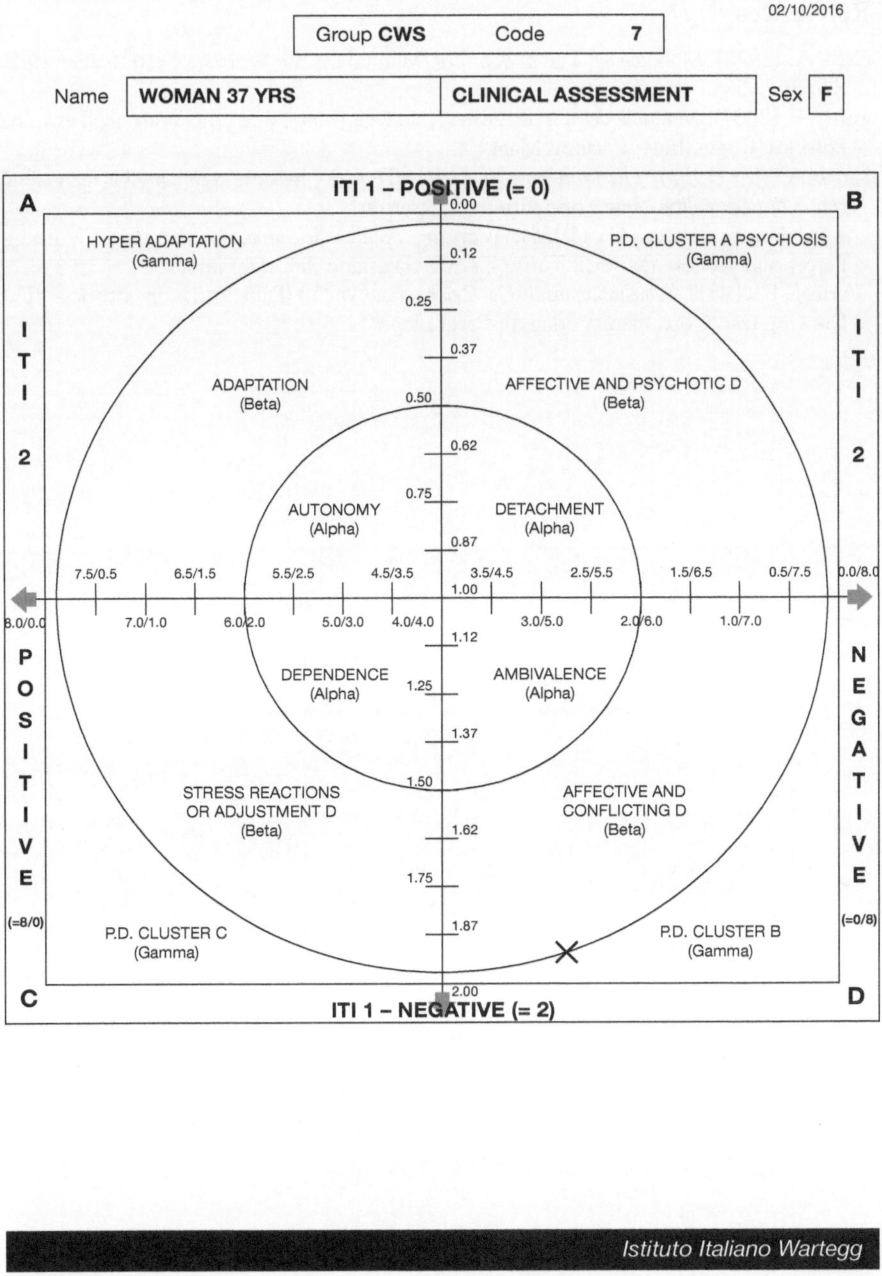

FIGURE 6.15 *Continued*

References

Crisi, A. (1998). *Manuale del Test di Wartegg* [Manual for the Wartegg Test]. Rome, Italy: Edizioni Magi.

Crisi, A. (2007). *Manuale del test di Wartegg, 2nd ed.* [Manual for the Wartegg Test, 2nd Edition]. Rome, Italy: Edizioni Magi.

Kinget, G. M. (1952). *The Drawing-Completion Test: A projective technique for the investigation of personality*. New York: Grune & Stratton.

Lossen, H., & Schott, G. (1975). *Wartegg: Analisi del processo percettivo* [Wartegg: Perceptual process analysis]. Turin: Centro Salesiano di Orientamento.

Wartegg, E. (1953). *Schichtdiagnostik-Der Zeichentest* (WZT) [Differential diagnostics—The Drawing test. Göttingen: Verlag für Psychologie.

7 Diagnostic Interpretation

The scoring elements (discussed in Chapter 5), through the calculation process (discussed in Chapter 6), result in an array of indices (i.e., computations, percentages, and ratios). These indices, in conjunction with the two additional tasks of *Picture Gallery* and *Choice of Drawings and Boxes*, provide a great deal of diagnostic information. Combined, all of these sources of information contribute to the formulation of the client's personality profile.

This chapter describes the psychodiagnostic meaning of each scoring element, including interpretation for both children and adults of the diagnostic values. In the cases where no difference between age groups is mentioned, descriptive interpretive information generally applies to both children and adults. Furthermore, it should be stressed, especially for readers not experienced in the field of psychological assessment, that all the diagnostic considerations described in this chapter should not be understood in a strictly narrow sense. That is, interpretive values are intended to be implicative rather than definitive. In the realm of psychodiagnostic assessment, the clinical value of an index or a ratio should never be interpreted in isolation from all other elements collected from the same test and from other tests, including the clinical interview. For example, an optimal value of FQ+% (81–100%) certainly indicates stability and self-control, but only when paired with an adequate A/F Ratio and in the absence of Special Scores (such as Contamination and Arbitrary Performance). Otherwise, although FQ+% is within the average range, disturbances of thought process or thought content could be present. Thus, readers are reminded and encouraged to always integrate inter- and intra-test data in order to reach an accurate diagnosis.

In structuring this chapter, the various indices are discussed in the same order in which they appear on the CWS Scoring Form (see Figure 5.1, Chapter 5). Scoring, computations, and interpretation are generally completed according to the following sequence:

1. each response of the completed WDCT Protocol is scored;
2. once the scoring is completed, the first set of indices to be derived is the Analysis of Sequence 1;
3. Analysis of Sequence 2 is completed;

4. computations, as discussed in Chapter 6, are completed;
5. with the calculations completed, the computed results for the Adaptive Area and the Affective Area are compared.

There are two exceptions to this proposed structure, the additional analytical tasks related to the *Picture Gallery* and *Choice of Drawings and Boxes*. These processes are described here first, as they relate to administration and do not rely on computations.

The Picture Gallery

Consideration of the *Picture Gallery* is especially important, as it allows for the analysis of the Wartegg response process (described in Chapter 4). Each response provided in the Picture Gallery must be carefully examined using the indices derived from the scoring in order to interpret which of the four levels of response prevailed when the client formulated the response. For example, if in Box 3 the client draws a stairway (i.e., a frequent response scored as Popular, P), this response has less personal meaning, integration, and differentiation, and it falls within response Level II (Evocative Character). However, if on the same box a different client makes a drawing with highly Original content (e.g., "The lanes of a running track seen from above"), then the interpretation must move toward Level III (Externalization) of response.

Choice of Drawings and Boxes

The *Choice of Drawings and Boxes* takes place at the end of the *Picture Gallery* verbalization phase. As explained below, in regard to the Analysis of Sequence, a decrease in the degree of preference that the client demonstrates for any of the eight boxes and stimuli of the Wartegg protocol is diagnostically significant. It provides information about: 1) the "intrapsychic placement" of the area, as reflected by the position of each specific box, within the psyche; 2) the extent to which the client accepts this area of the psyche; and 3) the extent to which this area of the psyche is functionally and flexibly integrated within the client's personality structure.

On a fundamental level, what we prefer relates to less conflictual areas of the psyche, whereas what we reject relates to more conflictual areas of the psyche. This idea reflects a basic concept of psychoanalysis, according to which our mind seeks pleasure and avoids psychic pain or anguish. This mechanism has previously been discussed as related to the Rorschach (Crisi, 1984), and was extended to interpretation of the CWS; that is, conducting an Analysis of Sequence allows us to identify areas of conflict within the client's responses to the WDCT. *As this topic is related to the Analysis of Sequence (described below), the reader may wish to review the section of this chapter regarding the Analysis of Sequence prior to continuing.*

Generally speaking, the client can demonstrate a degree of preference for both boxes and symbols (i.e., preferred vs. non-preferred), as well as a degree of consistency (i.e., consistent vs. inconsistent) between produced drawing and chosen boxes while completing the WDCT. This may indicate either optimal connection to the area of the psyche evoked by the box (in the case of consistency) or repression in the area of the psyche evoked by the box (in the case of inconsistency). More specifically, when there is a convergence between drawing and chosen box, indicated either as a major preference (e.g., the client reports that he likes the drawing made in Box 1 the most, and he also likes the symbol of Box 1 the most) or by a consistent non-preference (e.g., the client reports that she likes the drawing in Box 7 the least, and she also likes the symbol of Box 7 the least), this indicates, in the case of major preference, a close connection to the area evoked by the box; and in the case of non-preference, a great repression in those areas. When a discrepancy between the choices of drawing and boxes exists (e.g., the client reports that he likes the drawing in Box 5 the most, but likes the symbol in Box 5 the least), strong ambivalence toward the areas evoked by those boxes is present.

The Order of Sequence

It was noted before that clients' age inversely correlates with the number of clients who complete the Wartegg test following a "1 to 8" order of sequence, referred to as the Numerical Order of Sequence. The most recent data, derived from the last standardization of the CWS conducted in 2004 (Crisi, 2007), indicate that 7% of adults follow the Numerical Order of Sequence, versus 15% of children. Research data confirms Wartegg's argument that the client's demonstrated order of sequence on the WDCT is a highly personal and individualized "route" that must be interpreted on a case-by-case basis (Wartegg, 1953). In general, approximately 92% of adults and 80% of children complete the WDCT following an Individualized Order of Sequence.

Rather than an individualized sequence, approximately 8% of the adult population, and 20% of the child population, complete the WDCT utilizing one of the following four models: Numerical, Numerical Circular, Reversed, and Reversed Circular. Each is discussed below.

The Numerical Order of Sequence

The Numerical sequence is produced by individuals who are generally well balanced and well adjusted within their reality (environment) and cultural system. These are clients prone to self-control, which can possibly result, depending on the data obtained during the analyses of sequence, in emotional inhibition. These clients are characterized by general conformism, as well as by logic and predictability in their choices and behaviors. As reviewed in ►Appendix B (Table B.2), in children, as compared to the normative sample, the

Numerical sequence is found in 16% of stuttering clients, 25% of clients with learning disorders ($p < .05$), and 42% ($p < .0000$) of Deaf clients.

Table B.1 (see ►Appendix B) demonstrates that the presence of Individualized Sequences (i.e., completion sequences that do not follow the models of Numerical, Reversed, Numerical Circular, and Reversed Circular) varies consistently among the different groups studied: 80% in the non-clinical group, 69% in the learning disabled group ($p < .05$), 78% in the stuttering group, and 50% in the Deaf group ($p < .00$) as compared to the normative sample.

Furthermore, Table B.2 (see ►Appendix B) shows that in non-clinical subjects, the Numerical Order of Sequence tends to significantly decrease with age (from 19% in the 7-year-old group to 8% in the 14-year-old group, $p < .05$). This demonstrates how initial conformism develops into increasingly autonomous and individualized attitudes and behaviors as children mature. For all other groups, Numerical sequences tended to increase with age (i.e., slightly, in the case of the stuttering group—from 16% to 18%; more significantly in the case of learning disabled subjects—from 19% to 35%). Diagnostically, this indicates that in the non-clinical group, an increase in age leads to greater differentiation and adaptive plasticity, while in clinical groups, an increase in age may promote rigidity and stereotypical behavior.

The Numerical Circular Order of Sequence

The Numerical Circular sequence is typical of clients who, although well adjusted, demonstrate a higher degree of differentiation in their adaptation to reality as compared to those who demonstrate a Numerical sequence. For these clients, plasticity takes the place of rigidity; personal, individualized contents become more frequent. In these clients, there is greater integration and balance between cognitive and affective areas of the psyche. In children, this sequence is especially frequent in preschoolers (Caricchia, d'Angerio, & Lonoce, 2000) and is strongly related to circular graphic movement. After elementary school, this sequence becomes progressively less frequent, until it becomes almost absent in adults.

The Reversed Order of Sequence

The Reversed Sequence is typical of oppositional clients. These clients also tend to demonstrate strong analytical skills in comparison to their peers, but in most cases, these abilities manifest as overly critical, obstinate, stubborn and oppositional behavior. This is the kind of rigid and maladaptive stubbornness that reflects profound internal conflict projected onto others. The value of this finding is greater if the CWS protocol of these clients includes Reversed Boxes (RB), a high Impulsivity Index (IM), and either direct or indirect criticism toward the test, the testing situation, or the assessor. In children, the highest number of Reversed sequences (3%) has been found in stuttering clients (see ►Appendix B, Table B.1).

The Reversed Circular Order of Sequence

The Reversed Circular sequence is typical of clients with strong analytical skills. These clients have developed their own way of thinking. Such a way of thinking diverges from that of the other people because it is more original, more elaborated, and it demonstrates a higher degree of integration. It may relate to idiosyncratic thinking. As Table B.1 (See ►Appendix B) indicates, no statistically significant differences emerged among childhood groups.

If the client completes the WDCT by following one of the four orders of sequence described on page 167, the Test of Sequence is additionally administered (see Chapter 3 for instructions and details). In these cases, the assessor uses the Order of Sequence interpretive information described above to interpret the client's original sequence of completion. The assessor subsequently conducts the Test of Sequence, using this "new" sequence data to obtain important diagnostic information in the processes known as the Analyses of Sequence 1 and 2, described below.

Analyses of Sequence

In the past, several authors (Crisi, 1998, 2007; Kinget, 1952; Lossen & Schott, 1975; Wartegg, 1953) have focused on the Analysis of Sequence, reaching considerable agreement on the fact that the more divergent the client's approach is from the Numerical sequence, the greater diagnostic value it presents. Both the Analysis of Sequence 1 and 2 will be discussed below.

Analysis of Sequence 1

In considering the Analysis of Sequence 1, the six different Codes a box can be assigned will be reviewed, stressing the diagnostic meaning of each Code. As discussed in Chapter 6:

If the box is completed in the first half of the test (positions I–IV), it is coded as:

- *Choice (C)*: when EC + AQ > 1;
- *Ambivalent Choice (AC)*: when EC + AQ = 1;
- *Negative Compensation (NC)*: when EC + AQ < 1.

If the box is completed in the second half of the test (positions V–VIII), it is coded as:

- *Delay (D)*: when EC + AQ < 1;
- *Ambivalent Delay (AD)*: when EC + AQ = 1;
- *Positive Compensation (PC)*: when EC + AQ > 1.

Note about Global Rejections: Regarding the Analysis of Sequence, Global Rejections should be coded as Delays, marked on the Scoring Form in last place of the sequence, and scored as 0 for Evocative Character (EC), Affective Quality (AQ), and Form Quality (FQ). In the event of two or more Global Rejections, it is customary to mark them on the Scoring Form, at the end of the sequence in numerical order.

The following psychodiagnostic meaning is attributed to each box Code:

Choice (C)

Choice is the most positive code that a box can obtain. Choices indicate the most developed and integrated areas of the psyche. On the basis of these key elements, the client's personality structure evolved and matured. On one hand, a Choice indicates an area of preference, major attunement, and integration. On the other hand, very high scores (specifically, when EC + AQ = 2) can also indicate an excessive dominance of those areas in the client's personality. These areas' overdevelopment inevitably takes emotional energy away from other functions. For example, if Box 1 were completed first with EC and AQ of 1, this might represent security, awareness, and confidence in one's abilities, and might also represent traits of slight narcissism, a rigid egocentric personality structure, and relational difficulties (always in consideration with other aspects of the evaluation). In terms of prognosis, Choices represent the aspects of personality on which the therapeutic alliance can be founded.

Ambivalent Choice (AC)

Ambivalent Choice indicates that the client experiences a certain degree of ambivalence of which he/she is usually aware. Frequently the client experiences opposite feelings of equal intensity. For example, again in Box 1, an AC response indicates some indecision, insecurity, and a conscious tendency to self-deprecation, which is opposed by a desire for autonomy and agency. In other words, AC responses in Box 1 are indicative of some conflict on the dimension of dependence-autonomy.

Negative Compensation (NC)

Negative Compensation indicates a higher degree of ambivalence and sharp conflict within the area of the psyche that is evoked by the box. These feelings are generally not within the client's awareness, but instead are unconscious. NC responses are true compensations, and, as such, tend to carry a negative meaning. However, they should be understood from two points of view. On one hand, NC responses suggest profound conflict in the area in which they appear. On the other hand, they also suggest an adaptive attempt to find balance. Thus, for example, if a client draws Box 7 as first or second, but EC = 0 and AQ = 0, one possible meaning is that an unconscious strongly ambivalent and conflictual relationship with femininity and sexuality is experientially concealed at the behavioral level through mechanisms of overcompensation. For example, in the case presented in Chapter 8, this situation is described, and the client, as a result of profound trouble in his relationship with the mother, behaved like a "Lothario." While Ambivalent Choice (AC) responses can easily be confronted, because they fall within the client's awareness, NC responses require a greater degree of psychotherapeutic exploration. Thus, when many AC responses are present, cognitive or supportive psychotherapy may be appropriate recommendations. When NC responses dominate the protocol, psychodynamic psychotherapy is indicated.

Positive Compensation (PC)

Positive Compensation is the most positive among the codes of the second half of the WDCT sequence, as PC is defined by high scores on both EC and AQ. In the vast majority of cases, a PC response indicates that the area of the psyche associated with this box is equal to a Choice (C) in terms of its diagnostic value. It should be noted, however, that a code of PC is not always purely positive. For example, when negative elements are present, PC responses indicate mild to moderate complexity, including areas of conflict or difficulty. Inherent in this conflict, however, is latent potential that can function as the basis of therapeutic work directed at structural personality integration. In this way, PC responses can sometimes alert a therapist that the client is experiencing a problem, while also pointing toward the way to solve it. For example, Box 5 may be completed in the second half of the sequence, with a sum of EC and AQ higher than 1; however, other data may indicate less positive elements concerning the same area of the psyche, namely the integration of aggression into the client's personality (e.g., an Opposite Direction in Box 3 or an elevated Pd score on the MMPI-2). This presence of the PC in Box 5 would indicate that although the client's aggressive impulses are repressed and not integrated in an entirely functional manner, the prognosis for the client to resolve this conflict is good. It is by working on these same aggressive impulses that the client may become able to utilize them ego-syntonically. Therefore, a classification of PC indicates that the client has great potential (i.e., positive prognosis) in that area.

Ambivalent Delay (AD)

Ambivalent Delay is similar to Ambivalent Choice (AC). However, as opposed to AC, AD indicates that the conflict is unconscious. Similar to an actual Delay, AD indicates that unconscious ambivalence and conflict exist in a specific area of the psyche. These contents are deeply repressed, which may lead to generalized tension, reactive behaviors, and distress that govern the majority of the client's behavior. An AD suggests poor prognosis, and due to the absence of conscious awareness, indicates that psychodynamic psychotherapy is indicated.

Delay (D)

Delay represents the most negative code that a box may receive. It connotes that the client tends to repress and erase those elements represented by the box. These are, therefore, completely unconscious areas of the psyche that indirectly determine and affect all of the client's behaviors. Delays are conflictual areas that affect—mostly unconsciously—the entire personality functioning. The closer the score is to 0, the more indicative the Delay is of total repression of the related area of the psyche.

The above six categories represent a continuum from high degree of personality integration to a complete absence of integration; from a lesser degree of conflict, to a greater degree of conflict; and from a state of conscious awareness to the absence of conscious awareness. This information is summarized in Table 7.1.

TABLE 7.1 Analysis of Sequence 1—Characteristics of the 6 Codes

Code	*Level of Integration*	*Level of Conflict*	*Level of Awareness*
C	Extremely High	Absent	Present
AC	Medium/High	Low/Medium	Present/Subconscious
NC	Low/Medium	Medium/High	Absent
PC	Medium/High	Absent/Low/ Medium	Present/Subconscious/ Absent
AD	Absent/Low	High	Absent
D	Absent	Severe	Absent

As part of a valid assessment process, the above information must be integrated with the client's scores on other psychodiagnostic categories, and must be confirmed and contextualized by the formal CWS indices (Form Quality, Affective Quality, A/F Ratio, and Impulse Responses). For example, an AC response with a Form Quality score of 1 indicates greater rational control of the specific psychic conflict activated by the box than it would if the Form Quality score were 0. Similarly, for example, the diagnostic meaning of AD will be changed depending on whether or not it is accompanied by an Impulse Response (IR); when an IR accompanies AD, primary process mechanisms are likely; when AD is coded in the absence of IR, the prevalence of secondary process is suggested.

From this, we understand that the Order of Sequence, EC, and AQ are consistently utilized in determining the six types of valuation codes (C, AC, NC, PC, AD, D), whereas FQ, the A/F Ratio, and IR provide supplementary elements of interpretation. Below is a brief analysis of the diagnostic meaning of FQ, the A/F Ratio, and IR in the Analysis of Sequence 1.

FQ in the Analysis of Sequence 1

In general, FQ should always equal 1 because it represents: 1) The ability of the client to represent reality; and 2) The ability of the client to control affective states. (For further discussion of affective states, see A/F Ratio below.) Regarding the representation of reality, as FQ is based on the "evidence criterion" (discussed in Chapter 5), it provides significant information about the client's judgment, as well as the ability to determine what is useful and what is not. At the same time, a client whose drawings always are scored FQ = 1, except, for example, in Box 3 where FQ = 0, suggests that some psychological troubles in that area (Box 3) prevent positive performance.

The A/F Ratio in the Analysis of Sequence 1

The A/F ratio is calculated for each box. The values of the two parameters for each box include 0, 0.5, and 1. From the A/F Ratio, we derive information about how the affective and control elements relate to each other for the specific underlying area of the psyche elicited by each box. In the protocol of an adult non-clinical client, F should be greater than A for all boxes (e.g., 0.5/1 is an optimal ratio). Ratios in which A = F or A > F indicate emotional immaturity and limited or absent rational control over the specific area of the psyche.

Therefore, the A/F ratio for each box is an added assessment tool, which must be carefully considered in conjunction with all other CWS indices.

Impulse Responses in the Analysis of Sequence 1

As part of the Analysis of Sequence 1, the presence/absence of Impulse Responses is recorded on the last line of the CWS Scoring Form (see Figure 5.1, Chapter 5). The presence of IR in one or more boxes indicates difficulties in the corresponding areas of the psyche. As explained elsewhere, these responses should only be taken into account in interpretation when they are consistent with other formal indices.

Analysis of Sequence 2

Clinical and statistical findings contributed to further developments in the Analysis of Sequence, known as the Analysis of Sequence 2. Statistically, Boxes 1, 3, 6, and 8 appear significantly more frequently in the first half of the Order of Sequence than do Boxes 2, 4, 5, and 7 (See ►Appendix B, Tables B.25–B.35). Combining statistical considerations with the meaning that can be attributed to each box, the eight stimuli were organized into four pairs.

1–8: Box 1 elicits thoughts and feelings regarding the ego/Self. Box 8 provides information about the client's relationship to his/her environment.

3–6: Box 3 reflects the client's emotional resources and Box 6 reflects his/her ability to apply such resources adaptively.

2–4: Box 2 arouses existential dynamics of movement, and ultimately the relationship with the mother as the origin of life. Box 4 evokes dynamics of masculinity and issues related to the paternal figure. Therefore, these two Boxes are paired in light of their respective linkage with the maternal and paternal figures. (See Chapter 4 for a review of this information.)

5–7: Box 5 relates to the ability to overcome an obstacle and confront frustrating situations. It captures whether the client has access to aggressive energy that promotes survival of the species. Box 7 evokes dynamics of femininity, delicacy, and ultimately sexual energy. These two Boxes are grouped together as they represent psychic energy (in the form of aggressive impulses for Box 5 and libidinal impulses for Box 7).

The four pairs can be further grouped as follows:

Adaptive Area (1–8 & 3–6): These boxes closely relate to the client's consciousness. This includes several ego functions: perception and association, and executive functions (formation of concepts, memory, anticipation, planning, etc.); self-evaluation and self-esteem; interpersonal relationships; and the amount of energy available to the client to adapt to the environment (judgment, reality testing, etc.);

Affective Area (2–4 & 5–7): These boxes relate to affective aspects of personality that are not necessarily conscious and are sometimes completely unconscious.

In other words, four Boxes (1, 3, 6, and 8) have to do with the ego and with its adaptation process, and four Boxes (2, 4, 5, and 7) have to do with affect in its various forms.

Meaning of Analysis of Sequence 1 and 2

If the four pairs represent specific areas of the psyche, their relationships to each other can be understood in the following manner:

Choices consciously represent the main areas of affect, around which the client's personality is organized and adapted to reality.

Delays represent fully unconscious areas, repressed, that underlie the client's behavior; these represent areas of dissociated or split-off affect.

In the middle are Ambivalent Choices, Ambivalent Delays, Positive Compensations, and Negative Compensations. *Ambivalent Choices* and *Positive Compensations* represent conscious or preconscious areas, more closely related to Choices, and which contribute to the client's adaptation to his/her environment. *Ambivalent Delays* and *Negative Compensations* represent unconscious areas, more closely related to Delays, representing underlying conflict or difficulties.

Therefore, it is reasonable to hypothesize that for a non-clinical client, with a non-pathological personality organization, the Order of Sequence in the Wartegg should proceed as follows, with the optimal corresponding box Codes (depicted in Figure 7.1):

1. Boxes 1 and 8 are drawn in the first half and coded *Choices* (or possibly *Ambivalent Choices*);
2. Boxes 3 and 6 are drawn in the first half and coded *Choices* or at least *Ambivalent Choices*;
3. Boxes 2 and 4 are drawn in the second half and coded *Positive Compensations*;
4. Boxes 5 and 7 are drawn in the second half and coded *Positive Compensations*.

As shown in Figure 7.1, from a theoretical point of view, a non-clinical client should never demonstrate *Negative Compensations*, *Ambivalent Delays*, or *Delays*. Of course, in reality, this is not the case. Once again, this is only a heuristic model and, as such, it should be used only as a theoretical guide when interpreting the WDCT.

According to this model, the four pairs can be organized as presented in Figure 7.2. This model, based on theoretical expectations, and confirmed via statistical analyses (see ▶Appendix B), is the basis for the Analysis of Sequence 2.

Analysis of Sequence 1								
	I	**II**	**III**	**IV**	**V**	**VI**	**VII**	**VIII**
Expected Order of Sequence	1	8	3	6	2	4	5	7
Theoretical Coding	**C *or* AC**	**C *or* AC**	**C *or* AC**	**C *or* AC**	**PC**	**PC**	**PC**	**PC**

FIGURE 7.1 Theoretical Coding of WDCT Boxes According to Expected Order of Sequence in Analysis of Sequence 1.

Figure 7.1 details the expected Codes, by box, according to the theoretical model of the Analysis of Sequence 1 in a non-clinical individual, generally free from distress. Each box contains a positive (C or PC) or mild ambivalent (AC) Code, suggesting healthy functioning and integration.

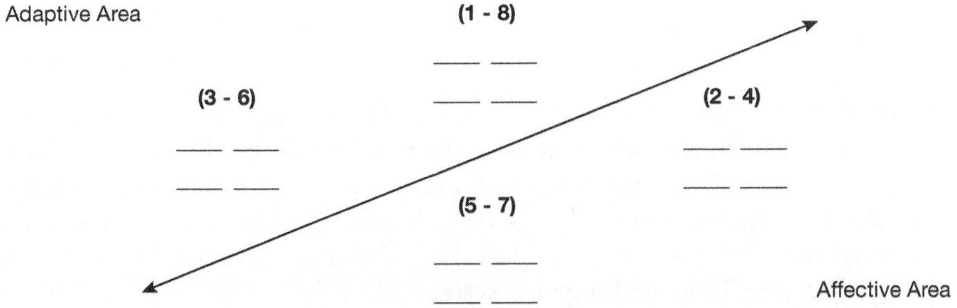

FIGURE 7.2 Example of Analysis of Sequence 2—Theoretical Order of Sequence Diagram.

Figure 7.2 provides a graphic description of the Analysis of Sequence 2, with parenthetically indicated numbers representing expected Order of Sequence according to the theoretically derived statistical model.

Here, pairs 1–8 and 3–6 represent the ego and society and fall in the realm of consciousness. Pairs 2–4 and 5–7 express affectivity, which may be conscious or unconscious. The initial hypothesis of statistical analyses was that Boxes 1, 3, 6, and 8 (boxes of ego functioning) would be more frequent in the first half of the Order of Sequence, while the other four "unconscious" boxes (2, 4, 5, 7) would be more frequent in the second half. This hypothesis was confirmed for all groups (see ►Appendix B, Tables B.18–B.19).

Interpretation of the Analyses of Sequence requires a dynamic, flexible approach on the part of the clinician. It is the clinician's job to uncover the dynamics that each box elicited in the client. Just as the human mind constantly fluctuates between conscious and unconscious content and between different modes of interacting with the environment, the same is true of CWS interpretation; the entire protocol must be interpreted in the context of the totality of varied elements available from the assessment. Only by taking this broader, flexible approach and perspective will the assessor begin to understand the appropriate meaning of each drawing.

A Note about the Analysis of Sequence in Children's Protocols

For protocols produced by children, clearly, the adult model described above cannot be rigorously adhered to. In children under 12 we expect the Order of Sequence to represent a current picture of: 1) The client's primary object relations (parents/caregivers): 2) Social adaptation; 3) Emotional development, including blockages or arrests in emotional development; and 4) An evolving picture of the clients' future adult personality organization.

Conclusions Regarding the Analyses of Sequence

In conclusion, the Analyses of Sequence are two of the interpretive tools used with the CWS that has, over time, come to be central to the assessment instrument. The Analysis of Sequence revolves around two separate, but connected levels of meaning:

- *Analysis of Sequence 1*: Assesses the degree of personality organization reached by the client in the various areas of the psyche reflected by each box. This process relies on the assessment of: Order of Sequence, Evocative Character, Affective Quality, Box Codes (Choice, Ambivalent Choice, Negative Compensation, Positive Compensation, Delay, and Ambivalent Delay), Form Quality, A/F Ratio, and Impulse Responses.
- *Analysis of Sequence 2*: Assesses how much each box diverges from the theoretical/ statistical model of functioning described in this chapter. The more a box diverges from the model, the more complex and noteworthy the client's personality structure is as regards the area of the psyche reflected by the box.

It is worth mentioning that the Analysis of Sequence is most informative when the client follows an Individualized Order of Sequence. The assessor is advised *not to complete the Analysis of Sequence* when the client produces a non-individualized approach to the test and the Test of Sequence (see Chapter 3) is unable to be administered. Examples of non-individualized orders of sequence include: Numerical; Reversed; Numerical Circular; Reversed Circular; whenever Boxes 1, 2, 3, 4 are completed first (in any order); whenever Boxes 5, 6, 7, 8 are completed first (in any order), and; any recognizable logical or methodical Order of Sequence (i.e., all even boxes first, etc.)

To illustrate the clinical interpretation of the Analyses of Sequence, two clinical examples have been included at the end of this chapter, one for each level of the Analysis of Sequence (see Figures 7.4 and 7.5). In an actual assessment report, the two levels would be integrated, but they are presented separately here to stress their respective characteristics and diagnostic power.

Major Interpretive Indices and Calculations of the Crisi Wartegg System

A summary of the major calculated indices of the CWS is presented in Table 7.2. Each index will be reviewed below, with frequencies and normative ranges presented, as well as differences between genders discussed. Considerations specific to the child/adolescent population will be provided.

Interpretive tables for major CWS indices, specifically for clinical use and interpretation, are also provided in Appendix G of this manual.

Evocative Character (EC+%)

The EC+% is representative of accurate perception and associative functions, adaptation to conventional thinking, and intact reality testing. It demonstrates the client's ability to relate to the environment. Its average value ranges from 56% to 81%. The average EC+% value is significantly higher in women than in men: 77.5% versus 74.5% ($p < .0001$).

EC+% values between 56% and 81% (produced by 76% of the normative population) indicate intact perceptive and associative functions, adaptation to conventional thinking, and adaptation to reality. These values suggest the subject's ability to relate to the environment.

EC+% values of 87% of higher are found in extremely sensitive clients, artists, and psychoanalytic patients.

Elevated values of EC+%, ranging between 94% and 100%, are found in approximately 6.5% of women and 1.3% of men. EC+% values this high are often found in severely disturbed clients who are extremely sensitive to their surroundings and external stimuli. They tend to lack appropriate filters and healthy defense mechanisms.

TABLE 7.2 Major Interpretive Indices and Calculations of the Crisi Wartegg System

Index	*General Interpretive Meaning*
Evocative Character (EC+%)	Accurate perception and associative functions; Adaptation to conventional thinking; Intact reality testing; Client's ability to relate to the environment; Sensitivity and permeability to the environment
Affective Quality (AQ+%)	Overall ability to be in touch with emotions/affect; Kind of affect that characterizes the client's life; Presence/absence of repression; Syntony with environment; Info about depression, interest in interpersonal relationships, available energy
Form Quality (FQ+%)	Quality of cognitive processes; Adequacy of reality testing; Ability to relate to environment; Soundness of judgment; Conscious self-control
Affective Stability Index (A/F)	Dynamics of personality structure; Affective balance/emotional stability; Rational thought process; Extroversion vs. introversion; Self-control; Maturity
Popular Percentage (P%)	Client's adaptation to reality; Conventional/Conformist/ Mainstream thinking
Popular with Good Form (P+%)	Ability to represent reality; Quality of adherence to mainstream thinking; Ability to perform adequate reality testing
Original Percentage (O%)	Creativity/Individuality; Interests and general fund of knowledge
Original with Good Form (O+%)	Creative abilities grounded in reality; Thinking challenges or bizarre thinking
Index of Inner Tension-1 (IIT-1)	Overall internal distress, inadequacy and emotional tension; State anxiety
Impulsivity Index (IM)	Ability to control thoughts, emotions and behavioral impulses; Internal conflict and distress
Anxiety Index (AI)	Indicates significant states of anxiety; Degree to which anxiety is well-managed
Index of Inner Tension-2 (IIT-2)	Degree of flexible personality integration and structure; Trait characteristics
Wartegg Index of Psychopathology (WIP)	Potential correlates of personality and functioning, including attachment style, symptoms, strengths, personality traits, and diagnoses
Movement Ratio (M/m)	Thought productivity; Energy level; Sexual identification; General level of cognitive functioning; Internalized tension/ anxiety/insecurity; Introspection ability; Defenses/Repression; Level of overall maturity
Primary Contents	Interests; Concerns; Difficulties; Strengths; Flexibility in thinking; Focus of cognitive energies; Propensity for treatment engagement/change; Overall energy/Cognitive effort
Special Scores	Thought productivity and cognitive level; Reality testing; Thought disturbance; Negative affect states; Psychic shock; Emotional conflict

TABLE 7.2 *Continued*

Index	*General Interpretive Meaning*
Index of Suicidal Tendencies (IST)	Constellation of scores indicating potential for self-harm or intrapunitive behaviors; Internal tension and coping
Adaptive vs. Affective Area Comparisons	Relationship of ego functioning and processes of adaptation to reality to quality and structure of primary relationships, aggressive and sexual impulses, and defenses (Ego adaptation vs. Affectivity)
Global Assessment	Severity of symptoms and functional impairments; 5 criteria indicate areas of strength and weakness

Scarpellini (1964, p. 87) reported an example in which a client, diagnosed with schizophrenia, produced a protocol that resulted in an EC+% that equaled 100%. In this example, the client was reported to have drawn the following on the WDCT:

Box 1: "Me, I am the center of a great mystery";
Box 2: "A sperm, isolated like a fish out of water";
Box 3: "A curve of my hopes and of my previous desires";
Box 4: "The black dot, the mole, of my identity";
Box 5: "The platform, the runway to re-launch my personality";
Box 6: "The blueprint in which I would like to frame my character";
Box 7: "Punctured hymen";
Box 8: "My baldness, which gives me a sense of inferiority."

EC+% values of 50% and below (produced by 5% of the population) indicate organic or cognitive deficits, adaptive rigidity, and lack of flexibility. Such low values usually occur in individuals that are poorly adjusted, and/or not inclined to social interactions.

In children, the EC+% index usually has a greater range. EC+% values for children also tend to be higher than in the adult group. The increase in value is inversely proportional to the child's age. This relates to a less structured personality that is not yet made rigid by social norms and conventions. Thus, extremely high values, up to the age of 9 or 10, should be interpreted more leniently in children than in adults.

Affective Quality (AQ+%)

The AQ+% index assesses how well the client's projections are attributed to well-structured, functional, and integrated dynamics. This applies to each box and, thus, to each area of the psyche. Overall, this index evaluates: the client's ability to be in touch with emotions; the kind of affect that characterizes his/her emotional life; the presence of repression; and the extent to which he/she can be syntonic with the environment.

The normative range for AQ+% spans from 50% to 69%. This should not be mistaken for an excessively low value. In fact, an AQ+% score of 100% is only theoretically possible. For the majority of people, four boxes (3, 4, 5, and 6) elicit projections with neutral content (i.e., OBJ, ARC, SIG). These contents are scored as 0.5, leading to a maximum AQ+% value of 75%. (This value is obtained by scoring Boxes 2, 4, 7, and 8 as 1 and the other 4 Boxes as 0.5. Thus, the total score is equal to 6, which translates into an AQ+% value of 75%.)

However, because nothing is ignored in the diagnostic process, those cases with an AQ+% value of 94–100 (produced by less than 1% of the normative population) may indicate: Severe cognitive deficits when the high values of this index are due to the perseveration of positive contents; Marked traits of immaturity and infantilism, and/or; Extroverted personalities dependent on interpersonal relationships.

The mean values of AQ+% are statistically different between the sexes. The mean value for females is 67.7%, whereas the mean value for men is approximately 60.6% ($p < .0001$). This is consistent with other tests, such as the Rorschach (see also A/F ratio).

AQ+% values lower than 50% (produced by 14% of the normative population) are indicative of depressive personalities that are scarcely interested in interpersonal relationships, unable to establish a connection with the environment, and/or repression of affect.

Elevated AQ+% values between 75% and 87% may be found in highly adjusted clients (3% of the normative population), who are accommodating in their interpersonal relationships and may use defenses such as denial. These values may also be indicative of high impulsivity and a tendency to act on emotions.

In a control group of children, the mean for the AQ+% was found to be 62%. This control group consisted of 282 clients, both male and female, between the ages of 6 and 14. This group included a sub-group of Deaf children. The Deaf group was the only experimental group showing a statistically significant difference from the control group (Deaf group, AQ+% = 58%).

It should be noted that the above interpretive statements regarding adults may also be applied to children with the necessary adjustments to statistical ranges made. Additionally, in evaluation of children, it must be remembered that average ranges (using the child statistics) will indicate expected developmental functioning for that age group (i.e., in children, some degree of immaturity, indicating less ability than adults in the corresponding adult average level, would be demonstrated).

Form Quality (FQ+%)

From a strictly cognitive perspective, FQ+% provides information about the quality of cognitive processes, on both a quantitative (i.e., intellectual level of the client), and qualitative level (i.e., quality of attention, concentration, planning, anticipation, concept formation, adaptation to secondary process, etc.). More generally, FQ+% assesses: Adequate reality testing; Ability to relate to the environment; Sound judgment; Defense mechanisms; and Conscious self-control.

Generally, the value of FQ+% falls between 81% and 100% (produced by 93.8% of the normative population), which indicates the individual's intact ability to use cognitive processes to manage emotions. While high levels of FQ+% are expected in the non-clinical population, when elevated values of FQ+% are found in clinical populations (concurrently with other signs of affective or personality dysfunction), these levels of FQ+% may also indicate depressive tendencies, paranoid personality traits, and obsessive-compulsive symptoms.

An FQ+% value of 75% must be carefully evaluated, especially in highly educated clients. This value is only found in 4.6% of the normal population. It must be closely analyzed in relation to Box 6. An FQ+% of 75% is indicative of cognitive deficits or a lack of self-control and poor reality testing. The lower the FQ+% value becomes, the higher the chance that the client is psychologically disturbed or cognitively limited.

In non-clinical clients, FQ+% tends to range between 94% and 100%. When this value is combined with an A/F ratio where the F side is much higher (such as 1/4), it is indicative of conformity, a lack of spontaneity and affective connection, excessively rigid defenses, and a proneness to develop psychosomatic symptoms.

For children, the mean FQ+% in the control group was 65%. This value steadily increases with age (56% at age 6–7; 67% at age 8–10; 75% at age 11–14). This confirms the diagnostic meaning of this index. That is, the value of FQ+% increases with the development of cognitive abilities, rational functions, control factors, and the experiences and knowledge of the individual.

Affective Stability Index—A/F Ratio

The comparison between Affective Quality and Form Quality, known as the Affective Stability Index, describes how affect relates to rationality in the client. More experienced assessors are likely to notice the similarity between this index and the EB index in the Rorschach Comprehensive System (Exner, 1997, 2003). By analyzing how the affective and rational aspects of an individual are organized within his/her personality structure, we are better able to understand the individual's inner life. This comparison allows us to determine how well these aspects of the personality are balanced, and which factor is dominant (i.e., extroverted versus introverted). This index tends to evolve as the person develops. Initially, Affective Quality tends to be greater than Form Quality (A > F), but this ratio shifts toward Form Quality (A < F) beginning in pre-adolescence.

The A/F Ratio demonstrates the presence or absence of emotional stability, affective balance, self-control, and maturity.

The A/F ratio has four main combinations:

1. A < F (with F greater than A by 1–2 points, such as 2/4): This ratio is the normative value, which is found in approximately 66% of the normal population. It indicates emotional stability and balance, as well as the ability to effectively manage feelings and emotions.
2. A << F (with F greater than A by more than two points, for example 1/4): This ratio is found in approximately 10% of the normative population. It indicates a tendency toward rigidity, inhibition, constriction, conformism, and a lack of spontaneity. As A decreases in value, these characteristics become more profound.
3. A ≈ F (this includes A = F, for example 3/3, or A < F by 0.5, for example 2.5/3). This ratio is found in approximately 23% of the normative population. It indicates the presence of sociability and spontaneity. However, depending on the clinical picture and implications of other test indices, it can also signify immaturity, dependency, and impulsivity.
4. A > F (A greater than F): This ratio is only found in approximately 2% of the normative population. It suggests a marked conflict in the area of affect, egocentrism, and a tendency to act out. These individuals tend to be "explosive," extremely immature, egocentric, and are unable to plan and organize activities. This is especially true when combined with low values of FQ+% and an absence of primary movement.

When both sides of the ratio are low, (with A ≤2 and F ≤2; for example, 1.5/2, 1/1.5, or lower) clients are likely limited cognitively, or demonstrate personalities have been inhibited by extreme conflict and/or depression.

The mean value of F in the A/F ratio is similar for men (3.9) and women (3.95), although statistically significant differences were noted ($p < .01$). The mean value of A in this particular ratio is significantly different for men and women, with a mean of 2.59 for males and 2.93 for females ($p < .0001$).

It has also been found that there are different frequencies for men and women in the four combinations of the A/F ratio mentioned above. For example:

A < F is found in 66.7% of males, and in 59.7% of females ($p < .01$);
A << F is found in 10.5% of males and in 5.3% of females ($p < .01$);
A ≈ F is found in 20.9% of males and in 33.5 % of females ($p < .0001$);
A > F is found in 1.8% of males and in 1.5% of females (no significant difference).

Therefore, an A < F or A << F ratio is found in 77.2% of male cases and in 63% of female cases, whereas an A/F ratio of A ≈ F and A > F is found in only 22.8% of male cases and 35% of female cases.

In a normative sample of children, differences tended to emerge depending on the age group. Specifically:

- children aged 6–7 show on average an A > F ratio (prevalence of affective aspects);
- children aged 8–10 show on average an A ≈ F ratio;
- children aged 11–14 show on average an A < F ratio.

The differences between the three groups were statistically significant (ranging from $p < .01$ to $p < .001$).

Frequency

Interpretation of Frequency in the CWS requires consideration of both Popular (P%) and Original (O%) responses, as well as the percentage of each of these types of responses that are accompanied by adequate Form Quality (P+%, O+%). Each is addressed below.

P% (Percentage of Popular Responses)

This frequency represents the extent to which the client adheres to mainstream thinking, and adaptation to reality.

Of Popular responses, Giambelluca, Parisi, and Pes (1995) have written:

> Popular responses are relevant in the assessment of the following areas: Functioning of perceptive-associative processes; Degree of automatism of perceptive-associative processes; Reality testing; Stereotypic thinking or flexible thinking depending on the percentage; Degree of adaptability; Recognition of objective data; Recognition of the other and object relations; Knowledge of social norms; Integration in one's environment; Defensive flight into depression and dullness for high percentages.
>
> (p. 318)

In the WDCT, Popular responses range on average from 12% to 31%. Higher percentages are generally found in clients with stereotypical thinking, who lack critical skills. High values can also be found in depressed individuals, and in conformistic clients.

When low percentages, such as 12% or below are combined with elevated values of FQ+% and O+%, this may indicate a tendency toward creativity. However, when combined with elevated values of O%, but low values of O+%, it tends to suggest a lack of reality testing with manic or psychotic symptoms potentially being present.

It should be noted that P% = 0 is only found in 10.7% of the normative population. Moreover, only 4.9% of individuals concurrently produced both P% = 0 and Human (H)% = 0.

The maximum value of P% cannot reach 100%. The upper limit of P% is 81.25% in children and adult males. This is because Boxes 1, 5, and 7 can only receive Semi-Popular [(P)] scores of 0.5. Popular responses cannot be scored in these three boxes. Therefore the maximum score that a client can obtain in terms of P% is:

	5	(obtained by giving a P response in Boxes 2, 3, 4, 6, and 8)
+	**1.5**	(obtained by giving a (P) response in Boxes 1, 5, and 7)
=	**6.5**	(which translates into a P% of **81.25%**)

In adult females, the upper limit of P% is 88%, as Boxes 5 and 7 can only receive Semi-Popular [(P)] scores of 0.5.

For children, the non-clinical group showed an average P% value of 26%, which was significantly higher than that of the clinical groups.

P+% (Percentage of Popular Responses with Good Form Quality)

In the WDCT, contents are scored as popular according to their statistical frequency. However, contents can be more or less positive depending on their associated Form Quality. In other words, the process of adaptation to reality and to mainstream thinking can be assessed not only quantitatively (with P%), but also qualitatively (with P+%). Therefore, this index reflects the client's ability to represent reality, the quality of his/her adherence to mainstream thinking, and his/her ability to perform adequate reality testing.

The value of P+% must not drop below 81%. For example, if a record shows P% = 25 and P+% = 87, we can argue that the person is well adjusted, with intact reality testing. However, if P% = 25 is combined with P+% = 40, we may say that this is an initial sign of social dysfunction or mental deterioration. In the severely mentally ill, with the exception of paranoid personality, both P% and P+% are low. Clients with paranoid tendencies or overt paranoia tend to use defense mechanisms such as rationalization and/or intellectualization in a rigid manner (and therefore their P% and P+% is typically higher).

In a normative sample of children, the P+% value was 72% compared to 65% in a stuttering group, 53% in a learning disabled group, and 55% in a Deaf group. This suggests that a child from the non-clinical population is more likely to conform to mainstream thinking and adhere to adequate reality testing. The clinical groups demonstrated some degree of adherence to conventional thinking, but with greater effort and less accuracy.

O% (Percentage of Original Responses)

O% represents the client's ability to individually and creatively elaborate on the stimulus. It also demonstrates the ability to move away from stereotypical thinking by creating original drawings, and it is linked to divergent thinking. Generally, O% assesses the direction of the person's interests and general fund of knowledge.

In regard to Original responses, Giambelluca, Parisi, and Pes (1995) wrote:

> Original responses contribute to the assessment of the following aspects: Characteristics of associative and perceptive processes; Use of primary and secondary process and their interaction; Level of intelligence; Specific pathological characteristics that relate to ego-functioning; Mood; Identification of primary defenses, centered on suppression or on repression; Specific differential diagnosis for personality disorders.
>
> (p. 321)

The O% value tends to range between 6% and 18% (produced by 48% of the normative population). Elevated values, equal to 25% or higher, indicate that the client has an excessive tendency to retreat into his/her own world, to limit interpersonal communication, and to rely on fantasy rather than reality.

Low values are often found in clients that demonstrate concrete thinking, are poorly educated, tend to rely on stereotyped associations, or are depressed.

In a normative sample of children, the O% was approximately 12%.

O+% *(Percentage of Original Responses with Good Form Quality)*

The O+% index measures a person's creative ability. Its value on average is above 81%. Thus, a creative person with high intelligence tends to show a medium to high O%, with an O+% of 81–100%. O+ responses often represent professional attitudes and individual interests. The content of original responses can also be related to highly conflictual areas in the individual's life. In this case, we will have a "highly individualized" response, with potentially significant psychodiagnostic meaning.

O+% values less than 81% (and more so for lower values) indicate either marked conflict in the area of functioning or bizarre thinking.

O% (with good Form Quality) and M (Primary Movement with good Form Quality) have primary significance in evaluating cognitive abilities. Higher values of O% and M generally indicate above average functional intelligence. 78.4% of normative subjects contemporarily showed O% = 0 and M = 0.

IIT-1 (Index of Inner Tension-1)

The Index of Inner Tension-1 is derived from the two most frequent special scores in the CWS, Anxiety Stroke (AS) and Crossed Border (CB). This index is indicative of non-specific emotional distress and describes the extent of *inadequacy* and *emotional tension* that the client experiences.

IIT-1 is based on the theoretical assumption, agreed upon by many authors, that AS and CB hold specific diagnostic meaning. AS indicates anxiety, insecurity, and indecision. CB indicates internal conflict and impulsivity. Furthermore, generally these two phenomena do not happen comparably in the same person. For these reasons, a combined index was developed, indicative of the overall internal distress experienced by the client. As explained below, the IIT-1, by nature of the Special Scores on which it is based, must be interpreted as an index that measures *State* (transient or episodic) distress, or distress felt in the moment. The value of IIT-1 is increased in the presence of movement of inanimate objects (MI), Animal Movement (FM), Facial Expressions (FE), Cloud Contents (CLD), and the special score Incomplete Drawing (ID) if related to FQ+% ⩾81%. (This is why the IIT-1 formula is adjusted in calculating the WIP; see Chapter 6 for more information.)

The value of IIT-1 usually ranges between .25 and .75; higher values indicate marked internal conflict and emotional distress.

When elevated values of IIT-1 are associated with elevated FQ+% and an A/F ratio where A<<F, psychosomatic disturbances may be present.

In children, the lowest value of IIT-1 is found in the normative (non-clinical) group (IIT-1 = .19). The clinical groups demonstrated statistically significant differing values of IIT-1 ($p < .001$): Stuttering group, .36; Learning disabled, .42; Deaf, .32.

IM (Impulsivity Index)

The Impulsivity Index is derived from the number of Crossed Border (CB) special scores contained in the client's protocol. The IM measures the client's ability to control emotions and behavioral impulses. Values below .25 are considered adaptive, and are not indicative of psychopathology. Higher values show heightened impulsivity. It must be noted that an elevated value of IM (for example IM > .5) alone is not sufficient to establish if behavioral impulsivity is present. In order to hypothesize the presence or absence of behavioral impulsivity, one must take into account: FQ+%, the A/F Ratio, and the number of Movement responses. Specifically:

- *Impulsivity* is usually consistent with: elevated IM, low FQ+%, A ≈ F or A > F and no M responses.
- *Repression* and *control of impulsivity* are usually consistent with: elevated IM, high value of FQ+%, A<<F and elevated number of M responses.

In assessing the Impulsivity Index (IM), the specific type of Crossed Border (CB) known as "Leaning Over" (i.e., when the client's drawing simply touches the side of the box, without actually crossing the border) must be considered differently from overt graphic strokes that cross the boundaries of a box. This less severe tendency can indicate either a need for safety and stability (when paired with other signs of insecurity, such as: H%, ARC%, and Self-Criticism), or a tendency to be excessively controlling (when paired with FQ+% = 100 and, more importantly, A < F).

In children, the highest average value of IM is found in learning disabled clients (.2), followed by stuttering clients (.15), Deaf children (.09) and finally by non-clinical clients (.03). Thus, the highest value of impulsivity is found in children that behaviorally mask their symptoms, showing "their distress and opposition through the silence of the drawings" (Bianchi di Castelbianco, Crisi, & Di Renzo, 1996, p. 149).

AI (Anxiety Index)

The Anxiety Index is derived from the special score Anxiety Stroke (AS). AI relates to experienced anxiety, and its average value ranges from 0 to .50. Scores above .75 indicate significant states of anxiety, whereas .63–.75 suggest low-level anxious symptoms. The degree to which the anxiety is or is not well managed is evaluated by analyzing the graphic quality of the response and other formal indices (mainly FQ+% and A/F Ratio):

- When the *anxiety is well managed*, the drawing shows well-defined, often light shadows.
- When the client is *not able to manage the anxiety*, the drawing is messy, lacks order, and shows heavy, non-defined shadows.

In forensic psychology (especially in cases of child custody), and in the field of personnel selection, highly elevated scores, between .75 and 1, are common.

In children, what has been described above in regard to IM also applies to discussion of AI. Values of AI for the normative (non-clinical) group are the lowest (.15). The clinical groups demonstrated the following average values of AI (ranging between $p < .05$ to $p < .001$): Stuttering, .21; Learning disabled, .2; Deaf, .2).

IIT-2 (Index of Inner Tension-2)

The IIT-2 is a non-specific assessment of the main factors around which the personality is structured. Each box in the Wartegg relates to a different area of personality. Therefore, positive box Codes (such as C and PC), should prevail in the Analysis of Sequence 1 of a non-clinical client. In other words, in a well-functioning individual, the IIT-2 should lean to the left side of the ratio, the side that refers to the positive Codes of the Analysis of Sequence (C and PC). The values on the negative right side, when present, should generally be AC (the least pathological among the remaining possible classifications).

Values considered positive on the IIT-2 are ratios such as 7/1 and 6/2. However, depending on the client's age, as well as the configuration of Codes present in the protocol (for example, a 5/3 configuration formed by 3 AC is less negative than one formed by 3 D), ratios of 5/3 and 4/4 can also indicate sufficiently integrated personality organization (for example, in adolescents).

The IIT-2 cannot simply be evaluated quantitatively. To the contrary, an attentive qualitative analysis of the composition of this index should be performed. For example, the same IIT-2 value of 5/3 takes on a completely different diagnostic meaning depending on what this value results from: (1C)+(4PC)/(3AC) or (4C)+(1PC)/(3D). In the first case, the index holds a positive diagnostic connotation; in the second case it holds a negative one. Similarly, special attention must be paid to the 8/0 ratio. These are excessively positive ratios, which might hide overly adjusted (hyper-adapted) personalities according to the "false-self model." This may suggest conscious attempts to present oneself as a conformist (as found in forensic cases, child custody evaluations, and in the field of personnel selection), personalities structured around denial, or narcissistic personalities.

The average normative values of the IIT-2 are 4.8/3.2 in males and 5.4/2.6 in females. A comparison between gender indicates a statistically significant difference in the left side values (4.8 in males versus 5.4 in females, $p < .0001$).

Furthermore, in terms of quantitative analysis of IIT-2, highly significant differences are found between genders, as presented in Table 7.3.

TABLE 7.3 IIT-2—Frequencies by Gender (N = 2,293)

IIT-2	*Male N*	*Male %*	*Cumulative %*	*Female N*	*Female %*	*Cumulative %*	*p*
8/0	25	1.3	1.3	19	5.6	5.6	.0001
7/1	189	9.7	11.0	54	15.9	21.5	.001
6/2	415	21.2	32.2	101	29.7	51.2	.001
5/3	537	27.5	59.7	75	22.0	73.2	.05
4/4	436	22.3	82.0	66	19.4	92.6	—
3/5	245	12.5	94.5	17	5.0	97.6	.0001
2/6	78	4.0	98.5	5	1.5	99.1	.05
1/7	25	1.3	99.8	3	.9	100.0	—
0/8	3	.1	100.0	0	.0	100.0	—

Just like the IIT-1, the IIT-2 is a non-specific index of distress or tension. However, being based on the calculations of the Analysis of Sequence, the IIT-2 provides a more accurate and subtle interpretation. The evaluations of the Analysis of Sequence represent more stable personality structures and personality "traits," and therefore, the IIT-2 can be interpreted to reflect *trait* characteristics. Conversely, being based mainly on the special scores of Crossed Border and Anxiety Stroke, the IIT-1 represents more transient elements, temporary conditions that are less deeply rooted in the personality. *That is, the IIT-1 describes "states," whereas the IIT-2 describes "traits."*

The Wartegg Index of Psychopathology (WIP)

First and foremost, it must be stressed that the values for the two indices reported here (IIT-1 and IIT-2) must be understood as having explanatory and interpretive purposes, rather than simply points on a graph to be concretely and quantitatively understood. That is, in clinical practice, as mentioned above, these indices must be also analyzed qualitatively. Similarly, it must be clarified that the diagnostic meaning of the Wartegg Index of Psychopathology (and the comparison between IIT-1 and IIT-2) must not be interpreted rigidly, but rather is intended to provide potential indications and correlates of a client's personality and functioning. As with all personality assessment measures, the WIP must be used in concert with other psychodiagnostic assessment tools.

Starting from what was discussed above (and briefly introduced in Chapter 6), the information derived from the IIT-1 relates to "states," whereas the information derived from the IIT-2 relates to "traits." Based on this assumption, the IIT-1 and IIT-2 scores are plotted on two intersecting axes. The scores fall on a continuum from a positive score (i.e., absolute absence of psychopathology) to a negative score (i.e., severe psychopathology). This procedure results in four different

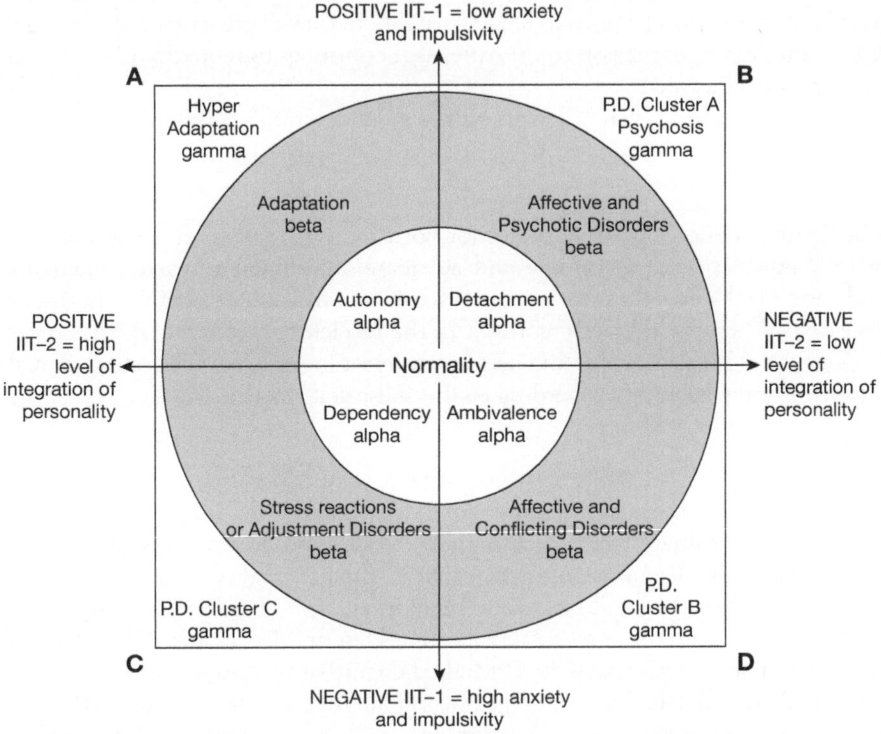

FIGURE 7.3 Wartegg Index of Psychopathology (WIP).

Figure 7.3 presents a graphic representation of the Wartegg Index of Psychopathology, depicting the IIT-1 as the vertical axis (experienced distress and tension), and the IIT-2 as the horizontal axis (personality flexibility and integration). Intersection of these indices results in four quadrants, each with personality correlates, attachment styles, and diagnostic indications.

quadrants: A, B, C, and D (pictured in Figure 7.3). Diagnostically, each quadrant identifies and describes different domains of functioning, with associated strengths and weaknesses, by which to conceptualize and understand the client.

In addition to the four quadrants, a second graphic categorization model has developed, which is overlaid on the first. Here, three "areas," beginning with a circle at the intersection of the axes, and proceeding in concentric circles outward, describe the severity or intensity of symptoms.

The central circle (known as area α) corresponds on one hand to "normality," intended as adequate psychosocial adjustment. On the other hand, this adjustment comes with certain psychological patterns of personality structure and attachment style. Thus, *autonomy* dominates quadrant A; *detachment* dominates quadrant B; *dependency* dominates quadrant C; and *ambivalence* dominates quadrant D.

In the next circle outward from the center (known as area β), quadrants B, C, and D show an exacerbation of the tendencies represented in the internal circle. The closer the scores get to the outermost border of the circle or to the external vertex of the section (known as area γ), the more they express psychopathology. Quadrant A is an exception to this rule, as it continues to represent efficacy and appropriate adjustment.

More specifically, each WIP quadrant can be described as follows.

Quadrant A

Quadrant A denotes positive scores for both indices. It represents "normality," with a prevalence of autonomy and adequate adjustment (area α). Elements indicating lack of balance, tension, and significant distress are completely absent (area β). When the subject's scores fit in the top left corner (area γ), the scores no longer hold positive value and take on the meaning of hyper-adaptation, denial defenses, and personality according to the "false-self" model.

Quadrant B

Quadrant B denotes positive scores for IIT-1, but not for IIT-2. Dynamics of detachment dominate this area (area α). Area β and area γ show progressive worsening of the diagnostic meaning; that is, the personality structure becomes clearly more disturbed and lacks functional integration. Furthermore, awareness and emotional pain for one's distress becomes less and less evident. This lack of awareness may be indicative of: a) Marked cognitive limitations; b) Personality organized around detachment, isolation, and fulfillment of fantasy (area β); or c) Cluster A (Schizotypal, Schizoid, Paranoid) or Cluster B (Antisocial) personality disorder; d) Psychosis (area γ).

Quadrant C

Quadrant C denotes positive scores for IIT-2 and negative scores for IIT-1. Dynamics of dependence prevail in this area (area α). Marked distress emerges in a personality organization that is otherwise quite balanced and that shows reactive behaviors typical of Posttraumatic Stress Disorder (PTSD) or, more generally, adjustment disorders (area β). In area γ, the client appears severely disturbed and Cluster C personality disorders may be present (i.e., Avoidant, Dependent—with the exception of Obsessive Personality that falls within quadrant D).

Quadrant D

Quadrant D denotes negative scores for both the IIT-1 and IIT-2. Patterns of ambivalence dominate this area (area α). The profound distress that emerges from this quadrant is of a chronic and long-standing nature, originating early in the client's development and impacting subsequent personality structure, and is accompanied by marked emotional pain and awareness of one's distress. When the client's WIP falls within area β, dynamics of immaturity and conflict—characteristic of this chronic "structural" distress—predominate. When the client's WIP falls within the area γ, the picture evolves toward Obsessive Personality Disorder (Cluster C) and Cluster B personality disorders (i.e., Borderline, Histrionic, Narcissistic—with the exception of Antisocial Personality disorder, which falls within Sector B).

Ratio M/m

Primary Movement (M) generally represents cognitive and introspective abilities, including coping resources. In the normative population, it is expected that Primary Movement will exceed Secondary Movement (m, comprised of FE, FM, and MI) with an anticipated ratio of M = 1–2/m = 0.

Secondary Movement (m) in adults generally represents inner tension and immaturity. If several m responses are present, especially if their number is greater than M (M $\leq$ m), this indicates an immature affectivity and represents a mask over unacceptable drives.

Contents

Contents reflect the client's interests, concerns, and difficulties. They are organized into two main categories: Primary and Secondary. For both groups, interpretation of Contents is based on two main criteria: 1) The number of categories; and 2) The percentage value obtained for each category.

Number of Primary Content Categories

On average, this number ranges between four and six Content categories. A lower number (i.e., three and below) can relate to stereotypical thinking, depression, low propensity for change, mental retardation, or restricted interests. A higher number (i.e., seven or eight) may indicate numerous and diverse interests;

however, higher numbers may also indicate the dissipation of energies that are not channeled toward achieving a purpose, including manic traits (in this case, the elevated number of contents is paired with low FQ+%).

The number of Primary Content categories must be interpreted on the basis of the overall quality of the CWS protocol. In this way, a high number, (i.e., six or more Content categories), in an overall positive protocol shows versatility, curiosity, and varied interests; however, the same number of Content categories, in an overall poor protocol, may indicate unstable thought processes, ideational hyper-productivity, manic traits, and aggression. Conversely, a low number of Primary Content categories (i.e., three or less) in a CWS protocol of good quality may suggest limited (but highly developed) interests, cultural and ideational poverty, and/or depressed mood; however, the same number of Content categories, in an overall poor protocol, may suggest inadequate associative processes, low intelligence, social isolation, depression, and anxiety.

Percentage of each Primary Content Category

These percentage values reflect the client's interests, concerns, and difficulties. The most frequent contents produced in the CWS are (in order from the most to the least frequent): OBJ, SIG, ARC, H, A, NAT, AST, and BOT. It must be noted that the frequency of each Content category differs depending on the box. Specifically:

- OBJ contents are most frequent in Boxes 1, 4, 5, 6, and 7;
- ARC contents are most frequent in Boxes 3, 4, and 6;
- H contents are most frequent in Boxes 2 and 8.

The most frequent CWS Content Categories are as follows.

OBJ%: OBJ contents represent 41.5% of responses, with a maximum peak in Box 5 (60% of responses), and the lowest number of responses in Box 2 and 3 (16% and 14% of responses, respectively). On all other boxes, values range between 26% and 42%. The Object Content category produces mean values that are quite different between males and females (females: 35.1%; males: 42.6%, $p < .0000$). OBJ responses are produced by approximately 97% of clients in the normative sample.

Object contents are indicative of the client's practical skills, and of a realistic attitude toward life and personal interests. The mean value ranges between 25% and 50%. 42.5% of males and 34.9% of females ($p < .0001$) fall within this average range. An elevated number of OBJ%, especially when paired with H% = 0, indicates tension in interpersonal relationships, traits of withdrawal, and an excessive tendency to retreat into oneself. Values higher than 62% are only found in 8% of clients.

Values < 25% indicate few practical aptitudes, as well as possible exaggerated abstract thinking tendencies.

SIG%: SIG contents represent 15% of responses, with the highest peak in Box 6 (34%, no difference between gender). In Box 2, SIG responses are quite rare (<2%). SIG contents are produced by approximately 28.2% of the normative sample.

An elevated number of SIG responses may indicate cognitive deficits or a strongly defensive attitude, which in some cases invalidates the test (in the most defensive clients it is not uncommon to find up to eight SIG responses).

In children, students in first and second grade may produce an elevation of SIG responses, which often represents a momentarily heightened interest for the unknown and fascinating world of writing and numbers. In discussing SIG% and children, a somewhat unique case provides an example: A learning disabled child (Dyslexic) drew what looked to be the letter "d" in Box 1. During the Picture Gallery he stated, "Like the initial of my name." As his name began with the letter "b," his drawing was determined to be inverted, appearing like the letter "d."

ARC%: 87% of clients of in the normative group produce ARC content on their CWS protocols. ARC contents represent 19.1% of CWS drawings, with a significantly elevated peak in Box 3 (60%). Elevated values are also found in Boxes 4 and 6.

The Architectural Content category produces mean values that are quite different between males and females (females: 18%; males: 19.5%, $p < .05$). Values higher than 25% (13% of normative population) may indicate conscious overcompensations and indicate internal insecurity and need for environmental approval, or dependency traits.

H%: Human contents represent approximately 12% of all responses (no difference between gender). They are the most frequent in Boxes 2 and 8, with peaks of 35% and 22% respectively. They also reach peaks in Boxes 1 and 7 of 11% and 19% respectively. On other boxes, they represent 2% to 7% of responses. H responses are produced by approximately 66% of individuals in the normative sample.

The normative mean value of H% ranges between 12% and 25% and its diagnostic meaning describes the client's inclination to be social, ability to relate to others, and level of gender identity. Surprisingly, in the normative group, approximately 1/3 of clients scored H% = 0 (34% of total group; 26% of females, 35% of males, $p < .01$). Despite the fact that such an elevated percentage of people show this score, a lack of H responses indicates difficulty with socializing (Crisi & Carlesimo, 2008) and a personality that is closed off, reserved, and scarcely inclined to social interaction. When H% = 0 and P% = 0 (or is low), social adjustment difficulties may be present. (H% = 0 and P% = 0 is present only in 4.9% of the normative group: female = 2.6%, male = 5.3%, $p < .05$).

Only 5.6% of clients show H% > 25%. This high value indicates marked social interest and empathy, but also suggests a strong need to lean on others and marked dependency traits.

In children, each Wartegg protocol with no human responses (H% = 0) must be carefully evaluated. This is a troublesome score, especially when paired with low percentage of Animal (A%) responses, and very high Object (OBJ%) frequency. Similarly, it is a shared opinion that a lack of human responses in the Rorschach should raise concerns.

A%: This category represents 4.7% of the responses to the CWS and the average is quite low (male = 4.3, female = 6.8, $p < .0001$); 31.8% of individuals in the normative sample produce A content. Animal responses in the CWS are not produced as frequently as in the Rorschach, for example, due to several differences between these measures. First, the symmetry of the Rorschach inkblots favors the perception of animal shapes, whereas the stimuli of the WDCT do not. Second, verbalizing animal content is significantly easier than drawing animal content (as compared to, for example, drawing a geometric figure or simple object). These factors combine to result in a lower A% on most CWS protocols.

The percentage of Animal responses must be interpreted on the basis of the overall quality of the CWS protocol. For example, an above average percentage (e.g., ⩾ 25%,) in an overall positive protocol suggests formalism, stereotypical thinking, and affective immaturity; however, the same value in a protocol of overall poor quality may indicate psychopathology (i.e., in psychotic clients, oftentimes A% = 100), depression, obsessiveness, passivity, and dependence.

In children, the A% mean tends to be higher, and until the age of 7 or 8, Animal responses may substitute for Human responses. After this age, the A% tends to reduce and the presence of Animal responses is interpreted similarly to those of adults.

NAT%: Natural contents represent approximately 5% of responses and are provided by approximately 37% of clients. Their mean value of NAT% is 4.8%, with no significant differences noted between male and female clients. The meaning of NAT%, somewhat similar to that of BOT%, relates to interpersonal sensitivity.

AST%: Astronomical content responses are found in 26.1% of clients in the normative group (no differences noted between gender). Responses represent 3.6% of total responses to the CWS. The diagnostic meaning of the AST content category is connected to a cool and/or detached affectivity that can hardly be expressed. If accompanied by an overall good quality of CWS protocol, AST responses may indicate depressive tendencies, affective and emotional poverty, and difficulties in social relationships; however, in protocols of overall poor quality, AST contents may indicate the presence of anxiety, emotional regression, and severe adaptation challenges.

BOT%: BOT responses comprise 4% of CWS responses, and were produced by 28.1% of individuals in the normative sample. The BOT content category produces mean values that are quite different between males and females (females:

7.8%; males: 3.5%, $p < .0001$). Botanical responses, more typical of the female population, indicate sensitivity and aesthetic interests. In males, 79% of the population (compared to 49% in females) produced CWS protocols containing no Botanical content (BOT% = 0). Elevated values in males, when corroborated by other indexes (such as AD or D), may indicate confusion or conflict related to gender identity.

All other Content categories appear quite rarely; however due to their relevant diagnostic meaning, important interpretations are possible when these Content categories are present. This less frequent group of Content categories is comprised of representations of Animal Content (AS), Abstract Content (ABS), Anatomical Content (ANA), Biological Content (BIO), Cloud Content (CLD), Explosions (EXP), Fire (FIR), Food Content (FD), Human Representation (HS), Ice Content (ICE), Mineral Content (MIN), Pathological Content (PAT), and Sexual Content (SEX). Interpretive guidelines for these "rare" Primary Contents are provided in Table G.16 (Appendix G).

Number of Secondary Content Categories

The number of Secondary Contents usually ranges between 0 and 2. It is rarely above 3. When the number is greater, if paired with an elevated number of Primary Contents, the index has decreased meaning, due to excessive diffusion of content.

In considering this expected number of Secondary Contents (between 0 and 2), it is important to note that this expected range refers only to "true" Secondary Contents (listed below; that is, those content categories that are only scored as Secondary Contents). While any Primary Content may also be scored in the secondary position, these are not considered when comparing Secondary Content categories to expected ranges.

Percentage of each Secondary Content Category

In adults, the most frequent Secondary Contents are weapons (WP, more likely to be produced by males); Figurative Art (FA), Religion (RE), and Clothing (CG, more likely to be produced by females).

In children, the most frequent Secondary Contents are Fairy Tale (FT), Science Fiction (SF), and Toys (TY).

Secondary Contents can be grouped for the purpose of interpretation. Interpretive guidelines for Secondary Content categories (by group) are provided in Table G.17 (Appendix G).

Total Number of Special Scores

Special Scores categorize unusual phenomena that may accompany the test sequence and produced protocol. The total number of Special Scores generally indicates the degree of the client's distress. Generally speaking, aside from Anxiety Stroke (AS)—the most frequent Special Score—only a few Special Scores are found in the non-clinical population. Thus, in addition to the importance of conducting a qualitative analysis of the recorded special scores, it is useful to examine quantitatively the *number* of Special Scores. Typically, in a normative protocol, between 8 and 10 Special Scores are likely (including both Anxiety Stroke and Crossed Border, the most frequent Special Scores). The higher the number of Special Scores, the more complex the client's state is likely to be. Special Scores always hold psychodiagnostic significance. Clinical experience suggests that the more rare a Special Score is, the more diagnostically relevant it is.

Type and Number of Special Scores

First and foremost, it is important to note that the presence of only one Special Score in a CWS protocol is almost never descriptively significant. The presence of only one Special Score most likely indicates that the client experienced some type of emotional disturbance when presented with a specific box. It is the repetition of a Special Score that indicates diagnostic severity.

It should be noted that Special Scores found in $\leq 2\%$ of the normative sample are considered to be rare.

According to their psychodiagnostic value, Special Scores can be organized in three groups, as follows:

Level 1—Expressions of Primary Process

- AP Arbitrary Performance
- CO Contamination
- DS Disproportion
- PA Personalized Answer
- TR Transparency

Level 2—Expressions of Cognitive Deficit

- AP Arbitrary Performance
- ID Incomplete Drawing (if FQ+% < 81)
- II Inadequate Integration
- MU Missing Union
- PP Perseveration
- SR Stimulus Repetition

Level 3—Expressions of Conflict

- AS Anxiety Stroke
- CB Crossed Border
- GD Global Rejection
- ID Incomplete Drawing (if FQ+% $\geq$81)

- IS Interpreted Stimulus
- MR Morbid
- OD Opposite Direction
- PD Partial Rejection
- RB Reversed Box
- SC Self-Criticism

Level 1—Expressions of Primary Process

Arbitrary Performance: The AP special score is typical of 2% of the normative sample. It has a similar interpretive meaning to the FABCOM Special Score in the Rorschach Comprehensive System. It always indicates reality distortions in the client. The more this response is arbitrary in quality, the more suggestive it is of cognitive or psychotic disturbances.

In children, beginning in the 2nd grade, this score always indicates poor reality testing.

Contamination: The CO special score is rare (found in only .1% of the normative sample). It indicates an interjection of primary process into the client's thinking process. True contamination is typically found in the protocols of schizophrenic patients, where several different elements are condensed in an unnatural or unrealistic manner. A less severe form of contamination is indicated by the depiction of mythological characters, science fiction characters, and similar representations.

The CO special score always indicates some degree of deficit in the area of concept formation. Its diagnostic meaning takes on a more negative connotation when the patient is not aware of the contamination and does not try to justify it to the assessor. Also, the more it is associated with low Form Quality, the more concerning this score becomes.

In children, the CO special score should be carefully evaluated, as children's books and TV shows are filled with "contaminated" creatures (that is, organisms or creatures with human, animal, and/or mechanical parts). As for adults, the weight of this score is reduced if the client acknowledges that he drew a comic or fictional character. When all human figures produced by the client are contaminated, the interpretive value of this score is strongly significant. In these cases, strong tensions with the environment, under-developed sexual identity, or difficulty controlling sexual and aggressive energies may be indicated. The more contaminations arbitrarily incorporate different and incongruent parts, the more severe they are considered.

Disproportion: The DS special score is found in 1.4% of the normative sample. It either indicates limited ability to draw or detachment from reality (i.e., weakened reality testing). A distinction must be made between two forms of Disproportion: 1) The first relates to a disproportion within the drawn object itself (e.g., the dot in Box 1 is the head of a big figure); and 2) The second relates to a drawing of disproportionate size in one box compared to the remainder of the protocol (e.g., in a Wartegg protocol of small/medium size drawings, one drawing takes up the whole box; see below, Noted Special Phenomena). The first form of DS is mostly interpreted as detachment from reality; the second form might indicate an expression of shock in response to the Evocative Character of the disproportionately drawn box.

In children, this special score is quite frequent until 2nd grade.

Personalized Answer: The PA special score is quite rare (2.4% of population). It always reflects a "projection of one's self" and a surfacing of primary process. A mild form of this phenomenon is found in egocentric, narcissistic, and emotionally immature clients. A marked presence of PA is found in clients with mental retardation or schizophrenia.

In children, PA is quite frequent up to 8 or 9 years of age. The presence of a PA response normally indicates a concrete experience from the child's life (with people or things), either positive or negative in nature. For example, a child with strong attachment to his father, in Box 4, drew "A paperweight, like the one that my dad has on his desk."

Transparency: The TR special score is found in 1.4% of the normative sample. It is to be expected up to the age of 6 or 7. After this age its presence must be carefully evaluated, as it is indicative of disturbances of thought process.

Level 2—Expressions of Cognitive Deficit

Arbitrary Performance: See description above.

Incomplete Drawing: Incomplete Drawing is considered an expression of cognitive deficit when it is accompanied by a Form Quality (FQ+%) less than 81%. The ID special score with FQ+% < 81 is found in only .2% of the normative sample. When Incomplete Drawing is scored repeatedly, and is paired with scores that indicate cognitive deficit, it indicates that the client's ability to represent reality is inadequate, partial, and not sufficiently grounded in the client's thought process.

In children, this special score becomes extremely rare past the ages of 6 or 7. If present, and supported by other indices and assessments, ID may indicate cognitive deficits.

Inadequate Integration: The II special score is found in 6% of the normative sample. It conveys more information than any other score about developmental cognitive delays and lack of reality testing. Again, in protocols containing only one instance of II, the score must be understood more as an expression of shock, rather than as one of cognitive deficit.

In children, II Special Scores are common until the age of 9 or 10. Past this age, the presence of even just one instance of the score must be carefully evaluated.

Missing Union: The MU special score is only found in Boxes 3, 5, and 6 (although it is also theoretically possible in Box 7), and it applies to .1% of the normative sample. In general this score indicates a struggle with Gestalt perception; thus it is not frequent. It suggests cognitive deficit and/or depressive inhibition of intelligence.

In Box 5, Missing Union reflects marked repression of aggressive impulses that are not sufficiently integrated in the person's personality structure. (This only applies to Box 5, given the Evocative Character of the stimuli.) For children, in Box 5, no significant differences were recorded between the normative (non-clinical) sample and the clinical samples.

In Box 6, Missing Union is more frequent (and statistically significant) in stuttering and learning disabled groups. In the learning disabled group, MU might be interpreted as the result of limited perceiving, planning, and foreseeing skills.

Perseveration: The PP score is found in 1.4% of the normative sample. It might indicate:

- specific interests of the client (when FQ+%≥94);
- guardedness toward the assessor (perseveration of SIG content);
- organic conditions (when it is paired with low FQ+% or the same content is repeated on almost all boxes);
- severe psychopathology (often accompanied by elevated FQ+% to indicate paranoid delusions).

The most severe form of content perseveration is found in clients that draw the same content in all eight boxes (i.e., "monotypical perseveration"). For example, a client in a manic state drew weapons in all Boxes.

In children PP it is normal up to 6 or 7 years of age.

Stimulus Repetition: The SR special score is characteristic of .2% of the normative sample. In its most severe form (presence on four or more boxes) it indicates a cognitive deficit or an organic condition. In its less severe form (presence in one or two boxes) SR indicates a low level of education or a dismissive attitude toward the test.

Level 3—Expressions of Conflict

Anxiety Stroke: AS is the most frequent Special Score, with almost 99% of all individuals in the normative sample producing at least one. AS signifies the presence of anxiety, and when more than six AS are present in a protocol, indicates significant (conscious) anxiety. Interpretation of AS is increased when paired with CLD contents, scary faces, or negative box Codes in Boxes 5 and 7. As it represents a transient distress state, AS may be especially elevated in assessments conducted for personnel selection or for forensic purposes (similar to what happens with the L scale in the MMPI).

In children, AS is found in 15% of boxes in the normative group. The clinical groups produced higher scores, ranging from 21% to 23%, without this difference being significant.

Crossed Border: CB is the second most frequent Special Score; 65% of the population produces between 0 and 2 CB, 15.2% produce three, and only 19.6% produce four or more CB within a protocol. When four or more CB are present, this indicates the likelihood of internal tension and conflicts. This score signifies that the client is in a reactive state. The lower the self-control indexes (FQ+% and A/F), the more likely it becomes that internal tension will be expressed behaviorally, especially when the CB score is elevated.

As mentioned in Chapter 5, even the smallest mark on the border is scored as CB. Therefore, the nature of each instance of CB must be carefully evaluated. For example, only one CB in Box 3 (where it is most common) is not scored at all (if the CB occurs on the bottom border of the box). Several minor CBs indicate a need for safety and stability, when paired with other signs of insecurity, such as elevated H%, FQ+% = 100, ARC% > 25%, and the presence of a Self-Criticism (SC) special score. Alternatively, when FQ+% = 100 and A < F, several minor CBs may signify a tendency to being excessively controlling and to discharge aggressive impulses in small, continuous doses. Three instances of CB, when consistent with the rest of the evaluation, may indicate the presence of manifest aggressive impulses.

In children, CB reaches only 4% of the total of the boxes in the normative (non-clinical) group, but the statistical differences with the other groups are significantly elevated ($p < .001$).

Global Rejection: The GR special score is the most evident expression of difficulty in responding to the Evocative Character of a stimulus. It indicates that the client is experiencing conflict around a particular area of the psyche.

In the normative sample, one or more Global Rejections are found in only 6.4% of clients, precisely in 7.1% of males and 2.7% of females ($p < .05$). They are most common in Boxes 7, 4, and 5. The lowest number of Global Rejections has been recorded in Box 8.

The meaning of the GR Special Score is more or less severe depending upon several factors:

- The frequency with which Global Rejection is recorded on a particular box, within a specific group. For example, in stuttering clients, the most rejected box is Box 5, whereas in learning disabled clients, it is Box 4.

- A rejection can be more or less severe depending on the general personality structure that emerges from the testing. For example, a box rejection within the context of relatively average indices tends to indicate conflict circumscribed to a particular area that otherwise does not greatly interfere with the client's personality structure. Conversely, when a rejection is recorded in the context of a more disturbed personality organization, it must be weighted more heavily. It indicates interference with ego functioning and the ability to adopt perceptive and associative mechanisms (for example, a female client diagnosed with schizophrenia rejected Boxes 1, 2, and 4).
- Clinical practice shows that Global Rejection carries different values depending on the box on which it is recorded. For example, in Box 1, GR often reflects identity issues; in Box 2, it indicates disturbed object relations with females; in Box 3, GR reflects a block in energy flow; in Box 4, it indicates disturbed object relations with males; in Box 5, GR is connected with repressed aggressive impulses; in Box 6, it reflects cognitive and adaptation difficulties; in Box 7, GR is connected with repressed libido; finally, in Box 8, it shows difficulties in relating with the environment.

In children, Global Rejection is quite rare, making the instances of its occurrence more diagnostically meaningful. The clinician must therefore carefully consider in what box it occurred and to what manifestations it is connected.

Incomplete Drawing: Incomplete Drawing is considered an expression of conflict when it is accompanied by a Form Quality (FQ+%) equal to or greater than 81%. The ID special score with FQ+% ⩾81 is found in 3.6% of the normative sample. When it appears in isolation and is not accompanied by other scores indicating cognitive deficit (e.g., II, SR, PP, MU, AP) it expresses neurotic conflict. It also indicates marked traits of insecurity, indecision, and fear of responsibility. Finally, ID is connected with expressions of anxiety, and it indicates the presence of a strongly defensive attitude (which, when especially marked, can border on paranoia).

Interpreted Stimulus: The IS special score is typical of .5% of the normative sample. It is a particular type of rejection that must be interpreted as a tendency to remove painful content from awareness. IS are often found in the protocols of poorly motivated clients, who may be either aware or unaware of their rejection of the task.

Morbid Contents: The MR special score in the CWS is similar to the Morbid special score in both the Rorschach Comprehensive System (Exner, 1997, 2003) and the Rorschach-Performance Assessment System (R-PAS; Meyer, Viglione, Mihura, Erard, & Erdberg, 2011). Specifically, as in these other systems, this score captures two distinct response phenomena: 1) When the client draws or verbalizes objects, people, or situations that are objectively damaged, abnormal, destroyed, deteriorated, or decomposing (often containing terms including, "broken," "ruined," "dead," "sick," "diseased," "mutated," "disabled," and/or "misshapen"; and 2) Indications of sadness, pain, distress, dysphoric mood or overt depression, gloominess, pessimism, or hopelessness. MR is not scored for aggressive or angry content. The CWS MR special score typically identifies depressive affect and symptoms in the client, and has been related to mood disorders via research.

Opposite Direction: The OD special score is infrequent and it is only scored in Boxes 3 and 5. It is found in clients that experience marked repression of aggressive impulses. In these clients, aggressive impulses are not integrated into the personality structure and can result in inappropriate and dysfunctional behaviors such as inadequate responses to frustration, lack of assertiveness, lack of zest, apathy, and depression. In cases of major depressive disorder, and when paired with other specific indexes (elevated Impulsivity Index, lack of M, low FQ+%, Morbid special score), Opposite Direction may be indicative of self-harming behaviors or an intrapunitive orientation.

In children, the same parameters listed for adults also apply.

Partial Rejection: The PR special score is typical of 1.2% of the normative sample. It is a less accentuated version of Global Rejection (GR); it indicates the presence of marked psychological conflicts, although these are experienced less significantly than in the case of GR, or with strong ambivalence. The presence of PR is similar to the diagnostic implications found in boxes valued as Ambivalent Delay (AD). That is, in its clinical meaning, PR can be related to Ambivalent Delay because both represent an ambivalent behavior toward the box. In other words, drawing something in a WDCT box without fully considering the symbol is representative of ambivalence toward the psychological area described by the box.

Reversed Box: The RB special score is found in 10.9% of the normative sample. Two or more instances of RB always indicate the presence of oppositional traits. Only one Reversed Box may indicate that the Evocative Character of the box caused a halt in the person's flow of free association, which led the client to attempt to modify the gestalt of the box. The interpretation of oppositionality is heightened by the client's completion of the WDCT utilizing the Reversed Order of Sequence.

In children, adolescents show the greatest expression of this Special Score. (For example, one client completed the sequence of boxes from Box 8 to Box 1, also reversing all boxes).

Self-Criticism: The SC special score is quite common. It indicates feelings of insecurity, indecision, and poor self-esteem. When self-criticism appears only at the beginning of the test it is evaluated much less negatively than when it is found throughout the protocol. The diagnostic meaning of self-criticism is magnified by an elevation of ARC%, by "Or" responses (see Noted Special Phenomena below), or by the presence of dotted lines.

Noted Special Phenomena

In additional to the formally scored Special Scores discussed above, some additional phenomena are found in reviewing WDCT protocols, including: Big Drawing (BD), Blackening (BL), Encapsulation (EN), Color Projection (CP), Conjoined Boxes (CJ), Disproportion between Boxes (DB), Human Content Negation (HN), Improper Description (IP), "Or" Answer (OA), Perspective Response (PS), and Small Drawing (SD). Diagnostic interpretive guidelines of these phenomena are provided in Appendix G, Table G.19.

Total Number of Impulse Responses

In the majority of Wartegg protocols, there are no Impulse Responses. Therefore, the presence of only one Impulse Response might take on specific meaning and provide a significant diagnostic contribution. Impulse Responses, according to Erikson's theory of development (1959, 1994), can illustrate the client's primary modes of interaction with the outside world.

Oral Impulse Responses are the most frequent, recorded in 5% of boxes in the normative sample.

Type of Impulse Response and Box in Which It Manifests

Impulse Responses tend to signify the presence of a current internal conflict or personality trait, which might be understood as fixations in phases of emotional development, lack of sexual identification, traits of emotional immaturity, or other dynamic processes. It must be remembered, however, that the presence of specific content categories only suggests possible interpretations (e.g., the possibility of dependency might be suggested in a protocol where a child draws food, but without corroborating evidence from other indexes, is not sufficient for interpretation). Therefore, once again, hazardous generalizations and rushed interpretations must be avoided. That is, elevated scores on a single index, not supported by other calculations, should not be included in the testing report.

Total Number and Direction of Primary Movement Responses

Primary Movement responses (M) represent 27.8% of all movement responses in the normative sample. The majority of clients (approximately 80%) tend to provide no M responses; 15% of clients provide one Primary Movement response. Only 5.5% of clients shows $M > 1$. The low frequency of this type of responses is partially due to the graphic nature of the test, and partially due to the strict rules for their scoring.

In considering the interpretation of M, $M > 1$ generally indicates optimal cognitive level and well-developed introspective abilities (especially when paired with O+%). An excessive number of M ($M > 3$) must be carefully evaluated, as it might reflect an excessive tendency to turn inward, toward introversion.

Type and Direction of Primary Movement Responses

Primary Movement responses are indicative of thought productivity and the capacity for introspection. They are strictly related to cognitive ability and quality of intelligence. M responses generally start emerging in the CWS protocols of clients around 6 or 7 years of age.

Furthermore, M responses can provide information about sexual/gender identity. In general, individuals produce movement responses representing clients of their same gender. Otherwise, this can be interpreted (even in isolation) as a sign of a poorly established sexual identity.

The direction of movement is also an important diagnostic element.

- *Active* M responses indicate strong-willed, action-oriented people, who are able to react to situations. This carries an important positive prognostic connotation.
- *Passive* responses indicate potentially unmotivated clients, with a tendency for giving up.
- *Blocked* and *Rotary* M responses suggest strong internal tensions.
- *Double* and *Indeterminate* M responses indicate ambivalence, indecision, and lack of self-confidence.

Total Number and Direction of Secondary Movement Responses

In the normative group, a little over half of the clients (approximately 52%) produced no Secondary Movement responses; 30% of clients produced only one Secondary Movement response; 18% of clients produced more than one Secondary Movement response.

It must be noted that this category of responses can be expressed through three types of movements: a) Animal Movement (FM); b) Inanimate Movement (MI); and c) Facial Expression (FE). These categories respectively carry the following meaning:

Animal Movement (FM): Animal Movement responses represent 19% of all movement responses and show spontaneous affect and a prevalence of repression as a defense mechanism. The direction of FM takes on the same meaning that it has for M. In adults, when occurring in isolation or in the presence of at least one M, it indicates an ability to show a "child-like" side and might reflect some ability to relate with children (i.e., in the field of personnel selection, this can be a positive indicator for positions that require working with children). If FM responses appear in conspicuous number, especially when FM > M, this may indicate arrested development at an infantile stage, immaturity, and concealed instincts that are otherwise intolerable to consciousness.

In children up to the ages of 7 or 8, FM responses fully substitute M responses (and must be interpreted as such). These responses do not express emotional immaturity, but instead the manner in which the client manifests feelings and drives. The negative psychodiagnostic interpretation of these responses increases with age.

Inanimate Movement (MI): Inanimate Movement responses represent the largest group of movement responses in the normative sample (47.6%). They express internal tensions and conflict that are better managed when the drawings represent mechanical objects and less well managed when the drawings represent astrological or elemental objects (i.e., planets) and climate conditions (i.e., rain, wind, rising smoke).

In terms of psychodiagnostic meaning, the direction of movement is especially important in MI responses:

- MI *active* responses indicate:
  - — energy that is not filtered through secondary process;
  - — use of primary process;
  - — internal zest;
  - — vivacious and exuberant affect;
  - — creative promptness.
- MI *passive* responses indicate a quality of answer that refers to more marginal personality traits. The possible psychodiagnostic interpretations of MI must also be confirmed by other data in the protocol. The following meanings have been described in the literature (Giambelluca, Parisi, & Pes, 1995, p. 286):
  - — tendency to become withdrawn;
  - — marked tendency to compulsive self-scrutiny;
  - — social isolation;
  - — resignation mixed with exhibitionism;
  - — generic and scarcely realistic ambitions.

Facial Expression (FE): In the normative sample, the representation of facial expressions, with the addition of emotional expression represents 15.7% of all movement responses. It indicates a need to connect and relate to people. It is often strictly related to the client's prevalent mood. Giambelluca et al. (1995) noted:

> When FE responses reach an elevated number, their perseveration reflects the significance of the specific problems that they represent. Psychodiagnostic indications refer to the following aspects: Punitive superego; Guilt; Fear of persecution; Fears and phobias; Problematic object relations; Suspiciousness and guardedness; Aggressive Impulses; Specific personality traits.
>
> (p. 285)

A Note about Movement Responses with HS, HDS, AS, and ADS Content

An extremely rare, but also extremely significant diagnostic connotation is the attribution of movement to AS, ADS, HS, and HDS contents ("stand ins" or representations; e.g., the responses: " the face of a sad puppet"; "a painting of a galloping horse"; or "A walking Robot"). In these cases, the respective movement category is scored as a tendency ("→"). For example, the above examples are scored respectively: → FE; → FM; and → M. Psychodiagnostically, these rare responses reflect a conflict between psychological attributes: On one hand, the emergence of unconscious contents; on the other hand, resistance working to maintain these contents repressed.

Comparison between the Adaptive Area (Adp-A) and the Affective Area (Aff-A)

As explained above, the adaptive area (Adp-A) consists of the boxes connected with the ego and its processes of adaptation to reality (which are summarized as: self-evaluation; levels of activity; rational control; and socialization). Furthermore, the four boxes of the Adp-A (1, 3, 6, 8) represent the relationship that the individual has established with the environment over the course of different developmental phases.

Conversely, the Affective Area (Aff-A) is connected with the ego and its affective or emotional processes. The Aff-A represents the boxes associated with the various phases of emotional development (which are summarized as: quality and structure of primary relationships; aggressive and libidinal impulses; and ego defense mechanisms). Therefore, the four boxes of the Aff-A (2, 4, 5, 7) are interpreted as the representation of the primary modes around which the client's affectivity developed.

Comparing the main indices and calculations of the two areas represents an important assessment tool. In general, it is expected that for an adult non-clinical client:

- the indices of both areas would be in the normal range;
- the Adp-A (adaptive) indices would prevail (i.e., demonstrate higher values) over the Aff-A (affective) indices.

Any deviation from the two points listed above is worth considering diagnostically, as it indicates unexpected individual dynamics.

In general, the absolute values of CWS indices must be considered during interpretation. That is, an AQ+% score of 62 (within the normal range) would mean something different than an AQ+% score of 87 (elevated and indicative of affective immaturity), or an AQ+% score of 25 (extremely low and indicative of repression of affect). Similarly, the absolute values of Adp-A and Aff-A indices must also be taken into account when comparing the two areas. For example, a case in which AQ+%[Adp-A] = 81 / AQ+%[Aff-A] = 75 is very different than a case where AQ+%[Adp-A] = 56 / AQ+%[Aff-A] = 37. In the former case, both areas are elevated indicating immaturity in both adaptive and affective areas. In the latter case, both areas are low indicating repression of affect in both domains.

Finally, in order to be diagnostically significant, the differences between indexes in the two areas must be greater than or equal to 25 percentage points (i.e., ⩾25%) for those indices interpreted via percentage ranges. For those interpreted as decimals, differences of .25 or greater are considered significant. Smaller discrepancies have limited or null value and if interpreted may misinform the diagnostic process. Particularly significant are those situations in which one area shows normal values on an index and the other area is extremely low indicating a significant interpretation in the low area (e.g., FQ+%[Adp-A] = 87 / FQ+%[Aff-A] = 38). It should be noted that when comparing Human content percentage (H%), that can only receive a score of 0 or 1, the possible percentage values (calculated for the four boxes of each area) are limited to 25, 50, 75, and 100. Due to this mathematical limitation, differences between areas in H% (i.e., H%[Adp-A] vs. H%[Aff-A], etc.) are interpreted only when the difference between areas reaches 50% (or greater). For this reason, special care should be taken in interpreting H% differences between Adp-A and Aff-A.

For the purposes of interpretation of the main indices (EC+%, AQ+%, FQ+%, P+%, O+%, H+%), it is recommended that an analytical approach be followed, looking at the four possible outcomes of the comparison: 1) the case of higher Adp-A values; 2) the case of higher Aff-A values; 3) the case where both values are above the average range; and 4) the case where both values are below the average range. Descriptions of the interpretation for each condition, in relationship to the major CWS indices, are provided in Appendix G (Table G.21).

Analysis of Sequence—Comparison between Adp-A and Aff-A

As explained previously, the complete theoretical model of the Analysis of Sequence is based on the idea that the sequence of the WDCT follows the order presented in Figure 7.1 above.

From the point of view of the Order of Sequence, comparing the client's performance on the Adp-A and Aff-A areas has great psychodiagnostic value. It must be noted that the elevated number of possible combinations makes it impossible to fully describe the various comparisons. For example, it is difficult to define the psychodiagnostic meaning of a case where C[Adp-A] > C[Aff-A] because one could imagine the following possibilities: the client obtained four C responses in the Adp-A and four PC responses in the Aff-A; the client obtained four C responses in the Adp-A which would then be outweighed by four D responses in the Aff-A; or four C in the Adp-A when the Aff-A is comprised of one D, two AD, and one PC. While there are still more possibilities not considered here, it can be seen that even in this brief example, diagnostic meanings could vary considerably.

Therefore, here, only a general consideration can be provided. According to the theoretical model, the only acceptable comparisons within the non-pathological range should be those involving C, AC, and PC. All other responses (NC, AD, D) are placed outside of expectations and, therefore, outside of the realm of "normality." They are instead placed on a continuum, from situations of minor conflict, to ones of manifest psychopathology. It is the assessor's responsibility to evaluate, case by case, the specific psychodiagnostic meaning of these comparisons.

Additional CWS Indices Available in the Computer Scoring Package

Three additional indices are available in the CWS, calculated by the computer scoring package due to their complexity and the potential for error in hand calculations: Index of Suicidal Tendencies (IST), Index of Validity (IV), and the Global Assessment classification.

Index of Suicidal Tendencies (IST)

The index of suicidal tendencies tells us about the presence of a cluster of symptoms that can be connected to a condition of depression with risk of suicide. The index has a score from 0 to 23 and the scores over 8 are very rare in the normal population (2.8%). Given this, 8 is considered the "clinical cutoff" for a positive IST, with a score above 5 suggesting potential concern for self-harm tendencies.

Of course, because of the difficulty of assessing and identifying a suicidal intent, the IST cannot be considered a pathognomonic sign but one of the numerous factors to take into consideration.

Indices included in the calculation of the IST include: EC+%; AQ+%; IM; CLD content; IIT-2 (adjusted); Codes of Boxes 1, 2, and 6; H%; P%; Opposition Direction special scores in Boxes 3 and 5; M, Affective Stability Index (A/F), and FQ+%.

Index of Validity (IV)

The Index of Validity (IV) tells us about the presence of a cluster of variables that can be connected to a condition of defensiveness, impression management, and/or tendency to exaggerate a symptom-free normative/common way of thinking. Used exclusively in selection and forensic cases, the IV alerts the assessor to potential coaching, significant defensiveness, or pervasive minimization of difficulties. The index, valuated via a constellation of other scores, has a range from 0 to 23 and scores over 8 are considered invalid and require closer evaluation.

Indices included in the calculation of the IV include: IIT-2 (adjusted); AQ+%; IM; AI; P%; O%; EC+%; Affective Stability Index (A/F), and the presence of Special Scores (except AS and CB).

Global Assessment

The Global Assessment provides an overall description of a client's experienced level of symptoms and impairments in functioning. Each client can be placed on one of five steps in an incremental scale ranging from absence of psychopathology and impairment (NOP) to significant psychopathology and impairment (PTL). These five categories, including associated level of symptoms and impairment, are described in Table 7.4.

The Global Assessment further provides a qualitative description of the client's functioning in five areas (five criteria). These Global Assessment criteria are described in Table 7.5.

TABLE 7.4 Global Assessment Classifications and Descriptions

Code	*Global Assessment Classification*	*Description*
NOP	**Not Pathological**	*Limited Symptoms/Impairment*. Well-structured processes of individual and social adaptation.
LSI	**Low Level of Symptoms/ Impairment**	Slight psychoaffective difficulties; however, these do not negatively impact the global efficacy of the client.
MSI	**Medium Level of Symptoms/Impairment**	Conflicting personality aspects are present that negatively impact the client's psychological balance.
SSI	**Severe Level of Symptoms/Impairment**	High levels of serious conflicting aspects that negatively impact the global behavior of the client.
PTL	**Pathological**	*Psychopathological Condition*. Significant symptoms and impairments are evident.

TABLE 7.5 Global Assessment Criteria and Descriptions

Criterion	*Description*
Overall Maturity Level	Well-balanced personality structure.
Emotional Regulation	Self-control and mood stability.
Cognitive Abilities	Critical analysis and judgment.
Social Skills	Effectiveness as a group member.
Group Affiliation	Flexibility and adaptiveness.

Each criterion, comprised of CWS indices, is qualitatively rated using the following symbols:

+ Functional; the client functions adequately in this domain;
+/– Partially Functional; some difficulties may be present in this domain;
– Area of Weakness; the client experiences severe challenges in this domain.

These qualitative evaluations supplement the overall Global Assessment classification, providing guidance in "adjusting" the Global Assessment classification (i.e., an MSI code with 3 – criteria and 2 +/– criteria might be better considered SSI; Conversely, an LSI code with 5 + criteria might be better considered NOP).

In evaluating the Global Assessment, negative scores (–) on the third criterion (Cognitive Abilities) are especially important because of their relatively rare frequency in the normative population. When this occurs, severe difficulties in thinking and global cognitive deficits may be present.

Indices included in the calculation of the Global Assessment classification include: H%; P% and P+%; AQ+%: presence of Reversed Boxes; presences of contents: OBJ%, HS% FD%; Affective Stability Index (A/F); EC+%; Index of Suicidal Tendencies (IST); FQ+%; Codes of Box 3, 5, and 7; IIT-1 (adjusted); Number of Primary Categories; and presence of special scores: PA, CO, TR, DS, AP, MR, GR.

Identifying Areas of Conflict

Sometimes, when the client is confronted with areas that reflect problematic aspects of his or her personality, he/she can experience distress expressed through various manifestations:

- an unusual verbalization;
- a variation in the performance;
- the rejection of a box (either global or partial);
- the perseveration of a particular content (not including Popular responses);
- a delayed response time (prior to starting a particular box);
- the presence of Impulse Responses;
- coding that is evidently different from the theoretical model described above;
- Small and Big Drawings;
- presence of a single instance of any type of Special Score (with the exception of AS or CB).

Each of these signs of distress is briefly discussed below. Based on clinical experience, deviation from the theoretical model is the most effective parameter in identifying difficulty in the discrepant area.

Unusual Verbalization

Unusual verbalizations refer to when clients make unusual, unexpected, or odd expressions during the WDCT administration, including in the *Picture Gallery* and the *Choice of Drawings and Boxes*. Many of these unusual verbalizations receive Special Scores (such as Personalized Answer or Contamination). For example, if, while choosing which boxes a client liked or didn't like, he/she says, "Box number 5 is the most unpleasant, because it is all weird." ("Weird?" the assessor asks.) "It looks like something that smashes something"; or, in Box 1, "This now! This dot in the middle, so isolated . . . it seems detached from all the others . . . it's agonizing." In these cases, the client's verbalizations are not scored, but are kept in mind for qualitative interpretation.

Variation in Performance

A significant variation in performance can be identified through the standardized CWS scoring. For example, when one response is scored FQ = 0, while all other responses demonstrate FQ = 1, a specific change in performance can be identified, with interpretations related to the specific box (i.e., in this case, the box with FQ = 0) hypothesized.

Rejection of a Box

The rejection of a box, either Partial (PR) or Global (GR), indicates, as explained previously, an emotional blockage of the client's associative processes reflected by that box.

Content Perseveration

Perseveration (PP) generally refers to any unusual specific content that the client draws two or more times within a protocol (e.g., a volcano in Box 1 and another volcano in Box 7). This form of perseveration, referring to cases when the same, identical content is produced, earns the Special Score PP (Perseveration). Popular contents, or other frequently observed contents, are not considered Perseveration due to their high frequency (i.e., repetition of human faces, geometric figures, or buildings should not be considered to represent perseveration).

Similar to formally scored Perseveration (PP) is the phenomenon of content perseveration. In these cases, many objects of a similar variety (i.e., three varied weapons: a sword, revolver, and knife), human beings, or natural elements (i.e., sun, moon, stars) are represented. This type of perseveration, content perseveration, is not scored; however, incidences of content perseveration are taken into consideration during interpretation as they can indicate the interests, as well as the conflicts or troubles, of the client.

Latency Time

When the client demonstrates a lengthy time delay in completing or initiating a drawing in a specific box of the WDCT, this can provide evidence of a disturbance in the processes associated with that box. For example, if extended latency time is recorded at the beginning of the test (the client hesitates to start the drawings), this may indicate an insecure client, who is looking for reassurance. If, instead, the delay occurs spontaneously within the administration, it is more likely the expression of difficulty related to the specific box where the delay occurs.

Impulse Responses

Impulse responses indicate a fixation at a specific stage of emotional development. For this reason, the presence of an IR might reflect the presence of difficulties related to that stage.

Box Codes that Differ from the Theoretical Model

According to the theoretical model described above, each box is expected to have a specific placement and Code in the Order of Sequence. When a box excessively deviates from one of these parameters (Order of Sequence or Box Code, per the theoretical model) it likely reflects the expression of difficulties or conflict in that area.

Small and/or Big Drawing(s)

As explained previously, the phenomena of Small and Big Drawings take on different meaning, depending on whether they appear in all boxes or in isolation. In the latter case, an isolated disproportionately sized drawing might indicate a masked shock and/or turmoil in that area. The opportunity to identify these active or potentially active difficulties in an area becomes an element of primary importance for both diagnostic and therapeutic purposes.

Solitary Special Scores

With the exception of Anxiety Stroke (AS) and Crossed Border (CB), the presence of any single Special Score (from any level) may indicate that the evocative character of the box interrupted the associative processes of the client.

Clinical Examples

Two clinical examples, one for each portion of the Analysis of Sequence, are provided below. In an actual assessment report, the two Analyses of Sequence would be integrated, but they are presented separately here to stress their respective characteristics and diagnostic power.

Clinical Example 1—Analysis of Sequence 1

Client Information: 20-year-old male, who completed the WDCT in the context of vocational counseling for college.

Figure 7.4 details the Scoring, Analysis of Sequence 1, Analysis of Sequence 2, and Basic Computations for Clinical Example 1.

The following psychodiagnostic assessment can be derived from the Analysis of Sequence 1 alone. As a general guideline for clinical practice, it is not advised to interpret the Analysis of Sequence alone, but rather in combination with calculated scores and indices, as well as other assessment-derived data (i.e., life history information, results from other test measures, etc.). This interpretation is provided as an example, to illustrate the added value of the Analysis of Sequence 1.

Box 3: This box is drawn as I (first in the Order of Sequence); it obtains an EC score of 0.5 and an AQ score of 0. Thus, it is coded *Negative Compensation (NC)*. This box evokes themes of directionality, the ability to invest energy outward. These scores show that the client's conflict in this area is masked by his tendency to keep himself busy, engaging in many activities, although he is likely to do so in a disorganized and inconsistent manner. The extremely low A/F Ratio (0:0), along with the relatively elevated IIT-1 (1.125), IM (.38), and AI (.75) scores indicate strong tensions that are discharged externally in a disordered manner, rarely aimed to accomplish a goal (i.e., evident disorganization, inability to complete tasks).

Box 2: This box is drawn as II (second in the Order of Sequence); it obtains an EC score of 0.5 and an AQ score of 1. Thus, it is coded *Choice (C)*. The maternal relationship is highly integrated into the personality structure and expressed through warm and positive affect. The EC score is 0.5 and the A/F Ratio leans toward the left (1.0:.5). This shows that the client is not always able to contain behavioral manifestations of affect, which might be at times expressed inappropriately (FQ is expected to be scored as 1. In this case, FQ = 0.5, considered too low given the affect evident in AQ = 1).

Box 5: This box is drawn as III (third in the Order of Sequence); it obtains an EC score of 1 and an AQ score of 0. Thus, it is coded *Ambivalent Choice (AC)*. As explained previously, this pattern indicates the presence of a conflict. Aggressive impulses are experienced ambivalently (A/F Ratio = 0:1) and they are subjected to strict control. Concordantly with what is described about Box 3, the client's energy is not managed in a functional and productive manner, but is expressed as inconsistent and ineffective behaviour.

Box 7: This box is drawn as IV (fourth in the Order of Sequence); it obtains an EC score of 0.5 and an AQ score of 1. Thus, it is coded *Choice (C)*. It is important to stress that this box is consistent with Box 2, also coded *Choice (C)*.

11/03/2017

Group **XXX** Code **4**

Name **MALE** **20 YEAR** Sex **M**

SCORING

* TEST OF SEQUENCE NOT PERFORMED *

Boxes	I	II	III	IV	V	VI	VII	VIII
Order of sequence	3	2	5	7	6	8	1	4

TEST execution time 9 Minutes **# Boxes completed** 8

Box	E.C.	A.Q.	F.Q.	Content		FR.	SPECIAL SCORES							Movement			I.R.
				PR.	SE.									M/m	g	d	
1	1,0	0,5	0,5	OBJ	FT	O	AS	SC									*
2	0,5	1,0	0,5	H		P	AS	II						M	m	a	
3	0,5	0,0	0,0	ARC		(O)	AP	AS									
4	1,0	0,5	0,0	SIG		P	CB										
5	1,0	0,0	1,0	OBJ	WP	P	CB										
6	0,0	0,5	0,5	SIG			AS	SC									
7	0,5	1,0	0,0	NAT		O	AS	SC									
8	1,0	1,0	1,0	BOT			AS	CB									

ANALYSIS OF SEQUENCE 1

	I	II	III	IV	V	VI	VII	VIII
Order of Sequence	3	2	5	7	6	8	1	4
Evocative Character	0,5	0,5	1,0	0,5	0,0	1,0	1,0	1,0
Affective Quality	0,0	1,0	0,0	1,0	0,5	1,0	0,5	0,5
Code	NC	C	AC	C	D	PC	PC	PC
Form Quality	0,0	0,5	1,0	0,0	0,5	1,0	0,5	0,0
A/F Ratio	0,0 : 0,0	1,0 : 0,5	0,0 : 1,0	1,0 : 0,0	0,5 : 0,5	1,0 : 1,0	0,5 : 0,5	0,5 : 0,0
Impulse Responses							*	

ANALYSIS OF SEQUENCE 2

Adaptive area
(1 - 8)
3 2
NC C

Adaptive area
(3 - 6)
5 7
AC C

Affective area
(2 - 4)
6 8
D PC

Affective area
(5 - 7)
1 4
PC PC

Istituto Italiano Wartegg

FIGURE 7.4 Clinical Example—Interpretation of Analysis of Sequence 1.

Figure 7.4 provides the scoring and calculations of the WDCT protocol completed by a 20-year-old male client. Interpretation of Clinical Case #1 refers to these scores and calculations, focusing on the Analysis of Sequence.

Source: CWS Scoring Platform;

11/03/2017

Group **XXX** Code **4**

Name **MALE** | **20 YEAR** | Sex **M**

 # Boxes completed 8

INDICES

E.C.+%	69	AQ.+%	56	FQ+%	44	A/F	3,5 / 1,5	P%	38	P+%	50	AC = 1 AD = 0
O%	31	O+%	20	I.I.T- 1	1,125	I.M.	0,38	A.I.	0,75	I.I.T - 2	5,0:3,0	NC = 1 D = 1

W.I.P. : Quadrant **AC** Area α Alfa

SECURE / PREOCCUPIED

M/m = 1 / 0

I.S.T. 3 / 23

I.V. 2 / 18

PRIMARY CONTENTS # 6

H%	13	A%	
OBJ%	25	ARC%	13
SIG%	25	AST%	
NAT%	13	BOT%	13
ABS%		ANA%	
AS%		BIO%	
FD%		EXP%	
FIR%		ICE%	
HS%		MIN%	
CLD%		PAT%	
SEX%			

SECONDARY CONTENTS # 2

AC%		H%		A%	
HR%		OBJ%		ARC%	
FA%		SIG%		AST%	
TY%		NAT%		BOT%	
MT%		ABS%		ANA%	
CG%		AS%		BIO%	
WP%	13	FD%		EXP%	
FT%	13	FIR%		ICE%	
SF%		HS%		MIN%	
MK%		CLD%		PAT%	
RE%		SEX%			

IMPULSE RESPONSES # 1

SPECIAL SCORES # 14

SC	3	PA		CB	3	CO		RB		AS	6
MR		ID		II	1	MU		PP		AP	1
GR		PR		SR		IS		DS		TR	
		Box 3 OD						Box 5 OD			

PRIMARY MOVEMENT

# M	GENDER m	GENDER f	GENDER i	DIRECTION a	DIRECTION p	DIRECTION b	DIRECTION d	DIRECTION r	DIRECTION i
1	1	0	0	1	0	0	0	0	0

SECONDARY MOVEMENT

# m	MI	FE	FM
0			

Istituto Italiano Wartegg

FIGURE 7.4 *Continued*

Thus, libidinal energy is well integrated and no difficulties emerge in intimate relationships. The A/F ratio, entirely in favor of AQ (1:0) shows a high degree of reactivity, but also a tendency to give in to feelings and emotions.

Box 6: This box is drawn as V (fifth in the Order of Sequence); it obtains an EC score of 0 and an AQ score of 0. Thus, it is coded *Delay (D)*. This box tells us about the client's ability to synthesize, structure, and adapt to reality. The fact that this box received the most negative code (D) stresses the negative connotation of what has been hypothesized thus far. It indicates that the client experiences great behavioral difficulties in terms of adaptation and reality testing. However, this is confirmed by a poor P+% (50%), suggesting difficulties adapting to the environment (also taking into account what has been said about Box 3). It is possible that this person manifests marked difficulties of concrete and practical adaptation to everyday life.

Box 8: This box is drawn as VI (sixth in the Order of Sequence); it obtains an EC score of 1 and an AQ score of 1. Thus, it is coded *Positive Compensation (PC)*. The A/F ratio shows a strong affective component (1:1) in the client's relationships with the environment and the people in it.

Box 1: This box is drawn as VII (seventh in the Order of Sequence); it obtains an EC score of 1 and an AQ score of 0.5. Thus, it is coded *Positive Compensation (PC)*. If consistent with other diagnostic findings, it can be derived that this person might experience lack of self-confidence, insecurity, and self-doubt. However, he potentially possesses optimal resources that could be activated in therapy. Form and control aspects prevail in this area (A/F Ratio = 0.5:1). An Impulse Response with oral content might reflect traits of dependency toward others.

Box 4: This box is drawn as VIII (eighth in the Order of Sequence); it obtains an EC score of 1 and an AQ score of 0.5. Thus, it is coded *Positive Compensation (PC)*. In the event that other diagnostic elements show conflict with authority figures, with therapeutic intervention, this client would appear to possess the potential to overcome these difficulties. The affective components prevail, as shown by the lack of a control factor, and emphasis on the left side of the A/F Ratio (.5:0).

Example 2—Analysis of Sequence 2

Client Information: This is a 23-year-old woman, referred for an anxious-depressive state, associated with obsessive traits. She participated in an interview and assessment battery. The interview clearly demonstrated that, beside her symptoms (reactive in nature), she possesses a well-organized personality structure, with good energy levels and reality testing. Furthermore, the client appears to lack assertiveness, and reports suggest that her mother is an overwhelming presence in her life. Her relationship with both parents is characterized by positive affect, but she complains about their excessive rigidity and severity, based, she believes, in their rigid and ultra-orthodox religious beliefs. She experiences guilt for her emotional and sexual life.

Figure 7.5 details the Scoring, Analysis of Sequence 1, Analysis of Sequence 2, and Basic Computations for Clinical Example 2.

The following psychodiagnostic assessment can be derived from the Analysis of Sequence 2 alone. As a general guideline for clinical practice, it is not advised to interpret the Analyses of Sequence 2 alone, but rather in combination with calculated scores and indices, as well as other assessment-derived data (i.e., life history information, results from other test measures, etc.). This interpretation is provided as an example, to illustrate the added value of the Analysis of Sequence 2.

The first element that stands out in the Analysis of Sequence 2 is the great extent to which this client's protocol resembles the theoretical model presented above, both in terms of her Order of Sequence, and in terms of the evaluation obtained on each box. Essentially, only the positions of Box 2 and Box 6 are switched. The switch of Boxes 5 and 7 is not relevant as it happened within the last two boxes (i.e., the "last pair"). Similarly, although Box 3 was drawn as #4 instead of as #3, it remains within the expected theoretical "second pair."

Regarding the Codes, the following interpretations can be made. Only the last box drawn (Box 5) does not receive the expected Code and is therefore relevant in terms of the final diagnostic assessment. The first four boxes (1, 8, 2, 3) are all coded *Choice*; Boxes 4, 6, and 7 are coded *Positive Compensation* (which is consistent with the theoretical model). The last Box, Box 5, is coded *Delay*, suggesting that the client experiences (as her major symptom) a profound repression of aggressive impulses, which are likely to be manifested behaviorally.

This conflict regarding aggressive impulses must be understood in the context of an overall well-integrated and adapted personality organization. She likely generally functions well in terms of self-esteem, relationship with the environment, levels of aspiration and activity, and relationship with the maternal figure (Boxes 1, 8, 3, and 2, respectively, valued as *Choice*). Meanwhile, functioning in the areas represented by Boxes 4, 6, and 7 (i.e., relationship with the paternal figure and with authority; ability to synthesize; and relationship to sexuality, respectively) appear positively integrated, but should be confirmed via other test data (both within the CWS and from other sources). In the case that other test data suggest impairments, she might be expected to present with behavioral difficulties including inconsistencies in demonstrated and expressed attitude toward male figures (Box 4) and sexual relationships (Box 7), as well as general difficulty in scheduling and managing her activities (Box 6). In terms of prognosis, if these hypotheses were to be confirmed by other diagnostic findings, these areas of reduced functioning still show potential to become well developed and integrated into the personality, through therapeutic intervention (given their coding as *Positive Compensation*).

11/03/2017

Group **MTH** Code **10**

Name **WOMAN** | **23 YEARS** Sex **F**

SCORING

* TEST OF SEQUENCE NOT PERFORMED *

Boxes	I	II	III	IV	V	VI	VII	VIII
Order of sequence	1	8	2	3	6	4	7	5

TEST execution time 7 Minutes **# Boxes completed** 8

Box	E.C.	A.Q.	F.Q.	Content PR.	Content SE.	FR.	SPECIAL SCORES	Movement M/m	Movement g	Movement d	I.R.
1	1,0	1,0	1,0	A			AS				
2	1,0	1,0	0,5	NAT			AS				
3	0,5	1,0	1,0	ARC		(P)	AS				
4	1,0	0,5	1,0	ARC			AS				
5	0,0	0,5	1,0	OBJ	WP		AS				
6	1,0	0,5	1,0	SIG		P	AS				
7	1,0	1,0	1,0	BOT			AS				
8	1,0	1,0	1,0	AST		(P)	AS				

ANALYSIS OF SEQUENCE 1

	I	II	III	IV	V	VI	VII	VIII
Order of Sequence	1	8	2	3	6	4	7	5
Evocative Character	1,0	1,0	1,0	0,5	1,0	1,0	1,0	0,0
Affective Quality	1,0	1,0	1,0	1,0	0,5	0,5	1,0	0,5
Code	C	C	C	C	PC	PC	PC	D
Form Quality	1,0	1,0	0,5	1,0	1,0	1,0	1,0	1,0
A/F Ratio	1,0 : 1,0	1,0 : 1,0	1,0 : 0,5	1,0 : 1,0	0,5 : 1,0	0,5 : 1,0	1,0 : 1,0	0,5 : 1,0
Impulse Responses								

ANALYSIS OF SEQUENCE 2

Adaptive area (1 - 8)
1 8
C C

Adaptive area (3 - 6)
2 3
C C

Affective area (2 - 4)
6 4
PC PC

Affective area (5 - 7)
7 5
PC D

Istituto Italiano Wartegg

FIGURE 7.5 Clinical Example—Interpretation of Analyses of Sequence 1 and 2.

Figure 7.5 provides the scoring and calculations of the WDCT protocol completed by a 23-year-old female client. Interpretation of Clinical Case #2 refers to these scores and calculations, focusing on the Analyses of Sequence 1 and 2.

11/03/2017

Group **MTH** Code **10**

Name **WOMAN** **23 YEARS** Sex **F**

\# Boxes completed 8

INDICES

E.C.+%	81	AQ.+%	81	FQ+%	94	A/F	4,0 / 4,0	P%	25	P+%	100	AC = 0 AD = 0
O%	0	O+%	N.D.	I.I.T-1	1,000	I.M.	0,00	A.I.	1,00	I.I.T-2	7,0:1,0	NC = 0 D = 1

W.I.P. : Quadrant **A** Area **β** Beta

SECURE

M/m = 0 / 0

I.S.T. 2 / 23

I.V. 8 / 18

PRIMARY CONTENTS # 7

H%		A%	13
OBJ%	13	ARC%	25
SIG%	13	AST%	13
NAT%	13	BOT%	13
ABS%		ANA%	
AS%		BIO%	
FD%		EXP%	
FIR%		ICE%	
HS%		MIN%	
CLD%		PAT%	
SEX%			

SECONDARY CONTENTS # 1

AC%		H%		A%	
HR%		OBJ%		ARC%	
FA%		SIG%		AST%	
TY%		NAT%		BOT%	
MT%		ABS%		ANA%	
CG%		AS%		BIO%	
WP%	13	FD%		EXP%	
FT%		FIR%		ICE%	
SF%		HS%		MIN%	
MK%		CLD%		PAT%	
RE%		SEX%			

IMPULSE RESPONSES # 0

SPECIAL SCORES # 8

SC		PA		CB		CO		RB		AS	8
MR		ID		II		MU		PP		AP	
GR		PR		SR		IS		DS		TR	
		Box 3 OD						Box 5 OD			

PRIMARY MOVEMENT

# M	GENDER m	f	i	DIRECTION a	p	b	d	r	i
0	0	0	0	0	0	0	0	0	0

SECONDARY MOVEMENT

# m	MI	FE	FM
0			

Istituto Italiano Wartegg

FIGURE 7.5 *Continued*

A second level of interpretation regarding divergence from the theoretical model can be added to the above, indicating:

- The pair of *Choices* (1–8) is drawn as I and II. As explained above, this means that levels of self-regard, self-esteem, and adaptation to the environment are intact and well developed;
- Box 6, of the pair 3–6, is postponed (coded PC), which might indicate a slight preference for affectively driven interpretations of reality as opposed to a more rational thoughtful approach. Box 3 (coded C) shows that activity levels and ego-strength characteristics are well organized;
- Box 2, of the pair 2–4, occurs earlier than expected, showing on one hand a positive relationship with the mother (C), and on the other hand indicating that the maternal figure may play an excessive role in the client's life (as this box was completed earlier in the sequence). The relationship with male figures might be difficult, and if so, could be an area of potential to build upon in therapeutic intervention (Box 4);
- The pair 5–7, drawn last, suggests marked repression of aggressive dynamics (Box 5, Delay) and potential difficulty in the organization of libidinal dynamics (Box 7).

It is evident, just from the Analysis of Sequence 2, how the client's problems revolve around a conflict between dependency and autonomy. Despite her great potential, this client appears stuck in her development, and is unable to assertively stand for what she believes. The strong repression of aggressive impulses requires further investigation. The level of conflict found in the client stresses the need for therapeutic intervention, specifically short-term psychodynamic psychotherapy.

References

Bianchi di Castelbianco, F., Crisi, A., & Di Renzo, M. (1996). *Il test di Wartegg nell'età evolutiva. Un contributo psicodiagnostico allo studio clinico della balbuzie, della sordità e dei disturbi dell'apprendimento* [The Wartegg Test in childhood. A clinical contribution to the study of stammering, deafness, and learning disorders]. Rome, Italy: Edizioni Magi.

Caricchia, F., d'Angerio, S., & Lonoce, G. (2000). Il bambino in eta prescolare all'esame del test di Wartegg [The preschool child examined by the Wartegg Drawing Completion Test]. *Babele*, *14*, 81–87.

Crisi, A. (1984). Una prova supplementare per l'interpretazione dei fenomeni di choc e di rifiuto nell'uso clinico del test di Rorschach [An additional test for the interpretation of the phenomena of shock and rejection in the clinical use of the Rorschach test]. *Studi Rorschachiani*, *1*(84), 95–107.

Crisi, A. (1998). *Manuale del Test di Wartegg* [Manual for the Wartegg Test]. Rome, Italy: Edizioni Magi.

Crisi, A. (2007). *Manuale del test di Wartegg, 2nd ed.* [Manual for the Wartegg Test, 2nd Edition]. Rome, Italy: Edizioni Magi.

Crisi, A., & Carlesimo, S. (2008, July). *The Human, Food, and Cloud contents: Discriminative ability in clinical personality assessment*. Paper presented at the meeting of the International Rorschach Society, Leuven, Belgium.

Erikson, E. H. (1959). *Identity and the life cycle: Selected papers. Psychological issues*. New York: International Universities Press.

Erikson, E. H. (1994). *Identity and the life cycle*. W. W. Norton & Company.

Exner, J. (2003). *The Rorschach: A comprehensive system. Volume 1: The Rorschach, basic foundations and principles of interpretation*. New York: Wiley & Sons. (1st edition, 1997).

Giambelluca, F. C., Parisi, S., & Pes, P. (1995). *L'interpretazione psicoanalitica del Rorschach: modello dinamico strutturale* [The psychoanalytical interpretation of Rorschach: A dynamic structural model]. Edizioni Kappa.

Kinget, G. M. (1952). *The Drawing-Completion Test: A projective technique for the investigation of personality*. New York: Grune & Stratton.

Lossen, H., & Schott, G. (1975). *Wartegg: Analisi del processo percettivo* [Wartegg: Perceptual process analysis]. Turin: Centro Salesiano di Orientamento.

Meyer, G. J., Viglione, D. J., Mihura, J. L., Erard, R. E., & Erdberg, P. (2011). *Rorschach Performance Assessment System: Administration, coding, interpretation, and technical manual*. Rorschach Performance Asessement Systems LLC.

Scarpellini, C. (1964). Diagnostic differentiel a travers deux tests de personalite: le Rorschach et le Wartegg [Differential diagnostic through two personality tests: The Rorschach and the Wartegg]. *Bulletin de Psychologie Scolaire et d'Orientation*, *13*, 79–92.

Wartegg, E. (1953). *Schichtdiagnostik-Der Zeichentest* (WZT) [Differential diagnostics—The Drawing test]. Göttingen: Verlag für Psychologie.

8 Conceptualization

Chapter 8 details the recommended interpretive strategy for a CWS clinical protocol, focusing on five domains of functioning: functional intelligence; organization of thought processes; available energy; social skills; and emotional functioning. In discussing these domains, the specific CWS indices and computations involved in interpretation are presented. A complete clinical example is provided to conclude the chapter.

CWS Approach to Conceptualization

After some brief and non-exhaustive general considerations, the process of conceptualization using the CWS will be described. This is a recommended model, but is not intended to be rigidly followed by the reader. Rather, what follows is a general structure within which to develop the final assessment report on the basis of the evaluation results.

In general, after listing the tests administered and the client's attitude toward testing and the examiner, reports may follow a general structure that takes into account a stepwise interpretation of five significant areas of personality:

1. Functional Intelligence
    a) quantitative evaluation
    b) qualitative evaluation
2. Organization of Thought Process
    c) presence and description of dysfunctional areas (when present)
    d) adherence to conventional thinking
3. Available Energy
4. Social Skills
5. Emotional Functioning, particularly in relationship to the concepts of maturity and affective stability.

Specific scores, ratios, and indices that inform interpretation for each of these five domains of personality are discussed later in this chapter.

After thorough review of each of the five domains, conclusions are presented, organized in three parts: 1) Descriptive Diagnosis; 2) Prognosis; and 3) Recommendations for Psychotherapy. Each is briefly described below:

Descriptive Diagnosis: Here, more concisely than in the body of the report, the relevant areas of the personality, with particular attention to problematic areas, are summarized.

Prognosis: Here, the overall findings of the personality testing are used to provide a prognosis, which takes into account evaluation of the client's potential, complexity of current circumstances, and degree of psychopathology.

Recommendations for Psychotherapy: Finally, when sufficient elements of evaluation are available, recommendations for the most adequate therapeutic approach, according to the client's emotional characteristics, are provided.

Indices Utilized in CWS Interpretation

Within this general structure of personality assessment, specific to the CWS, the following indices are taken into account for each of the steps listed above. It should be noted that the lists contained in this chapter are provided as guide-

TABLE 8.1 Main Indices of Reference for CWS Interpretive Domains

Functional Intelligence	EC+%; FQ+%; M; EC of Box 6; O%; 3rd Criterion (Cognitive Abilities); Lack of Special Scores related to intellectual deficit (2nd level); A/F Ratio; P+%; Number of Primary Content Categories
Organization of Thought Processes	Awareness of the interpretive attitude; Absence of Special Scores of 1st and/or 2nd level; FQ+%; EC of Box 6; 3rd Criterion (Cognitive Abilities); P%; P+%; Quadrant/Area; Verbalization; EC+%; O%; O+%; Number and type of the Primary Contents
Available Energy	Code of Boxes 3, 5, & 7; IST; FQ+%; first two boxes drawn; Absence of Rejections; Direction of M; Quadrant/Area; IIT-1; Number of Primary Contents; m < 2; Size of the drawings
Social Skills	Code and position of Box 8; H%; P%; AQ+%; Quadrant/Area; Comparison between Adp-A and Aff-A; Quality of H responses; Contents
Emotional Functioning	Global Assessment classification; WIP Quadrant/Area; IIT-2; Code of Box 1; presence of GR and PR; IST; Special Scores; EC+%; AQ+%; FQ+%; A/F Ratio; P%; H%; IIT-1; Balance between Adp-A and Aff-A; Movement responses; Number of Primary Content Categories

lines, with quantitative values of indices interpreted qualitatively; that is, not all indicators are necessary to reach a general conclusion. Clinicians should evaluate whether a preponderance of evidence exists, based upon the number of criteria met (as compared to those that are not met). In each case, scores and indices are presented from most relevant (and diagnostically important) to least relevant. Therefore, should a client's CWS protocol not meet the first several criteria on a list (but perhaps meets lower criteria), the clinician should use caution in making specific or definitive interpretations.

Table 8.1 details the main indices of reference for each of the five domains of CWS interpretation.

Non-Specific Pathological Indices

In interpreting the CWS, certain indices and values are indicative of various forms of distress. However, it is important to stress that no diagnosis can be derived from only one test. Interpretive data should be carefully examined in the context of a client's experiences, symptoms, history, and clinical presentation.

In general, specific markers in CWS protocols indicate a level of psychopathology, which then may be specified through further analysis and evaluation. When clinical protocols contain the following indicators, the clinician can infer that the client experiences difficulties or challenges, including mental health symptoms and impairments:

- ☐ Area β of Quadrant B, C, D; or area γ of all quadrants
- ☐ Global Assessment = MSI (if criteria mainly = – or ±), SSI or PTL
- ☐ 3rd criterion (cognitive abilities) = ± or –
- ☐ Box 1 = NC, AD, or D; or Box 1 last in the Order of Sequence
- ☐ FQ $\leq$ 75
- ☐ P+% < 81
- ☐ IST > 4
- ☐ Presence of GR and/or PR
- ☐ Significant differences between WIP: Quadrant [Adp] and WIP: Quadrant [Aff]
- ☐ More than 1 Special Score (except AS and CB), especially if 1st level
- ☐ Incongruency between indices
- ☐ Incongruency of scoring within the same index
- ☐ 3 or 4 boxes of AFF in the first half
- ☐ Ratio A/F with both sides $\leq$ 2
- ☐ Perseveration (thematic perseveration, or monotypical perseveration).

Functional Intelligence

Although the WDCT is not a cognitive test, and the CWS is not a cognitive system, it can provide important information about the client's functional cognitive abilities, which must be verified though other instruments.

Main Indexes of Reference

EC+%; FQ+%; M; EC of Box 6; O%; 3rd Criterion (Cognitive Abilities); Lack of Special Scores related to intellectual deficit (2nd level); A/F Ratio; P+%; Number of Primary Content Categories.

Level of Functional Intelligence

Given the indices noted in Table 8.2, high, medium, and low levels of intelligence can be summarized as follows:

HIGH INTELLIGENCE

- ☐ Box 6 valued C or PC with O+
- ☐ M > 1
- ☐ FQ+% = 94–100
- ☐ O% = 13–25 with O+%≥81
- ☐ M > m
- ☐ Number of Primary Content Categories = 5–7
- ☐ Adp-Area/Aff-Area comparisons between EC+%, AQ+%, and FQ+% without great differences (and values in the normal range)
- ☐ ABS Content
- ☐ Refined verbalizations

MEDIUM INTELLIGENCE

- ☐ Box 6 valued C or PC (also AC or AD if such valuation is because AQ = 0)
- ☐ FQ+% = 81–100
- ☐ M = 0–1
- ☐ EC+% = 56–81
- ☐ Absence of Special Scores of 2nd level (excepted ID)
- ☐ Presence of P% with P+% = 81–100
- ☐ O% = 0–6 with O+% = 81–100
- ☐ Adp-Area/Aff-Area comparisons between EC+%, AQ+%, and FQ+% without great differences (and values in the normal range)
- ☐ Presence of OBJ%
- ☐ Brief but adequate verbalization

LOW INTELLIGENCE

- ☐ Lack of understanding of the instructions (additional instructions were administered)
- ☐ Low awareness of the interpretive aptitude
- ☐ Box 6 with EC = 0.5 or 0
- ☐ FQ+%≤ 75

TABLE 8.2 Levels of Functional Intelligence as Indicated by CWS Indices

	Indices (most important → least important)									
Intellectual Level	**EC +%**	**FQ +%**	**M**	**EC Box 6**	**O%**	**3rd Criterion**	**SS II level**	**A/F**	**P +%**	**# Pr. Cont.**
High (IQ > 135)	94	100	2–3	EC=1 (with O+) SS Absent	18–38 FQ+% > 81	+	Abs.	A < F	100	6–7
Good (IQ = 110–135)	88	88–100	1	EC=1 SS Absent	6–13 FQ+%81	+	Abs.	A < F	88–100	4–5
Average (IQ = 90–110)	56–81	81–100	0–1	EC=1 SS Absent	0	+	Abs.	A < F	81	4
Low (IQ = 75–89)	50	75	0	EC=1, 0.5, or 0 SS Present	0–13 FQ+% < 81	±	Pres.	A≥F	< 81	< 4
Low MR* (IQ = 50–74)	44	63–69	0	EC=0 SS Present	18–25 FQ+% < 81	–	Pres.	A≥F	< 69	< 4
Medium/Severe MR* (IQ ≤ 50)	< 44	> 63	0	ED=0 SS Present	> 25 FQ+% < 81	–	Pres.	A≥F	< 63	1–2

Notes: The values of IQ are purely suggestive approximations. The WDCT is not a cognitive test, and does not provide a specific value of IQ. * MR = Mental Retardation; In the assessment of the MR *beware of perseverations* for H, ARC, and SIG contents that can distort many indices (including AQ+%, EC+%).

- ☐ EC+%≤ 50
- ☐ M/m = 0/0 (most importantly, M = 0)
- ☐ Quadrant B, area β or γ
- ☐ Presence of ID, II, MU, SR, AP, PP; mainly AP and II
- ☐ Low or absent AI
- ☐ Sometimes DS and/or TR
- ☐ A/F Ratio with A ≈ F or A > F
- ☐ P%≤13 or P% > 31 (if PP is present)
- ☐ Number of Primary Content Categories = 1–4
- ☐ PAT content
- ☐ SIG%≥50
- ☐ Adp-Area/Aff-Area comparisons between EC+%, AQ+%, and FQ+% without great differences (but lower than normal range)
- ☐ Sometimes O% > 25 but with O+% < 81
- ☐ Poor verbalization and drawings

Inhibition of Intelligence

Inhibition indicates when a client's intellectual abilities and capabilities are not fully realized due to psychological or depressive factors. In these cases, the performance of a client is generally less than his or her true potential.

Inhibition is generally indicated by *significant incongruity* between indices in Table 8.2. Two types of inhibition are described below:

PSYCHOLOGICAL (NEUROTIC) INHIBITION

- ☐ Presence of GR, PR, IS
- ☐ Quadrants C and D, areas β or γ
- ☐ CLD
- ☐ ID if FQ ≥ 81
- ☐ Lack of Special Scores of 1st and 2nd Level
- ☐ MI

DEPRESSIVE INHIBITION

- ☐ CWS indicators of depression (see Specific Pathological Indices below)
- ☐ Box 3 = AC, NC, AD, or D
- ☐ IST ≥ 5
- ☐ MR (1 or more)
- ☐ AQ = 0 in Box 6
- ☐ M = 0
- ☐ O% = 0 and P% medium-high (25% and 38%)
- ☐ OBJ+ARC% ≥ 50

Style of Intelligence

CWS indices can indicates a client's typical thinking style, whether that be practical, abstract, or intellectualized.

PRACTICAL INTELLIGENCE

Practical, or concrete, thinking indicates that the subject's thinking is oriented in a concrete, functional manner and he/she has good practical skills. The subject is generally able to master concrete skills and effectively perform practical activities.

- ☐ OBJ% + ARC% $\geqslant$ 50 (only Primary Contents)
- ☐ O+ in OBJ and/or ARC
- ☐ Numerical Order of Sequence
- ☐ Number of Primary Content Categories = 1–4
- ☐ O% and O+% Adp-Area > Aff-Area
- ☐ Sometimes A/F Ratio with A $\approx$ F or A > F

ABSTRACT INTELLIGENCE

Abstract intelligence indicates that the subject's thinking is primarily fluid and abstract; he/she generally views reality in an integrative manner. These individuals are more confident with theoretical, conceptual, and speculative manners of thinking, and such aptitude strongly influences the ways they view and interpret reality.

- ☐ Presence of ABS% and/or SIG% (but not geometrical figures)
- ☐ O+ in ABS, H, SIG, and NAT
- ☐ Individualized Order of Sequence
- ☐ Number of Primary Content Categories = 5–7
- ☐ O% and O+% Adp-Area < Aff-Area
- ☐ Sometimes A/F Ratio with A << F

HIGHLY INTELLECTUALIZED INTELLIGENCE

- ☐ Sophisticated verbalization
- ☐ FQ+% = 100
- ☐ M > 1
- ☐ Box 6 as 1st or 2nd in the Order of Sequence
- ☐ A/F Ratio: A << F
- ☐ Presence of IS
- ☐ H% = 0–13
- ☐ ABS > 13
- ☐ OBJ% > 50

Organization of Thought Process

Main Indexes of Reference

Awareness of the interpretive attitude; Absence of Special Scores of 1st and/or 2nd level; FQ+%; EC of Box 6; 3rd Criterion (Cognitive Abilities); P%; P+%; Quadrant/Area; Verbalization; EC+%; O%; O+%; Number and type of the Primary Contents.

Table 8.3 summarizes CWS indicators of intact and inadequate reality testing.

TABLE 8.3 CWS Indicators of Intact vs. Inadequate Reality Testing

Intact Reality Testing	*Inadequate Reality Testing*
☐ Good awareness of the interpretive attitude	☐ Absent or weak awareness of the interpretive attitude
☐ Adequate verbalization	☐ Strange, unusual, or absurd verbalizations
☐ No Special Scores of 1st and 2nd level mainly no AP and II (especially in Box 6)	☐ Presence of Special Scores of 1st and 2nd level and especially AP and II
☐ 3rd criterion (cognitive abilities) = +	☐ 3rd criterion (cognitive abilities) = ± or –
☐ FQ+% = 81–100	☐ FQ+%⩽75
☐ Box 6 EC = 1	☐ Box 6 EC = 0.5 or 0
☐ Box 6 FQ = 1	☐ Box 6 FQ = 0.5 or 0
☐ M with FQ = 1	☐ M with FQ = 0.5 or 0
☐ Box 6 with P or O (with P+% and O+%⩾81)	☐ Box 6 with P or O (with P+% and O+% < 81)
☐ O%⩽25 with O+% > 81	☐ O% > 25 with O+% < 81
☐ P% = 13–25 with P+% > 81	☐ P% = 0 or present with P+%⩽81
☐ OBJ% + ARC%⩾38	☐ OBJ% + ARC% < 38
☐ 3 Boxes of ADP area in the first half	☐ 3 Boxes of AFF area in the first half
☐ m = 0–1	☐ m⩾2

Disturbances in Thought Processes and Content

Differentiation between disturbances in thought process and content can be made utilizing CWS indices. Disturbance in thought process, generally related to organic or physiological factors, is evidenced by disruption in mental activities including conscious thought, reality orientation, problem solving, judgment, and comprehension. Disturbance in thought content is more likely reflective of thought disorder, including derailment, poverty of speech, tangential thoughts, illogicality, perseveration, neologism, thought blocking, and detachment from reality.

DISTURBANCES OF THOUGHT PROCESS

- ☐ Absent or weak awareness of the interpretive attitude
- ☐ Poor, inadequate verbalization and poor drawings
- ☐ Special Scores of 2nd level, especially AP*, II, and ID (if FQ+% < 81)
- ☐ Monotypical perseveration
- ☐ Box 6 EC = 0–.5
- ☐ FQ+%≤75
- ☐ EC+%≤50
- ☐ 3rd criterion (cognitive abilities) = ± or –
- ☐ Quadrant B, area β or γ
- ☐ M = 0
- ☐ P% = 0–6 and O% > 25 (with P+% and O+%≤ 81)
- ☐ Inability to describe one's own drawings
- ☐ Poor quality of drawings (consistent across boxes)
- ☐ Time of Performance > 10'
- ☐ Perseveration (PP)

* *In the disturbances of thought process, AP are mainly connected to the incongruity within the drawings; in the disturbances of thought content, AP are usually scored due to the client's verbalizations.*

DISTURBANCE OF THOUGHT CONTENT

- ☐ Absent or weak awareness of the interpretive attitude
- ☐ Strange, unusual, or absurd verbalizations
- ☐ Special Scores of 1st level (especially AP*, CO, and PA)
- ☐ Box 6 with AP
- ☐ FQ+%≤75
- ☐ EC+% = 75–94
- ☐ 3rd criterion (cognitive abilities) = ± or –
- ☐ Quadrant B, area β or γ
- ☐ M with FQ = 0.5 or 0
- ☐ P% = 13–25 and O% with O+% and P+%≤75
- ☐ Increased ABS%, SIG%, PAT% (higher than normal range)
- ☐ Sometimes PP
- ☐ Sometimes broken or damaged content
- ☐ Inconsistent performance across boxes (i.e., both good and poor performance; For example, EC = 1 and FQ = 1 in one box, EC = 0 and FQ = 0 in another box; Human content in one box, Blood content in another, etc.)

* *In the disturbances of thought process, AP are mainly connected to the incongruity within the drawings; in the disturbances of thought content, AP are usually scored due to the client's verbalizations.*

Thinking Style

CWS indices provide information about a client's general style of thinking, including degree of conventionality, conformism, and oppositionality.

ADHERENCE TO CONVENTIONAL THINKING

- ☐ Good awareness of the interpretive attitude
- ☐ P% = 6–25 with P+% ⩾81
- ☐ Presence of H%
- ☐ Positive Code in Box 6 (C or PC) with P+% or O+% > 81
- ☐ Area α of all Quadrants or area β of Quadrant A
- ☐ FQ+% = 81–100
- ☐ EC+% = 56–81
- ☐ Absence of Special Scores (except AS and CB)
- ☐ Presence of OBJ%
- ☐ O% = 6–25 with O+%⩾FQ+%

CONFORMISTIC STYLE

- ☐ Accentuated awareness of the interpretive attitude
- ☐ Numerical (or Numerical Circular) Order of Sequence
- ☐ Quadrant A, area γ
- ☐ H% > 25
- ☐ P% > 25
- ☐ ARC%⩾25
- ☐ Absence of O%
- ☐ H%[Adp] >> H%[Aff]
- ☐ P%[Adp] >> P%[Aff]
- ☐ Sometimes AQ+% > 69 with other signs of dependence (i.e., FD content)

OPPOSITIONAL STYLE

- ☐ Oppositional attitude and/or criticism toward the test/examiner
- ☐ Lack of effort and motivation
- ☐ Reversed (or Reversed Circular) Order of Sequence
- ☐ Presence of RB, especially in Box 4 and Box 8
- ☐ Incomplete or careless drawings
- ☐ Negative Code in Box 4
- ☐ Quadrant B, area α or β
- ☐ IM⩾.38 with A ≈ F or A > F
- ☐ Box 3 and/or Box 5 and/or Box 7 = Negative Code
- ☐ Absence of H%
- ☐ Absence of P%
- ☐ Anal Impulse Response (especially if FQ < 1)

☐ Short time of performance (< 4')
☐ SIG (only in case of group administration)

Available Energy

Main Indexes of Reference

Code of Boxes 3, 5, & 7; IST; FQ+%; first two boxes drawn; Absence of Rejections; Direction of M; Quadrant/Area; IIT-1; Number of Primary Contents; m < 2; Size of the drawings.

The CWS provides information related to the client's integration of aggressive and libidinal energies, and successful use of these energies to engage in productive, goal-directed behaviors.

ADEQUATE AND FUNCTIONAL ENERGY

☐ Positive and collaborative attitude toward the test/assessor
☐ Absence of GR (Global Rejection) and/or PR (Partial Rejection)
☐ Codes of Boxes 3, 5, and 7 = C or PC
☐ IST≤4
☐ Box 3 and/or Box 6 and/or Box 5 as 1st or 2nd in the Order of Sequence with positive scores (especially for EC and FQ)
☐ FQ+% = 81–100
☐ Active M and with FQ = 1
☐ O% presence with O+% > 81
☐ IIT-1 < 1.0 (not in Selection or Custody evaluations)
☐ Area α of all the Quadrants + area β of Quadrant A
☐ Number of Primary Content Categories = 4–6
☐ m = 0–1
☐ Short time (< 5') of performance with high FQ+%

Social Skills

Main Indexes of Reference

Code and position of Box 8; H%; P%; AQ+%; Quadrant/Area; Comparison Adp-Area/Aff-Area; Quality of H responses; Contents.

The CWS provides information related to clients' social skills and approach to interpersonal situations. Both positive indicators (Adequate Socialization) and indicators of social difficulties (Detachment and Isolation; Dependency) are presented below.

ADEQUATE SOCIALIZATION

☐ Box 8 Code = C or PC (and is 1st or 2nd in Order of Sequence)
☐ Presence of H

- ☐ P% = 13–31%
- ☐ AQ+% = 50–63
- ☐ Adequate A/F Ratio
- ☐ Area α of Quadrants A, C, and D; or Quadrant A, area β
- ☐ H%[Adp] = H%[Aff]
- ☐ P%[Adp] = P%[Aff]
- ☐ Positive Human contents
- ☐ Presence of NAT and/or BOT

DIFFICULTIES (DETACHMENT AND ISOLATION)

- ☐ Quadrant B, Area α or β
- ☐ Negative Code in Box 8 (and in the 2nd half of the Order of Sequence)
- ☐ H and/or P = 0
- ☐ Presence of HS% and/or AS%
- ☐ Presence of MK (Mask Secondary Content)
- ☐ AQ+%≤50 or ≥69
- ☐ A << F or A > F
- ☐ OBJ% > 50
- ☐ Indices Adp-Area < Aff-Area (particularly H and P)
- ☐ Presence of AST, MIN, ICE, SIG content (Primary Contents)
- ☐ Presence of SF (Science Fiction Secondary Content)

DIFFICULTIES (DEPENDENCE)

- ☐ Oral Impulse Response (IR)
- ☐ Quadrant C, area α and β; or Quadrant A, area γ
- ☐ Positive Code in Box 8 (C or PC; sometimes NC); Completed first in the Order of Sequence
- ☐ AQ+%≥69
- ☐ A/F Ratio with A ≈ F or A > F
- ☐ H% and/or P% > 25
- ☐ ARC%≥25
- ☐ Indices Adp-Area > Aff-Area (especially H% and P%)
- ☐ Childish Contents/identification in the H and/or M response
- ☐ Presence of FT and TY (Fairy Tale and Toy Secondary Contents)

Emotional Functioning

The CWS provides information related to affective functioning of the client, highlighting both adaptive functioning (Normative values indicating Overall Maturity and Stability) as well as indications of affective difficulties (Specific Pathological Indices). Each is presented below.

NORMATIVE VALUES INDICATING OVERALL MATURITY AND STABILITY

- ☐ Global Assessment = NOP or LSI (with criteria mainly = +)
- ☐ Area α of all Quadrants; or Quadrant A, area β
- ☐ C+PC >> AC+AD+NC+D; or C+PC ⩾ AC+AD+NC+D (with only AC in the right side of the equation)
- ☐ Analysis of Sequence 2: No more than 2 boxes of Aff-area in the first half
- ☐ Positive Code in Box 1 (C or PC); Not in 7th or 8th position in the Order of Sequence
- ☐ No GR and/or PR
- ☐ IST⩽4
- ☐ Special Scores absent; if present, only belonging to Level 3 (indications of conflict)
- ☐ EC+% = 56–81
- ☐ AQ+% = 50–63
- ☐ FQ+% = 81–100
- ☐ A/F Ratio: A < F (with F greater than A by 1–2 points)
- ☐ Presence of P
- ☐ Presence of H
- ☐ IIT-1 < 1.0
- ☐ IM⩽.25
- ☐ AI⩽.75
- ☐ Balance between indices Adp-Area/Aff-Area
- ☐ Individualized Order of Sequence
- ☐ M > m
- ☐ Number of Primary Content Categories = 4–6

Specific Pathological Indices

Specific pathological indices, as related to anxiety disorders, eating disorders, trauma, depressive disorders, mania, personality disorders, and psychosis are presented below.

Anxiety Disorders

GENERALIZED ANXIETY

- ☐ AI > .63
- ☐ CLD
- ☐ ID (if FQ+% > 81)
- ☐ Long time of performance (> 10')
- ☐ Small drawings
- ☐ SC > 1
- ☐ Presence of GR and/or PR
- ☐ Quadrant C, area α or β

- ☐ Dysphoric Contents
- ☐ OBJ% > 50

SOCIAL ANXIETY

- ☐ Absence of H% and P% in the Adp-Area
- ☐ AI [Adp] > AI [Aff]
- ☐ Box 8 Code = AC, NC, AD, or D
- ☐ Box 8 with AST, HS, AS, OBJ, SIG (Primary Content)
- ☐ Box 8 content suggesting detachment (i.e., animals from other elements, especially aggressive or dangerous; objects depicted far from earth or moving away from earth including UFOs, balloons, asteroids, etc.)
- ☐ Quadrant C, area β
- ☐ H content present in protocol, but not in Box 8

PHOBIC ANXIETY

- ☐ Presence of 2 or more HD content with FE
- ☐ Negative Code in Box 4 and/or Box 5 (AC, NC, AD, or D)
- ☐ Box 4 and Box 5 with aggressive content (i.e., dangerous objects, aggressive animals, weapon)
- ☐ Quadrant D, area β
- ☐ Σ HS/HDS > Σ H/HD
- ☐ Masks or masked figures (MK Secondary Content)
- ☐ Perspective drawings

OBSESSIVENESS*

- ☐ Quadrant D, area β or γ
- ☐ Box 6 with MI, FM, FE
- ☐ Box 6 with IR
- ☐ Meticulous and detailed drawings
- ☐ EC+% < 56 or ⩾81
- ☐ IR (mainly anal) with FQ = 1
- ☐ Concurrent M and MI in one or more boxes
- ☐ FQ+% = 100
- ☐ EC+%⩾88 + AQ+% < 50 in Aff area

**If majority of criteria indicate obsessiveness, evaluate A/F Ratio to clarify how obsessiveness manifests in client: if A ≈ F: compulsive behaviors; if A << F: obsessional ideation.*

HYPOCHONDRIASIS

- ☐ Quadrant D, area α or β
- ☐ Presence of ANA and/or PAT (medicine-related content)

EATING DISORDERS

- ☐ Quadrant D, area α or β
- ☐ Signs of Obsessiveness (see *Obsessiveness* above)
- ☐ Box 6 with Oral IR and/or MI
- ☐ A/F Ratio with A ≈ F or A > F
- ☐ Negative Code in Box 2 (AC, NC, AD, or D)
- ☐ CWS indicators of depression (see *Mood/Depressive Disorders* below)
- ☐ Box 1 and/or Box 8 with FD and/or OBJ/FD contents
- ☐ IR (Oral)

Trauma and Adjustment Disorders

INDICES COMPATIBLE WITH A HISTORY OF SEXUAL ABUSE/VIOLENCE

- ☐ Dysregulated performance (i.e., heightened emotionality, CB, AS, distraught verbalizations)
- ☐ Dysphoric and/or aggressive Contents (FIR, EXP, CLD, PAT, WP)
- ☐ MR (Morbid special score)
- ☐ Negative Codes in Boxes 4 and 7 (NC, AD, or D)
- ☐ Negative Code in Box 1 (NC, AD, or D)
- ☐ CWS indicators of depression (see *Mood/Depressive Disorders* below)
- ☐ m≥1
- ☐ Quadrant C, area β

POSTTRAUMATIC STRESS DISORDERS

- ☐ Quadrant C, area β

Mood/Depressive Disorders

REACTIVE DEPRESSION

- ☐ IST = 4–5
- ☐ Long time of performance (> 10')
- ☐ Global Assessment: NOP, LSI, or MSI (with criteria mainly = +)
- ☐ Quadrant A or C, area α or β
- ☐ Low AQ+% (44–50)
- ☐ Negative Code in Box 3 (AC, NC, AD, or D)
- ☐ OD in Box 3
- ☐ MR (Morbid) = 1
- ☐ Medium–high EC+% (75–88)
- ☐ H% = 0–13
- ☐ P% < 31
- ☐ IIT-1 > 1 (mainly due to AS)
- ☐ Positive IIT-2

- ☐ Number of Content Categories = 1–4
- ☐ M = 0–1
- ☐ Lack of effort or apparent motivation *without* GR and/or PR

MAJOR DEPRESSION

- ☐ IST≥6
- ☐ Long time of performance (> 15')
- ☐ Helplessness in completing test
- ☐ Global Assessment: MSI, SSI, or PTL (with criteria mainly = – or ±)
- ☐ AQ = 0 in Box 6
- ☐ AQ = 0 in Box 3
- ☐ Very low AQ+% (< 44)
- ☐ Quadrant B, area α or β
- ☐ Negative Codes in Box 3 and/or 5 and/or 7 (NC, AD, or D)
- ☐ OD in Box 5 (*This could be a sign of suicidal tendencies*)
- ☐ Lack of effort or apparent motivation *with* GR and/or PR
- ☐ MR (Morbid) > 1
- ☐ EC+% < 56
- ☐ H% = 0
- ☐ P% > 31
- ☐ IIT-1 > 1.0 (mainly due to AS)
- ☐ Negative IIT-2
- ☐ Passive FE
- ☐ Number of Contents < 4

MANIC STATES

- ☐ Box 3 & Box 5 as 1st or 2nd in the Order of Sequence (with negative Code, especially NC)
- ☐ Big drawings
- ☐ Short time of performance (< 3')
- ☐ Grandiose contents especially in Box 1
- ☐ Quadrant B, area β and γ
- ☐ A ≈ F or A > F
- ☐ Sometimes IST elevated (≥ 6)
- ☐ Increased O% but O+% < 81
- ☐ M > 1 (with FQ = 0.5 or 0)
- ☐ m≥3
- ☐ M < m
- ☐ P% = 6–18
- ☐ FQ+% < 81
- ☐ Number of Primary Content Categories > 6
- ☐ AQ+%≥69
- ☐ Sometimes PP

Personality Disorders

- ☐ Schizotypal, Schizoid, Paranoid, Antisocial: Quadrant B, area γ
- ☐ Avoidant, Dependent: Quadrant C, area γ
- ☐ Borderline, Histrionic, Narcissistic, Obsessive: Quadrant D, area γ

Psychotic Conditions

PSYCHOTIC WITHDRAWAL

- ☐ Quadrant B, area β and γ
- ☐ Global Assessment: SSI or PTL (with criteria mainly = – or ±)
- ☐ Special Scores of 1st level
- ☐ Presence of Inadequate Integration (II)
- ☐ Sometimes Perseveration (also monotypical record)
- ☐ High incongruency among boxes and/or indices
- ☐ FQ+%≤81
- ☐ AQ+% < 44
- ☐ H% = 0–13 and P% = 0–13
- ☐ A/F Ratio: both sizes≤2
- ☐ GR (especially in Boxes 1 and 8)
- ☐ IIT-1 < 1
- ☐ Presence of HS% or AS%
- ☐ OBJ%, ABS%, SIG% (greater than normal value)
- ☐ Sometimes broken or damaged content

PARANOID TRAITS

- ☐ Quadrant B, area β and γ
- ☐ EC+% > 81 or EC < 44
- ☐ EC+% > 81 with EC+%[Adp] >> EC+%[Aff]; or EC+% < 44 with EC+% [Aff] >> EC+%[Adp]
- ☐ FQ+% = 100
- ☐ A/F Ratio: A << F
- ☐ Paranoid contents (i.e., eyes, masked figures or menacing figures, target)
- ☐ Super-Ego contents (i.e., judge, policeman, etc.)
- ☐ Sensory contents (i.e., radar, periscope, surveillance camera, megaphone, etc.)

SCHIZOPHRENIA

- ☐ Absent or weak awareness of the interpretive attitude
- ☐ Bizarre verbalization
- ☐ Often total denial of the test
- ☐ Quadrant B, area β or γ

- ☐ Numerical Order of Sequence
- ☐ FQ+% < 81
- ☐ A/F Ratio: both sizes ≤ 2
- ☐ P% = 6–13
- ☐ P+% < 81
- ☐ Incongruency of FQ scoring with O% > 25 and O+% < 81
- ☐ Special Scores of 1st level
- ☐ M = 0 (or present but with FQ = 0.5 or 0)
- ☐ ABS%, OBJ% (greater than normative range)
- ☐ Broken or damaged contents
- ☐ Perseverations (also monotypical record)
- ☐ EC+% < 44
- ☐ Encapsulation
- ☐ Blackening
- ☐ High incongruency in the scoring within and between boxes

Sample Clinical Case—A Complete Wartegg Protocol

This manual concludes with the presentation of a clinical case. This client, previously diagnosed with Narcissistic Personality Disorder was assessed via a clinical interview and a standard battery of tests (Rorschach Inkblot Test, Draw-A-Person, WDCT, and MMPI-2, Short Version). Below is the CWS report.

Data Collection and Testing Materials

Mr. Smith is a 37-year-old married male. He has no children. Mr. Smith has a high school education and works as an architect. Mr. Smith sought assessment due to a desire to clarify the nature of his experienced depressive state. He elaborated two main reasons for pursuing mental health treatment at the time of assessment: 1) He was experiencing serious marital difficulties and "existential" suffering that impacted his interpersonal relationships, making him unsatisfied; and 2) Mr. Smith reported preoccupation with eating problems. Per his report, he manifested behaviors suggestive of Bulimia (i.e., he eats and then purposely induces vomiting, due to a conscious fear of gaining weight).

Mr. Smith's parents always had a conflictual relationship and were essentially separated, although they lived in the same household. After his mother passed away a few years ago, Mr. Smith's relationship with his father was almost completely severed, as the conflict in their relationship prevented contact. Mr. Smith reported that his relationship with all members of his family of origin was very poor, especially with his twin sisters (one of whom suffers from a severe mental illness).

Figure 8.1 presents Mr. Smith's WDCT protocol, administered per CWS administration guidelines. Figure 8.2 presents Mr. Smith's administration transcript.

The scoring report, generated by the CWS Scoring Platform (see ►Appendix E for more information) is provided in Figure 8.3 (pp. 349–354). This figure details

FIGURE 8.1 CWS Clinical Case Conceptualization Example—Mr. Smith's WDCT Protocol.

Figure 8.1 provides an example of a WDCT Client Form completed by a Mr. Smith, a 37-year-old male client.

the scoring, Analysis of Sequence 1, Analysis of Sequence 2, computations, descriptive classifications, comparison between the Adaptive and Affective areas, Global Assessment classification, and WIP placement for Mr. Smith's CWS protocol.

CWS Conceptualization—Five Domains of Interpretation

Reviewing the non-specific indicators of psychopathology, strong indicators of dysfunction are noted, primarily: WIP Quadrant D (area β), Global Assessment classification = SSI (severe symptoms and impairments), and the presence of Partial Rejection (PR) special score.

Functional Intelligence

Mr. Smith shows average to high average intellectual ability (FQ+% = 94; M = 1; Number of Primary Contents = 6 + 3 Secondary Contents; Box 6 EC = 1) with tendencies toward abstract thinking (SIG%; Primary Content categories = 6; A/F Ratio with F > A by two points).

Organization of Thought Processes

Mr. Smith presents with good judgment and intact reality testing (Box 6 Code = C). No disturbances of thought process emerged (absence of Special Scores, with the exception of a benign self-reference in Box 4). Mr. Smith, therefore, conforms to a conventional manner of thinking (P% = 25, P+% = 100) without clear signs of creativity and critical skills (O% = 0).

	I	II	III	IV	V	VI	VII	VIII
Order of Sequence	3	8	7	6	5	1	2	4

(Write here the order in which the client completed the 8 boxes)

Total Time of Performance: 7"

PINACOTECA	NOTES
B1. Saturn and some kinds of planets, or space, little planets that rotate around it.	
B2. A rabbit.	
B3. A series of skyscrapers.	
B4. A typical drawing of mine (E: What is it?) Nothing really, it is something that I doodle when I am on the phone or talk to others.	
B5. A stop sign with a car stopped.	
B6. A window.	
B7. A Panzer tank.	
B8. A bald Chinese man smoking.	

Which drawing do you like the most? 8 Why? Because it turned out better.

Which drawing do you like the least? 7 **Why? It is a weapon.**

(Using a new blank form) **Which stimulus do you like the most? 3 Why? It is the one that stimulated me the most.**

Which stimulus do you like the least? 4 Why? It did not suggest anything to me.

Succession Test: + 8 6 7 1 4 2 -

Did the subject turn the Wartegg during the performance? ☐ **Yes** ☒ **No**

If YES, which panels? n/a

Was it necessary to provide the additional instructions? ☐ **Yes** ☒ **No**

FIGURE 8.2 CWS Clinical Case Conceptualization Example—Mr. Smith's WDCT Administration Transcript.

Figure 8.2 provides the administration transcript of the WDCT protocol completed by Mr. Smith, a 37-year-old male client (presented in Figure 8.1).

11/03/2017

Group	CLN	Code	35

Name	MR.SMITH	37 YEAR OLD	Sex	M

SCORING

ORIGINAL ORDER OF SEQUENCE	3	8	7	6	5	1	2	4
Boxes	I	II	III	IV	V	VI	VII	VIII
Order of sequence	3	8	6	7	1	5	2	4

TEST execution time 7 Minutes **# Boxes completed** 8

Box	E.C.	A.Q.	F.Q.	Content		FR.	SPECIAL SCORES							Movement			I.R.
				PR.	SE.									M/m	g	d	
1	1,0	0,5	1,0	AST			AS							MI		r	
2	1,0	0,5	1,0	A			AS	CB									
3	0,5	0,5	1,0	ARC		(P)	AS	CB									
4	0,0	0,5	0,5	SIG			PA	PR									
5	0,0	0,5	1,0	SIG	OBJ		AS	CB						MI		b	
6	1,0	0,5	1,0	OBJ			AS	CB									
7	0,0	0,0	1,0	OBJ	WP	(P)	AS										
8	1,0	0,5	1,0	H	CLD	P	AS							M	m	p	*

ANALYSIS OF SEQUENCE 1

	I	II	III	IV	V	VI	VII	VIII
Order of Sequence	3	8	6	7	1	5	2	4
Evocative Character	0,5	1,0	1,0	0,0	1,0	0,0	1,0	0,0
Affective Quality	0,5	0,5	0,5	0,0	0,5	0,5	0,5	0,5
Code	AC	C	C	NC	PC	D	PC	D
Form Quality	1,0	1,0	1,0	1,0	1,0	1,0	1,0	0,5
A/F Ratio	0,5 : 1,0	0,5 : 1,0	0,5 : 1,0	0,0 : 1,0	0,5 : 1,0	0,5 : 1,0	0,5 : 1,0	0,5 : 0,5
Impulse Responses		*						

ANALYSIS OF SEQUENCE 2

Adaptive area
(1 - 8)
3 8
AC C

Adaptive area
(3 - 6)
6 7
C NC

Affective area
(2 - 4)
1 5
PC D

Affective area
(5 - 7)
2 4
PC D

Istituto Italiano Wartegg

FIGURE 8.3 CWS Clinical Case Conceptualization Example—CWS Scoring Report for Mr. Smith.

Figure 8.3 provides the scoring and calculations of the WDCT protocol completed by Mr. Smith, a 37-year-old male client (presented in Figures 8.1 and 8.2).

Source: CWS Scoring Platform;

11/03/2017

Group **CLN** Code **35**

Name **MR.SMITH** | **37 YEAR OLD** Sex **M**

Boxes completed **8**

INDICES

E.C.+%	56	AQ.+%	44	FQ+%	94	A/F	1,5 / 3,5	P%	25	P+%	100
O%	0	O+%	N.D.	I.I.T.- 1	1,625	I.M.	0,50	A.I.	0,88	I.I.T - 2	4,0:4,0

AC = 1 AD = 0
NC = 1 D = 2

W.I.P. : Quadrant **D** Area **β** Beta
UNRESOLVED

M/m = 1 / 2

I.S.T. 3 / 23

I.V. 4 / 18

PRIMARY CONTENTS # 6

H%	13	A%	13
OBJ%	25	ARC%	13
SIG%	25	AST%	13
NAT%		BOT%	
ABS%		ANA%	
AS%		BIO%	
FD%		EXP%	
FIR%		ICE%	
HS%		MIN%	
CLD%		PAT%	
SEX%			

SECONDARY CONTENTS # 3

AC%		H%		A%	
HR%		OBJ%	13	ARC%	
FA%		SIG%		AST%	
TY%		NAT%		BOT%	
MT%		ABS%		ANA%	
CG%		AS%		BIO%	
WP%	13	FD%		EXP%	
FT%		FIR%		ICE%	
SF%		HS%		MIN%	
MK%		CLD%	13	PAT%	
RE%		SEX%			

IMPULSE RESPONSES # 1

SPECIAL SCORES # 13

SC		PA	1	CB	4	CO		RB		AS	7
MR		ID		II		MU		PP		AP	
GR		PR	1	SR		IS		DS		TR	
		Box 3 OD						Box 5 OD			

PRIMARY MOVEMENT

# M	GENDER m	GENDER f	GENDER i	DIRECTION a	DIRECTION p	DIRECTION b	DIRECTION d	DIRECTION r	DIRECTION i
1	1	0	0	0	1	0	0	0	0

SECONDARY MOVEMENT

# m	MI	FE	FM
2	2		

Istituto Italiano Wartegg

FIGURE 8.3 *Continued*

11/03/2017

Group **CLN** Code **35**

Name **MR.SMITH** **37 YEAR OLD** Sex **M**

Number boxes filled 8

INDICES

INDEX	boxes 1-3-6-8	boxes 2-4-5-7
E.C.+%	88	25
AQ.+%	50	38
FQ+%	100	88
A/F	2,0 /4,0	1,0 /3,0
P%	38	13
P+%	100	100
O%	0	0
O+%	0	0
I.I.T- 1	1,750	1,500
I.M.	0,50	0,50
A.I.	1,00	0,75
I.I.T. - 2	3,0:1,0	1,0:3,0
WIP [Q/A]	C b	D g
H%	25	0
N. S.S.	6	7
N. GR ,PR	0	1
M	1	0
m	1	1
N. IR	1	0
C	2	0
AC	1	0
NC	0	1
PC	1	1
AD	0	0
D	0	2

INDEX	boxes I - II III - IV	boxes V - VI VII - VIII
E.C.+%	63	50
AQ.+%	38	50
FQ+%	100	88
A/F	1,5 /4,0	2,0 /3,5
P%	50	0
P+%	100	0
O%	0	0
O+%	0	0
I.I.T- 1	1,500	1,750
I.M.	0,50	0,50
A.I.	1,00	0,75
I.I.T. - 2	2,0:2,0	2,0:2,0
WIP [Q/A]	DC a	D b-
H%	25	0
N. S.S.	6	7
N. GR,PR	0	1
M	1	0
m	0	2
N. IR	1	0
C	2	0
AC	1	0
NC	1	0
PC	0	2
AD	0	0
D	0	2

INDEX	boxes 1-2-7-8	boxes 3-4-5-6
E.C.+%	75	38
AQ.+%	38	50
FQ+%	100	88
A/F	1,5 /4,0	2,0 /3,5
P%	38	13
P+%	100	100
O%	0	0
O+%	0	0
I.I.T- 1	1,500	1,750
I.M.	0,25	0,75
A.I.	1,00	0,75
I.I.T. - 2	3,0:1,0	1,0:3,0
WIP [Q/A]	C a-	D g
H%	25	0
N. S.S.	5	8
N. GR,PR	0	1
M	1	0
m	1	1
N. IR	1	0
C	1	1
AC	0	1
NC	1	0
PC	2	0
AD	0	0
D	0	2

Istituto Italiano Wartegg

FIGURE 8.3 *Continued*

11/03/2017

Group **CLN** Code **35**

Name **MR.SMITH** **37 YEAR OLD** Sex **M**

BOX VALUES

Boxes	Val.	Personality Description
Box 1 Self-evaluation	PC	Possible feelings of insecurity and lack of confidence in his/her abilities are limited but there is also great potential for emotional maturity.
Box 2 Female O.R.	PC	Stable affect and good ability to interact with the environment. Any social inhibition or interpersonal difficulties are limited and circumscribed to certain situations or particular emotional triggers.
Box 3 Available Energies	AC	Energy level is good and effectively directed to attain desired goals, but less efficient when highly stressed or emotionally triggered.
Box 4 Male O.R.	D	Difficulty accepting societal rules and norms. Widespread and fundamental conflict with authority.
Box 5 Aggressive Energies	D	Passive, indecisive, and inhibited, aggressive energy is repressed.
Box 6 Relation to reality	C	Able to structure and synthesize thoughts and actions. Reality testing is solid and effective. Judgment and logic is good (capable of mature decision making, rational thinking, and logic). Able to understand and interpret situational and emotional nuance.
Box 7 Sexual Energies	NC	Sexual dynamics and sexual relationships are a primary focus, possibly due to unconscious overcompensation related to sexual issues. The overcompensation may be positive, manifesting as emotional awareness, gentleness, and tact, or may take the form of obsessive-compulsive attitudes and/or behaviors.
Box 8 Social skills	C	Exceptional ability to relate to others, generally mature and appropriately adaptive. At times,. subject may be overly compliant and dependent in close interpersonal relationships.

Istituto Italiano Wartegg

FIGURE 8.3 *Continued*

30/05/2017

Group **CLN** Code **35**

Name **MR.SMITH** **37 YEAR OLD** Sex **M**

GLOBAL ASSESSMENT

SSI Quadrant D Area β Beta

I1)	Overall maturity level :	Well balanced personality structure	-
I2)	Emotional regulation :	Self-control and mood stability	±
I3)	Cognitive abilities :	Critical analysis and judgment	+
I4)	Interpersonal skills :	Effectiveness as group member	±
I5)	Group affiliation :	Flexibility and adaptiveness	±

Notes

Istituto Italiano Wartegg

FIGURE 8.3 *Continued*

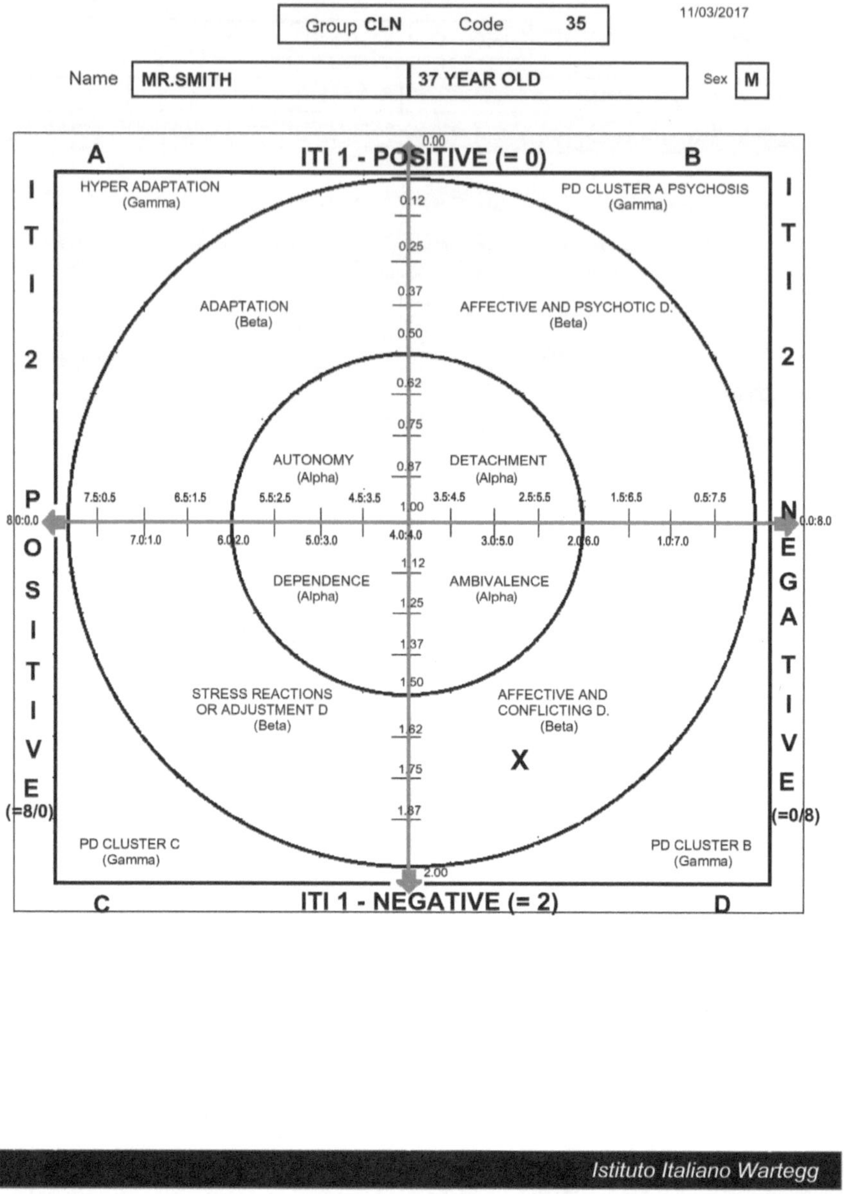

FIGURE 8.3 *Continued*

Available Energy

Available energy is elevated as demonstrated by the anticipation of Box 3 in the Order of Sequence and the number of Primary Content categories (6), although it is currently not functional or goal-directed (Box 3: EC = 0.5, AQ = 0.5, Code = AC). Behaviorally, this may translate into a dispersion of energy and interests, and into a tendency to engage simultaneously in multiple activities, without having carefully evaluated the realistic chances of carrying them out (6 Primary Content categories + 3 Secondary Content categories; Partial Rejection in Box 4). This heightened activity level is consistent with the intense anxiety that emerged on the WDCT (AI = .88; IIT-1 = 1.62; CLD content; m = 2 including one rotary movement and one blocked movement) and the fundamentally conflictual nature of his personality organization (IIT-2 = 4:4; presence of only 2 C; Boxes 4 and 5 valued as D; Box 7 coded NC).

Social Skills

Mr. Smith's interpersonal relationships are characterized by a high degree of discomfort (Global Assessment: Criterion 4 [Interpersonal Skills] and 5 [Group Affiliation] = +/–). He likely exhibits dependency traits (Oral Impulse Response in Box 8) combined with narcissistic traits (Self-Reference on Box 4) and with a strong tendency toward autonomy and independence (Box 1: EC = 1, AQ = 0.5, Code = PC). Additionally, a notable difference exists in WIP Quadrant and area between the Adaptive and Affective areas. In the Adaptive area, strong signs of a conflicting relationship with the environment are present, indicating adjustment difficulties and ambivalence (Quadrant C, area β), whereas in the Affective Area, Quadrant D, area γ typically indicates symptoms related to personality disorder including immaturity and emotional reactivity.

Taken together, these indices suggest that Mr. Smith lacks a genuine interest in interpersonal relationships and instead manifests a tendency to exploit others (i.e., aggressive dependency). This emerges from: 1) Comparison: H%[Adp-A] = 25 >> H%[Aff-A] = 0; and 2) Comparison: P%[Adp-A] = 38 >> P%[Aff-A] = 13. Furthermore, the analysis of the main comparisons between indices of the Adaptive Area and of the Affective Area are consistent with a personality type that is especially attentive to the formal aspects of relationships, but only for his own benefit and advantage (EC+% and AQ+% of the Adaptive Area > the EC+% and AQ+% of the Affective Area).

Emotional Functioning

Mr. Smith's CWS protocol produced a Severe (SSI) Global Assessment. His affective life is markedly constricted (AQ+% = 44; A/F Ratio = 1.5:3.5), characterized by strong internal tensions (2 Inanimate Movement responses), marked immaturity (Global Assessment: Criterion 1 [Overall Maturity Level] = –), and egocentrism (IIT-1 = 1.625; 4 CB; Rotary MI in Box 1 and Blocked MI in Box 5). In fact, both aggressive (Box 5: EC = 0, AQ = 0.5, Code = D) and sexual impulses (Box 7: EC = 0, AQ = 0, Code = NC) are greatly disturbed and Mr. Smith likely regulates them in a dysfunctional manner. He likely lacks adequate abilities for introspection and self-criticism, especially with regard to affect-related matters (EC+%[Adp-A] = 88; EC+%[Aff-A] = 25).

Affect-related dynamics that relate to aggressive impulses are repressed and outside of conscious awareness (Box 5 coded D, with Blocked MI), leading to inappropriately reactive behaviors that are not proportional to circumstances (Box 5 = D, but anticipated in the Order of Sequence; 4 CB).

Mr. Smith's affective dynamics that are linked to sexuality are also the source of marked conflict (Box 7: EC = 0, AQ = 0) and lead to a compensatory heightening of sexual behaviors (Box 7 is anticipated in the Order of Sequence, and coded NC). Hence, Mr. Smith's underlying conflict in female object relations likely leads him to actively seek potentially superficial and exploitative sexual relationships (Box 2 postponed in the Order of Sequence, and coded PC).

Overall the comparison between the IIT-2 of the Adaptive Area and of the Affective Area portrays a person capable of adapting to social and interpersonal situations (IIT-2 of the Adaptive Area = 3/1), but that is incapable of a true inner affective balance (IIT-2 of the Affective Area = 1/3). Accordingly, the values of the IIT-1 and IIT-2 (4/4, negatively affected by the presence of 1 NC and 2 D) place Mr. Smith in Quadrant D, area β of the Wartegg Index of Psychopathology (WIP). This area of the WIP is generally associated with long-standing patterns of ambivalence (including insecurity of attachment) accompanied by marked emotional pain and awareness of personal distress. In the β area, dynamics of immaturity and conflict predominate.

Additionally, Analysis of Sequence shows the following personality traits: Box 6 is valued as a Choice. This suggests that Mr. Smith may tend to utilize intellectualizing and rationalizing defense mechanisms in his personality organization.

Analysis of Sequence 2

Pair (1–8)—[Mr. Smith's Order of Sequence: I: Box 3 (AC); II: Box 8 (C)]

Box 3 is anticipated in substitution of Box 1. This indicates that Mr. Smith's available energy is heightened, though not in a productive manner. The client compensates his internal sense of inadequacy through action. This action, as shown by the AC Code (Box 3), is not always goal-directed, as confirmed by the fact that the drawing on Box 3 does not show a vertical progression of the marks within the stimulus (EC = 0.5). Mr. Smith tends to identify more with what he does, than with what he feels. Social interactions (Box 8) are characterized by ambivalence; the balance between dependency and autonomy presents as unstable and is likely a source of conflict. Also, the verbalization provided at the Picture Gallery for Box 8 ("A bald Chinese man smoking") involves several interesting content elements. The fact that the person drawn is from a distant country, and belongs to a different and foreign culture, shows that the client experiences a sense of detachment and alienation from the environment. The fact that the person is bald, hence has an "aesthetic defect," stresses the importance that Mr. Smith attributes to his physical appearance. Finally, the fact that the person is smoking introduces an element of dependency and social anxiety.

Pair (3–6)—[Mr. Smith's Order of Sequence: III: Box 6 (C); IV: Box 7 (NC)]

Box 7 is largely anticipated in the Order of Sequence and is coded NC. Negative Compensations indicate a significant degree of ambivalence and conflict. Hence, Mr. Smith likely experiences intense distress with regard to sexual dynamics, which is outside of his awareness and is masked by compensatory behaviors. The overall presentation of this box, along with the provided verbalization ("a Panzer tank"), suggests that an area of intense conflict was activated. Mr. Smith likely experiences inadequacy and lack of satisfaction in his sexual and interpersonal interactions with the opposite sex, although may demonstrate superficial hypersexual behaviors.

The Order of Sequence confirms Mr. Smith's tendency toward intellectual sophistication and suggests that he uses it in his interactions with the outside world (Box 6 = C, FQ+% = 94).

Pair (2–4)—[Mr. Smith's Order of Sequence: V: Box 1 (PC); VI: Box 5 (D)]

Box 5 is anticipated, but coded D. Aggressive impulses are entirely repressed and unconsciously determine and impact the client's behavior. It should be noted that the performance and the verbalization for this box ("Stop sign with a car stopped"), along with the presence of blocked MI reflect the client's stunted experience. This might be expressed behaviorally with attitudes and conduct of masked aggression, such as irony and sarcasm, which are consistent with the client's high level of education. Again in this Box, the D coding indicates a conflict or a poorly integrated area of personality.

Box 1 is delayed and coded PC suggesting that Mr. Smith has latent potential, with room for improvement via therapy, in the area of self-concept and identity.

Pair (5–7)—[Mr. Smith's Order of Sequence: VII: Box 2 (PC); VIII: Box 4 (D)]

Both Boxes 2 and 4 are delayed and are respectively coded PC and D. These boxes are drawn as the last two positions in the Order of Sequence, suggesting that Mr. Smith's relationship with his parents is more conflictual and less integrated into his personality functioning. This indicates, especially with regard to Box 4 (coded D), that his relationship with his father and authority figures is likely disturbed and may unconsciously determine Mr. Smith's behavior. This is confirmed by the presence of the special score Partial Rejection (PR) in Box 4.

Mr. Smith drew in Box 4 "A typical drawing of mine," coded D. This might symbolically reflect an obsessive thought about the father figure, which is, however, no longer in the client's awareness in terms of content. Similarly, the drawing in Box 2 is significant. The depicted rabbit introduces an animal element, which, as mentioned previously, often represents repressed impulses. On one hand, the rabbit evokes tenderness and need for affection. On the other hand, it represents insecurity, fear, and heightened sexuality (which is consistent with what is mentioned above about Mr. Smith's sexual dynamics).

Overall, Mr. Smith presents as markedly distressed, with traits of narcissistic personality disorder. This is expressed through compensatory behaviors that hide feelings of insecurity and dependency. In light of the two positive compensations and of the good intellectual and educational level, psychodynamic psychotherapy is recommended. His prognosis for change is moderately positive.

Appendices

APPENDIX D

CWS Form for Administration, Scoring, and Computation

I.I.W.

ISTITUTO ITALIANO WARTEGG

C.W.S

Crisi Wartegg System

ADMINISTRATION, SCORING AND COMPUTATION FORM

First Name .... Middle .... Last Name ....

Date of birth .... Age .... Male ☐ Female ☐

Grade in school/Highest education level achieved: ....

Profession: ....

Reason for assessment: ....

....

....

....

Date .... **Assessor** ....

FIGURE D.1 CWS Form for Administration, Scoring, and Computation.

Figure D.1 provides a sample CWS Form for Administration, Scoring, and Computation.

Source: Copyright by IIW, Rome, Italy). Reproduction of any kind is strictly forbidden. The form can be ordered at the Istituto Italiano Wartegg (www.wartegg.com). For inquires, please contact: iiw@wartegg.com.

	I	II	III	IV	V	VI	VII	VIII
Order of Sequence								

(Write here the order in which the client completed the 8 boxes)

Time of performance		

PICTURE GALLERY
(In numerical order, write here what the client drew in each box)

B1 ....

B2 ....

B3 ....

B4 ....

B5 ....

B6 ....

B7 ....

B8 ....

NOTES
(Starting on the first line, write here in chronological order everything that happens during the administration)

Which drawing do you like the most? .... Why? ....

Which drawing do you like the least? .... Why? ....

(Using a new blank form) Which mark do you like the most? .... Why? ....

Which mark do you like the least? .... Why? ....

Test of sequence: + ____ ____ ____ ____ ____ ____ –

Did the subject turn the Wartegg form during the administration? YES – NO

If YES, which panels? ....

Were the additional instructions necessary? YES – NO

FIGURE D.1 *Continued*

Box	EC	AQ	FQ	CONT. PR.	CONT. SE.	Fr.	SPECIAL SCORES					M/m M/m	M/m g	M/m d	IR
1															
2															
3															
4															
5															
6															
7															
8															

AoS 1 & 2	I	II	III	IV	V	VI	VII	VIII
Order of Sequence								
Evocative Character								
Affective Quality								
Code								
Form Quality								
Ratio A/F								
Impulse Response								

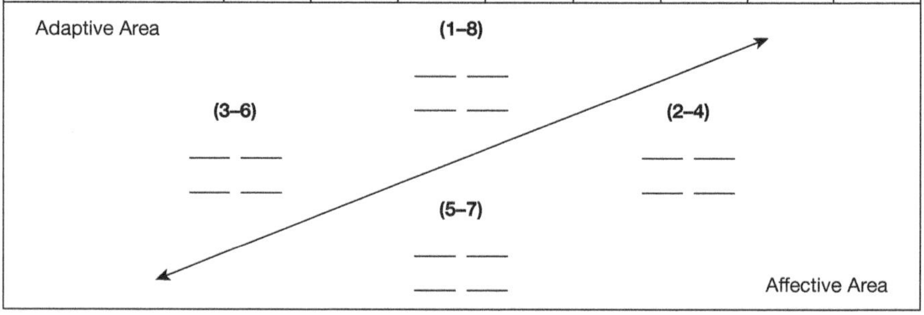

W.I.P.: Quadrant A B C D Area: α β γ

Notes

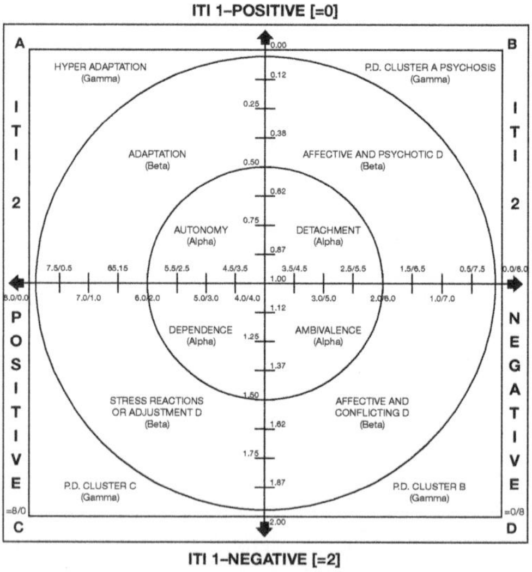

FIGURE D.1 *Continued*

INDICES

EC+% _____ AQ+% _____ FQ+% _____ A/F _____

P% _____ P+% _____ O% _____ O+% _____

I.I.T.–1 _____ IM _____ AI _____ I.I.T.–2 _____

W.I.P.: Quadrant A B C D Area: α β γ M/m=

AC ___
NC ___
AD ___
D ___

NUMBER OF PRIMARY CONTENT CATEGORIES (# = ______)

H% ______ A% ______ OBJ% ______

ARC% ______ SIG% ______ AST% ______

NAT% ______ BOT% ______ ....% ______

........% ______ ....% ______ ....% ______

NUMBER OF SECONDARY CONTENT CATEGORIES (# = ______)

.... % _____ .... % _____ .... % _____

.... % _____ .... % _____ .... % _____

TOTAL NUMBER OF SPECIAL SCORES (# = ______)

Type: ___ Number: ___ Type: ___ Number: ___ Type: ___ Number: ___

Type: ___ Number: ___ Type: ___ Number: ___ Type: ___ Number: ___

Type: ___ Number: ___ Type: ___ Number: ___ Type: ___ Number: ___

TOTAL NUMBER OF IMPULSE RESPONSES (# = ______)

Type: ________ Box: ______ Type: ________ Box: ______

Type: ________ Box: ______ Type: ________ Box: ______

Type: ________ Box: ______ Type: ________ Box: ______

COMPARISON	Adp-A	Aff-A
	Boxes 1-3-6-8	Boxes 2-4-5-7
EC+%		
AQ+%		
FQ+%		
A/F		
P%		
P+%		
O%		
O+%		
I.I.T.-1		
IM		
AI		
I.I.T.-2		
QR. Area		
H%		
# Sp.Sc		
# GR/PR		
M		
m		
# I.R.		
C		
AC		
NC		
PC		
AD		
D		

PRIMARY MOVEMENT (# = ______)

	m	f	i	Total
Active				
Passive				
Blocked				
Double				
Rotary				
Indeterminate				
Total				

SECONDARY MOVEMENT (# = ______)

	FM	MI	FE	Total
Active				
Passive				
Blocked				
Double				
Rotary				
Indeterminate				
Total				

FIGURE D.1 *Continued*

Report

....

....

....

....

....

....

....

....

....

....

....

....

....

....

....

....

....

....

....

....

....

....

....

Assessor ....

FIGURE D.1 *Continued*

APPENDIX F

CWS Scoring Tables

Evocative Character

TABLE F.1 Box 1 (Simple) Evocative Character—Centrality or Relevance

1-point responses: The client grasps the centrality or relevance of the mark and depicts responses where the stimulus is central and/or a major element in the drawing. The central placement of the stimulus must be appropriate based on either graphic or conceptual criteria.

Examples of 1-point responses include: the center (of a target, of a circle, of spokes in a wheel, of a clock, of flower petals, of a galaxy, of a constellation, of a spider web, of a car horn on a steering wheel); an eye (isolated or as part of a face), a nose or a mouth (these must always be part of a face, never isolated parts), a diamond solitaire ring, the vanishing point in a 1-point perspective drawing, the head of a small human-like figure, the nucleus of an atom, the center point of a spiral, a navel, the ace side of a die, the dot at the bottom of an exclamation or question mark, the dot above the letter "i."

0.5-point responses: The client only partially captures the mark's centrality or relevance, drawing something that includes the mark in a non-centralized way or attributing less important or secondary meaning to the mark.

Examples of 0.5-point responses are: the window of an airplane*, the porthole of a ship*, a star in a constellation*, a button on a shirt*, or an apple on a tree*.

* There is also a quantitative aspect to the EC in Box 1: drawings that include *between 2 and 5 items* (5 apples, 5 windows, etc.) earn an EC score of 0.5. Drawings that include more than five items (showing even less centrality or importance to each item) earn EC scores of 0.

0-point responses: The client does not capture the centrality or the relevance of the stimulus and draws:

1) responses in which the stimulus is simply repeated, without any meaning attributed to it;

2) responses that alter the stimulus itself (i.e., the mark is thickened/blackened to make it bigger); or

3) responses that include the stimulus in such a way that any sense of centrality or importance is lost (e.g., a dot on a spider web, on a line, or on an object; the apex of a geometric figure; the center of the letter "x"; snow flakes; rain drops; floating balloons or flying birds; a freckle on a face; confetti).

TABLE F.2 Box 2 (Simple) Evocative Character—Movement and Vitality

1-point responses: The client captures the mark's "pull" for movement and vitality. *Examples of 1-point responses include*: human figures or animals (either as entire figures or as parts of them, such as a face), objects that are alive (e.g., a tree, a flower, a plant), and inanimate objects that are in movement (e.g., a lit candle, a flame, smoke, rain, a wave, sun rays, a river, a flag blowing in the wind, the sea).
0.5-point responses: The client does not capture the suggestion of movement and vitality, but makes a drawing that includes the stimulus and its sense of plasticity, flexibility, and curviness. *Examples of 0.5-point responses include*: an arch, the curved edge of a lake or turn in a road, a bottle, a single leaf (not attached to tree), an ice-cream cone, an acorn, clothing (e.g., a hat, a dress shirt with buttons), a cloud, curved brackets or musical notations, decorations that repeat the stimulus, statues, dolls, a cruet, a piece of parchment, numbers, signs and words that follow the curviness of the stimulus, and lifeless human figures, animal figures, or botanical elements (e.g., a dead man, an animal corpse, a dead branch, a dead leaf).
0-point responses: The client does not capture the mark's movement or vitality, and does not even grasp a sense of plasticity or curviness. Instead, client draws rigid, mechanical, static drawings, including: buildings; geometric figures such as squares or rectangles; squared and mechanical objects; numbers, marks, or words that require an alteration of the stimulus. Additionally, isolated human or animal body details (e.g., an eyebrow, a mouth, an eye, a moustache, a beak, a finger, etc.) earn an EC of 0.

TABLE F.3 Box 3 (Complex) Evocative Character—Directionality and Progression

Recall that for Complex Boxes, the NECESSARY, BUT NOT SUFFICIENT CONDITION requires that the client perceives the two or more marks as belonging to the same entity, either conceptually or graphically. If this condition is not met, an EC score of 0 is automatic. **Special Considerations for Box 3:** Also note that in scoring the EC for Box 3, special attention must be paid to the client's age. As the skill of drawing in perspective only develops around 11–12 years of age, the younger the child is, the more leniently EC should be scored. Once the necessary condition has been met (i.e., the marks are graphically and/or conceptually linked to each other), EC is scored according to the following guidelines:
1-point responses: Responses that show a sense of direction and of dynamic progression toward the top right corner. Examples of 1-point responses include: stairs (or staircase), organ-pipes, a diagram, buildings of increasing height, runways, and objects (i.e., light-poles, trees, or bridges) in a perspective view. In order for the drawing to receive a 1-point EC score, the direction of the drawing must be *clearly oriented* (structurally and/or dynamically) toward the top right corner of the box, and should include a minimum of six lines of increasing height across the full width of the box. Some examples include: buildings that get taller and taller as they are closer to the top right-hand side of the box (structural), stairs going up toward the upper right side of the box (structural), cars going up a hillside toward the upper right side of the box (dynamic).
0.5-point responses: Examples of 0.5-point responses include all responses that: 1) Integrate the three consecutive lines of the stimulus without showing any sense of vertical progression (e.g., three flowers or three trees with no emphasis on height increases); 2) Integrate the three marks, but that continue horizontally after the third mark (e.g., stairs that lead to a landing); 3) Are initially directed upward but subsequently turn downward (e.g., a roof, a suspension bridge); 4) Suggest direction and dynamic progression toward the top right corner, but contain less than six lines of increasing height.
0-point responses: Examples of 0-point responses include all responses: 1) That involve a Reversed Box (upside down or sideways); 2) Where the three consecutive lines are not integrated but instead represent separate objects (e.g., one line is a broom, one is a cigarette, and one is a fishing pole); 3) In which the stimulus is extended primarily vertically (e.g., a person's legs, an animal's legs, a road or freeway drawn vertically); 4) In which a sense of progression or directionality is totally lost although the drawing may use the entire box (e.g., bars, a prison window, a net, graph paper, a checker board, keys on a piano, a picket fence, lists of numbers); 5) That while graphically pointing toward the top right corner, are clearly oriented toward the bottom left corner (e.g., a children's slide that faces left, a bridge from a perspective view-point, but with a car driving toward the bottom left corner). This last category describes examples of drawings that require the Special Score of Opposite Direction or OD (see below).

TABLE F.4 Box 4 (Simple) Evocative Character—Heaviness and Stability

1-point responses: The client's drawing grasps the concepts of heaviness, great weight, and/or stability—expressed in either a literal or symbolic manner. *Examples of literal 1-point responses include*: buildings, houses, towers, bridges, tunnels, railways, a tree, a boulder, a window, door, or brick (only as part of a house or of a wall), a robot, a fireplace, the sun, certain (heavy) modes of transportation NOT in motion (e.g., an airplane that is not in flight, a ship at dock, a stationary truck or car). Symbolic responses that express a sense of heaviness must refer to difficult objects or activities, complicated things that "make you think." Examples of symbolic 1-point responses include: plane or solid geometric figures, crossword puzzles, a rebus, chess pieces, chess or checkerboard, a computer.
0.5-point responses: *Examples of 0.5-point responses include*: 1) The client partially captures a sense of heaviness and/or stability and draws things including: a rock, a barbell, furniture such as a desk, dresser, or night-stand, a television, an isolated window or door (not as part of a structure), and some videogames (e.g., Minecraft in adults. In children, Minecraft is considered EC = 1. Videogames must be evaluated on a case by case basis; Most are scored 0.5, although in rare cases, a cognitively complicated videogame may be scored EC = 1); 2) Responses that represent heaviness, but not stability: a rolling boulder, and all drawings depicting moving means of transportation (e.g., a plane in flight, a ship in a storm, a moving train, truck, or car); 3) All responses that represent stability, but not heaviness, such as a billboard, a fence, or video camera tripod.
0-point responses: The client grasps neither heaviness nor stability and draws something representing the opposite of heaviness and stability. *Examples of 0-point responses include*: a kite, a die, a butterfly, a human or animal figure (except the ones typically associated with size and heaviness), videogames focusing on manual dexterity and not requiring significant cognitive effort (i.e., Pong, Tetris, etc.), food, a feather, a flower, jewelry, a cigarette, musical notes, a mattress spring, a single brick, a spiral, a computer keyboard or mouse, a remote control, a playing card, an hourglass.

TABLE F.5 Box 5 (Complex) Evocative Character—Overcoming Obstacles with Dynamic Progression Toward Center of the Box

Recall that for Complex Boxes, the NECESSARY, BUT NOT SUFFICIENT CONDITION requires that the client perceives the two or more marks as belonging to the same entity, either conceptually or graphically. If this condition is not met, an EC score of 0 is automatic. Once the necessary condition has been met (i.e., the marks are graphically and/or conceptually linked to each other), EC is scored according to the following guidelines:
1-point responses: *Examples of 1-point responses include*: 1) Drawings that point (even a little) past the more central diagonal line toward the center of the box (e.g., a kitchen utensil, a tool, an object, a kite, a bow and arrow pointing toward the center, a cross, a flashlight, a syringe with the needle pointing toward the center of the box); 2) Drawings of objects that are separate, but conceptually related (e.g., nail and hammer, bucket and spade, book and pencil, detached geometric figures); 3) Due to their high frequency, the following responses are exceptions to the above rules and are scored as 1-point responses: the letter "T," a hammer, and a steering wheel with a driver or cyclist on a bicycle or motorcycle.
0.5-point responses: *Examples of 0.5-point responses include*: 1) All responses in which the drawing is confined to the bottom left corner of the box (e.g., an open book, a house, a teepee, a tent, a roof) and does not move past the contraposed mark; 2) Responses in which the marks, although part of the same object, are graphically disconnected (e.g., an arrow in which the point is disconnected from the shaft). This "disconnect" rule also applies to the responses noted above (i.e., the letter "T," a hammer, and a steering wheel with a driver or cyclist on a bicycle or motorcycle) which are scored 0.5 if the two marks remain graphically disconnected.
0-point responses: *Examples of 0-point responses include*: 1) All responses involving a Reversed Box (upside down or sideways); 2) Responses in which the drawing is oriented laterally, either toward the right or toward the left (e.g., a person doing sit-ups, the yoga position "downward dog", a piano keyboard); 3) Responses in which the two marks are not integrated, graphically OR conceptually (e.g., a match and a nail; pencil and drinking glass); 4) All responses that express a total block of movement (e.g., two cars in a car crash, a car stopped at a stop sign, a maze, a railroad crossing with the bar down, a sunken anchor); 5) All responses that focus toward the bottom left corner of the box. These drawings may integrate the two marks and point toward the center of the box; however, the directional focus of the depicted objects is toward the bottom left corner (e.g., a syringe where the needle is the bottom mark, a man working with a jackhammer). This type of drawing meets criteria for the Special Score OD (Opposite Direction).

TABLE F.6 Box 6 (Complex) Evocative Character– Synthesis and Structure

Recall that for Complex Boxes, the NECESSARY, BUT NOT SUFFICIENT CONDITION requires that the client perceives the two or more marks as belonging to the same entity, either conceptually or graphically. If this condition is not met, an EC score of 0 is automatic.

Special Considerations for Box 6

As Box 6 has particular diagnostic relevance, it has specific rules for EC scoring. Sometimes, on Box 6, when the client conceptually and/or graphically joins the two marks, the structural quality of the drawing is insufficient (i.e., the two marks are rays of the sun). Thus, once the necessary condition is met, the assessor must closely evaluate the TYPE, AND QUALITY OF THE SYNTHESIS drawn by the client in order to properly score this box.

Once the necessary condition has been met (i.e., the marks are graphically and/or conceptually linked to each other), EC is scored according to the following guidelines:

1-point responses: The client grasps the ideas of "shared destiny," "proximity," and "similarity" of the two marks and demonstrates this either graphically and/or symbolically.

Examples of graphically demonstrated 1-point responses include: a plane or solid geometric figure (e.g., squares, rectangles, cubes, but not circles and spheres), buildings, automobiles, a painting, a window, an architectural blueprint of a house or room, a television, a gift box, a blow-dryer, and a rifle or gun. Examples of symbolically demonstrated 1-point responses include: a martini glass and shaker, two geometric figures, two buildings, a hammer and nail, a house and tree, a pair of boots.

0.5-point responses: *Examples of 0.5-point responses include*:

1) Responses in which the client understands synthesis, but leaves the structure partially incomplete by leaving a graphic disconnection, gap, or break in the two lines (e.g., a perspective view of a road left open as it comes "forward," a ship's bow);
2) All drawings that graphically deserve a score of 1, but that are not completely closed (e.g., squares that are clearly left with gaps at the corners) or drawings with the Special Score "Incomplete Drawing" (ID), discussed later in this chapter;
3) Drawings in which parts of objects are depicted rather than whole objects (e.g., part of a baseball infield, a battery that is cut off by the borders of the box.

0-point responses: *Examples of 0-point responses include*:

1) All drawings involving a Reversed Box (upside down or sideways);
2) All drawings that do not satisfy the necessary condition of graphic and/or conceptual linking (e.g., a telephone pole and a spoon);
3) All responses that ignore the "pull" of synthesis and structure, resulting in clear alterations of the stimulus (e.g., clouds, sky, flowers, non-squared geometric figures such as circles or spheres, faces or whole human figures, animals' snouts or whole animal figures such as a puffer fish or a whale, round objects such as a ball or a plate, the sun, the moon). Drawings such as these would earn the Special Scores of "Inadequate Integration" (II). In the case of Inadequate Integration, EC (in Box 6) is always considered EC = 0. In some cases, drawings in Box 6 also meet scoring criteria for "Arbitrary Performance" (AP; i.e., drawings depicted from multiple perspectives, but maintaining synthesis and structure), discussed later in this chapter. In the case of Arbitrary Performance, EC may range from 0–1, depending on the characteristics of the drawing.

TABLE F.7 Box 7 (Complex) Evocative Character—Delicacy

Recall that for Complex Boxes, the NECESSARY, BUT NOT SUFFICIENT CONDITION requires that the client perceives the two or more marks as belonging to the same entity, either conceptually or graphically. If this condition is not met, an EC score of 0 is automatic. **Special Considerations for Box 7** In scoring EC in Box 7, the Affective Quality score is considered, as the degree of pleasantness or agreeableness is an important factor in determining the score. Drawings described as graceful, gentle, soft, warm, light, or affectively pleasant are likely to have a corresponding positive EC in Box 7. Once the necessary condition has been met (i.e., the marks are graphically and/or conceptually linked to each other), EC is scored according to the following guidelines:
1-point responses: Responses that grasp delicacy along with sophistication, sensitivity, and aesthetic sense, either literally or symbolically. 1-point responses in Box 7 are always associated with AQ = 1 (in Box 7). *Examples of 1-point responses include*: 1) Drawings that literally or figuratively capture the concept of delicacy and are also scored Affective Quality = 1, including: soap bubbles, jewelry, a Christmas tree ornament, a flower, food content (with the exception of foods specifically mentioned below), pleasant animals, human figures, snowflake, the sun, symbolic hearts, a smile; 2) Dotted drawings that are scored Affective Quality = 1; 3) Drawings that evoke refinement, culture, sensitivity, and aesthetic taste (e.g., figurative arts, statues, historical monuments); 4) Due to statistical frequency, round geometric figures, wheels (either in isolation or as part of a car, truck, motorcycle, or bicycle).
0.5-point responses: Responses grasping the concept of delicacy but associated with AQ = 0.5. *Examples of 0.5-point responses include*: 1) Drawings that capture the concept of delicacy accompanied by Affective Quality of 0.5, including: a snail, a light bulb, ant, the moon, ball of yarn, computer loading symbol, letters and symbols follow the curve of the stimulus; 2) Dotted drawings that are scored Affective Quality = 0.5.
0-point responses: All responses that include the stimulus without grasping any sense of delicacy, and instead use it for something coarse, rigid, or hard; or responses that capture delicacy with associated AQ = 0. *Examples of 0-point responses include*: 1) Drawings in which the literal or figurative concept of delicacy is not captured, and instead hard, rough, rigid, aggressive, unpleasant, slimy, repellant, or dirty constructs are depicted. Examples include: buildings, weapons, mechanical objects, gears of any kind, unpleasant or aggressive animals or insects, tile, bench, floor, isolated human or animal parts (e.g., eyebrow, moth, mustache, beak, finger), roads, rocks, fishhook, bowling ball, leash, whirlpool, microphone, the handle of an umbrella, and all food content characterized by hard exterior (e.g., coconut, pineapple, watermelon, oyster, nuts). 2) Drawings in which the literal or figurative concept of delicacy is captured, but is paired with Affective Quality = 0, including: worm, snake, footprint, cloud, sad face, tears, spider web. 3) Dotted drawings that are scored Affective Quality = .0.

TABLE F.8 Box 8 (Simple) Evocative Character—Rounding and Closure

1-point responses: Client captures a sense of both rounding and closure. *Examples of 1-point responses include:* 1) Responses in which the client produces drawings depicting rounding and closure that include the stimulus mark (e.g., plane or solid round geometric figures, a face, the sun, rounded animals or people, most fruit (e.g., an orange, a lemon, an apple, a watermelon), a button, a ball, a clock); 2) Responses that are frequently provided (e.g., a parachutist with the parachute, an umbrella, a beach umbrella, the sun partially covered by mountains or by the ocean, a half-moon, and an isolated eye).
0.5-point responses: *Examples of 0.5-point responses include:* 1) The client understands the sense of rounding but only partially that of closure and draws things that close the stimulus either partially (e.g., a rainbow, a magnet, a bridge, a spiral), or only at its base (e.g., a helmet, slices of fruit, a turtle, a parachute); 2) The client understands the sense of closure, but only partially emphasizes the rounding of the stimulus (e.g., a curved-roof hut, an ice cream cone, an arched door, a bowler hat in absence of a head, a fish).
0-point responses: The client shows no sense of closure or rounding. *Examples of 0-point responses include:* 1) Isolated human or animal details, such as fingers, a mouth, bones, an arm (with the exception of the specific content "eye"), a building, squared things (e.g., boxes, tools); 2) Anything with a Reversed Box (a smiley face that is upside down).

Affective Quality

TABLE F.9 Affective Quality Scoring Guidelines

This table provides scoring guidelines for Affective Quality (AQ). Like contents are grouped in shaded areas, with notes provided regarding decision rules and considerations for children and adults.

General AQ scoring guidelines:

***Positive* AQ** (1): humans (H), animals (A), constructs related to Nature (NAT), botanical content (BOT), food (FD)

***Neutral* AQ** (.5): objects (OBJ), signs and numbers (SIG), minerals (MIN), architecture (ARC)

***Negative* AQ** (0): anatomy (ANA), weapons (WP), explosions (EXP), adverse meteorological conditions including clouds and rain (CLD), pathological content (PAT)

Clinicians are reminded that AQ scores should be adjusted in the positive or negative direction based upon client verbalizations that indicate positive or negative connotations.

Term	**Adult Scoring Guidelines/ Notes**	**Child Considerations/Notes** *(Children are considered ≤ 12)*
Aliens	0	
Alphabet letters	0.5	
Anatomy	0 *Note: includes anatomical hearts; if symbolic heart is drawn, AQ = 1*	
Angel	1	
ANIMALS / INSECTS		
Animals/Insects (positive, unless listed below)	1	
Animals/Insects (disliked or ambivalent) • *ant*** • *bear* • *bee* • *most birds** • *cat* • *caterpillar*** • *chameleon* • *chicken* • *cricket*** • *dinosaur* • *donkey* • *dragonfly***	0.5 ** birds and marine animals considered ambivalent because they live in a different element. (Exceptions: "Swallow" is scored 1)* *Note: If described specifically as pleasant, may be scored 1; If particularly unpleasant, may be scored 0*	** *ant, caterpillar, cricket, dragonfly, duck, guinea pig, hamster, millipede, penguin, snail are scored 1 for children*

TABLE F.9 *Continued*

• *duck*** • *eagle* • *fish* • *fox* • *goose* • *guinea pig*** • *hamster*** • *most marine animals** • *millipede*** • *mole* • *mollusk* • *monkey* • *ostrich* • *owl* • *parrot* • *penguin*** • *rabbit* • *sheep* • *shrimp* • *snail*** • *whale*		
Animals/Insects *(generally considered unpleasant or aggressive)* • *birds of prey* • *bull* • *cockroach* • *crab* • *crocodile* • *crow* • *dragon* • *flea* • *fly* • *frog* • *gorilla* • *grasshopper* • *hyena* • *jackal* • *jellyfish* • *leech* • *lion* • *mosquito* • *octopus* • *owl* • *pig*	0	

continued

TABLE F.9 *Continued*

• *rat* • *rhino* • *scorpion* • *shark* • *skunk* • *snakes* • *spider* • *tic* • *tiger* • *toad* • *vulture* • *wild boar* • *wolf* • *worm*		
Animals, Birds	0.5 *Note: If described specifically as pleasant, may be scored 1; If particularly unpleasant, scored 0.* *(Check list above for positive/negative animals)*	
Animal Details (drawn in isolation) • *beak* • *claw* • *eye* • *hair* • *hoof* • *paw* • *teeth*	0 *Note: This also includes Animal Faces missing important details (i.e., eyes, nose, or mouth)* *For scoring on Animal Faces not missing important details, refer to "Animals" above*	
Animals, Fish	0.5 *Note: If described specifically as pleasant, may be scored 1; If particularly unpleasant, scored 0.* *(Check list above for positive/negative animals)*	
Architectural Constructions • bridge • buildings • house • hut • soccer field • staircase	0.5 *Note: "Home" is scored 1; "Lighthouse" is scored 1*	
Arguments (verbalized)	0	

TABLE F.9 *Continued*

Artwork • drawings • masterpieces • mosaic • primitive cave art	1 *Note: Caricatures are scored 0.5; "Paint" (house paint or splotches not considered to be artistic) is scored 0.5*	
ASTRONOMICAL CONTENT		
Astronomical content (positive) • comets • constellations • earth • solar system • star (single) • sun • universe • world	1	
Astronomical content (neutral) • cosmos • moon • planets • space • stars (many)	0.5	
Astronomical content (negative) • black hole • eclipse • solar flare	0	
Atom	1	
Aurora Borealis	1	
Avalanche	0	
Bacteria	0	
Barriers (including fences, gates, and obstacles)	0.5	
Bars (of prison)	0	
Beehive	0	
Bell	0.5	
Birds	*(see Animals, Birds, above)*	
Blankets	1	
Blizzard	0	

continued

TABLE F.9 *Continued*

Bows	1	
Bubbles, soap	1	
Buildings	0.5	
Bullseye (target)	0 *Note: Weapon contents are scored 0.5 if clients are employed in the military or law enforcement*	
Bush/ Bushes	0	
Cage	0	
Campfire	1 *Note: "Fire" is generally scored 0.5; Destructive fires (i.e., house on fire) is scored 0*	
Candle	0.5	
Candy	1	
Caricature	0.5	
Carpet	0.5 *Note: "Flying Carpet" is scored 1*	
Cave/Cavern	0	
Cell (biological)	1	
Cemetery	0	
"Chaos"	0	
Chimney	0.5	
Christmas tree	1	
Church	0.5	
Cigar/Cigarette	0	
Circus	1	
Clay	1	
Cliff	0	
Clothing (general)	0.5	
Cloud(s)	0	
Clown	0.5	
Combat/Fighting scenes	0	
Comet	1	
Computer Loading Symbol	0.5	

TABLE F.9 *Continued*

Confetti	1	
Constellations (astrological)	1	
Constructions	0.5	
Cross	0.5	
Cyclops	0	
Debris	0	
Desert	0	
Deterioration (elaborated as deteriorated, spoiled, or damaged objects)	0	
Devil	0	
Diamond	1	
Dirt	0	
DNA	1	
Drawings without meaning	0.5	
Drugs, including medications	0	
Earth	1	
Easter Egg	1	
Eclipse	1	
Egg	1	
EMOTICONS		
Emoticon, positive • *"Smiley face"*	1	
Emoticon, negative • *"Frowny face"*	0	
Explosions	0	
Explosives	0 *Note: Fireworks are scored 1*	
Feather	1	
Fence (including gate, obstacle, and other barriers)	0.5	
Fetish items (sexual)	0	

continued

TABLE F.9 *Continued*

Fighting/Combat scenes	0	
Fingerprint	0	
Fire	0.5 *Note: Fires causing damage are scored 0 (see below, "Fires"); "Campfire" is scored 1*	
Fireplace	1	
Fires • house fires • forest fires • objects on fire	0 *Note: "Campfire" = 1*	
Fireworks • sparklers	1	
Fish	*(See [Animals, Fish], above)*	
Fish tank	1	
Flag (national)	1	
Flame	1	
Flowers	1	
Flying carpet	1 *Note: "Carpet" is scored 0.5*	
Food	1 *Note: Some exceptions apply; Lemon is scored 0.5. Food described as "spoiled," score 0*	
Footprints	0	
Forest	0	
Fossil	0.5	
Fountain	1	
Fruit	1 *Note: Some exceptions apply; Lemon is scored 0.5*	
Games/Toys *(including most videogames)*	0.5 *Note: For adults, 1 is scored if client verbalizes particular preference, affinity, or interest in game or toy*	1 *(if drawn by children)*
Gate (including fence, obstacle, and other barriers)	0.5	

TABLE F.9 *Continued*

Geometric figures	0.5	
Germs	0	
Ghost	0	
Giant	0.5	
Grass	1	
Grave	0	
Gun	0 *Note: Weapon contents are scored 0.5 if clients are employed in the military or law enforcement*	
Hail (Ice)	0	
HEARTS		
Hearts, symbolic or associated with Valentine's Day	1	
Hearts, anatomical	0	
Heater	1	
Hole	0	
"Home"	1 *Note: "House" is scored 0.5*	
Hook	0	
"House"	0.5 *Note: "Home" is scored 1*	
HUMAN/HUMAN REPRESENTATIONS		
Humans • *whole* • *busts including the head* • *profiles*	1	
Humans, arguing	0	
Humans, elderly	0.5	
Humans, in distress • *feeling unpleasant emotions* • *hurt/wounded* • *ill/sick*	0	

continued

TABLE F.9 *Continued*

Humans, seen from behind	0.5	
Humans, wearing mask	0.5	
Human Characters (real or fictional) with positive connotation: • *angel* • *E.T.* • *fairies* • *gnomes* • *positive Disney characters* • *positive fairy tale characters* • *superheroes*	1 *Note: For Mythological Figures (including half-human, half-animal figures), see "Mythological Figures" (below)*	
Human Characters from fairy tales, cartoons, literature (generally considered negative) • *Captain Hook* • *Cruella de Vil* • *Iago* • *The Joker* • *Hannibal Lecter* • *Voldemort* • *Slenderman* • *monsters* • *ogres* • *pirates* • *vampires* • *witches* • *zombies*	0 *Note: For Mythological Figures (including half-human, half-animal figures), see "Mythological Figures" (below)*	
Human Details drawn in isolation: • *ear* • *eye* • *finger* • *hair* • *leg* • *nose* • *teeth*	0	
Human Faces missing facial features (i.e., eyes, nose or mouth)	0	

TABLE F.9 *Continued*

Human Simulacrum (stand-ins or representations): • *aliens* • *devil* • *footprints* • *ghost* • *mannequin* • *Martian* • *puppets* • *scarecrow* • *shadows*	0	
Hurdles (or obstacles), for humans or horses	0.5	
Hut	0.5	
Ice	0.5	
Iceberg	0	
Ice cube (in drink)	1	
Imprints of things • fingerprints • footprints • shadows	0	
Insects	*See Animals/Insects (above)*	
Island	0.5	
Jail	0	
Jewelry	1	
Jungle	0	
Kite	1	
Labyrinth	0	
Lake	1	
Lamp	0.5	
Lamp, Aladdin's	1	
Landscapes/Natural Elements • lake • mountains • river • waterfall	1 *Note: Singular mountains are scored 0.5 (Mountains included in landscapes are scored 1)*	
Landslide	0	

continued

TABLE F.9 *Continued*

Leaf (solitary)	0 *Note: If leaves are part of larger botanical content, generally scored 1*	
Ledge	0	
Leisure and Sport activities • football • skis • snorkel	0.5 *Note: For adults, 1 is scored if client verbalizes particular preference, affinity, or interest in activity*	1 *(if drawn by children)*
Lemon	0.5	
Letters of the Alphabet	0.5	
Light	1	
Lightening	0	
Lighthouse	1	
Martian	0	
MASKS		
Mask (Carnival or Mardi Gras)	0.5	
Mask (Halloween or frightening)	0	
Mask (Surgical)	0	
Maze	0	
Meaningless drawings	0.5	
Medal	1	
Medication	0	
Minerals (including rocks)	0.5	
Mole (beauty mark)	0	
Molecules	0.5	
Moon	0.5	
Mosaic	1	
Mountain (singular)	0.5 *Note: Mountains included in landscapes are scored 1*	
Musical Instruments	0.5 *Note: For adults, 1 is scored if client verbalizes particular preference, affinity, or interest in the instrument*	1 *(if drawn by children)*

TABLE F.9 *Continued*

MYTHOLOGICAL FIGURES		
Mythological Figures (including half-human, half-animal figures) generally thought to be positive: • *Pan* • *Pegasus* • *mermaid* • *phoenix* • *unicorn*	1	
Mythological Figures (including half-human, half-animal figures) generally thought to be negative: • *Cyclops* • *Dragon* • *Hydra* • *Medusa*	0	
Natural Elements/Landscapes • lake • mountain • ocean scenes • river • waterfall	1	
Natural Wonders • Aurora Borealis • eclipse • sunrise	1 *Note: "Sunset" is scored 0.5*	
Night	0	
Numbers	0.5	
Objects in general	0.5	
Obstacles (including hurdles), for humans or horses	0.5	
Ocean	1	
Olympic rings	1	
Paint (not artistic) • house paint • splotches	0.5 *Note: If paint is considered artistic, scored 1 (see Art above)*	

continued

TABLE F.9 *Continued*

Photograph	0.5	
Pipe (used for smoking)	0	
Pirate	0	
Planets (anthropomorphic)	0.5	1 *(If drawn by children)*
Plants/Botanical content • flowers • trees	1 *Note: This does not apply to bushes, forest, woods, jungle which are scored 0*	
Play-Doh	0.5 *Note: For adults, 1 is scored if client verbalizes particular preference, affinity, or interest in game or toy*	*1 (if drawn by children)*
Podium	1	
Prescription medication	0	
Prison	0	
Puddle	0	
Puppet	0.5	
Raft	0	
Rain	0	
Rainbow	1	
River	1	
Robot	0	
Rock	0.5	
Rocket	0.5	
Roller Coaster	0.5	*Roller Coaster is coded 1 in children.*
Root	1	
"Sad Face" (or sad emoticon)	0	
Scar	0	
Scarecrow	0	
Seed	1	
Shadow	0	
Shell	1	
Signs/Signals	0.5	

TABLE F.9 *Continued*

Slide	1	
"Smiley Face" (or positive emoticon)	1	
Smoke	0	
Snail	0.5	1 *(if drawn by children)*
Snow	0	
Snowman	0.5	
Soap bubbles	1	
Solar system	1	
Sparklers	1	
Spider web	0	
Spirals • for hypnotism • reflecting "out of control" feeling	0	
Spoiled items, including food	0	
Sponge	0.5	
Stain	0	
Star, single	1	
Statue	0.5	
Storm	0	
Suitcase	0.5	
Sunrise	1 *Note: "Sunset" is scored 0.5*	
Sunset	0.5 *Note: "Sunrise" is scored 1*	
Swallow (bird)	1	
Symbols	0.5	
Syringe	0	
Target (Bullseye)	0 *Note: Weapon contents are scored 0.5 if clients are employed in the military or law enforcement*	
Tattoo	0	
Tear (crying)	0	
Thermometer (medical)	0	

continued

TABLE F.9 *Continued*

Tomb	0	
Torch	0.5	
Toys/ Games	0.5 *Note: For adults, 1 is scored if client verbalizes particular preference, affinity, or interest in game or toy*	1 *(if drawn by children)*
TREE/TREES		
Tree/Trees	1 *Note: If verbalized as "forest" or "woods," score 0*	
Tree (dry, dead)	0	
Trees (without leaves)	0	
Trophy	1	
Trunk	0.5	
Tunnel	0	
UFO	0	
Universe	1	
Virus	0	
Volcano	0	
Wall	0	
Wart	0	
Water	1	
Waterfall	1	
Wave	1	
Weapon • bow and arrow • gun • knife (if elaborated as weapon)	0 *Note: Weapons are scored 0.5 if clients are employed in the military or law enforcement*	
Weather, negative: • blizzards • earthquake • hurricane • monsoon • snow storm • thunderstorm • tornado • typhoon	0	

TABLE F.9 *Continued*

Whirlpool	0	
Wind	0	
"Woods"	0 *Note: Referring to forest or trees, not pieces of wood*	
World	1	
Wound	0	

Form Quality

TABLE F.10 Form Quality Scoring Guidelines

Score	*Scoring Guideline/Description*
1	The meaning of the drawing is obvious and immediately clear to the assessor, in most cases requiring no explanation or clarification by the client.
0.5	The meaning of the drawing is not immediately apparent or is open to multiple interpretations and requires client's explanation or description in order to be understood.
0	The meaning of the drawing is unintelligible, totally incorrect, or arbitrary and nothing (including the client's verbalizations) makes it identifiable or recognizable.

Contents

TABLE F.11 Primary Content Category Scoring Guidelines

Score	*Primary Content*	*Description/Scoring Guideline*
A	Animal	Whole animals.
ABS	Abstract	Abstract content or verbalizations (e.g., "Surreal painting," "happiness," "fear"); *Excluded from this category and NOT considered to be ABS are drawings in which the client says: "I didn't draw anything specific," "I don't know what that is," or "Nothing, really." Drawings such as those are coded as SIG (see below).*
AD	Animal Detail	Animal head or snout.
ANA	Anatomy	Internal parts of the human or animal body either in their natural form, or as X-rays, ultrasounds, etc.
ARC	Architecture	All man-made buildings and constructions, including houses, roads, stadium, bridges, buildings, towers, swimming pools, etc.). "Stairs" or "Staircase" in Box 3 is coded as ARC.
AS/ADS	Animal Simulacrum	Whole animal (AS) or animal head/bust (ADS) in the form of a replica, stand-in, or representation, including an effigy, statue, toy, stuffed animal, painting, photo. (With thanks to Professor Valentino Crisi for suggesting this category.)
AST	Astronomy	Stars, sun, comets, moon, planets, universe, cosmos, etc.
BIO	Biology	Constructs related to biology, including cells, cell culture dishes, DNA, etc.
BOT	Botanical	Flowers, leaves, branches, trees, woods, grass, lawn, etc.
CLD	Cloud	Elements of the environment from which the individual may be surrounded or enveloped like smoke, fog, clouds, rain, storm, wind, woods, jungle, rough sea, tornado, blizzard, bushes.
EXP	Explosion	Explosions, fireworks, eruptions, etc.
FD	Food	Solid or liquid foods or drinks.
FIR	Fire	Fire, flames, torches, bonfire, etc.
H	Human	Whole human figure.
HD	Human Detail	Human head, face, bust (from the waist up).
HS/HDS	Human Simulacrum	Whole human figure (HS) or human head (HDS) in the form of a replica, stand-in, or representation, including an effigy, toy, ghost, robot, alien, Martian, scarecrow, snowman, doll, painting, photo, footprint, fingerprint, reflection in mirror, snow angel, emoticon/emoji. Cartoon characters are scored H or A for children, HS or AS for adults.

continued

TABLE F.11 *Continued*

Score	*Primary Content*	*Description/Scoring Guideline*
ICE	Ice	Ice, snow, hail, iceberg.
MIN	Mineral	Minerals, stones, rocks, crystals, lava, dirt, etc.
NAT	Nature	Constructs considered as part of nature, including mountains, rivers, lakes, parks, etc.; Natural spectacles, including sunsets, waterfalls, landscapes, etc.; and Natural phenomena, including aurora borealis, rainbow, eclipse, etc.
OBJ	Object	Objects such as vehicles, furniture, clothing, inanimate "things", and architectural elements if drawn in isolation (e.g., a window, a door, a fence, a light pole, etc.).
PAT	Pathological	Constructs related to pathology and sickness, including wounds, bruises, scars, viruses, bacteria, sick people, etc.; Drawings of isolated human or animal details, including legs, hair, arms, fingers/toes, a mouth, an ear, tongue, navel, eyes, paws, horns, tail, hoof, teeth, etc.
SEX	Sexual	Explicit sexual content (*not including any symbolic interpretations of the drawings*).
SIG	Symbol	Letters, numbers, signals, symbols, marks, musical notes, geometric figures, the face of a compass, symbol on a road/street sign, etc.

TABLE F.12 Secondary Content Category Scoring Guidelines

Score	*Secondary Content*	*Description/Scoring Guideline*
AC	Archeology	Constructs related to archeology, including ruins, temple, ancient coins, etc.
CG	Clothing	Clothing, including articles of clothing (shirt, pants, dress, tie, shoes) and jewelry and accessories that are worn (hat, scarf, necklace, watch, sunglasses). *Accessories that are not worn (purse, briefcase, umbrella, luggage, backpack) are not scored as clothing responses.*
FA	Figurative Art	Paintings, statues, post cards, photographs, contents from movies and television programs, drawings and cartoons verbalized as such (i.e., "A drawing of my mother," or "A cartoon of Scooby Doo").
FT	Fairy Tale	Fairy Tale creatures, including elves, fairies, gnomes, goblins, ogres, witches, wizards, characters from cartoons or fairy tales.
HR	Heraldry	Heraldic constructs, including coats of arms, shields, noble characters such as kings, knights, etc.
MK	Mask	All masks (Halloween, Mardi Gras) including facemasks; Whole masked figures, clowns, caped or hooded people.
MT	Mythological	Mythological characters and objects (e.g., Zeus, Pan, Athena, Sphinx, Triton).
RE	Religion	Religious items and constructs, including sacred objects, religious symbols, religious clothing, churches, temples, mosques, and other religious buildings.
SF	Science Fiction	Aliens, extraterrestrials, spaceships, UFOs, etc.
TY	Toy	Childhood toys and games. (*This does not include athletic gear or adult hobbies/interests.*)
WP	Weapon	Weapons, armor, military-related content, war-related content.

Frequency (Popular)

TABLE F.13 Popular Responses in Italy (2005)—Child/Adolescent

	Ages 5–14 years, 11 months		*Ages 15–17 years, 11 months*	
Box 1	Flower (11%)	**(P)**	Human face (12)	**(P)**
	Human face (10)	**(P)**	Flower (11)	**(P)**
			Geometrical figure (11)	**(P)**
Box 2	Human face (21)	**P**	Human face (26)	**P**
	Slithering animal (14)	**(P)**	Whole human being (12)	**(P)**
Box 3	Staircase (19)	**P**	Staircase (28)	**P**
	Building (10)	**(P)**	Building (16)	**(P)**
			Trees, flowers (10)	**(P)**
Box 4	Building (25)	**P**	Building (23)	**P**
	Geometrical figure (19)	**P**	Geometrical figure (13)	**(P)**
Box 5	Hammer (12)	**(P)**		
	Tool (12)	**(P)**		
	Letter T (10)	**(P)**		
Box 6	Geometrical figure (37)	**P**	Geometrical figure (30)	**P**
	Building (17)	**(P)**	Building (18)	**P**
			Cars (12)	**(P)**
Box 7	Ball (14)	**(P)**	Wheel (10)	**(P)**
	Human being (14)	**(P)**		
	Geometrical figure (10)	**(P)**		
Box 8	Face (21)	**P**	Face (15)	**(P)**
	Ball (11)	**(P)**	Lonely eye (14)	**(P)**
	Geometrical figure (11)	**(P)**	Sun, sunset, moon (12)	**(P)**
	Sun, sunset, moon (10)	**(P)**		

TABLE F.14 Popular Responses in Italy (2005)—Adult

	Male Adult (18+ years)		*Female Adult (18+ years)*	
Box 1	Human being (whole or face)	**(P)**	Flower	**P**
			Human being (whole or face)	**(P)**
Box 2	Human being (whole or face)	**P**	Human being (whole or face)	**P**
	Animal	**(P)**	Animal	**(P)**
Box 3	Stairway	**P**	Building	**P**
	Buildings	**(P)**	Stairway	**P**
			Tree	**(P)**
Box 4	Building	**P**	Building	**P**
	Geometrical figure	**P**	Geometrical figure	**P**
Box 5	Tool	**(P)**	Letter T	**(P)**
	Letter T	**(P)**	Tools	**(P)**
Box 6	Geometrical figure	**P**	Geometrical figure	**P**
	Building	**P**	Building	**(P)**
	Vehicle	**(P)**	Vehicle	**(P)**
Box 7	Ball	**(P)**	Flower	**(P)**
	Vehicle (wheels)	**(P)**	Vehicle (wheels)	**(P)**
Box 8	Sun (dawn, sunset)	**P**	Sun (dawn, sunset)	**P**
	Human being (whole or face)	**P**	Human being (whole or face)	**(P)**
	Geometrical figure	**(P)**	Geometrical figure	**(P)**

Special Scores

TABLE F.15 Special Scores Scoring Guidelines

Code	Special Score	Description/Scoring Guideline
	Level 1—Expressions of Primary Process	
AP	Arbitrary Performance	Drawings that show a degree of arbitrariness, inadequacy, dissonance, or randomness (evident via position in space, graphic quality, or unusual verbalizations)
CO	Contamination	1) Two things that are interwoven or overlapping; 2) Part of the drawing holds two different meanings at the same time
DS	Disproportion	The response includes notably disproportionate elements within the same box
PA	Personalized Answer	The client introduces highly personal elements about his/her life, either while drawing or while describing the drawing
TR	Transparency	The drawing includes visible elements that would not be visible in reality
	Level 2—Expressions of Cognitive Deficit	
AP	Arbitrary Performance	Drawings that show a degree of arbitrariness, inadequacy, dissonance, or randomness (evident via position in space, graphic quality, or unusual verbalizations)
ID	Incomplete Drawing	The drawing is missing important parts, is unfinished or left incomplete, or only the outline of a figure was drawn without internal details
II	Inadequate Integration	The stimulus is included in the drawing in an inadequate manner, which contradicts reality
MU	Missing Union	*Scored in complex boxes only*. The client uses the marks as part of his/her drawing but does not conceptually connect the separate elements of the marks
PP	Perseveration	The same (non-Popular) content appears in two or more boxes
SR	Stimulus Repetition	The client simply re-draws or copies (one or more times) the stimulus and gives no meaning to the drawing
	Level 3—Expressions of Conflict	
AS	Anxiety Stroke	The response entirely or partially consists of areas that are emphasized with doubled or shaded pencil strokes
CB	Crossed Border	The drawing crosses over or touches the inside black border, or edge, of the box
GR	Global Rejection	The client does not draw anything in one or more boxes (and attributes no meaning)
ID	Incomplete Drawing	The drawing is missing important parts, is unfinished or left incomplete, or only the outline of a figure was drawn without internal details

TABLE F.15 *Continued*

Code	*Special Score*	*Description/Scoring Guideline*
IS	Interpreted Stimulus	The client attributes meaning to the mark(s), without having drawn anything
MR	Morbid	1) Drawings/verbalizations of objects, people, or situations that are damaged, abnormal, destroyed, deteriorated, or decomposing; 2) Indications of sadness, pain, distress, dysphoric mood or overt depression, gloominess, pessimism, or hopelessness
OD	Opposite Direction	*This special score only applies to Boxes 3 and 5*. The client draws something *opposite/contrary* to the box's EC
PR	Partial Rejection	1) The client draws something in a given box, but does not incorporate the stimulus; 2) The client graphically includes the stimulus, but states that he/she did not draw anything
RB	Reversed Box	The drawing is made and/or is intended to be viewed with the Client WDCT Form turned upside down or sideways
SC	Self-Criticism	The client *spontaneously* criticizes himself/herself, his or her ability to draw, and/or the drawings produced
	Other Noted Phenomena (Scored by Box)	
BK	Blackening	The client obscures or "blackens" the stimulus mark in a box completely without attributing meaning to the drawing
CJ	Conjoined Boxes	The client graphically joins two or more boxes within the same drawing
CP	Color Projection	The client attributes color qualities to the drawing (based on the client verbalizations)
DB	Disproportion Between Boxes	In a protocol of small/medium size drawings, one drawing completely fills an entire box
EN	Encapsulation	The client circles or encloses the stimulus marks without attributing meaning to the drawing
HN	Human Content Negation	The client depicts one or more human contents without verbalizing the presence of these human contents
IP	Improper Description	The client gives an incorrect or inaccurate description of the completed drawing in a box
OA	"Or" Response	The client points out at least two meanings for the same drawing, often separated by the word "or"
PS	Perspective Response	The client's drawing is characterized by a perspective view, with strong emphasis on depth
	Other Noted Phenomena (Scored at the Protocol Level)	
BD	Big Drawing	The majority of drawings in a protocol take up all or most of the box
SM	Small Drawing	The majority of drawings in a protocol are small, tiny, or microscopic

Movement

TABLE F.16 Primary and Secondary Movement Scoring Guidelines

Score	*Movement*	*Description/Scoring Guideline*
		Primary Movement
M	Primary (Human) Movement	Explicitly verbalized human movement
		Secondary Movement
FE	Facial Expression	Facial Expressions of Humans or Animals. Examples include: happy or sad faces, fierce or scared animal faces
FM	Animal Movement	Verbalized animal movement. Examples include: dogs running, climbing monkeys, flying birds
MI	Inanimate Movement	Movement of inanimate objects. Examples include: flags waving, explosions, fireworks, racing cars, flowing rivers, spraying fountains
		Gender Specifier *(For Primary Movement)*
f	Female	Verbalized female human content in motion
m	Male	Verbalized male human content in motion
i	Indeterminate	Human movement is verbalized without gender specification
		Direction Specifier *(For Primary and Secondary Movement)*
a	Active	Movement effected by the organism (human, animal, object) itself, unaided by external influences
b	Blocked	Movement indicating a tension state or blockage
d	Double	"Back-and-forth" or bi-directional movement
p	Passive	Movement imparted to an organism or any of its parts by external agency (including gravity)
r	Rotary	Movement indicating spinning or circular motion
i	Indeterminate	Verbalized movement with no clear directionality. Example: "Something moving"

Impulse Responses

TABLE F.17 Impulse Response Scoring Guideline

Score	*Movement*	*Description/Scoring Guideline*
OR	Oral Impulse Response	All direct and/or indirect references to food and nutrition, sources of food, objects containing food, organs connected with food, and situations related to food
AN	Anal Impulse Response	All direct and/or indirect references to excretory functions of the human and animal body, but also associated details such as rashes, mud, diapers, people or animals seen from behind, puddles, dirt, trash, dirty objects or unintentional messes (i.e., paint splotches, a spot of sauce, an oil stain), sewer, volcano, gas, etc.
PH	Phallic Impulse Response	All direct references to male or female sexual organs (human or animal), as well as references to human and/or animal sexuality

APPENDIX G

CWS Interpretation Tables

Tables G.1–G.21 present each of the major CWS indices and computations, providing normative ranges for interpretation. When applicable, specific considerations for child/adolescent norms are provided. When no distinction is made between adults and children/adolescents, no significant difference was noted between groups (and the adult interpretive ranges are applicable). Frequency (percentage of adults) within the normative sample is indicated parenthetically for each interpretive range.

This appendix is not designed to be comprehensive, and clinicians are encouraged to refer to Chapters 7 and 8 for additional interpretive and conceptualization guidelines.

TABLE G.1 EC+%—Frequencies and Interpretive Ranges

EC+% is representative of accurate perception and associative functions, adaptation to conventional thinking, and intact reality testing. It demonstrates the client's ability to relate to the environment. Its average value ranges from 56% to 81%. The average EC+% value is significantly higher in women than in men: 77.5% versus 74.5% ($p < .0001$).	
≥ 50	(5%) Indicates organic or cognitive deficits, adaptive rigidity, and lack of flexibility. Such low values usually occur in individuals that are poorly adjusted, and/or not inclined to social interactions.
56–81	(76%) Intact perceptive and associative functions, adaptation to conventional thinking, and adaptation to reality; Ability to relate to the environment.
> 81	(19%) High or excessive permeability to external stimulation and influences; Great sensitivity; Delicacy and fragility; Extremely sensitive subjects, artists, and also psychoanalytic patients. Elevated values of the EC+%, ranging between 94% and 100%, are found in approximately 6.5% of women and 1.3% of men. EC+% values this high are often found in severely disturbed clients who are extremely sensitive to their surroundings and external stimuli. They tend to lack appropriate filters and healthy defense mechanisms.
In children: The EC+% index usually has a greater range in children. EC+% values for children also tend to be higher than in the adult group. The increase in value is inversely proportional to the child's age. This relates to a less structured personality, which is not yet made rigid by social norms and conventions. Thus, extremely high values, up to the age of 9 or 10, should be interpreted more leniently than in adults.	

TABLE G.2 AQ+%—Frequencies and Interpretive Ranges

Overall, AQ+% evaluates: the client's ability to be in touch with emotions; the kind of affect that characterizes his/her emotional life; the presence of repression; and the extent to which he/she can be syntonic with the environment. The mean of females = 67.7; men = 60.6 ($p < .0001$).	
< 50	(14%) Indicative of depressive personalities that are scarcely interested in interpersonal relationships, unable to establish a connection with the environment, and/or repression of affect.
50–63	(59%) Good awareness and integration of feelings, emotions, and affect.
69–75	(23%) Excessive adaptation to surroundings and environmental requests/expectations; Dependence and imitation of the other behavior; (69 = 16%; 75 = 7%).
81–88	(3%) May be found in highly adjusted clients, who are overly accommodating in their interpersonal relationships and/or may use defenses such as denial. These values may also be indicative of high impulsivity and a tendency to act on emotions.
94–100	(1%) Severe cognitive deficits when the high values of this index are due to the perseveration of positive contents; Marked traits of immaturity and infantilism; Extroverted personalities dependent on interpersonal relationships.
In children: In a control group of children, the mean for the AQ+% was found to be 62%. It should be noted that the above interpretive statements regarding adults may also be applied to children with the necessary adjustments to statistical ranges made.	

TABLE G.3 FQ+%—Frequencies and Interpretive Ranges

FQ+% provides information about the quality of cognitive processes, on both a quantitative (intellectual level of the client), and qualitative level (i.e., quality of attention, concentration, planning, anticipation, concept formation, and adaptation to secondary process). More generally, FQ+% assesses: Adequate reality testing; The ability to relate to the environment; Sound judgment; Defense mechanisms; and Conscious self-control.	
< 75	(1.6%) Mental retardation or thought trouble; The lower the FQ+% value becomes, the higher the chance that the client is psychologically disturbed or cognitively limited.
75	(4.6%) Must be carefully evaluated, especially in highly educated clients. It must be closely analyzed in relation to Box 6. Generally, FQ+% of 75% is indicative of cognitive deficits or a lack of self-control and poor reality testing.
81–100	(93.8%) Indicates the individual's intact ability to use cognitive processes to manage emotions; Ability to exercise cognitive control over manifestations of affect; Adequate reality testing. In non-clinical individuals, FQ+% tends to range from 94–100%. When this value is combined with an A/F ratio where the F side is much higher (such as 1/4), it is indicative of conformity, a lack of spontaneity and affective connection, excessively rigid defenses, and a proneness to develop psychosomatic symptoms. In clinical clients, elevated values of FQ+% are often found in depressed patients, patients with paranoid personality, and obsessive-compulsive patients.
In children: the mean FQ+% in the control group was 65%. This value steadily increases with age (56% at age 6–7; 67% at age 8–10; 75% at age 11–14). The value of FQ+% index increases with the development of cognitive abilities, rational functions, control factors, and the experiences and knowledge of the individual.	

TABLE G.4 A/F (Affective Stability Index)—Frequencies and Interpretive Ranges

A/F describes how affect relates to rationality in the client. By analyzing how the affective and rational aspects of an individual are organized within his/her personality structure, we are better able to understand the individual's inner life. This comparison allows us to determine how well these aspects of the personality are balanced, and which factor is dominant (i.e., extroverted versus introverted).

Initially, Affective Quality tends to be greater than Form Quality (A > F), but this ratio shifts toward Form Quality (A < F) beginning in pre-adolescence. A < F demonstrates the presence/absence of emotional stability, affective balance, self-control, and maturity.

	A Value	2–3 < 2 > 3	71% 15% 14%	**F Value**	< 3 3–4	4% 96%

A < F	(66%) A < F (*with F greater than A by 1–2 points, such as 2/4*): Normative value, found in approximately 66% of the normal population. Indicates emotional stability and balance, as well as the ability to effectively manage feelings and emotions. [60 % (♀) and 67 % (♂) dss.]
A << F	(10%) A << F (*with F greater than A by more than 2 points, for example 1/4*): Indicates a tendency toward rigidity, inhibition, constriction, conformism, and a lack of spontaneity. As A decreases in value, these characteristics become more profound. [5% (♀) and 10% (♂) dss.]
A ≈ F	(23%) A ≈ F (*this includes A = F, for example 3/3; and A < F by 0.5, for example 2.5/3*): Indicates the presence of sociability and spontaneity. However, depending on the clinical picture and implications of other test indexes, can also signify immaturity, dependency, and impulsivity. [33 % (♀) and 21% (♂) dss.]
A > F	(2%) A > F (*with A greater than F*): Suggests a marked conflict in the area of affect, egocentrism, and a tendency to act out. These individuals tend to be "explosive," extremely immature, egocentric, and are unable to plan and organize activities. This is especially true when combined with low values of FQ+% and an absence of primary movement. [1.8% (♀) and in 2.2% (♂) no dss.]

Note about Low Values: When both sides of the ratio are low (*with A ≤ 2 and F ≤ 2, for example 1.5/2 or 1/1.5, or lower*) cognitive limitations, or personalities stunted by conflictual, or depressive dynamics are likely.

In children: In the non-pathological sample, differences emerge depending on the age group:
6–7-year-olds show on average an A > F ratio (prevalence of affective aspects);
8–10-year-olds show on average an A = F ratio;
11–14-year-olds show on average an A < F ratio (prevalence of cognitive control).

TABLE G.5 P%—Frequencies and Interpretive Ranges

P% represents the extent to which the client adheres to mainstream thinking, and adaptation to reality.	
0	(10.7%) It must also be noted that P% = 0 is only found in 10.7% of the examined population. Only 4.9% of subjects contemporarily showed P% = 0 and H% = 0.
6–12	(5.3%) With elevated values of FQ+% and O+%, this may indicate a tendency toward creativity. When combined with elevated values of O%, but low values of O+%, it tends to suggest a lack of reality testing (manic or psychotic symptoms potentially being present).
13–31	(75%) Normative range; Good adaptation to reality and the conventional way of thinking.
> 31	(9%) Subjects with highly stereotypical thinking, who lack critical skills; Depressed, formal, conformist individuals.
For children: The non-clinical group showed an average P% value of 26%, which was significantly higher than that of the clinical groups.	

TABLE G.6 P+%—Frequencies and Interpretive Ranges

P+% reflects the client's ability to represent reality, the quality of his/her adherence to mainstream thinking, and his/her ability to perform adequate reality testing.	
< 81	Initial sign of social dysfunction or mental deterioration. In the severely mentally ill, with the exception of paranoid personality, both P% and P+% are low. Clients with paranoid tendencies or overt paranoia tend to use defense mechanisms, such as rationalization and/or intellectualization, in a rigid manner.
≥ 81	(90%) Well adjusted, with perfectly intact reality testing.
In a normative sample of children: The highest P+% value was 72% compared to 65% in a stuttering group, 53% in a learning disabled group, and 55% in a Deaf group. This suggests that children from the non-clinical population are more likely to conform to mainstream thinking and adhere to adequate reality testing. The clinical groups demonstrated some degree of adherence to conventional thinking, but with greater effort and less accuracy.	

TABLE G.7 O%—Frequencies and Interpretive Ranges

O% represents the client's ability to individually and creatively elaborate on the stimulus. It also demonstrates the ability to move away from stereotypical thinking by creating original drawings, and it is linked to divergent thinking. Generally, O% assesses the direction of the person's interests and general fund of knowledge.	
0	(48.5%) Low values are often found in clients that demonstrate concrete thinking, are poorly educated, tend to rely on stereotyped associations, or are depressed.
6–19	(48.5%) With elevated values of FQ+% and O+%, may indicate a tendency toward creativity. When combined with elevated values of O%, but low values of O+%, it tends to suggest lack of reality testing with manic or psychotic symptoms potentially being present.
> 19	(2%) Indicates that the client has an excessive tendency to retreat into his/her own world, to limit interpersonal communication, and to rely on fantasy rather than reality.
Relationship between O% and M: O% (with good Form Quality) and M (Primary Movement with good Form Quality) have primary significance in evaluating cognitive abilities. Higher values of O% and M generally indicate above average functional intelligence. 78.4% of subjects contemporarily showed O% = 0 and M = 0.	
In children: O% is approximately 12%.	

TABLE G.8 O+%—Frequencies and Interpretive Ranges

The O+% index measures a person's creative ability, while maintaining reality testing, rational thought control, and connection to the environment.	
< 81	O+% values less than 81% (and more so for lower values) indicate either marked conflict in the area of affect or bizarre thinking.
≥ 81	O+ responses often represent professional attitudes and individual interests. The content of original responses can also be related to highly conflictual areas in the individual's life. In this case, we will have a "highly individualized" response, with potentially significant psychodiagnostic meaning.

TABLE G.9 IIT-1—Frequencies and Interpretive Ranges

This index is indicative of non-specific emotional distress and describes the extent of *inadequacy* and *emotional tension* that the client experiences (as evidenced by AS and CB). AS indicates anxiety, insecurity, and indecision. CB indicates internal conflict and impulsivity. The value of IIT-1 usually ranges between .25 and .75, with higher values indicating marked internal conflict and emotional distress. When elevated values of IIT-1 are associated with elevated FQ+% and an A/F ratio where A << F, psychosomatic disturbances may be present.
In children: The lowest value of IIT-1 is found in the normative (non-clinical) group (IIT-1 = .19). The clinical groups demonstrated the following values of IIT-1 ($p < .001$): stuttering group, .36; learning disabled, .42; Deaf, .32.

TABLE G.10 IM—Frequencies and Interpretive Ranges

The Impulsivity Index is derived from the number of Crossed Border (CB) special scores contained in the client's protocol. IM measures the client's ability to control emotions and behavioral impulses. Values below .25 are considered adaptive, and are not indicative of psychopathology. Higher values show heightened impulsivity. It must be noted that an elevated value of IM (for example IM > .5) alone is not sufficient to establish whether behavioral impulsivity is present. In order to hypothesize the presence or absence of behavioral impulsivity, one must take into account: FQ+%, the A/F ratio, and the number of movement responses. Specifically: • *Impulsivity* is usually consistent with: elevated IM, low FQ+%, A ≈ F or A > F, and few M responses. • *Repression* and *control of impulsivity* are usually consistent with: elevated IM, high value of FQ+%, A << F, and elevated number of M responses. In assessing IM, the specific type of Crossed Border (CB) known as "Leaning Over" (i.e., when the client's drawing simply touches the side of the box, without actually crossing the border) must be considered differently. This tendency can indicate either a need for safety and stability (when paired with other signs of insecurity, such as: H%, ARC%, and self-criticism), or a tendency to be excessively controlling (when paired with FQ+% = 100 and, more importantly, A << F).	
0–.25	(75%) Normal frequency.
.37	(13%) Border value.
> .37	(12%) Manifest impulsivity or strong inner conflict.
In children: the highest average value of IM is found in learning disabled clients (.2), followed by stuttering clients (.15), Deaf children (.09) and finally by non-clinical clients (.03).	

TABLE G.11 AI—Frequencies and Interpretive Ranges

The Anxiety Index is derived from the special score Anxiety Stroke (AS). AI relates to anxiety, and its average value ranges from 0 and .50. Scores of .75 and above indicate significant states of anxiety. The degree to which the anxiety is or is not well managed is evaluated by analyzing the graphic quality of the response and other indices (mainly FQ+% and A/F Ratio):

- When the *anxiety is well managed*, the drawing shows well-defined, often light shadows.
- When the client is *not able to manage the anxiety*, the drawing is messy, lacks order, and shows heavy, non-defined shadows.

In forensic psychology (especially in cases of child custody), and in the field of personnel selection, highly elevated scores, between .75 and 1, are common.

0–.5	Normal value; absence of anxiety.
.63–.75	Low anxiety level.
> .75	Manifest anxiety state. Very common in forensic and selection fields.

TABLE G.12 IIT-2—Frequencies and Interpretive Ranges

The IIT-2 is a non-specific assessment of the main factors around which the personality is structured. Each box in the WDCT relates to a different area of personality. Therefore, positive Codes (such as C and PC), should prevail in the Analysis of Sequence-1 of a non-clinical client. In other words, in a well-functioning individual, the IIT-2 should lean to the left side of the ratio, the side that refers to the positive Codes of the Analysis of Sequence (C and PC). The values on the right side, when present, should generally be AC (the least pathological among the remaining possible classifications).

Values considered positive on the IIT-2 are ratios such as 7/1 and 6/2. However, depending on the client's age, as well as the configuration of codes present in the protocol (e.g., a 5/3 configuration formed by 3 AC is less negative than one formed by 3 D), ratios of 5/3 and 4/4 can also indicate sufficiently integrated and harmonious personality organization (for example, in adolescents). Special attention must be paid to the 8/0 ratio. These are excessively positive ratios, which might hide excessively adjusted personalities according the false-self model, conscious attempts to present oneself as a conformist (as found in forensic cases, child custody evaluations, and in the field of personnel selection), personalities structured around denial, or narcissistic personalities.

The average normative values of the IIT-2 are 4.8/3.2 in males and 5.4/2.6 in females. A comparison between the sexes indicates a statistically significant difference in the left side values (4.8 in males versus 5.4 in females, $p < .0001$). In quantitative analysis of IIT-2, highly significant differences are noted between the sexes (see Table G.13).

TABLE G.13 Distribution of IIT-2 in the Italian Normative Sample ($N = 2,293$)

IIT-2	*Male*	*(%)*	*Cumulative (%)*	*Female*	*(%)*	*Cumulative (%)*	*p*
8/0	25	1.3	1.3	19	5.6	5.6	.0001
7/1	189	9.7	11.0	54	15.9	21.5	.001
6/2	415	21.2	32.2	101	29.7	51.2	.001
5/3	537	27.5	59.7	75	22.0	73.2	.05
4/4	436	22.3	82.0	66	19.4	92.6	—
3/5	245	12.5	94.5	17	5.0	97.6	.0001
2/6	78	4.0	98.5	5	1.5	99.1	.05
1/7	25	1.3	99.8	3	.9	100.0	—
0/8	3	.1	100.0	0	.0	100.0	—
Total	1,953	100.0	100.0	340	100.0	100.0	

TABLE G.14 Wartegg Index of Psychopathology—Interpretive Guidelines

Quadrant	*Area*	*Interpretation*
A	**Area α**	"Normality," with a prevalence of autonomy and adequate adjustment.
	Area β	Elements indicating lack of balance, tension, and significant distress are completely absent.
	Area γ	When the subject's scores fit in the top left corner, the scores (e.g., IIT-1 = 0, IIT-2 = 8/0) no longer hold positive value and take on the meaning of hyper-adaptation, denial defenses, and personality according to the "false-self" model.
B	**Area α**	Dynamics of detachment dominate this area.
	Area β	Progressive worsening of personality structure, with limited awareness of distress; Marked cognitive limitations; Personality organized around detachment, isolation, and fulfillment of fantasy.
	Area γ	Cluster A (Schizotypal, Schizoid, Paranoid) or Cluster B (Antisocial) personality disorder; Psychosis.
C	**Area α**	Dynamics of dependence prevail in this area.
	Area β	Marked distress emerges in a personality organization that is otherwise quite balanced and that shows reactive behaviors typical of Posttraumatic Stress Disorder (PTSD) or, more generally, adjustment disorders.
	Area γ	The client appears severely disturbed and Cluster C personality disorders may be present (i.e., Avoidant, Dependent—with the exception of Obsessive Personality that falls within Quadrant D).
D	**Area α**	Patterns of ambivalence dominate this area. The profound distress that emerges from this quadrant is of a chronic and long-standing nature, originating early in the client's development and impacting subsequent personality structure (e.g., IIT-2 = 2/6), and is accompanied by marked emotional pain and awareness of one's distress (e.g., IIT-1 = 1.37).
	Area β	Dynamics of immaturity and conflict—characteristic of chronic "structural" distress—predominate.
	Area γ	Obsessive Personality Disorder (Cluster C) and Cluster B personality disorders (i.e., Borderline, Histrionic, Narcissistic—with the exception of Antisocial Personality disorder, which falls within Quadrant B).

TABLE G.15 Frequent Primary Content Categories-—Frequency and Percentages

<table>
<tr><th colspan="2">Animal Content (A%)</th></tr>
<tr><td colspan="2">A responses are found in 31.8% of clients in the normative group (no difference between gender). A contents represent 4.7% of all responses to the CWS.</td></tr>
<tr><td colspan="2">Animal responses in the CWS are not produced as frequently as in the Rorschach, for example, due to several differences between these measures. The mean A% is quite low (male = 4.4, female = 7.0; $p < .0001$).

The percentage of Animal responses must be interpreted on the basis of the overall quality of the CWS protocol. For example, an above average percentage (e.g., $\geq 25\%$) in an overall positive protocol suggests formalism, stereotypical thinking, and affective immaturity; however, the same value in a protocol of overall poor quality may indicate psychopathology (i.e., in psychotic clients, oftentimes A% = 100), depression, obsessiveness, passivity, and dependence.</td></tr>
<tr><td colspan="2">In children: the A% mean tends to be higher, and until the age of 7 or 8, Animal responses may substitute for Human responses. After this age, the A% tends to reduce and the presence of Animal responses is interpreted similarly to those of adults.</td></tr>
<tr><th colspan="2">Architectural Content (ARC%)</th></tr>
<tr><td colspan="2">ARC responses are found in approximately 87% of clients in the normative group. ARC contents represent 19.1% of WDCT drawings, with a significantly elevated peak in Box 3 (60%). Elevated values are also found in Boxes 4 and 6.</td></tr>
<tr><td colspan="2">The mean value ranges between 12% and 25%. The Architectural Content category produces mean values that are quite different between males and females (female = 18.0%, males = 19.5%; $p < .05$).</td></tr>
<tr><td>0–25</td><td>(86%) Normative value.</td></tr>
<tr><td>> 25</td><td>(13%) Values higher than 25% may indicate more or less conscious overcompensations and indicate internal insecurity and need for environmental approval, or dependency traits.</td></tr>
<tr><th colspan="2">Astronomical Content (AST%)</th></tr>
<tr><td colspan="2">AST responses are found in 26.1% of clients in the normative group (no difference between gender). AST Responses represent 3.6% of the responses to the CWS.</td></tr>
<tr><td colspan="2">The diagnostic meaning of AST content category is connected to a cool and/or detached affectivity, which can hardly be expressed. If accompanied by an overall good quality of CWS protocol, AST responses may indicate depressive tendencies, affective and emotional poverty, and difficulties in social relationships; however, in protocols of overall poor quality, AST contents may indicate the presence of anxiety, emotional regression, and severe adaptation challenges.</td></tr>
<tr><th colspan="2">Botanical Content (BOT%)</th></tr>
<tr><td colspan="2">BOT responses are found in approximately 28.1% of clients in the normative group and they represent about 4% of all responses.</td></tr>
<tr><td colspan="2">BOT produces mean values that are quite different between males and females (female = 8.2%, males = 3.5%; $p < .0001$).</td></tr>
</table>

TABLE G.15 *Continued*

<table>
<tr><td colspan="2">BOT responses, more typical of the female population, indicate sensitivity and aesthetic interests. In males, 79% of the population (compared to 49% in females) produce CWS protocols containing BOT% = 0. Elevated values in males, when corroborated by other indexes (such as AD or D Codes), may indicate confusion or conflict related to gender identity.</td></tr>
<tr><td colspan="2">Human Content (H%)</td></tr>
<tr><td colspan="2">H responses are found in approximately 66.2% of clients in the normative group (no difference between gender). H contents represent about 12% of all responses. They are the most frequent in Boxes 2 and 8, with peaks of 35% and 22% respectively. They also reach peaks in Boxes 1 and 7 of 11% and 19% respectively. On other boxes, they represent 2% to 7% of responses.</td></tr>
<tr><td>0</td><td>(31%) In the normative group, approximately one third of clients scored H% = 0 (34%; females = 26%, males = 35%, $p < .01$). A lack of H responses indicates difficulty with socializing (see Crisi & Carlesimo, 2008, reviewed in ►Appendix C) and a personality that is closed off, reserved, and scarcely inclined to social interaction. When H% = 0 and P% = 0 (or is low), interpersonal adjustment difficulties may be present. (H% = 0 and P% = 0 is present only in 4.9% of the normative group: female = 2.6%, male = 5.3%, $p < .05$).</td></tr>
<tr><td>12–25</td><td>(63%) The normative mean value of H% ranges between 12% and 25% and its diagnostic meaning describes the client's inclination to be social, ability to relate to others, and level of gender identity.</td></tr>
<tr><td>≥ 38</td><td>(5.6%) Indicates marked social interest and empathy, but also suggests a strong need to lean on others and marked dependency traits.</td></tr>
<tr><td colspan="2">In children: WDCT protocols with no human responses (H% = 0) must be carefully evaluated. This is a troublesome score, especially when paired with low percentage of Animal (A%) responses, and high Object (OBJ%) frequency.</td></tr>
<tr><td colspan="2">Nature Content (NAT%)</td></tr>
<tr><td colspan="2">NAT contents are found in 37% of clients of the normative group. NAT contents represent 4.8% of responses. The meaning of NAT%, somewhat similar to that of BOT%, relates to sensitivity, although this sensitivity is more controlled and adapted to conventional thinking than the sensitivity expressed by BOT responses. Natural content is most frequent in Box 2 (11.7%) and 8 (11.2%), and least frequent in Box 4 and 6.</td></tr>
<tr><td colspan="2">The NAT content category produces mean values that are different between males and females (female = 5.3, male = 4.7; not significant).</td></tr>
<tr><td>0–13</td><td>(94%) Normal value.</td></tr>
<tr><td>> 25</td><td>(6%) Indicates extreme sensitivity to the environment and other people.</td></tr>
<tr><td colspan="2">In children: NAT is more frequent until age 10, normalizing to adult ranges after this age.</td></tr>
</table>

continued

TABLE G.15 *Continued*

<table>
<tr><td colspan="2">Object Content (OBJ%)</td></tr>
<tr><td colspan="2">OBJ responses are found in approximately 97% of clients in the normative group. OBJ contents represent 41.5% of responses, with a maximum peak in Box 5 (60% of responses), and the lowest number of responses in Box 2 and 3 (16% and 14% of responses, respectively). On all other boxes, values range between 26% and 42%.</td></tr>
<tr><td colspan="2">Object contents are indicative of the client's practical skills, and of a realistic attitude toward life and personal interests. The mean value ranges between 25% and 50% (female = 35.1%, male = 42.6%; $p < .0001$).</td></tr>
<tr><td>0–12</td><td>(7%) No practical aptitudes, possible tendency to exaggerate abstract thinking.</td></tr>
<tr><td>25–50</td><td>(65%) Practical abilities and realistic view of the world.</td></tr>
<tr><td>62</td><td>(19%) Critical value.</td></tr>
<tr><td>75–100</td><td>(8%) An elevated number of OBJ%, especially when paired with H% = 0, indicates tension in interpersonal relationships, traits of withdrawal, and an excessive tendency to retreat into oneself (values higher than 62% are only found in 8% of clients). Excessive interest in objects, rather than people.</td></tr>
<tr><td colspan="2">Symbol Content (SIG%)</td></tr>
<tr><td colspan="2">SIG contents are found in 28.2 % of clients of normative group. SIG contents represent 15% of responses, with the highest peak in Box 6 (34%). In Box 2, SIG responses are quite rare (< 2%).</td></tr>
<tr><td colspan="2">The SIG Content category produces mean values that are quite different between males and females (females = 4%, males = 5%; tendency toward significance).</td></tr>
<tr><td>0–25</td><td>(75%) Normal value.</td></tr>
<tr><td>> 25</td><td>(25%) An elevated number of SIG responses may indicate cognitive deficits or a strongly defensive attitude, which in some cases invalidates the test (in the most defensive clients it is not uncommon to find up to 8 SIG responses).</td></tr>
<tr><td colspan="2">In children: Students in first and second grade may produce an elevation of SIG responses, which often represents a momentarily heightened interest for the unknown and fascinating world of writing and numbers.</td></tr>
</table>

TABLE G.16 Rare Primary Content Categories—Frequency and Percentages

Abstract Content (ABS%)
ABS responses are found in approximately .7% of clients in the normative group (no difference between gender). ABS contents represent about .2% of all responses. Abstracted responses generally have the same meaning as SIG responses, indicating the defensive abilities of the client. Diagnostic meaning can vary from the possible presence of an unreal, autistic thought process (in this case, the FQ is low, Special Scores are present, or the response is completely inadequate compared to the box in which it occurs) to creative and divergent thinking (if paired with high FQ, Original responses, lack of Special Scores). The meaning of ABS% is therefore linked to the quality of the entire protocol.
In children: ABS responses are very rare. Their production by children can be a sign of "adultification" and/or excessive intellectualization.
Anatomical Content (ANA%)
ANA responses are found in approximately .1% of clients in the normative group (no difference between gender) and they represent about .01% of all responses. Their diagnostic significance varies from mental deterioration (when paired with FQ ≤ 75) to normal "contamination" based upon a client's professional training (i.e., doctors, nurses, etc.). Between these two extremes, ANA responses may indicate hypochondriacal or actual concerns related to health, a tendency to somaticize, or the need to appear intelligent and clever. Within the category of ANA, skeletal responses suggest desolation and abandonment concerns.
In children: ANA responses are extremely rare.
Animal Simulacrum Content (AS%)
AS responses are found in 1.1% of clients in the normative group (no difference between gender) and they represent about .1% of all responses; therefore, the AS% mean value is quite low (.01%). In adult clients, the presence of AS responses is always indicative of difficulties understanding and positively utilizing emotions. The diagnostic power of AS responses increases when they are accompanied by OBJ% > 63 and AQ+% ≤ 50.
In children: AS responses are more frequent than in adults; however, the diagnostic meaning is reduced if AS content is comprised of dolls, puppets, or other types of toys.
Biological (BIO%), Ice (ICE%), and Mineral (MIN%) Contents
BIO%, ICE%, and MIN% share common interpretive characteristics. BIO responses are found in approximately .7 of clients in the normative group (no difference between gender) and they represent .08% of the responses to the CWS. ICE Responses are found in approximately .9% of clients in the normative group (no difference between gender) and they represent about .01% of all responses. MIN responses are found in approximately .3% of clients in the normative group (no difference between gender) and are about .04% of all responses.

continued

TABLE G.16 *Continued*

The common diagnostic meaning of these content categories suggests cool and/or detached affectivity, which can hardly be expressed. If accompanied by an overall good quality CWS protocol, this group of responses may indicate depressive tendencies, affective and emotional poverty, and difficulties in social relationships; however, in protocols of overall poor quality, these contents may indicate the presence of anxiety, emotional regression, and severe adaptation challenges.
Cloud Content (CLD%)
Cloud contents are found in 5.1% of clients (no differences between gender) and they represent about .7% of all responses. The presence of Cloud content is most often associated with states of acute distress. Their diagnostic value is heightened by an elevated number of AS (Anxiety Stroke) and by the presence of MI (inanimate movement).
Explosion (EXP%) and Fire (FIR%) Contents
Contents related to fire and explosions are relatively rare (EXP in 1% of clients, FIR in 2%) and they are present respectively in about .12% and .15% of all responses. They may indicate the presence of primitive drives. Their negative diagnostic value increases in the presence of elevated IM, low FQ+% value, or an A/F ratio with high A values ($A \approx F$ or $A > F$).
Food Content (FD%)
Food responses are found in approximately 11.3% of clients in the normative group (female = 2.1, male = 1.5, $p < .01$) and they represent about 1.5% of all responses. Food responses generally relate to dependency, oral dynamics, passivity, eating disorders, and immaturity. Their diagnostic value is heightened when H% and P% are elevated (> 25%).
Human Simulacrum Content (HS%)
HS responses are found in 8.1% of clients in the normative group (no difference between gender). HS contents represent about 1% of all responses. The presence of this type of response is always indicative of problems with interpersonal relationships. The diagnostic power of HS responses increases when they are accompanied by H% = 0, P = 0, OBJ% > 63.
In children: the highest score recorded on any Box is 9% (Box 4, where the response "Robot" or "Robot face" is common for children).
Pathological Content (PAT%)
PAT responses are found in approximately 10.3% of clients in the normative group (female = 16% male = 9%; $p < .001$). PAT responses represent about 1.3% of all responses. Diagnostically, PAT responses must be divided into two categories: 1) medical/pathology-related responses (i.e., wounds, hematoma, etc.), related to states of profound distress (mostly found in severely disturbed clients); 2) isolated human or animal details, generally associated with cognitive limitations and/or emotional inhibition.

TABLE G.16 *Continued*

Sexual Content (SEX%)
SEX responses are not found in the normative group. Diagnostic value of SEX% is heightened when present prior to the age of 12. In adults, SEX% increases, although remains low compared to total responses. SEX% responses may contribute to the following diagnostic interpretations: Sexual maturity; Particular sexual characteristics; Type and level of affectivity; Type and level of object relations; Sexual identity. It must be noted that diagnostic meaning also depends on which box receives a sexual response. Box 7 is the "libidinal" box on the WDCT; thus, a sexual response on this box must be evaluated more positively. A SEX response in the more "mechanical" boxes (Boxes 3, 4, 5, and 6) suggests a more negative connotation. SEX contents are almost completely absent in children, generally up to the age of 12.

TABLE G.17 Secondary Content Categories—Frequency and Percentages

Archeological (AC%), Mythological (MT%), Religious (RE%)
Archeological, mythological, and religious contents may indicate deep personal interests. Religious content may further be related to guilt.
Clothing (CG%), Heraldry (HR%), Mask (MK%)
Contents related to clothing and heraldry may indicate gender identity confusion and emotional lability. Masks may indicate tendencies to emotionally manipulate others, possibility of exploitation of others in interpersonal relationships, exhibitionistic behaviors, and/or suspiciousness.
Figurative Art (FA%)
Figurative art contents are interpreted in a similar manner as the Primary Content categories HS and AS (representations of humans and animals). Moreover, FA content may also indicate defense mechanisms, cultural interests, and a tendency to intellectualize.
Fairy Tale (FT%), Science Fiction (SF%), Toy (TY%)
Contents related to fairy tales, science fiction, and toys suggest association or affiliation with child-like concepts of play and expressivity. In the event of healthy personalities, including those individuals who professionally work with children or are parents of children, these contents may indicate comfort with the childhood world or character traits that enable playful expression. Conversely, in the absence of this professional and parental association with children, these contents may indicate emotional immaturity, childish and self-centered attitudes, inhibition of personality, strong avoidant defenses, and narcissistic tendencies toward avoidance of responsibility.
Weapon (WP%)
Weapon contents are generally interpreted similarly to Primary Contents related to explosions (EXP) and fire (FIR). Weapon content is very frequent in children, specifically males.

TABLE G.18 Special Scores—Frequency and Interpretive Guidelines

Total number of Special Scores The total number of Special Scores generally indicates the degree of the client's distress. Generally speaking, aside from Anxiety Stroke (AS)—the most frequent Special Score—only a few Special Scores are found in the non-clinical population. The higher the number of Special Scores, the more complex the client's state is likely to be. Special Scores always hold psychodiagnostic significance. Clinical experience suggests that the more rare a Special Score, the more diagnostically relevant it is. **Type and Number of Special Scores** It is important to note that the presence of only one Special Score in a CWS protocol is almost never descriptively significant. The presence of only one Special Score likely indicates that the client experienced some type of emotional disturbance when presented with a specific box. It is the repetition of a Special Score that indicates diagnostic severity. On average, 6–11 Special Scores (including AS and CB) are considered Normal (60% of population fall within this range).	
LEVEL 1—EXPRESSIONS OF PRIMARY PROCESS	
AP	**ARBITRARY PERFORMANCE.** AP is typical of 2% of the normative sample. It always indicates reality distortions in the client. The more this score is arbitrary in quality, the more suggestive it is of cognitive or psychotic disturbances. **In children**: Beginning in the 1st grade, this score always indicates poor reality testing.
CO	**CONTAMINATION.** CO is rare (found in only .1% of the normative sample). It indicates an interjection of primary process into the client's thinking process. True contamination is typically found in the protocols of schizophrenic patients, where several different elements are condensed in an unnatural or unrealistic manner. A less severe form of contamination is indicated by the depiction of mythological characters, science fiction characters, and similar representations. This special score always indicates some degree of deficit in the area of concept formation. Its diagnostic meaning takes on a more negative connotation when the patient is not aware of the contamination and does not try to justify it to the assessor. Also, the more it is associated with low FQ, the more concerning this score becomes. **In children**: CO should be carefully evaluated, as children's books and TV shows are filled with "contaminated" mutants (organisms or creatures with human, animal, and/or mechanical parts). As for adults, the weight of this score is reduced if the client acknowledges that he drew a comic or fictional character. When all human figures produced by the client are contaminated, the interpretive value of this score is strongly significant. In these cases, strong tensions with the environment, under-developed sexual identity, or difficulty controlling sexual and aggressive energies may be indicated. The more contaminations arbitrarily incorporate different and incongruent parts, the more severe they are considered.

TABLE G.18 *Continued*

DS	**DISPROPORTION.** DS is found in 1.4% of the normative sample. It either indicates limited ability to draw or detachment from reality (i.e., weakened reality testing). A distinction must be made between two forms of Disproportion: 1) The first relates to a disproportion within the drawn object itself (e.g., the dot in Box 1 is the head of a big figure); and 2) The second relates to a drawing of disproportionate size in one box compared to the remainder of the protocol (e.g., in a WDCT protocol of small/medium size drawings, one drawing takes up the whole box; see *Noted Special Phenomena*, Table G.19). The first form of DS is mostly interpreted as detachment from reality; the second form might indicate an expression of shock in response to the Evocative Character of the disproportionately drawn box. **In children:** This special score is quite frequent under the age of 9.
PA	**PERSONALIZED ANSWER.** PA is quite rare (2.4% of normative sample). It always reflects a "projection of one's self" and a surfacing of primary process. A mild form of this phenomenon is found in egocentric, narcissistic, and emotionally immature clients. A marked presence of PA is found in mentally retarded and schizophrenic clients. **In children:** PA is quite frequent up to 8 or 9 years of age. The presence of a PA response normally indicates a concrete experience from the child's life (with people or things), either positive or negative in nature.
TR	**TRANSPARENCY.** TR is found in 1.4% of the normative sample. It is to be expected up to the age of 6 or 7. After this age its presence must be carefully evaluated, as it is indicative of disturbances of thought process.
LEVEL 2—EXPRESSIONS OF COGNITIVE DEFICIT	
ID	**INCOMPLETE DRAWING.** ID is considered an expression of cognitive deficit *when it is accompanied by a Form Quality (FQ+%) less than 81%* (this combination is found in only .2% of the normative population). When ID is scored repeatedly, and is paired with scores that indicate cognitive deficit, it indicates that the client's ability to represent reality is inadequate, partial, and not sufficiently grounded in the client's thought process. ID may also indicate shock, neurotic tendencies, and anxious distress (*see Level 3, below*). **In children:** ID becomes extremely rare past the ages of 6 or 7. If present, and supported by other indices and assessments, ID may indicate cognitive deficits.
II	**INADEQUATE INTEGRATION.** II is found in 6.1% of the normative sample. It conveys more information than any other score about developmental cognitive delays and lack of reality testing. Again, in protocols containing only one instance of II, the score may be understood more as an expression of shock, rather than as one of cognitive deficit. **In children:** II is common until the age of 9 or 10. Past this age, the presence of even just one instance of the score must be carefully evaluated.

continued

TABLE G.18 Continued

MU	**MISSING UNION.** MU can only be found in Boxes 3, 5, and 6 (although it is also theoretically possible in Box 7), and it applies to .1% of the normative sample. In general this score indicates a struggle with gestalt perception. It suggests cognitive deficit and or depressive inhibition of intelligence. In Box 5, MU reflects marked repression of aggressive impulses that is not sufficiently integrated in the person's personality structure. For children, in Box 5, no significant differences were recorded between the normative (non-clinical) sample and the clinical samples. In Box 6, Missing Union is quite frequent (and statistically significant) in stuttering and learning disabled groups. In the learning disabled group, MU may be interpreted as the result of limited perceiving, planning, and foreseeing skills.
PP	**PERSEVERATION.** PP is found in 1.4% of the normative sample. PP suggests: • specific interests of the client (when FQ+% is elevated or extremely elevated); • guardedness toward the assessor (perseveration of SIG content); • organic conditions (when it is paired with low FQ+% or the same content is repeated on almost all boxes); • severe psychopathology (often accompanied by elevated FQ+% to indicate paranoid delusions). The most severe form of content perseveration is found in clients that draw the same content in all 8 boxes ("monotypical perseveration"). **In children:** PP it is normal up to 6 or 7 years of age.
SR	**STIMULUS REPETITION.** SR is characteristic of .2% of the normative sample. In its most severe form (presence in 4 or more boxes), SR indicates a cognitive deficit or an organic condition. In its less severe form, SR indicates a low level of education or a dismissive attitude toward the test.
AP	**ARBITRARY PERFORMANCE.** *See above, Level 1.*
LEVEL 3—EXPRESSIONS OF CONFLICT	
AS	**ANXIETY STROKE.** AS is the most frequent Special Score. It generally signifies the presence of anxiety. It may also indicate actual states of distress when paired with CLD contents, scary faces, or negative assessments in Boxes 5 and 7. As it represents a transient distress state, AS may be especially elevated in assessments conducted for personnel selection or for forensic purposes. **In children:** AS is found in 15% of boxes in the normative group. The clinical groups produced higher scores, from 21 to 23%, without this difference being significant.
CB	**CROSSED BORDER.** CB is the second most frequent Special Score. It indicates the presence of internal tensions and conflicts. This score signifies that the client is in a reactive state. The lower the self-control indexes (FQ+% and A/F), the more likely it becomes that internal tension will be expressed behaviorally, especially when the CB score is elevated.

TABLE G.18 *Continued*

	Even the smallest mark on the border is scored as CB. Therefore, the nature of each instance of CB must be carefully evaluated. Several minor CBs indicate a need for safety and stability, when paired with other signs of insecurity, such as elevated H%, FQ+% = 100, and the presence of Self-Criticism (SC) Special Scores. Alternatively, when FQ+% = 100 and A << F, several minor CBs may signify a tendency to being excessively controlling and to discharge aggressive impulses in small, continuous doses. **In children:** CB reaches only 4% of the total of the boxes in the normative (non-clinical) group, but the statistical differences between groups are significant ($p < .001$).	
REJECTION	GR	**GLOBAL REJECTION.** GR is the most evident expression of difficulty in responding to the Evocative Power of a stimulus. It indicates that the client is experiencing conflict around a particular area of the psyche. In the normative sample, one or more GR are found in only 6.4% of clients (female = 2.7%, male = 7.1%; $p < .05$). GR is most common in Boxes 7, 4, and 5. The lowest number of GR has been recorded in Box 8. The meaning of GR is more or less severe depending upon several factors: 1) The frequency with which Global Rejection is recorded on a particular box, within a specific group. For example, in stuttering clients, the most rejected box is Box 5, whereas in learning disabled clients, it is Box 4. 2) A rejection can be more or less severe depending on the general personality structure that emerges from the testing. For example, a box rejection within the context of relatively average indexes tends to indicate conflict circumscribed to a particular area, which otherwise does not greatly interfere with the client's personality structure. Conversely, when a rejection is recorded in the context of a more disturbed personality organization, it must be weighted more heavily. It indicates interference with ego functioning and the ability to adopt perceptive and associative mechanisms. 3) Clinical practice shows that Global Rejection carries different values depending on the box on which it is recorded. For example, in Box 1, GR often reflects identity issues; in Box 2, it indicates disturbed object relations with females; in Box 3, GR reflects a block in energy flow; in Box 4, it indicates disturbed object relations with males; in Box 5, GR is connected with repressed aggressive impulses; in Box 6, it reflects cognitive and adaptation difficulties; in Box 7, GR is connected with repressed libido; finally, in Box 8, it shows difficulties in relating with the environment. **In children**: Global Rejection is quite rare, making the instances of its occurrence more diagnostically meaningful. The clinician must therefore carefully consider in what box it happened and to what manifestations it is connected.

continued

TABLE G.18 *Continued*

REJECTION	PR	**PARTIAL REJECTION.** PR is typical of 1.2% of the normative sample. It is a less accentuated version of Global Rejection (GR), indicating less severe psychological conflict, or strong ambivalence. The presence of PR is similar to the diagnostic implications found in Ambivalent Delay (AD) responses. That is, in its clinical meaning, PR can be related to Ambivalent Delay because both represent an ambivalent behavior toward the box.
	IS	**INTERPRETED STIMULUS.** IS is typical of .5% of the normative sample. It is a particular type of rejection, which must be interpreted as a tendency to remove painful content from awareness. IS are often found in the protocols of poorly motivated clients, who may be either aware or unaware of their rejection of the task.
ID	**INCOMPLETE DRAWING.** When ID is *paired with FQ+%≥81*, appears in isolation, and is not accompanied by other scores indicating cognitive deficit (e.g., II, SR, PE, MU, AP) it expresses neurotic conflict. ID indicates marked traits of insecurity, indecision, and fear of responsibility. Finally, ID is connected with expressions of anxiety, and it indicates the presence of a strongly defensive attitude (which can border on paranoia). ID can also indicate cognitive deficits (*See Level 2, above)*.	
MR	**MORBID.** Similarly to MOR coding on the Rorschach, MR on the WDCT indicates the likely presence of depressive affect, mood difficulties, and dysphoria.	
OD	**OPPOSITE DIRECTION.** OD is infrequent and it is only scored in Boxes 3 and 5. It is found in clients that experience marked repression of aggressive impulses. In these clients, aggressive impulses are not integrated into the personality structure and can result in inappropriate and dysfunctional behaviors, such as inadequate responses to frustration, lack of assertiveness, lack of zest, apathy, and depression. In cases of depressive disorders, and when paired with other specific indices (elevated IM, lack of M, low FQ+%), Opposite Direction may be indicative of self-harming behaviors or self-punishment.	
RB	**REVERSED BOX.** RB is found in 11% of the normative sample. Two or more instances of RB indicate the presence of oppositional traits. One RB may indicate that the Evocative Character of the box caused a halt in the flow of free association, which led the client to attempt to modify the gestalt of the box. The interpretation of oppositionality is heightened by the client's completion of the WDCT protocol utilizing the Reversed Order of Sequence. **In children**: Adolescents show the greatest expression of RB.	
SC	**SELF-CRITICISM.** SC is quite common. It indicates feelings of insecurity, indecision, and poor self-esteem. When self-criticism appears only at the beginning of the test it is evaluated much less negatively than when it is found throughout the protocol. The diagnostic meaning of self-criticism in magnified by an elevation of ARC%, by "Or" responses (see *Noted Special Phenomena* below, Table G.19), or by dotted lines.	

TABLE G.19 Noted Special Phenomena—Interpretive Guidelines

In additional to the formally scored Special Scores discussed above, some additional phenomena are found in reviewing WDCT protocols. Below is the diagnostic interpretation of these cases that, although not formally included in the scoring, provide diagnostic information.
***Big Drawing (BD)*:** This phenomenon is associated with elevated self-esteem and inflated ego. It indicates increased activity levels. It must be considered in relationship to FQ+%. When paired with positive FQ+%, it indicates a tendency to action, determination, and self-confidence. When paired with negative FQ+% it suggests dispersion of energy, manic states, and omnipotence.
***Blackening (BL) and/or Encapsulation (EN)*:** This phenomenon is typically produced by psychotic clients or significantly impaired individuals. This represents an attempt to avoid the Evocative Character of the stimulus and erase, obscure, suppress, or avoid the psychic area evoked by the box in which it occurs.
***Color Projection (CP)*:** This phenomenon is generally a sign of a denial defense mechanism in which underlying depression is hidden by assuming a false or overly positive affective tone or behavior.
***Conjoined Boxes (CJ)*:** This phenomenon reflects diametrically opposite diagnostic interpretations. Its meaning is therefore entirely dependent on Form Quality and on the general diagnostic picture. In other words, Conjoined Boxes can stem from an act of extreme creativity typical of a person of above average intelligence and great originality. "A landscape from a perspective view," which functionally connects all boxes to each other with optimal form quality and creativity. Conversely, Conjoined Boxes may indicate severe thought disorder and difficulty with reality testing.
***Disproportion between Boxes (DB)*:** This phenomenon is a clear sign of psychic shock or turmoil/conflict occurring in the specific psychological area in which it is noted.
***Human Content Negation (HN)*:** This phenomenon represents a strong sense of ambivalence toward human relationships.
***Improper Description (IP)*:** This phenomenon may represent a sign of carelessness and inattention toward the test (low), anxiety (mild), to significant disturbances in thought process and conceptual organization (severe). IP must be carefully evaluated when working with children and individuals with lower levels of schooling where this type of verbalization may be more common. If IP occurs in isolation, it may represent shock in the area of personality.
***"Or" Answer (OA)*:** Especially when paired with Self-Criticism (SC), "Or" Answers indicate indecision, lack of self-confidence, and need for reassurance and support from the environment.
***Perspective Responses (PS)*:** This phenomenon indicates that the client is putting distance between himself/herself and the task, activating his/her defense toward the psychological domain underlying a specific box. It must be noted that in Boxes 3, 5, and 6, Perspective Responses are somewhat facilitated by the nature of the stimuli themselves. Therefore, on these boxes, this phenomenon may be indicative of logic, rationality, maturity, critical skills, and ability to establish social connection. Some authors consider Perspective Responses in Boxes 1 and 4 as an index of psychopathology.
***Small Drawing (SD)*:** This phenomenon is typical of clients who lack self-confidence and self-esteem, have limited aspirations, and experience inhibition and constriction of affect. It is often a substitute for AS (Anxiety Stroke) in showing elevated levels of anxiety.

TABLE G.20 Primary and Secondary Movement Responses—Frequency and Interpretive Ranges

<table>
<tr><th colspan="2">PRIMARY MOVEMENT (M)</th></tr>
<tr><td colspan="2">Primary Movement responses (M) represent 27.8% of all movement responses in the normative sample. The majority of clients (approximately 80%) tend to provide no M responses; 15% of clients provide 1 M response. Only 5.5% of clients shows M > 1. The low frequency of this type of responses is partially due to the graphic nature of the test, and partially due to the strict rules for their scoring.</td></tr>
<tr><td>0–1</td><td>(95%) Normal value; Thought productivity, sexual identification; qualitative evaluation of intellectual level.</td></tr>
<tr><td>2</td><td>(3.5%) Indicates optimal cognitive level and well-developed introspective abilities (especially when paired with O+).</td></tr>
<tr><td>> 2</td><td>(1.5%) An excessive number of M (M > 3) must be carefully evaluated, as it might reflect an excessive tendency to turn inward, toward introversion.</td></tr>
<tr><td colspan="2">The direction of movement of M responses is also an important diagnostic element:
• Active M responses indicate strong-willed, action-oriented people, who are able to react to situations. This carries an important positive prognostic connotation.
• Passive M responses indicate potentially unmotivated clients, with a tendency for giving up.
• Blocked and Rotary M responses suggest strong internal tensions.
• Double and Indeterminate M responses indicate ambivalence, indecision, and lack of self-confidence.</td></tr>
<tr><th colspan="2">SECONDARY MOVEMENT (m)</th></tr>
<tr><td colspan="2">In the normative group, approximately 52% produce no m (m = 0) responses. 30% of clients produce only 1 m (m = 1) response. 18% of clients produce more than one m (m > 1) response.

It must be noted that this category of responses can be expressed through three types of movements: Animal Movement (FM); Inanimate Movement (MI); and Facial Expression (FE). These categories respectively carry different meaning, described below.</td></tr>
<tr><td>FM</td><td>FM responses represent 19% of all movement responses and show spontaneous affect and a prevalence of repression as a defense mechanism. The direction of FM takes on the same meaning that it has for M. In adults, when occurring in isolation or in the presence of at least one M, it indicates an ability to show a "child-like" side and might reflect some ability to relate with children (i.e., in the field of personnel selection, this can be a positive indicator for positions that require working with children). If FM responses appear in conspicuous number, especially when FM > M, this may indicate arrested development at an infantile stage, immaturity, and concealed instincts that are otherwise intolerable to consciousness.

In children: Until age 7 or 8, FM responses fully substitute for M responses (and must be interpreted as such). These responses do not express emotional immaturity, but instead the manner in which the client manifests feelings and drives. The negative psychodiagnostic interpretation of these responses increases with age.</td></tr>
</table>

TABLE G.20 *Continued*

MI	IM responses represent the largest group of movement responses in the normative sample (47.6%). They express internal tensions and conflict that are better managed when the drawings represent mechanical objects and less well managed when the drawings represent astronomical or elemental objects (i.e., planets) and climate conditions (i.e., rain, wind, rising smoke). In terms of psychodiagnostic meaning, the direction of movement is especially important in MI responses: **MI *active*** responses indicate: Energy that is not filtered through secondary process; Use of primary process; Internal zest; Vivacious and exuberant affect; Creative promptness. **MI *passive*** responses indicate a quality of answer that refers to more marginal personality traits. The possible psychodiagnostic interpretations of MI must also be confirmed by other data in the protocol: Tendency to become withdrawn; Marked tendency to compulsive self-scrutiny; Social isolation; Resignation mixed with exhibitionism; Generic and scarcely realistic ambitions.
FE	In the normative sample, the representation of facial expressions, with the addition of emotional expression, represents 15.7% of all movement responses. It indicates a need to connect and relate to people. It is often strictly related to the client's prevalent mood.
Verbalized movement in Human or Animal Simulacrum Content: An extremely rare, but also extremely significant diagnostic connotation is the attribution of movement to AS, ADS, HS, and HDS contents. Psychodiagnostically, these rare responses reflect a conflict between psychological tendencies: on one hand, the emergence of unconscious contents; on the other hand, resistance working to maintain these contents repressed.	

TABLE G.21 Comparison between Adaptive Area Boxes (1, 3, 6, 8) and Affective Area Boxes (2, 4, 5, 7)—Interpretive Guidelines

In order to be diagnostically significant, the differences between most indices in the two areas must be *greater than or equal to 25 percentage or decimal points* (i.e., $\geq$ 25% or $\geq$ .25). For significance, differences between areas in Content (i.e., H%) percentages are interpreted only when the difference between areas reaches $\geq$ 50%.

EC+%

EC+%[Adp-A] > EC+%[Aff-A]
The client is able to grasp formal aspects of social interactions, perceiving their practical and functional aspects more than their affective components. They understand social rules and behavior.

EC+%[Adp-A] < EC+%[Aff-A]
The client is in touch with his/her emotions and has a tendency to look inward. He/she also has a tendency toward introversion. When consistent with other indexes, this outcome might indicate limited predisposition toward socialization.

Above Average Scores in Both Adp-A and Aff-A
The client is excessively permeable and sensitive to both environmental and emotional situations. The client is sensitive and excessively vulnerable to frustrations, disappointments, and obstacles.

Below Average Scores in Both Adp-A and Aff-A
The client is rigid and guarded both in adaptive and in affectively loaded situations. He/She has limited flexibility for adaptation and therefore struggles with social integration

AQ+%

A+%[Adp-A] > A+%[Aff-A]
Both areas are equipped and enriched with adequate affectivity, without conflict. Aspects of social dependence might be present. Superficial affect prevails; true emotional openness toward others is missing.

A+%[Adp-A] < A+%[Aff-A]
If both areas fall within the average range, both are equipped and enriched with adequate affectivity, without conflict. The affective tone leans toward spontaneity, and vivaciousness. When the values on the right side are much higher (with **AQ+% [Adp-A] << AQ+%[Aff-A]**), this outcome indicates impulsivity and immaturity.

Above Average Scores in Both Adp-A and Aff-A
The client experiences excessive, expansive, uncontrollable affect, suggesting a tendency toward action and issues of emotional conflict.

Below Average Scores in Both Adp-A and Aff-A
The client experiences generalized repression of drive, which may reflect a depressive state. When the values on the right side are lower, strong emotional inhibition is likely.

TABLE G.21 *Continued*

FQ+%
FQ+%[Adp-A] > FQ+%[Aff-A] The client shows appropriate ability for self-control. The lower the values on the right side, the more difficulty the client experiences in handling emotionally charged and tense situations. **FQ+%[Adp-A] < FQ+%[Aff-A]** The client shows adequate ability to manage affect, though marked insecurity and social anxiety can determine a decrease in this ability in social and work-related circumstances. **Above Average Scores in both Adp-A and Aff-A** This outcome is not possible. **Below Average Scores in Both Adp-A and Aff-A** The client experiences marked difficulties with controlling emotions, and emotional reactions. He/she tends to act-out behaviorally. The negative connotation of this outcome is accentuated by a lack of M responses and an inadequate A/F ratio. With lower values on the right side, the client may demonstrate difficulty behaving rationally with increased tendencies for inadequate and dysfunctional emotional reactions.
A/F Ratio (Affective Stability Index)
The A/F Ratio index provides valuable information on the client's degree of emotional stability, affect balance, self-control, and maturity. Thus, in an adult client, it is reasonable to expect a dominance of the right side (F) for both areas (Adaptive and Affective).
P%
P%[Adp-A] > P%[Aff-A] This is the most common outcome, indicating greater participation in conventional thought in the Adp-A compared to the Aff-A, as well as due to technical considerations. Values in the average range indicate adequate adhesion to conventional thought. Any relational or affect problems experienced by the client do not prevent or interfere with the client's adherence to conventional ways of thinking. **P%[Adp-A] < P%[Aff-A]** The client experiences fundamental emotional dependence on others, but unconsciously compensates for this dependence by enacting social behaviors of self-assurance and determination. **Above Average Scores in Both Adp-A and Aff-A** This outcome indicates excessive and non-critical adherence to conventional norms, with marked tendency to imitate behaviors in order to fit in or please others. With higher values on the right side, unpredictable mimicking of others' behavior (excessive dependence) is possible.

continued

TABLE G.21 *Continued*

A *note about* P+%
Because P+% indicates the quality of adaptation to conventional thought, in order to take on a positive connotation, this index must exceed 75–81%. Therefore, both areas showing values < 75 must be looked upon as an extremely relevant negative sign. Only one of the areas showing a value < 75 (with the other > 75) indicates a particularly problematic conflict within the lower area.

O%

The O% index might be seen as a sign of creativity. When its values are excessively elevated, they indicate bizarre thinking, extravagance, and excessive detachment from conventional thinking. O% must always be considered along with O+%. The comparison between these two indexes in both areas might be of interest in terms of vocational counseling and personnel selection.

O%[Adp-A] > O%[Aff-A]
The ability for originality and creativity are mostly related to concrete and operational activities.

O%[Adp-A] < O%[Aff-A]
The ability for originality and creativity is mostly related to art and the humanities.

Above Average Scores in Both Adp-A and Aff-A
If this outcome is paired with O+% values above 81, it indicates creative, even gifted personalities; if paired with O+% values < 75, it indicates bizarreness, extravagance, detachment from reality, and arbitrariness of thought.

Below Average Scores in Both Adp-A and Aff-A
This outcome is not possible.

A *note about* O+%
In order to take on a positive connotation, the O+% index must exceed 75–81%. Therefore, both areas showing values < 75 must be looked upon as an extremely relevant negative sign. Moreover, when only one of the areas shows a value < 75 (with the other > 75), this indicates a particularly problematic conflict within the lower area.

IIT-1

The following only applies when the value of *at least* one area is > .75.

IIT-1[Adp-A] > IIT-1[Aff-A]
This outcome indicates the presence of anxiety and tension in social and work environments. This anxiety is thus directly connected with the adaptation process.

IIT-1[Adp-A] < IIT-1[Aff-A]
This outcome indicates tensions, internal distress, and/or internal emotional conflict. This is a normal state during adolescence, but abnormal in adults.

IIT-1[Adp-A] = IIT-1[Aff-A]
This outcome indicates generalized anxiety. It represents a serious condition that involves all areas of personality.

TABLE G.21 *Continued*

IM
The following only applies when the value of *both* areas is > .50. **IM[Adp-A] > II[Aff-A]** This outcome indicates the presence of social conflict, which determines more or less conscious attitudes that are socially oppositional, oppositional, or in violation of social rules and norms. **IM[Adp-A] < II[Aff-A]** This outcome indicates the presence of emotional conflict, which, in emotionally laden situations, might lead to lack of behavioral control and overt acting out (depending on the values). It must be noted that, in isolation, this index is not sufficient to determine the presence of behavioral difficulties. **IM[Adp-A] = II[Aff-A]** This outcome shows the presence of general conflict, with possible lack of behavioral control (when both values are > .5).
AI
The following only applies when the value of *at least* one area is > .75. **AI[Adp-A] > AI[Aff-A]** The client experiences states of social anxiety at work, and in the general context of interpersonal relationships. **AI[Adp-A] < AI[Aff-A]** When faced with emotionally charged situations, the client experiences anxiety, which is caused by internal conflict and emotional ambivalence. **AI[Adp-A] = AI[Aff-A]** This outcome indicates generalized anxiety, involving all areas of personality.
IIT-2
The IIT-2 describes some traits of the client's personality. In the comparison between the two areas, the left side of the ratio is always expected to prevail. On the right side of the ratio, AC evaluations are expected to prevail. In the Adp-A, values of 4/0 and 3/1 are expected. In the Aff-A, depending on the client's age and on the prevalence of AC evaluations, 2/2 and 1/3 ratios are considered acceptable.
H%
H%[Adp-A] > H%[Aff-A] This outcome indicates a tendency to lean on others and experience limited autonomy. H% = 0 in the Aff-A suggests a tendency to exploit others (i.e., aggressive dependency).

continued

TABLE G.21 *Continued*

H%[Adp-A] < H%[Aff-A]
This outcome indicates a relational life characterized by spontaneity, altruism, and sincere interest for others. This outcome is also compatible with aspects of dependency.

Above Average Scores in Both Adp-A and Aff-A
This outcome indicates that the client's behavior is completely structured around dependency and social imitation. With higher values on the right side, the client's affective life completely revolves around relationships with others.

Below Average Scores in Both Adp-A and Aff-A
This outcome is not possible.

Number of Special Scores/Number of Rejections

Number of Special Scores
In general, Special Scores relating to primary thought process and cognitive deficits tend to present homogeneously, without significant differences between Adp-A and Aff-A. Special scores relating to conflict tend to be more varied between the two areas, related to specific individual problems.

Number of Global and Partial Rejections
These indices represent the most blatant example of Special Scores related to conflict. As such, they take on different meaning, depending on the area in which they present. In general, a prevalence of rejections in the Adaptive Area relates to difficulty with adaptation in the work place and within relationships. Great attention must be paid to the cases in which rejections present in Box 6. This might be indicative of disturbance of thought or of a severe form of depressive inhibition of intelligence. A prevalence of rejections in the Aff-A is mostly connected with conflict originating in the client's emotional development.

M (Primary Movement)

For an exhaustive psychodiagnostic picture of this category, the direction and type of movement must be considered.

Primary Movement[Adp-A] > Primary Movement[Aff-A]
This outcome indicates that the client is capable of higher performance and creativity when faced with practical, work-related issues (when M responses are active).

Primary Movement[Adp-A] < Primary Movement[Aff-A]
This outcome indicates that the client's productivity is primarily an artistic one.

Primary Movement[Adp-A] = Primary Movement[Aff-A]
This outcome indicates that the client is productive in both practical and artistic areas.

m (Secondary Movement)

When comparing the two areas in this scoring category, it must be noted that Secondary Movement can be expressed through three types of movement: Animal Movement (FM); Inanimate Movement (MI); and Facial Expression (FE). Because each one of these movements has a particular diagnostic meaning, it is important to

TABLE G.21 *Continued*

assess the impact that each has on each area of the personality. It is also important to consider the direction of Secondary Movement.

Secondary Movement[Adp-A] > Secondary Movement[Aff-A]

- *A prevalence of FM in the Adp-A*: This might indicate traits of immaturity, avoidance of responsibility, and inadequacy in dealing with social relationships. This stems from the fact the FM responses represent the activation of a displacement defense (i.e., displacing onto an animal, rather than onto a human figure, is much less emotionally demanding).
- *A prevalence of MI in the Adp-A*: This indicates tensions and conflicts that are expressed consciously, and that are directly related to the workplace or social relationships (i.e., actual adaptation difficulties).
- *A prevalence of FE in the Adp-A*: This indicates excessive attention to others' opinion.

Secondary Movement[Adp-A] < Secondary Movement[Aff-A]

- *A prevalence of FM in the Aff-A*: This might indicate a certain degree of immaturity in the client's emotional development.
- *A prevalence of MI in the Aff-A*: This shows that internal conflicts cause tensions that are outside of the client's conscious awareness and therefore lead to significant distress.
- *A prevalence of FE in the Aff-A*: This indicates that the client might tend to project outward. The degree of projection may vary from empathy for others, to interpretive projection of paranoid states (i.e., seeing everyone as against them or out to get them).

Impulse Responses

Impulse Response[Adp-A] > Impulse Response[Aff-A]
This suggests inaccessible material that re-emerged as the result of a cracking in the defense mechanism of repression (Levine & Spivack, 1964). This outcome might show the importance of specific personality traits (oral, anal, or phallic) in the client's way of relating to the outside world (Erikson, 1959, 1994).

Impulse Response[Adp-A] < Impulse Response[Aff-A]
The affect-related repressed material tends to surface in moments of high emotional stress. In the absence of adequate self-control and emotional stability indexes, it can unconsciously affect the client's behavior, which becomes reactive and non-functional to the achievement of a goal.

Impulse Response[Adp-A] = Impulse Response[Aff-A]
The mechanism of repression cracks in a generalized way, manifesting its contents both on a conscious level and at a more unconscious level. The outcome is a generalized state of uneasiness, which might be expressed through distress.

References

Crisi, A., & Carlesimo, S. (2008, July). *The Human, Food, and Cloud contents: Discriminative ability in clinical personality assessment*. Paper presented at the meeting of the International Rorschach Society, Leuven, Belgium.

Erikson, E. H. (1959). *Identity and the life cycle: Selected papers*. Psychological issues. New York: International Universities Press.

Erikson, E. H. (1994). *Identity and the life cycle*. London: W. W. Norton.

Levine, M., & Spivack, G. (1964). *The Rorschach index of repressive style*. Oxford: Charles C. Thomas.

Index

Note: Page references in *italic* refer to Figures; page references in **bold** refer to Tables; and page references in ***bold italic*** refer to Boxes.